THE NINE BOOKS

OF THE

HISTORY OF HERODOTUS,

TRANSLATED

FROM THE TEXT OF THOMAS GAISFORD, D.D.

DEAN OF CHRIST CHURCH, AND REGIUS PROFESSOR OF GREEK.

WITH

NOTES, ILLUSTRATIVE AND CRITICAL,

AND

A GEOGRAPHICAL INDEX,

DEFINING THE SITUATION OF EVERY PLACE MENTIONED BY HERODOTUS.

TO WHICH ARE PREFIXED,

A SUMMARY OF THE HISTORY,

AND AN INTRODUCTORY ESSAY.

BY PETER EDMUND LAURENT,

TRANSLATOR OF " THE ODES OF PINDAR" INTO ENGLISH PROSE,
AUTHOR OF " A MANUAL OF ANCIENT GEOGRAPHY,"
&c. &c.

THIRD EDITION:

WITH NUMEROUS AND IMPORTANT CORRECTIONS,
ADDITIONAL NOTES, &c.
AND
A MAP OF THE WORLD OF HERODOTUS.

IN TWO VOLUMES.

VOL. I.

OXFORD:
HENRY SLATTER, HIGH STREET.
1846.

BAXTER, PRINTER, OXFORD.

ADVERTISEMENT.

On revising the first Four Books of this History for a new Edition, the Translator was satisfied of the justice of a Reviewer's remark respecting some Gallicisms and Archaisms, which had escaped notice. To chasten the style, therefore, and to render the whole work more acceptable, he decided on a NEW TRANSLATION of the *First Volume;*—and having accomplished this laborious task, he trusts the present Translation will be found so greatly improved, as to induce the Readers of Herodotus to peruse these Four Books more attentively.—The Notes have also been more strictly attended to; and every deficiency supplied, to assimilate the plan of both volumes.

As the chronology of the First Book is considered of paramount importance, some observations have been incorporated in the Notes, with the intention of furnishing students with a comprehensive idea of Ancient Chronology—of its authenticity—and of the means by which the data may be deduced from the texts of Classic Authors themselves. This was particularly necessary in *Clio;* where the histories are much varied, and extend over so wide a field. In the other Books, the chronology is not equally important; every date having been previously ascertained by many illustrious scholars, with all possible accuracy, as far as respects the History of Greece.

ADVERTISEMENT.

In the Text of the *Second Volume,* which has been honoured with the approbation of the Literary Public, the Translator has adopted a few alterations, approaching more closely to the English idiom, without affecting the sense of the original; and to the Notes he has made considerable additions.

To render the present Edition more acceptable, an accurate Map of the World as known to Herodotus has been expressly engraved; and the Latitude and Longitude of every important place added to the *Geographical Index,* so that the exact position may be readily found in the Eton Atlas.

CONTENTS
OF
VOL. I.

SUMMARY of the Nine Books of Herodotus.

INTRODUCTION: Page

Life of Herodotus	i
Plan and Object of the History	vi
Digressions of the History	xiv
Moral Character of Herodotus	xx
His Religious Character	xxvi
His Industry	xxix
His Veracity	xxxi
His Political Principles	xxxvi
His Style	xxxviii
Conclusion	xxxix

BOOK		
I.	CLIO	1
II.	EUTERPE	105
III.	THALIA	195
IV.	MELPOMENE	275

SUMMARY

OF THE

HISTORY OF HERODOTUS.

BOOK I. CLIO.

HERODOTUS, intending to develope the causes of the hostility between the Greeks and the Barbarians, in the first place records the mutual rapes of women committed by the two parties: that of Io, 1; that of Europa and Medea, 2; that of Helen, 3: in doing which, he states the accounts given both by the Persians and the Phœnicians. Then, as Crœsus, king of the Lydians, was the first to attack the Greeks with arms, 5, he enters on the Lydian history, 6. The first kings of the Lydians, then, sprang from Atys; the second dynasty from Hercules, 7; the last of whom, Candaules, having been killed by Gyges, 8—12, the kingdom is transferred to the Mermnadæ. Then follows the history of Gyges, 13, 14; that of Ardys, 15, under whose reign the Cimmerians made an irruption into Asia, and took Sardis, 15; that of Sadyattes, 16; that of Alyattes, 18, 25, who expelled the Cimmerians from Asia. Digressions are interposed, relating to Thrasybulus, the tyrant of Miletus; and Periander, the tyrant of Corinth; cotemporary with whom was Arion, saved by a dolphin, 20—24. Alyattes is succeeded by his son Crœsus, 26, who subjugates the Asiatic Greeks, and extends his power over the whole of Asia, as far as the Halys, 26—28. Crœsus is admonished unsuccessfully, by Solon of Athens, to hold no one happy, until he have ended life in happiness, 29—33. Crœsus is visited with great calamity; his son Atys is killed, unwittingly, in the chase, by Adrastus, a Phrygian refugee, 34—45. The Medes having been conquered by Cyrus, Crœsus, alarmed at the growing power of the Persians, first sends round to make trial of the oracles of the Greeks, 46—52; and then consults about levying war against Cyrus: an ambiguous answer is returned, which Crœsus interprets as favourable to himself; and therefore undertakes the expedition, first sending to court the alliance of the Greeks, the chief nations of whom, at that time, were the Athenians and Lacedæmonians: the former sprung from

SUMMARY.

the Pelasgi, the latter from the Hellenes, 56 seq. The empire of the Athenians was then held by Pisistratus, 59—64: the Lacedæmonians had received excellent laws from Lycurgus, 65, and conquered the Tegeans, 66 seq. The Lacedæmonians frame an alliance with Crœsus, 69. Crœsus crosses the Halys, and engages Cyrus with dubious success in the Pterian plain, 75 seq. Returning from Sardis, he sends for assistance from the Egyptians, Babylonians, and Lacedæmonians, 77. Cyrus meanwhile follows rapidly on the heels of Crœsus; conquers the Lydian army before the town; besieges Sardis, which he takes, together with Crœsus himself, 79—85. The country and manners of the Lydians are briefly described, 93 seq. The history then passes to Cyrus, 95. The empire of Asia had been five hundred and twenty years in the hands of the Assyrians: the Medes were the first to assert their freedom: their example was followed by other nations. The Medes, after eleven years of anarchy, choose Deioces for their king, 95—101. He is succeeded by Phraortes, 102. Phraortes is succeeded by Cyaxares, who expels the Scythians, who had taken possession of Asia; and subjects the Assyrians, 103—106. Astyages the son of Cyaxares, admonished by a dream, gives his daughter Mandane in marriage to a Persian, Cambyses: he delivers the child born of that marriage to Harpagus, with orders to put it to death: Harpagus gives the child to a herdsman, with orders to expose it; but the herdsman, prevailed upon by his own wife, educates the child as his own. Cyrus, thus preserved, having reached his tenth year, is recognised by his grandfather, Astyages, and sent safe into Persia: Harpagus, however, is punished in a most cruel manner, 107—121. Harpagus, desirous of being avenged of the injury he had received at the hands of Astyages, prompts Cyrus to rise up against his grandfather: Cyrus excites the Persians to rebellion, 122—126. The Medes are routed in two battles, and Astyages himself is taken prisoner, 127—130. The manners of the Persians are described, 131—140. After conquering Crœsus, Cyrus directs his arms against the Asiatic Greeks: but before the Historian describes the war, he gives an account of the situation of Ionia, the origin, institutions, and manners of its inhabitants, 142—148; the same with respect to Æolis, 149. Cyrus having once more subdued the Lydians, who had rebelled, 154—160, sends Harpagus against the Ionians; among whom, the Phocæans and Teians forsake their towns, and establish themselves elsewhere: the rest submit: 162—170. Caria and Lycia are next

SUMMARY.

subdued, 171—176. In the mean time, Cyrus in person subdues Upper Asia: description of Babylon, and history of Semiramis and Nitocris, 177—187. Cyrus conquers the Babylonians in battle; drives them within the city, which he besieges, and captures by stratagem, 188—191. In this place, the territory of the Babylonians, their institutions, laws, manners, diet, &c. are described, 192—200. At last, Cyrus, carrying war against the Massagetæ, crosses the Araxes, and is slain by Queen Tomyris, 201 to the end.

BOOK II. EUTERPE.

CAMBYSES, having succeeded his father Cyrus on the throne, undertakes, in the fifth year, an expedition against the Egyptians. But, before the Historian relates that expedition, he describes the country of the Egyptians, and the nature of the Nile, 2—36, the manners, rites, and mode of living of the people, 37—98. The series of their kings is given, 99—150. The affairs of Egypt become better known after strangers are admitted into the country by Psammitichus, 151 seq. He is succeeded by Necos, 158; who is succeeded by Psammis, 160; who is succeeded by Apries, 161. Apries is deprived of the crown by Amasis, 162, (here the seven castes of the Egyptians are described, 164 seq.) 172 to the end.

BOOK III. THALIA.

THE causes of the war between Cambyses and the Egyptians, 1—9. King Psammenitus, son of Amasis, is conquered near Pelusium, 10 seq. After the surrender of Memphis, the Africans, Cyrenæans, and Barcæans surrender of their own accord, 13. Psammenitus is at first treated liberally; but soon after, being caught intriguing, is put to death, 14, 15. Having subjugated Egypt, Cambyses resolves to carry war against the Carthaginians, Ammonians, and Ethiopians; but the Phœnicians refuse to carry war against the Carthaginians, their fellow citizens: the expedition, therefore, is dropped, 19. Spies are sent from the Ichthyophagi to the Ethiopians, 20: they bring back a threatening answer from the king. The army, marching against the Ethiopians, is compelled to return by famine, 25. Those sent against the Ammonians are swallowed up, under mountains of sand, 26. Cambyses is wroth against the rites and the priests of the Egyptians, fancying that the Egyptians rejoice on account of his failure, 27 seq. He refrains not even from his own subjects; but puts to death his brother Smerdis, and his sister, who was likewise his wife; slaughters many,

SUMMARY.

both of the Persians and Egyptians; and gives various other proofs of his insanity, 30—39. In this place is inserted the history of Polycrates, tyrant of the Samians, against whom the Lacedæmonians undertook, about this time, an expedition, 39 seq. The Corcyræans assist in this expedition, in consequence of a grudge against the Samians from the time of Periander: concerning Periander, 49 seq. In the mean time, Smerdis, the Magus, takes possession of the Persian throne, 61: he sends a herald into Egypt, to summon the troops to abandon the standard of Cambyses, 62. Cambyses, seized with great anger, is about to lead his army against the Magi; but is accidentally wounded, as he is leaping on his horse, and dies, 64 seq. The cheat of the Magus having been discovered by the daughter of Otanes, seven of the chief men among the Persians conspire the death of the usurper, 68 seq. The Magi are put to death, 78. A consultation is held on the most expedient form of government to be adopted; and finally, Darius, the son of Hystaspes, is pointed out king by the neighing of his horse, 80 seq. He divides the empire into twenty satrapies; the revenue from each of which is stated, 89, 96. Some other nations furnish free gifts to the king; among whom the Indians, whose country and manners are described, 98—101. The advantages of Arabia are then enumerated, 107—113; as well as those of Ethiopia, and the distant tracts of Europe, 114 seq. Intaphernes, one of the seven conspirators, is put to death by Darius's order, 118 seq.; and afterwards Orœtes, 128, who had compassed, by perfidy, the death of Polycrates, the tyrant of Samos, 120—125; who had likewise put to death Mitrobates, a noble Persian, together with his son Crasaspes, and had ordered the murder of a messenger to him by Darius, 126. Democedes, a physician of Croton, having been found among the slaves of Orœtes, (125,) cures the king and Atossa: he is sent as a guide with some Persians, to reconnoitre Greece and Italy: he makes his escape: and the Persians who had accompanied him are taken, and ransomed by Gillus, an exile of Tarentum, 129—138. The manner in which the Persians took Samos, 139—149. But, at the same time, the Babylonians secede; and, after a siege of twenty months, are subdued by the art and valour of Zopyrus, 150 to the end.

BOOK IV. MELPOMENE.

AFTER the capture of Babylon, Darius marches against the Scythians, because they had invaded Asia, and held possession of

SUMMARY.

it for twenty-eight years, 1. The country and the origin of the Scythians, 5—36. Concerning the three quarters of the world, Asia, Libya, and Europe, 37—45. Concerning the rivers of Scythia, 47—57. Darius, having started from Susa, crosses the Thracian Bosphorus by a bridge of boats; compels the Thracians to submit to his yoke; (digression concerning the Getæ and Zalmoxis, 94—96;) crosses the Ister, and, leaving the Ionians to guard the floating bridge over the river, marches up the country, 83—98. The situation and dimensions of Scythia: its various tribes, 99—117. The art by which the Scythians elude the efforts of Darius, 118—134. After pursuing the Scythians without success, the king at last returns to the Ister; from whence he passes over into Asia, 134—143. At the same time, another army of the Persians attacks Barce, in order to avenge the death of Arcesilaus, king of the Cyrenæans, and son of Pheretime. The Historian takes the opportunity of inserting the history of Cyrene, from the time that a colony was settled in Libya by the Minyæ of the island of Thera, 145—164. A description of the tribes of Libya, 168—199. The Barcæi are taken by the perfidy of the Persians; and Pheretime cruelly avenges the death of her son. The Persians make a vain attempt on Cyrene; and, on their return into Egypt, are harassed by the Africans, 201 to the end.

BOOK V. TERPSICHORE.

AFTER the failure of the Scythian campaign, Megabazus, who had been left by Darius in Europe, first subjects the Perinthians, 1; afterwards the Thracians, 2, whose country is described, 3—10. He transfers the Pæonians out of Europe into Asia, 12—16; after which he receives the submission of the Macedonians, 17—21. In this place the family of the kings of Macedonia is commemorated, 22. Darius, having appointed Artaphernes satrap of Sardis, returns to Susa, taking with him Histiæus, whom he has recalled from Myrcinus, (a town which he had given him, 11,) lest he should plan any measures against him, 23—25. Megabazus is succeeded by Otanes, who subjects Byzantium and some other cities, Lemnos, Imbros, and some other islands, 26, 27. At that time the chief men of Naxos, being expelled their country by the commons, go over to Aristagoras, (who had been left by Histiæus as vice-governor of Miletus,) and beseech his assistance, 30. Aristagoras persuades Artaphernes to seize the opportunity of subjecting to the King, Naxos, and the rest of the Cyclades islands: the King approves the project; in consequence of which, Arista-

SUMMARY.

goras, accompanied by Megabates, departs for Naxos: but a quarrel arises between the two commanders; whereupon Megabates betrays the intentions of the Persians to the Naxians, who therefore make the due preparations for an obstinate resistance; in which they succeed so well, that the enemies are compelled to return into Asia, without gaining their ends, 31—34. Aristagoras, however, prompted by fear of receiving punishment from the Persians, and by the advice of Histiæus, excites the Ionians to rebellion, 35—37; and proceeds to Sparta and Athens, in order to solicit assistance, 38: in this place, the states of the cities of Sparta, 39—48, and of Athens, from the death of Pisistratus, 55—96, are described. Aristagoras, not succeeding in his request with the Spartans, goes to Athens, and easily persuades the people to vote the Ionians a supply of twenty sail, to which the Eretrians add five triremes, 97—98. Strengthened by this assistance, the Ionians take Sardis, all but the citadel; but, retreating at the approach of a Persian army, are routed in battle, near Ephesus, 99—102. The Athenians return into Greece: the Ionians, however, continue their revolt, and add to themselves the arms of Caria and Cyprus, 103—104. The Persian leaders, after reducing Cyprus, Caria, and the towns of the Hellespont, direct their arms against Ionia and Æolis, 105—124. Aristagoras flees to Myrcinus; in a sally from which, he is slain by the Thracians.

BOOK VI. ERATO.

The Ionian fleet is beaten off Lade, Miletus is taken, and Ionia once more reduced, 6—25. Histiæus (who, having been sent by Darius to Sardis, had fled over to the island of Chios, 1—5) crosses over to the main land for forage; when he is routed, taken, and put to death, by Artaphernes, 26—30. The Persians subject the European side of the Hellespont. In this place is inserted a digression concerning the Thracian Chersonesus and the dominion of the first Miltiades son of Cypselus, and that of the second Miltiades son of Cymon, 35—40. The latter (in fear, on account of the counsel he had given to break asunder the bridge over the Danube, iv. 137) flees to Athens, 41. Good order is restored in Ionia, 42. Mardonius, with vast forces, marches against Greece, to wreak vengeance on the Athenians and Eretrians; but the fleet is wrecked off Mount Athos, and the land-army is worsted by the Thracians; in consequence of which, he returns into Asia, 43—45. Darius then sends ambassadors into Greece, to demand earth and water, 48. All the islanders accede to the demand; and, among

SUMMARY.

others, the Æginetæ, whom the Athenians and Lacedæmonians prepare to punish: but Cleomenes, one of the kings of Sparta, having gone over to the island for that purpose, is compelled, by the arts of the other king, Demaratus, to return without success, 48—51. Then follows a digression concerning the Spartan kings, 52—60. But Cleomenes, irritated against Demaratus, proves to the Spartans that he is not their lawful king, since not born of Ariston: Demaratus, in consequence, is obliged to abdicate; and, being insulted by his successor, Leotychides, flees over into Asia, to the King, 61—70. Cleomenes, however, passes over once more into Ægina, seizes the chief inhabitants of the island, and delivers them into the keeping of the Athenians: but the fraud with which he had circumvented Demaratus being detected, he escapes from Sparta, is afterwards received back again in the state, falls mad, and lays violent hands on himself, 73, 74. The causes assigned for his madness are enumerated, 76—78. The Æginetæ, after claiming to no purpose their citizens from the Athenians, levy war against Attica, 93. Meanwhile Datis and Artaphernes, appointed to the Persian command in place of Mardonius, cross over into Greece, and, after subjecting the islands, take Eretria by treachery: they pass over into Attica; but being routed at Marathon, by the Athenians under the command of Miltiades, retire back into Asia, 94—116. Herodotus, in exculpating the Alcmæonidæ from the charge of a treacherous compact with the Persians, engages himself in a digression respecting the fortunes of that family, 121—131. After the battle of Marathon, Miltiades attacks Paros; but being compelled, in consequence of a bodily accident, to raise the siege, is indicted at Athens: the victory of Marathon and the conquest of Lemnos save him from capital punishment, but not from a fine, 132—136. Then follows a digression concerning Lemnos and its inhabitants, the Pelasgi, 137 to the end.

BOOK VII. POLYMNIA.

DARIUS prepares for another expedition against Greece. Egypt meanwhile rebels; and the King dies, having previously appointed Xerxes his successor, 1—4. Xerxes, having ascended the throne, commences by subduing Egypt, 7: then, prompted by the advice of Mardonius, the Aleuadæ, and the Pisistratidæ, 5, 6, although dissuaded by Artabanus, 10—19, he prepares to invade Greece. Having made the due preparations, 20—25, Xerxes and his army

SUMMARY.

enter upon their march, and cross the Hellespont by a bridge of boats, 56. The various tribes in the army are enumerated, 61—99. The march of Xerxes, and the nature of the countries he crosses, are described, 108. Several of the Grecian nations submit to his power: the partisans of freedom resolve to punish them, at the termination of the war, 131. On the arrival of the tidings, that Xerxes is on his march against Greece, the greatest firmness and courage is shewn by the Athenians, 139: according to the advice of an oracle, 140—143, they resolve to forsake their city, and to embark aboard the ships which Themistocles, with admirable foresight, had persuaded them some time before to build, 144. The Argives refuse to join the Greek confederacy, 148—152. Ambassadors are sent by the Greeks to Gelo, tyrant of Syracuse (whose origin and history are narrated, 153—156), in order to beseech his assistance. Gelo refusing to send any succours, unless the whole, or at least one half, of the command be given to him, the ambassadors withdraw, after a fruitless negociation, 162: nevertheless, Gelo sends a person into Greece, to watch the events of the war, 163 seq. The Sicilians give another reason for the refusal of assistance; to wit, the threatened invasion of their country by the Carthaginians, who, a little time after, did in effect make an inroad on Sicily, but were conquered by Gelo, and Theron of Agrigentum, about the same day that the Greeks defeated the Persians at Salamis, 165—167. Neither can any assistance be obtained, whether from the Corcyræans or Cretans, 168—171. The Greeks make choice of the pass of Thermopylæ, and the roadstead of Artemisium, to receive the invaders, 175 seq. The fleet of the barbarians is shattered by a dreadful storm off the coast of Magnesia, and the Greeks have some little success, 177—195. Xerxes marches, through Thessaly, to Thermopylæ: the situation of the countries is described, 196—200. A chosen handful of the Greeks (202 seq.) under Leonidas (204 seq.) keeps the enemy at bay for several days, until a path leading round the mountain is treacherously shewn to the Persians: the Greeks, thus surrounded, perish to a man on the field, 210 to the end.

BOOK VIII. URANIA.

The Greeks off Artemisium engage the barbarians three times, with doubtful success; but hearing of the discomfiture at Thermopylæ, retire to the inner parts of Greece, 1—23. Xerxes, having passed through Phocis (where a part of his army makes a

SUMMARY.

vain attempt on the temple of Delphi, 35—39), enters Bœotia, which is in his interests, 34. The Greek fleet, after quitting Artemisium, makes for Salamis: the Athenians abandon the city, 41. Enumeration of the nations of Greece which sent ships to Salamis: their origin is briefly described, 43—48. The barbarians break into Attica, put all to fire and sword, capture the deserted city, and storm the citadel, garrisoned by a few obstinate Athenians, 50—55. The majority of the Greek admirals, terrified by the news, are desirous of proceeding to the isthmus of Corinth, but are restrained by the arguments and threats of Themistocles, 56—63. In the mean time, the barbarian fleet touches at Phalerus: it is then resolved in council, notwithstanding the contrary advice of Artemisia, 68, to attack the Greek fleet stationed at Salamis, while the land army is to march towards the isthmus, which is carefully fortified by the Peloponnesians, who are enumerated, 72. Themistocles, fearing lest the Greek fleet should proceed to the defence of the isthmus, advises Xerxes that the Greeks are meditating a retreat, and persuades him to envelope them with his fleet, 76. Aristides, having brought news that the manœuvre had been performed by the Persians, the Greeks make ready for battle. An engagement ensues, and the Persians are conquered, 84—96. Xerxes (approving the advice of Mardonius, 100) orders the fleet to stand for the Hellespont, 107: the Greeks, desirous of pursuing the fugitive ships, are retained by Eurybiades, seconded even by Themistocles, 108 seq. Xerxes himself leaves three hundred thousand men with Mardonius, and, accompanied by the rest of his army, retreats by land towards the Hellespont: after losing the major portion of his followers by hunger and disease, and finding the bridges swept asunder by a tempest, he crosses over to Abydos on ship-board, 120. The offerings of the Greeks to the gods are commemorated, the division of the spoil, and the honours paid to Themistocles at Sparta, 121—125. Artabazus, who had escorted the King with a body of Mardonius's army, falls upon the Olynthians at his return, but is grievously discomfited in his attack on the Potidæatæ, 126—129. In the mean while, the Persian fleet assemble at Samos, to keep watch over the Ionians; and the Greeks, invited by the Ionians to deliver them from slavery, proceed, under Leotychides, as far as Delos, but dare not advance any further, through fear of the Persians, 132. During winter, Mardonius consults the oracles of the Greeks; and sends Alexander of Macedonia with proposals of peace to

SUMMARY.

Athens, 136 (in which place the origin and genealogy of the Macedonian kings are interposed, 137—139); the Athenians, however, spurn the conditions of Mardonius, and exhort the Spartans to come speedily to their assistance, 140—144.

BOOK IX. CALLIOPE.

MARDONIUS, at the opening of spring, marches into Attica, and takes Athens once more, although deserted, 1—3. He renews in vain his solicitations to the Athenians, to make peace with the King, 4 seq.; but as the Spartans, after long delay, send at last assistance, 10, 11, and all the forces of Peloponnesus are pouring towards the isthmus, he returns into Bœotia, and pitches his camp in the Theban territory, 15. Soon after, the Greeks come up, and pitch their camp at Erythræ, 19: afterwards, having engaged with success the barbarian horse, they shift their station to the Platæan territory, 25. Some days are passed, during which the two armies remain in view, the victims boding success to neither party, in the case of an engagement: at last, Mardonius, in spite of the victims, prepares to give battle, 26—42: his design is communicated to the Greeks, by Alexander of Macedonia, 44. The Greeks, deprived of water and victuals, resolve to shift their station at night, but are attacked by the barbarians: a bloody battle ensues, in which Mardonius is slain, and the Persians are driven back to their camp: Artabazus alone escapes, with forty thousand men, into Phocis, 69. The camp of the barbarians is stormed, and a dreadful slaughter ensues, 70 seq. The movers of the Theban defection to the Medes are delivered up to Pausanias, the leader of the Spartans, and put to death, 88. In the mean time, the naval forces of the Greeks, according to the invitation of the Samians, take their departure from Delos, 90—92. A digression concerning Evenius of Apollonia, the father of Deiphonus, the divine of the Greeks, 93 seq. The Persians, informed of the approach of the Greek fleet, haul up their ships on the strand of Mycale, and fortify them with a wall. The Greeks, pursuing them, debark, and overcome the Persians in a sharp engagement: they capture the camp, and set fire to the ships. Ionia once more secedes from the Persians, 96—107. The Peloponnesians return into Greece: the Athenians, also, after capturing Sestos, return into Greece, 114 to the end.

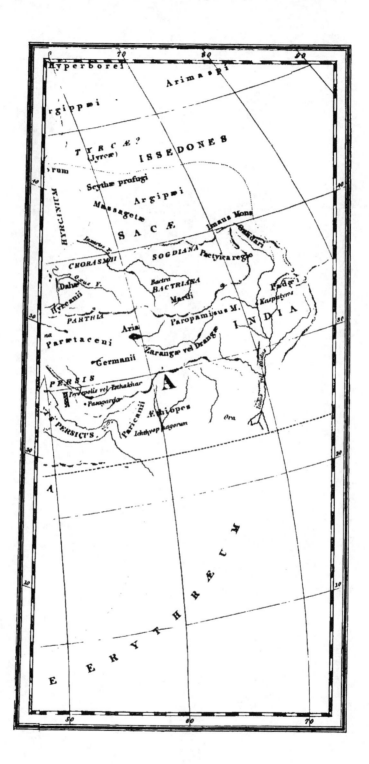

INTRODUCTION.

LIFE OF HERODOTUS.

HERODOTUS was born at Halicarnassus[1], a considerable town of Asia Minor, four hundred and eighty-four years before the Christian era: he was, therefore, about four years of age at the time that Xerxes quitted Sardis, on his expedition against Greece[2]. He was of an illustrious family, originally Dorian, and both his parents were of high rank in the state[3]. Among his relations was Panyasis, an uncle either by the father's or mother's side: the works of this person have, unfortunately, not reached our day; although he was so celebrated, that some of the ancients[4] do not scruple to assign to him the second rank after Homer, in poetical excellence. Soon after Herodotus had reached the age of early manhood, he entered, it appears, on a course of travelling: it cannot now be determined, whether he adopted this plan of practical education in the design of giving to the world the result of his researches, after the examples of some writers who had preceded him, all of whom came from the same quarter of the world as himself[5], and whose success in the field of History may be reasonably supposed to have stimulated the ambition of a youth, whose natural endowments were evidently great, and much improved, no doubt, by the education which an illustrious birth placed within his reach: or, whether he merely quitted his country in order to gratify that curiosity which, in minds created for

---

[1] The Preface to Clio. [2] Wessel. Herod. Vita.
[3] Suidas in 'Ηρόδοτος. [4] Suidas in Πανύασις.
[5] Hecatæus of Miletus, Xanthus, Hellanicus of Miletus, and Charon of Lampsacus. See Wessel. Herod. Vit.

LIFE OF HERODOTUS.

the contemplation of human nature, is an irresistible passion. Be that as it may, to his travels he was indebted for many of the fascinating beauties scattered over his works; from which we gather, that he visited all the most remarkable parts of the world then known—Egypt[6], Syria[7], Palestine[8], Colchis[9], probably Babylon[10] and Ecbatana[11], the northern parts of Africa[12], the shores of the Hellespont, the Euxine Sea[13], and Scythia[14]. He pursued, in all those countries, his researches with unwearied industry: convinced that circumstances, which at the first view appear trifling, are frequently the cause of that variety which human nature assumes in different climates, he dedicated the same patient attention to the religion, the history, the morals, and the customs, of all the nations he visited.

On his return to Halicarnassus, he found that his uncle Panyasis had been put to death by the tyrant Lygdamis, grandson of the celebrated Artemisia, who accompanied Xerxes in his disastrous campaign[15]. Thinking, perhaps, his life not secure in his native country, Herodotus withdrew to the neighbouring island of Samos. This voluntary exile gave him leisure, of which it is fair to presume he profited, to arrange the researches he had made in his travels, and to form the plan of his History. But the love of liberty, innate in the Greek, combined with a justifiable desire of vengeance for the death of his kinsman, inspired him with the idea of overthrowing the tyrant, and restoring freedom to his country. Halicarnassus was not wanting in citizens discontented with the tyranny of Lygdamis; the talents and experience of Herodotus gave decision and unanimity to the counsels of the malcontents; and when his plans were ripe for execution, he appeared once more in his native land, and at the head of a formidable party.

---

[6] Lib. ii. passim. [7] Lib. ii. 44. [8] Lib. iii. 5. and ii. 106.
[9] Lib. ii. 104. [10] Lib. i. 193. [11] Lib. i. 98.
[12] Lib. ii. 181. [13] Lib. iv. 86. [14] Lib. iv. 168, 43, 195, 196.
[15] Suidas voc. Ἡρόδοτος.

LIFE OF HERODOTUS.

The tyrant was dethroned, and Halicarnassus might have been free; but the motives which urged the Historian to make this attempt were shared by few among those who had joined in the execution. The men of rank and the wealthy had been eager to overthrow the tyrant, in order they might get the government in their own hands, and establish an aristocracy. The people presently discovered, that the assumed enthusiasm for liberty was but a pretext to subject them to a yoke still more galling. The virtuous republican, too honest to join the aristocratic party, was looked upon by them with a jealous eye: on the other hand, he was insulted by the people, as the author of a change which they found ruinous to themselves. The natural simplicity and honesty of his own heart had probably hitherto blinded the Historian to the fact, that patriotism and love of freedom are the cloaks under which men are wont to hide the deformities of a selfish nature: convinced now by experience, and disgusted, he bade farewell for ever to his ungrateful country[16].

He proceeded to Olympia[17]: the games were then celebrating, and he read to an illustrious meeting in the Opisthodomus[18] some portions of his History. Although the circumstance is not immediately connected with his life, it must not be omitted to observe, that among his hearers was Thucydides, then about fifteen years of age: the youth, swelling with noble ambition, burst into tears: " Olorus," said Herodotus to the boy's father, " thy son " burns with the desire of knowledge[19]." The compositions of the Historian were much applauded. Encouraged by the wages most gratifying to a high and well-formed

---

[16] Suidas in 'Ηρόδοτος.   [17] Aul. Gell. Noct. Attic. xv. 23.

[18] The Opisthodomus was a large hall in the back part of the temple of Olympian Jove at Elis; where Herodotus recited, during the celebration of the Olympic Games, a part of his History, in the presence of the men the most distinguished by their talents and acquirements, who had collected from all parts of Greece. *Lucian. in Herodoto*, i. quoted by Geinoz.

[19] 'Οργᾷ ἡ φύσις τοῦ παιδὸς τοῦ πρὸς τὰ μαθήματα. Marcell. Vit. Thucyd. Wess. Herod. Vit. Dodwell, Apparat. ad Annal. Thucydid. 18.

LIFE OF HERODOTUS.

mind, he dedicated the next twelve years of his life to the improvement of a work destined by Providence to survive long after his own death, and to remain, for future generations, an inexhaustible mine of useful knowledge and practical wisdom. He recommenced his researches and his travels with renovated ardour; and, as he had before directed his attention more particularly to the nations and countries which acknowledged the supremacy of the Persian empire, he now travelled with the same patience of investigation over the various provinces of Greece, collecting the records of the most illustrious families of the different towns of any note.

Having thus brought his work to a degree of perfection more satisfactory to his own mind, he presented himself before the Athenians at the Panathenæa[20], a festival celebrated in the summer. He again read some extracts from his History; and that enlightened people not only applauded the work, but presented the writer with ten talents[21] from the public treasury. Soon after this second triumph, he joined a band of adventurers, who quitted Athens to found a colony at Thurium[22], near the ancient site of Sybaris, in the south of Italy.

On his arrival at Thurium, Herodotus was forty years of age; and here, it is probable, he passed the remainder of his days, making various improvements in his History: indeed, several passages are pointed out by the commentators, which were evidently added to the body of the work[23] subsequently to his coming to reside in Italy; more particularly the revolt of the Medes against Darius Nothus, which must have been inserted, according to good chrono-

[20] Corsini Fast. Attic. tom. ii. 357. Larcher, Vie d'Hérodote, lxxxv.
[21] Plutarch. de Malig. Herod.
[22] Plin. Hist. Nat. xii. 4. Larcher, Vie d'Hérodote, lxxxvi.
[23] 1. The Lacedæmonian invasion of Attica, in the first year of the Peloponnesian War, lib. ix. 72. 2. The calamitous lot of the Lacedæmonian ambassadors sent into Asia in the second year of the Peloponnesian War, vii. 137. 3. The desertion of Zopyrus the son of Megabyzus, to the Athenians, iii. 160.

LIFE OF HERODOTUS.

logists, after he had completed his seventy-sixth year[34]. The period, the manner, and the place of his death are alike unknown; although it seems unquestionable that his tomb, or at least his cenotaph, was shewn on the Cœle, just without one of the gates of Athens, among the monuments of Cimon's family, and near that of Thucydides[35].

The admirers of Herodotus are disappointed to find that so few details of the life of this great and virtuous man can be gathered from the works of the ancients that have reached our time. It would, indeed, be gratifying to the curious, and instructive to the world at large, particularly in the present age, to be informed by what process of education, and what series of accidents in life, this Historian was brought to unite the highest feeling of devotion and religion with the faculty of penetrating the human causes of events, and to join that patience of research, which spurned not even the most trifling details of human nature, to such depth of thought and quickness of perception. But it is useless to repine at the absence of what was never possessed: it will be more prudent to direct our attention to his writings; in which he may be said, more perhaps than any other of the ancient authors, to be still living; for he dispenses instruction with such a delightful alloy of amusement, and, at the same time, discovers the principal features of his character with such amiable artlessness, that it is impossible to study his pages without feeling a sort of friendly attachment to the man, or picturing to the imagination almost a personal idea of the writer.

In order, however, to form a just estimate of the art and character of this Historian, it is necessary, first of all, to understand well the method which he has followed; for so extensive and numerous are the subjects which he has handled, that while some can compare him only to Homer,

---

[34] Larcher, Vie d'Hérodote, lxxxix.; and Herod. lib. i. 130.
[35] Marcell. Vit. Thucyd. p. ix.

in the art with which he has blended so many heterogeneous parts into one beautiful whole, others deny that he had any fixed plan at all, and emphatically observe, that his History is no sooner read than it is forgotten. To point out all the instances of the nicety of art by which Herodotus has contrived to insert in a narrow compass a panorama, as it were, of the whole world, would be a subject sufficiently extensive for an interesting work. It will not, however, be irrelevant, to give in this place the broad lines of Herodotus's plan of history; leaving the attentive and sagacious reader to supply the deficiencies by his own exertions in the study of the original author.

PLAN AND OBJECT OF THE HISTORY.

The ultimate object, therefore, in the History of Herodotus, is, to commemorate the glorious struggle between the Greeks and the Persians; in which the former successfully defended their liberties against the incredible multitudes brought into the field, from all parts of the world, by the latter, whose dominion extended over the whole of Asia and Africa then known, and some parts of Europe. The account of the immediate causes of the war, and the events which ensued after its breaking out, commences at the Fifth Book, and is thence continued to the end of the work; occasionally interrupted by digressions, or rather episodes, which serve to relieve the reader's attention, by diverting it for a while from the direct course of the History, and thus, by instructing, to amuse. Such however is the nicety with which most of those digressions, as they are called, are fitted into the body of the work, that, in almost every case, the History would lose by their suppression, not only in interest, but even in perfection as a whole.

The most remarkable events, tending directly towards the ultimate scope of the History—and they are all contained in the five last Books—may be summed up in a few words. The Ionians, having ensured the assistance of the

Athenians[26], revolt from the Persian empire[27]: the Athenians send a few ships to the succour of their descendants: they obtain possession of Sardis, and fire its buildings[28]. Darius, king of Persia, informed of the share the Athenians have had in the capture and destruction of Sardis, swears that he will wreak vengeance on them[29]: he commences by reducing once more the Ionians[30], and then despatches a formidable army against Athens[31]. The Persians are beaten at Marathon[32]. Enraged at the tidings of this defeat, Darius makes still greater preparations[33]; but his vengeance is suspended for a time by the rebellion of Egypt[34], one of his provinces, and finally checked for ever by death[35]. Xerxes, his son and successor, prompted, as is natural in a young man, by ambition, and the counsels of the imprudent, instead of confining his designs to the punishment of Athens, resolves to subdue the whole of Greece[36]: determining to march in person against the enemy, he levies the most numerous and formidable army ever heard of[37]; he mans a considerable fleet[38]; and establishes, for this immense multitude, magazines of corn and provisions on the frontier of Greece[39]; and finally, after two years of incessant preparations, commences his march in the spring of the third[40]. He first receives a check at Thermopylæ[41]; and, his fleet being afterwards defeated at Salamis[42], he returns into Asia, covered with disgrace[43]. Mardonius, his chief general, is however left in Europe[44], with the ablest part of the forces: in the following year, Mardonius is conquered at Platæa[45]; and, by a singular coincidence, on the very day of the battle of Platæa, another battle is fought by the forces on board the Grecian fleet, against a Persian army stationed at

[26] Lib. v. 97. [27] Lib. v. 99. [28] Lib. v. 100, 101.
[29] Lib. v. 105. [30] Lib. vi. [31] Lib. vi. 43.
[32] Lib. vi. 112, &c. [33] Lib. vii. 1. [34] Lib. vii. 1.
[35] Lib. vii. 4. [36] Lib. vii. 19. [37] Lib. vii. 20, 60.
[38] Lib. vii. 89. [39] Lib. vii. 25. [40] Lib. vii. 37.
[41] Lib. vii. 233, &c. [42] Lib. viii. 84, &c. [43] Lib. viii. 117.
[44] Lib. viii. 113. [45] Lib. ix. 63.

Mycale[46], in Caria of Asia Minor; and here likewise the Greeks win a signal victory.

It has already been observed, that these events are the most remarkable of those tending towards the object of the History, and that they are all contained in the five last Books: this is so true, that those whose inclination and curiosity do not extend beyond the desire of obtaining some knowledge of the manner in which the valour of the West, aided by an inscrutable Providence, succeeded in repelling the countless tribes of the East, generally confine their study of Herodotus to the Books which contain the description of the course of the war; and few historians would probably have carried their researches any further. But Herodotus, whose genius for expatiating eminently qualified him for the investigation of causes, while his natural simplicity of character inclined him to devote his talents to the service of his fellow-creatures, saw that, if he confined his History within such narrow limits, the Greeks would form but an indistinct idea of the difficulties with which their ancestors had to contend. It was necessary to shew them, that the heroes of Marathon, of Thermopylæ, of Salamis, of Platæa, of Mycale, had conquered the conquerors of the world: it was therefore indispensable to present to their view the history of the Persians. Hence the history of that extraordinary and highly-civilized people forms the connecting chain throughout the whole of the Nine Books; to the various links of which, Herodotus, with most surprising art, attaches the histories of the other barbarians, the manners and customs of foreign nations, the wonders of distant lands, and even the antiquities and early traditions of the Greeks themselves. This leads us to a contemplation of the more complicated machinery of the First Book.

Clio opens, accordingly, with the writer's declaration of his intention to commemorate the actions of the barbarians

---

[46] Lib. ix. 98. 104.

and the Greeks, and likewise to record the causes of the hostility between those two races of men[47]. It seems, at first, rather extraordinary, that he should have gone so far back into the annals of time, as to produce the mutual rapes[48] of women committed by the Europeans and the Asiatics, which led, in the end, to the Trojan war[49]. But this objection is answered by the Historian himself[50]. It seems, in fact, to have been a principle of the Persian polity, that any insults offered to the countries under the Great King's sceptre, even centuries previous to their being united to his empire, were held as insults to his own person: this principle is illustrated by a curious anecdote in the Ninth Book[51], and was indeed the ostensible motive of Darius in undertaking the Scythian campaign[52]. Absurd as it may appear, it was unquestionably founded on good political reasoning: for when once a country like Persia, in her glory, is inspired with the spirit of conquest, and therefore has enormously aggrandized her territory, it becomes absolutely necessary that pretexts for distant warfare should be always at hand, in order to occupy those restless characters, who otherwise would, in all probability, busy themselves in fomenting rebellion in their own country.

Herodotus, however, evades giving his opinion upon events of so early a date[53]; and, choosing a period of time nearer his own day, declares his intention of pointing out the prince whom he knew was the first, in times comparatively modern, to commence hostilities on the Greeks: after which, he will enter upon the course of his History. Deeply convinced that the noblest attribute of History is to instruct mankind by attracting their attention to the mutability of human affairs, he informs us, that he shall commemorate alike the feeble and the powerful states:

[47] The Preface to Clio. [48] Lib. i. 1, &c. [49] Lib. i. 5.
[50] Τὴν γὰρ Ἀσίην καὶ τὰ ἐνοικέοντα ἔθνεα βάρβαρα οἰκηιοῦνται οἱ Πέρσαι, τὴν δὲ Εὐρώπην καὶ τὸ Ἑλληνικὸν ἥγηνται κεχωρίσθαι. Lib. i. 4.
[51] Lib. ix. 116. [52] Lib. iv. 1. [53] Lib. i. 5.

"for those," says he, "which of old were great, most of "them have now become small; while those which in my "time were great had previously been small: convinced, "therefore," he continues, in a strain of deep moral feeling, "that human greatness is ever variable, I shall com-"memorate both alike." Ere therefore we are presented with the records of the victory won by the Greeks over the Persians, we shall have to contemplate a long course of human events, by which we shall be enabled to understand better the real bearings of the question with regard to the importance of the Grecian stand for freedom, and, at the same time, be improved in heart and mind by the numerous examples of the instability of worldly greatness.

Crœsus, then, was the first who commenced hostilities on the Greeks[54]: he it was who subjected the colonies of that nation residing in Asia. But who was this Crœsus? The consideration of this question affords an opportunity of going back to the early ages of the Lydian empire[55]: nor can we blame the Historian for taking advantage of the opportunity, particularly if we consider that the subject must have been fraught with interest to the people for whom he professedly wrote. In order, however, that the object of the History may not be lost sight of, the origin and progress of the kingdom of Lydia are dismissed in a few words, and Crœsus is again brought before the reader[56]. He is represented as uneasy at the growing power of Cyrus, king of the Persians, who had already subdued the kingdom of the Medes, and was marching from conquest to conquest[57]: he draws upon himself the arms of the Persian hero[58]: he is taken prisoner, and his country subdued[59].

"The history now proceeds to inquire who this Cyrus "was, that overturned the kingdom of Crœsus; and in "what manner the Persians came to obtain the supremacy "of Asia[60]." The conquest of Lydia had proved them to be a people of some importance: they had, however, but

[54] Lib. i. 6.   [55] Lib. i. 7.   [56] Lib. i. 26.   [57] Lib. i. 46.
[58] Lib. i. 80.   [59] Lib. i. 86.   [60] Lib. i. 95.

lately shaken off the yoke of the Medes: the Historian therefore goes back to the early history of the Medes[61], of which he gives a sketch down to the destruction of that empire, by the victory which Cyrus won over Astyages[62]. But the Medes themselves had been formerly dependent on the Assyrians, who possessed the supremacy of Upper Asia during five hundred and twenty years[63]; it was therefore natural that Herodotus should give some account of that remarkable people; but had this been done at the place where they first appear in this historic scene, the reader's attention would have been too much diverted from the history of the Persians, which must now be regarded as the main stream, flowing through the whole work, into which all the others are made to fall: add to which, that an excellent opportunity occurs for completing the vast picture in the account of Cyrus's subsequent enterprises[64].

Cyrus, having conquered Media, and overthrown Crœsus, king of Lydia, left to his generals the task of subduing the Asiatic Greeks[65]; and marching in person against the Babylonians[66] and their dependent nations, compelled them to submit to his power. Herodotus tarries awhile only on the most important and interesting subjects: hence he does not mention the Bactrii and Sacæ, whom Cyrus did, we know, reduce[67]: and if the Historian expatiates somewhat on the Massagetæ[68], it is only because the war against that nation was unsuccessful, and led to the death of the founder of the Persian monarchy[69].

Cyrus was succeeded by his son Cambyses[70]. Proud of his power, this latter marched into Egypt. That country was in those days the most interesting in the world; and it was here that the learned among the Greeks suspected that their arts, sciences, and religion, had their rise: it is,

[61] Lib. i. 96.   [62] Lib. i. 128.   [63] Lib. i. 95.
[64] Lib. i. 178, &c.   [65] Lib. i. 153.   [66] Lib. i. 178.
[67] Larcher, Préface, xxviii.   [68] Lib. i. 215, &c.
[69] Lib. i. 214.   [70] Lib. ii. 1.

therefore, fair to assume that the Greeks must have looked upon Egypt with nearly the same feelings as we do on Greece and Rome: the Greeks, moreover, were now beginning to visit Egypt, from motives of commerce, instruction, and curiosity. It was consequently of the utmost importance to give the Grecians a correct idea of that portion of the world: Herodotus, therefore, consecrates the whole of his Second Book to the history of the kings of Egypt, and an account of the productions and curiosities of that extraordinary region, together with the manners and religion of the inhabitants. This history is traced, in a succinct manner, from the most early period, down to that of the invasion by Cambyses; when it merges into the history of the Persians.

After the conquest of Egypt, Cambyses marched against the impostor Smerdis[71], who had usurped the throne of Persia: his death was caused by an accident. Soon after the decease of Cambyses, the cheat of Smerdis the Magus was discovered[72]: he was put to death, and Darius was elected King[73]. This prince subdued once more the Babylonians, who had revolted[74]. These events of the Persian history form the groundwork of Thalia, the Third Book.

Prompted by ambition, or more probably by the necessity of employing the restless spirits of his vast dominions, Darius formed the design of enslaving the Scythians[75]. Those tribes were but little known, excepting to their neighbours, and the Grecians settled in the towns on the frontier of Scythia: it is natural, however, to suppose that the Greeks must have been desirous of having some information respecting that curious people, particularly as there were already some Grecian colonies settled in Thrace, and on the European and Asiatic shores of the Euxine Sea. Moreover, the Scythians were in that state of barbarous society, to the accounts of which men of all ages, who enjoy the blessings of civilization, listen with

[71] Lib. iii. 64.   [72] Lib. iii. 69.   [73] Lib. iii. 86.
[74] Lib. iii. 159.   [75] Lib. iv. 1.

a natural eagerness of curiosity. The Historian's description is framed so as to give a rough but clear idea of the government of the Scythians, their manners, and the nature of their country. The Scythians adopted a system of warfare which compelled Darius to retreat into his own states[76].

But at the time that Darius was carrying on an unsuccessful war against the Scythians, another mighty expedition[77] was undertaken, by the Persians stationed in Egypt, against the town of Barce, on the northern coast of Africa. This affords the Historian an opportunity of touching on a subject which must have been no less interesting than instructive to his countrymen : it is, the foundation of the Greek colonies in Libya, which began then to assume an important station. This history he likewise traces from its beginning, and continues down to the time of the inroad of the Persians on the Libyan territory. Herodotus knew, also, too well the instruction which civilized nations may derive from contrasting their situation with that of men cramped beneath the oppressive weight of barbarism, to neglect the opportunity now before him of giving some account of the vagrant hordes resident on the north coast of Africa.

All the events here mentioned are necessarily and intimately connected with the history of the Persians; and perhaps equally so with that of the Grecians, inasmuch as they enable us better to appreciate the importance of the noble victories which they won over the Persians; and not only the valour of the other Greek confederates, but more particularly that of the Athenians, who, to use the Historian's emphatic language, " engaged the Persian at " Marathon single-handed, fought and conquered six and " forty nations[78]."

[76] Lib. iv. 120, &c. [77] Lib. iv. 145. [78] Lib. ix. 27.

DIGRESSIONS OF THE HISTORY.

Such, then, are the principal lines of the plan of History adopted by Herodotus: and if we consider the probable motives which may have induced him to choose so vast a field, we shall, no doubt, trace them to that thirst of universal acquaintance with human nature which enabled him to face the hardships of travel in so many and distant countries. Happily for mankind in general, to the thirst here alluded to is always united an equally irresistible desire of communicating the knowledge obtained. Nor is this turn of mind perceptible only in the general outline of the method: it characterizes the execution of each individual part of the History. The anxiety of the writer to explain and expatiate, and by his explanations to instruct, is every where too visible to escape notice; and one is sometimes tempted to think that the work must have been composed by some mathematician, accustomed to define as he advances. Hence the numerous digressions from, and interruptions of, the narrative, which are met with in the course of the History; many of these are naturally introduced by the subject in hand, while others, according to his own fair avowal, are rather far-fetched: προσθήκας γὰρ δή μοι ὁ λόγος ἐξ ἀρχῆς ἐδίζητο[n].

But having touched on the subject of the digressions of Herodotus, it will be proper to extend a little farther our observations; particularly as the objections made to the History on this score, unlike most others, proceed frequently from persons whose talents entitle their opinion to some respect. Many minds are naturally endowed with a fretful curiosity to see the sequel and termination of the events announced by a history: hence their judgment condemns whatever obliges them to lose sight for a moment of the object of their sole interest: to such persons, Herodotus must always appear exceedingly garrulous; and

---

[n] Lib. iv. 30.

indeed the reader must be a very prejudiced admirer of the Historian, who can see his attention diverted, in the middle of the brilliant description of the battle of Thermopylæ, to the marriage of a Persian lady, and the amount of her dowry[20], and yet deny that he is at least annoyed. But examples of such preposterous interruptions are very few: presuming that his reader has the time and inclination to attempt a perfect knowledge of the country he is going to travel over, the Historian disdains to whirl him along the straight and sandy road, but leads him, by the hand, over hill and dale.

The digressions then of Herodotus may be divided into two classes; those naturally suggested by the subject, and those which are not so. The object of the first is, the antiquities of nations, their manners, customs, and religion; the constitution of states; the geographical definition of countries; the fulfilment of oracles and predictions; the origin of the worship of the gods, and of the Grecian mysteries. These subjects were all of high interest to the Greek people, who could not but hold themselves indebted to the writer who attached so much useful information to the narrative of their deeds of glory. The art with which some of those digressions are linked on to the whole is truly surprising. Darius, in his expedition against Scythia, goes to contemplate the Euxine: the Historian seizes the opportunity to describe that sea[21]. Aristagoras of Miletus is about to answer the question of Cleomenes, king of Sparta, how far it is from Ionia to Susa: he is interrupted in his reply; and the Historian, having thus whetted the curiosity of the reader, takes up the subject, and describes himself the road[22]. The consideration of the Hyperboreans leads the Historian to consider the opinion of those who held that the world was round as a shield: he refutes their opinion, in a digression, rich of geographical knowledge[23].

[20] Lib. vii. 224. [21] Lib. iv. 85. [22] Lib. v. 50—52.
[23] Lib. iv. 36, &c. The expression of the Historian is, οἱ 'Ωκεανόν τε ῥέοντα γράφουσι πέριξ τὴν γῆν, ἐοῦσαν κυκλοτερέα ὡς ἀπὸ τόρνου: the usual translation given is, "as if turned by a lathe." The mistake of the

xvi   DIGRESSIONS OF THE HISTORY.

Crœsus, desirous of repressing the power of the Persians, seeks the alliance of the Greeks: this introduces the earliest history of Sparta and Athens[84]. Aristagoras of Miletus, intending to levy war against the Persian empire, goes to Lacedæmon, to solicit assistance: the Historian seizes the opportunity of continuing the history of Sparta[85]. The same individual proceeds on the same errand to Athens; when the history of that state is likewise continued[86]. In the account of the Libyan tribes, the Historian has occasion to mention an island, where, according to the statement of the Carthaginians, the girls procure gold sand by dipping bunches of feathers daubed with pitch into the mud of a lake: Herodotus signifies his unwillingness to decide whether the tale is correct or not, but takes the opportunity of describing, as an eye-witness himself, a phænomenon in the island of Zacynthus, where bitumen is obtained from a lake by a similar contrivance; and thus conveys a piece of information which would be despised by none but the hermit of the closet[87]. The above are but a very few instances of the art of Herodotus, the illustrations of which, as has been observed before, would fill a volume; and every where this astonishing skill of execution is to be traced to a desire of instructing: this art even sometimes borders on cunning. Sosicles, the Corinthian deputy, opposes the tyrannic principles of the Spartans: Herodotus grasps the opportunity of placing in his mouth the history of the Cypselidæ[88].

translators might be excused, but not the sneer of ignorance which some indulge at the idea that Herodotus should have laughed at those who represented the world as globular. The fact is, that Herodotus probably had no idea of the world being spherical: " he derides those who make " the world like a shield, with the ocean surrounding the flat circle " of the earth." See the Tabulæ Herodoteæ. I had not seen the prefatory observations to that valuable little book when I translated that part of Melpomene: I am glad, however, to find my explanation corroborated by this authority. See vol. i. p. 285, note 4; where I have shewn that τόρος means a *compass*.

[84] Lib. i. 56—69.   [85] Lib. v. 39.   [86] Lib. v. 55.
[87] Lib. iv. 195.   [88] Lib. v. 92.

Leotychides, addressing the Athenians, is represented as producing an old Spartan tradition[89], which can hardly be said to bear on the question: and, to speak the truth, even the brazen plate of Aristagoras[90] seems to have been introduced only to afford an opportunity of giving geographical information to a people, who, but a few years before, were so ignorant of the state of the world, that many among them fancied Samos was as far from Delos as the pillars of Hercules[91].

But these digressions stand in need of no defence: all patient readers will be grateful for the instruction which the Historian thus finds the means of conveying; and, far from regarding them as superfluous ornaments, will deem them an essential part of the History itself; which may be compared to a vigorous tree, well set with branches, and adorned with rich foliage; an object truly more gratifying to the eye than a dry trunk with two or three leafless stems. It is not, however, so easy to account for those of the second class; in which the writer has evidently strayed out of his road, in search of an opportunity of introduction. The study of history and of foreign countries having engaged the mind of Herodotus in a constant and deep consideration of human nature, he must necessarily have framed a system of morality and religion, which he himself no doubt thought the best, and the principles of which none can deny that it was not only his right, but his duty, to record, and, when possible, to exemplify, in the course of his work. This appears to be the only reasonable grounds on which we can account for several digressions, that have no relation, either in point of time, or in their other bearings, to the thread of the narrative. The fate of Periander[92] of Corinth was too striking an illustration of the chastisement of the wicked, even in this world, for Herodotus not to wish to shew his readers, by a detail of that tyrant's domestic misfortunes and miserable

[89] Lib. vi. 86.
[91] Lib. viii. 132.
[90] Lib. v. 49.
[92] Lib. iii. 50, &c.

end, that power and wealth united cannot make man happy, unless accompanied by virtue. But the reign of Periander was many years anterior to the events which constitute the subject of the Third Book, and is totally unconnected with the object of the History. The art with which this beautiful moral lesson is introduced is therefore deserving of some consideration. The History is engaged in the account of some Samians, who, in order to assert their freedom, attract the arms of the Lacedæmonians on their island, to which are united those of the Corinthians[93]. This portion of the History is itself a digression, which Herodotus takes the opportunity of introducing in this place, because some of the Samians had been sent by their tyrant Polycrates to assist Cambyses, and because the dates of the Persian expedition against Egypt, and of that of the Lacedæmonians against Samos, were coincident[94]. The interference of foreign nations in civil wars may generally be attributed to one of two motives; either to an honest desire of ensuring the success of one party, or to a crafty design of weakening the country itself for some political reason, by entangling the quarrel, and adding to the horrors of the struggle: it is not therefore surprising, that two causes should have been alleged for the alacrity with which the Lacedæmonians joined the republican party; the Samians asserting that it was out of gratitude for a former favour, while the Lacedæmonians themselves declared it was from a desire to be avenged on the Samians for some acts of piracy which they had committed on their nation[95]. With regard to the Corinthians, Plutarch, in his Treatise of the Malignity of Herodotus—the prototype of those compositions, improperly termed criticisms, with which modern literature is infested—takes for granted that they acted from the pure and praiseworthy desire of putting down tyranny: it is to be hoped, for the honour of human nature, that such was really the case. Hero-

---

[93] Lib. iii. 48. [94] Lib. iii. 39, 44. [95] Lib. iii. 47.

dotus, however, states, that the Corinthians meddled in the civil war out of a desire of vengeance, and in order to punish the Samians for an insult received at their hands, when some Corcyræan boys, being sent by Periander to Asia for a most infamous purpose, in order thereby to punish the Corcyræans who had murdered his son, were rescued by the Samians[96]. It is very true, that when we consider the time elapsed between the rescue of the boys and the Samian revolution, and, likewise, when we consider that the rescue, if an insult at all, was an insult not on the Corinthian people, but on the Cypselidæ their tyrants, a family at this period recollected only with feelings of detestation by the descendants of their subjects[97], this motive does at first appear extremely improbable: but the Historian, foreseeing, as it were, the objection, gives a very good reason why the Corinthians should have considered the service rendered by the Samians to the Corcyræans as an insult on their whole body; the Corinthians and Corcyræans had, in fact, been at variance from the very foundation of the island: Νῦν δὲ αἰεὶ, ἐπεί τε ἔκτισαν τὴν νῆσον, εἰσὶ διάφοροι ἐόντες ἑωυτοῖσι[98]:—and surely this is not the only instance of gross anomaly in conduct produced by national animosity. Whether Herodotus is right in the motive which he attributes to the merchants of the Isthmus, is however a question of little importance, and perhaps somewhat foreign to the object of these remarks: the mention of the tradition which he adopts, whether true or false, makes room for an account of Periander himself, and affords an opportunity of attaching to the historical digression a moral episode: the tyrant had murdered his wife, but neither power nor wealth could shield him from the vengeance of Providence, which smote him while yet alive: one of his sons was an idiot: the other, seeing in his father the murderer of his mother, made use of the powerful qualifications with which nature had endowed his mind to

[96] Lib. iii. 48.   [97] Lib. v. 92, passim.   [98] Lib. iii. 49.

torment an aged parent by obstinate disobedience: the young man at last meets his death in Corcyra; and Periander, at the edge of his grave, finds himself reft of any useful posterity, and completely miserable. Such indeed is the art of the Historian, that he not unfrequently takes advantage of some obscure tradition, or even some most improbable report, to narrate events which may illustrate his moral principles; and, as before has been observed, it is upon this ground that the insertion of not a few digressions must be accounted for.

MORAL CHARACTER OF HERODOTUS.

This likewise leads us to the consideration of a subject both important and interesting, namely, the moral and religious philosophy which pervades the History of Herodotus. The principles of the system are submitted to the reader at an early stage of the work, and represented as proceeding from the lips of Solon[90]: 1. Power and wealth are not sufficient to constitute happiness; for the man in possession of a moderate fortune is oftentimes happier than the sovereign on his throne. 2. Every thing is subject to the laws of destiny, which not even the gods can avert. 3. The divinity is jealous of the pride and vanity of men[1], and loves to abash those that raise themselves too high. 4. Consequently, no man can be predicted to have been truly happy until he has ended life in happiness. To which may be added two other maxims, which are repeatedly illustrated in the course of the History: 5. The divinity visits great crimes with punishment in this world. 6. The divinity is wont to interfere directly in human affairs. Any remarks on these maxims would be inconsistent with the scope of these observations: it will suffice, to prove that such were the ideas of Herodotus, in order that, in reading the History, the attention may be directed towards their illustration.

---

[90] Lib. i. 32.
[1] The authorities concerning the τῶν φθονερῶν are, i. 32. iii. 40. and vii. 46.

The first maxim, that power and wealth are not sufficient to constitute happiness, is strikingly displayed in the account of Crœsus himself, who, soon after the departure of the Athenian sage, is plunged into the deepest domestic misery: his son, the only darling of his hope, is killed by the hand of a person whom he had comforted in misery and cherished as it were in his bosom[2]. The same principle is likewise remarkably illustrated in the Seventh Book. The account of the wreck of the Persian fleet off the Sepiad foreland leads the writer to mention an individual who much enriched himself by the quantities of gold and silver plate thrown up by the sea on his estate: men are wont to listen with a sort of envious and eager curiosity to the narratives of wealth thus obtained by chance: those feelings, however, are in this instance benumbed; for the Moralist carefully observes, that even this individual was visited with sorrow, which embittered his days, λυπεῦσα καὶ τοῦτον[3], to use his own expressive language. The same maxim is illustrated in the history of Polycrates[4], of Periander[5], and indeed almost every high personage brought to the reader's view.

Hardly less numerous are the illustrations of the second maxim—that every thing is subject to the laws of destiny; or, as he makes the Pythoness reply to the remonstrances of Crœsus, τὴν πεπρωμένην μοῖραν ἀδύνατά ἐστι ἀποφυγέειν καὶ θεῷ[6]. This principle sheds a considerable degree of dramatic interest on several portions of the work, more particularly, perhaps, on the misfortunes and death of Adrastus[7]; a tragedy which, by the effects it produces on the finer feelings of our nature, may be placed on a level with those written by the best masters, purposely for the stage. Nor must we omit to observe the art with which the Historian avails himself of this principle to rivet the attention of his reader: Cambyses, wounded accidentally to death, finding that he has mistaken

---

[2] Lib. i. 43.   [3] Lib. vii. 190.   [4] Lib. iii. 120, 124.
[5] Lib. iii. 50, &c.   [6] Lib. i. 91.   [7] Lib. i. 45.

the oracle, and that the Ecbatana, which he understood of Media, alluded to an obscure town in Syria of the same name, exclaims, " Here is the fated spot for Cambyses, the son of Cyrus, to die[8]!"—no person can read this passage without having the same searching feeling as is produced by a similar stroke of art in Shakspeare's Macbeth. Xerxes, in the pride of youth and power, has brought the myriads of Asia across the Hellespont: hardly has he set foot on the European shore, than various tokens forebode his disasters[9]: the Persian prince passes them unheeded: not so the reader, who is prepared to contemplate, during the whole account of the expedition, the imbecility of human power, when acting contrary to the decrees of fate. The same art, if art it may be called, is displayed in the narrative of the death of Polycrates: the dream of the daughter previous to the departure of her father to meet the treacherous Orœtes, the earnestness with which she is represented foreboding her parent's calamity, and the simplicity with which she prefers to abide long unwedded rather than to lose a dear father, excite an awful interest in the reader[10].

The third maxim, that the divinity is jealous of the pride and vanity of man, and loves to abash those that raise themselves too high, is too frequently laid down in the course of the History for any one to doubt that such was the idea of Herodotus. Solon produces it, in his discourse, to humble the pride of Crœsus[11]: Amasis, in his letter to Polycrates, wherein he endeavours to set his friend on his guard against too great a reliance in his own good fortune[12]: and Artabanus, when, taking advantage of the young King's state of mind, he makes a last effort to bring him to some feelings of humility[13]. To illustrate this principle, the Historian, previous to recounting the disastrous expedition of Cyrus against the Massagetæ, his death, and the ignominious treatment of

[8] Lib. iii. 64.   [9] Lib. vii. 57.   [10] Lib. iii. 124.   [11] Lib. i. 32.
[12] Lib. iii. 40.   [13] Lib. vii. 46—50. ἐᾷ τὰ ὑπερέχοντα κ. τ. λ.

his body by Tomyris, informs the reader, that Cyrus thought himself something more than a man, and that no nation could resist his power[14]: thus the chastisement which he receives corroborates the truth of the maxim placed in the mouth of Solon.

The fourth maxim, that no man can be predicated to be happy until he has ended life in happiness, is a necessary consequence of the preceding principles. Artabanus developes it, in his speech to Xerxes, just now alluded to; and the History exemplifies it, in passages too numerous to specify. No where, however, is its truth enforced more directly, than when Crœsus, fixed on the pyre, calls out, " Solon! Solon! Solon[15]!" In this part of the work, the sympathy of the conqueror, the raging of the flames in spite of all efforts to quench them, the miserable state of the Lydian king, from which he is rescued only by a miracle, constitute a living picture, admirably adapted to humble the proud, and painted in such vivid colours, that, when once viewed, it remains for ever fixed in the memory.

Herodotus seldom permits any opportunity to slip of impressing his reader with the belief that the divinity visits great crimes with great punishment : it will be sufficient to adduce one or two instances. After proving practically that the Trojans could not be in possession of Helen, who had indeed been ravished by Paris, but was in Egypt during the war, he accounts for the disbelief shewn by the Greeks to the assertions of the Trojans : " No faith was put in what they said: the cause of " which, in my opinion, was, that Providence arranged " that the destruction of the Trojan nation, by one general " massacre, should convince all men, that for great mis- " deeds, great are the punishments at the hands of the " gods"—ὡς τῶν μεγάλων ἀδικημάτων μεγάλαι εἰσὶ καὶ αἱ " τιμωρίαι παρὰ τῶν θεῶν[16]." Pheretima, having glutted her desire of blood and vengeance, dies a most miserable

[14] Lib. i. 204.   [15] Lib. i. 86.   [16] Lib. ii. 120.

death; her body swarming, while yet alive, with maggots: Herodotus observes, *Ὡς ἄρα ἀνθρώποισι αἱ λίην ἰσχυραὶ τιμωρίαι πρὸς θεῶν ἐπίφθονοι γίνονται* [17]. The same principle leads the Historian, despite of the other reasons reported, to regard the madness of Cleomenes as a punishment inflicted on him by Providence, for having tampered with the prophetess of Delphi, and procured the ruin of Demaratus [18].

We now proceed to the sixth and last principle of this moral philosophy; namely, that the divinity is wont to interfere directly in human affairs. To the adoption of this maxim, Herodotus was no doubt conducted by the natural course of his studies: for the more we contemplate the world, whether in active life or the pages of history, the more convinced we are of the futility of attempting to account for every thing solely by human agency. This principle, however, in a mind guided only by the light of nature, may be reasonably supposed to superinduce something of superstition, and consequently credulity: it would be a folly to deny, that Herodotus is entirely free from those failings. He is of opinion, that tokens forebode the approach of calamities to nations and cities: *Φιλέει δέ κως προσημαίνειν εὖτ' ἂν μέλλῃ μεγάλα κακὰ ἢ πόλι ἢ ἔθνεϊ ἔσεσθαι* [19]. As the Grecian forces were marching up to the Persians, on the strand at the foot of Mycale, a report pervaded the army, that Pausanias had defeated Mardonius at Platæa that same day; and a caduceus, or herald's wand, was related to have been seen on the shore. It would certainly have been a good stroke of policy in the Grecian leaders to animate their men by such a representation: the Historian, however, prefers attributing it to divine agency; characteristically observing, *Δῆλα δὴ πολλοῖσι τεκμηρίοισί ἐστι τὰ θεῖα τῶν πρηγμάτων* [20]. Hence, likewise, the repugnance which he exhibits, in the Second Book, to enter into any discussion on the Egyptian mysteries [21]. Let it not, however, be

---

[17] Lib. iv. 205.   [18] Lib. vi. 84.   [19] Lib. vi. 27.
[20] Lib. ix. 100.   [21] Lib. ii. 3, 48, 171.

supposed, that this superstition has induced him to suppress any thing that might be used as an argument against his own principles. A little previous to the account of the battle of Salamis, he quotes a prediction of Bacis, the seer, which had been remarkably fulfilled: the comment deserves attention, as it decidedly proves that Herodotus did believe in the oracles which are so thickly scattered over his pages: "When I consider these events, and reflect that " Bacis has spoken so distinctly, I dare not myself say any " thing in contradiction of oracles, nor do I approve it in " others[22]." Yet the Historian does not scruple, in another part of his work, to unfold the avaricious views of the Pythoness herself[23]; and to give it as his opinion, that those who had corrupted her were the real authors of the deliverance of Athens from the tyranny of the Pisistratidæ[24]. But enough has been said on this subject to minister to the depraved appetite of those persons who love to fix on the failings of great men. The reader, who recollects that Herodotus was a pagan, and considers the immense difficulty, or, more strictly speaking, the utter impossibility, of the human mind, in that state of spiritual darkness, keeping itself properly balanced between the extremes of universal scepticism and disgusting superstition, will admire the spirit of true devotion which pervades the whole work. One striking instance, among many, may be brought forward: he has been considering the state of the Greek nations at the time that tidings were brought of Xerxes' intention to invade and subjugate the country; and shews, with great political skill, that Greece was indebted for her freedom to the decisive measures adopted by the Athenians: thence he concludes, that it was they who effectually did repel the King, next, at least, he adds—fearing the Grecian reader may be induced by the preceding political and shrewd statement of the facts to forget that he was to

---

[22] Lib. viii. 77. [23] Lib. v. 63: compare, likewise, lib. vi. 66.
[24] Lib. vi. 123.

thank the gods for the victories won by his forefathers—next, at least, to the gods—αὐτοὶ οὗτοι ἦσαν οἱ βασιλέα μετά γε θεοὺς ἀνωσάμενοι[35]. Providence did not ordain that this virtuous man should have the privilege of acquiring the principles of a pure and revealed religion; but that same Providence has permitted that his works should survive the lapse of centuries, and the wreck of ancient literature; so that we, who, through the Divine mercy, have the straight road pointed out to us, are enabled to avoid the errors into which the greatest men, when left to the light of nature, have fallen; and haply may be brought to a conviction of our unworthiness, when we contrast our own feelings of devotion with those even of an ethnic philosopher, whose soul was cramped under the trammels of unavoidable superstition.

RELIGIOUS CHARACTER OF HERODOTUS.

But as the religion of Herodotus may be attacked, at the present period, without any danger to the worldly interests of the critic, there are many passages of the History produced as proofs of superstition and credulity, which might more fairly be regarded as arguments of a very praiseworthy feeling of religion and morality. Artabazus, in his attack on the Potidæatæ, loses a good portion of his troops by a wonderful ebb and flow of the sea in the Thermaic gulf: the Historian assents to the belief of the natives, that this was a miracle wrought by Neptune, in order to punish the barbarians for having violated his temple and sacred image[36]. The battle of Platæa was fought near a grove sacred to Ceres: Herodotus states it to be an extraordinary fact, that none of the barbarians fell within the precinct, but that all the bodies were found on profane ground: he gives it as his opinion, that this likewise was a punishment at the hands of the goddess, because the Persians had violated her fane at Eleusis[37]. The commentators do not fail to direct the

[35] Lib. vii. 139. [36] Lib. viii. 129. [37] Lib. ix. 65.

reader's attention to the superstition of the writer: it would certainly be more honest to refer to that noble portion of the work, where Herodotus explains the moral view that he takes of sacred matters. Cambyses, in his invasion of Egypt, had insulted and derided the temples, the gods, and the rites of the inhabitants: Herodotus concludes that he must have been completely reft of his senses, οὐ γὰρ ἂν ἱροῖσί τε καὶ νομαίοισι ἐπεχείρησε καταγελᾶν[a]— a principle which, as a practical philosopher, he proves by an interesting and instructive anecdote. Eloquent and poetical as the opponents of superstition may be in their descriptions of the evils which it produces on the human mind—and the subject is one that affords an easy opportunity of displaying the ornaments of oratory, and working on the passions of men—still they will unquestionably allow that sacrilege, under whatever form, and among whatever people it may occur, is a very wicked crime; so wicked indeed, that one is tempted to regard it, like suicide, as one too horrible to enter the mind of any but a madman: and certainly that historian should not be jeered as superstitious himself, who takes every opportunity of exciting public detestation against such impious deeds: if mistaken in the religious view of the subject, he is, as a pagan, entitled to the compassion of the wise; but the solidity of the moral principle cannot fail to claim their admiration, however it may be railed at by the foolish and inexperienced. Those, on the other hand, who accuse Herodotus of too much credulity, and of attaching implicit faith to the traditions he collected in the various countries he visited, are bound, in justice, to produce classical instances of his believing in the reports he indites. The most instructive mode of conveying an idea of the state and history of any nation, particularly at the time when the Muses were written, was to give fairly the various legends, traditions, and reports credited by the inhabitants, and to leave

[a] Lib. iii. 38.

the reader to judge for himself: this task Herodotus undertook and performed[29], quoting invariably, with the utmost scrupulousness, his authorities[30]: it sometimes indeed happens, that he does give his own opinion, in words which imply much modesty and diffidence[31]; but in none of those cases can he be accused of credulity; on the contrary, those parts of the work are, perhaps, without one exception, so many proofs of his good sense and sound judgment. One of the practical advantages resulting from this manner of handling the subjects is, that the reader certainly obtains, from a perusal of Herodotus, a far more complete knowledge of the state of civilization among distant nations than he would have from reading any philosophical treatise on their character that could have been penned. We must therefore beware, particularly when we consider the object and plan of the whole work, and the success attending its execution, of accusing the Historian too lightly of credulity; for surely it would be not only absurd, but highly dishonest, to stigmatize a modern traveller as sharing in the base and barbarous superstition of the South of Europe, because he affirms that at Naples the common people bring forward many instances of the progress of volcanic torrents and the horrors of a protracted drought being checked by the exposition of St. Januarius's blood. Nor would the indignation of the accused be much diminished, were he told, that he ought to have strung together some common places about superstition, in order to shew that he did not approve of Catholic bigotry. But perhaps more has been said on this subject than is strictly necessary, particularly when we consider the many proofs of sound judgment and critical

[29] Proof: Τοῖσι μὲν νυν ὑπ' Αἰγυπτίων λεγομένοισι χράσθω ὅτῳ τὰ τοιαῦτα πιθανά ἐστι· ἐμοὶ δὲ παρὰ πάντα τὸν λόγον ὑπόκειται, ὅτι τὰ λεγόμενα ὑπ' ἑκάστων ἀκοῇ γράφω. Lib. ii. 123.

[30] Among many other instances, see lib. ii. 32. i. 191. iv. 195. ix. 16. iii. 55. more particularly iv. 32. Perhaps also vi. 117. concerning which last passage the reader may consult Mitford's History of Greece.

[31] ὡς ἐμοί γε δοκέει, lib. vi. 95. and in other passages too numerous to quote.

discrimination which a person well acquainted with the works of Herodotus may bring forward, from the text of his History. He expresses his disbelief of the god's nightly visits to the Babylonian temple[32]: he endeavours to explain physically the curious tradition of the Dodonæans[33]: and over and over again, after the relation of some wonder-working report, we meet with the phrase, Ἐμὶ μὲν νυν ταῦτα λέγοντες οὐ πείθουσι, or something similar[34].

Up to this point of these observations, the object has been, to give some idea of the art and character of Herodotus, considered as a man and a philosopher: it now remains to investigate his qualifications in a cognate though more confined view as an historian: in which therefore it will be necessary to inquire, whether, in his accounts of so many and different nations, and in the commemoration of events extending over such a long range of time, he has exhibited due industry and judgment of research; strict veracity, in inditing the result of his inquiries; and lastly, whether he had adopted such a mode of conveying his information, as may please, interest, and allure his readers. For without much industry and patience, corroborated by a sound judgment, it is impossible that man should ever arrive at historical truth: without truth, history is but a novel: and again, unless truth is decked with the ornaments of a pleasing diction, mankind too frequently turn aside from it with indifference.

INDUSTRY OF HERODOTUS.

Of Herodotus's industry, the History, in its whole, and in each of its parts, bears the most irrefragable proof: he travelled over almost all the countries which it was necessary he should mention, examining with scrupulous attention, as we have before observed, their geographical situations, their productions in all the kingdoms of nature, the

[32] Lib. i. 182.   [33] Lib. ii. 57.   [34] Lib. iv. 105. ii. 121, 5, &c.

manners and religion of the inhabitants; he consulted their monuments, and inscriptions, and historical chronicles; and carefully collected their traditions. He measured himself the Propontis and Euxine Sea[35]; examined carefully the ancient monuments of Egypt, in order to be able to describe them as an eye-witness[36]; and, when he had not the opportunity of personal observation, he consulted the best-informed natives of the countries he visited. Cautious of adopting traditions without sufficient authority, he spared no pains to obtain all possible evidence to warrant a correct inference: thus he travelled, he tells us, from Memphis to Heliopolis, and from Heliopolis to Thebes, expressly to ascertain whether the priests of the last two places would agree with those of Memphis: θέλων εἰδέναι εἰ συμβήσονται τοῖσι λόγοισι τοῖσι ἐν Μέμφι[37]. The Second Book affords likewise another remarkable instance of his anxiety to come at the truth, and of the patience which he exposed to all the obstacles that stood in his way. He had heard from the priests of Egypt an account of the antiquity of the worship of Hercules, which was calculated to startle a Greek: desirous of arriving at the truth in a point so important, as connected with the religion of his country, he proceeded to Tyre, and from thence to the island of Thasos, two places celebrated for the antiquity of their temples of Hercules: finding that the traditions of the Egyptian, Tyrian, and Thasian priests pretty nearly agreed, he concluded, with good reason, that those Greeks acted more consonantly to probability who possessed two temples of Hercules, one of the hero, and the other of the god[38]. Another equally convincing proof of the care and industry with which Herodotus pursued his historical researches may be deduced from the evident attention with which he examined almost all the celebrated temples existing in his day; most of which he describes as an eye-witness[39]. For in those ancient

---

[35] Lib. iv. 86. [36] Lib. ii. 148, et passim. [37] Lib. ii. 3.
[38] Lib. ii. 44. [39] See lib. i. 51. viii. 33, &c.

times, almost all remarkable events were transmitted to posterity by means of inscriptions engraved on durable monuments, and tripods dedicated in the temples. As an example of the judgment with which those researches were conducted, it will suffice to refer to that part of the History where Herodotus discusses the probability of the use of writing having been introduced in Greece by the Phœnicians[40].

VERACITY OF HERODOTUS.

It can hardly be doubted, that one who took such pains to ascertain the truth, would be equally scrupulous in offering nothing but the truth to his reader; and indeed, strange as it may sound to those who have been in the habit of hearing Herodotus stigmatized as a liar, by persons who ought to know better, there probably is no author, whether ancient or modern, (the inspired writers excepted,) who deserve to be placed before him in the scale of truth and accuracy. Not, however, that it is to be supposed, that every thing contained in the Nine Books is strictly true, or even was thought to be so by the author himself. " It is my duty," he says in one place, " to relate " all that is reported; although I am not, at all events, " obliged to give credit to every thing: this observation " I would have to be applied throughout this History:" Ἐγὼ δὲ ὀφείλω λέγειν τὰ λεγόμενα, πείθεσθαί γε μὲν ὦν οὐ παντάπασι ὀφείλω· καί μοι τοῦτο τὸ ἔπος ἐχέτω ἐς πάντα τὸν λόγον[41]. It is therefore, in all fairness, necessary, that before we accuse Herodotus of a wish to deceive in any particular passage of his History, we should first ascertain whether he is speaking on his own authority, or on that of others: for this the original text must be referred to; because the modern languages not admitting of that syntactical flexibility by which a long narration may be governed by one verb at the beginning, it must often happen that the translator is obliged to represent Herodotus as

[40] Lib. v. 57—61.   [41] Lib. vii. 152. Compare lib. ii. 123.

xxxii VERACITY OF HERODOTUS.

speaking in his own name, while he really is only relating what he has heard from others: for instance, in the long tale about Rhampsinitus, king of Egypt, and the sons of the architect, a person who would only consult a modern translation might naturally be led to believe that the whole is stated by Herodotus on his own authority; whereas in the Greek, the structure of every sentence recalls to the reader's attention, that the writer is only repeating what he had heard from the Egyptian priests; or, to use the grammatical terms, that each infinitive is governed by ἔλεγον at the head of the chapter[42].

The interior evidence, therefore, of the veracity of the History of Herodotus consists in the visible care with which he always quotes his authorities[43]; his attention to mark his own opinion, whenever he thinks proper to offer it[44]; and his upright and frank avowal of being unable to give any certain information to his reader, when his researches have not enabled him to obtain any that he could rely upon[45]. This evidence is so convincing, that it is by no means to the honour of the ancients that so many among them should have treated the Historian as a fabulist: that the pretended learned, however, among the moderns should cherish a similar opinion, can only be accounted for on the supposition that their ignorance equals their presumption. D'Anville and Rennell, among geographers; Shaw, Parke, Browne, Belzoni, among travellers; Cuvier, among naturalists; all bear their powerful testimony to the astonishing accuracy of the Father of History. It is now too late to laugh at Herodotus, when he asserts that Africa is a peninsula[46], or when he states that the Niger was reported to flow from the west[47]. His descriptions of the crocodile[48], the hippopotamus[49], the method of embalming bodies[50], are all found to be perfectly exact, by modern

---

[42] Lib. ii. 121. [43] See note 30, p. xxviii. [44] See note 31, p. xxviii.
[45] οὐκ ἔχω ἀτρεκέως εἰπεῖν, i. 57, 160. ii. 103. viii. 8, &c.
[46] Lib. iv. 42. [47] Lib. ii. 32. [48] Lib. ii. 68, seq.
[49] Lib. ii. 71. [50] Lib. ii. 86.

naturalists: it is even now said, that the ants mentioned in the Third Book[51], as throwing up the gold sand, have been recognised lately in the animal called the *corsac*[52], a sort of dog or fox: so true is the remark made by the illustrious Boerhaave, in shewing the possibility of the account of the fountain in the country of the Macrobian Ethiopians[53] being true : " Hodiernæ observationes probant fere omnia MAGNI VERI dicta[54]." Those, therefore, who join in the trite and old cry of falsehood against Herodotus, in this day, give no slight evidence of their own vanity and presumption: in ancient times, indeed, when the world was little known, men might be excused, if they brought the accusation against an author, who was not only a great traveller, but likewise too honest to follow the poet's precept:

Οὔ τοι ἅπασα κερδίων
φαίνοισα πρόσωπον ἀλάθει᾽ ἀτρεκής.
Καὶ τὸ σιγᾶν πολλάκις ἐστὶ σοφώ-
τατον ἀνθρώπων νοῆσαι[55].

But, in examining how far an historian is entitled to the confidence of his readers, there are two questions, to which the attention must be particularly directed; namely, 1. Whether he is blindly partial to any particular country? 2. Whether he is inclined to favour any particular system of political government? Patriotic and political prejudices, however necessary to tighten the bonds of human society, ought to be carefully excluded from history; the main object of which is, to unfold the nature of man, as acted upon by different religions, climates, and governments. When, however, the writer of history starts with

[51] Lib. iii. 102. [52] Miot. Traduction d'Hérodote. p. xxiv.
[53] Lib. iii. 23. [54] Boerhaave, Elementa Chymiæ, quoted by Wesseling.
[55] Pind. Nem. Carm. v. 30, seqq. Herodotus was aware of the prudence of the maxim: ἐκ δὲ αὐγχρου καὶ ευτάμου ἔστι τι δένδρον μέγεθος γίνεται, ἕξαιρευτάμενοι, μνήμην οὐ ποιήσομαι· εὖ εἰδὼς ὅτι τοῖσι μὴ ἐντυχμέναισι ἐς τὴν Βαβυλωνίων χώρην, καὶ τὰ εἰρημένα κάρτα ἐχόμενα ἐς ἀπιστίην πολλὴν ἀπίκται. Lib. i. 193.

the design of shewing the superiority of any particular society of men, or of any particular form of government, it generally happens, that the love of system gives a tincture to statements, even accurate in themselves, which hinders the reader from detecting the truth. It is another merit of Herodotus, that his work is free from such defects: he praises and censures by turns all the nations he has to mention, and leaves the reader to frame his own judgment respecting their comparative ranks in the scale of moral and political discipline. He has been accused of harbouring a grudge against the Corinthians: that people of merchants was not, probably, an object of great interest to a man of elegant acquirements and refined taste; and, from the eagerness with which Herodotus seems to seize every opportunity of producing such facts as may deteriorate the respect for their national character, one might also be tempted to suppose that the charge brought against him was not entirely unfounded. But even the parts of the History connected with this people afford ample evidence of his honest and upright mode of dealing: the Corinthians are represented as playing by far the most honourable and decisive part in the conference of the Lacedæmonian confederates, respecting the expediency of replacing the Pisistratidæ in the tyranny of Athens:—" If you persist," says the Corinthian representative to the hankerers after universal power, " if you " persist in endeavouring to replace Hippias on his " throne, know that the Corinthians will not second you:" ἴστε ὑμῖν Κορινθίους γε οὐ συναινέοντας[56]. Again, after pourtraying in vivid colours, perhaps indeed too vivid, the dastardly conduct of Adimantus, the Corinthian admiral, at the battle of Salamis, he takes care to state, that he speaks from the authority of the Athenians, whose report was contradicted by the universal testimony of Greece[57].

[56] Lib. v. 92.   [57] Lib. viii. 94. See likewise ix. 102.

But perhaps, after all, the greatest proof that can be adduced of the veracity and impartiality of Herodotus is the recitation of his History at the Olympic games. This event seems to be too well authenticated to admit of any doubt: its probability is likewise not a little increased by the evident marks which the History itself bears of having been composed for the purpose of recitation: hence those pleonastic sentences so often occurring at the termination of the different branches of the narrative; such as, τοσαῦτα μὲν θυωμάτων πέρι εἰρήσθω[58], and many others too frequent to enumerate: they are in Herodotus much more numerous than might even be expected in an author that wrote before paragraphic divisions came into vogue; and can only be accounted for under the supposition, that they were intended to direct the attention of the hearer to those parts where the narrative changes its subject. Now, at the time that Herodotus read his History at the Olympic games, it was only one hundred years since Cyrus had destroyed the empire of the Medes; not more than ninety-seven since he had conquered Crœsus; not more than seventy since Cyrus himself had died; and about thirty-six years since Xerxes commenced his expedition against Greece. It may therefore be assumed, that, among the persons composing the audience of the Historian, there must have been some individuals who had actually shared in the war, and many who were acquainted, by immediate tradition, with all the events of that glorious struggle: unless, then, Herodotus had stated the truth, particularly in every thing respecting the Greek nations, there can be no doubt that some person would have been found to have contradicted the eloquent but false narrator: had that been the case, some of the detractors, whom the well-earned fame of Herodotus excited against him in subsequent times, would not have failed to make proper use of a circumstance so favourable to their own designs: but Plutarch, the

---

[58] Lib. iii. 112.

most bitter of the critics of Herodotus, who even grasps at the opportunity afforded by the use of equivocal terms[59] to ground his accusation against Herodotus of malignity, and whose disgraceful tract subsists to this day, mentions no such circumstance: it is therefore highly probable that no such contradictor was found. The whole of Greece assembled must consequently have been convinced of the veracity of the History; and surely modern readers cannot require a safer warrant of its authenticity, so far at least as the Grecian history is in any respect concerned.

POLITICAL PRINCIPLES OF HERODOTUS.

As to the political principles of Herodotus, he has explained them too clearly for the most careless reader to be in doubt what they really were: he was a republican: this is proved, not only by the events of his life, but likewise by his own words: δηλοῖ δὲ οὐ κατ' ἓν μοῦνον, ἀλλὰ πανταχῇ, ἡ ἰσηγορίη ὡς ἔστι χρῆμα σπουδαῖον[60]. The truth of which observation he illustrates by the rapid rise of the Athenian commonwealth, after the expulsion of the tyrants. We must beware, however, of attributing an improper and too extensive sense to the word *isagoria*: it certainly means, in Herodotus, nothing more than the even-handed award of justice according to law, and the equal right, possessed by all citizens, of raising themselves to rank in the state, by the proper cultivation of the talents with which Providence may have blessed them. This liberty was incompatible with the existence of the τύραννος, who was obliged to ensure the possession of an usurped throne by the partiality of favour shewn to his own creatures: it might, however, be co-existent with the βασιλεύς, as at Sparta for instance, where, although there were two kings[61], the law was the sole master, both over the kings and the subjects[62]. The Historian even appears anxious,

---

[59] See Wesseling's note on lib. ix. 63, 3. vol. iv. p. 1090. Gaisford's edit.
[60] Lib. v. 78.   [61] Lib. vi. 52.   [62] Lib. vii. 104.

in different places, to impress on the Grecian readers a fact which they seem to have been unwilling to believe; namely, that the Persian nation were not without the true feelings of liberty. In the Third Book, the seven grandees, having put the Magi to death, hold counsel on what form of government it will be expedient to adopt, now that the direct line from Cyrus is extinct: the respective speakers shew the advantages of a democracy, of an aristocracy, of a monarchy: the proposal of retaining the monarchical form of government at last prevails. It would be the height of folly to suppose that the very words written by the Historian were really spoken by the orators: the intention of Herodotus was, no doubt, to shew the Greeks, that people who have as good ideas of the advantages of liberty as those on which the best republicans are wont to pride themselves, may choose, owing to various circumstances, to subject themselves to a monarchy: indeed, have we not seen the reasoning of Darius exemplified, in its minutest details, by the Revolution of France? This fact, however, some of the Grecians were unwilling to allow: hence the strong expression of the Historian— καὶ ἐλέχθησαν λόγοι ἄπιστοι μὲν ἐνίοισι Ἑλλήνων, ἐλέχθησαν δ' ὦν[63]. Mardonius, the Persian satrap, gives a democratical constitution to the Ionian states; an extraordinary circumstance in the eyes of the Greek republicans; which Herodotus takes care[64] to produce, as a corroboration of the probability of the sentiments placed in the mouths of the conspirators against the Magi. Although a republican, therefore, by principle, Herodotus was willing to allow that every nation knew best what government was fitting for itself: "For," says he, in one place, "were one "to offer all nations to make their choice of the best laws "out of all codes, they would each, after mature reflection, "select their own; so convinced in every nation that its "own institutions are much the best[65]." It must not be

[63] Lib. iii. 80. [64] Lib. vi. 43. [65] Lib. iii. 38.

inferred, however, that Herodotus approved that pliable maxim, which travellers have not unfrequently made the excuse for disgraceful conduct; namely, to fit one's behaviour to the customs of the country one may happen to be residing in for a time; or, according to the foolish proverb, "To do at Rome, as Rome does." Herodotus mentions the courageous manner in which the Spartans, sent to Xerxes as a satisfaction for the heralds who had been murdered, upheld the dignity of their national usages[66], with as much high-minded pride as an Englishman could relate the very same conduct exemplified in the ambassador of his own nation to the court of China.

STYLE OF HERODOTUS.

It can scarcely be necessary to say any thing on the beauties of the diction of Herodotus, as on this subject both the ancients and moderns are all agreed. Dionysius of Halicarnassus, a good judge on these points, assigns to Herodotus the same rank and class in style among historians, as to Homer among the epic poets, to Sophocles among the tragedians, and to Demosthenes among the orators. Herodotus wrote for the people; his object, therefore, was to instruct; hence simplicity and clearness are the main and distinctive features of his style: if he has to describe any place, he takes, as it were, the reader by the hand, and leads him over it: in his descriptions of the actions of men, he selects precisely the language befitting their station, their age, and their rank; and in the art of making his personages display character in their discourses, he has been excelled by none but Shakspeare, although perhaps equalled in the modern day by the author of the Scotch novels. In short, in his language, as well as in every thing else, Herodotus gives manifest proof that his knowledge was acquired by actual and direct intercourse with mankind, and not with books. It was this

[66] Lib. vii.

practical knowledge that enabled him to discover and believe that the Phœnicians had circumnavigated Africa, and that the Caspian was a sea of itself; two important truths, which Strabo, a most respectable and learned writer of later times, could not be brought to admit. To this practical knowledge he was likewise indebted for the easy freedom and sweet simplicity of his style; which, compared with the studied elegancies of some writers, are as much superior, as the healthy breeze of the open field is to the perfumed air of a confined apartment.

CONCLUSION.

In this Translation of the Works of Herodotus, the object has been, to give a correct version of the original, in as simple and clear language as possible; simplicity and clearness being regarded as the most striking characteristics of style in the original. The Notes have been composed in the two-fold view, of illustrating the meaning of the Historian, and of explaining the grammatical construction of his language. The comments of the latter class have been written principally with the view of directing the attention of the student in Greek to the peculiarities of structure in the text; lest, prompted by indolence, he should imagine that a perusal of a translation may answer the purpose of a careful study of the author himself.

P. E. L.

BOOK I.

CLIO.

SUMMARY OF BOOK I.

HERODOTUS, *intending to develope the causes of the hostility between the Greeks and the Barbarians, in the first place records the mutual rapes of women committed by the two parties: that of Io, 1; that of Europa and Medea, 2; that of Helen, 3: in doing which, he states the accounts given both by the Persians and the Phœnicians. Then, as Crœsus, king of the Lydians, was the first to attack the Greeks with arms, 5, he enters on the Lydian history, 6. The first kings of the Lydians, then, sprang from Atys; the second dynasty from Hercules, 7; the last of whom, Candaules, having been killed by Gyges, 8—12, the kingdom is transferred to the Mermnadæ. Then follows the history of Gyges, 13, 14; that of Ardys, 15, under whose reign the Cimmerians made an irruption into Asia, and took Sardis, 15; that of Sadyattes, 16; that of Alyattes, 18, 25, who expelled the Cimmerians from Asia. Digressions are interposed, relating to Thrasybulus, the tyrant of Miletus; and Periander, the tyrant of Corinth; cotemporary with whom was Arion, saved by a dolphin, 20—24. Alyattes is succeeded by his son Crœsus, 26, who subjugates the Asiatic Greeks, and extends his power over the whole of Asia, as far as the Halys, 26—28. Crœsus is admonished unsuccessfully, by Solon of Athens, to hold no one happy, until he have ended life in happiness, 29—33. Crœsus is visited with great calamity: his son Atys is killed, unwittingly, in the chase, by Adrastus, a Phrygian refugee, 34—45. The Medes having been conquered by Cyrus, Crœsus, alarmed at the growing power of the Persians, first sends round to make trial of the oracles of the Greeks, 46—52; and then consults about levying war against Cyrus: an ambiguous answer is returned, which Crœsus interprets as favourable to himself; and therefore undertakes the expedition, first sending to court the alliance of the Greeks, the chief nations of whom, at that time, were the Athenians and Lacedæmonians: the former* sprung from the Pelasgi, the latter from the Hellenes, 56, seq. The empire of the Athenians was then held by Pisistratus, 59—64; the Lacedæmonians had received excellent laws from Lycurgus, 65, and conquered the Tegeans, 66, seq. The Lacedæmonians frame an alliance with Crœsus, 69. Crœsus crosses the Halys, and engages Cyrus with dubious success in the Pterian plain, 75, seq. Returning from Sardis, he sends for assistance from the Egyptians, Babylonians, and Lacedæmonians, 77. Cyrus meanwhile follows rapidly on the heels of Crœsus; conquers the Lydian army before the town; besieges Sardis, which he takes, together with Crœsus himself, 79—85. The country and manners of the Lydians are briefly described, 93, seq. The history then passes to Cyrus, 95. The empire of Asia had been five hundred and twenty years in the hands of the Assyrians: the Medes were the first to assert their freedom: their example was followed by other nations. The Medes, after eleven years of anarchy, choose Deioces for their king, 95—101. He is succeeded by Phraortes, 102: Phraortes is succeeded by Cyaxares, who expels the Scythians, who had taken possession of Asia; and subjects the Assyrians, 103—106. Astyages, the son of Cyaxares, admonished by a dream, gives his daughter Mandane in marriage to a Persian, Cambyses: he delivers the child born of that marriage to Harpagus, with orders to put it to death: Harpagus gives the child to a herdsman, with orders to expose it; but the herdsman, prevailed upon by his own wife, educates the child as his own. Cyrus, thus preserved, having reached his tenth year, is recognised by his grandfather Astyages, and sent safe into Persia: Harpagus, however, is punished in a most cruel manner, 107—121. Harpagus, desirous of being avenged of the injury he had received at the hands of Astyages, prompts Cyrus to rise up against his grandfather: Cyrus excites the Persians to rebellion, 122—126. The Medes are routed in two battles, and Astyages himself is taken prisoner, 127—130. The manners of the Persians are described, 131—140. After conquering Crœsus, Cyrus directs his arms against the Asiatic Greeks; but before the Historian describes the war, he gives an account of the situation of Ionia, the origin, institution, and manners of its inhabitants, 142—148; the same with respect to Æolis, 149. Cyrus, having once more subdued the Lydians, who had rebelled, 154—160, sends Harpagus against the Ionians, among whom the Phocæans and Teians forsake their towns, and establish themselves elsewhere: the rest submit: 162—170. Caria and Lycia are next subdued, 171—176. In the mean time, Cyrus in person subdues Upper Asia: description of Babylon, and history of Semiramis and Nitocris, 177—187. Cyrus conquers the Babylonians in battle; drives them within the city, which he besieges, and captures by stratagem, 188—191. In this place, the territory of the Babylonians, their institutions, laws, manners, diet, &c. are described, 192—200. At last, Cyrus, carrying war against the Massagetæ, crosses the Araxes, and is slain by Queen Tomyris, 201 to the end.

THE

FIRST BOOK OF HERODOTUS.

CLIO.

HERODOTUS of Halicarnassus[1] here makes known the result of his researches and inquiries[2]: in order that the deeds of men may not be obliterated by time, nor the great and wonderful works, achieved by both Hellenes and barbarians, be reft of renown: among other subjects, he will explain the cause that gave rise to the spirit of war between them[3].

The Persians, skilled in history[4], assert, therefore, that the Phœnicians were the original authors of this feud. For these people, having migrated from the Erythrian sea, as it is called, to the Mediterranean[5], and settled in the country that they now inhabit, applied forthwith to long navigations: exporting Egyptian and Assyrian merchandize, they touched at various places; among others, at Argos, a town which, in those days, surpassed, in every respect[6], all in the country now called Hellas[7]. Having arrived at this town

---

[1] Matt. Gr. Gram. 273.
[2] Literally: " this is the narrative or history of Herodotus."
[3] See Schweigh. Not. Herod. vol. iii. p. 4.
[4] Λέγουσι δὲ τῆς ἱστορίης ἔμπειροι. Hesych.
[5] " This sea;" that is to say, the Mediterranean. ' The Erythrian' or Red Sea; answering to the present Indian Ocean, and comprising the present Red Sea or Gulf of Arabia, the Persian Gulf, and the Bay of Bengal. Herod. iv. 39. vii. 89.

[6] Matt. 404. 6. προέχω, to excel, to surpass; with the genitive of that over which it excels, and the dative of the thing in which it excelled. Schweigh. in Lex. Herod.—Larcher translates, " That town surpassed then all those in the country, &c."; and, in a note, observes, that in the phrase προεῖχε ἔργοισι τῶν ἐν τῇ Ἑλλάδι, τῶν is necessarily governed by ἔργων.
[7] Thucyd. i. 2, 3. βάρβαρος, " an alien—a non-Hellenian." Herod. ii. 158.

of Argos, the Phœnicians, we are told, spread forth their cargo; and on the fifth or sixth day from their coming, when they had nearly disposed of their cargo, several women came down to the sea-side; among whom was the king's daughter, whose name, according to the Phœnicians as well as the Hellenes, was Io, daughter of Inachus. While these women were standing near the stern of the vessel, and chaffering[8] such wares as took most their fancy, the Phœnicians, shouting to one another, made a sally on them: the consequence was, although most of the women made their escape, the sailors seized Io, together with a few others, threw them on board the vessel, and set sail for Egypt[9]. Thus, varying from the Hellenic account, the Persians describe the departure of Io into Egypt; and to this refer the first beginning of unlawful violence. Subsequently, they say, certain Hellenes—for they are unable to produce their names—landed at Tyre in Phœnicia, and carried off the king's daughter, Europa. These men were, in all probability, Cretans. In so acting, they certainly did no more than like for like: but after these events, the Hellenes were the authors of the second instance of violence: for they came, in a long ship[10], to Æa, on the river Phasis, in Colchis; from whence, after despatching the other business for which they had come, they carried off the king's daughter, Medea. The Colchian prince[11], in consequence, sent into Hellas a herald, to demand justice of the rape, and claim back his daughter: the Hellenes, however, made answer, that as those of Asia had not given satisfaction for the violence shewn to Io of Argos, so neither would they, on their part, give any to them. It is also said, that, in the second generation following these events, Alexander[12] the son of Priam, having heard of these occurrences, determined to procure himself, by force, a wife out of Hellas; being fully convinced that he should not be compelled to make any reparation, inasmuch as the Hellenes themselves had not done so. Alexander, accordingly, stole Helena; and the Hellenes thought proper to send instantly messengers to reclaim Helena, and demand justice for such an outrage; but the other party

---

[8] Matt. 342. Herod. v. 6.
[9] Matt. 554.
[10] " Long ship;" built long and narrow, for the purpose of velocity: the merchant vessels were more round, for stowage. The long vessels were vessels of war; the round vessels, merchantmen and transports. Πλοίῳ στρογγύλῳ. φορτηγῷ ὁπλοντοτι· μακρὰ γὰρ τὰ πολεμικὰ ὀνομάζουσιν. Ulpian. in Orat. Dem. contra Lept. p. 599, E. *Larcher.*
[11] " The Colchian:" understand, ' ruler,' ' sovereign,' or ' prince.'
[12] More generally known by the name of Paris.

replied to the proposers[13], by "objecting the rape of Medea; "that, not having themselves given satisfaction, nor made "the required restitution, they should expect such redress "from others." Until then, therefore, nothing had occurred between the two races, say the Persians, with the exception merely of a few rapes: but, from that period, the Hellenes were, in truth, greatly to blame; being the first to levy war against Asia, ere they of Asia made any attack on Europe: now they hold it to be the crime of a wicked man, to ravish women; but that of a simpleton, to trouble one's self about revenge; for prudent men ought to take no account of such females; since it is evident, that, without their own consent, they could not be forced: the Persians consequently declare, that they of Asia never troubled themselves about women that are stolen away; whereas the Hellenes, for the sake of a Lacedæmonian girl, collected an immense fleet, and then, passing over into Asia, overthrew the power of Priam. From that time, they have considered the Hellenic race as their foes: for the Persians claim[14] Asia, and the there residing foreign tribes, as belonging to themselves; while they regard Europe, and the Hellenic people, as wholly distinct.

Such is the account of the Persians; and to the capture of Troy they attribute their antipathy to the Hellenes. The Phœnicians, on the other hand, do not assent to the Persian statement concerning Io: they affirm, they made no use of violence[15] to remove her into Egypt; but that, having formed a connexion with the master of the merchant-vessel, she found herself with child; and dreading, in consequence, the rebukes of her parents, sailed away, of her own accord, with the Phœnicians, to avoid detection. The above, therefore, are the accounts of the Persians and the Phœnicians. It is not my intention, however, to decide whether things were so, or otherwise; but I shall now, after previously pointing out the man I myself know to have been the first to commit deeds of violence against the Hellenes, proceed on the sequel of my History, touching alike the small and the large estates of men: for of such as were of old and mighty, many have become weak; while of those flourishing in my day, many were originally insignificant: conscious, therefore, of the universal frailty of human prosperity, I shall commemorate both impartially.

---

[13] προϊσχομένων, instead of the dative agreeing with σφι. So, a little below, occurs a similar anacolouthia, ἀπαιτέοντων for ἀπαιτέουσι. See Schweigh. Not. Herod. vol. iii. p. 9.
[14] οἰκηιοῦνται, "claim for themselves." See Herod. i. 94. ix. 15.
[15] Matt. 413.

6   Crœsus was by birth a Lydian, son of Alyattes, and had usurped[16] the supremacy over the nations within the Halys, a river that runs between the Syrians[17] and Paphlagonians, from south to north, and falls into the Euxine sea. This Crœsus was the first of the aliens, we know of, that subjected any of the Hellenes to the payment of tribute, and united others to himself by alliance. He not only reduced the Ionian, Æolian, and Dorian settlers in Asia, but also framed a treaty of friendship with the Lacedæmonians. Previous to Crœsus's empire, all the Hellenes had been free; for the expedition of the Cimmerians, which was anterior to Crœsus, although directed against Ionia, was not so much a subjugation of states, as an irruption, having rapine for its object[18].

7   The empire, which had previously been in the possession of the Heraclidæ, passed over to the line of Crœsus, called the Mermnadæ, in the following manner. Candaules, named Myrsilus by the Hellenes, was tyrant of Sardis, and a descendant of Alcæus the son of Hercules: for Agron son of Ninus, grandson of Belus, great-grandson of Alcæus, was the first king of Sardis on the Heraclid line, and Candaules son of Myrsus the last. The previous rulers of this country, predecessors of Agron, were the progeny of Lydus son of Atys; from whom the whole nation, originally called Mæonians, took the name of Lydians. The Heraclidæ, sprung from a female-slave of Jardanus and from Hercules, having been entrusted with the affairs[19] by the above family, seized the power, according to an oracular behest: they ruled for twenty-two generations[20] of men, five hundred and five years; the son inheriting the throne from the father, down to Candaules

8   the son of Myrsus. This Candaules, therefore, was enamoured of his wife: impelled by his love, he fancied to himself that she was by far the most beautiful of all women. I must first observe[21], that one of his body-guards, Gyges

---

[16] τύραννος, the usurper over a people once free or under a βασιλεύς: it applies sometimes even to a ruler invested with conditional power only: "Omnes autem et habentur et dicuntur *tyranni*, qui potestate perpetuâ in eâ civitate, quæ libertate usa sit." Cor. Nep. Miltiad.

[17] The Syrians (not to be confounded with Tyrians), or Leuco-Syri, are the same as the Cappadocians. Herod. i. 72.

[18] The irruption here alluded to occurred under the reign of the Lydian Ardys. Herod. i. 15.

[19] ἐπιτραφθέντες, aor. i. pass. of ἐπι-τρέπομαι, *meæ curæ traditur—mihi committitur*: ᾧ λαοὶ ἐπιτετράφαται, Hom. Il. ii. 25. *cui populi commissi sunt*. Herodotus often uses this expression: ii. 121. iii. 155, 157, etc. *Larcher.*

[20] The word γενεά is, apparently, here taken in a sense somewhat different from what it bears in other places (Herod. ii. 143); but, for the actual reigns from father to son, twenty-three years each, on an average.

[21] Concerning this hyperbaton, consult Matt. 613. iv; and more particularly Schweigh. Not. Herod. vol. iii. p. 22, at the bottom.

the son of Dascylus, was his particular favourite; to whom he was wont to confide his more important affairs, and exaggerating especially his consort's beauty to this person. Candaules, after a brief lapse of time, (for he was doomed to be miserable,) addressed Gyges in these words: "Gyges, I think "you give me no credit, when I attempt to describe to you "the beauties of my wife: the ears of men, we know, are "more incredulous than their eyes: I will have you see her "naked." Gyges, uttering a loud exclamation, replied: "My lord! what unseemly language do you hold, enjoining "me to cast my eyes on my naked queen! At the same "time woman strips off her garments, she casts off her "modesty also. Our fathers of old devised the maxims of "virtue, and it is our duty to follow them: among these is "this saying, 'Let every man look to his own concerns.' I "firmly believe this lady to be the most beautiful in the "world, but entreat you not to exact any thing wicked²²." By this reply, Gyges sought to combat the proposal, dreading 9 that some harm might accrue to himself. But the king resumed in these words: "Take courage, my Gyges: be not "fearful that I have any design to tempt you by this dis- "course: be not alarmed at any disagreeable consequences "to yourself, on the part of my wife. First and foremost²³, "I will take care she shall not even know that she has been "seen by you. I will place you in the room we sleep in, "behind the open door; and when I enter, and my wife fol- "lows me to bed, there stands hard by the entrance an arm- "chair²⁴, on which she will lay each of her garments, as she "casts them off: there, at your leisure, you may take the op- "portunity of looking at her; and when she steps from the "chair towards the bed, you will be at her back: then, have "a care, and mind she do not get a glimpse of you, as you go "out by the door." Gyges was unable to evade: he held him- 10 self therefore ready. Candaules, on the other hand, when he thought it was time to go to bed, took Gyges into the sleeping-chamber; and immediately after, the lady made her appearance, and Gyges saw her as she came in and laid her clothes on the chair: the lady, turning then her back to him, stepped forward to the bed; and he crept softly out; but she spied him as he went away. She saw what her husband had been doing; but modesty restrained her from crying out, nor did she shew any emotion²⁵, being determined to have revenge on Can-

---

²² See Herod. iii. 44. Matt. 330, 332.
²³ ἀρχὴν, without the article, for ἐν ἀρχῇ.
²⁴ θρόνος, an arm-chair with a foot-board; the seat of dignity, the king's throne, the judge's bench.
²⁵ Rather, "she pretended total ignorance of what had occurred."

daules: for among the Lydians, and even almost all other foreign nations, it is held a great disgrace, for a man even, to 11 be seen naked. She accordingly held her peace for the time, and made nothing known; but as soon as day dawned, she ordered such of her household as she saw were the most attached to her person to be ready, and summoned Gyges to her presence. He, fancying she knew nothing of what had taken place, came as soon as he was called: indeed, he was wont, even before, to attend whenever the queen sent for him. As soon as Gyges arrived, the lady addressed him thus: " Here, Gyges, I give you your choice of two ways, " that are open to you: take which you like: for, either " you shall put to death Candaules, and take possession of " myself and the Lydian throne, or you shall yourself perish " by the hands of these[26]: thus, obeying Candaules in all " things, you may hereafter behold no more what is not " lawful to you. Therefore, either he that gave such counsel " shall be cut off; or you, who have seen me naked, and have " done what is not decent." Gyges stood some time amazed at this speech: then he besought the queen not to chain him down to the necessity of such a choice: he was, however, unable to persuade, but saw before his eyes the necessity in which he was placed, either to destroy his master, or to be destroyed himself by others: he elected, therefore, to survive; and so put the following question: " Since you compel me, " however against my will, to murder my lord and master, " come, let me hear also in what manner we shall lay our " hands on him." The queen resumed, and said: " The onset " shall be from the very spot where he exhibited me naked: 12 " the blow shall be struck when he lies asleep." The plot thus laid, at nightfall (for she would not let Gyges go, and he had no mode of escape, being forced either to kill Candaules or be himself killed) he followed the lady to the bedroom: she put a dagger in his hand, and concealed him behind the same door: some time after, when Candaules was asleep, Gyges crept up to him, and, inflicting a mortal thrust, won both the woman and the kingdom. [Of this event, Archilochus, who flourished about this period, has made 13 mention, in an iambic trimeter poem.] Gyges obtained, accordingly, the power; in which he was confirmed by the authority of the Delphian oracle; for the Lydians, exasperated at the murder of Candaules, were up in arms; and the partisans of Gyges came to these terms with the rest of the

[26] οὕτω, " thus:" she seems to have pointed to her attendants; who stood prepared to kill him, if he hesitated to accept the proposal.

Lydians, that if the oracle should declare Gyges king of the Lydians, he should rule; if not, he was to give back the power again to the Heraclidæ. Accordingly, the oracle acknowledged Gyges, and so he became king: it must be observed, however, that the Pythia added, 'Vengeance would be vouchsafed to the Heraclidæ on the fifth generation of Gyges;' but of this prophecy neither the Lydians nor their kings took any account, until it was fulfilled[27].

Such, therefore, was the way in which the Mermnadæ possessed themselves of the supreme power, and deprived the Heraclidæ. Gyges, become sovereign, sent no inconsiderable gifts to Delphi; most of the silver offerings at that shrine are his[28]: but, besides the silver, he dedicated also abundance of gold; and, among the rest, what[29] is especially deserving of mention, are the wine-bowls[30] of gold, consecrated by him, six in number. These wine-bowls stand in the treasury of the Corinthians, and are thirty talents in weight.—Correctly speaking, however, this treasury does not belong to the whole Corinthian people, but is that of Cypselus son of Eetion.—This Gyges was the first alien, we know of, that made any dedications at Delphi, with the exception of Midas son of Gordius, king of Phrygia; for that prince dedicated the royal throne on which he sat in judgment, an object worthy of being looked at. This throne lies in the same place as the wine-bowls of Gyges. The gold and silver presented by Gyges are by the Delphians denominated Gygads[31], from the founder's name. This prince, after his accession to the throne, made also an inroad on Miletus and Smyrna, and captured the fort of Colophon. He performed no other great action, during his reign of forty years, all but two; I shall therefore dismiss him, having said thus much. I must however mention Ardys, the son and successor of Gyges: he took Priene, and invaded Miletus. During the time that he ruled[32] at Sardis, the Cimmerians, driven from their seats by the Scythians, came into Asia, and obtained possession of Sardis, the citadel excepted.

Ardys, after a reign of fifty years, all but one[33], was succeeded by his son Sadyattes, who occupied the throne during

---

[27] See Herod. i. 94.
[28] The construction is perhaps this: ἀλλ' ἴσα μὲν ἐστιν ἀναθήματα ἀργύρεα ἐν Δελφοῖς, τούτων τὰ πλεῖστα ἐστιν οἱ. But see Matt. 445, c.
[29] ἐῶ for οὗ. Matt. 291.
[30] The crater was a bowl in which water and wine were mixed: it was usually placed on a tripod: but sometimes was made with a foot or stand, like a goblet.
[31] Matt. 414. 2, b.
[32] Matt. 337. Comp. Herod. i. 23, 59.
[33] Matt. 141. obs. 1.

twelve years: Sadyattes was succeeded by Alyattes. This prince [Alyattes] waged war against Cyaxares[34], a descendant of Deïoces, and against the Medes: he drove the Cimmerians out of Asia: he took Smyrna, a city peopled from Colophon, and invaded Clazomenæ: from this last, however, he came off, not as he wished[35], being sorely beaten. The other actions most deserving of description, performed by this 17 king during his reign, are these. He inherited from his father[36], and followed up, the war against the people of Miletus, overrunning and harassing their territory in the manner I am going to relate. At the time the fruits were ripe on the ground, he marched his troops into the country, to the sound of fifes and stringed instruments, and of flutes masculine and feminine[37]. When Alyattes entered Milesia, he would not pull down the farm-houses scattered about the fields, nor set fire to them, nor wrench the doors, but left them standing as they were: on the other hand, he never returned until he had destroyed all the plants and fruits of the earth; for this reason, that the Milesians prevailing by sea, a blockade by the land-forces would be impracticable. The motive, however, that led the Lydian prince not to pull down the houses, was, that the Milesians might come from the city to till and sow the ground; so that, when he renewed his inroads, he should, in consequence of their husbandry, 18 have something to plunder. Acting thus, he carried on the war eleven years; in the course of which, two great defeats befel the Milesians; one at the battle of Limenaïum in their own territory, the other in the plain of the Mæander. During six years, therefore, of the eleven, Sadyattes the son of Ardys still occupied the throne of Lydia, and was, in that period, the leader of these inroads on Miletus; for Sadyattes it was that began the war: but during the five years subsequent to the six, Alyattes the son of Sadyattes, inheriting (as I just observed[38]) the war from his father, prosecuted it

---

[31] Herod. i. 74. Phraortes, father of Cyaxares, ruled over Media in the days of Ardys, the grandsire of Alyattes. This was the second irruption of the Cimmerians: see Herod. i. 6.

[35] οὐκ ὡς ἤθελι ἀπήλλαξι. Such is the manner in which the Greeks expressed themselves, in order to soften, in some measure, what might be too harsh in a narration. In the Andromache of Euripides, the Chorus, addressing itself to Peleus (to whom they were bringing the corpse of his grandson), says, "Unfortunate old man! you receive in your palace the son of Achilles, *not as you could wish.*" *Larcher.*

[36] See Matt. 588.

[37] The masculine and feminine flutes or fifes were probably two different sorts of musical instruments. The τυσσλὶ was an ancient instrument, the invention of the Lydians, described as παλύχορδον καὶ πολυκρότισον: it was in later times confounded with the λύρα.—Concerning the power of ἐπὶ, see Matt. 592, β.

[38] See Herod. i. 17.

vigorously[39]. None of the Ionians, however, afforded any help to the Milesians, saving the people of Chios, who came to their assistance, in return for a similar service[40]: for, at a former period, the Milesians had taken the part of the Chians, in the war against the Erythræans[41]. In the twelfth year, the harvest being again set on fire by the army, the following accident occurred: as soon as the halm was lighted, the flames, fanned by the wind, caught a temple of Minerva, called the Assesian: the temple, thus set on fire, was burnt to the ground. At the immediate time, no notice was taken of this; but after the return of the expedition to Sardis, Alyattes fell sick: the disease lasting a considerable time, he sent some person to consult the oracle at Delphi—whether counselled by somebody, or himself conceiving the idea, to send and inquire of the god concerning his malady: the Pythia, however, refused to make any response to the persons who came to Delphi, until they had rebuilt the temple of Minerva, which they had set on fire at Assesus in the territory of Milesia. So far I know what took place, by the information I obtained from the Delphians. To which the Milesians add the following particulars: That 'Periander[42] the son of Cypselus, who was a most intimate friend of Thrasybulus, then the ruler of Miletus, having ascertained what answer the oracle had made to Alyattes, sent off a messenger to report it to Thrasybulus, so that, knowing all beforehand, he might take some counsel for the present conjuncture. Alyattes, apprised by his messengers, forthwith sent a herald to Miletus, requesting to make a truce with Thrasybulus and the Milesians till such time as he should have rebuilt the temple: the herald, therefore, went his way to Miletus; and meanwhile Thrasybulus, authentically informed of all particulars, and knowing what were the intentions of Alyattes, devised the following artifice: He collected in the market-square all the wheat there was in the place, the property of himself and others, and notified to the Milesians that, when he gave the signal, they should all fall to drinking and eating among themselves[43]. This was arranged and commanded by Thrasybulus for the purpose that the Sardinian herald, after witnessing the vast quantity of corn heaped up, and the inhabitants enjoying themselves,

---

[39] Hostilities against Miletus began with the dynasty of the Mermnadæ; and continued under every king of that house, with various interruptions (i. 14, 15, 17).

[40] Literally, 'giving back the like.'

[41] The citizens of Erythræ, one of the Ionian states. See Herod. i. 142.

[42] Concerning Periander, see Herod. iii. 48.

[43] Matt. 413.

should report accordingly to Alyattes. And so indeed matters came to pass; for the herald, having seen these things, and communicated the message from Alyattes to Thrasybul·us, went back to Sardis; and I am informed that the reconciliation was brought about by this, and nothing more: for Alyattes had hoped that a severe famine was raging in Miletus, and that the people were ground down to extreme misery; but now he heard from the herald, returned from Miletus, a statement so directly opposite to what he had pictured to himself. Soon after, a reconciliation took place between the two parties: a treaty was framed, on the condition" they should be mutual friends and allies. Alyattes built two temples of Minerva at Assesus instead of one, and he himself recovered from sickness.

23 Periander, the person who gave notice to Thrasybulus of the oracle, was the son of Cypselus; he was sovereign over Corinth: in his lifetime, there occurred an astonishing prodigy, according to the account of the Corinthians, which is borne out by that of the Lesbians; That Arion, a native of Methymna, was conveyed by a dolphin to Tænarum: he was second to no cithern-player[44] of that age[45], and was the first man, we know of[47], that invented, named, and performed the
24 dithyrambus at Corinth[46]. It is asserted, that this Arion, after spending a considerable portion of his time[49] at the court of Periander, conceived a wish to cross over into Italy and Sicily: having there accumulated, by his profession, great wealth, he determined to return back to Corinth. He took his departure, in consequence, from Tarantum; and confiding in none more than Corinthians, he freighted a merchant-bark, manned by a crew of that nation. The mariners however, when at sea[50], conspired to throw Arion overboard, and take to themselves his money: the musician, aware of their project, entreated that they would spare his life, offering to deliver up to them his money; but he was unable to prevail upon them; the sailors ordering him either to lay violent hands on himself, so that he might find sepulture on shore, or to jump instantly into the sea. Arion, reduced to this strait, requested, since such was their pleasure, to be permitted to stand at the poop, in full attire, and sing: he pledged

---

[44] ἐπ' ᾧ. Matt. 585, β.
[45] The κιθαρῳδὸς played the cithar or cithern, accompanying himself with his own voice.
[46] Matt. 273, c. and 334.
[47] Matt. 473.

[48] διδάσκω δρᾶμα, ' docere (in scenam producere, agere) fabulum.'—Schweig. Lex. Herod. Matthiæ, 473.
[49] Matt. 442, 2.
[50] πέλαγος, " the deep sea," in contradistinction of θάλασσα, closer in land.

himself to make away with his own life, when he had sung. The sailors—for they felt what a pleasure it would be to hear the first musician in the world sing—[51] retired from abaft to midships. In the mean time, Arion put on his whole attire, and, standing on the poop, took his cithern and went through the orthian strain: having come to the end of his tune, he threw himself headlong into the sea, with all his apparel on: meanwhile, the sailors made away for Corinth. But a dolphin, it is represented, picked up the musician, and bore him off to Tænarus, where he landed, and proceeded on to Corinth, still in full attire: on his arrival there, he narrated all that had happened. Periander, however, discrediting the report, put Arion under guard, hindering him from going away, and watched narrowly[52] for the sailors: as soon therefore as they made their appearance, he summoned them before him, and inquired what they had to say about Arion: they replied, that he was safe in Italy, and they had left him flourishing at Tarentum; thereupon Arion suddenly appeared before them, just as he was when he leaped overboard: the men, thus abashed and confounded, had nothing to say in denial of their guilt. Such, therefore, are the accounts of the Corinthians as well as the Lesbians: there is, moreover, at Tænarum, a small brass offering—a man astride on a dolphin.

Alyattes the Lydian, who carried through this protracted war against the Milesians, died some time after, having reigned fifty-seven years. At his recovery from sickness, he became the second benefactor of his family[53] to Delphi; for he dedicated a magnificent wine-bowl in silver, together with its saucer of iron, inlaid; an object worthy, before all offerings[54] at Delphi, to be inspected. It was a work of Glaucus, a native of Chios, the only man in the world that ever found out the art of inlaying iron[55]. 25

At the decease of Alyattes, Crœsus his son, then in the thirty-fifth year of his age, succeeded to the kingdom. This prince, accordingly, attacked first of all, among the Hellenes, the people of Ephesus: at which time the citizens, being besieged by Crœsus, placed their city under the safeguard of Diana, stretching, for that purpose, a rope from the temple to the city wall. The distance between the old town, then 26

---

[51] See note 1. to chap. viii. See also Matt. 394, c.

[52] ἀνακῶς ἴχειν, equivalent to ἐπιμελεῖσθαι, Herod. viii. 109. See also Matt. 604.

[53] That is to say, of the Mermnadæ. See Herod. i. 7. and 14.

[54] Matt. 580, e.

[55] The inlaying or damascening of iron consists in making incisions and filling them up with gold or silver wire.

besieged, and the temple is seven stades⁵⁶: these, therefore, were the first that Crœsus laid his hands upon. He afterwards attacked, in turn, each of the Ionian and Æolian settlements: alleging various pretexts against various states; producing, wherever he could find them, serious complaints against them, and, in many instances, having recourse to frivolous motives. Having thus reduced the Hellenic settlers in Asia to the payment of tribute, he next bethought himself to construct ships and attack the islanders. All things being got ready for the building of the ships, Bias of Priene came to Sardis: some say it was Pittacus of Mitylene; and being asked, by Crœsus, if there was any thing new⁵⁷ from Hellas, put a stop, by the following answer, to all further ship-building: "Sire, the islanders are collecting a vast body of "horse, having it in contemplation to enter the field against "you and Sardis." Crœsus, supposing his visitor to be serious, exclaimed: "May the gods put such a thought into "the heads of the islanders, as to face the sons of the "Lydians⁵⁸ on horseback." The other, then resuming, said: "Sire, I see you earnestly pray that you may meet the "islanders mounted, and on the main land: your hopes are "rational. But do you think the islanders themselves can "pray more fervently for any thing, when they hear you "are fitting out a fleet against them, than to catch the "Lydians out at sea, under full sail⁵⁹, where they may re-"venge on you the Hellenes settled on the continent, whom "you have enthralled⁶⁰?" Crœsus was highly pleased with the point in this observation; thinking the visitor spake to the purpose, he took the advice, put a stop to ship-building, and accordingly entered into a league of alliance with the Ionians resident in the islands.

28 In the course of time, and when nearly all the nations dwelling within the Halys river were reduced;—for, with the exception of the Cilicians and Lycians, Crœsus held all in subjection; and they were, Lydians⁶¹, Phrygians, Mysians, Mariandynians, Chalybians, Paphlagonians, Thracians, both

---

⁵⁶ ἔστι ἡ [τὸ διάστημα] μεταξὺ, &c.
⁵⁷ Matt. 457, 3: likewise 273.
⁵⁸ Matt. 430, 6.
⁵⁹ Schweigh. Not. Herod. vol. iii. p. 25: see also the Lex. Herod. Ἀείρω. The reading proposed by this intelligent scholar is ἀιρόμενοι (understand the accusative τὰ ἱστία) Ἀελόντε ἐν θαλάσσῃ. The anacoluthia of ἀιρόμενοι, referring to ποιεῦνται, is accounted for by the following instances of false concord, Herod. i. 56. οὐδ' ἦν αὐτός οὐδὲ οἱ ἐξ αὐτοῦ, παύσεσθαι; by iv. 15. and 137.
⁶⁰ Matt. 496, 6. and 559, b.
⁶¹ Crœsus certainly inherited the states of Lydia: still, he was an usurper or τύραννος, being the descendant of Gyges, the assassin of Candaules. This is the reason, perhaps, why Lydia appears so conspicuous in this list of enthralled nations.

the Thynians and Bithynians, Carians, Ionians, Dorians, Æolians, Pamphilians;—all these had been reduced and annexed to Lydia under Crœsus, when the different wise men[63], who flourished in those days in Hellas, visited Sardis, which had now soared to the highest pitch of opulence; each coming at his own convenience[63]. Among the rest, was Solon, a native of Athens; who, after drawing up a code of laws for the Athenians at their own request, had expatriated himself for ten years; departing under the pretence of seeing the world, but, in reality, in order not to be compelled himself to abrogate any of the statutes he had enacted[64]; a thing which the Athenians dared not to do themselves, being bound, by solemn oaths, to observe for ten years the laws that Solon might institute for them[65]. Solon, therefore, one of these wise men, emigrating from the above motive, as well as for the purposes of study and contemplation, proceeded to the court of Amasis, in Egypt, and more particularly to that of Crœsus. On his arrival at the latter, he was received hospitably by the king: the third or fourth day after, Solon was, by the command of Crœsus, conducted by some attendants over the treasuries, and shewn all that was great and luxurious. When he had seen and contemplated sufficiently[66] every thing, Crœsus put this question to him: "My Athenian friend, the great celebrity has reached even "to us[67], which you have gained for your wisdom, and the "travels you have undertaken for the purpose of visiting "many countries and contemplating them as a philosopher: "and therefore I feel anxious to know[68] from you, who is "the most happy being you have yet seen." He asked this question because he fancied he was himself that happiest being. But Solon, not at all adulatory, and referring to experience[69], said: "It was, sire, Tellus of Athens." Crœsus was astonished at the answer. "For what reason," asked he, pettishly, "do you judge Tellus to have been the happiest?" "Tellus," resumed he, "in the first place, belonged to a "flourishing town[70]; his sons were handsome and good; and "he saw children born to them all, and all living. In the

[63] Herodotus gives the name of σοφιστὴς to Pythagoras, iv. 95. The same epithet occurs ii. 49. where it cannot be interpreted in any other sense than 'sage,' 'wise man.' This appellation was at first honourable, but became afterwards odious. Xenophon defines the sophist, one who sells his knowledge, for money, to the first comer. *Larcher.*
[65] Matt. 521.
[64] Matt. 519.
[66] Matt. 527. obs. 1.
[66] Matt. 581.
[67] See note 21, in p. 6 of this Volume.
[68] Literally, *A desire, therefore, has now come to me, &c.*
[69] τῷ ἐόντι χρεώμενος, *making use of the truth*: τὸ ἐὸν, id quod res est.—*Schweig. Lex. Herod.*
[70] Matt. 315, last parag.

" second place, being in comfortable circumstances, accord-
" ing to our ideas, he met with the most brilliant termina-
" tion of life that could befal man: for he had gone to the
" support of the Athenians, in a battle with their neigh-
" bours of Eleusis; there he turned the foe into complete
" rout, and died gallantly. The Athenians entombed him at
" the public cost, on the spot where he fell, and honoured
" him magnificently."

31 Solon having thus admonished[71] Crœsus by descanting thus much on the felicity of Tellus, the king again asked, who was the next to Tellus, he had seen[72]; expecting surely to obtain the second rank, at least. "Cleobis and
" Biton," replied the Athenian: " they were natives of Argos,
" supplied with a sufficiency for life; and, moreover, both
" were endowed with such strength, that each alike con-
" quered in the lists. It is related of them, that one day,
" the festival of Argeian Juno, their mother was, by law, to
" be conveyed in a chariot to the temple[73]: the oxen came
" not from the field in time: the youths, pressed by their
" delay[74], placed themselves beneath the yoke, and dragged
" the car in which their mother rode: proceeding thus for
" five-and-forty stades[75], they reached the temple. After
" they had achieved this feat, in the sight of the assembled
" spectators, the best of ends was vouchsafed them; the
" deity, by their example, showing that death is a greater
" boon to man than life[76]. For the Argeian by-standers
" extolled the strength of the youths, while the women of
" Argos blessed her as the mother of such sons[77]. The
" mother, transported with joy by the deed as well as by the
" glory, stood before the sacred image, and poured forth her
" prayers, that the goddess would vouchsafe whatever was
" best to befal man unto Cleobis and Biton, her own sons,
" who honoured her so nobly. After this prayer, when the
" sacrifice and holy banquet were over, they fell asleep
" within the sacred precinct itself: they never awoke more,
" but so found their final repose. The citizens of Argos
" had their statues carved[78], and dedicated them at Delphi."

32 Solon, accordingly, allotted to these young men the second rank in felicity. Crœsus, vexed at this, exclaimed: " What!

[71] See Schweig. Not. Herod. vol. iii. p. 29. See also Lex. Herod. προτρί-τισθαι.

[72] Matt. 501.

[73] She was the priestess of Juno Argiva, and, as such, could not lawfully absent herself from the sacred ceremonies.

[74] ἐκκλησίομενοι τῇ ὥρῃ, tempore exclusi, i. e. quum nihil temporis eis reliquum esset; urgente hora. *Schweig. Lex. Herod.*

[75] Matt. 424, 2. Forty-five stades are about four miles and a half.

[76] Matt. 458.

[77] Matt. 363. and 480. *obs.* 3.

[78] Matt. 492, c.

"my Athenian friend, is our happiness thus scorned, and
"held as nothing by you; so much even, that you have
"ranked us less worthy than mere subjects[79]?" The Athenian replied: "Crœsus! is it concerning worldly riches you
"ask the opinion of a man who is convinced the divinity
"looks on such things with indignation and proneness to
"change[80]? Let me first observe, that, in the long lapse of
"time, many things must be witnessed, many suffered, such
"as one might not wish. For I set the bourn of human
"life at seventy years[81]. Those seventy times twelve
"months comprise five-and-twenty thousand two hundred
"days, without reckoning the intercalatory months. Now,
"if every other year shall be made longer by one month, in
"order that the seasons may properly agree in coming
"round, then the intercalatory months in the seventy years
"are thirty-five; the days of these months are one thou-
"sand and fifty. The sum total of all these days, making
"up the seventy years, is twenty-six thousand two hundred
"and fifty days[82], of which not one produces one single
"thing exactly the same as another. Thus, then, man,
"O Crœsus! is but the sport of circumstance[83]. I am, no
"doubt, convinced[84] that you are immensely rich; that you
"are king over many nations; but, in respect of what you
"inquire[85] now of me, I cannot satisfy myself, until I shall

---

[79] Ἰδιώτης, 'one who holds no public office;' not a king; but a mere dependant, in comparison with the rich and mighty Crœsus.

[80] Literally. 'Dost thou ask me, O Crœsus, about human affairs—me, who know how indignant and turbulent the deity ever is?' In chap. 34, the Historian tells us, ἔλαβε ἐκ θεοῦ νέμεσις μεγάλη Κροῖσον. This proves that τὸ θεῖον is used synonymously with ὁ θεός; and is corroborated by the words attributed to Artabanes (Herod. vii. 10.), φιλέει γὰρ ὁ θεὸς τὰ ὑπερέχοντα πάντα κολούειν.

[81] The days of our years are threescore and ten. Psalm xc. 10.

[82] It is known, that in 235 lunar months there are no more than very nearly 228 solar months: 228 solar months are the same as 19 solar years; therefore, since 235—228 =7, it is necessary to add 7 lunar months to 19 lunar years, in order that the solar and lunar periods may coincide. The Greek calendar intercalates thus the seven lunar months in nineteen lunar years:—

Years of 12 lunar months: 1, 3, 5, 7, 8, 9, 11, 13, 15, 16, 17, 19.
Years of 13 lunar months: 2, 4, 6, 10, 12, 14, 18.

This was the mode in which Meton taught the Greeks to reckon, so as to secure a correct return of the seasons every year. Herodotus probably was unacquainted with Meton's reform of the Greek calendar; but it is difficult to conceive how such an intelligent observer as Herodotus should have strayed so wide of truth, as to adopt an average year too long by ten days.

[83] See Schweigh. Not. Herod. vol. iii. p. 35. on the meaning of συμφορή. Consult also Lex. Herod. συμφορή.

[84] φαίνεαι. Solon had examined at leisure all the riches of Crœsus: he could not, therefore, say properly, *You appear to me to be*, &c. Viger remarks, that φαίνομαι is often taken in the sense of *liquere, constare, manifeste compereri ac teneri.*—Larcher.

[85] Matt. 411.

"have ascertained that you have ended your life com-
"fortably. For the mighty rich man is not so much hap-
"pier than he who earns his daily bread, unless, indeed,
"good fortune accompany him through life, to its end[86], in
"the possession of every enjoyment. Many most opulent
"men are miserable; while many in moderate circum-
"stances are blessed with good-fortune. He, therefore,
"who possesses vast riches, and yet is miserable, surpasses
"only in two respects him who is blessed with good-fortune;
"while the latter exceeds, in many respects, the wealthy and
"miserable. The former is better empowered to gratify
"desire, and to bear up against heavy calamity: the latter
"soars above him in these particulars; he is not equally
"empowered to contend with desire and accident, but
"good-fortune averts these from him; he is whole of limb,
"unafflicted with disease, inexperienced of sorrow[87], blessed
"with good children of comely features: if, in addition to
"these advantages, follows a happy death[88], he is the man
"you seek for, worthy to be called happy[89]: until he be dead,
"however, it behoves us to refrain from calling him happy[90],
"but fortunate[91]. Still, it is not possible that one human
"being unite all these advantages; as no country suffices
"to produce for itself every thing, but furnishes some while
"reft of others, and that which gives the most is best; so
"no human being is complete in his accomplishments; one
"he has, another he has not: he who continues to the end in
"possession of the most[92], and then terminates his life in
"peace, that man, sire, deserves[93] to bear the name of
"happy. In all, it behoves never to lose sight of the end;
"for to many has the divinity vouchsafed a glimpse of
33 "happiness, and then scathed them to the root[94]." Solon,
addressing Crœsus in this language, was in no way compli-
mented, but dismissed: he was considered a very untutored
man, who passed over present good, and advised to keep in
view the termination of every thing[95].

34 After the departure of Solon, the dire indignation[96] of the

[86] Matt. 535, d.
[87] Matt. 322.
[88] Matt. 523, obs.
[89] "Ὄλβιος· ὁ διὰ τοῦ ὅλου βίου μακαρισθείς. Hesych.
[90] Matt. 544.
[91] Judge no man blessed before his death. Eccles. xi. 8. quoted by Larcher.
[92] Matt. 552.
[93] Matt. 296.

[94] La vita al fin, e'l dì loda la sera. Petrarca.
[95] Matt. 480. obs. 1.
[96] νέμεσις is, it seems, synonymous with φθόνος of chap. 32. Herodotus therefore uses the term φθόνος, not for 'envy,' but for that virtue which Aristotle places between φθόνος, 'envy,' and ἐπιχαιρεκακία, 'gratification at destruction;' a virtue which the philosopher calls νέμεσις, and is the opposite of ἔλεος.

gods visited Crœsus, in consequence, it may be presumed, of his presumption that he was the most happy of men. Forthwith, a vision stood over him in his sleep, which portended the truth respecting the calamities that were about to befal his son: for Crœsus had two sons; one of whom was grievously afflicted, being dumb[97]; the other, however, was by far the first in all things, among all his cotemporaries; his name was Atys. This Atys, accordingly, it was, whom the dream pointed out to Crœsus, that he should lose him, pierced by a sharp point of iron. When the king awoke, and turned over in his mind the occurrence, he dreaded the accomplishment of the dream, and took a wife to the youth; and although hitherto wont to place him at the head of the Lydian forces, he no longer sent him on such business: spears, javelins, and all such instruments as men use in war, he removed from the men's apartments, and laid up in the back chambers, lest any suspended weapon might fall down upon his son[98]. At the time he was busied with his 35 son's wedding, a man arrived at Sardis, oppressed with calamity; his hands were sullied; and he was by birth a Phrygian, one of the royal family. This person entered the palace of Crœsus, and supplicated to receive purification[99], according to the common laws. Crœsus purified him;—the ceremonies of expiation are nearly the same with the Lydians as with the Hellenes;—when therefore he had performed the accustomed rites, he inquired of the suppliant whence he came, who he was, addressing him thus: "Good man! who " are you? and from what part of Phrygia have you come " to my hearth? what man or what woman have you slain?" " I am, sire," answered[100] the fugitive, " the son of Gordius,

---

[97] Κωφὸς, 'obtuse,' and therefore afflicted in intellect, in hearing, in sight, in speech. With the more ancient writers, this word signifies only *dumb*. Among the more modern, *deaf*.

[98] Matt. 392, A.

[99] The scholiast of Homer informs us, (see ver. 48, last Book of the Iliad,) that it was customary amongst the ancients, for whoever had committed an involuntary murder, to leave his country, and fly to the house of some powerful individual. There, covering himself, he sat down, and entreated to be purified.—No author has described more minutely or exactly the ceremonies observed at the expiations than Apollonius Rhodius. The guilty person sits down on the hearth, fixes his eyes on the ground, and sticks the instrument of the murder in the earth. The person whose protection he implores discovers by these signs that he wishes to be expiated of a murder. He then takes a suckling pig, slaughters him, and smears the hands of the suppliant with the blood. He next uses lustral waters, invoking Jove the Expiator. Every thing that had served for the expiation is then removed out of the house. Cakes are then burnt, water poured out, and the gods invoked, to appease the anger of the Furies, and to propitiate Jove. *Larcher.*

[100] ἱστίοισι, Ion. for ἑστίοισι, which the scholiast of Apollonius Rhodius explains, very properly, ἐπὶ τῇ ἑστίᾳ ὄν, *one that stands at the hearth,* i. e. a

"and grandson of Midas; I am named Adrastus: unwittingly
"I have slain my own brother: driven away by my father,
"and reft of all, I stand here." Crœsus answered in these
words: "You are the child of my friends, and you are come
"to your friends: abide in my palace[100], where you shall know
"no want: and bear with this calamity as meekly as you
"can; you will be the greatest gainer." Adrastus, accordingly, took up his residence in the palace of Crœsus.

36 At this same time, a huge monster of a boar[102] made his appearance in the Mysian Olympus: rushing down from that mountain, he ravaged the cultivated lands of the Mysians. The inhabitants had repeatedly gone out against this animal: they could do him no harm, but were compelled to suffer his devastations: at last, a deputation from the Mysians came before Crœsus, and spoke thus: "Sire, a vast monster
"of a boar has appeared in our land, and devastates our
"cultivated fields: we have endeavoured to catch him, but
"cannot. We therefore now entreat you[103], send with us
"your son and some chosen youths, together with dogs, so
"that we may drive him out of the land." Such was their petition: to which Crœsus, remembering the warning of his dream, replied thus: "Make no more mention of my son[104]:
"I shall not send him with you; for he is but just married,
"and for the present has to attend to that[105]. However, I
"will send with you some chosen Lydians, together with my
"whole pack; and give those that go, my commands to assist
"you in extirpating the savage monster from your country."

37 Such was his answer, with which the Mysians were content; when the son of Crœsus happened to come in: having heard what the Mysians petitioned for, and that Crœsus had refused to send his son with them, the youth thus addressed his father:
"Father, formerly it was deemed most befitting and worthy
"of my blood to frequent the wars and the chace, there to
"gain renown[105]: now you exclude me from both these exer-
"cises, without having observed any cowardice on my part,
"or any want of spirit. With what eyes must I now appear
"to you[106], stalking to and from the market? What idea
"shall I give of myself to my fellow-citizens? To what a man
"will my bride say she is united? Either, therefore, permit

---

suppliant. We have in Homer a very remarkable instance of this custom.—Ulysses, after imploring the assistance of Alcinoüs, seats himself on the ashes near the hearth. Odyss. vii. 153.

[101] Matt. 379.
[102] Matt. 430.

[103] Matt. 332.
[104] Matt. 325.
[105] ταῦτα, sc. τὰ τοῦ γάμου. Matt. 535. p. 809.
[106] According to Valckenaer's reading, τῷ τῳ (for σῳ) etc., instead of τι. See Herod. vol. iii. p. 39.

"me to join this hunting-party, or convince me by some
"reason that you are justified in doing as you do." "I have 38
"not seen in you, my son," replied Crœsus, "either coward-
"ice, or any thing to displease me; it is not on that account
"I act thus: a vision has appeared before me in a dream,
"when I was buried in sleep, and warned me that you will
"have but short time to live, for you will be destroyed by a
"point of iron. In consequence of this vision[107], I have
"hastened this marriage; and have refused to send you on
"the present enterprise, having care to preserve you, if by
"any means I can, during my life; for you are my only son:
"the other, afflicted in his hearing, I reckon not as mine."
The young man replied: "To have beheld such a vision, 39
"dear father, is indeed an excuse for keeping such a watch
"over me: but you misunderstand the dream; you do not
"see its real meaning: and it is right[108] I should explain to
"you. You say that the dream boded I was to die by a
"point of iron; but where are the hands of a boar? where
"the point of iron that alarms you? Were I indeed to die
"by a tusk, or something of that kind, it would have been
"prudent in you to do as you do[109]. Again, as to my dying
"by a spear; this is no battle with men; therefore do give
"me leave to go." "My son," replied the king, "it is true: 40
"you beat me here in the interpretation[110] of my dream:
"you have conquered; I give up, and allow you to go."

As soon as Crœsus had done speaking, he sent for the 41
Phrygian, Adrastus, whom he addressed thus: "At the time,
"Adrastus, that you were smitten with a dreadful[111] cala-
"mity—not that I reproach you with that—I then expiated
"you, received you into my family, and ministered to all
"your wants. Now therefore—for it is your duty to make
"me a return for the service I have rendered you[112]—I re-
"quest you to be the guardian to my son, who is going to the
"chase, lest on the road some skulking thieves make their
"appearance to your detriment. It becomes you, moreover,
"to go where you may make yourself conspicuous by your
"deeds; for that you inherit from your fathers, to which you
"add bodily strength." "Sire," said Adrastus, "I would 42
"not have taken any part in this enterprise; for it is not
"meet that one visited with my misfortune[113] should join

---

[107] Matt. 591, β.
[108] Matt. 296.
[109] Matt. 510.
[110] ὃ ναί, ἔστι τῇ, for ταύτῃ, 'hoc in loco') με νικᾷς, etc. See Lex. Herod. τῇ, 3.
[111] ἀχάρι, the contracted dative of ἄχαρις, for ἀχάριτι. The nominative neuter of ἄχαρις is ἄχαρι, with the accent on the first syllable. See Herod. vol. iii. p. 41. Schweig. not. 1.
[112] Matt. 561, b. See chap. 178.
[113] Matt. 556, 8.

"with his more happy compeers, nor have I the wish;
"frequently even I have refrained myself: but now, as you
"yourself urge me, and it becomes me to oblige you—for I
"am bound in gratitude to make a return—I am ready to
"do as you desire. I pledge myself to bring back your son,
"whom you command me to watch over, safe and sound, as
"far as depends on his guardian[114]."

43 After Adrastus had returned this answer to Crœsus, they departed, provided with chosen youths and dogs: arriving at Mount Olympus, they tracked the game, and found the boar; then standing round him, they hurled their spears: at that moment, this very man who had been purified of blood, he called Adrastus, levelled his spear at the boar, missed his mark[115], and hit the son of Crœsus: the youth accordingly, wounded by the spear, fufilled the warning of the dream. Some one ran off to announce the tidings to Crœsus, and, reaching Sardis, communicated an account of the hunt and 44 the fate of his son. Crœsus, horror-stricken at the death of his son, was still more exasperated that the deed should have been done by the very hand that he had purified of blood: sorely deploring his calamity, he invoked Jove the Expiator, attesting what he had suffered at the hands of his guest: he called also on Jove as the god of Hearths and of Mutual Friendship[116];—as the god of Hearths, because, by admitting a stranger among his household, he had unwittingly harboured and fed the assassin of his son[117];—as the god of Mutual Friendship, because, having sent him as a guard, he had 45 found him his most cruel enemy. Soon after appeared the Lydians, bearing the dead body: behind followed the homicide; he advanced in front of the corse, and, stretching forth his hands, gave himself up to Crœsus, bidding the king sacrifice him on the dead body: then he alluded to his first misfortune, owned that he after that misfortune[118] had been the instrument of death to him that had purified him, and that he deserved no longer to live. Crœsus heard the words of Adrastus, although absorbed in domestic sorrow: he took pity on him, and spoke to him thus: "My friend, you have "made full reparation to me, by thus devoting yourself to "death: you are not the cause of this misfortune, saving so

---

[114] Matt. 576.
[115] Matt. 368.
[116] Jupiter was adored under different titles, according to the place and circumstance of his different worshippers. Hence those expressions, Ἀγοραῖος Ζεὺς, Μειλίχιος, Ἱστίος, Ἐφέστιος.

Φίλιος, &c. Larcher.
[117] Matt. 552, 2.
[118] ἐπ' ἐκείνῃ (τῇ συμφορῇ). Præter illam calamitatem. Æ. Portus, Lex. Ion. post illam calamitatem. Schweig. Lex. Herod.

"far as you were the unwilling instrument, but some god,
"who long since foreshowed me what was to come to pass."
Crœsus therefore performed the funeral of his son with
the beseeming honours. Adrastus, on the other hand, the
slayer of his own brother, the slayer also of his expiator,
convinced that he was the most calamitous of men, went to
the sepulchre, when mankind had retired to rest, and slew
himself on the tomb. Crœsus, during two years, sat down[119]
in deep mourning, bewailing his son.

Some time after, the empire of Astyages son of Cyaxares 46
being overthrown by Cyrus the son of Cambyses, and the
increasing power of the Persians, put an end to the mourning of Crœsus: it occurred to his mind, whether he could
check the growing power of the Persians, before they became
too formidable. Having conceived this idea, he forthwith
proceeded to make trial of the oracles; not only those in Hellas, but also that in Libya. For this purpose, he despatched
various persons to various places; some to Delphi, some to
Abæ in Phocis, some to Dodona; others were sent to Amphiaraus and Trophonius: others to Branchidæ in Milesia:
the above, therefore, were the Hellenic oracles which Crœsus
sent to consult. Others, also, were sent to consult the oracle
at Ammon in Libya. These deputations Crœsus sent for
the purpose of ascertaining what the oracles respectively
knew; in order that, if he found they knew the truth, he
might a second time consult them, whether he should hazard
a war against the Persians. Before he sent the Lydians to 47
make trial of the oracles, he gave them these orders; They
were to consult the different shrines on the hundredth day
from that of their departure from Sardis, and to inquire of
each what Crœsus son of Alyattes and king of the Lydians
was at that moment doing:—whatever responses might be
respectively given, they were to write down, and bring to
him. As far as the replies from the other oracles are concerned, nothing is related by any body: but in the case of
Delphi, no sooner had the Lydians consulted the god, and
put the questions prescribed, than the Pythia, in hexameters,
spoke thus:

"I ken the number of the sand, the dimensions of the sea; I
"understand the dumb, and I hear him that speaketh not[120].
"On my senses strikes the smell of the heard-sheathed turtle,
"boiling in brass with flesh of lamb: brass stretches beneath:
"over all stands brass."

[119] καθῆστο, *sat down*; i. e. attended to no business. *Schweig.*   [120] Matt. 327. *obs.* 2.

48 The Lydians having written down the above words that had fallen from the oracular Pythia, went their ways back to Sardis. When all the rest, who had been despatched around, had arrived, bringing the dictates from the different shrines, Crœsus unrolled each manuscript, and looked over what was written in them; but none came up to his expectations[121]: when, however, he had read[122] that from Delphi, forthwith he adored and approved it; being convinced that the oracle at Delphi alone was the true one, as it had discovered what he had done. Because, on the appointed day, from the departure of the messengers for the various shrines, having first considered what would be the thing most difficult to guess and describe, he hit upon the following contrivance: he cut up a tortoise and a lamb, and boiled them together himself
49 in a brass caldron with a coverlid of brass. Such, therefore, was the answer to Crœsus, returned from Delphi: as to that from the shrine of Amphiaraus, I cannot quote exactly what was said to the Lydians, who performed the accustomed rites round the holy precinct; nothing is related on that subject: at all events, however, Crœsus acknowledged that oracle also to be falseless.
50 After this, he propitiated the god of Delphi with magnificent sacrifices: he offered up three thousand head of cattle fit for sacrifice, and of each kind[123], together with gilt and silvered table-couches, gold flagons, purple shawls and garments; and building up a lofty pile, burnt it down; fancying that, by so doing, he should especially conciliate the god. He had likewise given previous notice to all Lydians, to offer up whatever victim each might happen to possess, to the same divinity. When the sacrifice was ended, he melted down a great quantity of gold, which he run into lingots; making each lingot six inches long, three inches broad, and one inch thick; the number of which was one hundred and seventeen: four of them, of refined gold, weighed each two talents and a half[124]: the other lingots, of pale gold, weighed each two talents. He made likewise the figure of a lion of pure gold, of the weight of ten talents[125]. This lion, at the

---

[121] τῶν μὲν δὴ οὐδὲν προσίετό μιν —Ion. and καὶ ὑπαλλαγὴν, for τῶν μὲν δὴ οὐδὲν αὐτὸς προσίετο. Horum tamen [oraculorum] nullum ad ipsum ibat, ad ejus animum accedebat, ei placebat, instead of nullum tamen horum ipse probabat. —Æ. Port. Lex. Ion. The usual signification of προσίεσθαι is, to allow, to approve, to believe, i. 75. i. 135. vi. 123.

[122] Compare the beginning of c. 125.

[123] κτήνεά τε γὰρ τὰ θύσιμα πάντα—πάντα is here equivalent to ἑκάστου γένους, of each kind. So in ix. 80. Παυσανίῃ δὲ πάντα δίκα ἐξαιρέθη. Larcher. Schweig. Comp. 2 Chron. vii. 5.

[124] Matt. 141.

[125] This lion was, perhaps, in commemoration of the singular tradition mentioned chap. 84.

time of the conflagration of Delphi, fell off the lingots on which it was placed as a pedestal; and now lies in the treasury of the Corinthians, weighing six talents and a half, three and a half being melted off. Crœsus having completed 51 these articles, sent them to Delphi, together with the others following: two wine-bowls of immense size[126]; one gold, the other silver: that of gold laid on the right as you entered the temple, and that of silver on the left; but these also were removed at the time the temple was burnt down; and the golden one now is found in the treasury of the Clazomenians, weighing eight talents and a half, and twelve minæ above. The silver bowl in one corner of the vestibule is of the capacity of sixty amphoræ; in consequence of which, it is used by the Delphians for mixing the wine with the water, at the Theophanian festivals. Some of the Delphians say that this was the work of Theodorus of Samos: in which I agree with them; for indeed the workmanship appears to me of no common order[127]. Crœsus sent also four silver casks; and dedicated two lustral vases, one of gold, the other of silver: on the golden one there now stands the inscription ΛΑΚΕΔΑΙΜΟΝΙΩΝ, who are represented as the dedicators; but falsely so, for that also is from Crœsus: the inscription was cut out by one of the people of Delphi, who wished to gratify the Lacedæmonians: I know the man's name, but need not mention it: the boy however, through whose hand the water flows, is, in reality, a gift of the Lacedæmonians; but certainly neither of these vases for aspersion. Crœsus sent, moreover, many other votive offerings, distinguished by no marks; among which were some round water-ewers of silver[128]; and especially a gold statue, three feet high, of a woman; said, by the Delphian people, to be the image of Crœsus's baking-woman: besides these things, he sent also the necklace and girdles of his wife[129].

Such were the presents he made to Delphi: to Amphi- 52 araus, having ascertained his virtue and sufferings, he dedicated a buckler wholly of gold, together with a spear of solid gold, head and shaft alike[130]. Both these were, in my time,

---

[126] Matt. 613, iv.

[127] ἐντυχὶς ἔργον, opus vulgare.— Æ. Port. Lex. Ion.

[128] χέρνιβα ἀργύρεα. It is not certain that plates are here meant: the χέρνιβα, however, formed a part of the vases put on the table. Larcher.— χέρνιψ, equivalent to πρόχοι, a vase to contain the water that is poured on the hands of the guests: the aiguière of the French, and giesskanne (pouring-can) of the Germans.

[129] Barthélemy makes the value of the presents of Crœsus amount to 21,109,140 French francs. Voy. du jeune Anach.

[130] The head of the spear was similar to that of a French pike or halbert, which is not unlike a fleur-de-lis, having three points.

deposited at Thebes, in the temple of Ismenian Apollo, belonging to that city.

53 To the Lydians commissioned to escort these gifts to the temples, he gave it in charge to inquire at the shrines, whether Crœsus ought to levy war against the Persians? and whether he should unite to his own forces those of any other nation? On the arrival of the Lydian deputies, they appended the offerings; and then inquired at the respective shrines; saying, " Crœsus, king of the Lydians and other nations, convinced " that this is the only oracle in the world, has given you " these presents, worthy of your discoveries; and now in- " quires at your hands, whether he shall levy war against " the Persians, and take the troops of any nation as his " allies?" Both oracles agreed completely in their opinions; predicting to Crœsus, that " if he attacked the Persians, he " would overthrow a mighty empire;" and advised him to adopt as allies those of the Hellenes he should find to be the
54 most powerful. When these decisions of the god were brought, and made known to Crœsus, he was beyond measure delighted with the oracles: fully confident that he should destroy the empire of Cyrus, he sent again to Delphi, ascertained the number of the inhabitants of the town, and gratified every citizen with two gold staters a head: In return for which, the Delphians bestowed on Crœsus and the Lydians the privilege of first consulting the oracle, exemption from scot and lot, priority of seats, and permission for ever, to such as chose to avail themselves thereof, of being citizens
55 of Delphi. Crœsus having gratified the people of Delphi, consulted for the third time the oracle;—for when once he had admitted the veracity of the oracle, he never tired of it: he now again consulted the shrine therefore, and inquired whether his dynasty would be of long duration: the Pythia pronounced to him this warning:

" So soon as a mule becomes the Medic king, then, soft-footed
" Lydian, o'er pebbly Hermus hie thee: tarry not, nor blush to
" be a dastard."

56 When this communication reached Crœsus, he was more than ever delighted; fancying that a mule, instead of a man, could never rule over the Medes; and that, in consequence, neither he himself nor his descendants[131] would ever cease to hold the sway. Immediately after, he directed his attention towards ascertaining who were the most powerful of the Hellenic nations, whom he should adjoin to himself. Making his inquiries, he discovered that the superior nations were

---

[131] αὐτὸς and οἱ in the nominative, instead of the accusative.

the Lacedæmonians and the Athenians; the former of Dorian blood, the latter of Ionic: for these were, from old, the two most distinguished races; this a Pelasgic people, that Hellenic: the former[132] had scarcely ever changed their residence: the other had wandered far and wide; for the progenitors of the Lacedæmonians[133], under king Deucalion, inhabited the territory of Pthiotis: and, under Dorus the son of Hellenus, the country at the foot of Ossa and Olympus, called Histiæotis: driven out of Histiæotis by the Cadmeians, they settled at Pindus[134], and were called Macedni; from thence again they crossed into Dryopis, and so from Dryopis came into Peloponnesus, where they took the name of Dorians.

I cannot, for a certainty, affirm what language the Pelasgi 57 used[135]; but if it be permitted to speak from the inferences that may be deduced from the Pelasgians that still exist to this day—those Pelasgians, I mean, that reside above the Tyrrhenians, in the town of Crestone[136], and once were borderers of the people now designated Lacedæmonians, and at that period dwelt in the lands at present called Thessaliotis;

---

[132] καὶ τὸ μέν. The Pelasgians of Attica, not the Pelasgians in general, whose migrations were various and distant.

[133] I have expanded the sense, to obviate all confusion.

[134] If Herodotus had meant that they withdrew on Mount Pindus, he would have used the article, ἐν τῷ Πίνδῳ. The omission of the article proves that the town and territory of Pindus are here meant.—*Larcher.*

[135] Ἴσασι: a little lower down, the same thing is expressed ἥτις ἵεσι. Matt. 559.

[136] According to Herodotus, the Pelasgians had in early times settled in Attica; the inhabitants of which were still of the same stock, although they had forsaken the language of their forefathers for the Hellenic. The Pelasgians, in this passage of the text, are not those of Attica, but a colony from the main Pelasgic body, originally placed in Argolis. This colony had migrated into Tyrrhenia (Tuscany) in Italy; from which, desolated by famine, contagious disease, and internal broils, they passed into various countries: some reached Attica. The Athenians received hospitably the emigrants; to whom they allotted a portion of land at the foot of Hymettus, on condition they should erect the wall around the acropolis of Athens. These terms were acceded to, and the Pelasgians prospered during forty-four years; at the expiration of which, an untoward quarrel ensued between the Athenians and Pelasgians (Herod. vii. 187): the Pelasgians were expelled for ever from Attica. They withdrew to Lemnos. Miltiades, son of Cimon, subsequently drove them out of that island: some then founded in Asia the towns of Placia and Scylace: others took refuge in the peninsula of Athos: lastly, a few proceeded to the coast of Thrace, and founded, a little inland, the town of Crestone.—*Larcher.*

The Tyrrhenians, a branch of the Pelasgic stock, settled in Lemnos and Imbros: they afterwards occupied various parts of the Chersonesus and Hellespont, as well as the foot of Athos (Thucyd. iv. 109). Above these was the Crestonic nation, and *perhaps* a city called Crestone, which, in the time of Thucydides, was, for the most part, alien to the Hellenes, and βαρβάρων. They are mentioned by Herodotus, vii. 124; viii. 116.—*Wesseling.*

those likewise settled on the Hellespont, at Placia and Scylace, who were once co-resident with the Athenians[137]; and indeed all Pelasgic communities whatever that now exist, although they may have altered their appellation—if, I say, we are allowed to infer from these, the Pelasgians spoke a language distinct from the Hellenic: if, therefore, this was the case with the whole Pelasgian race, the Attic nation, which is Pelasgic, must have forsaken their own language also when they turned into Hellenes; for it is well known, that neither the Crestoniats use the same language as the people that dwell around them, nor the Placianians either, and yet both Crestoniats and Placianians have one and the same speech: this proves then, that, when they migrated to those parts, they brought with them their characteristic language,

58 which they still preserve. The Hellenic race, however, from its origin, has used the same speech—such the fact appears to me; nevertheless, distinct from the Pelasgians, insignificant as they were, and proceeding at first from a small beginning, they have increased to a multitude of nations, mainly by the admixture of many races distinct from their own: so, accordingly, it is the general opinion, and I join in it, that the Pelasgian race, remaining unamalgamated, never increased to any extent[138].

59 Croesus accordingly found, on inquiry, that the Attic people, one of the above nations, was oppressed and distracted under Pisistratus the son of Hippocrates, at that time tyrant of Athens. A great prodigy occurred to Hippocrates, who was then in no public situation[139], while present as a spectator at the Olympian games. He had sacrificed a victim, and the caldrons, full of flesh and water, stood by his side; when, without the assistance of fire, they bubbled and ran over. Chilon of Lacedæmon happened to be present, and, witnessing this phænomenon, advised Hippocrates, in the first place, not to take into his house a breeding wife; and, in the second place, if he had already such a consort, to send her away; and also, if he had a son, to disclaim him. Nevertheless, Hippocrates would not be persuaded, by this exhortation from Chilon. Some time after this, Pisistratus

---

[137] We are informed, in vi. 137, that the Athenians expelled them from their habitations, because they offered violence to the young women who went to draw water at the nine fountains.

[138] The construction of the last sentence of chap. 58 may be explained thus: ὡς δὴ ὦν (δοκέω), ἐμοί τι δοκέει, τὸ Πελασγ. etc.

The meaning of Herodotus is, that the Pelasgi, having remained separate, and as it were insulated, and not having incorporated themselves with other nations, could not increase as the Hellenes.—*Larcher.*

[139] See Lex. Herod. *Ἱππocrάτης.*

was born to him; who, at the time of the altercation between the people of the sea-side, headed by Megacles son of Alcmæon, and the people of the plain of Athens headed by Lycurgus Aristoclaïdes, roused a third party, with a view of usurping supreme power. He collected some partisans, and, under pretence of heading the mountaineers, devised the following artifice: he wounded himself and his mules; and then drove to the public square, as if just escaped from his enemies who forsooth wanted to assassinate him as he was riding into the country. He entreated the commons to give him certain persons, to serve as a guard of his life; for, in fact, he had before obtained much renown, in heading the expedition against Megara and capturing Nisæa, and had also displayed other deeds of valour. The commons of Athens, deceived by this, chose from the citizens those men he had pointed out; and gave them to him, not to act as javelin-men, but rather as club-bearers to Pisistratus; for they were to follow behind him, bearing staves in their hands. These men rose up conjointly with Pisistratus, and took possession of the acropolis: then, accordingly, Pisistratus assumed the government of Athens; without, however, disturbing the magisterial offices, or making any alteration in the laws: on the contrary, he ruled the state according to the enactments, and adopted a good and liberal policy. Not long 60 after, the partisans of Megacles on one side, and Lycurgus on the other, made up their differences, and drove out Pisistratus. Thus, therefore, Pisistratus got possession the first time of Athens; and this power not having yet struck deep root, he lost it. But they who had driven him out again renewed their mutual quarrels; and Megacles, tired out by the faction, sent a herald to Pisistratus, to ask if he would consent to take Megacles' daughter to wife, under condition of receiving back the power[140]. Pisistratus closed with the offer, and consented to the terms: accordingly, to ensure his return, they had recourse to a scheme, which, I think, was by far the most foolish ever heard of; particularly as the Hellenes were from early times, as a race, esteemed, by foreigners, more acute, and farther removed from absurd simplicity; and more particularly still, as they played off this trick upon the Athenians, said to be, of the Hellenes, the first in wisdom. In the Pæanian district there was a woman called Phya, four cubits all but three fingers in height[141], and

[140] Matt. 585, β.
[141] (κατὰ) μέγαθος ἀπολείπουσα τρεῖς δακτύλους ἀπὸ τεσσέρων πηχέων. Literally, *In stature, leaving three digits out of four cubits*; that is to say, six feet all but about two inches.

in other respects handsome: they dressed this woman in a complete suit of armour, placed her in a chariot, and, having previously instructed her how to play her part in the most graceful manner[142], drove to the city. They had sent heralds on before, who, entering the town, proclaimed these prescribed words: "Athenians, receive, with gracious spirit, "Pisistratus; whom Pallas herself, esteeming most of all "men, is now conducting back to her citadel!" Forthwith the report spread, in all quarters, that Minerva was bringing in Pisistratus; and the people of the town, persuaded that the woman was the goddess herself, bowed down in worship to a human form, and received Pisistratus.

61 Pisistratus, having recovered the power in the manner above described, married, according to agreement, Megacles' daughter: but as he had already sons grown up, and the Alcmæonidæ were said to be contaminated[143], not desirous, in consequence, of having any children by his new-married bride, he conversed with her unnaturally. The lady accordingly kept this, at first, secret; but some time after, whether questioned or not, discovered it to her mother, who communicated it to the father. He was exasperated at being thus dishonoured by Pisistratus[144]: filled with indignation, he reconciled himself to his partisans: and Pisistratus hearing what was machinating against him, departed wholly from the country: he went to Eretria, and held counsel with his sons. The opinion of Hippias prevailed, that the tyranny should be recovered: they levied, therefore, free gifts from such cities as were in any manner indebted to them for former services[145]: several contributed large sums of money, but the Thebans exceeded all by the liberality of their gift. In short, time glided on, and every thing was provided for their return: for a body of mercenaries joined them from Argos in Peloponnesus; and a native of Naxos, called Lygdamis, displayed the greatest ardour, bringing money and

62 men[147]. Sailing from Eretria, they came back in the eleventh year of their absence, and first took possession of Marathon. In this place they encamped, and their partisans from the city came and joined them: others also from the various

---

[142] καὶ προδείξαντες σχῆμα οἷόν τι ἔμελλε εὐπρεπέστατον φανεῖσθαι ἔχουσα. And first shewing (her) what demeanour she should have, to appear most decorous.

[143] ἐναγέων explained in Herod. v. 70.

[144] Matt. 541.

[145] προφέρεσθαι· Ion. for προφέρεσθαι, from προαιδεῖσθαι. Προαιδεῖσθαί τι τινι, To owe some mark of gratitude to some one, for a benefit conferred.

[146] Matt. 543.

[147] προθυμίην πλείστην παρείχετο.— Translated by Larcher, Redoubla leur ardeur par un secours volontaire de troupes et d'argent.

districts flocked to them, all indeed by whom tyranny was cherished more than freedom[148]. The citizens of Athens, however, took no account of Pisistratus, either when he was levying funds, or, again, when he made himself master of Marathon: but as soon as they ascertained that he was about to advance against the town, they at last prepared to repel him from their country; and marched, with all their forces, to meet the invaders. In the mean time, Pisistratus's party[149] marched from Marathon, and proceeded against the city: falling all into one body, they reached the sacred enclosure of Minerva Pallena, opposite to which they pitched their tents. Here, inspired by godly impulse, Amphilytus the Acarnanian, a prophetic seer, stood in the presence of Pisistratus, and, advancing before him, prophesied in hexameter verse:

"The net is cast, the meshes are spread:
"In the moon-shine night the tunnies will pour in."

Thus, filled with the god, he spoke. Pisistratus, catching the sense of the oracle, and saying he took the warning, marched onwards his troops. But the Athenians had at that hour addressed themselves to supper; and after that meal, some were amusing themselves at dice, others were preparing for sleep; when Pisistratus and his followers fell upon them, and put them to the rout. Now, as the Athenians were running away, Pisistratus made use of a very ingenious expedient to stop the Athenians from rallying[150], and make them remain dispersed: he mounted his sons on horses, and sent them on before his van; and they, coming up with the fugitives[151], spoke to them as was prescribed by Pisistratus, bade the men be of good cheer, and go every one to his own house. The Athenians took the advice; and thus, therefore, for the third time, Pisistratus obtained possession of Athens; and now rooted firmly his power, by the help of many subsidiaries, and receipts of funds, some of which flowed in from the country itself, others from the Strymon river[152]. He seized as hostages the sons of the Athenians

[148] Matt. 450. obs. 1.
[149] Matt. 271.—ἐς τωὐτὸ συνιόντες. Larcher's translation: "Pisistratus and his partisans having departed from Marathon, *all in one united body*, approached the city. They arrived near the temple of Minerva Pallena, opposite to which they pitched their camp."—This translation may be adopted by such as do not assent to the meaning that Schweighæuser gives to ἐς τωὐτὸ συνιόντες.

[150] ἀλισθῶσι, from ἀλίζων. Literally, *That the Athenians might not be collected.*
[151] Acolouthia, καὶ λεγόντες λαοντες.
[152] There were silver-mines at Laurium and Thoricus (iv. 99) in Attica. The country between the Strymon and Nestus abounded in mines of gold and silver: the Athenians had settlements in that quarter, especially Amphipolis.

who had stood their ground[153] in the battle, and did not immediately take flight: these he banished to Naxos (which Pisistratus had already subdued, and turned over to Lygdamis): besides which, he purified the island of Delos, according to the oracular behests. The purification he performed thus: he dug up the dead bodies, as far as the eye could reach from the sacred enclosure, and transported them to another quarter of the island[154]. Pisistratus was now tyrant over Athens: but many of the Athenians fell in the battle; while others fled from their homes, with the son of Alcmæon[155].

65 Such therefore were the circumstances of the Athenians, at the time Crœsus made his inquiries: concerning the Lacedæmonians, he was informed that they had escaped from great calamity, and had at last become superior to the people of Tegea in matters of war: for under the reign of Leo and Hegesicles, at Sparta, the Lacedæmonians, although successful in their other wars, were defeated by the Tegeans only. For a long time before this, they had been almost the worst-constituted state among the Hellenes, averse to communication with one another and with strangers: but had afterwards altered for a good government, as I am going to describe.—Lycurgus was a man much venerated by the Spartans: he had come to Delphi for the purpose of consulting the oracle; and immediately he entered the holy fane, the Pythia spoke thus:

" Thou hast come, Lycurgus, to my sumptuous[156] temple, thou
" friend to Jove and all that dwell in the mansions of Olympus!
" —I doubt whether to greet thee, from the shrine, god or man;
" but rather god, I ween, O Lycurgus!"

Some persons accordingly say, that the Pythia not only pronounced this salutation, but also dictated the constitution now established among the Spartans: but, by the account of the Lacedæmonians themselves, Lycurgus, being appointed guardian to his nephew Leobotas[157], king of the Spartans, brought that code from Crete: for they relate[158], that no sooner was he appointed guardian, than he reformed all the laws, and took measures to prevent the violation of the new

---

[153] Larcher translates, " Qui avaient tenu fermes dans la dernière action." Schweighæuser also explains *εὐκα-μίνες, præsto manere dum illi pugnant*.
[154] Thucydid. iii. 104.
[155] " Son of Alcmæon;" that is to say, Megacles: see chap. 59.
[156] *κίων δόμος* (Odyss. ix. 35) is 'a magnificent and sumptuously-furnished residence.'
[157] There is scarcely a doubt that Charilaus was intended, instead of Leobotas. Larcher shews that Lycurgus was guardian to Charilaus, about 884 B.C. and promulgated his code 866: Chronol. p. 489.
[158] *δὲ γὰρ*: understand *λέγουσι*. Compare chap. 58. Schweigh. note 53, 3.

ones. After which, Lycurgus settled every thing belonging to war, the enomotiæ and triacades and syssitia[159]: he instituted also the ephori and senators. Thus the Lacedæmonians exchanged their bad laws for good; and have erected a holy enclosure to Lycurgus, and honour him magnificently. As they inhabited a good soil numerously peopled, they quickly grew up and flourished. Being no longer content to live in peace and quiet, and fancying themselves better men than the Arcadians, they consulted the oracle at Delphi about conquering the whole of Arcadia: the Pythia's response was this:

"Thou askest me all Arcadia?—It is a large request; I cannot
"grant it thee. Many acorn-eating men there are in Arcadia,
"who will repel thee. A part I will not grudge thee: I will
"give thee foot-trod Tegea, to dance there; and the fair mead,
"to measure out by the rod[160]."

When this answer was reported, the Lacedæmonians gave up their views on the whole of Arcadia; but, taking fetters with them, marched to attack Tegea; putting their trust in an ambiguous oracle, and confident they should enthral the Tegeans. But they were themselves defeated in battle; and such as survived, and were made prisoners, were compelled to till the ground, bearing the fetters which they had themselves brought, and measuring their task by the rod, on the plain of Tegea. These same fetters, in which they were bound, were still in my time extant at Tegea, hanging around the temple of Minerva Alea.

During the first war, therefore, the Lacedæmonians had constantly fought with adverse fortune against the people of Tegea: but in the days of Crœsus, and under the reign of Anaxandrides and Aristo over Lacedæmon, the Spartans had already become superior in the war: this happened in the following manner. Being constantly worsted in battle by the

---

[159] ἐνωμοτία, 'a certain number of sworn soldiers;' the quarter of a λόχος, which, generally speaking, was of 100 men, divided into four enomotiæ, each of twenty-five men, commanded by an enomotiarch.—τριακάς, a civil division, by which each φυλή was divided into thirty γένη, called the τριακάδες.—συσσίτια, the daily meals in common of all citizens in their respective divisions.—γερουσία, 28 senators not less than sixty years old.—ἔφοροι, five overseers, constituting a council, to restrain and balance the power of the two kings (βασιλεῖς). These were the springs of Lycurgus's constitution, both military and civil. The words τὰ ἐς πόλεμον ἔχοντα refer to ἐνωμοτία only.

[160] The schœnus in Greece, like the pertica in Italy, was a measure, by which the shares of conquered land were apportioned to the settlers: it was likewise used as a measure of the daily labour of a slave at field-work. —σχοῖνος is a Greek word, signifying 'a rush:' hence, a basket, mat, cord for drawing water from a well, for measuring the extent of labourers' work done, &c.

Tegeans, they sent deputies to consult the Delphian oracle; and inquired, which of the gods they ought to propitiate, in order to become superior to the Tegeans in the war. The Pythia charged them, from the shrine, to take home the bones of Orestes the son of Agamemnon. But, as they were still unable to discover the coffin of Orestes, they sent once more a deputation[161] to inquire of the god what spot Orestes' bones lay in: to this question, put by the consulters, the Pythia gave this answer:

"In Arcadia's level plain stands a town, Tegea: there, by stern
"compulsion, two winds breathe; the blow and the counter-
"blow; wo on wo lies. There the fertile earth contains
"Agamemnon's son: convey him home, and thou wilt conquer
"Tegea."

On hearing this, the Lacedæmonians were as far off as ever from finding what they wanted, although they searched on all sides. At last, Lichas, one of the Spartans called Agathoergi, made the discovery. These Agathoergi are certain citizens, the five seniors of the knights which go out every year in rotation: during that year in which they go out of the body of the knights, they are not suffered to remain idle, but are sent respectively to various places by 68 the Spartan commonwealth. Lichas, who was one of these persons, made the discovery at Tegea, partly by chance, partly by his own ingenuity. At that time, communication with Tegea was allowed; and Lichas went into a smith's forge[162], where he saw iron welded: he was surprised at what he saw done; and the smith, remarking how astonished he was, stopped working, and said: "How greatly then, my "Spartan friend, would you have been astonished, had you "seen what I saw, particularly when you are so surprised "to see how iron is welded[163]! I wanted to make a well in "my yard, and, in digging, I came down to a coffin seven "cubits long. Not believing that men were ever any taller "than they are now, I opened the coffin, and saw the body, "which was as long as the coffin; I took the measure, and "covered it up again." Such was the man's description of what he had seen. Lichas turned the thing over in his mind; and conjectured that, according to the oracle, this must be Orestes: he came to that conclusion by the following

---

[161] Understand τομπὴν, between τὴν and ἐς θεὸν.

[162] εἰς χαλκήιον, *a brazier's shop.*— Brass was discovered and forged before iron. "Prior aëris erat quam ferri cognitus usus:" *Lucret.* v. 1292.

"They tilled the earth with brass," says Hesiod, "as there was not then any iron." When iron became common, such is the force of habit, they still called a smith χαλκεύς.—*Larcher.*

[163] Matt 413. *obs.* 5; and 599.

reasoning: seeing the smith's two bellows, he inferred they were the two winds; the beetle and the anvil, the blow and counter-blow[164]; the iron that was being welded, the wo lying on wo; figuring to himself it was such, because iron was found to the injury of man[165]. Having formed this conclusion, he went to Sparta; where he related every thing to the Lacedæmonians;—who brought against him a fictitious charge, and he was banished. Lichas then came back to Tegea, and explained to the smith how unfortunate he had been; offering him a remuneration for his yard[166], which the man refused: however, after some time, he altered his mind; and Lichas took possession, opened the grave, collected the bones, and carried them to Sparta. From that time, whenever the Spartans and Tegeans tried their strength, the Lacedæmonians were always uppermost in the war; and already most part of Peloponnesus was likewise subjected to them.

Crœsus having been informed of all these particulars, sent 69 ambassadors to Sparta, with gifts, and a request of mutual alliance: what they were to say was prescribed to them; and, on their arrival, they spoke thus: "Crœsus, king of the "Lydians and other nations, has sent us, to say as follows: "Ye Lacedæmonians! the god has, through his oracle, bade "me connect myself with some Hellenic friend. I under- "stand you are the first in rank of Hellas; therefore, in "obedience to his oracle, I invite you to be my willing "friends and allies, without let or fraud." This was the communication that Crœsus made through the ambassadors. The Lacedæmonians, who had themselves heard of the oracle given to Crœsus, being much gratified at the arrival of the Lydians, swore the oaths of alliance and mutual friendship. Indeed, certain favours had already been previously shewn them by Crœsus: for the Lacedæmonians sent some agents to Sardis, who were to purchase gold, which they wanted to use about a statue of Apollo which now stands at Thornax in Laconica; but, as they were trying to strike a bargain, Crœsus gave it to them as a gift. From 70 this motive, as well as from his selecting them in preference before all the rest of the Hellenes, the Lacedæmonians

---

[164] τύπος, *type*, coming from τύπτω, *verbero*, expresses pretty well 'the hammer,' in the enigmatic language of the Pythia; and ἀντίτυπος, the 'anvil,' because it repels the stroke.—*Larcher.*
[165] "Ast homini ferrum letale incude nefanda Produxisse parum." Juv. Sat. xv. 165: quoted by Wesseling.
[166] The force of the imperfect should be observed: ἐμισθοῦτο does not signify, *he hired*, but *he wished to hire*. So, in the following chapter, χρυσὸν ὠνέοντο, *they wished to purchase gold*.—*Larcher.*

accepted the treaty of alliance. In the first place, accordingly, they held themselves in readiness for the earliest call: in the second place, they made a wine-bowl of brass, covering the outside, up to the rim, with various figures of animals and other objects[167], and of such dimensions as to hold three hundred amphoræ[168]: this they sent, intending it for a present to Crœsus: but the wine-bowl never reached Sardis; the reasons for which are stated in these two ways. The Lacedæmonians, on the one hand, assert, that when the wine-bowl, on its road to Sardis, was opposite to Samos, the Samians, informed of its coming, pushed off with some ships of war, and took it away by force. On the other hand, the Samians declare, that when the Lacedæmonians, who were conveying the wine-bowl to Sardis, found they were too late, and that Crœsus was a prisoner, they disposed of the wine-bowl in their island; where it was purchased by some private individuals, as an offering for Juno's temple: they add, that probably the sellers, on their return to Sparta, might have said that it was taken away by the Samians[169]. So much, therefore, for the wine-bowl[170].

71 Crœsus, misunderstanding the oracle, prepared for a campaign against Cappadocia; expecting he should overthrow Cyrus, together with the Persian power. When he had provided every thing for war with the Persians, one of his Lydian subjects, previously noted for his wisdom, but who, in consequence of the advice he now gave, obtained a very great name among the Lydians, counselled the king in these words—the name of this person was Sandanes:—"Sire! you "are about to engage in war with a people who wear nothing "but hose[171] and other garments of leather; who feed not "on what they like, but on what they have; and they have a "rugged soil: add to this, they use no wine, but drink wa- "ter: they have no figs[172] to eat, nor any thing that is good: "should you, therefore, conquer them, what can you take "from those that have nothing? But, on the other hand, "if you should be conquered, know what blessings you throw "away. As soon as they will have tasted of our good things, "they will cleave to them; nor will they be easy to shake

---

[167] ζῶα signifies not only *animals*, but *figures of every kind*, whether animals, flowers, fruits, &c.—*Schweigh.*

[168] The *amphora*, according to Arbuthnot, is seven gallons, one pint, and a little more; that is to say, rather less than a bushel.

[169] Matt. 514. Comp. iii. 47.

[170] The Greek text adds: κατὰ μὲν τὸν κρητῆρα οὕτως ἔσχε: So it was, then, *with regard to the crater.*

[171] ἀναξυρίδας, literally, *breeches.*

[172] Figs and olives constitute the chief food of the lower classes in the Levant.

"off. I give, therefore, thanks to the gods, that they have "not inspired the Persians with the thought of bringing "war upon the Lydians." Sandanes however failed to persuade Crœsus by this discourse. What he said was true enough; for, previous to the subjection of the Lydians, the Persians possessed nothing delicate or good. The Cappadocians are called Syrians by the Hellenes: before the rise of the Persian power, they had been subject to the Medes: they now were subjects of Cyrus; for the river Halys served as the boundary between the Medic and Lydian empires: that river flows out of Armenia, through Cilicia; then continues its course, having the Matianians on the right, and the Phrygians on opposite banks; below which, flowing up[173] to the northward, it divides the Syrian Cappadocians from the Paphlagonians on the left. Thus the Halys river skirts nearly the whole of Lower Asia from the sea opposite Cyprus to the Euxine sea: it marks, as it were, the neck of that whole division of Asia; the way across which occupies five days to a well-girt[174] man.

The following were the motives that induced Crœsus to invade Cappadocia: first, the desire of getting possession of a country which he would fain annex to his own states: chiefly, however, his confidence in the oracle, and the wish to be avenged of Cyrus for his treatment of Astyages. For Cyrus the son of Cambyses had subjugated Astyages son of Cyaxares, a relation by marriage[175] to Crœsus. He had become related to Crœsus in the following manner. A party of Scythian nomades, in consequence of a feud, had quitted their country, and secretly entered[176] Media: at that time, Cyaxares son of Phraortes, grandson of Deïoces, ruled over the Medes; who at first received these Scythians humanely, as being his suppliants: at last, he conceived so

---

[173] ἄνω ῥέω, flowing up; i. e. up, in relation to the cardinal points; for it runs from the south, towards the north pole, which is the most elevated.

[174] εὔζωνος, well-girt, expeditious: so the Latins say succinctus, from which we have derived the word succinctly. See Eton Atlas, Pl. 18. The principal head of the Halys is at the junction of the Paryadres and Camisena mountains in Armenia Minor (between 39 and 40 lat., 38 long.) The second head is in the range of Taurus, on the confines of Cilicia (between 37 and 38 lat., 34 long.) Herodotus apparently confounds these heads: what he says, applies only to the course of the branch running west from Armenia Minor. The length of what the Historian calls the neck is ascertained, by modern research, to be about 300 German miles; equivalent to Eratosthenes' estimate, which was, according to Strabo, 3000 stades.

[175] γαμβρός. This word is not confined to one meaning only, 'son-in-law:' in this case, it signifies 'sister's husband,' or what is generally called 'brother-in-law.'

[176] ὑπεξέρχομαι, clam exire. Æ. Port. Lex. Ion.—Excedere suis sedibus, et alio se conferre.—Schweigh. Lex. Herod.

much esteem for them, that he entrusted some boys to learn from them their language, and the art of shooting with the bow. In the course of time, the Scythians, making it their constant practice to hunt, and always bringing home something, it one day so happened, that they took no game: as they returned empty-handed, Cyaxares—for he was, as he proved, inclined to anger—treated them pretty harshly, with abusive language. The Scythians, having suffered usage at the hands of Cyaxares which they considered not deserved by them, determined among themselves to cut up one of their pupils; and, dressing the flesh as they were wont to do the animals of the chace, serve it up, as if forsooth it were game; and, immediately after they had taken it in, to proceed to Alyattes, son of Sadyattes, at Sardis. This was accordingly done: in fact, Cyaxares, and his guests of that day, ate of the flesh; and the Scythians, who had committed this offence, became suppliants to Alyattes. After this occurrence—for Alyattes refused to give back the Scythians, when claimed by Cyaxares—war raged for five years between the Lydians and Medes; during which, the Medes frequently defeated the Lydians, and the Lydians frequently defeated the Medes: among these[177], occurred a sort of nightly engagement. Being hitherto equal in war, a meeting took place in the sixth year, where, as the battle began to grow warm, day was all at once changed into night. This change of the day had been foretold to the Ionians by Thales of Miletus, who had fixed its occurrence in the year that it actually took place. The Lydians, as well as the Medes, seeing the day become night, ceased fighting; and both parties hastened in good earnest to establish peace between themselves. The mediators between them were Syennesis, the Cilician prince, and Labynetus[178], the king of Babylon: these princes hastened to tender the oaths, and arranged an interchange of connubial connexions; for they ordained that Alyattes should give his daughter Aryenis to Astyages the son of Cyaxares; because without the powerful tie of necessity, they knew the peace would not be of itself strong enough. These nations perform the ceremonies of taking an oath nearly after the same manner as the Hellenes; with this addition, that, after making a slight

---

[177] ἐν ᾗ. In full, it would be, ἐν ταῖς ἄλλαις μάχαις. Larcher observes, that the particle μὲν indicates, that during the first five years the success was equal on both sides. ἐν ᾗ proves that the author is then going to speak of the sixth year.

[178] This Labynetus (for others of the same name occur, ch. 77 and 118) is supposed to be the Nebuchadnezzar of Scripture.

incision in the upper skin of their arms, they lick up one another's blood.

Cyrus had therefore, for a reason which I shall point out in the sequel[179], dethroned this Astyages, who was his grandfather by the mother's side. Crœsus, laying this to the charge of Cyrus, had sent to the oracles, to inquire whether he ought to undertake war on the Persians: an answer accordingly came; and he, fancying it to be in his own favour, determined to attack a portion of the Persian appurtenances. When he came to the Halys, he marched his army across the river by the same bridges that are now[180] there. Such is my opinion; but, according to the report general among the Hellenes, Thales the Milesian was the person that got the troops over for him: it is related, that Crœsus, doubting how he should cross the river with his forces—for the above-mentioned bridges were not in existence at that time—Thales, who was in the camp, planned for him some works on the river, so that the stream running on the left of his army might flow on its right. The work was this: beginning some distance above the camp to dig a deep canal in the shape of a crescent, so as to enclose the back of the camp in the situation where it then stood, the river, being turned off from its old bed into the canal at the above place, and thus passing along the camp, would fall again into the old bed[181]. Thus, as soon as the river was split into two streams, it became fordable in both. Some say, indeed, that the old bed was completely drained of water; but that I can never assent to; for, in such a case, how could they ever have effected a passage, on their return home? Crœsus, however, passed over with his army, and came to a place called Pteria in Cappadocia: this is the

---

[179] See ch. 121 of this Book.

[180] Wyttenbach proves satisfactorily, that τὰς λοιπὰς γεφύρας signifies *the bridges which are now there*, and not such bridges as are now used.

[181] Schweighæuser proposes the following construction. Ὅπως ἂν (for Ἵνα) [ὁ ποταμὸς], ταύτῃ, ἱστρατοπέδευτο ἐκ τῶν ἀρχαίων ῥείθρων, λάβῃ τὸ στρατόπεδον κατὰ νώτου, καὶ αὖτις ἐκβάλλῃ ἐς τὰ ἀρχαῖα, παραμειβόμενος τὸ στρατόπεδον.

CAPPADOCIA.

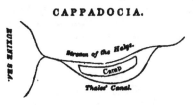

PHRYGIA.

strongest position in that quarter, situate not far[182] from Sinope, a town on the Euxine sea: there he pitched his camp, and devastated the fields of the Syrians: he captured also the town of the Pterians, and sent them into captivity: he took possession, also, of all the neighbouring places; and compelled the Syrians, although guiltless, to leave their country. Cyrus, however, mustered his own soldiers, and enlisted all dwelling on his road to Cappadocia, where he faced Crœsus. Previous however to commencing his march, he sent heralds to the Ionians, summoning them to secede from Crœsus: but the Ionians refused. Cyrus, notwithstanding, proceeded, and pitched his tents opposite to Crœsus, in the vicinity of Pteria, where he was resolved to make essay of the strength of both parties. A bloody battle ensued; and great numbers having fallen on both sides, they at last separated, neither having conquered, at the fall of night. Such was the result of the engagement between the two armies.

77 Crœsus, laying the blame to the numbers of his own army[183]—for the troops engaged were far inferior to those of Cyrus—and seeing Cyrus on the following day was not inclined to renew the attack, marched back to Sardis; with the intention of summoning the Egyptians, conformably to the treaty of alliance he had framed with Amasis king of Egypt, previously to that with the Lacedæmonians; of sending for the Babylonians, with whom he had also entered in alliance, under the reign of Labynetus; and of letting the Lacedæmonians know at what appointed time they should be present. He thought to spend the winter at home, and to open with the spring a campaign against the Persians, after having collected the above allies, and mustered his own forces. In this view, on his arrival at Sardis, he sent heralds to the different members of the alliance, giving them notice to assemble before the end of five months. The present army, that which had just been engaged with the Persians, and which consisted of foreign mercenaries, he disbanded completely, and dispersed; not once giving it a thought, that Cyrus, having been so nearly beaten[184], might

78 march against Sardis. While Crœsus was forming these projects, the suburbs were completely swarmed with ser-

---

[182] μάλιστά κη. Like the Latin adverb *maxime*, the Greek μάλιστα is put for *almost, nearly*: when taken in that sense, Herodotus generally adds the particle κω or κη.—*Schweig. Lex. Herod.*

[183] Construe: Κροῖσος δὲ, μεμφθεὶς τὸ ἑαυτοῦ στράτευμα κατὰ τὸ πλῆθος.

[184] ἀγχωμάχισιος αὐτοῦ παρεκτλησίως· Qui ita æquo Marte pugnasset.— *Schweig. Ver. Lat.*

pents; at the appearance of which, the horses, forsaking the pastures, came and devoured them. Crœsus saw this, and considered it, as it was in fact, a prodigy: forthwith, he despatched some persons to consult the soothsayers of Telmessus: the persons thus sent, arrived, and learnt, from the Telmessians, what the prodigy portended; but had not the opportunity to report it to Crœsus; for before they could complete their voyage back to Sardis, Crœsus had been taken prisoner. The declaration of the Telmessians was, that Crœsus should expect a foreign host within his territory, and they would come to subjugate the natives; for, said they, the serpent is the son of the earth, whereas the horse is a foe and alien. This answer the Telmessians gave to Crœsus, when he had already been taken prisoner; although they knew nothing about Sardis, or Crœsus himself.

Cyrus, however, immediately after the departure of Crœ- 79 sus, subsequent to the engagement at Pteria, learnt that Crœsus had retreated, for the purpose of disbanding his troops: he considered the matter; and found that the best thing he could do, would be, to march as quickly as he could upon Sardis, and anticipate the levying a second time of the Lydian forces: no sooner thought than done; for he directly marched into Lydia, and came his own messenger to Crœsus. Crœsus, now thrown into great embarrassment, events turning out so contrary to his expectation, nevertheless led out the Lydians to battle; and in those days, there was no nation in all Asia more valiant and warlike than the Lydian: their mode of fighting was from the backs of horses[185]: they carried long javelins, and were good riders. The two armies met 80 in the plain that stretches before the citadel of Sardis, which is extensive, and not encumbered with trees[186]—several rivers flowing through it, among which is the Hyllus, pour their waters into the largest stream, called the Hermus, which rises in the sacred mountain of mother Ceres, and falls into the sea by the city of Phocæa—where Cyrus, who was alarmed at the sight of the Lydian horse drawn up in battle array, acted, after the suggestion of Harpagus, a Mede, in the following manner: He collected all the camels that followed in the train of the army, carrying provisions and munitions; he took off their burdens, and mounted upon them soldiers accoutred as cavalry: having made these preparations, he drew them up in the van of the whole army, opposite to Crœsus's cavalry, and commanded the infantry to

---

[185] Matt. 573.
[186] ψιλὶς, nudus, indicates that the plain had neither trees nor bushes.— *Larcher.*

follow on and support the camels: in the rear of the infantry he arrayed the whole of his own cavalry. Having thus formed all his forces in line, he recommended them not to spare any of the Lydians, but to cut down every man that stood up against them: not, however, to slay Crœsus, not even if, when overpowered, he should still resist. The reason that induced him to place the camels opposite to the enemy's horse, was, because the horse has a dread of the camel, and cannot bear to look at the figure or snuff the smell of that animal[187]. For this purpose, therefore, Cyrus had recourse to the above expedient, that he might make Crœsus's cavalry of no use, by which the Lydian prince expected to perform many brilliant achievements. As soon as the armies joined battle, the horses, instantly smelling the camels, and seeing them before them, reared back, and the hopes of Crœsus were blasted. Nevertheless, the Lydians behaved not as cowards, but, as soon as they saw what had occurred, leaped off their horses, and engaged the Persians foot to foot. After some time, many having fallen on both sides, the Lydians were turned to the right-about, and, shut up within their walls, were blockaded by the Persians.

81 Siege was accordingly laid to the Lydians. But Crœsus, who thought that the blockade would last some time, sent, from within the ramparts, other messengers to the allies: as those formerly despatched had given them notice to assemble in the course of the fifth month, Crœsus sent the present persons to request assistance as speedily as possible, he himself being already besieged.

82 He sent more particularly, of all his allies[188], to the Lacedæmonians; but just at that very time the Spartans themselves happened to be engaged in a quarrel with the Argians, on the subject of a place called Thyrea, which, although a portion of the domain of Argos, the Lacedæmonians had appropriated. To the Argians also belonged the whole country westward down to Maleum, both on the land, and Cythera, together with the rest of the islands. The Argians proceeded to the defence of their own property, thus abstracted: then both parties met, and came to an agreement, that three hundred men on each side should engage battle, and that the disputed

---

[187] I can see no objection to the veracity of this anecdote: the confusion of the Lydian cavalry arose from a very natural cause—the fact, that the Lydian horses now beheld for the first time the uncouth figure of the camel: the Historian was well aware that the camels of Cyrus were not an object of such abhorrence to his own horses, in consequence of the long and close connexion between the two races, in the countries under the Persian sway.

[188] Matt. 429, 1.

ground should be that of which every party survived: it was also settled, that the mass of the army on both sides should retire homeward, for this purpose, that neither army being present, they might not, seeing their own party give way, rush to their assistance. After they had agreed to these terms, they respectively withdrew: the chosen champions on both sides, left to themselves, joined battle: they fought with such equal valour, that, out of the six hundred, three alone remained; Alcenor and Chromius on the part of the Argians; Othryades on that of the Lacedæmonians: these were the combatants remaining, when night came: the two Argians accordingly, as having conquered, ran off to Argos; while Othryades the Lacedæmonian stripped the dead bodies of the Argians, and, having carried their arms to his camp, stood at his post. On the second day, both parties came to ascertain the result: for some time, accordingly, each party persisted that they had conquered: on one side, it was said that the greater number of their men had survived: the others contended, that the two that disappeared were runaways, and that their one survivor stripped the dead bodies of the others: at last, from words they came to blows: many fell on both sides: the Lacedæmonians gained the day. From that time, therefore, the Argians have shaved their heads, although previously obliged by necessity to wear long hair; and enacted a law accompanied with curses, on such as violate it, that no Argian man should let his hair grow, and that the women should wear no jewels of gold till such time as they should recover Thyrea. The Lacedæmonians, on the other hand, enacted a law quite the contrary: for though, until then, they had never worn long hair, from that time it was suffered to grow[189]. As to Othryades, the one Spartan that remained out of the three hundred, he, being ashamed to return to Sparta, all his fellow-champions having fallen, made away with himself at Thyrea. At the time affairs were in this confusion at Sparta, the Sardian herald arrived, and requested them to come to the assistance of the besieged Crœsus: the people nevertheless, when informed by the herald, prepared to start to his assistance; when, as they had all got ready, and their ships were equipped, another message came, that the Lydian citadel had been taken, and Crœsus made prisoner: consequently, sympathizing deeply with the Lydians, they ceased their exertions.

Sardis was taken in the following manner: on the fourteenth day that Crœsus had been besieged, Cyrus sent round

[189] Matt. 534, c; and 555. obs. 1.

some horsemen, to proclaim to the whole army, that he would give a reward to the first man that would scale the wall: in consequence, the whole army having made the attempt without success[190], all gave up, but a Mardian soldier, who determined to try if he could climb up: the man's name was Hyrœades: on that quarter of the citadel no guard was stationed, because there was no fear of the fort being ever carried in that place; for in this part the citadel was abruptly perpendicular, and inaccessible: this was the only part around which Meles, one of the former kings of Sardis, had not carried the lion which his concubine brought forth; the Telmessians having decided, that if this lion were conveyed around the fortifications, Sardis would be impregnable: and Meles, after carrying the lion about the rest of the wall, where it might be possible to storm the citadel, refrained from doing the same by this place, regarded as impregnable and precipitous: this quarter of the town lies towards Tmolus. This Hyrœades therefore, the Mardian, had the day before seen one of the Lydians descend by this way, pick up a helmet that had rolled down, and carry it up: he observed what was done, and turned it over in his mind: accordingly, he ascended then himself, and was followed by some other Persians: great numbers having gone up, Sardis was thus taken, and the whole town abandoned to pillage.

85 I will now relate what happened to Crœsus himself. He had a son, whom I have before mentioned, in other respects well endowed by nature, but dumb: in the foregone days of prosperity, Crœsus had done every thing for him possible: he had recourse to many expedients; more particularly, he sent a deputation to Delphi, in order to consult the oracle: the answer returned by the Pythia was this:

"Thou Lydian-born, king of many, mighty simple man that
"thou art, Crœsus! long not to hear the much-besought voice
"of thy son, within thy halls: that were far better for thee
"indeed! for in a hapless day thou wilt first hear him."

The fortifications had been carried[191]:—one of the Persians, not knowing Crœsus, was about to kill him: Crœsus saw the man rushing on: absorbed in his present calamity, it made no difference to him whether he died under the stroke; but his son, the dumb boy, saw the Persian rushing to the attack: pressed by terror and misery, he burst a passage to his voice: "Soldier, kill not Crœsus!" he exclaimed. This was,

---

[190] ὡς οὐ προχώρει (τὸ πρῆγμα): As the thing did not succeed.—*Schweig. Lex. Herod.*

[191] ἥτι γάρ. Matt. 613, vii. See ch. 8, of this Book.

therefore, the first word he ever uttered; but from that time, ever after, throughout life, he had the use of his speech. The Persians had possession of Sardis; and took Crœsus alive, having reigned fourteen years, and been besieged the same number of days: he had thus, according to the oracle, put an end to his own mighty empire. The Persians, who had made him prisoner, carried him before Cyrus; who collected a huge pile, on which he placed Crœsus, bound in fetters, and, by his side, twice seven of the sons of Lydians: whether having it in contemplation accordingly to offer up these firstlings to one of the gods, or wishing to fulfil some vow; or perhaps, having heard that Crœsus was a devout worshipper of the divine powers, he placed him on the pile only to ascertain whether any of the divinities would rescue him from being burnt alive. They relate, that as Crœsus was standing on the pile, and, notwithstanding the deep misery he was in, recalled to his mind the saying of Solon, pronounced as it were by divine inspiration, that " No one, yet in life, is happy." When this occurred to him, he broke his deep silence: breathing from the bottom of his heart, and sighing, he called out three times, " Solon." Cyrus heard him, and commanded the interpreters to ask Crœsus whom he called thus [192]: they approached, and put the question. Crœsus, however, although repeatedly asked, held for some time his peace: at last, from compulsion, he said: " One, whom " to see converse with all kings, I should prefer before great " wealth [193]." As what he said was unintelligible to the interpreters, they again inquired what he said: as they persevered in urging him to speak, he said, ' That once upon a time, Solon, a native of Athens, came to his court, and, having seen all his blessings, despised them:'—he accordingly stated, ' that Solon had told him every thing exactly as had occurred to him, and would say no more in respect of him than of the rest of mankind, and such especially as conceived themselves to be happy.'—Thus Crœsus spoke: the pile was already lighted, the flames caught the outside, and Cyrus heard from the interpreters what Crœsus had said: he now relented: and recollecting, that he, being himself a man, was giving up alive to the flames a man who had been not less fortunate than himself; dreading, moreover, retribution, and considering that nothing pertaining to man

[192] Matt. obs. 4.

[193] τὸν ἂν ἐγὼ πᾶσι τυράννοισι προτεί- μησα μεγάλων χρημάτων ἐς λόγους ἐλθεῖν. Larcher gives this construction, προ- τίμησα μεγάλων χρημάτων (οὐσῶν) πᾶσι τυράννοισι. Another translation may be given: *One, such that I should prefer before great wealth, his conversing with all tyrants.*—*Schweig.*

is stable, gave order that the burning fire should be quenched as speedily as possible, and that Crœsus, as well as those with him, should be lifted down from the pile. They endeavoured to obey the orders, but were yet unable to master the flames: then, it is related by the Lydians, that Crœsus, perceiving the change in Cyrus's resolution, and seeing all the people endeavour to quench the flames but not able to repress their violence, invoked aloud Apollo, if ever any grateful gift had been presented to the god by him, that he would come to his assistance, and rescue him from impending death. Weeping, it is said, he thus called on the god: instantly, from its being a clear and tranquil sky, clouds gathered, the storm burst, and rain poured down in torrents, to extinguish the fire. This was sufficient proof to Cyrus that Crœsus was a pious and good man: he caused him to be taken down from the pile: " Crœsus," said he to the king, " who in the world ever induced you to invade a country " that belongs to me, and to be my foe, instead of being my " friend." " Sire," he replied, " what I have done is to your " good fortune[194], to my misfortune: the promoter of these " things was the god of the Hellenes: he it was that spurred " me to war:—for no man is so reft of common sense, as to " prefer war before peace[195]; since in peace sons bury fa- " thers, while in war fathers have to bury sons. But it " pleased the gods that things should thus come to pass."

88 When he had thus spoken, Cyrus took off his fetters, and seated him near himself, and behaved to him with great respect: he, as well as his attendants, were astonished at the sight of the Lydian monarch: Crœsus himself, absorbed in thought, stood silent: after a time, he turned round and saw the Persians sacking the Lydian capital. " Sire," said he to Cyrus, " am I allowed to communicate any thoughts to " you[196], or must I be silent now in my present state?" Cyrus bade him be of good cheer, and say what he chose. " Tell me then," said Crœsus, " what is all this crowd occupied " at so earnestly ?" He was answered: " They are sacking " your city, and plundering your riches." " Not my city," retorted Crœsus, " not my riches, are they sacking: none of " these things belong to me any longer; it is your property 89 " they plunder and bear away[197]." Crœsus's words had a striking effect on Cyrus: he dismissed all his attendants, and

[194] Matt. 403, b.
[195] Matt. 479. obs. 1.
[196] Matt. 553. obs. 4.
[197] ἀλλὰ φέρουσί τε καὶ ἄγουσι τὰ σά.— ἄγειν καὶ φέρειν signifies, properly, ' to pillage;' but with this difference, that ἄγειν is said of flocks which are driven before, and of the men that are led away as slaves; while φέρω is used of moveables, and such things as it is necessary ' to carry away.'

then asked Crœsus what he thought should be done in the present conjuncture. " Since the gods have given me a slave " to you," said Crœsus, " it becomes my duty, when I observe " any thing that escapes you, to point it out. The Persians, " by nature presumptuous, are poor: if, therefore, you per- " mit them to plunder and retain this great wealth, you may " expect the issue to be this: he who gets the greatest " booty, be assured, will revolt. Now therefore, if my pro- " posal be agreeable to you, adopt this plan: place at each " gate some of your body-guards, as sentinels; let them stop " those that are carrying off the valuable booty, and say to " them, that they must absolutely pay the tithe to Jupiter: " thus you will not incur the hatred of taking away the " property; and the soldiers, confessing the equity of your " proceedings, will willingly accede." Cyrus was exceed- 90 ingly gratified to hear these words: he thought the suggestion very expedient, praised it highly, and gave orders to his guards to do what Crœsus intimated: then he addressed him in these words: " You are resolved, Crœsus, like a true " king[188], to shew yourself wise in action and in word: de- " mand whatever gift you may desire, at this very moment." " My lord," said Crœsus, " most highly would you gratify " me, by giving me leave to send the god of the Hellenes, " whom I have honoured the most of all the gods, these " fetters, and ask if it is his custom to lead astray his bene- " factors." Cyrus asked why he made such a charge, and why such a request. Crœsus then related to him all his projects, the answers of the oracles, and dwelt especially on the offerings; and again observed, that, urged by the oracle, he had waged war against the Persians. Having said so much, he concluded by supplicating that he might reproach the god with this behaviour[189]. Cyrus burst into laughter, and said: " Not only shall you receive that boon from me, but whatever else you may at any time want." Crœsus heard this; and sent the Lydians to Delphi, prescribing to them to lay the fetters on the temple-sill, and ask the god if he was not ashamed to have, by his oracles, incited Crœsus to attack the Persians, as he would put an end to Cyrus's dominion; and such were the firstlings of the contest: they were to make those inquiries, and at the same time ask whether it was the custom with the Grecian gods to be ungrateful. The Lydians 91 arrived, and spoke as was prescribed: it is related, that the

---

[188] ἀληθὴς βασιλεὺς, as a man king. ἀνὴρ is put pleonastically: this expression is familiar to the Greeks. 'Ἀνὴρ δὲ βασιλεὺς ἰχθὺν ἡγεῖται τόδε, A king regards them as foes. Eurip. Supp. 526.—*Larcher*.
[189] Matt. 345.

Pythia's reply was this: "It is beyond the power of a god "even to evade[200] the fated doom. Crœsus has made reparation for the wicked deed of his fifth progenitor[201], who, "being but a guardsman to the Heraclidæ, abetting a woman's fraud, murdered his sovereign lord, and grasped a "dignity which in no manner appertained to him. Apollo had "indeed earnestly wished that the fall of Sardis might come "to pass under the sons of Crœsus, and not under Crœsus "himself; but he was not equal to the task of relenting the "fates. As much as the fates would give, he obtained, and "transferred the boon to him: he retarded three whole "years the capture of Sardis: let Crœsus know, that he was "made a prisoner three years later than was fated. In the "second place, Apollo brought salvation when he was about "to be consumed by fire. As far as concerns the oracle, "Crœsus brings forward a false accusation: Apollo declared, "if he waged war against the Persians he would overthrow a "mighty empire: had he been anxious to take good counsel, "it behoved him to send and inquire which empire was "meant, his or that of Cyrus: as he neither comprehended "the oracle, nor repeated his inquiry, let him take the blame "to himself. In the last oracle, pronounced at the shrine, "he again misunderstood the words that Apollo spoke about "a mule; for Cyrus was that mule, as he was born of parents "of different nations; the mother superior, the father inferior; "she a Mede, and daughter of Astyages the king of the "Medes; he a Persian, vassal of the Medes, and lower than "any Mede, was united to his sovereign mistress."—This was the answer returned by the Pythia to the Lydians: it was brought back to Sardis and communicated to Crœsus, who, having heard it, confessed the fault to be his, and not the god's. Such is the history of the rule of Crœsus, and the first subjugation of Ionia.

92 It is to be observed, however, that there are a great number of offerings from Crœsus in Hellas, besides those only mentioned heretofore. In Thebes of Bœotia is a gold tripod[202], which he dedicated to Ismenian Apollo; in Ephesus, both the golden oxen and several of the pillars; in the Pronaïa at Delphi, a large buckler of gold: all these objects

---

[200] Matt. 443.

[201] The Greeks considered, in their genealogies, the father as the second generation, the grandfather as the third generation, and so on: Gyges was, therefore, the fifth progenitor of Crœsus; thus: 1st, Crœsus; 2d, Alyattes; 3d, Sadyattes; 4th, Ardys; 5th, Gyges.

[202] The tripod was a vase, standing on three legs: they were of two sorts, some being used at banquets for mixing the wine and water; others being intended to boil water.—*Larcher.*

were still in existence in my day: some others, however, had been lost; those at Branchidæ, for instance, in Milesia, equal, I am told, in weight, and similar to those at Delphi. Those offerings which he presented to Delphi and Amphiareus were his own property, and the firstling of his paternal inheritance: the other offerings were the produce of the spoils of his enemy, who, previously to Crœsus's accession, had revolted, exerting himself to raise Pantaleon to the throne, a son of Alyattes, but by the same mother as his brother Crœsus: for Crœsus was the offspring of a Carian wife of Alyattes, but Pantaleon came from an Ionian woman. When, by the will of his father, Crœsus attained to the royal power, he put his adversary, the supporter of Pantaleon, to death, tearing to shreds his flesh, by a rack made like a fuller's thistle[203]. As he had previously dedicated the property of this individual to sacred purposes, he presented out of it the offerings just mentioned.

Lydia does not present many wonders for description, like some other countries, if we except the gold-dust brought down from the Tmolus. This country, however, exhibits an immense work, ranking next to those of the Egyptians and Babylonians: you see there a monument to Alyattes, father of Crœsus, the basis of which consists of large stones, the rest is made of accumulated earth: this mound was wrought by the tradesmen, the mechanics, and the prostitutes: five bourns, still remaining in my time, are placed on the top of this monument; on which inscriptions are carved, stating how much of the work was done by each of the above classes: from the measures, it is evident that the largest portion was the work of the prostitutes: for the daughters of the Lydian lower orders all make a traffic of their persons; and thus collect money for their portions, until, by so doing, they have got enough to marry: these girls have the right of choosing their own husbands. The monument is six stades and two plethra in circumference[204]; the breadth across is thirteen plethra. Adjoining[205] this monument is a wide lake, which the Lydians represent as always full: it is called the Gygæan lake.

The people of Lydia have pretty nearly the same customs as the Hellenes; excepting, of course, that the latter do not prostitute their females. They are the first nation, we know

---

[203] Κνάφος, according to Suidas, Hesychius, and Timæus, is an instrument armed with points, not unlike the thistles which fullers use: it was a sort of rack, on which criminals were torn to death.—*Larcher*.
[204] That is to say, 598 fath. 2 ft. 10 in. French, in circumference; not quite a mile round.
[205] Matt. 365.

of, that introduced and circulated gold and silver coin; and were the first venders by retail. According to the statement of the Lydians themselves, all the games likewise, now in vogue among themselves and the Hellenes, were inventions of their own: the epoch of this discovery is said to have been coincident with that of their colonization of Tyrrhenia: they give the following account of these matters: Under the reign of Atys son of Manes, a great famine pervaded the whole of Lydia: for a long time the Lydians bore patiently with this scourge; but no cessation taking place, they sought for remedies to the evil. Various persons devised various expedients: at that time, accordingly, the different kinds of games were discovered; dice, round-bones, ball, and all except drafts[305], the invention of which the Lydians do not claim to themselves[307]. The following was also invented as an expedient against the dearth—to play the whole of one day in order not to feel the hankering after food; on the next, to eat, and refrain from play. In this manner they passed eighteen years; at the end of which, the evil, far from relaxing, had acquired greater virulence: accordingly, their king divided the whole Lydian nation into two portions, and then drew lots which should remain, and which forsake their country[308]: on the party allotted to remain, he appointed himself king: at the head of the emigrants he put his own son, whose name was Tyrrhenus: those, whom fortune had doomed to abandon their country, went down to Smyrna, built ships, and, stowing on board all their useful articles of furniture, sailed away in search of land and food: at last, after coasting many states, they reached the Ombrici, where they erected for themselves towns, and dwell to this day. They have, however, altered their name from Lydians, to that of the king's son who headed the expedition; according to which they have given themselves the name of Tyrrhenians.—Thus the Lydians were enthralled by the Persians*.

[305] The games here enumerated are: the ἀστραγάλαι, 'the bone on which the heel springs,' those of sheep in particular, used in the game called πενταλίζειν, or placing five pebbles or round-bones on the back of the hand, throwing them up, and catching them all in the palm of the hand; 'the game of the huckle-bone or cockal;' in French, le jeu des osselets;—σφαίρα, 'the ball;'—πεσσοί, a kind of 'draught-board,' divided into 36 places by five lines drawn lengthways and breadthways: the middle line was called the ἱερὰ γραμμή.

[307] Comp. ch. 4, note 1, of this Book.
[308] Matt. 413.

* CHRONOLOGY OF LYDIA, FROM THE TEXT OF HERODOTUS.

1. The decease of Darius, son of Hystaspes, occurred four years after the Battle of Marathon. (Herod. vii. 1.)

Our history from this place proceeds, accordingly, to in- 95
quire who the Cyrus was that overthrew the power of Crœsus;
and in what manner the Persians obtained the supremacy of
Asia. This I shall describe, therefore, on the authority of
some Persian writers; who shew an anxiety, not so much to
embellish the adventures of Cyrus, as to speak the truth. I
am acquainted, nevertheless, with three other different ways
of presenting the life of Cyrus[209].—The Assyrians had been
lords over Upper Asia during five hundred and twenty

> 2. The Battle of Marathon, from undoubted authority, took place about 17th August, 490 B.C. The death of Darius consequently happened in 485 B.C.
> 3. Darius reigned (vii. 4.) 36 years; Smerdis the Magus (i. 68.) 8 months; Cambyses, 7 years and 5 months (iii. 66.); Cyrus (i. 24.) 29 years. The sum of these reigns is 73 years and 1 month; which, added to 485, gives, for the first of Cyrus's reign, 559.
> 4. The date of the capture of Sardis is no where clearly defined by Herodotus: it is presumed, however, that this event occurred in the second year of Cyrus's reign, B. C. 557. This assumption receives a powerful corroboration from the chronology of Media, which will be explained hereafter.
> 5. Departing from B.C. 557, the assumed date of the capture of Sardis: Crœsus reigned 14 years (i. 86.); Alyattes (i. 25.) 57 years; Sadyattes (i. 16.) 12 years; Ardys (i. 16.) 49 years; Gyges (i. 14.) 30 years. The sum of the reigns in the House of the Mermnadæ amounts to 170; which, added to the date of the capture of Sardis, gives for that of Gyges' usurpation, B. C. 727. The Heraclidæ held the sway previously for 505 years; so that Agron, the first prince of that line, ascended the throne B. C. 1232.

		B.C.
1st Dynasty: Atyadæ, in the fabulous times.		
2d Dynasty: Heraclidæ:	First King, Agron son of Ninus.	1232
	Last King, Candaules, murdered by Gyges.	
3d Dynasty: Mermnadæ:	1. Gyges usurps the throne.	727
	2. Ardys succeeds.	689
	He takes Priene.	
	Invades Miletus.	
	The Cimmerians, displaced by Scythian Nomades, come into Asia, and take possession of Sardis, all but the citadel.	
	3. Sadyattes succeeds.	640
	Pursues war against Miletus.	
	4. Alyattes succeeds.	620
	He makes war five years with Cyaxares, which terminates in consequence of a great eclipse.	
	Drives the Cimmerians out of Asia, takes Smyrna, and fails in an attack on Clazomenæ.	
	Continues the war against Miletus for five years.	
	5. Crœsus succeeds.	571
	Cyrus, already sovereign of Asia above the Halys, captures Crœsus, and takes possession of Sardis.	557

[209] Among the Greeks, there were three modes of narrating the life of Cyrus; those of Herodotus, Xenophon, and Æschylus.

years, when the Medes first seceded from their allegiance: in the struggle with the Assyrians for freedom, they became, it appears, a valiant and warlike race[210], and, shaking off the yoke of servitude, recovered their liberty: subsequently, the other dependent nations followed the example of the Medes. All the nations of the continent were then their own masters; but they again fell under usurped dominion: in what manner 96 this came to pass, I shall now describe. Among the Medes was an intelligent man, whose name was Deïoces, son of Phraortes: this individual, enamoured of royalty, endeavoured to attain his object, by the following means. The Medes were scattered about in villages: in his own, Deïoces had already made himself conspicuous, by his earnest application to the distribution of justice: he acted thus, principally, on account of the general lawlessness that pervaded Media, and from the conviction, that, by all honest people, the violators of justice are regarded as enemies[211]: the Medes of that village observed the disposition of Deïoces, and elected him their judge. He, still bearing in view the sovereign power, conducted himself uprightly and honestly, by which means he obtained no slight praise at the hands of his fellow-citizens: in consequence of this, the inhabitants of the other villages, having ascertained that Deïoces was the only man that pronounced fair decisions and sentences, having themselves before met with unjust judgments, hastened joyfully, when they heard this, to submit their disputes to Deïoces' adjudication: at last, no litigant would apply to any other 97 judge. The crowd of applicants constantly increasing[212], as people became aware that justice was distributed according to truth, Deïoces, who knew that every thing depended upon himself, would no longer occupy the seat from which he had heretofore pronounced judgment: he refused to fill any longer the office of judge, as it did not suit his interest to neglect his own affairs, and attend the whole day to the adjudication of those of others: in consequence, rapine and wickedness pervaded the villages still more even than before: the Medes therefore assembled, and debated on their present circumstances. The friends of Deïoces spoke, I presume, in some such language as this: "As it is wholly

---

[210] *ἐγένοντο ἄνδρες ἀγαθοί* may be perhaps translated, simply, 'behaved gallantly;' as in chap. 169 of this Book.

[211] Deïoces, aiming to usurp the sovereign power, sought prudently to make a party among the honest and respectable members of the community: he therefore shewed himself to be an unrelenting prosecutor of lawless malefactors; and thus made good his ends, being at last elected by the good and virtuous, to be their ruler.

[212] Matt. 269.

"impossible for us to live in this country, if we are treated in this manner, let us, without delay, establish a king over us[213]: by such means the country will be well managed and governed, and we ourselves shall be able to attend to our business, without being disturbed by the violation of the laws." By such discourses, they persuaded the assembly 98 to adopt a kingly government. Immediately after that decision, the subject for debate proposed was, whom should they appoint king: Deïoces was by every one present greatly preferred and extolled; so that, at last, all approved his appointment as king. Deïoces insisted, they should build for him a palace worthy of the royal power, and insure his safety by appointing a body-guard for him. This the Medes acceded to, and built him an extensive and strong palace in that part of the country that he himself pointed out: they also deferred to him the privilege of choosing his body-guards from among the whole Medic population. Now therefore, being in possession of the power, he compelled the Medes to build one single city, attend to the fortifications and embellishment of that, and take less account of the others. The Medes again obeyed: they built vast and substantial walls at the place now called Ecbatana, rising up one circle within another. This fortification was so contrived, that each circle was higher than the preceding by the battlements only; to which the hilly situation contributed in some degree, although its effect was mainly due to art. The circles are seven in number: within the last and highest is the royal palace and treasuries. The most extensive of these walls is very nearly equal to the circumference of Athens in length. The battlements of the first circle is white; of the second, black; of the third, purple; of the fourth, blue; of the fifth, scarlet: these battlements are all painted of those colours: the two last are coated respectively with silver and gold[214].

Such, therefore, were the fortifications, that Deïoces erected 99 around himself and his palace: to the rest of the people he assigned the space about the walls for their residence: when all these buildings were completed, he established, for the first time, the following state etiquette—that nobody should dare to come into the immediate presence, but that all business should be transacted through messengers: in addition to this, that it should be held at least disgraceful, in all per-

[213] Valckenaer proposes (ἵνα) ἡμῶν αὐτῶν.
[214] This party-coloured architecture is still frequently seen in the towns of China and India.

sons whatever[215], to laugh or spit in his presence. He cast about himself this mantle of veneration, for the purpose that his compeers, who had been brought up with him, and were not of baser blood than himself, or behind him in valour, should not, from seeing him frequently, envy his elevation, and conspire against him; but that, unseen, he should seem 100 to them a being of another nature. After he had established all these forms and ceremonies, and seated himself firmly in the throne, he continued to keep a vigilant watch on the distribution of justice: the complainants wrote down their depositions, and sent them in to the king, who, after deliberating on the contents, and coming to a judgment, sent them back; such was his arrangement in respect of justice: all the other details of government were settled by himself: if he ascertained that any of his subjects had presumed to contravene the law, he sent for him, and awarded the proper sentence for every offence: for this purpose, he kept spies and eavesdroppers, in every part of his dominions.

101 Deïoces therefore contented himself with collecting together the Medes only; and over them he ruled. The following are the Medic tribes: the Busæ, Paretaceni, Struchates, Ari- 102 zanti, Budii, Magi.—Deïoces had one son, Phraortes, who at the decease of his father, after a reign of fifty years, inherited the throne. Invested with royal power, this prince was not content to rule over the Medes only; but attacked the Persians, and, reducing them, gave the first subjects to the Medes. After this achievement, being master of those two nations, both of them very powerful, he subdued Asia, passing from one nation to the other; until, having made an attack on the Assyrians, that is to say, the Assyrians that occupied Nineveh, and had previously been supreme over all, but were now reft of their allies, who had abandoned them, and, although standing by themselves, were even now a flourishing nation—Phraortes, I say, having marched against this people, there perished, after two and twenty years' reign, together with the greater part of his army.

103 At the death of Phraortes, Cyaxares, the son of Deïoces, succeeded: this prince is represented as having been far more valiant than his progenitors; and the first that divided the Asiatics into military departments, and first separated the javelin-men, bowmen, and horsemen, who in former days were all, without distinction, confused and mixed together. This was the same king that was fighting with the

---

[215] καὶ increases the meaning of ἄνευ, ' all without exception.'—*Schweig.*

Lydians at the time day was converted into night over the combatants[216], and that subjected the whole of Asia above the Halys river. He collected forces from all parts of his dominions; and invaded Nineveh, with the intention not only to avenge his father, but also to get possession of that city: he had defeated the Assyrians in an open engagement; and was encamped before Nineveh, when a large army of Scythians, headed by their king Madyes, the son of Protothyes, passed over into Asia, having driven the Cimmerians out of Europe: in their pursuit of the fugitives, they came into Media. There is indeed a road of thirty days, for an expeditious walker, from the Palus Mæotis to the Phasis river and Colchis; from Colchis to Media is no great distance; only one nation, that of the Saspires, intervening; passing through which, you find yourself in Media. But the Scythians did not make their entrance by this route: they turned, far northward, into a much longer road, keeping the Caucasian mountains to their right[217]: there the Medes engaged with the Scythians: they were defeated in the battle, and reft of the empire, while the Scythians ruled over all Asia. From Media they proceeded on to Egypt; and when they had reached Palestine in Syria, Psammitichus, king of Egypt, met them with gifts and prayers, and diverted them from advancing any farther: in their march back, they passed through Ascalon of Syria: most of the Scythians proceeded on their way, without stopping to pillage: some few however lagged behind, and stripped the holy precinct of Celestial Venus. This holy precinct, I find, by inquiry, is the most ancient of all palaces consecrated to this goddess; for that in Cyprus was a branch from this, as the Cyprians themselves confess; and that in Cythera was built by Phœnicians, who came from this same Syria. The goddess, however, smote with a female disease those Scythians and their posterity who had rifled her temple at Ascalon: the Scythians assert, that for the same reason they are still afflicted, and travellers visiting their country may witness how these people are afflicted[218]: the Scythians call them Enarees. For eight and twenty years, therefore, did the Scythians hold the sway, and every thing was turned upside down by their presumptuous and haughty conduct; for not only did

104

105

106

---

[216] See i. 74.

[217] The Cimmerians took the way along the shore of the Euxine, and burst into Asia by the Caucasian defile: the Scythians, in their pursuit, missed their way, and came, by the Caspian gates, upon Media.

[218] The ingenious explanation of this extraordinary disease, hereditary in certain families, even in England, may be consulted by the curious, in Valckenaer's note on Herod. iv. 67, 3.

they extort from every body what tribute they chose to impose, but, independent of all that, they galloped about, ransacking whatever the people might have [219]. Accordingly, Cyaxares and the Medes invited most of them to a banquet, where, after overpowering them with wine, they massacred them all: in that manner, then, the Medes recovered the power, and, as before, extended their dominion over the rest of Asia: they took also Nineveh—the siege of which I shall describe in a different history [220]; and enthralled all the Assyrians, with the exception of the Babylonian territory. After these exploits, Cyaxares, who, including the time that the Scythians predominated, had reigned forty years, departed life.

107 Astyages the son of Cyaxares [221] succeeded to the throne: he had a daughter called Mandane, who, he dreamed, discharged such a quantity of urine, that it not only filled his capital, but even inundated the whole of Asia. He communicated his dream to the magians, that profess to interpret such visions: he was greatly alarmed, when informed by them of every particular. Some time after, dreading the accomplishment of the dream, he avoided giving this daughter, then already marriageable [222], to any of his Medic grandees; but united her to a Persian, whose name was Cambyses, and whom he knew to be of a respectable family and a quiet disposition: he considered such a man as vastly inferior to a Mede, even of the middle order.

108 In the first year of Mandane's union with Cambyses, Astyages had another vision: it seemed to him as if a vine grew up from his daughter's womb, and spread all over Asia. Having beheld this vision, and communicated with the interpreters of dreams, he sent for his daughter, who was pregnant and near her time, out of Persia: from the time of her arrival, he kept a watch on her, being determined to destroy her offspring; for the magian interpreters had pointed out to him, from his dream, that the progeny of his daughter would reign in his stead. Astyages, therefore, watched in this manner, until Cyrus came into the world: he then called Harpagus, one of his relations, the most loyal of the Medes, and the confidant of all his affairs. "Harpagus," said he to him, "by no means neglect the business that I am about to

---

[219] χωρὶς μὲν γὰρ 'for not only' φέρον ἐνεγκόντες 'they extorted tribute' παρ' ἑκάστων (Matt. 588) τὸ (κατὰ τὸ) ἐπιβάλλειν, χωρὶς δὲ φέρον 'but, over and above tribute' ἤρπαζον, etc. The first χωρὶς is an adverb; the second, a preposition.—*Schweig.*

[220] Probably the History of Assyria, supposed to be a work of Herodotus, destroyed by time.

[221] Matt. 273.

[222] Matt. 317.

"charge you with. Let me be exposed to no danger, by "any deception: consult not the interest of others, lest you "work your own destruction hereafter[223]. Take the son "that Mandane has just brought forth; carry him to your "house, and put him to death; and then bury him, in what "manner you yourself may think proper." Harpagus made the following answer: "Sire, hitherto, never have you witnessed in the man that stands before you any ingratitude: "be assured, that, for the time to come, I shall still have a "care not to offend you. If, therefore, it is your pleasure "that it should be done, as far, at all events, as I am concerned, it is my bounden duty to perform diligently what "you command." Harpagus having given the above answer, 109 the babe was delivered over to him, sumptuously clad in its shrowd, for death[224]. He proceeded home, weeping: at his entrance, he related to his wife all the conversation he had had with Astyages. "And what, then, do you now intend "to do?" said the lady. "Not indeed, what Astyages prescribes," answered he, "not even were he more raving and "distraught than he now is, would I, at all events, accede to "his desire, or lend myself to such a murder. I have many "reasons not to be his butcher: not only is the child my "own relation, but Astyages himself is now an old man, "and has no male issue: at his decease, should[225] the crown "descend to this daughter, whose son he wishes to massacre "by my hand, what then can I expect, but the most dreadful "danger[226]? Yet my own safety requires that the child "shall die: let, then, one of Astyages' own people be the "assassin; none of mine." So he spoke; and forthwith des-110 patched a courier to one of Astyages' herdsmen, who he knew grazed his cattle on pastures exceedingly well adapted for his purpose, being in mountains greatly infested with wild beasts: the man's name was Mitradates: he was married to a fellow-servant: the name of the woman who was his partner was Cyno, in Hellenic; or Spaco, in Medic, for the Medes use the word *spaca* for 'dog.' The mountains, at the foot of which this herdsman accordingly grazed his cattle, lay northward of Ecbatana, facing the Euxine sea: that quarter of Media, on the confines of the Saspireo, is very mountainous, lofty, and covered with forests: the rest of

---

[223] μὴ σοὶ (al. σὺ) ἑαυτῷ σφαλείης· ne tua ipsius culpa in malum incidas; ne tibi ipse causa sis exitii. *Schweig. Lex. Herod.* Matt. 489, ii.

[224] Understand αἴρεσιν after τὴν. Matt. 487, 8.

[225] πλέου. It is proper to observe, that in Herodotus, and others, δίλω and ἰδίλω are often redundant, and joined to inanimate objects.—*Larcher*.

[226] Matth. 487, 8. Constr. τί ἄλλο λείπεται μοι ἢ ὁ μέγιστος τῶν κινδύνων.

Media, however, is all level ground. On the arrival, accordingly, with all speed, of the herdsman; as soon as he was summoned, Harpagus addressed him in these words: "Astyages commands you to take this new-born child, and "expose him on the bleakest part of your mountains, so that "he may quickly perish. He has likewise given his com- "mands, that you should be informed, that if you do not "procure the immediate death of this infant, but in any "manner contribute to his preservation, you shall be visited "with the most horrid of deaths. I myself have it in com- "mand to see the body exposed." The grazier heard these orders: he took the new-born child, returned by the same way he had come, and arrived at his farm; where his own wife, who was expecting every day to go to bed[227], had happened just then to be delivered, while he himself was gone to town. Both man and wife had been uneasy on each other's account: he was alarmed about her approaching delivery: the woman, on the other hand, was not less alarmed for her husband, as it had never been the custom with Harpagus to send for him. At his return, the woman, seeing him thus unexpectedly, first inquired what Harpagus had sent to him for in such haste. "O wife!" said the man; "when I got to "the town, I there beheld and heard what I fain never "would have wished to see, nor to have befallen our mas- "ters: the whole house of Harpagus was filled with mourn- "ing: terrified that I was, I entered: no sooner had I "stepped in, than I behold a new-born babe lying on the "ground, palpitating and crying, clad in cloth of gold[228]. "Immediately that Harpagus saw me, he ordered me to "take directly the babe, carry him away with me, and ex- "pose him on the mountain that abounds the most in wild "animals: he observed, at the same time, that Astyages was "the person that charged me with this commission, and "threatened me with dreadful punishment if I failed to "execute it. I then took away the infant; and was bringing "him here, supposing that it was the child of one of the "servants of the house; for I could not guess whence he "came: yet I was surprised to see him clad in cloth-of-gold "garments, and still more at the mourning evident through "the house of Harpagus. Soon after, however, on my road "home, I was informed of the whole business, by the servant "who was to escort me out of the town, and give the child

[227] πᾶσαν ἡμέραν, signifies, *from day to day*, not the whole day; ὠδίνει, *near her delivery*.

varied robe of gold cloth; it is an example of the figure called by the grammarians ἓν διὰ δυοῖν.—*Larcher*.

[228] χρυσῷ τε καὶ ἐσθῆτι ποικίλῃ.

"into my hands—that he was the son of Astyages' daugh-
"ter, by Cambyses the son of Cyrus; and that Astyages
"commanded he should be destroyed:—and now, here he is."
So saying, the herdsman uncovered the child, and showed 112
him to his wife: she, seeing the infant of good size and handsome features, shed tears; and embracing the knees of her
husband, she besought him, by all means, not to expose the
infant: but he denied the possibility of doing otherwise; for
inspectors were to come, on the part of Harpagus, who would
destroy him by the most cruel of deaths, if he did not obey
his orders. Not succeeding in persuading her husband, the
wife once more addressed him thus: "Since I cannot then
"obtain from you not to expose this infant, I beseech you
"to act as follows: if it is absolutely necessary a child
"should be seen stretched on the mountain, I also have
"been delivered and have brought forth a still-born infant.
"Carry the dead body out, and expose that; and let us bring
"up the son of Astyages' daughter as though he were one
"of our own: in that manner you cannot be convicted of
"disobedience to your masters, and we shall take no bad
"counsel to ourselves; for the lifeless child will receive a
"kingly funeral, and the surviving babe will not be reft of
"life." The herdsman thought his wife spoke quite to the 113
purpose, and instantly proceeded to do as she said: the child
that he had brought[29], for the purpose of putting it to death,
he consigned to his wife: his own lifeless child he deposited
in the cradle that he brought the other in, and, adorning it
with all the finery of the living child, carried it to the bleakest mountain, and there exposed it. On the third day of the
body lying there, the herdsman set off for the city, leaving
one of his hinds on the watch. He arrived at Harpagus's
residence, and declared that he was ready to exhibit the dead
body of the infant: Harpagus, accordingly, sent some of the
most faithful of his guards, through them saw the infant,
and interred the herdsman's son. Thus the still-born child
was buried; and the grazier's wife took the boy subsequently
called Cyrus and suckled him, giving him some other name,
different from Cyrus.

When, accordingly, the boy had reached his tenth year, the 114
following accident disclosed his birth to the world: he was
playing in the same village where the cattle-stalls were, along
with the boys of his own age, in the road: his comrades,
accordingly, in sport, elected for their king this herdsman's
son, as he was called. He appointed some of his playmates to
be superintendants of the buildings; others, to be his body-

[29] مل repeated. Matt. 606, 3.

guards; one of them, to be the king's eye; to another he assigned the office of bringing in all messages; determining according to his own judgment the duties of each respectively. One of these boys, therefore, who was joining in the game—he was the son of Artembares, a Medic nobleman—refusing to obey the orders of Cyrus, the mock-king gave his orders that the boy should be taken into custody by the others: he was obeyed, and Cyrus handled the youth pretty sharply with the whip. The boy, immediately he was released, being highly affronted to have undergone such unworthy treatment, hastened to the city, and complained bitterly to his father of the treatment he had received from Cyrus—not that he made use of that name, for he was not known by it then—but, from the hands of the son of Astyages' herdsman. Artembares, in anger, went, on the spot, to Astyages, taking his son with him, and complained of the intolerable treatment he had met with: then shewing the boy's shoulders, he said, " Thus, my king, are we presump-" tuously insulted by your slave, the son of a herdsman."

115 When Astyages had seen and heard the case, wishing to have some reparation made to the honour of Artembares, he sent for the herdsman and the boy. When they were both come into his presence, Astyages fixed his eyes on Cyrus: " How, then, have you the audacity," said he, " you, the son " of so humble a man as this, to treat with such indignity " the son of that gentleman, the first nobleman in my court?" " My lord," replied the boy," what I did was in justice : for " the other lads in the village, to which I belong, had elected " me as king, in play, over them ; as I appeared to be the " best adapted for that office. The rest of the boys obeyed " my orders; but this youth, without assigning any reason, " refused to obey, and consequently was punished[220]: if, on " that account, I am deserving of blame, here I stand before

116 " you." As the boy spoke these words, a thought struck Astyages that he recognised him[231]: he fancied to himself that his countenance was something similar to his own: the time of the exposing seemed also to agree with the lad's age. Startled at these thoughts, he stood some time silent: at length, when he recovered, he said, with a desire of getting rid of Artembares, and in order to be able to examine the herdsman all alone: " Artembares, I will take care " to arrange matters, so that neither you nor your son shall " have to complain." Thus he dismissed Artembares: at

[220] I, *i*, " quare," " quapropter:" see Book ii. 16.

[231] Literally, *The recognition of him entered* the mind of Astyages.

the order also of Astyages, Cyrus was taken, by some attendants, into the inner part of the palace. Then the herdsman alone remained; and Astyages questioned him, unaccompanied by witnesses, from whence he got the boy, and who had given him to him? The man affirmed that the lad was his own-begotten son, and the mother that had borne him was still living with him. Astyages observed to him, that he had not taken prudent counsel, and wished to bring himself into great trouble: as he pronounced these words, he beckoned to his guards to lay hold on him: when brought to the rack, the man discovered the truth; and beginning from the beginning, went through all the true particulars; and concluded by prayer, beseeching the king to shew mercy to him[28]. Astyages however, now that the herdsman had discovered the truth, was indifferent as to what became of the man: but attaching great blame to Harpagus, he ordered the guards to summon him. As soon as Harpagus made his appearance, Astyages put this question to him: "Harpagus, "to what kind of death did you put the son born of my "daughter, whom I delivered into your hands?" Harpagus, who caught sight of the herdsman in the inner part of the palace, would not recur to falsehood, lest he should be detected and convicted; but explained as follows: "Sire, when "I had received the new-born child, I revolved in my mind "how I might act according to your pleasure, and yet re-"main blameless in your eyes as well as in your daughter's, "without dipping my own hand into his blood for you: "I then did as I will now tell you: I sent for this herdsman, "to whom I delivered the new-born infant, telling him that, "by your command, it was to be put to death: in so saying, "at all events, I told no falsehood, for such were your in-"junctions: I then delivered the child to him, with orders "to place him on some bleak mountain, and remain by him, "on the watch, until he died. I threatened the man with all "sorts of torture, if he did not do this effectually. When he "had properly executed these orders, and the infant was "dead, I sent the most faithful of my eunuchs, and, through "them, saw, and buried the corse. Thus, sire, things passed "in this business, and such was the fate of the child."

Harpagus, therefore, told the honest truth: but Astyages, smothering the anger that possessed him at what had been done, repeated to Harpagus the account as he had heard it from the herdsman; and, when he had finished the rehearsal,

[28] Construction: καὶ (καταβαίνει) κι-λεύει αὐτὸν ἔχειν συγγνώμην ἑαυτῷ. The verb καταβαίνει in this sense is constantly construed with the participle.

concluded by saying: "The lad is still living, and the result "is as it ought to be: for," continued he, "I suffered greatly "on the boy's account, and I took much to heart[222] the re- "proaches of my daughter: however, as things have turned "out so lucky, you must send us your own son, to keep com- "pany with the young stranger: besides, as I intend to offer "sacrifice, as a thanksgiving for the preservation of the boy, "to the gods to whom that honour belongs, you will attend 119 "yourself at my table." Harpagus, on hearing this invitation, prostrated himself, and kissed the ground: congratulating himself that his disobedience was followed by such a favourable result[223], and that he was invited to the royal board under such auspicious circumstances, he went home: as soon as he entered—(he had an only son, at most thirteen years of age)—he sent him out, bidding him go to Astyages, and do what he should tell him: and then, full of gladness, went and told his consort all that had happened. But, at the arrival of Harpagus's son, Astyages slaughtered the youth, cut him up into joints, and roasted some of the flesh, the rest he boiled: having properly cooked the whole, he held it in readiness: at the dinner-hour, together with the other guests, came Astyages also: before Astyages and the rest, tables were placed[224], replete with mutton; but they served up to Harpagus all the parts of his own son, with the exception of the head and extremities, that is, the feet and hands; these were deposited apart, in a basket, carefully covered up. When Harpagus seemed to have eaten a sufficiency of the meat, Astyages asked him if he had enjoyed his feast. Harpagus, having returned for answer that he had greatly enjoyed it, some persons, appointed for the purpose, brought him the head of his son, together with the hands and feet, and, standing before Harpagus, bade him lift up the covering, and take what he chose. Harpagus assented: he lifted up the cover, and beheld the remnants of his son. Not at all shaken off his guard, he kept his presence of mind. Astyages asked him if he knew of what game he had eaten: he replied, that he was perfectly aware; and whatever a king may do, it is always pleasing. Having made this answer, he picked up the remaining bits of flesh, and went home; intending, I suppose, to collect and bury all he could.

120 Such was the punishment Astyages inflicted on Harpagus.

[222] οὐκ ἐν ἐλαφρῷ (ἐλαφρῶς) ἐποιεύμην, "haud leviter tuli." *Schweig.*

[223] ἡ ἁμαρτὰς οἱ ἐς δέον ἐγεγόνει · peccatum ei in id quod debuit (commode, recte) cessit.—*Schweig. Lex. Herod.*

[224] It appears that every guest had his own separate table, or tray; which is the case now, sometimes, in Eastern countries.

Then, taking into his consideration what should be done with Cyrus, he convened the same magians who had interpreted his dream in the manner I have already described. When they were come, Astyages asked them what was the interpretation they had put upon his dream: they answered, saying, That the child would reign, if he survived, and had not previously died. "The child is, and still survives," said Astyages to the magians: "he has been brought up in the " country, where the lads of the village have made him king. " He has performed all things exactly as kings in reality do: " for he has appointed guards, ushers, and messengers, and " made all the other arrangements. Tell me, what you think " these things tend to?" The answer on the part of the magians was: " If the child does survive, and has in fact " reigned, without any premeditated object, you may cease " to feel alarm on his account: resume a stout heart, for he " will not rule a second time: indeed, many of our declara-" tions have ended in insignificant results. At all events, " dreams, and the like, frequently bring, in conclusion, very " simple accomplishments." To this Astyages made reply: " I also, magians, am chiefly of the same opinion, that the " child having been nominated king, the dream is fulfilled, " and he may no longer be an object of terror to me. Never-" theless, it is my wish, that you should carefully weigh the " matter, and advise me what will be the safest way of pro-" ceeding, for the advantage of my family and yourselves." To which the magians spoke as follows: " Sire, it is of high " importance to ourselves, to support your throne: for if the " empire be thus alienated, passing over to this child, a Persian, " even we Medes shall be enthralled, and held in no account " by Persians, as being foreigners. But so long as you are " king, you our fellow-citizen, even we ourselves participate " in some measure of your government, and we receive great " honours at your hands: thus, therefore, the welfare of " yourself, and the security of your throne, must be the con-" stant objects of our vigilance: and did we see at present " aught to fear, be assured we would not fail to inform you. " Now the dream has been thus innocently accomplished, we " ourselves take heart, and exhort you to do as much. We " advise you, sire, to send this child away, from before your " eyes, to his father and mother[225], in Persia." Astyages listened to this answer, which gave him much pleasure. He called Cyrus into his presence: "My son," said he to him, " I " confess that I have done unjustly by you, in consequence of a

---

[225] Matt. 570.

" vain dream; you have escaped the lot that was intended for
" you: now, therefore, go into Persia: I will send an escort
" with you. When you get there, you will find your father and
" mother, who are nothing like [226] Mitradates and his wife."

122 Astyages having thus spoken, sent Cyrus away. On
his arrival at the house of Cambyses, he was received by
his parents, who embraced him with transports of joy when
informed who he was, having been hitherto convinced that
he had died immediately at his birth. They inquired in
what manner he had been saved: he related to them, saying
that he knew nothing before, but had been under a great
mistake: on the road, however, he had been informed of all
his adventures; for, previous to that time, he thought he
was the son of Astyages' herdsman: on the road from
Media, he had been made acquainted with the whole history,
by his escorters. He described how he had been brought
up by the herdsman's wife; and praised her, in preference
of all[227]; Cyno was every thing to him in his discourse[228]:
in consequence, his parents, availing themselves of that
name, and in order that the preservation of the child might
appear to the Persians more clearly the work of the
gods, put about the report that Cyrus, when exposed, was
suckled by a bitch: from thence the tale had its origin.

123 When Cyrus approached to manhood, and became the most
gallant and beloved of the young men of his day, Harpagus
sent him gifts, and courted him to take revenge on Astyages;
for he himself, being but a subject, saw no prospect of ever
obtaining reparation by his own influence: regarding, therefore, Cyrus as one grown up and educated to be his avenger[229],
he sought to make him his confederate, comparing the sufferings of Cyrus with his own; but previously he made the
following preparations. The behaviour of Astyages to the
Medes being generally very harsh, Harpagus had communication with the various chief noblemen among the Medes,
and persuaded them to stand up for Cyrus, and put an end
to the rule of Astyages. Having effected this object, and
being now ready, he was accordingly desirous to make
known his ideas to Cyrus, who was then resident in Persia:
but, as the roads were watched, and he had no other mode of
so doing, he devised the following artifice: he took a hare,
and ripping up its belly, without discomposing any thing or

---

[226] Matt. 581, b.
[227] Matt. 180. Schweig. takes διὰ παντὸς in the sense of ἀεί. See like-wise Matt. 559, c. on the circumlocu-tion.
[228] Matt. 438.
[229] Supply, after ἐντετραφότιτα, the word τιμωρόν, from the foregoing τιμωρίαν.—*Wyttenb.*

tearing any of the hair, slipped in a letter, containing what he had to say: then, sewing up again the hare, he gave it, together with some nets, to the most faithful of his servants, dressed as a sportsman; whom he sent over into Persia, prescribing to him *vivâ voce*, to tell Cyrus, in delivering the hare, to paunch it himself, and let nobody be present when he did so. This was therefore done: Cyrus took the hare, and ripped 124 up the skin: he found the letter there deposited: he took it and read it: the letter ran thus: " Son of Cambyses—as[240] " the gods watch over you: for otherwise you might never " have attained such good-fortune—I beseech you now to " wreak vengeance on Astyages, your murderer: according " to his intentions, you would have long since died: aided " by the gods, and me, you survive. You have erewhile, me- " thinks, been informed how he behaved towards you, what " sufferings I underwent myself at the hands of Astyages, " because I did not slaughter you myself, but gave you to " the herdsman. Now, then, if you will hearken to me, you " shall rule over the same empire that Astyages now reigns " over. Do you, therefore, persuade the Persians to stand; " march them upon the Medes. And whether I myself, or " any other noble Mede, be appointed commander against " you, be assured every thing will be as you wish; for all " these will be the first to stand up against him and for you, " and to depose Astyages: as all is here, at least, prepared, " do as I say, and do quickly."

Cyrus, having received this information, considered what 125 would be the most prudent manner to persuade the Persians to rebel: after turning the matter over, he found that the most expedient mode would be to act thus: he wrote a letter, comprising what he thought proper to indite, and then mustered the Persians: in the presence of the assembly, he unrolled the letter, and, reading it out, said that Astyages appointed him leader of the Persians. "Now," continued he, "Persians, I command you to assemble, each bringing " with him a sickle." This was Cyrus's proclamation.—The Persian tribes are numerous; some of which Cyrus collected together, and persuaded to secede from the Medes: they are those from whom all the rest of the Persians take their origin; Pasargadæ, Maraphians, Maspians: of these the Pasargadæ are the most noble: among them is the branch from which the Persic kings spring, called the Achæmenidæ. The rest of the Persian tribes are as follow: Panthialæans, Derusiæans, Germanians, all of whom are husbandmen: the

[240] The hyperbaton, οἱ γὰρ etc. See ch. 24 of this Book.

remainder are nomades: Daians, Mardans, Dropicans, Sagartians. When they were all assembled, provided with the prescribed instruments, Cyrus proposed to them to clear that day
a certain tract of land situate in Persia, and overrun with
bushes, the extent of which, every way, was about eighteen
or twenty stades: as soon as the Persians had completed the
prescribed task, he ordered them to muster again on the following day, and previously wash themselves. In the interval,
Cyrus collected together the flocks and herds of his father,
slaughtered and cooked them, for the purpose of regaling the
Persian body. In addition to this, the proper rations of wine
and bread were prepared. At the arrival of the Persians on
the next day, Cyrus bade them stretch themselves on the turf,
and feasted them. After the repast was at an end, he asked
them which of the two was preferable, in their opinion;
whether the treatment of the preceding day, or the present:
the men replied, that there was a vast difference between the
two; the day before, they had experienced nothing but hardships of all kinds; on the present day, they had tasted nothing but sweets. Cyrus took advantage of the expression,
and laid before the assembly the whole naked plan: " Men
" of Persia," said he, " thus matters stand with you: if you
" will hearken[241] to me, these and ten thousand other sweets
" are yours, and you have no slavish toil: if you hesitate to
" hearken to me, toils beyond number, like those of yester-
" day, await you. Now, therefore, follow my orders, and
" be free. I myself, methinks, am born, by divine blessing,
" to place this boon within your hands: you, I hold not be-
" hind the Medes in valour, either in war or other things.
" Since such is the case, rise up directly against Astyages."
The Persians, thus provided with a leader, although they
had long since abhorred the Medic rule, now longed for
liberty. Astyages, acquainted with the projects of Cyrus,
sent a messenger, to summon him to his presence: Cyrus
ordered the messenger to report, that he would come, and
meet him, sooner than Astyages himself could wish. At
this intelligence, Astyages armed all his Medes; and, as if
driven astray by the divine power, placed Harpagus at
their head, unmindful how he had exasperated the feelings
of that person. Accordingly, the Medes engaged with the
Persians: some of them, not implicated in the plot, fought;
the rest either passed over, of their own accord, to the Persians, or, acting as willing cowards, fled in great numbers.
As soon as Astyages heard of this disgraceful rout of the

---

[241] Matt. 340. ' Mihi obtemperare, credere.'— *Wyttenb.*

Medic army, he exclaimed, threatening Cyrus: " No, Cyrus, " you shall not, at all events, rejoice at so cheap a rate." Having so said, the first thing he did was to impale the magian interpreters of dreams, who had induced him to send away Cyrus: next, he armed the Medes that had been left behind in the capital, young and old: these he led out, engaged the Persians, and was defeated. Astyages himself was taken prisoner, and lost all the Medes under his command. Before Astyages, thus a prisoner, Harpagus now 129 presented himself: he insulted with cutting gibes, and triumphed over his fallen enemy; saying to him many heart-rending things, and, among others, questioned him, in reference to the repast at which he had feasted him with the flesh of his own son, " How he relished his present thraldom, " instead of his former sway." But the prisoner looked up, and asked, in return, whether he attributed to himself the achievement of Cyrus: and Harpagus observing, that, as he himself had written, the credit of the thing was his due; Astyages proved to him, beyond doubt, that " he was both
" the most foolish and the most iniquitous of men: certainly,
" if when the opportunity offered him to be himself king,
" and if, as he pretended, he was the agent in the present
" conjuncture, he must have been most foolish to have given
" the power to another; and most iniquitous, to have, for the
" sake of that repast, enslaved all the Medes: for granting[20]
" it was absolutely necessary that the royal power should be
" transferred to other hands, and he himself could not hold
" it, it would have been more fair and equitable to have
" given that boon to some native Mede, and not to a Persian:

[20] Matt. 555. *obs.* 2.

CHRONOLOGY OF THE MEDES, ACCORDING TO HERODOTUS.

1. The date of the deposition of Astyages, or the first year of the reign of Cyrus, constitutes the foundation of this chronology: Herodotus places this date, as we said before, in B. C. 559.
2. Astyages reigned 35 years (i. 130); Cyaxares 40 years, including 28 years of the Scythian rule; Phraortes 22 years (i. 102); Deïoces 53 years. Sum of the years of the dynasty of Deïoces, 150 years. Add 150 to 559, the first year of Cyrus's reign, the result is B. C. 709, the first year of the usurpation of Deïoces.
3. But the power of the Medes had existed in Upper Asia 128 years in all; to which 28 years of Scythian supremacy must be added. The Assyrians, therefore, had lost the supremacy of Upper Asia 156 years before the deposition of Astyages (i. 130). As the dynasty of Deïoces lasted only 150 years, it is inferred, that during six years, intervening between the origin of Medic independence and Deïoces' usurpation, the Medes were in that state of *abrurípua* described i. 95.
4. The Assyrian supremacy previous to the Medic independence had endured 525 years (i. 95). Therefore,

Assyrian

"but now, the Medes, wholly guiltless of what he complained "of, were, from masters, to become servants; while the Per- "sians, from being formerly servants to the Medes, were "now to be exalted into masters."

130 Astyages was accordingly, after a reign of five-and-thirty years, thus deposed: the Medes, who had ruled over Asia above the Halys during one hundred and thirty years, all but two, excepting the time that the Scythians held the power, bowed to the Persians, in consequence of the harsh rule of Astyages. In later days, however, they repented them to have so done, and rose up against Darius; but, conquered in battle, they were a second time subjugated: at this period, however, the Persians, headed by Cyrus, rose up against the Medes under Astyages, and from that day have been the rulers of Upper Asia. Cyrus kept Astyages by him until his decease, without doing him any further injury. Therefore Cyrus, thus born and educated, came to the throne; and subsequently to these events, as I have already described, subdued Crœsus, the author of the first provocation: after deposing the Lydian prince, he obtained the sovereignty of all Asia.

131 The following observations on the manners and customs of the Persians I know to be correct. It is not the custom with them to erect statues or temples or altars; they reproach with folly such as do so. Their reason for this appears to be, that they do not, after the example of the Hellenes, regard the gods as participating in the nature of man. They are in the practice of ascending the loftiest of their mountains, there to make sacrifice to Jove, calling by that name the whole ambient sky. They offer up sacrifice to the sun and moon, to the earth, water, fire, and winds; and those

---

B C.
Assyrian supremacy commences under Ninus 1235
Origin of the independence of Media 715
Last year of democracy (i. 95)
    1. Deïoces usurps the throne— } 709
       His government confined solely to the Medes.
    2. Phraortes succeeds 656
       Conquests begin: Persia; Upper Asia, except the Assyrians.
    3. Cyaxares succeeds 634
       War of five years with Lydia.
       Twenty-eight years of Scythian oppression.
       Capture of Nineveh.
    4. Astyages succeeds 594
       Deposed by his grandson Cyrus 559

The origin of the Assyrian supremacy being attained by Ninus, he, in the second year, it appears, of his reign, places his son Agron on the throne of Lydia, B. C. 1232. The same result is obtained from the assumption of the date of the capture of Sardis: this is a strong corroboration of the accuracy of both the Lydian and Medic chronologies.

are the only gods they have worshipped from the earliest times: they have now, however, learnt to offer sacrifice to Venus Cœlestis; borrowing the custom from the Assyrians and Arabians; the former of whom call this goddess Mylitta; the latter, Alitta; and the Persians, Mitra. Sacrifice, with the Persians, to the above deities, is conducted in the following manner: they raise no altars, kindle no fires, when about to offer a victim: they make no use of libation, or flute, or labels[243], or roasted barley[244]: every one that wishes to offer up sacrifice, takes the victim to a clean spot of ground, and invokes the deity, his tiara[245] decked generally with myrtle-branches: no one that presents a victim is permitted to pray for blessings on himself alone; he must supplicate for the welfare of all the Persians and their king, in which number he himself is necessarily included: he then carves the sacrificed victim into joints, boils the flesh, and, spreading abundance of herbage, more particularly trefoil or shamrock, displays thereon the meat. When this has been properly laid out, comes a magus, who chaunts over the meat a *theogonia*, the name they give to the hymn: without such magus it is not lawful for them to offer any sacrifice. After tarrying a short time, the sacrificer carries away the flesh, and does with it whatever his fancy prompts. Of all days, that which they are wont to honour most is the birth-day of each; on that day they hold it necessary to serve up more provision than on others. At such times, the opulent Persians put on their board, an ox, a horse, camel, and an ass, roasted whole in ovens. The poor people make a display of the smaller kinds of cattle. They eat little at dinner; but are fond of sweetmeats of all kinds, served up separately, not all together[246]. And it is on that account, they say, " that " the Hellenes, when they have once eaten, cease to be " hungry, because, after dinner, nothing of any account is " brought in; but if any delicacies were to be produced, " they would no longer cease to eat[247]." They are exceedingly addicted to wine; but it is forbidden them to vomit, or

132

133

---

[243] The labels are two long strips of wool, hanging down from the ears, on the shoulders and along the breast.

[244] ούλαί, understand κριθαί: coarse ground barley, roasted: it was strewed between the horns of the victim.

[245] Herodotus makes τιάρα masculine.

[246] This custom still holds in the East: pipes, coffee, and sweetmeats are brought in to visitors at all hours of the day.

[247] I take the meaning of this remark to be, " that the Hellenes eat to " complete satiety at one single meal, " and therefore take no refreshment " between meals; whereas the Per- " sians do not eat at one meal to their " fill, but reserve some appetite for " repeated refreshments at every hour " of the day."
The Persians consider this custom of eating more grateful and sanitory than that of the Hellenes.

to make water, in the presence of another. These customs are still now in vogue. They are in the practice, also, of debating, when intoxicated, the most important affairs: whatever may have met with their approbation at these debauches is proposed to them fasting, on the day following, by the landlord at whose house the council is held; and if their decisions still meet with their approbation when thus fasting, they adopt them. The resolutions entered into while fasting are, on the other hand, submitted to them when they 134 are under the influence of wine. When Persians meet one another on the highways, any spectator can ascertain whether the individuals that come in contact are equal in rank, by this sign: before they accost each other, they kiss on the lips: if one is a little inferior to the other, they kiss on the cheeks: if one of the parties is greatly below the other, he prostrates himself and kisses the ground. As a nation, they honour, immediately after themselves, those that reside next to them; those further on are the second in their estimation; and so by degrees, as they advance further from themselves, apportion their honours, holding in account the least of all such as reside at the greatest distance from Persia; thinking themselves, of all nations, the most worthy in every respect; and all others inferior in virtue, according to the proportion above described; the most distant from themselves being the worst of all. Under the empire of the Medes, one nation even ruled over another; the Medes over all, generally speaking, and particularly over those resident next to themselves: these, over the nations on their boundaries; they again, over the more removed. In the same order the Persians also distribute their honour and respect; for they 135 are themselves an ancient and superior race. The Persians are of all nations the most prone to adopt foreign manners and customs: for instance, they wear the Medic costume, fancying it more handsome than their national dress: in war, they adopt the Egyptian cuirasses; and indulge in all voluptuous luxuries they become acquainted with: a particular example of which is, that they have adopted from the Hellenes an infamous practice; they marry each several lawful wives, but at the same time keep many concubines. 136 Next to gallant conduct in battle, the most manly qualification is deemed to be the possession of a numerous offspring: the king every year sends gifts to him that exhibits the greatest number of children: number is regarded as force. Their children are brought up, commencing from the fifth year and continuing to the twentieth, in three things alone; horse-riding, use of the bow, and speaking the truth: previously to the fifth year, the children never come in the presence of the father, but pass their whole time with the women: the motive for this custom is, that if the child happen to die in his infancy, he may not give any uneasiness to his father.

The above custom I approve of: as I do also of the next following; which is, that not even the king himself is allowed to put to death any person for one crime only; neither is it lawful for any Persian to inflict any very severe punishment[248] on one of his slaves, before he has carefully considered and ascertained whether his misdeeds are more numerous than his good services, in which case he may gratify his anger. They deny that any human being ever murdered his own father or mother; but assert, that whenever such things have taken place, if matters were properly looked into, it would be necessarily found that they are committed by supposititious or adulterine children: for it is unnatural to suppose, they say, that the lawful and real parent of a child should be killed by that same child. The things that it is unlawful for them to do, they may not mention: lying is, they hold, the most disgraceful of vices: next to which is the contracting of debts, for many reasons: but especially because, they say, it is absolutely necessary that a debtor should tell lies. Whosoever of the natives has the leprosy, or morphew, is forbidden to enter a town, or to have any communication with the rest of the Persians: they pretend that all afflicted with those distempers must have sinned against the sun: many of them even drive out of the country every stranger that may have caught these diseases: they likewise drive away all white pigeons, attributing to them the same infections. They never make water in rivers, nor spit nor wash their hands in them; but prevent others from so doing, and in all respects venerate highly their streams. They have another peculiarity, which the Persians themselves do not take notice of, but which we fail not to observe: it is, that their names, allusive to the body and to grandeur, end all in one and the same letter, that called *San* by the Dorians, and *Sigma* by the Ionians. If you examine the names of the Persians ending in that letter, you will find they all do so, invariably[249]. The above things being perfectly known to me, I am able to speak positively of them. The following particulars, relating to the dead, are

---

[248] Matt. 409, b.
[249] Another observation equally frivolous occurs chap. 148. Instances of the final *s* in the Persian names are, Cyrus, Cambyses, Smerdis, Darius, Xerxes, etc.

mentioned not so authentically, being kept secret. The dead body of a Persian is never interred until it has been lacerated by some bird or dog: that the magians do thus, I am confident, for they do it openly: the Persians then case the body in wax, and conceal it under ground. The magians, however, differ exceedingly from other men, and from the Egyptian priests in particular: for the latter kill nothing that breathes, with the exception of the victims that they sacrifice; whereas the magians, with their own hands, kill all animals, except man and dog: they display even great ardour in the destruction of ants and serpents, and of all other creeping and flying things. But be this custom observed as it has been from the first, I now return to my former subject.

141 The Ionians and Æolians sent ambassadors to Cyrus at Sardis, immediately after the subjection of the Lydians: they were desirous of being subjects to Persia, on the same terms as they had been, before, to Crœsus. Cyrus having heard the purport of what they proposed, related to them this fable: " Once upon a time," said he, " a piper seeing some fishes in " the sea, began to pipe, in the expectation of their coming " out of the water, on land. He was disappointed of his " hopes[250]; so he took a casting-net, threw it on a numerous " shoal of the fishes, and hauled them up. Seeing them " bound on the shore, he said to them, 'Cease now your " dancing; since, when I piped, you chose not to come out to " dance.'" Cyrus related this parable to the Ionians and Æolians, for these reasons; that the Ionians, when he before had, by his deputies, employed them to shake off the yoke of Crœsus, had refused to take his advice; but now the work was done, they were ready enough to hearken to him: in consequence of this, irritated at their behaviour, he gave them the above fable for answer. At the receipt of this intelligence, which was communicated to all the cities, each state fortified themselves, by building walls around their towns; and all met together at the Panionium, with exception of the Milesians, the only state with which Cyrus entered into the same treaty as the Lydian sovereign had done before. The rest of the Ionians agreed unanimously to
142 send ambassadors to Sparta and implore assistance. The Ionians, to whom also the Panionium belongs, have erected their towns under the finest sky and sweetest climate in the world, that we know of: for no country approaches to Ionia in these blessings, neither above nor below, nor west

[250] Matt. 316.

nor east; some of which are oppressed by cold and wet; others, by heat and drought. These Ionian states have not all one and the same language: it divides into four different branches[251]. Miletus, the first of these states, lies south; next to which are Myus and Priene: these three places are situate in Caria, and use one common dialect. The states in Lydia are, Ephesus, Colophon, Lebedus, Teos, Clazomenæ, Phocæa: these settlements do not at all agree, with the others mentioned above, in language; they speak a dialect common to themselves. There are three more Ionian states; two of which, Samos and Chios, occupy islands: the third stands on the main land, Erythræ. The Chians, accordingly, and the Erythræans, speak one and the same dialect: the Samians have a form of language peculiar to themselves. These make up the four characteristic branches.

Among these Ionians, therefore, the Milesians were under shelter from any alarming danger, as they had already framed a treaty: there was no cause for terror, either, to the islanders; for the Phœnicians were not as yet subjected to the Persians, neither were the Persians themselves any thing of sailors. The Milesians had seceded from the rest of the Ionians for the following and no other reason, that, feeble as the Hellenic corporation was in those days, the Ionic was, of all the Hellenic tribes, the weakest and most insignificant, by far[252]; for, Athens excepted, they possessed not one state of any renown. The other Ionians accordingly, together with the Athenians, shunned the name, and would not be called Ionians: I know many of them, even now, that blush at the name. These twelve states, however, prided themselves on the appellation, and established for themselves, separately, a holy precinct, to which they affixed the name of Panionium. They decreed, that this temple should not be shared by any other of the Ionians; nor, indeed, did any crave for admittance, unless the Smyrnæans. In the same manner, the Dorians of the present Pentapolis, the same territory as formerly bore the name of Hexapolis, take care not to admit any of the neighbouring Dorians into the temple of Triopium; and even have excluded from participation[253] such as have violated the sacred institutes. For in the Triopian list, brass tripods were, of old, proposed as prizes to the victors: it being understood, that those who should win them would

---

[251] They were all corruptions of the old Attic. The sense of τρόπους παραγωγὴν and χαρακτῆρες γλώσσης is one and the same, 'varieties,' 'branches;' nor, in this passage at least, changes in gender or cases.

[252] Matt. 461.

[253] The word μετοχῆς, twice repeated in this chapter, signifies, properly, participation in the sacrifices and religious ceremonies. *M. de St. Croix*, quoted by *Larcher*.

not take them away from the temple, but leave them there, as offerings: accordingly, an inhabitant of Halicarnassus, called Agasicles, being conqueror, infringed the law, and carried his tripod home, where he hung it up: in consequence of which, the five cities, Lindus, Ialyssus, Cameirus, Cos, and Cnidus, excluded from their communion the sixth town, Halicarnassus: such was, therefore, the punishment 145 they imposed on the people of that place. I am inclined to believe that the Ionians founded twelve cities; and would not admit any more, from the following motive: when they resided in Peloponnesus, they consisted of twelve portions: such is the case now with the Achæans, who expelled the Ionians, and are divided also into twelve states;—Pellene, the first towards [253] Sicyon; next Ægira, and Ægæ (in which is seen the ever-flowing Crathis, from which the river in Italy has borrowed its name); Bura, and Elice (at which the Ionians, routed in battle by the Argians, took refuge); Ægium, Rhypes, and Patrees; together with Pharees, and Olenus (where flows the extensive river of Peirus); besides which, 146 the only inland towns, Dyma and Tritæes. Such, at the present day, are the twelve divisions of the Achæans; and such were those of the Ionians, at all events: and, in consequence, the Ionians made for themselves twelve towns in Asia also: for it would be exceedingly foolish to contend that these Ionians of Asia are in the slightest degree at all superior to the other Ionians, or of any purer origin. No small portion of them, in fact, are Abantes, out of Eubœa, who have no connexion, but the name, with Ionia: the mixture comprises Minyans from Orchomenus, Cadmeans, Dryopians, Phocidian emigrants, Molossians, Arcadian Pelasgians, Dorian Epidaurians, together with other nations, many and various. Those among them that came from the prytaneum of Athens, and imagine themselves the purest of the Ionians, brought no wives with them to their new settlement; but took to themselves Carian women, after they had killed all the men belonging to them. In consequence of this massacre, these women established a law, which they bound themselves to by oath, and bequeathed to their daughters— that they would never eat with their husbands, nor call them by that name; because they had slain their fathers, husbands and children, and, after so doing, had taken them to live with 147 them. These events took place at Miletus. These Ionians elected for their kings, some of them Lycians, descendants of Glaucus and Hippolochus; others chose Cauconian Pylians,

---

[253] πρὸς, with the genitive, usually πρὸς μεσαμβρίης, towards the south,— signifies towards, on the side of, &c. Larcher. Matt. 590, γ.

from the family of Codrus and Melanthus; some elected their kings from both houses. But then it is argued, that these Ionians are more attached to the name than the other Ionians. We will grant, that these Ionians of Asia are, then, of unsullied origin: still, all are Ionians, that descend from the Athenians, and celebrate the Apaturia festival: now, all celebrate that festival, except the Ephesians and Colophonians, who are the only Ionians that refrain from so doing; and they are excluded on some excuse of murder[254]. The Panionium, however, 148 is a sacred spot at Mycale, looking northward, and erected by the Ionians in common, to the honour of Heliconian Neptune. Mycale, here mentioned, is a headland of the continent, jutting out westward towards Samos, on which Ionians, congregating from the various states, celebrated the feast called Panionia; for not only the Ionian festivals, but those of all the Hellenes without exception, end in one and the same letter, similar to the Persian names[255]. Such, 149 then, are the Ionian states. Those belonging to the Æolians are, Cyma, called also Phriconis, Larissæ, Neon-teichos, Temnos, Cilla, Notium, Ægiroessa, Pitane, Ægææ, Myrina, Grynia: these eleven towns are the ancient Æolian states; for one of them had been taken away by the Ionians, the number of those on the continent being twelve before that. These Æolians possessed a better soil than the Ionians, but as to the temperature of the seasons did not come near them. The Æolians lost Smyrna in the following manner. The 150 Smyrnæans had received certain inhabitants of Colophon, who had been worsted in a tumult there, and cast out of their country: some time after, the Colophonian fugitives, having watched the opportunity of the Smyrnæans being outside of the walls, busy in celebrating the feast of Bacchus, shut to the gates, and took possession of the town. All the Æolian forces came to the relief of their fellow-countrymen; and an agreement was made between the two parties, that the Ionians should restore the moveable property, and the Æolians would abandon Smyrna. The Smyrnæans acceded to this: the eleven cities divided them among themselves respectively, and created them all citizens. The above, 151 therefore, are the Æolian towns situate on the main land of Asia; without reckoning those in Mount Ida, as they were distinct from this confederation. The following states are found on islands: five towns are inhabited by Æolians in Lesbos; for the sixth town there, Arisba, was enslaved by the Methymnæans, although of kindred blood. One city belongs to the Æolians on Tenedos; and in the parts called Hecaton-

[254] Matt. 471, 7.   [255] Comp. with chap. 139 above.

nesi, they have another. The Lesbians, accordingly, and the Æolians at Tenedos, similarly situated to the Ionian islanders, had nothing to fear: the rest of the states decided, of one accord, to follow the Ionians wherever they might lead the way.

152 The ambassadors from the Ionians and Æolians, on their arrival at Sparta—for all these matters were transacted with great celerity—elected for their common orator a citizen of Phocæa, whose name was Pythermus: he put on a purple cloak, with a view that as many as possible of the Spartans might be informed and assemble: he then stood up, made a long discourse, beseeching them to assist his countrymen. But the Lacedæmonians, without listening to what he had to say, decidedly refused to give any assistance to the Ionians. The deputies therefore retraced their steps. The Lacedæmonians, however, although they had rejected the Ionian ambassadors, sent, at the same time, some men on board a penteconter, for the purpose, I have no doubt, of reconnoitring the affairs of Cyrus and the Ionians. On the arrival of these people at Phocæa, they sent up to Sardis the most approved man in the party, whose name was Lacrines: he repeated to Cyrus the warning of the Lacedæmonians, " that " Cyrus should beware of attacking any city standing on Hel- " lenic ground, as they did not intend to be idle spectators."

153 The herald having pronounced these words, Cyrus is related to have inquired, of the Hellenes who were present, " Who " were[226] these Lacedæmonians, and what their numbers, that " they dared to accost him in such a manner." Having received the information he wanted, he addressed the Spartan herald in the following words: " Never yet was I afraid of " such people as have an appointed space in the middle of " their town, where they congregate to cheat one another by " false oaths. If I preserve my health, they shall have to " chatter about their own sufferings, not so much about those " of the Ionians." Cyrus threw out this taunt against all the Hellenes, because they have markets where they practise buying and selling: for the Persians themselves are not wont to have any such marts; a market is a thing unknown with them. Some time after, Cyrus appointed Tabalus, a Persian, as governor of Sardis; and made choice of Pactyas, a Lydian, who was to superintend the conveyance of the gold taken from Crœsus and the other Lydians: he then directed his march towards Ecbatana, taking with him Crœsus; at first, regarding the Ionians as of no importance. The

---

[226] Matt. 567.

great obstacles, in his career, were, Babylon, the Bactrian people, the Sacæ, and the Egyptians: he proposed himself to head the forces against these latter, and send some other general against the Ionians. As Cyrus was on his way from Sardis, Pactyas stirred up the Lydians to revolt from Tabalus and Cyrus: being in possession of all the gold found at Sardis, he went down to the sea-coast, where he hired mercenaries, and prevailed on the people of the out-ports to join him in the expedition: he then marched his troops against Sardis, and besieged Tabalus, who was shut up in the citadel.

Cyrus received intelligence of this, while on his road: and addressed Crœsus. "Crœsus," said he, "what will be the "end of these proceedings? The Lydians, it seems, will "never cease to cut out work for themselves and me. I "really think the best thing I can do is, to sell them off at "once into slavery. For now, indeed, every body must see, "that, at all events, I have acted just as if I had cut off the "father, and spared the children: since I am carrying away "you, who were something more than a father to the Ly-"dians, while I trust the city to Lydians themselves: and "then I am astonished that they stand up against me!" These words discovered what Cyrus contemplated: Crœsus dreaded lest he should utterly destroy Sardis. "Sire," replied he, "what you say, is agreeable to reason. But, let "me beseech you, yield not to the impulse of your mind "wholly! destroy not an ancient city, guiltless of any former "offences, or even of the present events. I myself was the "author of the former grievance, and my head pays the "forfeit: in the present rebellion, Pactyas is the culprit; "Pactyas, to whom you confided Sardis[257]: let him, then, pay "the penalty. Shew mercy to the Lydians; do by them as I "will tell you; to the end, they shall never more rebel, "never more be an object of terror to you. Send to them, "and say, they shall no longer have in their keeping any "weapons of war: bid them put on linen shirts beneath their "cloaks, and bind buskins on their legs: command them to "sweep the cithern strings, to dance, to teach their sons to "chaffer; and forthwith, mighty king, you will see them "converted from men into women, so that you will never "have to fear rebellions on their part[258]." Crœsus, accord-

---

[257] According to Larcher, the construction is: οὗτος (i. e. Pactyas) ὅσω τω λόγω τῷ (i. e. Tabalus) ἐπιτρέψας Σάρδις. Schweighæuser is of opinion, however, that Crœsus uses the construction followed in this translation, to impress on the Persian conqueror, that, in confiding to Pactyas all the treasures of Sardis, was equivalent to giving a Lydian supreme power over the capital.

[258] Matt. 294.

ingly, gave this advice; feeling that such treatment of the Lydians would be preferable to their being sold into bondage: moreover, he knew perfectly well, that if he did not bring forward some feasible proposal, he should not be able to alter Cyrus's determination. He dreaded, also, lest the Lydians, even should they escape the present storm, would again rise up against the Persians, and be utterly destroyed. Cyrus was pleased at the suggestion, relaxed his anger[259], and said that he would follow Crœsus's counsel. He then called to his presence Mazares, a Mede; ordered him to convey these commands to the Lydians, such as Crœsus proposed: and, over and above this[260], Mazares was commissioned to sell into captivity all the others who had joined the Lydians in the attack on Sardis, but by all means to bring
157 Pactyas to him alive. Cyrus having, accordingly, given these orders on his way, proceeded to the seats of the Persians. Pactyas finding that an army was coming after him, was seized with fear, and fled to Cyma. Mazares the Mede marched, however, his forces against Sardis, having under his command a very slight proportion of Cyrus's army: as he found Pactyas's party were no longer in Sardis, he, in the first place, put into execution Cyrus's orders, and compelled the Lydians, according to the royal behest, to change completely their mode of life. Having accomplished this, Mazares sent ambassadors to Cyma, summoning the citizens to deliver up Pactyas. The people of Cyma resolved to apply to the god at Branchidæ for advice on the subject; for at that place stood a shrine, built in early times, which the Ionians and Æolians were in the pratice of consulting:
158 this spot lies above Lake Panormus, in Milesia. The Cymæans, therefore, sent some persons to consult the god at Branchidæ: they asked: "What would the gods be pleased that they should do with Pactyas?" The answer returned to these inquirers, from the shrine, was: "To deliver up Pactyas to the Persians." This declaration was brought and communicated to the citizens of Cyma, who prepared to deliver up the fugitive: but, although the people had come to that decision, Aristodicus the son of Heraclides, a man in great repute among the citizens, restrained[261] the Cymæans from committing such an action; not himself giving any credit to the oracle, but fancying it to be an invention of the persons sent to consult. Finally, other consulters, of whom Aristodicus himself was one, went to inquire a second time

---

[259] Matt. 316.
[260] καὶ πρὸς· the general expression would be, καὶ δὲ πρὸς, insuper.
[261] Matt. 533, 3.

about Pactyas. Arrived at Branchidæ, Aristodicus, in the name of all, addressed the shrine, and made the following inquiry: "Sovereign lord! Pactyas, a Lydian, has come to "us, a suppliant; flying a violent death at the hands of the "Persians: they claim him, and summon the Cymæans to "deliver him up. We, however, dreading as we do the Per- "sian power, have not dared to deliver up, hitherto, a sup- "pliant, before we ascertain, beyond all doubt, from you, "whether we ought to do so." Such was the question put: the answer from the oracle was again the same, enjoining to deliver up Pactyas to the Persians. Then Aristodicus, as he had before determined, proceeded to act as follows: he walked all round the holy precinct, and pulled down the nests built in the temple by the sparrows and various other kinds of fowl: as he was occupied in this work, a voice, it is said, issued from the sanctuary, addressed to Aristodicus, saying: "Most nefarious of men! dare you commit such deeds as "this? Do you thus tear my suppliants from my temple?" Aristodicus, not at all thrown off his guard, replied: "Sove- "reign lord! you protect your own suppliants, but command "the Cymæans to deliver theirs?" "Yes," retorted the voice, "yes, I do command you so, that such ungodly "wretches should, at all events, be forthwith swept away, "that henceforth you may not come and ask at the shrine "about the delivering up of suppliants." As soon as the people of Cymæ received this answer brought from Bran- chidæ, they sent off the fugitive to Mytilene; not wishing to bring down destruction on their heads by delivering up Pactyas, nor to subject themselves to a siege for keeping him with them. But the Mitylenæans, when a message was sent to them by Mazares to give up Pactyas, were prepar- ing to do so, for some remuneration: what the remuneration was to be, I cannot say for certain, as the agreement was never completed; for the Cymæans, having received an inkling of what the Mytilenæans were about, sent a ship to Lesbos, and conveyed Pactyas away to Chios. But there he was torn from the temple of Minerva Poliouchos, by the Chians, and betrayed: the Chians betrayed the suppliant, in return for Atarneus, a district in Mysia, opposite to Lesbos. Pactyas, therefore, being now in the hands of the Persians, was kept under watch, to be delivered over to Cyrus: but it was a very long time before any of the Chians would offer to the gods any libation of roasted barley from Atarneus, or would take any pastry of the flour of that quarter, all productions from that country, of every sort, being carefully excluded from all holy precincts. The Chians, therefore, betrayed Pactyas. Mazares afterwards attacked the people who had joined to besiege Tabalus: on the one hand, he sold the Prienians as slaves; on the other, he overran the plain of the Mæander, abandoning all to the fury of his soldiery: Magnesia was ravaged in the same manner: soon after which, Mazares died of disease.

162 At the decease of this general, Harpagus came down to assume the command of the troops: he was also a native Mede, the same whom Astyages, king of the Medes, had feasted at the abominable banquet; the same also that assisted Cyrus in attaining to the throne. This individual, appointed by Cyrus to head the army, came into Ionia, where he captured the various cities by means of earthen mounds: for after he had compelled the citizens to shut themselves within their ramparts, he proceeded next to scale the walls, by throwing up excavations alongside of them [261]: the first place he took in Ionia, was Phocæa.

163 These Phocæans were the first of the Hellenes that performed any long voyages by sea: they were the discoverers of the Adriatic and Tyrrhenian seas, of Iberia and Tartessus. They sailed not in merchants' craft, but in fifty-oared galleys: on their coming to Tartessus, they became favourites of the king, called Arganthonius: he was ruler over Tartessus eighty years, and lived, in all, one hundred and twenty years. The Phocæans became such great favourites of this old man, that he exhorted them at first to forsake Ionia, and come and live in his country, wherever they chose [262]: afterwards, not being able to prevail on the Phocæans to accede to his advice [263], and informed that the Mede [264] was growing in strength in their neighbourhood, he gave them money to erect a wall around their city [265]; and gave it with no sparing hand, for the walls are not a few stades in circuit, all built of immense blocks nicely joined

164 together. The Phocæan walls had been accordingly built in the above manner, when Harpagus brought on his forces, and besieged them; first proffering terms, " that he would " be satisfied [266] if the Phocæans would throw down only " one of their battlements, and consecrate one house to the " king's service [267]." The Phocæans, abhorring thraldom, said, " they wished for one day to hold counsel, when they

---

[261] These heaps of earth would probably serve as inclined planes, by which the besiegers might scale the walls in great numbers at once.

[262] Matt. 507, 3. 1st parag.

[263] Matt. 413.

[264] τὸν Μῆδον, " the king of the Medes;" that is to say, Cyrus, as in c. 206.

[265] Matt. 425.

[266] Matt. 507, 3. 2d parag.

[267] This is the probable meaning: it cannot be, " dedicated to the gods:" see c. 131.

"would return an answer: they stipulated also, that, during
"the time they were debating, he should conduct his army
"to a distance from the walls." Harpagus observed, that
"he knew perfectly well what their intentions were, but he
"would permit them to hold council." At the appointed
time, therefore, Harpagus led his troops away from the
walls; and the Phocæans meanwhile launched their fifty-
oared galleys, placing on board their children, wives, and
moveables, together with the images of the temples and
other votive offerings, except articles of stone, or brass, or
painting: having stored all these things, and embarked
themselves, they took their departure for Chios: and the
Persians took possession of Phocæa, thus deserted by its inhabitants. The Chians refused to part with the Œnyssæ 165
islands; which the Phocæans wished to purchase, being
afraid lest that station should become a staple for trade, and
exclude their own island: the Phocæans, therefore, determined to make for Cyrnus, where they had, twenty years
previous to this, erected, in obedience to the behest of the
oracle, a city called Alaia: Arganthonius being at that time
no longer alive. Previous to sailing for Cyrnus, they steered
back to Phocæa; where they put to the sword the Persian
garrison appointed by Harpagus to guard the city: after
they had done this, they pronounced horrid imprecations
on such as should desert the fleet: they let down, also, a
red-hot peg of iron into the sea; and swore "they would
"never come back to Phocæa, before that peg of iron came
"to light again." When, however, they were about to set
sail for Cyrnus, more than one half of the citizens were
seized with a longing affection for their town, and dwellings
in the country: they broke their oath, and sailed back to
Phocæa: while those who kept their oath, hove anchor,
and stood away from the Œnyssæ isles. On their arrival at 166
Cyrnus, they resided for the first five years in common with
the earlier settlers, and built some temples: but as they
made a practice of ravaging and plundering all their neighbours, the Tyrrhenians and Carthaginians accordingly agreed
to fit out together sixty ships, and make a combined attack
upon them: the Phocæans, on their part, manned their
ships, sixty in number, and proceeded to face their adversaries in the Sardinian sea: they engaged the combined
squadrons, and met with a most disastrous defeat[287]; for
forty of their ships were utterly destroyed; and the other
twenty rendered useless, by having their points at the prow

---

[287] In the text, "a Cadmean victory," one like that of Eteocles and
Polynices; attended with great disasters to both parties.

blunted. They returned back to Alalia; where they took on board their wives and children, together with what property they could stow; and then, forsaking Cyrnus, stood for
167 Rhegium. As to the men belonging to the ships destroyed, the Carthaginians as well as the Tyrrhenians divided the far greater portion of them, and took them on shore, where they stoned them to death[207]. After this, every citizen of Agylla, that passed by the spot where the slaughtered Phocæans lay, was seized with contortions, falling off of the limbs, and palsy: nor were these diseases confined to men only; the sheep and oxen suffered in the same manner. The people of Agylla, anxious to wipe off the sinful stain, sent to Delphi, to consult the oracle: the Pythia, in reply, ordered them to do as they now do; that is to say, pay magnificent honours to the dead, and open a list for gymnic sports and chariot-races. Such was the fate of this portion of the Phocæans: the others, that had fled to Rhegium, quitted that place, and built in the land of Œnotria a town now called Velia; in consequence of information which they received from a citizen of Posidonium, that the Pythia, in her response, alluded not to Cyrnus the island, but to Cyrnus the hero, to whom they were to erect
168 a statue. The people of Teos acted nearly in the same manner as the Phocæans: for when Harpagus had, by means of his excavations, become master of their citadel, they embarked on board of their ships, and sailed away to Thrace; where they built the town of Abdera, on the site before chosen by Timesias of Clazomenæ; who, however, did not enjoy his acquisition, being expelled by the Thracians. He now received honours, as a hero, from the Teian settlers of Abdera.
169 The above, therefore, were the only Ionians, who, rather than brook thraldom, forsook their countries: the rest of the Ionians, with the exception of the Milesians, gave battle to Harpagus[208]; and proved themselves gallant men, as well as those who had left their country, each fighting for his own: they were, however, defeated and subdued: each remained in his respective country, and paid the appointed impost. The Milesians, as I said before[209], had entered into a treaty with Cyrus himself: they enjoyed peace. Thus, therefore, Ionia was, for the second time, deprived of freedom; and when Harpagus had completely subjugated the

---

[207] αὐτῶν refers to the Phocæans, and not to the Carthaginians and Tyrrhenians. This sentence is followed by an exceedingly abrupt transition to Agylla, the situation of which is left wholly undefined by the Historian. Agylla, however, is known to be a town of Etruria. See also Matt. 363, obs.
[208] Matt. 580, e.
[209] Herod. I. 140.

Ionians on the continent, those settled on the islands, dreading the same treatment, gave themselves up to Cyrus. Oppressed by calamity as they were, the Ionians did not 170 cease to hold assemblies at Panionium: I understand that Bias, of Priene, broached here a very wise proposal to the Ionians; which, had they accepted, would have made them the most happy and flourishing of the Hellenes: his advice was, " to heave anchor, and to sail, in one combined " squadron, to Sardinia, and there build one town for all " Ionians: thus they would secure their happiness, far re-" moved from slavery, respected as the most extensive of " the islands, and supreme over the others: whereas, if they " remained in Ionia, he declared he could not see any pro-" spect of there ever being freedom." This suggestion was made by Bias of Priene to the Ionians, when already subjugated. Previously to their destruction, a wholesome counsel was given likewise by Thales, a Milesian, and of Phœnician extraction; who advised that the Ionians should establish a common council, which should sit at Teos, that being the central point of Ionia; and the various settlements might nevertheless still be governed as independent states.

Harpagus having subdued Ionia, invaded Caria, Caunia, 171 and Lycia, taking both Ionians and Æolians in his ranks. The Carians, one of the above nations, consisted originally of emigrants from the islands: for of old they were subjects of Minos, and called Leleges: they held the islands, and paid no tribute, as far as I can ascertain, by inquiry respecting so remote a period. They manned the ships of Minos, whenever he required their services: as Minos accordingly subjected a great extent of country, and was successful in war, the Carians became the most noted of all nations by far, in those days: to them the Hellenes are indebted for three inventions which they have adopted; the Carians were the first to set the example of putting crests on helmets and devices on shields; they were likewise the first that made handles for bucklers: until their time, all who carried a shield was accustomed to manage it by means of the leather thongs, with which it was slung round the neck, over the left shoulder[170]. A very long time after this, the Ionians and Dorians drove the Carians out of the islands; and so they came to the continent. Such is, therefore, the account that the Cretans gave of the Carians; very different, at all events, from what the Carians themselves declare: they consider themselves as aboriginally belonging to the continent, and

[170] Matt. 421.

as having borne always the same name as they now do. They point to the ancient temple of Jupiter Carius at Mylasa, which is shared by the Mysians and Lydians, as kinsmen to the Carians; for it is related, that Lydus and Mysus were brothers of Car. The above temple is shared, by all who, though of a different nation, agree in their language with the Carians: all others are excluded. The 172 Caunians are also aboriginal, in my opinion; yet they themselves assert that they proceed from Crete: either they have approximated to the Carians in language, or the Carians have done so to them—that is a question I cannot decide; but it is certain that they differ greatly in their manners and customs from all men, as well as from the Carians. With the Caunians, for instance, it is looked upon as very proper and decent to men, women, and children, that, according to age and friendship, they should meet together in crowds, to drink: they had once erected temples to foreign gods, but afterwards, changing their minds, determined to worship none but their paternal deities; when the Carian youth, clad in armour, and beating the air with their spears, followed up to the Calyndic mountains the foreign gods, 173 saying, they were expelling them from the land. The Lycians, however, sprung in early times from Crete, which of old was entirely occupied by barbarians: a feud having arisen in Crete respecting the throne, between Sarpedon and Minos, the sons of Europa, Minos overcame the faction opposed to him, and drove out of the island both Sarpedon and his partisans: the exiles came into the land of Milyas, in Asia; for the country now occupied by the Lycians was then called Milyas: and the Milyans of those days bore the name of Solymoi. So long as Sarpedon ruled over them, they were designated by the name Termilæ, which they had brought with them, and by which the Lycians are still called, among their neighbours. But from the time that Lycus son of Pandion, exiled from Athens by his brother Ægeus likewise, came to the court of Sarpedon in the country of the Termilæ, the Lycians have in time come to be called after the name of Lycus. Their manners and customs are partly Cretan and partly Carian[271]: one custom is peculiar to them, in which they differ from every other nation; they take their mothers' names, not those of their fathers: if any one ask them about their kindred, who they are, they reckon from themselves to their mother, and then rehearse their mother's mothers[272]. Moreover, if a free

---

[271] Matt. 288, b.   [272] Matt. 503, 4.

woman marry a slave, the offspring is looked upon as pure and free; but if a free-man take for wife a strange woman, or cohabit with a concubine, the children are deemed infamous.

The Carians therefore performed no brilliant achievements, but were enslaved by Harpagus: this observation applies not only to the Carians, but likewise to the Hellenes settled in that quarter: among those resident here are the Cnidians, Lacedæmonian settlers, whose territory, jutting into the sea, is called the Triopeum: beginning from the Bybassian peninsula, the whole of Cnidia, with exception of a small space, is surrounded by the sea; for it is bounded north by the Ceramic gulf, while to the south stretches the sea of Syme and Rhodes: that narrow portion, therefore, about five stades in length, the Cnidians were excavating at the time that Harpagus was subjugating Ionia, with a view to converting their territory into an island. Within that, all belongs to them; for the Cnidian territory extends to the isthmus they were now cutting through. The Cnidians had set many hands at the work; and as the workmen, it was found, were more frequently and unaccountably wounded in the face and all other parts, particularly about the eyes, by the chips of the stone, they sent to Delphi some deputies to ask for a remedy: the Pythia, according to the Cnidians, spoke thus in trimeter verse:

> On the isthmus, erect no tower, nor delve:
> Jove would have made it an island, had he willed.

In consequence of this answer from the Pythia, the Cnidians stopped their excavation, and, without a blow, delivered themselves up to Harpagus, as soon as he made his appearance with his army. Above Halicarnassus, inland, were the Pedases: when any evil is to fall on these people or their neighbours, the priestess of Minerva acquires a long beard: three times has this occurred. These were the only people about Caria that stood any time[773] against Harpagus: they gave a great deal of trouble, by fortifying a mountain called Lida: but the Pedases even were, after a time, captured. But when Harpagus led his army into the Xanthian plain, the Lycians came forth, and, engaging an enemy far superior to their small band, displayed prodigious bravery: defeated and shut up in their city, they collected in the citadel their wives and children, their property and servants, then set fire to the whole, and burnt it to the ground: having so done, they bound each other by terrible oaths;

---

[773] Matt. 424, b.

and, sallying, every Xanthian died fighting. Most of the Lycians, now said to be Xanthians, are new-comers, with the exception of eighty families, which happened at that time to be away from home, and consequently were not present. Harpagus thus possessed himself of Xanthus: he likewise reduced, after the same manner, nearly the whole of Caunia; for the Caunians, generally speaking, followed the example set by the Lydians.

177 Harpagus therefore reduced the lower parts of Asia: in the upper parts, Cyrus himself subjugated every nation, without one exception. Most of these conquests we shall pass over. I will, however, commemorate those which gave him the greatest trouble, and are likewise the most deserving of mention.

178 Cyrus having subjected to his dominion all the other parts of the continent, now directed his arms against the Assyrians. Assyria comprises, besides many other extensive towns, one of the most renowned and best fortified; and there the seat of government was established, after the fall of Nineveh: this city is Babylon, of which the following is a description:—The city stands on a wide plain, and is of a quadrangular shape, each side being one hundred and twenty stades in extent: the four sides of the city, therefore, constitute a circuit of four hundred and eighty stades in all [274]: such are the dimensions of the city of the Babylonians: moreover, it is built and adorned with a magnificence not found in any other great city that we know of. In the first place, a moat, deep and broad, full of water, runs round the whole; next to which rises a wall, fifty royal cubits in thickness, and in height two hundred: the royal cubit is longer 179 by three fingers' breadth than the average cubit. I must not neglect to explain how the clay dug up for the moat was consumed, and in what manner the wall was wrought. At the same time they were excavating the moat, they moulded the clay, thrown up in the works, into bricks: when a sufficient quantity of bricks was cast, they baked them in kilns: next, making use of hot bitumen in the place of mortar, and spreading on each of the thirty bottom courses of brick a layer of wattled reeds, they first built up the edges of the moat, and then went on with the wall itself in the same manner: at the edges of the top, and on opposite sides, they erected, all round, uniform turrets [275], leaving between

---

[274] Nearly fifty miles.

[275] *περίσκεπος* this word, according to Schweighæuser's observation, may be taken in the same sense as *μονάδις*, or *οἱ πανίλος*; and, consequently, *μονάπολα εἰκμαρα* may mean *domuncula uniformes, simillimam cunctæ frontem præferentes*.

every two a space sufficient to turn a four-horse chariot. The gates leading through the wall, all around, are of solid brass, as well as the jambs and lintels. At eight days' journey from Babylon, there is a town called Is, on a small river of the same name, which discharges its stream into the Euphrates: this river Is, accordingly, brings down with its waters abundance of flakes of bitumen, from whence the bitumen used on the wall of Babylon was brought[276]. Such, then, was the mode in which Babylon was walled around. The city consists of two parts, divided by the Euphrates, which flows through the middle. This river rises in Armenia, is large, deep, and rapid: it disembogues in the Erythræan sea. Hence the wall of each of these two parts runs to an elbow on the river side: from those elbows, following the curves on each side of the river, runs a wall of baked bricks. The city itself, full of houses, three and four stories high, is cut into rectilinear streets; some parallel to the river; others, crossing the above at right angles, conduct to the bank[277]: in each of the latter streets, a small door opens, through the masonry, over the stream: they are in number equal to the streets themselves, are made of brass, and take down to the water. The outer wall, above described, is the main rampart to the town; but this latter, ranging in the interior, is scarcely inferior in strength to the other, although narrower[278]. In each portion of the city stood a vast building, occupying the centre: in one, the palace, surrounded by a long and well-fortified inclosure: in the other, the brazen-gated precinct of Jove Belus, yet standing in my day, of a square shape, in each direction two stades: in the middle of the precinct rises a massive tower, one stade in length and breadth: on that rises another tower; and so on, up to eight. The road up to the top of this building runs spirally round the outside of all the towers: somewhere about the middle[279] of the ascent, there is a place where resting-benches stand, on which those going up may sit down and take breath. In the last tower stands a magnificent temple; in which is placed a bed, sumptuously fitted up; and, by its side, a table of gold. No statue has been erected on this spot; nor does any person pass the night here[280], except only a native woman, elected by the god himself: so

---

[276] The abundant sources of bitumen in these countries are noticed by modern travellers: about Bagdad, it is suffered to flow into the Tigris, where it floats on the surface, and is frequently set on fire by the mariners; thus presenting the singular appearance of a river of fire.—*Malte-Brun.*

[277] This translation is on the authority of Schweighæuser.

[278] Matt. 487, 5.

[279] Matt. 331, c; the last parag. See also 390, b.

[280] Matt. 424, 3.a.

182 say the Chaldees, who are the priests of Belus. These same individuals assert—not that I give any credit to what they say—that the god himself comes to the temple, and reposes in the bed, just in the same manner as the Egyptians say is the case at Thebes in Egypt; for, in fact, a woman there also lies in the temple of Thebaic Jove: both women, we are told, have no communication whatever with men. Exactly the same thing takes place at Patres, in Lycia, with the woman that propounds the oracle, when there is a god there; for there is not constantly an oracle at that place: in such case as there is, the woman lies with the god at night,
183 within the temple. There is another temple, besides, in the Babylonian precinct below. Here is seen a colossal statue of Jove, seated; close to which stands a gold table: the flight of steps up to the throne, and the throne itself, are of gold; and, according to the Chaldees, all these articles are computed to be eight hundred talents of gold. Outside of the temple is a golden altar; together with another large altar, where all full-grown sheep are sacrificed, none but sucklings being allowed to be sacrificed on the golden altar. On the larger of these altars, annually, the Chaldees burn one thousand talents of frankincense, when they celebrate the feast of this god Belus. There was at that time, also, in the precinct, a statue of twelve cubits of solid gold;— not of course that I ever saw it: what I say, I repeat on the authority of the Chaldees. Darius the son of Hystaspes coveted this statue, but durst not seize it: Xerxes son of Darius, however, took it away, and killed the priest that warned him not to move the image.—Thus have I described how the holy precinct was decorated. I must add, there were abundance of private offerings.
184 Several sovereigns, at different times, have ruled over Babylon, whom I shall mention in my Assyrian history: they were the builders of the walls and sacred edifices. Two of them, especially, were women: she who reigned the first, was many generations anterior to the second; her name was Semiramis: this princess accomplished several works on the plain, that are worthy of contemplation: previously to her reign, the river was wont to inundate, and make a sea
185 of the whole plain. The second queen, that flourished after Semiramis, bore the name of Nitocris: her genius was greater than that of the queen before her: she left, as a memento, the works which I shall presently describe: in the next place, seeing the Medes' empire great and never at rest, and observing, among other cities, that of Nineveh captured by that power, she adopted beforehand every

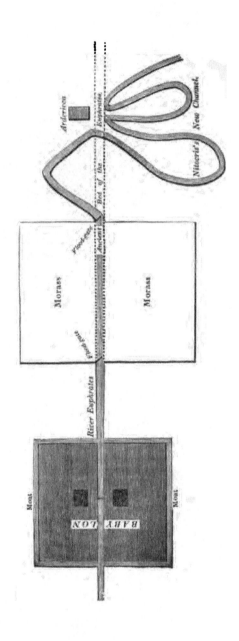

possible expedient for preservation. First, then, by making deep excavations high up the stream, she so altered the course of the Euphrates which passes through Babylon, that, from straight that it was, it became so winding as to touch three times at one and the same village in Assyria, as it flows down: the name of this village is Ardericca; and even to this time, those that, travelling from the Mediterranean shore down to Babylon, embark on the Euphrates, pass three times, within three successive days, at this spot: this was, therefore, one of the things she accomplished. She threw up, on both sides of the river, a prodigious mound, astonishing by its magnitude and height: she effected, a long distance above Babylon, a reservoir for a lake; which she placed not far from the river, digging for the depth till she came to water, and making its extent the circumference of four hundred and twenty stades: the earth thrown out in this excavation she expended in forming an embankment on the sides of the river. When the lake was finished digging out, she brought stones, with which she ran a case all round. These two works—I mean the windings of the stream, and the whole excavated marsh—were performed for the purpose of lengthening the course of the river; breaking its force in many windings, and making the passage to Babylon intricate; and that travellers, on quitting their barks, might still have to make the long circuit of the lake. In this manner she threw up these vast works in that part of the country where the shortest road from Media enters Babylonia, in order that the Medes might cease to communicate with the Babylonians, and spy into her affairs. These fortifications 186 completed, Nitocris added the following performance, the effectual success of which was the consequence of her previous works. The town being divided into two districts, by the river flowing between, whoever, under former reigns, wished to pass over from one to the other, was obliged to cross in a boat: and that, I conceive, must have been an annoyance. Nitocris provided for this. After she had dug out the basin for the lake, she determined to leave another monument of the utility of the works thrown up on the Euphrates. She caused large blocks of stone to be hewn: when they were ready, and the basin had been excavated, she turned the whole stream of the river into the hollow she had dug. While that was filling, the original bed of the river became dry: seizing the opportunity, the queen built up, with baked bricks, the banks of the river within the city, and the steps leading down from the smaller gates to the river, after the same fashion as the great wall had been put together. Besides this, about the middle of the city she constructed a bridge of cut stone, fastened together with lead and iron. During the day, square floors of wood were laid from pier to pier, by which the Babylonians crossed over: but at night these boards were taken away, for the purpose of preventing people from going across, in the dark, and committing robberies. When the hollow had been replenished by the river, and the bridge was finished, Nitocris brought the stream of the Euphrates back again, into its old bed, out of the lake. Thus the hollow, becoming a marsh, proved itself adapted for the purpose intended; and the inhabitants were accommodated with a bridge. This same queen, Nitocris, planned the following deception. Over the gate, which is the greatest thoroughfare of the city, she erected her own sepulchre, high above the gate itself; and engraved on it an inscription to this purport:—" Whoever " may, after me, be the ruler of Babylon, if in want of cash, " let him open[220] this sepulchre, and take what he chooses: " not, however, unless he be truly in want, let him open " it[221]: for it would be no good." This sepulchre remained untouched, until the throne came to Darius. That king conceived, that it was absurd he should not be able to make use of that gate, nor touch the money there deposited; money, too, that seemed to invite his grasp. The reason that induced him not to make use of this gate, was, that if he went through, there would be a dead body over his head. He opened the sepulchre: instead of money he found nothing but the skeleton, and a scroll, purporting: " Had you not " been so greedy of money and disgraceful pelf, you would " not have broken into the sojourn of the dead."

188 It was against the son of this queen that Cyrus was accordingly directing his next attack: this Babylonian king inherited the name of Labynetus, and the Assyrian empire, from his father. When the great king goes to war, he travels provided with provisions well preserved, and cattle, from home: he takes, especially, with him, water from the Choaspes, a river that flows by Susa, of which, and no other, the king drinks. A vast number of four-wheel waggons, drawn by mules, follow in his train, wherever he goes: they are loaded with the Choaspes' water, boiled previously, and stored in silver vases. In his march to Babylon, Cyrus came to the Gyndes[222], a river that rises in the Matianian mountains, flows athwart the land of the Dardanians, and

---

[220] Matt. 494, 2.   [221] Matt. 508, b.
[222] See, concerning the Gyndes, v. 52.

falls into another river, the Tigris, which, rolling its waters through the city of Opys, disembogues in the Erythræan sea. As Cyrus, therefore, was endeavouring to get across this river Gyndes, which is only passable in barges, one of the sacred white horses, full of mettle, rushed into the stream, and tried to swim over: but the torrent seized the animal, and, whirling him under the surface, dashed him down the stream. The Persian king was much enraged by this insult on the part of the river; and pronounced a threat, that he would pull down his strength, so that for evermore even women should cross him readily, without wetting the knee. This threat pronounced, he suspended the campaign against Babylon, and divided his troops into two bodies: this being done, he marked out, by line, one hundred and eighty channels on each side of the river, diverging from the direction of the Gyndes in all quarters. He then stationed the men, and commanded them to dig. With such a multitude of hands, the work was indeed brought to a completion: the troops, nevertheless, passed at that place the whole of the summer in the task[289]. Cyrus having wreaked his vengeance on the Gyndes river, by distributing its stream into three hundred and sixty channels, proceeded, at the first gleam of spring, to march on to Babylon. The Babylonians, encamped on the field, awaited his onset: the Persian leader brought his army near the city, where the Babylonians gave battle; and, being routed, shut themselves within their walls. But, as they were long before convinced that Cyrus would never rest, and saw him fall on every nation indifferently, they collected beforehand provisions for many years. They cared, therefore, nothing for the blockade. Cyrus, however, found himself in difficult circumstances; a long time having slipped away, without his affairs making any progress. Whether, therefore, any person suggested the thing to him in the midst of his difficulties, or he himself conceived a plan of acting, he did as I will now describe. He stationed the greater part of his army at the opening by which the river enters the town, placing also a few companies at the opposite opening by which the river makes its exit: he then gave his orders to the men, that when they found the stream fordable, they should push into the town: having thus dispersed his army, and given the above directions, he himself marched away with the unarmed train of his army. He came to the

---

[289] The Historiad attributed this undertaking of the Persian hero to a ridiculous grudge against the Gyndes. The fact was, it seems, that this laborious work was undertaken for the purpose of rendering this part of Assyria more easily accessible by a vast army, in subsequent progresses.

lake, the work of the queen of the Babylonians, and did the same by the lake and the river as she had done before; that is to say, opening the sluice into the lake, then a morass, and turning in the waters of the river, made the old bed fordable. This being the case, the Persians stationed on that service close to the Euphrates, which now had sunk to at least the mid thigh of a man, made their ingress into Babylon. If, therefore, the Babylonians had been apprised beforehand, or had heard of what Cyrus was about, which they did not, they might have handled their foes in the most dreadful manner: they would have closed all the little gates leading down to the river, and, mounting themselves on the quays stretching along both sides of the stream, would have caught them as in a net: but in this instance the Persians took them by surprise. It is related by the people who were then residing at Babylon, that, in consequence of the immense extent of the town, the extreme limits of the city had been taken before the people dwelling in the centre of Babylon knew any thing of the capture; but—for it was with them a festive day—they were dancing at the very time, and enjoying themselves, until they also were at last brought acquainted with the truth. Thus was Babylon captured for the first time.

192 The most cogent proof I can give, among many others, of the resources of the Babylonians, is this one thing: the whole extent of lands over which the rule of the great king stretches, besides tributes, furnishes the sovereign and his army with provisions for food: the Babylonian district supplies this during four months of the twelve: the eight remaining months are provided by all Asia together. Thus the Assyrian soil possesses one third of the resources of the whole of Asia. Moreover, the superintendence of this province, called satrapy by the Persians, is, of all the governments, the most lucrative. When Tritantæchmes, son of Artabazus, held that government from the king, his daily income was a full artaba of silver[94]—the Persian measure, called artaba, contains above the Attic medimnus three Attic chœnixes. The horses belonging to himself personally, besides the army horses, were eight hundred stallions, and sixteen thousand mares; one stallion for twenty mares. So numerous were his packs of Indian dogs that he kept, that four large villages in the plain, which were relieved from all other taxes, were appointed to supply their food. Such were

193 the advantages accruing to the governor of Babylon. The

---

[94] According to Arbuthnot, four pecks and ten pints.

land of the Assyrians is visited with little rain, and that little water is what feeds the root of the corn: the crop, however, is made to grow up to give a harvest, by constant irrigation from the river: this irrigation does not take place, as in Egypt, by the spontaneous overflow of the river on the lands, but is done by the hand or swipe; for the whole of Babylonia is intersected by canals, the same as Egypt: the largest of these canals is navigable, and stretches in the direction of the winter sun-rise: it communicates from the Euphrates, with the Tigris, at the spot where Nineveh stood: this is, of all the lands we know any thing of, by far the best[295] for the produce of Ceres' gifts: other plants do not even make a show of growing in this quarter, neither the fig, nor the grape, nor the olive; but the wheat it bears is beautiful in the extreme: it returns, on an average, two-hundred-fold; but when it produces its best, the return is three-hundred-fold[296]. The blades of wheat and barley acquire easily a breadth of four fingers. Although I am well aware to what size of tree the sesame seed does grow, I shall not mention it; being fully convinced, that, to those who have never been in Babylonia, what I have already said of its products will be considered too exaggerated to be given credit to. They make no use of olive-oil, but make theirs from sesame. Palm-trees spring up all over the plain: most of these are fructiferous; and from the fruit they procure bread, wine, and honey; they cultivate them in the same manner as fig-trees, particularly as to what concerns the male palms, as the Hellenes call them; the fruit of which they tie about the branches of the date-bearing trees, in order that the fly may come out and enter into the dates, and so prevent the fruit of the palm from falling off; for the male palms have flies in their fruit, just like our wild figs[297].

The greatest wonder of all things here, next of course to the city, is, in my opinion, what I am now going to explain[298]. Their boats, that ply down the river to Babylon, 194

---

[295] Matt. 461.
[296] Matt. 460.
[297] The date-tree, a sort of palm, has the male and female on different plants: the pollen from the male is carried to the female, either by the hand of man, the bees and flies, or by the soft breeze. The fig-tree of Greece, Malta, and the Levant, are of two kinds, the cultivated and wild; the latter of which is not eatable, but serves as a receptacle for a sort of jet-black fly: the peasants make chaplets of the figs of this wild plant, called the *caprificus*, and append them to the branches of the fruitful fig-tree: the black fly hatches in these chaplets, and, issuing from thence, proceeds to pierce the eye of the cultivated fruit, in which they are said to fertilize the flowers enclosed within the fruit, by burrowing among them for food. Herodotus neglected, in this case, it seems, to search for accurate information, with his usual patience and perseverance.

[298] Matt. 556, 7.

are all circular, and consist of leather: after making the frames in Armenia, which lies above Assyria, from the osiers they cut in that country, they stretch on the outside a leather covering, in the room of planking; making no distinction between stem or stern, but perfectly round, like a buckler. They line the inside of this craft with straw, launch it into the river, and then stow it with merchandise. Their freight consists principally of casks filled with date-wine: they are managed, with two poles, by two men standing erect; one of whom hauls his pole in, while the other shoves his out[289]. Very large barges are made on this pattern, and so are smaller craft: the largest of all are of five thousand talents' burthen. On board of every barge there is seen a live ass: in the larger barges there are several. When they have floated down to Babylon, and disposed of their cargo, they put up to auction the ribs of the bark, and the straw; and the skins are piled on the pack-saddle of the ass, who is driven back into Armenia. To re-ascend the river, in the same manner, is out of the question, so rapid is the current; in consequence of which, also, they are obliged to make their boats of leather, and not of wood. When they have driven their asses back to Armenia, they construct other

195 barges in the same manner.—The costume of the Babylonians consists of a cotton shirt, reaching down to the feet; over which they throw a woollen cloak, and a close white cape: their covering for the feet is after a fashion peculiar to this country, closely approaching to the Bœotian clogs. Their flowing hair they bind up under a mitre, and anoint the whole body with perfumes. Every individual has a seal; and a staff, made by hand, on every one of which is carved an apple, a rose, a lily, and so forth: for they are not allowed to carry a stick, unless it bear some mark.

196 The following are some of their customs: the wisest in my idea is this, which I understand holds[290] also among the Venetians of Illyria. Once every year the following scene took place in every village: whatever maidens might be of marriageable years[291], were all collected, and brought into one certain place, around which stood a multitude of men. A crier called up each girl separately, and offered her for sale: he began with the prettiest[292] of the lot; and when she had found a rich bidding, he sold her off; and called up another, the next he ranked in beauty. All these girls were

---

[289] The mode of steering a barge on the Seine, when that river is highly swollen, is exactly the same as this description of Herodotus.

[290] Matt. 550, obs. 3.
[291] Matt. 317.
[292] Matt. 389.

sold off in marriage: the rich men, that were candidates for a wife, bade against one another for the handsomest: the more humble classes, desirous of getting partners, did not require absolutely beauty, but were willing to take even the ugly girls for a sum of money. Therefore, when the crier had gone through the list of the prettiest women, and disposed of them, he put up the ugliest, or some one that was a cripple, if any there were, and, offering to dispose of her, called out for the bidder that would, for the smallest sum, take her to live with him: so he went on,. till he came to her that he considered the least forbidding. The money for this was got by the sale of the pretty maidens; so that the handsome and well shaped gave dowries to the ugly and deformed. It was not lawful for any one to give his daughter to whom he chose; nor for a person to take a girl away that he had purchased, without giving bond that he verily proposed to marry her; when he might take her with him. If the couple could not agree, the law permitted the money to be returned. It was also allowed to any man coming from another village to make a purchase, if he chose. This was the best of their institutions. Lately, they have hit upon an expedient, that their daughters might not be maltreated or carried off to some other town: for since they have been conquered, they are illtreated and ruined by their lords; and all the lower orders, for the sake of getting a livelihood, prostitute their female offspring. The following is another of their institutions. They bring out into the public square all their sick; for they have no regular doctors. The persons that meet the sick man, give him advice; and exhort him to do the same that they themselves have found to cure such a disease, or have known some other person to be cured by. They are not allowed to pass by any sick person, until they have asked him what ailing he has.—They embalm the dead in honey: their lamentations are nearly the same as in Egypt. Every Babylonian that has conversed with his own wife sits down near the smoke of burning perfumes; the woman, on her part, does the same; and at dawn of day both wash; for until they have done so, they will not touch any vase: the same practice holds with the Arabians.

The most disgraceful of the Babylonian customs is this: every native woman must, once in her life, sit down in the holy precinct of Venus, and have communication with some stranger. Many of these women disdaining to mix with the others, and inflated by their riches, go to the temple in covered carriages, followed by a numerous retinue of servants. But the majority act in the following manner:

they seat themselves in the temple of Venus, wearing on their heads a wreath of cord: some are coming, others are going: paths are set off by line in every direction through the crowds of women, by which the strangers pass and make their choice. When a woman has once taken her seat there, she cannot return home until some stranger casts a piece of silver on her knees, and enjoys her person outside of the temple. When he throws the money, he is to say this much: "In the name of the goddess Mylitta." The Assyrians call Venus, Mylitta: the piece of silver may be ever so small; it will not be refused, for that is not lawful; but that coin is deemed sacred. The woman follows the first man that throws: she refuses no one[293]. After surrendering her person, the goddess being satisfied, she returns home; and from that time, however great a sum you may give her, you will not obtain her favours. Such girls as are endowed with beauty and grace soon return home; others, that are deformed, tarry a long time, finding themselves unable to fulfil the law: some even have remained three or four years. In many parts of Cyprus the same custom, nearly, is in vogue. Such, then, are the customs with the
200 Babylonians. There are three tribes among them that eat nothing but fish; which, after they have caught and dried it, they prepare thus: they put it into a mortar, bray it with a pestle, and drive it through a sieve; and whoever chooses, may make frumenty, or bake it into bread.
201 Cyrus having done with this nation also, conceived the desire of subjecting to his dominion the Massagetæ. This people is described as both great and warlike, dwelling eastward, towards the rising sun, beyond the Araxes river, and opposite to the Issedones: there are even some persons
202 who assert that this nation is Scythian. The Araxes is represented as both larger and smaller than the Ister: there are islands, thickly studded, on this stream, and nearly as considerable in size as Lesbos: on these islands are found men that in summer live upon roots of all sorts, which they grub up; but store up also, as food, the ripe fruits they get from the trees, and upon which they live in winter: they have also discovered a particular kind of tree, bearing fruit of a peculiar quality: at times, they collect together in large parties, kindle a fire, and, sitting in a ring around, throw some of this fruit into the flames. By inhaling the fumes of the burning fruit they have thrown in, they become intoxicated by the smell, as the Hellenes are by wine: the

[293] Matt. 516, b.

more fruit they throw on, the more inebriated they are; till at last they get up to dance and sing. Such their mode of life is said to be[294]. The river Araxes flows from the Matianian mountains—the same that the Gyndes rises in, which Cyrus dispersed into the three hundred and sixty channels: the waters of the former gush out of forty springs; all of which, with the exception of one, discharge themselves into swampy marshes[295], where men are said to reside that live on raw fish, and wear seal-skin garments. That one stream of the Araxes I have mentioned, flows, without impediment, into the Caspian sea. The Caspian is a sea of itself; that is to say, it does not mix with any other sea: for all that sea which the Hellenes navigate, and the Atlantic without the Pillars, together with the Erythræan sea, are all one and the same. But, as I have said, the Caspian is a different sea of itself; which, in length, is a fortnight's voyage in a row-boat; and in breadth, at its widest part, a week's voyage[296]. On the western shore of this sea stretches the range of Caucasus, the largest and loftiest of mountains. Many and various races inhabit the regions of Caucasus, the majority of whom live on the wild products of the forest; among which are trees that supply leaves, which, when rubbed and mixed with water, give a dye, with which their garments may be stained with all sorts of figures. The figures never fade, but last as long as the stuff itself, just the same as if it were inwoven at first: it is said that among these people the sexual intercourse takes place openly, as with cattle. The Caucasus, therefore, serves as a boundary to the Caspian sea in the west: on the east, and towards the rising sun, a plain succeeds, the extent of which is far beyond the stretch of the eye. A considerable portion of this heath is occupied by the Massagetæ, against whom Cyrus projected war: motives, numerous and powerful, incited and urged him on: in the first place, his birth, which he considered as something more than human; secondly, the good fortune that had attended him in his wars: for wherever Cyrus directed his arms, it was wholly impossible for that nation to escape.

The preceding king's widow, called Tomyris, was the queen over these Massagetæ. Cyrus despatched to her an ambassador, under pretence of paying his addresses, and

[294] Compare iv. 75.
[295] This translation is on the authority of Schweighæuser: *Ἀναβύσιαι* signifies *to burst* from a spring or source, quite the contrary *to discharge* its waters into the sea: this establishes the certainty that Herodotus, in this passage, at all events, does not mean what we now call the *Volga*.
[296] Matt. 460.

offering marriage; but Tomyris, aware that it was not herself, but the kingdom of the Massagetæ, that he courted, forbade his approach. Cyrus, thus thwarted in his attempt to deceive, marched to the Araxes, and made open preparations for war with the Massagetæ, by erecting a bridge over the river, and building floating castles to convey the troops across [297]. While the Persian chief was thus employed, Tomyris sent a herald to him, who was to say: "King of the "Medes, cease your great haste [298]; for you cannot yet know "whether this will end to your advantage. Cease, then, "once more: rule over your own dominions; and contem-"plate, with a peaceful eye, my government over what is "mine. If you will not hearken to this advice, but prefer "every thing before quietness and repose—if you are so "excessively anxious to make trial of the Massagetæ— "come; spare yourself the trouble of throwing a bridge "across the river. We will retire three days' march from "the river: meanwhile, do you cross into our territory: but "if you had rather receive us on your own ground, do you "the same." When Cyrus heard this proposal, he called a meeting of the chief Persians: the assembly convened, Cyrus laid the business before them, asking their opinion as to how he should act. They unanimously agreed in advising him to admit Tomyris and her army on his own soil. Crœsus was present: the Lydian prince disapproved the counsel; took up the opposite side of the question; and said: "Mighty "king, I have already observed to you, that since Jove has "given me into your hands, whatever misfortune I may see "impending over your house, to use all my exertions to "turn it aside. My sufferings, bitter as they are, have been "a lesson to me. If you consider yourself and your army "immortal, there can be no need of my explaining to you "what my opinion is: yet, if you are convinced that you "yourself even are but a man, and those you rule over "nothing more, be in the first place apprised of this—the "wheel of human life is ever revolving, and will not allow "the same mortal to be constantly successful. Now, there-"fore, the opinion I hold on the matter in question is "wholly contrary to that of this assembly. If we resolve to "receive the foe on our own ground, I say that there is this "danger in so doing; if on one hand you are defeated, you "will lose, besides, your whole empire; for it is clear the "Massagetæ, if conquerors, will not retrace their steps, but "will dash forward, into the heart of your dominions: if, on

[297] Matt. 431. [298] Matt. 417, σπεύδων. See also 337.

"the other hand, you conquer, still is your conquest not so
"complete as if you had your foot on their soil, had con-
"quered the Massagetæ, and were pursuing the fugitives: for
"I shall still object to this assembly, that after routing your
"adversaries you will directly press on into the interior of
"Tomyris's dominions. And, moreover, is it not disgraceful
"and intolerable that Cyrus the son of Cambyses should
"retire before a woman, on his own territory? My opinion
"therefore is, that you should cross the Araxes, and go as
"far as they retire; and having so done, endeavour to gain
"the day upon them. The Massagetæ, I am told, know of
"none of the Persian delicacies, and are inexperienced of
"the comforts of life. For such men, therefore, slaughter
"abundance of cattle, dress the flesh, and spread it forth in
"our camp; add vases filled to the brim with wine un-
"mixed with water, and all sorts of dishes. Having done
"this, leave the worst portion of your army behind; let the
"rest return again to the river; and, if I am not mistaken,
"the enemy, seeing all these good things, will fall to and
"devour them; and it will remain for us to achieve a mighty
"work."

Such were the plans proposed on both sides. Cyrus re- 208
jected the former, and adopted that of Crœsus: he made
known to Tomyris, that she might retreat, and he would
cross the Araxes to give her the meeting: she retired, according to her previous stipulation; and Cyrus, placing
Crœsus in the hands of Cambyses, to whom he bequeathed
the kingdom, earnestly prescribed to his son to honour and
shew every attention to the captured prince, in case the
campaign against the Massagetæ should be a failure.
Having given these injunctions, and sent Crœsus and Cambyses off to Persia, he crossed the river with his forces.
Arrived on the opposite bank of the Araxes, at the fall of
day he beheld, as he slept in the land of the Massagetæ, a
vision: it was this: Cyrus fancied in his sleep that he beheld
the eldest son of Hystaspes with wings on his shoulders, one
of which shadowed Asia, the other Europe. The eldest son
of Hystaspes the son of Arsames, one of the Achæmenides,
was Darius, then at best but twenty years of age: this son of
his was left in Persia, not being of age to join the expedition.
When Cyrus awoke, he considered within himself about his
dream; and, as the token seemed important, he sent for
Hystaspes; and, taking him aside, said: "Hystaspes, I have
"detected your son plotting against me and my throne:
"I am certain of it, and will tell you how: the gods watch
"over me, and forewarn me of all things that are to come.

"Now, this very night, in my sleep, I beheld the eldest
"of your sons with wings on his shoulders; one of which
"covered Asia, the other Europe, with shade. There cannot
"be the slightest doubt, from this dream, that the youth is
"conspiring against me. Go back, therefore, as speedily
"as you can to Persia; and manage so, that when I return
"there from the present expedition, you may produce your
210 "son before me, to examine." Cyrus spoke thus in the
conviction that Darius was plotting against him; but the
divinity foreshowed to him, that he would himself be killed
in the campaign, and that his kingdom would descend
to Darius. Hystaspes' answer was accordingly in these
words: "Sire, lives there a Persian that would conspire
"against you: if so, let him forthwith die: for you have
"made the Persians, from being slaves, to be free men; in
"place of being lorded by all, to rule over all[a]. If any
"dream has announced to you that my son broods any
"disturbance against you, I pledge myself to deliver him
"into your hands, to do by him what you choose." Hystaspes
having returned the above answer, repassed the Araxes; and
proceeded into Persia, to take his son into custody, and bring
him before Cyrus.

211 Cyrus having advanced one day's march from the banks
of the Araxes, proceeded to act according to the suggestion
of Crœsus. Having done as he advised, Cyrus, and the
efficient part of the Persian army, marched back to the
Araxes, leaving the inefficient forces behind: the third
division of the Massagetic army coming up, put to death
the men that composed the body he had left behind, and
that resisted: then, seeing the provisions spread out, they
stretched themselves on the turf, and feasted, after routing
their enemies. Filled with food and wine, they dropped to
sleep: and the Persians coming up, put many to the sword,
but took a much greater number prisoners: among the rest,
the leader of the Massagetæ, son of queen Tomyris, called
212 Spargapises. Tomyris, informed of what had happened to
her army and to her son, sent a herald to Cyrus, to say:
"Cyrus, you that are never satiate of blood, boast not of
"what has taken place; for it was the juice of the grape—
"which causes you yourself, when filled with it, to rave so,
"and sinks down into your body but to throw back a tide of
"insolent abuse—it was by that poison you deceived my
"son, and not in fair battle. Now, listen to some good
"advice, which I offer in good part: restore to me my son,

---

[a] Matt. 541. obs. 1. note.

" and depart unpunished from this land, although you have
" so cruelly treated the third of my army. If you refuse to
" do this, I swear by the sun, the god of the Massagetæ, that,
" insatiate as you are, I will glut you with blood!" Cyrus
took no account of this message; and Spargapises, having
recovered from the influence of wine, and seen the extent of
his misfortune, begged Cyrus to liberate him from his fetters,
which was granted: no sooner was he released, however, and
had regained the use of his hands, than he put an end to his
life. Such was the fate of the son; but Tomyris, not being
listened to by Cyrus, called all her forces together, and gave
battle to Cyrus.—I take it this engagement was the most
bloody of battles that ever took place between foreign
nations: I have heard the following description of the fight.
First, it is related, that, at a distance from one another, the
two armies fought with their bows and arrows: when their
arrows were all shot away, they closed, and engaged with
javelin and cutlass, man to man: for a long time the battle
raged; neither party would give way; but at last the Massagetæ got the upper hand: most part of the Persian army
was cut to pieces on the field; and there also fell Cyrus, after
a reign of nine-and-twenty years. Tomyris filled a skin
with human blood: she caused the body of Cyrus to be looked
for among the slain of the Persians: it was found: she
plunged his head into the skin, and reviled the dead body[200],
saying: " Although I live, and have conquered thee in battle,
" thou hast ruined me for ever, by ensnaring my son. But
" I will gorge thee, as I threatened, with blood."—This account of the death of Cyrus, of the many that are given out,
appears to me the most authentic.

The Massagetæ wear the same costume as the Scythians, and have the same mode of life: their forces consist of horse and foot; both join in battle: there are bowmen and javelin-men, who are wont to carry battle-axes. They make great use of gold and copper: in what concerns the spear-head, arrow-head, and battle-axe, they make all of copper: all that belongs to the helmet, girdle, and coat of mail, is ornamented with gold: in the same manner, they put copper mail on the cruppers of their horses; but the bridle, bit, and head-trappings, are of gold: they use no silver or iron; for those metals are not found in their country, which abounds, however, in copper and gold. Their manners and customs are as follows: every man marries one woman, but all the women are in common; for it is the Massagetæ, not the

---

[200] Matt. 384.

Scythians, as the Hellenes assert, that have this practice. Whatever female a Massagetan man feels a desire to enjoy, he has only to hang his quiver on her waggon, and do what he wishes at his ease. No limit is set to human life; but when a man becomes exceedingly infirm by age, his nearest kinsmen all meet, and sacrifice him, together with other cattle: they then boil the flesh, and feast on it: this is considered the happiest mode of ending life. Such as die of disease are not eaten; but are placed under ground, their friends lamenting that they did not reach the age to be sacrificed. They sow no pulse; but live on their cattle and fish, which abound in the Araxes: their beverage, also, is milk. They worship the sun alone, to whom they offer up horses: the reason of which custom is, that they think it right to consecrate the swiftest of mortal creatures to the swiftest of the gods.

BABYLONIAN CHRONOLOGY.

The kingdom of Babylon began, according to Ptolemy's Canon, with Nabonassar, 747 B. C.; who was followed by twelve kings, down to Nabopolassar.

	B.C.
Nabopolassar	627
Nebuchadnezzar	604
Evilmerodach	561
Neriglissar	559
Labynetus	555
Cyrus captures Babylon	538

BOOK II.

EUTERPE.

SUMMARY OF BOOK II.

CAMBYSES, *having succeeded his father Cyrus on the throne, undertakes, in the fifth year, an expedition against the Egyptians. But, before the Historian relates that expedition, he describes the country of the Egyptians, and the nature of the Nile, 2—36, the manners, rites, and mode of living of the people, 37—98. The series of their kings is given, 99—150. The affairs of Egypt become better known after strangers are admitted into the country by Psammitichus, 151 seq. He is succeeded by Necos, 158; who is succeeded by Psammis, 160; who is succeeded by Apries, 161. Apries is deprived of the crown by Amasis, 162, (here the seven castes of the Egyptians are described, 164 seq.) 172 to the end.*

THE SECOND BOOK OF HERODOTUS.

EUTERPE.

At the decease of Cyrus, Cambyses succeeded to the throne: he was a son of Cyrus, by the daughter of Pharnaspes, Cassandane; whose previous death Cyrus not only mourned deeply himself, but commanded all that he ruled over likewise to mourn. Cambyses, the son of this princess and of Cyrus, considered the Ionians and Æolians as hereditary slaves[1]; and when about to open a campaign against Egypt, took men, not only from the other nations under his rule, but also from those Hellenes that had been conquered.

The Egyptians, prior to the reign of Psammitichus, regarded themselves as the most ancient of mankind. But that prince, having come to the throne, resolved to ascertain what people were the first in existence: from that time the Egyptians have allowed that the Phœnicians existed before them, but that they themselves are anterior to all others. Psammitichus, finding it impossible to ascertain, by inquiry, any means of discovering who were the first of the human race, devised the following experiment. He delivered over to a herdsman two new-born children of humble parents, to rear them, with his flocks, after this manner: his orders were, that no one should ever pronounce a word in the presence of the children, who were to be kept by themselves in a solitary apartment; at certain hours[2], goats were to be brought to them; the herdsman was to see they sucked their fill of milk, and then go about his business. This was done and ordered by Psammitichus for the purpose of hearing what word the children would first utter, after they left off the unmeaning cries of infancy. And such accordingly was

---

[1] Matt. 569, 2, last parag.   [2] Matt. 424, 3, a.

the result. For the pastor had continued during the space of two years to act according to these orders, when one day opening the door, and entering, both the children fell upon him, crying 'becos,' and stretching out their hands. The first time that the shepherd heard this, he accordingly kept quiet; but the same word occurred repeatedly, every time he came to attend to them: he therefore let his master know, and was ordered to bring the children into his presence. Psammitichus heard himself the word; and inquired what people it was that called, in their language, any thing 'becos:' he was informed that the Phœnicians give that name to 'bread.' In consequence, the Egyptians, having deliberately weighed the matter, gave place to the Phœnicians, and granted they were more ancient than themselves.

3 It was by the priests of Vulcan, at Memphis, that I was informed things occurred as I have thus described[3]. The Hellenes, however, add many other nonsensical things; for instance, that Psammitichus cut out the tongues of some women, and, by their assistance, succeeded in bringing up the children:—so far for the account of the education of these children[4]. In my conversations with the priests of Vulcan, I heard many other traditions at Memphis; and even proceeded to Thebes and Heliopolis, on their account, being desirous to know whether the traditions there would coincide with those at Memphis; for the Heliopolitans are represented as the most skilful antiquaries among the Egyptians. Of those traditions that relate to divine things, and which I may have heard, it is not my intention to mention any thing more than the mere names; for I think all men equally wise upon these matters. If I should casually mention such things, it will be only when necessitated, by the course of the narrative.

4 So far, then, as concerns human matters, they agree among themselves in the statements I am going to present. That the Egyptians were the first people in the world to discover the year, and distribute over it the twelve parts of the four seasons; a discovery, they said, deduced from the stars: (so far, in my opinion, they act more wisely than the Hellenes; for the Hellenes intercalate every other year one month, on account of the seasons[5]: the Egyptians, on the

---

[3] Matt. 374, first parag.

[4] This experiment was renewed in the fifteenth century, by James IV. king of Scotland, who shut up two children in the isle of Inchkeith, with a dumb attendant to wait upon them.

[5] Comp. Herod. I. note.—If their year had been exactly three hundred and sixty-five days; far from the seasons always coming at the same time, the winter months would at the end of some centuries come in the spring, and so on with the others. Diodorus Siculus asserts, that the inhabitants

other hand, reckon twelve months of thirty days, and add to every year five days above that number, so that the circle of the seasons comes round to the same point.) They assert, likewise, that the Egyptians were the first to adopt and bring into use the names of the twelve gods; a practice which the Hellenes borrowed from them[6]: they were likewise the first to erect altars, as well as images and temples, and to invent the carving of figures on stone: of the authenticity of these statements, they, in most cases, brought proofs from facts. The priests stated, also, that Meues was the first of mortals[7] that ever ruled over Egypt: to this they added, that in the days of that king, all Egypt, with the exception of the Thebaïc nome, was but a morass; and that none of the lands now seen below Lake Mœris then existed: from the sea up to this place is a voyage, by the river, of seven days. I myself am perfectly convinced the account of the priests in this particular is correct: for the thing is evident to every one who sees and has common sense, although he may not have heard the fact, that the Egypt to which the Hellenes navigate is a land annexed to the Egyptians, and a gift from the river; and that even in the parts above the lake just mentioned, for three days' sail, concerning which the priests relate nothing, the country is just of the same description[8].

The nature of the Egyptian soil is, therefore, such as I will now relate. In the first place, as you make for that country, and when you are yet one day's sail from land, if you cast the sounding-lead, you will bring up mud, and find yourself in eleven fathoms' water: a proof this, that so far the alluvion extends. The breadth of this part of Egypt, washed by the

of Thebes, in Egypt, intercalated, at the end of each year, five days and a quarter. Larcher supposes there were in Egypt two sorts of years: the civil one, of three hundred and sixty-five days; and the astronomical one, known only to the priests, by which they regulated their festivals, and conciliated to themselves the respect of the people. This last year was not known to Herodotus; and indeed it was with great difficulty that Plato and Eudoxus, who lived thirteen years with the Egyptian priests, could draw from them this discovery, of which they made a great mystery. The mode in which the additional months were intercalated in the cycle of nineteen years, represented by asterisks, is 1, 2, *3, 4, 5, *6, 7, 8, *9, etc. which accounts for the intervals being designated *trieteris*, rather than, more accurately, *deteris*. See Corsini, quoted in the Oxford edition.

[6] The Greeks did not borrow the very names from the Egyptians; but took from them the practice of giving each of their many gods some particular name. The Pelasgians, who had borrowed this usage from the Egyptians, and transmitted it to the Greeks, worshipped many gods in earliest times, but knew of no nominal distinction between them. Herod. II. 52.

[7] In contradistinction of the gods his predecessors: II. 99.

[8] All, who visit Egypt, confess that they feel convinced of this fact.

sea, is sixty schœni; for I reckon the coast from the gulf of Plinthinetes to Lake Serbonis, near which Mount Casius rises, to belong to Egypt. From that place, therefore, the sixty schœni are taken:—for the people, whose land is scanty, measure it by the fathom: those less confined in that respect measure by stades; such as have an extensive territory, by parasang: lastly, in the case of a very vast country, the measure is estimated in schœni. Now, the parasang is equivalent to thirty stades; each schœnus, the Egyptian measure, contains sixty stades: consequently, the coast of Egypt
7 is of three thousand six hundred stades[9]. From the coast, up to Heliopolis in the interior Egypt, is wide, all on a gradual slope, without fresh water, and swampy. The way from the sea up the river to Heliopolis[10] is pretty nearly equal in length to the road from Athens; that is to say, from the altar of the twelve gods, and leading to Jove's temple at Pisa: not but a person actually measuring these two ways might detect some little difference or inequality between them[11]; not more than fifteen stades, however; for the road from Athens to Pisa wants but fifteen stades to be fifteen hundred: on the other hand, the distance
8 from the sea to Heliopolis is full that number. As you continue going up above Heliopolis, Egypt becomes narrow: on one side extends the range of the Arabian mountain, running from the north to the south, and continuously stretching up to the Erythræan sea, as it is called. In this

[9] The modern maps exhibit the coast of Egypt pretty nearly equal to the number of common stades mentioned by Herodotus; measuring from headland to headland, as was customary with the mariners from whom our Historian obtained his information. See the *Eton Atlas*.

[10] In ascending the river, the mariners, no doubt, took into account the windings and reaches of the river; as the number of days' navigation was the only information which their experience enabled them to supply.

[11] There are many reasons to doubt whether Herodotus uses in this Book the Pythic stade, instead of the common or Olympic stade, which is of about ten to a British mile: such, however, is the general opinion of the commentators in general: of this, the following quotation from the work of Major Rennel exhibits a palpable proof: -

"In the report of Herodotus respecting the extent of Egypt, he has made use of a stade which is totally different from that which he uses when he refers to Greece or Persia. This appears in a remarkable instance, where he assigns an equal number of stades, within 15, to the space between Athens and Pisa, as between Heliopolis and the sea-coast of Egypt; although the former be about 105, the latter 86 G. miles only; the one giving a proportion of 775, the other of 1012 to a degree. So that he appears to have used stades of different scales, without a consciousness of it." *Rennel*, p. 427.

Upon this opinion of the illustrious geographer, I may be permitted to remark, that the difference (19 miles) between the two distances mentioned by Herodotus may perhaps have proceeded from the Historian not taking, like Major Rennel, the measures in a linear direction; but computed them from days' journeys, and days' navigation along the coast.

chain are seen the quarries where the stones were cut for the pyramids at Memphis[12]; and where the mountain, ceasing its former course, bends away east to the sea above mentioned[13]. Here also, in its extreme length, the road from east to west, I am told, takes up two months: the eastern part of this mountain constitutes the boundary of the incense country: such, therefore, is the Arabian range. Between Libya and Egypt extends another mountain-chain, composed of rock, on which the pyramids stand, and covered with sand: it follows a direction parallel to that part of the Arabian chain which runs to the south. From Heliopolis, therefore, the territory belonging to Egypt is not considerable, as the country remains very narrow during four days' navigation up the stream: the land however, between the two above-mentioned mountains, is level; and in the narrowest part, the distance from the Arabian chain to the ridge, called the Libyan, did not appear, at most, but two hundred stades: above this spot, Egypt again expands. Such, accordingly, is an outline of this country. From Heliopolis to Thebes, is a voyage of nine days; the length of which, in stades, is four thousand eight hundred and sixty, or eighty-one schœni. If we collect these measures in stades, the breadth along the shore is, as I have already explained, four thousand six hundred: next, the distance from the sea, inland, as far as Thebes, is, namely, six thousand one hundred and twenty stades[14]; and from Thebes to the city of Elephantine, one thousand eight hundred.

Most part of the country, thus described, appeared to me, in accordance with the statement of the priests, to be an adjunction to Egypt. For the space between the above-mentioned mountains, situate beyond the town of Memphis, was evidently to me, at some time or other, a gulf of the sea; after the same manner, in fact, as the country about Troy and Teuthrania, and Ephesus and the plain of the

---

[12] Two places are mentioned by Herodotus, from which two different sorts of stone, used in the construction of the pyramids, are taken: the common stone was obtained from quarries not far from Memphis, on the opposite bank of the Nile: the hard Ethiopic stone was procured at a much greater distance, higher up the river, in the vicinity of Elephantine: the latter quarries are those alluded to in the text.

[13] *In this place* (where the quarries are) *the mountain range ceasing* (that is to say, no longer stretching from the north to the south), *bends to the above-mentioned quarter* (that is to say, the Erythræan sea); *and gradually rises* (along that sea, towards the summer east, and continues its progress to the incense-bearing countries).

[14] The Historian is at variance with himself: he now puts 6120 stades for the distance from the sea-side to Thebes; while he has before stated the distance from the sea to Heliopolis at 1500 stades, and that from Heliopolis to Thebes at 4860.

112   EUTERPE. II. 11, 12.

Mæander; to compare little things with great[15]: for not one of the rivers, whose deposits have formed those countries, can be put into comparison, as to size, with even one mouth of the Nile, divided into five as the stream of that river is. But there are other rivers, not equal in size to the Nile, which have wrought great works: I might mention their names; and among others, not the least, those of the Achelous, which, flowing through Acarnania, falls into the sea, and has already converted one half of the Echinades islands
11 into continent. There belongs also to the territory of Arabia, not far from Egypt, a gulf of the sea that stretches inland from the Erythræan sea, the length and breadth of which I will here describe: the length of the voyage, beginning[16] from the innermost recess, and proceeding to the open sea, takes up forty days with oars; and in the broadest part of this gulf presents a passage of half a day. In this arm of the sea, an ebb and flow of the waters takes place daily. Now, in my mind, Egypt was, at one time, another similar bosom of the sea; this latter penetrating from the northern[17] sea, towards Ethiopia; and the former flowing from the southern ocean, towards Syria; working, by their respective bays, almost into one another, and leaving but very little land between them. Now, then, were the Nile to turn his stream into the aforesaid Arabian gulf, and continue such deposits, what could hinder him from filling it up, within, say even twenty thousand years? I am myself certain that it would take less than ten thousand. How, then, I ask, in the time that elapsed before I came into the world, might not a gulf, at all events much larger than this of Egypt, have been absorbed by the deposits of so great a river, and one so capable of working changes?
12 Therefore, I do not discredit what the priests relate concerning Egypt; but am completely of their way of thinking, when I see Egypt project beyond the neighbouring coasts into the sea, shells appearing on the mountains, and a salt efflorescence, that even eats into the pyramids; and that mountain also above Memphis, the only one that is covered with sand in Egypt[18]: add to which, that Egypt, in its soil, resem-

[15] Matt. 543.
[16] Matt. 390, b.
[17] That is to say, the Mediterranean sea: the southern sea is the Erythræan.
[18] It is very certain, that shells are found upon the mountains of Egypt; but this by no means proves the existence of the Egyptian gulf. Shells also are found upon mountains much higher than those of Egypt, in Europe, Asia, and America. This only proves, that all those regions have in part been covered by the waters of the sea, some at one time and some at another. I say, in part; because it is certain, from the observation of the most skilful naturalists, that the

bles neither Arabia on its frontier, nor Libya, nor Syria (for there are Syrians that occupy the sea-shores of Arabia): the Egyptian earth is black, chapped, and clammy, being swept from Ethiopia by the river, and deposited here; but the ground in Libya is, we know, of a reddish colour and sandy nature; while that of Arabia and Syria is more clayey and flinty.

The following fact affords a great proof of the origin of this country: this was communicated to me also by the priests: they asserted, that, under king Mœris, whenever the river rose at least eight cubits, its waters irrigated Egypt below Memphis; and at the time I received this information from the priests, nine hundred years had not passed from the time of the death of Mœris. But in the present day, unless the waters of the river rise at least sixteen or fifteen cubits[19], they do not overflow the land. It appears therefore to me, that if this soil continues to grow according to the same proportion in height, and the river to furnish the same deposits for the increase[20], the Egyptians dwelling in what is called the Delta, and in the rest of the countries below Lake Mœris, in consequence of the land not being flooded by the Nile, must for ever after suffer the very same calamity which they boded once to the Hellenes: informed that all the soil of the Hellenes is refreshed by rain, and not, as theirs, by the river floods, they observed: " Some day, the " Hellenes, deceived in their hopes, will be miserably afflicted " with the horrors of famine." The purport of this observation was, " that if God did not vouchsafe [21] rain to them, but " sent a drought, the Hellenes would be taken off by famine; " as it seemed they had no resource for water, excepting " Jove only." And in so saying to the Hellenes, the Egyptians are perfectly right: but let us, on the other hand, remember what would happen to the Egyptians themselves: if, as I said before, the lands below Memphis, which are those that increase, should in time to come grow in height

---

highest mountains have not been covered with water. These, in the times of such general inundations, appeared like so many islands.

In every part of Egypt, on digging, a brackish water is found, containing natrum, marine salt, and a little nitre. Even when the gardens are overflowed for the sake of watering them, the surface of the ground, after the evaporation and absorption of the water, appears glazed over with salt.—*Volney.*

[19] Pococke's suggestion is, that both statements of the necessary rise of the waters of the Nile are the same; the first being taken from the usual surface of the stream, the second from the bottom. The fact is, matters stand now pretty nearly the same as they did in the time of the Historian.

[20] It is difficult to make sense of this passage, if ἡ χώρη αὕτη be regarded as the nominative of both verbs, ἐπιδιδοῖ, ἀέξηλαι.

[21] Matt. 525, 7, b.

in the same proportion, what could save the Egyptians of those parts from the same calamity of famine? when their soil will not be refreshed, at all events, by rain, and the river will no longer be able to overflow their fields. Now, indeed, these people certainly procure the fruits of the earth with less labour than any other in the world, and even than the rest of the Egyptians: they have not the toil of breaking open the furrows with the plough, nor of hoeing, nor of any other work which the rest of men must perform in cultivating a crop. On the contrary, when the river, of its own accord, has flowed over and watered the fields, and then, returning, forsaken them, each sows his own field, and drives into it the swine: after the seed has been trodden in by these animals, the crop remains the season through untouched: at last, the husbandman threshes the corn by means of the swine, and carries it to his garner[22].

15 If, therefore, we choose to adopt the opinion of the Ionians concerning Egypt, who declare that the Delta alone constitutes Egypt, and say that its shore stretches from the watchtower of Perseus to the Pelusiac Tarichæa, a space that is equal to forty schœni; that from the sea, inland, it stretches up to the city of Cercasorus, where the Nile divides, flowing in two streams, one to Pelusium and the other to Canobus; and add, that the other parts of Egypt belong to Libya and to Arabia;—if, I say, we adopt the Ionian system, we may prove that the Egyptians had originally no territory of their own, and this by the following reasoning;—their Delta, as the Egyptians themselves say, and I share in their opinion, has flowed together, and come to light in late times, to use such an expression: if therefore they had no territory at all, what an idle thing it was to fancy that they were the oldest race in the world! surely they had no need of recurring to the experiment of the children, to determine what language they would speak[23]! But I do not believe the Egyptians to be co-original with the Delta, as it is called by the Ionians, but that they have existed from the time that mankind has been: that, as the soil increased, many of them were left behind, while others proceeded lower down; and therefore Thebes was, of old, called Egypt[24], being in circumference 16 six thousand one hundred and twenty stades. If, then, my

---

[22] Almost every commentator affirms, that so gluttonous an animal can never have been used for the purpose here alluded to: hence different readings have been proposed and adopted, at the whim of editors. It may be asked of these sage inquirers, whether the swine might not have been muzzled.

[23] See c. 2. of this Book.

[24] Matt. 304.

opinion about these matters is correct, the Ionians have very erroneous conceptions about Egypt: if, on the contrary, the opinion of the Ionians is correct, I will prove that neither the Hellenes nor the Ionians themselves know how to reckon, when they say the whole earth consists of three parts, Europe, Asia, and Libya: for they ought undoubtedly to add a fourth part, the Delta of Egypt; since, at all events, it belongs neither to Asia nor to Libya. For it is clear, that, according to this account, the Nile is not the boundary[25] between Asia and Libya; as that river divides at the vertex of this Delta, so as[26] to place it between Asia and Libya. But let me dismiss the opinion of the Ionians, and say what I have to say about these things[27]; which is this:—The whole of the country inhabited by Egyptians should be Egypt; like that of the Cilicians, which is Cilicia; and that of the Assyrians, which is Assyria. I know of no boundary, correctly speaking, to Asia and Libya, unless it be the frontier of the Egyptians: but if we follow the custom of the Hellenes, we shall consider all Egypt, commencing from the cataracts[28] and Elephantine, as divided into two parts, and participating in the names of both; one part belonging to Libya, and the other to Asia: for the Nile, reckoning from the cataracts, flows on to the sea, dividing Egypt in the middle. As far, then, as the town of Cercasorus, the Nile has but one stream: from that city, however, it breaks into three directions[29]: one of these turns eastward; it is called the Pelusiac mouth: another proceeds westward, and is called the Canobic mouth: lastly, the direct path of the Nile is this[30]; rolling down from the upper countries, it comes to the vertex of the Delta; from thence it continues its course, dividing the Delta down the middle; and discharges into the sea, not by any means the most insignificant or least-renowned portion of its waters; this mouth is called the Sebennytic. Two more mouths diverge from the Sebennytic, and go down to the sea: their names are, one the Saïtic[31], the other the Mendesian. The Bolbitine and Bucolic mouths are excavations, not the work of nature.—An oracle, pronounced at Ammon, serves likewise to corroborate all that I have here demonstrated on the subject of Egypt: this argument was communicated to me after I had formed my own opinion of the nature of this country[32]. The inhabitants of Marea and Apis,

[25] Matt. 331, c. obs.
[26] Matt. 485.
[27] ἡμεῖς δέ κ. τ. λ.; lit. "but we say thus of them."
[28] i. e. at the second cataract: the large one is in Ethiopia.
[29] σχίζεται τριφασίας ὁδοὺς, for εἰς τριφασίας ὁδοὺς. Schweig. Lex. Herod.
[30] Matt. 392, g, 1.
[31] Matt. 306.
[32] Matt. 451.

who are situated on the confines of Libya, fancied they were Libyans, not Egyptians; and being discontented with the rites that concern victims, would fain be no longer restricted from the use of cow's flesh: they sent accordingly to Ammon, and represented, that " there was nothing com-" mon between them and the Egyptians; as they dwelt " without the Delta, and used not the same language[23]; and " wished to be allowed to eat of all things." But the god denied the request, saying, that " all the country which the " Nile reached, and overflowed, was Egypt; and that all who " dwelt below Elephantine, and drank of the waters of the " river, were Egyptians." Such was the answer returned.—

19 The Nile, when full, overflows, not only the Delta, but also other parts of the country, said to belong to Libya and Arabia; in some instances, for two days' journey on either side, more or less.

Concerning the nature of the river, I was unable to obtain any information, whether from the priests or from others: I was very desirous, nevertheless, of ascertaining, through them, the following particulars;—why the Nile fills and overflows, during one hundred days, beginning from the summer solstice; and why, as it approaches to that number of days, it forsakes the fields, and retires to its bed[24]; so that the stream remains, throughout winter, shallow, until the return of the summer solstice. These were, accordingly, things concerning which I could not get any information whatever from the Egyptians, when I inquired of them what was the reason that the Nile differed so widely in its nature from all other streams. Not only was I anxious to know something about the above particularities, but I also made inquiry wherefore this is the only river in the world that 20 sends forth no fresh gales blowing from its surface. Some of the Hellenes, however, desirous of making a display of their wisdom, have proposed three different ways of explaining the phænomena of this river: two of these systems are undeserving of mention, except for the purpose of shewing that such ever existed. One of these asserts, that the etesian

---

[23] καὶ οὐκ ὁμολογέειν αὐτοῖσι. Wesseling, and, after him, Larcher, understand ὁμολογέειν of the 'language,' as in i. 142. Schweighæuser translates " nec sibi cum illis convenire."

[24] Larcher understands πιλέσας of the increase of the river; " having risen during that number of days." Schweighæuser disapproves this translation, and renders " expleto fere hoc numero dierum." I think Larcher's version is more agreeable to good sense; since Herodotus has just observed, that κατέρχεται ὁ Νεῖλος πληθύων ..... ἐπὶ ἑκατὸν ἡμέρας, and would now contradict himself in some manner, by saying that its increase does not continue " quite one hundred days." But consult Schweig. Not.

gales are the cause of the rise[25] in the river, by impeding the discharge of the Nile into the sea. But, frequently, the etesian winds have not blown, and nevertheless the Nile still presented the same effects: moreover, if the etesian winds were the cause, that cause would act also on the other rivers that flow in a direction opposite to the said winds, and consequently they would undergo the same changes as the Nile itself; indeed, so much the more still, as they are smaller, and their currents not so strong. Now, there are many rivers, both in Syria and Libya, which are not subject to such alterations as the Nile. The next system is indeed less 21 entitled to credit than the above; but more marvellous, to use that expression. It asserts, that the Nile, flowing out of the ocean, is the cause, and that the ocean flows all round the earth[26]. The third explanation is by far the most plausible, 22 but also the most deceptious. This system destroys itself[27], by affirming that the Nile proceeds from melted snow; for that river flows out of Libya, through Ethiopia, and thence passes into Egypt. How, then, can it come about, that it should flow from snow; coming, as it does, from the hottest quarters into cooler? Many things occur, to a man capable of reasoning on such a subject, to shew why it is not probable this river can come from snow[28]. The first and grand proof is afforded by the winds that blow hot from those regions: the second is, that the soil is never wetted by rain, nor is ice known there: if, however, snow were to fall, rain must necessarily succeed within five days: so that if it snowed, it would likewise rain in these countries[29]. The third proof is, that the men in that country become black, from the burning heat: kites and swallows abide there throughout the year; cranes, flying from the rude climate of the Scythian tract, seek their winter-quarters in this country: if, therefore, ever so little snow were known to fall in these regions, through which the Nile flows, and from which

[25] πλυθύων, without the genitive article τοῦ. See Matt. Gr. Gram. 819; or sect. 541, note.

[26] This explanation seems to be as follows: the ocean, which the ancients regarded as composed of fresh water, encompasses the earth: when the periodical N.E. or etesian gales blow, a great body of water is driven down towards the S.W. quarter of the ocean, where it opens into the Nile; the consequence is, that the superabundant waters rush into the channel of the river, and cause it to overflow the neighbouring country;—a theory, in truth, savouring highly of the absurd and marvellous.

[27] Lit. " says nothing."

[28] τῶν τὰ πολλά. Wesseling supplies τεκμήρια, or μαρτύρια: " quorum, paullo ante scriptorum, indicia multa adsunt viro," &c. Schweighæuser, with that ingenuousness which distinguishes him and Heyne, observes that Wesseling's explanation would do very well if the reading was τῶν πολλά ἐστι, " sed turbat adjectus τὰ articulus, qui quid huc faciat non video."

[29] Which is not the case: see iii. 10, in fin.

it springs, none of the above things could take place, as ne-
23 cessity demonstrates. As for the person who talks about the
ocean, he does not think about proving, but refers his decision to some fable enveloped in the dark: for I never knew
of any river, at all events, called the Ocean; but suppose
that Homer, or some of the earlier Poets, found the name,
and so introduced it into poetry.

24 But if, after criticising the above opinions, it becomes me to
explain my own opinion on these obscure subjects, I will describe what I conceive to be the cause of the Nile's swelling
in summer. The sun, driven from his former path by the
storms at the winter season, proceeds to the upper parts of
Libya. Thus, therefore, to explain as briefly as possible, all
is said; for the nearer this god is to any tract of land, there
the lack of water will, according to reason, be the greatest,
25 and the native river-streams will be dried up. But, to develope things more in detail[40], the case is this: the sun, passing through the upper part of Libya, produces the following
effect: the atmosphere being at all times clear in those
countries, and the ground heated through, in consequence of
the absence of cold winds, the sun, in passing over, does just
the same as he does to other countries in summer-time, when
his path is along the middle of the firmament; that is to say,
he draws to himself the water, and scatters it in the higher
regions of the air, where the winds take it up, diffuse and
dissolve it: so that, as one might reasonably expect, the
south and south-west winds, blowing from these quarters,
are by far the most rainy of all. It is not, however, my belief that the sun throws away all the annual supply of water
from the Nile, but some of it abides round him[41]. The winter
becoming milder, the sun comes back into the middle of the
heavens; and from that situation and time, he attracts water
equally from all the rivers in the world: until then, those
rivers have abundant streams from the admixture of rain-
water, the soil being rained upon and torn by torrents; but
in summer, the rains no longer pouring down, these rivers
become weak, from that cause, as well as from the attraction
on the part of the sun: the Nile, however, which receives no
rain, and yet is attracted by the sun, is the only river that at
these times is shallower than in summer[42]; for in summer it
is attracted in the same proportion as all the rest of rivers,
whereas in winter it is the only one that is made to contribute. Thus I conclude that the sun is the cause of these

---

[40] Matt. 543, first parag.
[41] It was a general opinion, that the sun's food was water.
[42] Matt. 452, first parag.

things. The same cause, in my opinion, produces the dry air 26
in this country, the sun burning all on its passage⁴³: summer,
in consequence, ever reigns over the upper parts of Libya.
But if the stations of the seasons were to be interchanged,
and the quarter of the heavens, where the north and winter
now reside, were to be occupied by the south-west and south,
and the north took the position of the south⁴⁴; if, I say, such
a change were made, the sun, driven away from the middle
of the firmament, would pass over to the upper parts of Europe, as it now does to those of Libya. Passing, then, through
all Europe, he would, I conceive, produce on the Ister just
the same effect as he does now on the Nile. The absence of 27
all breezes from the Nile is accounted for, in my mind, by
this reason; that from exceedingly hot countries it is not at
all likely any should blow; for such a breeze is wont to proceed from some cool region.

Let these matters, therefore, remain as they were at the 28
beginning. Of all Egyptians, Libyans, and Hellenes, that I
ever conversed with, not one professed to know any thing
about the sources of the Nile, except the steward of the sacred things in Minerva's temple at Saïs in Egypt; and he,
to all appearance, was, at best, only joking me, when he said
that he knew perfectly well. His statement was as follows:
" Two mountains, rising each to a peak, are situate between
" the city of Syene in Thebaïs, and Elephantine; the name
" of these mountains are, one Crophi, the other Mophi.
" Between these rise the sources of the Nile, which are bot-
" tomless: one-half of the water runs north to Egypt, the
" other half south to Ethiopia. Psammitichus, king of Egypt,
" he said, proved, by actual experiment, that the springs are
" bottomless: he caused a rope, many thousand fathoms
" long, to be twisted and let down, and it never came to the
" bottom." Thus, therefore, this steward, if indeed he spoke
at all to the fact, induced me, by his description, to infer
there were at that place strong eddies and a whirlpool; so
that the water buffeting against the rocks, the sounding-line
could not find its way to the bottom. Nothing more was I 29
able to get from any person: but with respect to my further
research in the most distant part of this river, I went up myself to the city of Elephantine: so far I speak as an eyewitness; beyond that, my account proceeds from what information I collected by hearsay. As you ascend from Elephantine, the country is very rugged: here your boat must
be fastened with a rope on both sides, as you would harness

---

⁴³ αὐτοῦ for λαυροῦ. ⁴⁴ Matt. 606, 3.

an ox⁴⁵; and thus you proceed: but if the cords snap, the boat is carried off by the force of the current: this sort of country lasts during four days' navigation; in which the Nile winds as much as the Mæander. After this, you will come out into a smooth plain, where the Nile rolls around an island, the name of which is Tachompso: immediately above Elephantine you begin already to meet with resident Ethiopians, and they occupy one-half of the island; the other half is inhabited by Egyptians: close to the island is an extensive lake, round which some Ethiopian nomades rove: after you have crossed this lake, you enter again into the bed of the Nile, which discharges itself therein: you are then to land, and perform a forty days' journey along the river side; as sharp rocks there rise in the Nile, and many shoals occur, which make it impossible to navigate: after you have completed your forty days' land-journey, you embark again in a different boat, and continue your navigation for twelve days, which brings you to a great city, called Meroë. This city, it is said, is the metropolis of the rest of the Ethiopians: its inhabitants worship only Jove and Bacchus among the gods, and these they honour magnificently. They possess an oracle of Jove; and wage war when and where the god appoints, through his warnings. Ascending the river above this city, you will reach the Emigrants (Automoli), in another space of time equal to what you come in from Elephantine to the Ethiopian metropolis. These emigrants are denominated the Asmach; a word that signifies, when translated, the men that stand on the king's left hand. These two hundred and forty thousand Egyptians, of the war-caste, came over to the Ethiopians from the following motives: under king Psammitichus they were placed in the city of Elephantine, as a defence and guard against the Ethiopians; another party was placed at Daphnæ Pelusiacæ, against the Arabians and Syrians; a third was stationed at Marea, to face Libya; and still, in my day, the garrisons of the Persians were distributed in the same order as they were under Psammitichus; for Persians are garrisoned now at Elephantine and Daphnæ. These Egyptians, therefore, who had been three years on duty, were not relieved by any new garrison: they, in consequence, held council, and unanimously came to a resolution, to secede all from Psammitichus, and go over to Ethiopia. The king, aware of this, pursued the deserters:

---

⁴⁵ I conceive the meaning to be, that a rope is fastened on both sides of the boat, as you would harness an ox to the plough; by means of which, she is towed up from both banks.

when he came up with them, he implored them, saying a great deal, and begged them not to forsake their paternal gods, their children, and their wives. One of the deserters is represented to have then displayed his secret parts, and said: "Where that is, we shall find plenty of women and children." When these Egyptians arrived in Ethiopia, they gave themselves up to the king of the Ethiopians: he made this return to them. Certain Ethiopians were opposed to the king: he ordered the Egyptians to drive out these, and take possession of their land. In consequence of their settling among the Ethiopians, that nation became more civilized, learning the Egyptian manners.

For the space of a navigation and journey of four months, 31 the Nile is therefore known, besides that portion of its course that comprises Egypt: such is the number of months that is found in adding up the days spent in going from Elephantine to the country of these emigrants. There the Nile flows from the west and setting sun. Concerning the still higher parts, no one can give any correct account; that country being desert, by reason of the broiling heat. I have 32 heard, however, the following statement from some natives of Cyrene; who relate, that they went upon a time to the oracle of Ammon, and there had an interview with Etearchus, the king of the Ammonians: and how, after other subjects of conversation, they fell upon a discourse about the Nile—that nobody knew its sources. And that Etearchus said, some Nasamonians came once to visit him:—this nation is Libyan: they occupy the Syrtis, to the east of which they extend for a small distance:—that at the arrival of these visitors, they were asked if they had any fresh information to communicate respecting the deserts of Libya; and they replied, that some daring youths, the sons of powerful men, had grown up among them: these young men, having reached men's estate, devised various extraordinary feats; and among others, was, to choose, by lot, five out of their number, who should go and reconnoitre the deserts of Libya, and try whether they could make any further discoveries than those who had visited the most distant parts.— It must be observed, that in the portion of Libya which stretches along the Mediterranean sea, beginning from Egypt, and reaching to Cape Soloïs, which is the extremity of Libya, the whole country is occupied by Libyans, divided into various nations; excepting, however, the territories occupied by the Hellenes and Phœnicians. In the parts above the sea-shore, and higher up than the inhabitants of the coast, Libya is infested with wild beasts: above the wild-

beast tract, all is sand, dreadfully scant of water, and wholly uninhabited.—" Accordingly, the young men deputed by " their companions, well provided with water and provisions, " had passed first through the inhabited country; then came " to the tract infested with wild beasts; and, crossing over to " the desert, commenced their journey towards the west. " After going over much sandy ground, in a march of " many days, they at last saw some trees, growing in a " plain. They went up to them, and plucked the fruit that " hung from the branches: but, while they were thus occu- " pied in gathering the fruit, some diminutive men, less than " the common standard, laid hold of them, and carried " them off. The Nasamonians did not understand the lan- " guage of these people, nor did the conductors understand " that of the Nasamonians. They were accordingly taken " through some vast morasses; after which, they came to a " town where all the inhabitants were of the same size as their " conductors, and black in colour. A great river flowed by the
33 " town, in which crocodiles were seen."—So far, then, I have reported the discourse of Etearchus the Ammonian prince; except that, according to the Cyrenæans, " he said, the Nasa- " monians returned; and that the people they thus came to, " were all necromancers." With respect to this river flowing by the town, Etearchus conjectured it to be the Nile; indeed, reason shews that it is so: for the Nile flows out of Libya, and divides that country; and (as I assume, inferring the unknown by the known) proceeds parallel to the Ister[46]. The Ister is a river that, rising in the country of the Celts, and at the town of Pyrene, flows, dividing the whole of Europe. The Celts are outside the pillars of Hercules; they confine on the Cynesians, who inhabit the most western parts of all the Europeans. The Ister ends by flowing through Europe into the Euxine sea, at the spot where stands the Milesian
34 settlement of Istria. The Ister therefore runs through in- habited lands, and is known to many; while no one can say any thing about the sources of the Nile; because Libya, through which it flows, is both uninhabited and desert: as far as it was possible to carry inquiry, it has been described. Near its end, it enters Egypt: that country lies almost

[46] τῷ Ἴστρῳ ἐκ τῶν ἴσων μέτρων ὁρμᾶται I have followed Schweighæuser's Latin version: the learned scholar observes, however, that, after reconsidering the passage, he inclines to the opinion of Valckenaer; namely, " that Herodo- tus conjectured that the course of the Nile, from its head to the place where it discharges its waters in Egypt, was equal in length to that of the Ister, from its source to its mouth in the Euxine sea." See Schweig. Lex. Herod. voc. μέτρον.—Larcher's translation is, " Je pense qu'il part des mêmes points que l'Ister."

opposite Cilicia Montana: from this latter to Sinope, on the Euxine sea, is a straight road, five days' journey for a speed-courier on foot. Now Sinope lies exactly opposite to the place where the Ister falls into the sea: so that I consider that the Nile, crossing the whole of Libya, extends to the same length as the Ister.—So much then for the Nile.

I am now going to extend my account of Egypt; because it possesses more wonders, and exhibits more curiosities, beyond the powers of description [47], than any other country in the world; and for that reason, more must be said about it. The Egyptians not only have a climate peculiar to themselves, and a river differing in its nature from all other rivers: they have also many customs and usages wholly opposite to those of other men. Among them, the women go to market, and deal; but the men stay at home, and weave: in weaving, other nations throw the woof up the warf, but the Egyptians throw it down: the men carry burthens on their heads, the women on their shoulders [48]: the women stand erect when they discharge their urine, the men crouch down: they eat out of doors; but satisfy the other wants of nature within their houses, alleging, that what is unseemly, but necessary, should be done in secret; but what is not unseemly, in open view: no woman can serve the holy office, either for god or goddess; but men can for both: no necessity compels sons to support their parents, unless they choose: the daughters are compelled to do so, even against their will. The priests of the gods elsewhere wear long hair; but in Egypt they have it shorn: in other nations, it is customary, in mourning, for the nearest connexions to shave their heads; the Egyptians, in case of death, suffer their hair to grow [49]: with other nations, also, it is the practice to live separate from their cattle; with the Egyptians, it is the contrary; they live together with their domestic animals [50]. The food of most others consists of wheat and barley: among the Egyptians, every one is held very infamous that does so; and all make their bread of spelt [51]. They knead the dough with their feet, but pick up dung and filth with their hands. All

35

36

---

[47] Matt. 451; and 455. obs. 1, a: 591, γ.

[48] Matt. 504, 2, a.

[49] Construction: τίμας [ἰστί] ἅμα αὐτοῖ πακάρθαι τὰς κεφαλὰς τοῖς μάλιστα ἰωίστως [τὸ πᾶθος] Schweig. Lex. Herodot. That is to say, the nearest relatives.

[50] Larcher gives to δίαιτα the signification of repast, meal: Schweighæuser denies that the word is ever taken by Herodotus in that confined sense.

[51] The *triticum spelta* of Linnæus.—Martyn, in his note upon Georg. i. 73, is of opinion that " the ζιὰ or ζιὰ of the Greeks is what we call *spelt*, a sort of corn very like wheat; but its chaff adheres so strongly to the grain, that it requires a mill to separate them, like barley."

nations leave their private parts as they are; except such as have learnt otherwise from the Egyptians, who are circumcised. Every man wears two garments; every woman one. Other people fasten outside the rings and sheets of sails; the Egyptians fasten them inside: they write letters, and sum numbers with pebbles, from right to left; and, in so doing, say they go right-ways, and the Hellenes left-ways[52]. They have two sorts of letters; one sort called the sacred, the other demotic.

37 They are the most exceedingly devout of all men, and follow the practices here stated. They drink from brass mugs, which they scour out every day without exception; and wear cotton garments, constantly fresh-washed, attending to this most carefully. They circumcise themselves from motives of cleanliness, deeming it better to be clean than handsome[53]. The priests shave their whole bodies every third day[54], in order that no louse or any other vermin may be found upon them when attending upon the gods: the priests also wear nothing but cotton, and shoes of byblus[55]: no other garments or shoes are they allowed to wear. They wash themselves twice every day in cold water, and twice every night; and observe ten thousand other ceremonies, to use the expression. But, on the other hand, they enjoy no slight advantages; they consume none of their private property; are exposed to no expense; sacred bread is baked for them; a good supply of beef and geese is furnished to each every day; and wine from the grape[56] is allowed them: fish they must not touch. As for beans, the Egyptians not only refrain from sowing them on their land, and also from eating raw those that come up spontaneously[57], but will not taste them, even when boiled: the priests, especially, abhor the sight of that vegetable, regarding it as an impure husk. Every one of the gods is attended, not by one, but by several priests, over whom is a

38 rector; and whenever a priest dies, his son succeeds. The pure male kine[58] are held sacred to Epaphus; and, on that

---

[52] The fact is, it seems, the Egyptians spoke of the right side of the paper, and not the right side of the writer, as the Hellenes. I have heard the same remark made by Turks, and other Levantines, with regard to the European mode of writing.

[53] Matt. 456, first parag.

[54] Matt. 580, d.

[55] The bass or interior bark of the papyrus.

[56] In contradistinction of barley-wine or beer. See chap. 77.

[57] ἐρώγων, anciently used solely of things eaten raw or uncooked.

[58] Wesseling is of opinion, that the word καθαροὺς has been omitted, by negligence. One of these is the Apis of the Egyptians, chap. 133. Understand δοκιμάζων, to govern βοῦνας.

account, they ascertain which are so, in the following manner: if the examiner descry even one black hair, the animal is deemed impure. One of the priests appointed to the office examines the steer, both when standing, and when lying on the back: he pulls out his tongue, and sees whether it is pure of the prescribed marks, which I shall mention elsewhere[59]: he looks at the hairs of the tail, whether they grow naturally. If the steer is pure in all these respects, he puts a mark on him, by twisting a piece of byblus round the horns, and spreading some sealing-earth, which he stamps with his signet, and then drives him away. He who sacrifices an unmarked victim is punished with death. Such is the mode of ascertaining the purity of the victim. Their manner of sacrificing is this: they lead the animal, properly marked, to the altar, where they are going to sacrifice, and kindle fire: this being done, they pour wine on the altar[60], and invoke the god; then slaughter the steer, and cut off the head. They next flay the animal's body; and having pronounced many imprecations on the head, those who have a market-square, and among whom many Hellenic merchants reside, carry it to that market, and accordingly dispose of it: those that have no Hellenes resident among them cast the head into the river. The imprecations they pronounce on the heads are in these words:—" Whatever evil is about to " fall on the sacrificer himself, or on the whole of Egypt, " may it be diverted upon this head." In respect to the heads of the slaughtered animals, and the libations of wine, the Egyptians universally practise the same ceremonies alike in all sacrifices: and in consequence of this custom, no Egyptian will ever taste of the head of any animal. The disembowelling and burning are variously performed, in various sacrifices. I will describe, therefore, the practice for the deity whom they consider the greatest, and in whose honour they celebrate the most magnificent festival. After they have stript off the skin of the steer, with prayer, they take out all the intestines of the belly[61], leaving in the body the heart, liver and lights, together with the fat: they then cut off the legs and the extremity of the hind-quarter, with that of the fore-quarter and neck. After they have done this, they fill the body of the steer with white bread, honey, raisins, figs, incense and myrrh, together with other per-

---

[59] That is to say: B. iii. 28.
[60] ἐπ' αὐτοῦ, that is βωμοῦ.
[61] Ἐξελὼν πᾶσαν κοιλίην κοιλίης: the particle ἐν is pleonastically inserted between the preposition and the verb, as is frequent in Herodotus. Schweighæuser regards κατὰ κοιλίαν as equivalent to κοιλίαν, the belly, that part of the inside between the ribs and the haunch.

fumes: having thus stuffed the belly, they burn it, pouring out abundance of oil. This sacrifice they perform fasting; and while the holy things are being consumed, they all beat their breasts: when they have ceased this, they spread, as food, what remains of the victims.

41 All Egyptians, therefore, sacrifice pure male kine and calves: they are not allowed, however, to sacrifice cows, which are sacred to Isis: for the image of Isis is a woman's figure with cows' horns, the same as the Hellenes depict Io. All Egyptians alike have even a much greater veneration for cows than for any other cattle; that is the reason that no Egyptian man or woman will hardly kiss an Hellenic man on the lips[62], or make use of an Hellene's knife, or spit, or saucepan; nor will they taste of the flesh of a pure ox which has been carved by an Hellenic knife. The kine that die are buried in the following manner: the females are thrown into the river: the males are put underground, by each proprietor, in the suburbs: leaving above the surface one or both horns, as a mark[63]. After the body has rotted away, and when a certain time has elapsed, a barge, from the island of Prosopitis, comes to each city:—this island is situated in the Delta; it is nine schœni in circumference, within which are several cities, but especially one from which a great number of the barges come that collect the skeletons of the oxen: the name of this town is Atarbechis, where a temple to Venus has been erected:—from this town, accordingly, many persons go to different places, dig up the bones, convey them away, and bury them all in one place. In the same manner as the oxen, they bury all other cattle that die: such is their custom; for the Egyptians kill none of

42 these[64]. Those who belong to the temple built to Theban Jove[65], or are of the Theban nome, refrain all from sheep, and sacrifice goats; for all Egyptians do not worship the same gods alike, excepting Isis and Osiris, whom they accordingly call Bacchus: these they all worship alike. But those who belong to the temple of Mendes, or the Mendesian nome, refrain from goats, and sacrifice sheep. The Thebans therefore, and such as refrain from sheep after their example[66], account for that usage in the following manner: "that Hercules was exceedingly desirous of seeing "Jupiter, and Jupiter did not wish to be seen by him: as "Hercules persisted, Jupiter devised this: he skinned a ram;

---

[62] Matt. 514: and 516, obs.
[63] Matt. 427. b.
[64] ἀντίκουσι γὰρ δὴ οὐδὲ ταῦτα.—Lit. for neither do they slaughter even these, i. e. the other kinds of animals.
[65] Θρωνται is equivalent to θρήσκων ἴχουσι, or θρήσκοις ἱεροῖς.—Schweig.
[66] Matt. 580, 2.

"cut off the head, which he held before him; then wrapped "himself in the fleece; and so exhibited himself to Her- "cules." In consequence of this, the Egyptians make the image of Jupiter in the shape of a ram-face: and from the Egyptians the same practice has been taken by the Ammonians, who are descendants from the Egyptians, and speak a language between that of both those nations: in my opinion, the Ammonians took also their name from this circumstance, as the Egyptian word for Jupiter is Amoun. The Thebans do not, for this reason, sacrifice rams, but hold them sacred; except on one day only in the year, the festival of Jupiter, when they slaughter a ram, skin him, and wrap the fleece around the image of Jupiter; they then bring another image alongside of it, that of Hercules: having so done, the worshippers, assembled in the temple, beat their bosoms all in mourning for the ram[67], and afterwards bury him in a holy crypt[68].

By the account given me of this[69] Hercules, he is one of the twelve gods: concerning the other Hercules, known among the Hellenes, I was no where able to hear any thing about him in Egypt. And, indeed, I have many different proofs, to demonstrate that, at all events, the Egyptians did not adopt from the Hellenes the name of their Hercules, but rather that the Hellenes adopted it from the Egyptians; those Hellenes, I mean, who imposed the name on Amphitryon's son: for instance, this is one; that Amphitryon and Alcmene were of Egyptian origin; and because the Egyptians say that they are ignorant of the names of Neptune and the Dioscuri, and never admitted them among their other gods;—now it is certain, that if they had admitted the name of any deity from the Hellenes, they must, at all events, have thought of them the first, not the last[70]; for even in those days the Egyptians made some voyages, and there existed Hellenic sailors; and I myself have every reason to think[71] that the Egyptians would have been acquainted with the names of the above gods long before they heard of Hercules. But the Hercules of the Egyptians is one of their ancient gods; and, according to their statement, it was seven thousand years prior to Amasis's reign, when from the eight

43

---

[67] "With the middle verbs τύπτεσθαι, ἀλοιᾶσθαι, properly, 'to strike one's self, to bewail,' as in Latin *plangi*, the object of the grief is put in the accusative." Matt. 419, 5.

[68] θήκη signifies, in Herodotus, a repository or apartment, in which there is room for several sarcophagi.— Schweig.

[69] i. e. the Hercules to whom the Egyptians offer sacrifice.

[70] Matt. 463.

[71] ἡ ἐμὴ γνώμη αἱρέει is a stronger expression than ἔλπομαι; it signifies, an opinion founded upon proofs.— *Wesseling*.

gods came twelve gods, of whom they regard Hercules as
44 one. Anxious to get authentic information from whence I
could obtain it, I undertook a voyage to Tyre in Phœnicia,
where I had heard there was a temple of Hercules much venerated; and I saw that sacred edifice richly stored with
various and numerous offerings; and in the inside stood
two pillars, one of pure gold, the other of emerald stone[72],
which shone brilliantly at nights. I entered into conversation with the priests of the god, and inquired of them how
long it was since the temple was erected; and I found that
they also differed from the Hellenes, as the priests gave for
answer, that the temple of the god was built at the same time
Tyre itself was; and that from the building of Tyre it was
two thousand and three hundred years. I saw also another
temple, at Tyre, to Hercules, with the cognomen of Thasian[73]:
to Thasos therefore I proceeded, where I found a temple of
Hercules, built by the Phœnicians, who, navigating in search
of Europa, laid the foundation of Thasos; an event that
occurred five generations of men before the Hercules son of
Amphitryon was born in Hellas. The result, therefore, of
these researches makes it clear, beyond all doubt, that Hercules was an ancient god; and those Hellenes appear to me
to act the most properly, who have erected two sorts of
Heracleum[74]; one for the original Hercules, to whom they
offer sacrifice, as immortal, and under the name of Olympian Hercules; the other, for him to whom they give honours
45 as to the hero. But the Hellenes relate many other things
thoughtlessly: this, for instance, is a silly fable they tell of
Hercules; that, "on his arrival in Egypt, the inhabitants
" crowned him, and took him in procession[75] to be sacrificed
" to Jupiter; that for some time Hercules kept quiet; but
" when, at the altar, they began the sacrific solemnities, he
" exerted his strength, and slew them every one." Now, such
people as say this sort of things strike me to be totally unacquainted with the nature and the customs of the Egyptians;
for with that people it is not lawful to sacrifice even cattle,
excepting sheep, and such steers and calves as happen to be
pure: I must add geese also: how could they, then, sacrifice
human beings? Besides, Hercules was but one, and, as yet,
no more than a man: how could he, then, as they say, have
the power to slay many thousands? Be mercy shewn, at

---

[72] Supposed to have been green glass.
— λάμποντος τὰς νύκτας μεγάλως. To make
sense of the passage, μεγάλως must be
taken adverbially, as if for μεγάλως,
shining greatly at nights.— *Schweig.*

[73] Matt. 282. ὅπου superfluous.
[74] Tempho, or precincts to Hercules.
[75] Matt. 592, β.

the hands both of gods and heroes, to us, that say such things about them!

But, as to the reason why the above Egyptians do not sacrifice bucks or goats, the Mendesians think that Pan was one of the eight original gods: these eight gods, they say, existed prior to the twelve gods; and, accordingly, like the Hellenic painters and statuaries, they represent the images of Pan with a goat's face and buck's legs: they do not, however, fancy that Pan is such, but consider him similar to the other gods: for what purpose they represent him in this way it is not easy [76] for me to explain. But the Mendesians venerate all goats, and the males more than the females; and, with them, goat-herds are held in great honour; one especially, among the bucks; who, when he dies, is deeply mourned, according to custom, every where, by the Mendesian. The buck, likewise, is called Mendes in Egyptian; and so is Pan, the god. In my time, a prodigy occurred in this nome; a buck had connexion with a woman in open day, which came under the observation of all persons. The pig is considered, by Egyptians, as an unclean animal: in the first place, if any one passing by a pig should touch the beast with his garments, he forthwith goes down to the river and plunges in [77]: secondly, the swine-herds, although native Egyptians, are the only people of the country that never enter a temple; nor will any person give one of them his daughter in marriage; nor will he take a wife from among them: but the swine-herds take and give in marriage among themselves. The Egyptians, therefore, dare not offer swine to any other gods than Diana (the Moon) and Bacchus: to whom, at the same time, that is to say, at the same full moon, they sacrifice pigs, and afterwards eat of the flesh. Why they abhor pigs at every other festival, and sacrifice them at that one, is accounted for by Egyptians: although I am aware what the reason is, it is more becoming I should say nothing about it [78]. This sacrifice to the Moon is thus performed: after the sacrificer [79] has slaughtered the victim [80], he puts together the tip of the tail, the milt, and the caul; then covers them with all the fat found upon the belly of the animal: this is afterwards consumed by fire. The remainder of the flesh is eaten during the full moon in which the sacrifice is offered up: on no other day would it hardly be even tasted [81]. The poor

---

[76] Matt. 457, 3.
[77] Or, according to another punctuation, "plunges in with all his clothes on." Matt. 400, f.
[78] [λόγος] μωλ οὐκ εὐσχημονεστερος ἐστι λέγεσθαι, the comparative again being used instead of the positive. Matt. 457.
[79] Supply τὶς, or ὁ θύων, or ὁ ἱερεὺς, before ἐπεὰν.—Schweig.
[80] Matt. 294.
[81] Matt. 514.

people among them, from their want of means, make pigs of dough, which they bake and offer up as sacrifice. On the eve of the festival of Bacchus, every one slaughters before his door a young pig; and then returns the victim to the swine-herd who supplied it, that he may carry it away. The rest of the festival, with the exception of the pigs, is celebrated by the Egyptians, in almost all its details, after the same manner as by the Hellenes: in the place of phalli, is substituted an invention of their own; images about a cubit in height, moved by springs, which are paraded about the towns and villages by the women; the member scarcely any smaller than the whole body, nodding continually[63]: a piper heads the procession; and the women follow, singing the praises of Bacchus. A religious reason is assigned for the member being so disproportionate, and for its being the only part of the body that moves. I presume, therefore, that, even in those early times, Melampus the son of Amythaon, far from being ignorant of this mode of sacrifice, was perfectly acquainted with the usage[68]: for Melampus was the person who introduced among the Hellenes the name of Bacchus, his ceremonies, and the procession of the phallus. He did not, however, lay open the whole; but the sages that followed him have given more copious explanations. Melampus, therefore, was the institutor of the procession of the phallus to Bacchus; and from him the Hellenes learned to do as they now do. For my part, I am of opinion that Melampus, a wise man, endowed with the gift of prophecy, in consequence of information obtained from Egypt, introduced various things among the Hellenes, and more particularly, with some slight alterations, the worship of Bacchus; for I can by no means allow that the ceremonies performed in honour of Bacchus, both in Egypt and among the Hellenes, should so coincide by chance[64]; in which case they would be consonant to Hellenic customs, and not have been so lately introduced: neither can I admit that the Egyptians borrowed either this practice from the Hellenes, or any other usage. My opinion is, that Melampus obtained most of his information respecting Bacchus from Cadmus the Tyrian, and from his followers out of Phœnicia into the country now called Bœotia.

50 Nearly all the names of the gods came from Egypt to

---

[63] Coray is of Reiskius's opinion, that we should read νεύοντα, to agree with ἀγάλματα. If we read νεῦον, I think ἴχνετα must be understood.—Larcher.

[63] Matt. 324.

[64] Schweighæuser takes the verb συμπίπτειν in the sense of ' to happen or exist at one and the same time:' Gronovius, Wesseling, and Larcher, give it the signification of ' to agree or coincide *by chance*.'

Hellas: for I am convinced, by my own inquiries, that they must have proceeded from some people not of Hellenic race: accordingly, I think they came, for the most part, from Egypt. Indeed, with the exception of Neptune and the Dioscuri, as I before observed[65], and of Juno, Vesta, Themis, the Graces, and Nereïds, the names of all the other gods have for ever been in existence among the Egyptians: this I say from the authority of the Egyptians themselves. As to those names which they are not acquainted with, they were, I have no doubt, inventions of the Pelasgians[66]: Neptune, however, must be excepted; which god the Hellenes borrowed from the Libyans; for none but Libyans originally possessed the name of Neptune, a god whom they have always worshipped. The Egyptians have no ceremonies instituted in honour of heroes[67]. The above, therefore, and several other things 51 likewise, which I shall by and by explain, have been adopted[68] by the Hellenes from the Egyptians. As to the practice of representing the images of Mercury with the member erect, that was not learned from the Egyptians, but from the Pelasgians: the first of all the Hellenes that adopted this custom were the Athenians, whose example the rest followed; for the Pelasgians were neighbours of the Athenians, at that time already reckoned Hellenes: and from thence the Hellenes first took this practice. Whoever has been initiated in the mysteries of the Cabiri, which the people of Samothrace have adopted from the Pelasgians and now celebrate, will know what I mean; for these Pelasgians who had previously been the neighbours of the Athenians, dwelt, of old, in Samothrace; and from them the Samothracians adopted the mysteries. The Athenians were accordingly the first of the Hellenes that, borrowing the custom from the Pelasgians, made their images of Mercury with the member erect: for which the Pelasgians assigned a sacred reason, explained in the mysteries at Samothrace[69]. Originally, the Pelasgi 52

---

[65] See chap. 43.

[66] τῶν δὲ - - - ὄντα δέ. See, with regard to the repetition of the particle, Matr. 606, 3.

[67] I think this is the true sense of the words νομίζουσι δ᾽ ὦν Αἰγύπτιοι οὐδ᾽ ἥρωσι οὐδέν. The Latin translator has improperly rendered them, ' sed heroas Ægyptii nullo cultu prosequuntur.' This term appears to me consecrated: every one knows what the Greeks meant by the term τὰ νομιζόμενα, which is found every where.—Larcher.

[68] See B. iv. 27. παρὰ Σκυθίων νενομί-

κασιν.—νενομίκασι, before which must be understood μαθόντες, παραλαβόντες, or some other verb.

[69] Τὰ is for κατά. Herodotus more usually has the expression κατὰ σέ. Τὰ is Ionically for ἅ, and κατὰ for κατά. This may be explained also by the figure called enallage, in grammar: in that case, τὰ will relate to ἅπερά ἐστι, which was in the author's mind, and instead of which he has written ἱρὸν τινα λόγον. Larcher. τὰ ἐν ἐοῦσι ἐν Σαμ. must be regarded as equivalent to κατὰ τὰ or ὡς. Wess.

sacrificed all kinds of victims[90], and offered prayers to the gods (such was the information I obtained at Dodona); but attached no name, or cognomen, to any one of those gods; for as yet they had never heard of any. They called them *gods*[91] on this account, that they had arranged and distributed all things with such order. After a long time had intervened, they became acquainted with the names of all the gods imported from Egypt; except that of Bacchus, which they heard of at a later period. Soon after, they consulted the oracle at Dodona concerning the names:—that oracle is deemed the most ancient of all in Hellas, and was, at the time we are speaking of, the only one:—the Pelasgians, therefore, having consulted the Dodonæan oracle, " whether they were to adopt[92] the names coming from abroad;" the oracle gave the answer, " to adopt them." From that period, they made use of the names of the gods, in their devotions; a practice imitated some time later, from the Pelasgians, by the Hellenes. As to whence each of the gods sprung; whether they had all existed from eternity; what they were, as to form; such things were only known of yesterday, or the day before[93], to use a trivial expression: for I consider Homer and Hesiod older than myself by four hundred years, certainly not more: they were the poets that framed[94] the Hellenic theogony, gave distinctive names to the gods, distributed among them honours and professions, and pointed out their respective forms. The poets said to have flourished before the above two were, it is my belief, really posterior to them. My authority for the assertions in the first part of these statements is the Dodonæan priestesses: it is on my own authority I speak of Hesiod and Homer.

[90] Understand θύματα with ἱερὰ δὲ πάντα.

[91] Clement. Alexand. Θεὸς δὲ παρὰ τὴν θέσιν εἴρηται, καὶ τάξιν, καὶ τὴν διακόσμησιν: quoted by *Wesseling*. This alludes to the etymology of θεὸς, which is said to be derived from (θέω) τῶ, the original root of τίθημι.

[92] Matt. 525, 6, b.

[93] πρώην τε καὶ χθὲς, is a proverbial expression for *lately*.

[94] The signification of ποιεῖν, in this passage, is a subject of dispute: Wesseling, and after him Larcher, take it to mean, ' to describe in verse.' This interpretation is combatted by Wolfius; who denies that ποιεῖν, when taken in that sense, can be followed by a dative. Schweighæuser follows the opinion of Wesseling; it being absurd to suppose that Herodotus ever had an idea of attributing to Homer or Hesiod the vast fabric of Grecian superstition. I have used the English word ' framed,' because I think the meaning of Herodotus to be, that Homer and Hesiod collated in one body what was related in various writings, concerning the birth, shape, &c. of the gods, and their *mythi*: in the same manner we might say that Mahomet framed a new religion, although it is well known that the Koran is little more than patches of the works of the Jews, the Christians, and the Idolaters. See Schweig. quotation from Heine, in note to ii. 53.

Concerning the two oracles, that of the Hellenes, and the 54 other in Libya, the following account is given by the Egyptians. The priests of Thebæan Jupiter assert, "That two "consecrated women⁹⁵ were carried off by Phœnicians; that, "it was ascertained, one of them was sold, to be taken into "Libya⁹⁶; the other was disposed of to the Hellenes: that these "women were the original foundresses of the oracles, in the "said nations." I asked, how they could know so positively that this was the case: to which their reply was: "that dili- "gent search was made by them after those women; but they "were unable to find them; and were subsequently made "acquainted with what they had accordingly stated concern- "ing the two women." Such, therefore, was the account I 55 heard from the priests at Thebes: the following, however, is stated by the women that pronounce the oracles at Dodona. "Two black doves flew away from Thebes in Egypt: one "reached Libya; the other directed her flight to them. That "the dove perched in an oak-tree⁹⁷, and, with human voice, "proclaimed, it behoved an oracle of Jove should be there "established. They took this to be a divine token to them, "and did accordingly.—They add, that the other dove ar- "rived in Libya, and ordered the Libyans to found the "oracle of Ammon," which is also one of Jupiter's. The priestesses of Dodona said the same; both the eldest, named Promenia, and the juniors, called Timarete, and Nicandra: and all the Dodonæan people belonging to the holy precinct agreed with them. My opinion of these things is, that if it 56 was true that the Phœnicians did carry off the consecrated women, and that they were sold, one into Libya, and the other into Hellas, I presume that the latter was disposed of to some people of Thesprotia, now a part of Hellas, previously called Pelasgia; and that, reduced to slavery, she erected a temple to Jupiter under a green oak⁹⁸; as it was natural for a servant in the temple of Jupiter at Thebes to think of the place from which she came: and from this arose the oracle,

---

⁹⁵ If we read ἱρίας, Herodotus manifestly contradicts his statement, c. 35. Valckenaer proposes γυναῖκας ἱρὰς [as in c. 56], which will signify 'sacred women;' such, probably, as were employed to attend the temple and the priests, but were not admitted to the honour of priesthood.—*Larcher.*

⁹⁶ ἐς Λιβύην ἐπρήθησαν. The preposition ἐς, with the accusative, expresses motion: it would therefore be incorrect to translate 'was sold in Libya.'—*Larcher.*

⁹⁷ The φηγὸς of the Greeks is not the same with the *fagus* of the Latins. The latter is the beech; the former a species of oak.—*Larcher.* Schneider considers it to be the *quercus esculus* of Linnæus.—*Schneid. Gr. Ger. Lex.*

⁹⁸ Schweighæuser proposes 'under a real oak,' inferring that the other particulars of this tradition were allegorical.

when the woman had attained a knowledge of the Hellenic language; and the report originated with her, that her sister had been sold in the same manner by the Phœnicians, to go
57 into Libya. I presume, likewise, that the women were called doves by the people of Dodona; for this reason, that they were foreigners, and appeared to them to chatter like birds: after a time, they say, the dove spoke with human voice; that was, when the woman began to speak intelligibly: so long as she spoke a foreign tongue, they imagined she chattered as a bird; but how could a dove, of all things, speak like a human being? By saying that the bird was black, they give us to understand the woman was an Egyptian[99]. The oracle at Thebes of Egypt, and that at Dodona, resemble each other very closely.—The practice of divination by the victims in temples came likewise from Egypt.

58 Festive congregations[100], processions, and thanksgivings[101] to the gods were first introduced by the Egyptians, from whom the Hellenes learned the same practices: the early adoption of these rites by the Egyptians, and their comparatively modern establishment among the Hellenes, afford suffi-
59 cient proof of my assertion[102]. The Egyptians have festive meetings more than once in every year: the greatest and the most rigidly-observed festival is that of Diana, at Bubastis; the second, that of Isis, at Busiris: the largest temple of Isis is in this town, which stands in the centre of the Egyptian Delta: Isis, when translated, signifies Ceres. The third festival is celebrated at Saïs, in honour of Minerva; the fourth at Heliopolis, to the Sun; the fifth at Buto, in honour of
60 Latona; the sixth at Papremis, to Mars. Those, accordingly, who come by water to Bubastis act in the following manner. Men and women embark together; vast numbers of both sexes are seen in every barge: some of the women have rattles, with which they make a noise[103], some of the men also play on the fife, in every boat: the rest of the women and men sing, and clap their hands. When, in their progress, they arrive at any town, they push their bark to land; where some of the women do as I have described, while others scoff and scream at the women belonging to the place: some also dance; while others, standing forth, pull up

[99] The Egyptians were black: see chap. 104.
[100] Πανήγυρις, Panegyris, Festorum dierum celebratio. *Schweig. Lex. Herod.*
[101] Herodotus gives to *προσαγωγὰς* the meaning of 'solemn sacrifice' and 'feast,' called, in later times, *τελετὰς. Schneid. Lex.*
[102] φαίνονται .... πευθόμενοι. This mode of speech does not express a doubt; it rather contains an affirmation. *Larcher.* See Viger. sect. xiii. Reg. 1. Matt. 548, 5.
[103] The *κρόταλον* was a sort of rattle, made of a splitten reed, *κάλαμος ἐσχισμένος.*

their clothes and exhibit their persons. The same thing takes place at every town on the river-side: and when they have reached Bubastis, they celebrate the feast, and offer up great sacrifices: more grape-wine is consumed at this feast than in all the rest of the year besides. The congregated multitude of men and women, without reckoning the children, amounts, the people of Bubastis say, to seven hundred thousand. In what manner the feast of Isis is kept at Busiris has been already described by me[104]: there, accordingly, after the sacrifice, all the men and women, to the amount of many myriads, beat themselves on the breast, to the honour of whom I am not at liberty to divulge[105]. The Carians that are settled in Egypt carry their zeal still farther, inasmuch as they slash their faces with their knives; shewing thus, that they are not Egyptians, but foreigners. At Saïs, after the people have collected to be present at the sacrifices[106], all the inhabitants, on a certain night, kindle a great number of lamps, in the open air, around their houses: the lamps are small flat saucers filled with salt and oil, on the surface of which floats a wick that burns through the whole night; and hence the feast is called the lighting up of lamps[107]. The Egyptians who cannot join this festive congregation observe the night of sacrifice, and every one lights up lamps; so that the illumination is not confined to Saïs alone, but extends all over Egypt. A religious reason is assigned for this night being so honoured, and the illumination that accompanies it. At Heliopolis and Buto the people come merely, and attend the sacrifices: but at Papremis, not only are the sacrifices offered up, and the holy ceremonies performed, as in the other towns, but, about sunset, a few of the priests are employed about the image, while the greater part, armed with bludgeons, stand in the portal of the sacred edifice: other men, determined to accomplish certain vows they have made, and more than a thousand strong, each provided also with a bludgeon, stand in a mass opposite: (the image, placed in a small wooden chapel, all gilt, is conveyed the day before to some other holy sojourn:) the few left about the image drag a four-wheel vehicle, with the chapel containing the image: the priests stationed in the portal refuse admittance:

---

[104] Chap. 40.

[105] See the end of chap. 4.—τὸν ἢ τύπτονται. This is an example of the middle verb, taken in a reflective sense. The preposition ἐπὶ must be understood with τὸν ἢ. *Larcher*. See likewise Matt. 419, 5. In this case, as in several others, Herodotus refrains, through religious scruples, from stating the origin of this ceremony.

[106] Matt. 393, 5th parag.

[107] This reminds us of the Feast of Lanterns, in China.

the devotees, rushing to the assistance of the god, fall on the opponents with their bludgeons: then begins a furious struggle with clubs: they break one another's heads, and many must, I conceive, die of their wounds, although the Egyptians themselves deny that this ever is the case. The people of Papremis assert, that the reason for thus celebrating the feast is this: that the mother of Mars resided in the temple; her son, educated at some distant spot[108], having come to manhood, wished to pay a visit to his mother; but the attendants, who had never before seen him, refused him admittance, and drove him away. Mars therefore collecting men from the other part of the city, handled the servants very severely, and forced an entrance to his mother. In consequence of that event they declare that this sort of combat is instituted on his festival.

The Egyptians were also the first to establish the custom, that all communication with women in the sacred places should be prohibited, and that men who had been connected with females should not enter the temples unwashed. For with nearly all nations, except the Egyptians and Hellenes, men may either sleep with women within the sacred edifice, or, rising from a female partner, enter the temple unwashed. These people put mankind on a level with the brute creation; for, say they, other animals and various birds are seen coupling in the shrines, temples, and sacred precincts[109]; and, consequently, if this was displeasing to the god, the brute creatures even would not do it. The persons that endeavour to excuse, by such reasoning, the above behaviour, do not by any means meet with my approbation. The Egyptians observe, with scrupulous care, all religious ordinances, and especially the above mentioned.

65 Although Egypt confines on Libya, it is not very abundant

---

[108] ἀνότροφον, μακρὰν τεθραμμένον. Hesych. The whole of this passage may be translated in another manner; as the reader will see, if he consults the commentators.

[109] This paragraph affords an instance of the three different terms ἱερὸν, ναὸς, τέμενος. The ἱερὸν was the whole of the sacred inclosure: it must, in some cases, have been very extensive, for that of the temple of Æsculapius, at Epidaurus, the limits of which may to this day be pretty clearly ascertained, contained several hundred acres, and was adorned with theatres, amphitheatres, baths, and other buildings. The ναὸς was the cell itself of the deity, in which the sacred image was deposited. The τέμενος was a part of the ἱερὸν, consisting of various edifices, surrounding the ναὸς, and peculiarly consecrated, or, as it were, cut off, for the service of the divinity. The reader will no doubt call to his recollection, that even the deeds of brutal licentiousness, mentioned i. 199, took place ἔξω τοῦ ἱεροῦ. The nice distinction that I have just explained can hardly be attended to in the language of a country which a merciful Providence has long since delivered from the tyranny of superstition.

in animals [110]: those found in this country are all held to be sacred, whether domesticated by men or otherwise. Were I to mention the reasons why they are considered holy, I should be descending in my narrative to religious matters, which I wish, above all things, to avoid [111]: even the few I have superficially spoken of, were mentioned from necessity [112]. The practice with the Egyptians, in respect of animals, is this: curators are appointed for feeding every kind separately: they are Egyptian men and women: and the son inherits the dignity of his father. The inhabitants of cities acquit themselves in the following manner of the vows they have made to the gods: when they pray to the god to whom the animal may be consecrated, they shave either the whole heads of their children, or the half, or the third only of their heads: they weigh the hair in scales against silver: whatever that weight may be, they give it to the curator of the animals; in return for which, she cuts up some fish, and gives it as food to them: such, accordingly, is the appointed mode of feeding them. Whoever kills one of these animals, if wilfully, the punishment is death [113]: if accidentally, the culprit is bound to pay what fine the priests may impose: it is understood, however, that he who kills an ibis or a vulture, whether wittingly or unwittingly, must necessarily be put to death. Although the domesticated animals are numerous, their 66 numbers would be still greater, were it not for what takes place with the cats. When the females have littered, they no longer seek the company of the males, who, finding it impossible to gratify their desires at that time, have recourse, in consequence, to this artifice: they take away, secretly, the kittens from the females, and, carrying them off, kill them: in so doing, however, the males do not devour the young. The female cats, deprived of their kittens, and desirous of others, seek again the company of the males; for the cat is much attached to her offspring. When a fire occurs, a surprising prodigy takes place among the cats: for the Egyptians, not heeding the conflagration, stand at some distance, and give their whole attention to the cats: those animals however slip between, and leap over the ranks of men, to rush into the fire: at this, great sorrow takes possession of the Egyptian. When a cat dies, in a house, of a

---

[110] Libya abounded in wild animals of all kinds: it might perhaps have been inferred, that the case was the same with Egypt: this assumption the Historian contradicts.

[111] This passage, coupled with a similar one in c. 3, in fin., accounts for the scrupulousness with which Herodotus avoids stating the reasons of the various ceremonies he has described.

[112] Comp. chap. 3.
[113] Matt. 481. obs. 2.

natural death[114], the inmates all shave their eyebrows: but those with whom a dog dies, shave the whole body, together with the head. The deceased cats are carried to Bubastis, where they are embalmed, and buried in holy vaults. As for the dogs, all that die are buried in sacred cells, by the respective persons to whom they belonged, and in their own towns. The ichneumons are buried in the same manner as the dogs[115]: but shrew-mice and vultures are taken to Buto; the ibises to Hermopolis; the bears, which are not very abundant, and the wolves[116], not much larger than foxes, are buried wherever their carcases may be found.

68 The following is a description of the crocodile. During the four winter months he eats nothing: he is four-footed, and amphibious: this animal is oviparous: the female lays her eggs in the ground, and there leaves them. The crocodile passes the greater part of the day on the dry land; but the whole night in the water, because at that time the water is at a higher temperature than the atmosphere or the dew. Of all living things we are acquainted with, the crocodile is that which, from the smallest, grows to be the largest; for the crocodile's egg is not much larger than that of the goose; and the newly-hatched animal is proportioned to the egg he comes from, but gradually increases in size, till he reaches a length of seventeen cubits, and even still more. He has the eyes of a pig; large teeth and tusks in proportion to his body: is the only animal that has no tongue; the only animal, also, that does not move the lower jaw, but

---

[114] I was a long time in doubt, whether I should translate ἀπὸ τοῦ αὐτομάτου, 'by accident,' or 'naturally.' I adopt the latter, from the authority of Aulus Gellius, who says, αὐτόματος θάνατος, 'quasi naturalis et fatalis, nullâ extrinsecùs vi coactus venit.' *Noct. Attic.* xiii. 1. It is the same as what the Latins call 'mori suâ morte.' Not, however, but that ἀπὸ τοῦ αὐτομάτου may signify 'by chance,' as in the following passages from Xenophon: τούτων δὲ μάρτυρες οἱ σωθέντες ἀπὸ τοῦ αὐτομάτου, 'I have for witnesses of it those who have saved themselves by chance.' *Hellen.* i. 7. ἀπὸ τοῦ αὐτομάτου χθὲς ἥκοντος πλοίου, 'a vessel having arrived yesterday by chance.' *Cyr. Exp.* vi. 4, 12.—*Larcher.*

[115] Matt. 386, 3. Ἰχνεῦται, οἱ τῶν ἰχνευμένων λεγόμενοι. *Hesych.* This animal is found both in Upper and Lower Egypt. It creeps slowly along, as if ready to seize its prey: it feeds on plants, eggs, and fowls. In Upper Egypt, it searches for the eggs of the crocodile, which lie hid in the sand, and eats them, thereby preventing the increase of that animal. It may be easily tamed, and goes about the houses like a cat. It makes a growling noise, and barks when it is very angry. *Hasselquist.*

[116] Wolves are not found, it is said, now-a-days, in Egypt: Sonnini, therefore, supposes that Herodotus, in this instance, confounds the wolf with the chacal or jackal. Our Historian was a native of Asia Minor, where wolves are very frequently seen; and jackals are so numerous and noisy, that the traveller finds great difficulty to enjoy at night the necessary refreshment of sleep, amid a din ten thousand times greater than the caterwaulings on a summer night in a populous town.

brings the upper jaw down to the lower. He is armed with strong claws; his skin covered with scales, impenetrable on the back: blind in the water, exceedingly quick-sighted on land: passing so much of his time in the water, the inside of his mouth is always beset with leeches. All other beasts and fowls fly before him; but he is at peace with one sort of water-bird, called the trochilus, which assists him greatly; for when he gets out of the river on land, and opens his jaws (which he is wont always to do towards the west), the trochilus enters his mouth, and devours the leeches. The crocodile is grateful for this service, and does no harm to the bird[117]. The crocodile, therefore, is sacred 69 with some Egyptians: by others, far from being sacred, he is pursued as an enemy. The people residing about Thebes and Lake Mœris consider crocodiles to be highly sacred: each of these people feeds one crocodile in particular, brought up so tame as to allow himself to be handled: they put in his ears, crystal and gold gems[118]; bracelets on his fore paws; and give him appointed and sacred provisions, and treat him handsomely while he is alive; when dead, they embalm him, and inter him in a holy cell. The people at Elephantine, and the environs, eat these reptiles, conceiving them far from sacred. These animals are not in Egyptian called crocodile, but 'champsæ:' the Ionians have given them the former name, from an idea of their resemblance in shape to the lizards or newts of the hedges, which they thus denominate[119]. The modes of catching them 70 are many and various: that which accordingly appears to me at least the most deserving of description, I shall describe. They[120] bait a hook with the chine of a pig, and let it down the middle of the stream: the fisherman holds, on the bank of the river, a live hog, which he beats: the crocodile, hearing

---

[117] The mistakes detected in this description of the crocodile, by modern naturalists, are—The crocodile has a tongue, that is to say, the flesh and muscles of a tongue; but the skin that covers it extends all over the lower jaw, and connects itself with that of the sides of the mouth: the lower is the only moveable of the jaws of the crocodile, as well as other animals; the difference in the crocodile is, that the lower jaw is endowed with a double motion from top to bottom, and from right to left; all the teeth are pointed, and curved towards the throat: when the animal closes his mouth, the teeth of the upper and lower jaws lock in together, so tightly as to present the appearance of a barrier of bone.

[118] λίθινα χυτά. 'works of melted stone.' I cannot decide whether Herodotus means glass, enamel, or any other artificial stone. The use of glass is very ancient, but its origin cannot be determined.—*Larcher.*

[119] The hedge-lizard, or eft, [*Lacerta stellio* Linn.] was known by the name of the κροκόδειλος χερσαίος.

[120] Supply, from the preceding ἄγρας, the substantive ἀγρεὺς (literally, "hunter,") to govern the verb ἑλίσσῃ. See Matt. 294.

the squeaks, comes to the sound, and, meeting with the chine, gorges the bait. The men now haul him in; and, when the animal is drawn up on the land, the first thing the fisherman does is to plaster his eyes over with mud: this being done, the rest is easily effected: so long as this remains undone, the difficulties are great. The hippopotamus, also, is held sacred in the nome of Papremis, but not so by the rest of the Egyptians. This animal may be thus described: he is a quadruped; his foot is armed with claws; his hoof is that of the ox: he has a pug-nose, and a horse's neck; jutting teeth; the tail and the neigh of a horse. His size is that of the largest sort of oxen; and his hide is so tough, that, when dry, javelins are made from it [121]. Otters, likewise, are met with in the Nile: they hold them to be sacred, as well as, among fish, the lepidotus and eel: they affirm that the above sacred animals are the property of the Nile [122]: and so, among birds, the fox-goose.

73 There is another sacred bird, called the 'phœnix;' which I myself never saw, except in a picture; for it seldom makes its appearance among them; only every five hundred years, according to the people of Heliopolis. They state, that he comes on the death of his sire: if at all like his picture, this bird may be thus described, in size and shape. Some of his feathers are of the colour of gold; others are red. In outline [123], he is exceedingly similar to the eagle, and in size also. This bird is said to display an ingenuity, which to me does not appear credible: he is represented as coming out of Arabia, and bringing with him his father to the temple of the Sun, embalmed in myrrh; and there burying him. The manner in which this is done, is as follows:—In the first place, he sticks together an egg of myrrh, as much as he can carry, and then tries if he can bear the burden: this experiment achieved, he accordingly scoops out the egg, sufficiently to deposit his sire within; he next fills with fresh myrrh the opening in the egg by which the body was enclosed: thus the whole mass, containing the carcase, is still of the same weight. Having thus completed the embalming, he transports him into Egypt, and to the temple of the Sun.

[121] ξυστὰ ἀνίεται. Herodotus here joins the words ξυστὸς and ἀνίετων, the former of which is an adjective, and, when used alone, signifies 'a javelin,' on account of the substantive ἀνίετων being understood. It would, therefore, have been better, instead of 'polita jacula,' which I have used in my translation, to have put simply 'jacula.'—*Schweig.*

[122] Matt. 371, 1.

[123] περιηγησιν, according to Wesseling, signifies 'formam et diligentem ejus descriptionem.' I take it to be what we should call, in French, 'la contour.'—*Schweig.*

In the vicinity of Thebes, a kind of serpents are sacred, 74 that never do any harm to men[124]. They are diminutive in size; and carry two horns, springing from the crown of the head. All these serpents, that die, they bury in the temple of Jupiter, to whom it is said these reptiles are consecrated. But close to the environs of Buto, there is a spot belonging 75 to Arabia; which I visited, in consequence of information I received concerning some winged serpents. On my arrival there, I beheld such quantities of prickly bones as it would be impossible to describe: there were heaps of these spinal bones[125], some large, others small, others again still smaller: all in great quantities. The spot where the bones are accumulated, may be thus described: it is a gorge, between two steep mountains, and leads to a wide plain, which is connected with the Egyptian plain. And report says, that, with the spring, the winged serpents fly out of Arabia, towards Egypt; but the ibis, a sort of bird, takes his post at the defile, opposes the passage of the serpents, and destroys them. For this service, the Egyptians, according to the Arabians, give great honours to the ibis; and the Egyptians themselves confess that such is their motive for honouring these birds[126]. The following is the description of the ibis. 76 He is all of a deep black; his legs are like the crane's; his bill is strongly curved; his size that of the crex: such is the description of the black ibis, the champion that fights against the serpents. The other sort (for there are two kinds of ibis), more frequently met with[127], are naked on part of the head and the whole of the neck: the plumage is white, excepting the few feathers on the head and throat, on the tips of the wings, and the extremity of the tail, all of which are jet black. The legs and bill are similar to the other species. The winged-serpent is similar in shape to the water-snake: his wings are not covered with feathers, but completely similar to those of the bat[128].—So much for the description of the sacred animals.

Of the Egyptians with whom I have had an opportunity 77 to be acquainted, those inhabiting the arable parts of Egypt

---

[124] Matt. 322, 1.

[125] ἄκανθα signifies not only the back-bone, but all the bones of a fish or serpent: it is equivalent to the French word 'arête,' the fish-bone, that is, like that of the sole, for instance.—*Larcher.*

[126] See B. iii. 107.

[127] Constr. τῶν ἐν τοῖς εἰλουμένων (ἰβίων) ταῖσι ἀνθρώποισι (ἴβη) ψιλὴ κ. τ. λ. .... εἰλουμένων from εἰλεῖσθαι 'versari.' *Schweig.* τὰ ἐν ποσί are 'common things,' such as one frequently meets on one's road.—*Larcher.*

[128] Matt. 462, last parag. but one. The particle ἄν, on to μάλιστα, is pleonastic.

are the most distinguished of the world in their exertions to preserve the memory of events[129], and, beyond all doubt, the most skilful historians. As to their mode of diet, they take purgatives three successive days in every month; and look for health by means of emetics and clysters, being convinced that all the diseases incident to man have their origin in the food that he takes. In fact, next to the Libyans, the Egyptians are the most healthy in the world; an advantage, I think, to be attributed to the seasons, which are always the same; for disease most frequently attacks the human frame at the changes of the seasons. They are eaters of bread in the form of spelt loaves, which they call 'cyllestis.' They make use of wine, brewed from barley; for their soil produces none from the grape. They live on fish, raw, but sun-dried, or steeped in brine: they eat also raw quails and ducks, and the smaller birds, salted beforehand; and all the rest boiled or roasted; but refrain from the birds

78 and fishes which are regarded as sacred. In the wealthier classes of society, and at their convivial banquets, a man carries round a wooden image of a dead body, exactly carved and painted to represent a corpse, although in its whole height[130] not more than one or two cubits. The person, that shews it round, says: "Look on this; drink and be jovial; for when you are dead, such will you be." This is their mode of managing their feasts.

79 They have their own national airs, and adopt none others: among various compositions highly deserving of praise, there is, more especially, one song, which is sung in Phœnicia and Cyprus, and in other places; it bears different names in different nations, but coincides with what the Hellenes call Linus, and which they sing[131]. Among the many wonderful things that I have observed in the Egyptians, this is one, Whence did they get the Linus[132]? They have apparently sung it from time immemorial. The Linus is called, in Egyptian, Maneros. The Egyptians represent, that Maneros was the only-begotten son of the first king of Egypt; and that, on the occasion of his untimely death, he was

---

[129] This is taken by Valckenaer and Wesseling to signify 'the exercise and cultivation of the faculty of memory.' Larcher is of the same opinion; but Schweighæuser regards μνήμην as alluding to 'the memory of past events,' 'historical records.'

[130] πάντη is used by Herodotus to signify, "in each direction;" a meaning which does not make sense in this passage.

[131] Matt. 535, d.

[132] *Linus*, a hero, the son of Urania, on whose fate the Greeks had a song, which was frequently chaunted at their feasts, and was called Λίνος. *Schneider, Lexic.*

honoured with these mournful strains by the people: and this lay was the first and only one they had in early times. In the next following particular, the Egyptians assimilate to none of the Hellenes, except the Lacedæmonians. The young people, meeting their elders, give way, and turn out of their path; and, at their approach, rise up from their seats. The following custom, however, is not known to any Hellenic nation whatever: instead of accosting one another in words on the ways, they salute by sinking the hand to the knee. They wear cotton under-garments, with fringes about the legs, and call them ' calasiris:' over these they throw mantles of white flannel; but they take no woollen clothing whatever into their temple, nor do they use shrouds of wool for the dead: that would be contrary to law. In this respect they agree with the Orphic and Bacchic rites, which are the same as the Egyptian and Pythagorean: in the above mysteries, none of the initiated is allowed to be buried in winding-sheets of wool. For which institutions, a religious reason is assigned.

These again are inventions made by the Egyptians: Every month, and every day, is consecrated to one of the gods; and, according to the birth-day of any person, is determined what shall befal him, how he shall end his days, and what will become of him. The Hellenic Poets have made use of this science: they have found out more signs and tokens than all the rest of mankind put together; for whenever any prodigy occurs, they observe and note down, in writing, the result; and if at any time a nearly similar thing should happen, they conclude that the same result will ensue. In respect of divination, the following practice holds: The art is vouchsafed to no mortal man, but to some of the gods. Accordingly, there are oracles of Hercules, of Apollo, Minerva, Diana, Mars, and Jupiter; together with that of the greatest repute, the oracle of Latona at Buto. The practice of medicine is thus distributed among them: Every physician confines himself to one disease only, no more: all places abound in doctors: some are doctors for the eyes; others respectively for the head; teeth; and for the belly, and the parts about it, for the inward disorders.

Their mode of mourning and performing funeral ceremonies is this: At the death of any person of distinction belonging to the family[133], all the females of the house accordingly daub their heads and faces with mud, leave the corpse in the house, and parade the town; and, after tying a

---

[133] Matt. 527. obs. 2.

girdle round their waists, expose their bosoms, and beat their breasts[134]: they are accompanied also by all their female relations. The men, on the other hand, beat their breasts, and gird their waists. When these ceremonies have been performed, they carry away the dead body, for the purpose of having it embalmed. For this business, certain persons are specifically appointed[135], and exercise it as a profession: when the corpse is brought to them, these artists shew to the bearers of the body some wooden models of dead bodies, painted to imitate nature; and first explain to them the most-carefully executed of these patterns, the name of which in this business I deem it improper to mention. They next shew the second pattern, considerably inferior to the former, and cheaper; and then the third, which is the cheapest of all. They then inquire according to which model the people wish to have the body prepared: when the relations present have agreed for the price, they withdraw; while the artists, who work at home, proceed to embalm the body in the following manner, which is also the most sumptuous. In the first place, with an iron hook, they draw out the brain through the nostrils; not the whole, but a part only; which they replace with certain drugs. Next, with a sharp Ethiopian stone, they make an incision down the flank, by which they draw out the whole of the intestines: having cleansed the abdomen, and rinsed it with palm-wine, they then sprinkle the inside with pounded perfumes[136]. After they have filled the belly with genuine pounded myrrh, casia, and other perfumes, frankincense excepted, they sew up again the aperture: having so prepared the body, they put it in natron[137], where they steep it for seventy days:

[134] The women undid the top of their garment, in order to open their bosoms; and, lest the robe should drop, and so discover them naked to the spectators, they tied it up with a girdle round their middle. This is the meaning of ἐπιζωσμέναι. *Larcher, from Wyttenbach.*

[135] ναυτίεται, Ion. for *καθηνται*. This term, although general, is particularly applied to those who work at the trades called, by the Latins, *artes sellulariæ*, " sedentary arts." *Larcher.*— I have followed Schweighæuser's version, " constituti sunt:" he states, however, that *ναυίεται* may also be rendered simply " sedent." *Schweig. Lex. Herod.* voc. *ναυίεται.*

[136] The following is the translation of Larcher: " They extract, by this opening, the intestines, cleanse them, and rinse them in palm-wine: they rinse them again in pounded aromatics: after which, they fill the belly with myrrh," &c. A difficulty then occurs: What did they do with the intestines, after they had taken so much trouble to cleanse them?— Schweighæuser is of opinion, that ἐξαιρέων τὴν κοιλίην means, " to take the bowels out of the belly," (as in c. 40, κοιλίην αυτὴν πᾶσαν ἐξ ὧν εἶλον,) and proves that κοιλίη and νηδὺς are synonymous. By this interpretation, the difficulty disappears. See *Schweig. Not.* and *Lex. Herod.*

[137] Larcher sufficiently proves that λίτρον should not be translated "nitre," but " natrum," a fixed alkali, which would blend with the lymphatic and oily juices and the fat.

more than that time it is unlawful to keep the body in pickle. When the seventy days are gone by, they wash the corpse, and wrap the whole body in bandages of cotton cloth, smeared with the gum[138], which the Egyptians generally use instead of paste: the dead body is then taken back by the relations; who have a wooden case, made in the shape of a man, in which they put the corpse; and then, closing it, deposit the whole in a sepulchral chamber, placing the case upright against the wall. This is the most costly mode of preparation. For such as wish to go to a moderate expense, and avoid all extravagance, the embalmers prepare the bodies thus: They fill their syringes with oil made from the cedar, and inflate the abdomen of the corpse, without making any incision or taking out the intestines, but merely apply their injections by the anus of the dead body: they stop the passage by which the injection might flow out, and so put the body into pickle for the prescribed number of days; on the last of which they let out from the abdomen the cedar oil, by injecting which they had begun their operation: the power of this drug is so great, that it dissolves and brings out with it the bowels and other intestines[139]. The natron consumes the flesh; and consequently nothing remains of the body but skin and bone. When this has been done and completed, the embalmers return the body, without doing any thing more. The third mode of embalming, which is used only for the very poor, is this: they inject the abdomen with radish-juice[140], steep the body the seventy days in pickle, and then give it to the relations when they come to fetch it. As for the wives of great people, they are not delivered to the embalmers immediately after death; neither are such women as have been particularly beautiful, and the subject of great notice: they are entrusted to the embalmers three or four days after death: this is done in order that the workmen may not abuse the persons of the deceased females; for they say that one of these persons was caught in the very act, having been informed against by a brother workman. Every person seized by a crocodile, no matter whether he be Egyptian or alien, and all brought to death by the river itself, on whatever territory the body may float to, must by law be embalmed, adorned in the most magnificent manner, and entombed in a sacred coffin. No one

---

[138] Gum-arabic, probably.

[139] νηδύς, in this case, signifies the bowels or intestines: τὰ σπλάγχνα are the nobler viscera, i. e. the heart, lungs, &c.—*Schweig.*

[140] It is not determined what sort of liquid is meant by συρμαία. The same word occurs in c. 125, where Pliny translates it in a sense which cannot apply here.

dare touch him, whether relation or friend: the priests of the Nile bury the body with their own hands, as being something more than that of a man.

91 The Egyptians have a great aversion to the Hellenic customs, and, generally speaking, to all the usages of other nations. This aversion pervades all Egypt, with the exception of Chemmis, a large town in the Thebaïc nome, not far from Neapolis. At this place there is seen a quadrangular temple to Perseus the son of Danaë, around which palm-trees have been planted: the propylæa of the edifice is very extensive, and built of stone; upon the top of which stand two colossal statues. Within this precinct stands the temple itself, where the image of Perseus is seen. The people of Chemmis assert that Perseus has frequently appeared to them on earth; frequently, likewise, within the temple; and that one of the sandals that he wears, two cubits in length, is sometimes found: and after this appearance, Egypt is throughout blessed with abundance. In imitation of the Hellenic ceremonies, they open, to the honour of Perseus, a gymnic list for all sorts of sports and combats[141]; proposing as prizes, heads of cattle, cloaks, and skins. When I inquired how it was that Perseus was wont to make his appearance to them alone, and why they departed so widely from the Egyptian customs as to celebrate gymnic games, the answer given to me was: " that Perseus was originally " of their town; for Danaus and Lynceus, who were natives " of Chemmis, came, by sea, from thence to Hellas:" then recapitulating the genealogy of these two men, they brought it down to Perseus: and next proceeded to say in answer: " Perseus had come to Egypt, for the same purpose as the " Hellenes themselves represent; that is to say, to bring " away from Libya the Gorgon's head: he paid them also a " visit, and acknowledged all his kindred:—that, informed by " his mother, he had heard of the name of Chemmis before " he came to Egypt; and that according to his injunction " they celebrated the gymnic games."

92 All the above customs hold among the Egyptians that reside above the morasses: those that occupy the morasses themselves have the same institutions as the rest of the Egyptians; among others, that, like the Hellenes, of every man having but one wife. But, as respects the domestic customs

---

[141] ἀγῶνα γυμνικὸν διὰ πάσης ἀγωνίας ἔχουσι, " ludos gymnicos qui per omnia certaminum genera obtinent, locum habent," i. e. " celebrantur," equivalent to " ludos gymnicos omnium certaminum genera complectentes." *Schweig. Lex Herod.* vocc. ἔχω and ἀγωνία. Larcher, after Wesseling, translates, " qui de tous les jeux sont les plus excellens;" which, of all games, are the most excellent. See *Gaisford's Herod.*

relating to provisions, they have discovered many things conducive to their comfort. For instance, when the river has swollen to its highest, and has swamped the meadows, an abundance of lilies springs up in the water, which are called by the Egyptians 'lotus:' they gather these plants, dry them in the sun, and then thresh out the pods in the middle of the lotus, which are similar to those of the poppy, and make loaves of the seed, and bake them: the root of this lotus is also edible, and of a delicate sweet taste; it is globular, and of the size of an apple[142]. There are, moreover, other lilies, similar to roses, that grow in the river; the fruit of which shoots up from the root in a calyx, supported on an independent stalk, and is very like a wasp's comb: within this calyx are contained several eatable kernels, about the size of an olive-stone: these are eaten, both fresh and dried[143]. The annual plant called the 'byblus' is pulled up in the marshes: the top of the plant is cut off, and put to various uses: the lower part, about a cubit long, they eat, and make an object of sale: those who are desirous of having the byblus very deliciously prepared, put it into a hot oven[144], and eat it without any seasoning[145]. Some of these people live entirely on fish, which they catch, gut, and dry in the sun; and, when properly cured, use them as food.

The gregarious sorts of fish are seldom found in the 93

---

[142] This plant is the water-lily of Egypt, not unlike our own water-lily: its flowers and fruit sink under water for the night, and make their appearance again at sun-rise. The root and seed of this plant constituted part of the food of the Egyptians.

[143] This plant is a kind of Colocasia or Arum, similar to the Calla Æthiopica of our green-houses. The Egyptian colocasia has leaves about the size of a cabbage-leaf, full of viscous juice: stalk, three feet high, and of the size of the thumb: the flowers are monopetalous, in the shape of an ass's ear, of a purplish colour. The flower-stalk ends in a pistil, which in time becomes a cylindrical fruit, composed of several berries, not unlike a wasp's nest when dug up.

[144] ἐν κλιβάνῳ διαφανεῖ πνίξαντες. Wesseling has properly explained διαφανεῖ, by *hot, red hot*: the expression is elliptical, and ἐν πυρὶ must be understood; as Herodotus expresses himself, iv. 73, λίθους ἐκ πυρὸς διαφανέας.

Larcher.—The signification of πνίγω is "suffocare;" but this word is also used to express a certain mode of cooking, thus described by Casaubon (ad Athen. ii. p. 65, l.) "The meat is cooked in its own juice, inclosed in a pot or pan, so that no steam may exhale; a mode of dressing which our cooks also call ' suffocation,' (i. e. bruising.)" From this it is evident that Herodotus cannot mean by κλίβανος a fixed large oven, but a pot, pan, or some other culinary vase: and we gather from Athenæus, that the κλίβανος was sometimes brought to table with its contents. *Schweig. Lex. Herod.* voce. πνίγω and κλίβανος.

[145] This is the Cyperus papyrus, or water-plant; consisting of a tuft of stalks without leaves, each terminating in an umbel of flowers very elegant and airy. The inner bark of this plant served the ancients instead of paper.

river: they grow to their natural size in the lakes[146]; and, when nature excites them to procreation, proceed in shoals to the sea: the males lead the way, shedding their milt; and the females, following in the rear, eagerly swallow it up, and are thus milted. When all have been fecundated in the sea, they return back, each to his own ground: the males, however, no longer take the lead; the females swim at the head of the shoal, and, as the males did before, eject now their spawn, which is about as large as millet-seed; the males, following behind devour greedily these seeds, which are themselves all fishes. The seeds that escape, and are not devoured, grow up, and become fishes. Those that are caught in their descent to the sea all bear marks of friction on the left of the head; those taken on their return have the marks on the right. This proceeds from the following circumstance: going down to the sea, they keep close to the land on their left; and at their return up the river, keep up to the same bank, and hug and scrape the land lest they should be thrown out of their way by the force of the current. As soon as the Nile begins to swell, and the hollows in the land and the quagmires near the river first begin to fill with the water oozing through the banks from the river, immediately those pools fill, vast quantities of little fishes swarm on all sides. How this comes to pass, may, I conceive, be thus explained: when, the preceding year, the Nile forsook the lands, the fish that had spawned in the marshy grounds withdrew at the same time; but when, in the course of time, the water again rises, fishes hatch forthwith, from those very eggs.

94 The Egyptians residing in the marshes use an oil extracted from the seeds of the ricinus, or palma-christi, which they call 'cici'[147]. They cultivate this plant (which in Hellas grows spontaneously wild) on the banks of the river and lakes; by which means it bears a greater crop, but sheds a vile smell. When they have harvested the seed, they tread it out; and some put it under the press, while others grill or boil it, and collect the matter that it discharges: the extract is fat, and not inferior to olive-oil for burning in lamps, only

95 that it sends forth such an abominable smell. As a defence against the musquitoes, which are in vast swarms, they resort to the following expedients: the people residing in the

---

[146] That is to say, the *canals derived from the Nile.—Reiske.*

[147] This is the "Ricinus" of the Latins, and the "Palma Christi" of our gardens, the seeds of which furnish the castor-oil of the apothecary. *Larcher.*

marshes themselves take advantage of the lofty towers they are obliged to inhabit, and sleep on the top; which the musquitoes are hindered, by the winds, from attaining, in their flight. But the people that reside on the sides or in the neighbourhood of the marshes substitute another expedient for the towers: every man possesses a net, with which he catches fish in the day, and makes the following use of in the night: around and over the bed he sleeps on he casts the net; he then creeps under, and lays himself down. The musquitoes, which, even if he were to wrap himself in a linen cloak when in bed, would bite through all, do not so much as even try the net.

The craft they use for the freight of merchandise are con- 96 structed of a kind of thorn[148]; I mean the thorn that resembles the Cyrenæan lotus[149], and the exudation of which constitutes gum. Out of this tree they cut wooden planks, about two cubits in length, and arrange them brick-fashion; proceeding thus in their ship-building. They fasten together the planks around with many long tree-nails[150]; and, when they have thus completed the hull, they lay across the top some beams of the same materials: they have no recourse to ribs: and caulk the seams with byblus in the inside: they fit on only one rudder[151], which passes through the keel; rig

---

[148] The Acacia, a thorny tree, from which exudes what we call gum-arabic. See Matth. 375.

[149] The Libyan lotus is very different from the Egyptian, just described. See Book iv. c. 177. See likewise Matt. 375, 2.

[150] γόμφος signifies, a 'peg,' or 'pin,' as in Homer, Odyssey, Book v. 248.—Ζυγά are pieces put across, to form a deck: 'transtra' is used in this sense, also, by the Latins. Ἐνδέσμευσαν cannot signify *inferciunt*. He is not speaking, in this place, of stopping up the interstices with papyrus, as with oakum. but of *strengthening* the structure; that is the meaning of the verb ἐνδέσμευσαν. Eustathius very properly explains it καταπφαλίζονται. Larcher. —Schneider, however, translates this passage, "sie verstopften die Fugen d. Pap:er," Gr. Germ. Lex. voc. παινύω.—Schweighæuser translates it, in the same sense, " Commissuras navium intus obturant byblo." This authority, and a reference to the sense in which Herodotus uses καταπαντός, v. 16, have induced me to English ἐμπαπτόν by to ' caulk.' πρὸς γόμφοις συνέβησαν τὰ ξύλα, lit. " they fasten the planks around *gomphi*." I am aware that the translation I have given above is any thing but literal: I have carefully consulted Schneider's erudite article on the word γόμφος, but must confess that I see no signification which will answer the purpose of combining grammatical accuracy with a good sense: the passage remains unintelligible to me. Perhaps the baris was a sort of raft, and the γόμφος a tie or bandage fastening the blocks together; but if that be the case, what shall we do with ἰκρίω ῥ - - - - τῇ ξύβλῳ?

[151] Lit. " They make one rudder, and that is driven through the keel." The ships of the ancients were very different from those of the present day. The helm or rudder consisted of two broad oars (πηδάλια) jutting out on either side of the stern: these were fastened together by a cross-bar, (ζευγηρία, Act. Apost. xxvii. 40,) so that one tiller (οἶαξ) moved both rudders. The helm of the baris appears to have been pretty nearly of the same kind as that adopted in modern navi-

a mast from the same sort of thorn; and hoist cotton sails. These craft are unable to stem the current, unless it blow a fresh gale, and are towed off land. When they go down stream, they manage them thus: A square frame is made of tamarisk[152] beams, wattled with reeds: a stone is likewise procured, bored through the middle, and in weight about two talents. The frame is now fastened to a hawser; and let down from the prow, to be carried out by the stream: the stone[153] is let down at the stern, and fastened to another hawser. Accordingly, the frame, falling in with the current, drives down pretty fast, with the 'baris' in tow—that is the name given to this craft: the stone trailing at the stern, and along the bottom of the river, serves to steady the vessel. There are vast numbers of this sort of barks, some of which are of many tons' burden. When the Nile overflows the land, the cities only are to be seen above its surface, somewhat similar to the islands in the Ægæan sea; for at those times all the other parts of Egypt are under water: so that they navigate, when this is the case, not only along the riverstream, but even over the middle of the plain: thus, if you are making the voyage up from Naucratis to Memphis, your course will pass close to the pyramids: this is not, however, the general road[154], which is to the vertex of the Delta, and the city of Cercasorus. As you sail from the sea up to Naucratis, you also cross the Canopic plain, and pass by the town of Anthylla, and that called the city of Archandros. The former of these, a respectable town, is set apart expressly for the shoes of the wife of the reigning king of Egypt; a

gation; but being no different from those in general use at the time the Muses were written, it is no wonder Herodotus should think it deserving of mention, "that the baris had but one rudder (πηδάλιον), and that close to the keel."

[152] The μυρίκη is the *tamarix* Linn.—θρᾶ is used to signify a board, or *tabulatum* of boards, longer than it is broad. *Schneid. Gr. Germ. Lex.*—πσυρραμμίνη, lit. 'sewed together.'

[153] This stone certainly could not have been of any avail towards steering the vessel; nor did Herodotus think so, since he has previously mentioned the rudder. I conceive the use of this weight at the poop to have been to serve as a sort of shifting or moveable ballast, the advantages of which are obvious;—in the case of the current bearing very hard on the frame or hurdle, they let the weight drag at the bottom of the river: the resistance thus procured would hinder the hurdle from hauling the prow under water, and swamping the boat; a misfortune which otherwise must, in all probability, have happened. I have therefore translated ναυτίλλω or ναυτίλλω as allusive to the position, and not to the course of the vessel. Such as disapprove of this manner of rendering the Greek verb, may, with Schweighæuser, Larcher, Beloe, &c. translate, "the stone dragging at the poop, and sinking to the bottom, steers the vessel."

[154] It is evident that οἷα οὗτος must be taken as signifying the usual and ordinary course, *i. e.* that followed when the river flows between its banks.—*Schweig.*

practice which has been instituted since Egypt was subjected to the Persians. The latter town appears to me to take its name from Danaus's son-in-law, Archandrus son of Phthius, grandson of Achæus; for that place is called Archandrus. There may, indeed, have been another Archandrus; but, at all events, the name is Egyptian.

Up to this part of my account of Egypt, the narrative is drawn from what I have seen myself, and my own ideas of things: what follows was composed from the information I gathered in my communications with Egyptians, accompanied by some particulars from my own observations. The priests stated, that Menes, the first that ever ruled over Egypt, threw up, in the first place[155], the dyke that protects Memphis[156]: for, previously, the whole of the stream flowed along the sand-covered mountain ridge fronting Libya; but Menes, beginning about one hundred stades above Memphis, filled in the elbow made by the Nile in the south; and thus, not only exhausted the old bed, but formed also a canal by which the river was made to flow in the mid-space between the [Libyan and Arabian] mountains. Even at the present day, this ancient elbow, repelling the Nile in his course[157], is attended to and watched with great care by the Persians, and fortified every year with additional works; for should the river rise over and burst this dyke, the whole of Memphis would be exposed to the danger of being swept away. When the part reclaimed from the river had become firm land, Menes, this first king, built in the first place, as I have said before, on this spot, the town now called Memphis (for Memphis is situated in the narrow part of Egypt); and without the town excavated a lake, communicating with the river, in the north and west quarter: for Memphis being washed to the east by the Nile, it was not possible to effect these works on that side. In the second place, he erected next[158], in the same town, the temple of Vulcan, which is a vast building, and well

---

[155] To this τοῦτο μὲν answers τοῦτο 22, §. 9; but as the intervening phrases are too long, τοῦτο μὲν is repeated, §. 7. *Schweig.*—See Matt. 288, *b*.

[156] ἀναγειρομένων, 'aggeribus munire,' *Schweig.*—The reader is here advertised, once for all, that most of the infinitives of the subsequent chapters are ruled by οἱ ἱρέες ἔλεγον: the observation is indispensable; since, in a modern version, it is incompatible with the necessary fluency of language to preserve at all times the same construction as in the original; the consequence of which has been, and may be again, that a person referring only to a translation sometimes fancies that Herodotus states, from his own authority, what he meant to be understood as the traditions of the sacerdotal officers.

[157] ἧς (ὁ ἀγκὼν τοῦ Νείλου) ἀπεργμένος ῥέει: lit. "which, excluded *from its former bed*, flows."

[158] τοῦτο μὲν, ἐν αὐτῇ οἱκοι κτίσαι, as well as its apodotic, τοῦτο δ, τοῦ Ἡφαίστου τὸ ἱερὸν ἱδρύσασθαι, relate to οἱ ἱρέες ἔλεγον.—*Larcher.*

100 deserving of commemoration. As successors to Menes, the priests quoted from a manuscript the names of three hundred and thirty other kings. In so many generations of men, there occurred eighteen Ethiopian kings, and one native queen: all the rest were Egyptian kings. The name of the woman, who thus held the sceptre, was Nitocris, the same as that of the Babylonian queen. According to the report of the priests, she avenged her brother, who had preceded her on the throne, but was put to death by the Egyptians: after committing this deed, the nation presented the empire to this woman, his sister. In revenge of her brother, she destroyed many of the Egyptians by artifice. She built herself extensive subterraneous apartments; and under the pretence of inaugurating the edifice [159], but really with a very different purpose, invited to a banquet many of the Egyptians whom she knew to have participated in the murder; and when they were seated at table and enjoying themselves, she let in the river waters, by means of a large concealed drain. Nothing more is related concerning this queen by the priests, except that, having effected her purpose, she threw herself into a room full of ashes, in order to evade retribution [160].

101 No display of works or splendour of action was mentioned of any of the other kings, with the exception of the last, Mœris [161]: this sovereign erected, as a memorial, the north portal of Vulcan's temple; and dug a lake, the dimensions of which I shall hereafter explain: he erected also the pyramids within the lake, the size of which I shall likewise describe, when I come to the subject of the lake itself [162]. Such were the achievements of Mœris: none were left by any of the others.

[159] καινόω, in Herodotus ii. 100, is equivalent to εινωείκεν, 'to consecrate,' καινίζω, Schneid. Gr. Germ. Lex.—As Schweighæuser approves this interpretation of Schneider's, I have not hesitated to admit it in my version.

[160] The anonymous author of a 'Treatise on the women who have made themselves illustrious in war by their prudence and valour,' speaking of Nitocris, uses the following reading: ἑαυτὴν δὲ εἰς οἴκημα, σποδοῦ πλήρες, ἐνέβαλεν. If we adopt this reading, it will be necessary to make a very slight alteration in the text of Herodotus, which consists in putting a comma after οἴκημα and changing πλέον into πλέως. The Historian's meaning then becomes, 'that, covered with ashes, she threw herself into her apartment, in order to evade retribution.' This no doubt admits of an easy explanation; but there remains a little difficulty: is πλήρης or πλέως σποδοῦ equivalent to πεφορμένος σποδῷ? Larcher, quoting Bibliot. der alten Lit. etc. Götting. 1789.

[161] The construction is rather intricate; it may be thus unravelled: τοὺς δὲ ἄλλους βασιλέας κατ' οὐδὲν ἵναι λαμπρότητος ἔλεγον, οὐ γὰρ αὐτῶν οὐδεμίαν ἀπόδεξιν ἔργων εἶναι, πλὴν ἰδὲ τοῦ ἐσχάτου αὐτῶν, Μοίριος. The words κατ' οὐδὲν ἵναι λαμπρότητος seem to be equivalent to ἐν οὐδενὶ λαμπροὺς ἵναι Gaisford.

[162] Chap. 149.

I shall therefore pass over all the above monarchs; and 102 make mention of a king that came after them, and whose name was Sesostris. The priests represented Sesostris as the first that, embarking on long ships, proceeded out of the gulf of Arabia into the Erythræan sea, and subjected the inhabitants of the shore: they added, that, wishing to penetrate still further, he arrived at last into a sea unnavigable, by reason of the shoals; and thence sailed back into Egypt; where, according to the same priests, he levied a mighty army, and marched over the whole continent, subjecting every nation he fell in with. In the territories, accordingly, of such as fought gallantly, and strove hard for freedom[163], he erected pillars, with inscriptions describing his own name and country, and in what manner he had subdued the inhabitants with his forces: but in the lands of such as yielded up their towns as dastards, without a struggle, he set up pillars with the same inscriptions as for the valiant nations; to which he added a representation of the secret parts of a woman, intending thereby to signify that they were soft and effeminate. So doing, he traversed the continent of Asia; 103 then, crossing over into Europe, subdued the Scythians and the Thracians: these were the most distant, it is my opinion, to whom the Egyptian army reached[164]: in that quarter the pillars are found, but not any further on: here, therefore, the troops wheeled back, to return. When they came to the Phasis river, either the king himself, Sesostris, (for I cannot say to a certainty,) divided a portion of his army, which he left to settle in that country; or some of the men, weary of this long migration, chose to remain on the banks of the Phasis. Indeed, it is manifest[165] that the Colchians are 104 Egyptians: this I assert, not only from my own previous conjecture, but also from what I heard of others; for, as I felt an interest in this subject[166], I made inquiries both of Egyptians and Colchians: the latter had a clearer remembrance of the Egyptians, than the Egyptians had of the Colchians. The Egyptians, however, said, that they considered the Colchians as having proceeded from Sesostris's army: and I inferred the same thing, not so much because the Colchians are black and curly-headed, (which amounts to nothing, since there are other races of that kind,) but chiefly

---

[163] Matt. 328.
[164] Matt. 464.—Lit. 'The Egyptian army appears to me to have reached to these (i.e. *the Thracians*), the furthest point of their progress in *Europe*.' Some read καὶ οὐ προσωτέρω: in which case, προσωτέρω will afford an instance of the superlative put for the comparative.
[165] Viger. neot. xiii. reg. i.
[166] " Quum vero curæ mihi hæc res esset."

from the following proofs; that, of all mankind, the Colchians, Egyptians, and Ethiopians, are the only nations that, from the first, have practised circumcision: the Phœnicians, and Syrians of Palestine, even confess they learned the custom from the Egyptians; while the Syrii (Cappadocians) about the Thermodon and Parthenius rivers, as well as their neighbours the Macrones, acknowledge that they have but lately adopted the practice. Now, the above are the only races of circumcised men; and, in this respect, they all evidently act in the same manner as the Egyptians; but the two nations, Ethiopians and Egyptians, which of these learnt it from the other, is a point I cannot decide upon, for it is clearly a very ancient custom [167]. The opinion, that it was learnt by communication with Egypt [168], is, I think, proved beyond doubt, by this fact: such of the Phœnicians as have any traffic with the Hellenes, no longer imitate the Egyptians, but leave their children uncircumcised. I will now mention [169], also, an additional instance of similitude between Colchians and Egyptians. The Colchians and the Egyptians weave cloth in the same manner, but different from all the world besides: the whole life, the language, are one and the same, in both nations. The linen woven by the Colchians is called Sardonic: that made in Egypt is, however, designated as Egyptian [170]. As to the pillars erected in the various countries by Sesostris king of Egypt, most of them have evidently perished [171]: I saw, however, one of these in Syria of Palestine, bearing the inscription as above, with the characteristic of the female sex. On some rocks in Ionia there are engraved images of this prince: one is on the road by which you go from Ephesia to Phocæa, and the other between Sardis and Smyrna. In both these places the image of a man has been cut out, four cubits and a half high [172], bearing in his right hand a spear, in his left a bow,

---

[167] ἀρχαῖον signifies a custom coëval with the origin of the nation, established from time immemorial: ' institutum ab ipsâ primâ gentis origine susceptum.' *Larcher*.

[168] ἐπιμεμογήμενον cannot relate to the Ethiopians; for in that case, Herodotus would contradict what he has just asserted; namely, that he did not know which of those two nations had taken circumcision from the other.—This word must therefore refer to the other nations that had communicated with the Egyptians. *Larcher*.

[169] Φέρε νυν, ' age vero.' See Viger.

sect. xiii. reg. vi.

[170] The Egyptians had then some peculiar manner of manufacturing linen. Herodotus has mentioned, ch. 35, that, in weaving their cloth, they shot the woof or weft downwards; whereas other nations drive it upwards. This is, perhaps, the custom he alludes to in this place. *Larcher*.

[171] Matt. 426, 2. and 474, c.

[172] Comp. B. i. c. 50. See also Matt. 141.—The σπιθαμή is *half a cubit*. We have seen before, i. 50, that τρίτον ἡμιτάλαντον signifies two talents and

and so on with the whole attire, which is half Egyptian and half Ethiopian: from shoulder to shoulder, athwart the breast, a line of sacred Egyptian characters is carved, the purport of which is: I HAVE WON THIS LAND BY MY OWN SHOULDERS:—who, or whence he is, Sesostris does not hint here, but explains elsewhere. Some persons, who have seen these relics, have conjectured them to be images of Memnon: in this, however, they are greatly deceived.

The priests go on to state, that when this Egyptian Sesostris, on his return with many men from among the various subdued nations, reached Daphnæ of Pelusium, being by his own brother, whom he had set over Egypt, invited to be present at a banquet, himself and his sons, wood was piled up on the outside of the edifice, and set on fire. Sesostris, informed of this, immediately consulted his wife, who had accompanied him thither: the advice she gave him, as they had six sons, was, to stretch two across the fire, and thus, making a dyke against the flames, seek salvation. Sesostris did so; and in this manner two sons were consumed by the fire, while the rest, together with their father, made their escape [172]. After Sesostris's return to Egypt, and when he had taken revenge on his brother, he employed the multitude of prisoners brought from the subdued countries in the following works: not only were they set to drag the huge masses of stone, which, under the reign of this king, were brought to Vulcan's temple, but were likewise obliged to dig all the canals now seen in Egypt: thus, they were compelled, by force, to work such an alteration in the face of the country, that the whole territory, previously well adapted for horse-riding and the use of chariots, became useless for those purposes; because from that time, in Egypt, which is all level land, horses and carriages were no longer used: the cause being, the numerous canals in all directions. The motive that induced the king to intersect in this manner the country, was, that all the Egyptians, whose cities do not stand on the river-side, but lie at some distance, suffered from drought when the floods left them, and the inhabitants were obliged to procure a brackish beverage [174] from their wells. It was also related, that this king divided the soil among all the Egyptians, giving to each individual an equal quadran-

a half, and ἱδμων ἡμιτάλαντον six talents and a half: it is therefore clear that σίμντα σνδαμἡ must signify four cubits and a half. *Schweig.*

[173] This chapter, as almost all the others, bears evidence of a direct interpretation of the figure carved on the walls of Vulcan's temple: whether the priests knew of the allegoric meaning, or wished to withhold it from Herodotus, is a matter of mere conjecture.

[174] Hesychius explains ἁλυκὺ ὕδωρ by τὸ ἀλμυρὸν: voc. ἁλυκύ. *Larcher.*

gular portion; and from thence drew his revenues, enacting what contribution should be made every year: and if the river should sweep away any portion, the proprietor was to come to him, and report what had happened; when he would send surveyors and measurers, to ascertain to what extent the soil was diminished, so that thereafter the appointed contribution should be proportionately decreased[175]. Hence, in my opinion, land-surveying took its origin, and subsequently extended to Hellas: for it was from the Babylonians that the Hellenes learnt the use of the clock and sun-dial.

110 This king was accordingly the only Egyptian that ever ruled over Ethiopia. He left, as memorials of himself[176], some stone statues in front of Vulcan's temple: two, thirty cubits each, himself and his wife: their sons, four, each twenty cubits. A long time after, one of the priests of Vulcan warned Darius, the Persian king, from setting up his own statue before these; observing, that "Darius had not "achieved deeds equal to those of Sesostris the Egyptian: "for Sesostris had conquered no fewer nations than Darius "had subdued; and had, moreover, overpowered the "Scythians, a thing which the Persian could not compass: "therefore it was not fair he should place his own statue[177] "before those offerings[178], unless he had surpassed in "exploits." Darius, accordingly, by their account, excused the boldness of the priest.

111 At the decease of Sesostris, the power, it is said, was assumed by his son Pheron. This prince displayed no inclination for war: he was afflicted with blindness, in consequence of the following event[179]: the river having swollen eighteen cubits, an enormous height for those days, and covering the arable lands, a gale of wind arose, and the river was agitated by waves; when the king, impiously grasping a spear, hurled it in the midst of the eddies of the stream: forthwith he was taken with ophthalmia, and became blind: and the affliction, accordingly, lasted during ten years: but in the eleventh year, an oracle came to him from the city of Buto, declaring, "that the period of his visita- "tion was at an end; and he would recover sight, by bath- "ing his eyes in the urine of some woman who had never

---

[175] Construction: ἴσως τοῦ λοιποῦ τελίων (μέρος) τῆς τεταγμένης ἀναφορᾶς κατὰ λόγον.

[176] μνημόσυνον is a monument intended to preserve the memory of something.—*Larcher.*

[177] Understand ἱστάναι αὐτὸν, ἀνάθημα or ἀνδριάντα —*Schweig.*

[178] The statues that were erected to any person were invariably offered or dedicated to the gods, to the end, that, being under the protection of religion, no one should dare to throw them down.—*Larcher.*

[179] Matt. 423, 4.

" gone astray from her lawful husband, and was innocent
" before all men excepting him." The king, therefore, made
the first trial on his own wife; but seeing no better after
that, he persisted in making the experiment on all women:
having at last been restored to sight, he collected in one
town, called Erythrebolus, all the women whom he had made
trial of, excepting her by whose urine he was cured; and
consumed them all by fire, together with the town itself.
Her, to whom he was indebted for his sight, he took to himself as wife. Having thus escaped from the disease in his
eyes, Pheron made magnificent offerings to all the celebrated
temples; but the most particularly deserving of our admiration, no doubt, are the beautiful works dedicated at the
temple of the Sun, namely, two stone obelisks, each cut out
of one single block, and each of a hundred cubits in length
by eight in breadth.

He was succeeded, the priests said, in the kingdom, by a 112
native of Memphis, whose name, in Hellenic, is Proteus: his
sacred grove, a beautiful and well-adorned spot, is still extant at Memphis, lying south of the Vulcanian fane: the
environs are inhabited by Tyrian Phœnicians; and the whole
of this quarter is known by the name of the Tyrian camp.
Within the sacred grove of Proteus stands the temple of
Foreign Venus: this is, I presume, the temple of Helen the
daughter of Tyndarus, who, I have been told, lived with
Proteus, and bore the name of Foreign Venus; for, among
all other temples of Venus, there is none elsewhere having
the name of Foreign[180]. The priests, when I inquired 113
into the history of Helen, told me that matters passed in
the following manner:—Paris, having stolen Helen from
Sparta, steered for his own country; but, when he was on
the Ægean sea, an adverse gale drove him from his course,
into the sea of Egypt; from whence—for the storm did not
slacken in violence—he came to Egypt; and landed at
Taricheæ, on the mouth of the Nile, now called the Canopic.
On that shore stood a temple, the same that is seen there at
present; where, if a slave, belong to whom he may, takes
refuge, and gives himself up to the god, by having certain
sacred marks impressed on his body, no one can lay hands
on him. This custom continued still in force in my time,
exactly as it was at the beginning. The attendants of Paris,
consequently, when informed of the practice that held in

that temple, forsook their master, and, setting down as suppliants of the god, accused Paris, with a view of doing him an injury; and described how he had behaved to Helen, and his iniquity towards Menelaus. This deposition was made to the priests, as well as to the governor of that mouth, the name of whom was Thonis. On the receipt of this intelligence, Thonis sends instantly a message to Proteus at Memphis, conceived in these words: " A stranger of Trojan race " has arrived here, after committing a nefarious deed in " Hellas; for he carried off the wife of his host; and has " come hither, bringing the woman, with great treasure, " being driven by the winds to your shore. I ask, Whether " we shall allow this stranger to take his departure unmo- " lested; or shall I seize his property before he goes away [181]?" Proteus returned for answer: " Arrest this man, whoever " he may be, that has dealt so wickedly with his host: send " him to me, that I may see what he has to say for himself." Thonis, having received these orders, seized the person of Paris, and put an embargo on his ships; and then sent off the prisoner to Memphis, together with Helen and his treasures: the suppliants were also despatched to the same place. When all were arrived, Proteus examined Paris, as to whom he was, and from whence he had sailed: the prisoner mentioned his family, and stated what was the name of his country; and, more particularly, described his voyage, and the port he had sailed from. Then Proteus questioned the prisoner on the manner he got possession of Helen. Paris, prevaricating in his answers, and not speaking the truth, the men, who had become suppliants, confronted him, and went through the history of his iniquities. At last, Proteus pronounced this sentence on him:—" Did I not hold it of para- " mount importance not to put to death any stranger " whatever that may come to my shores weather-bound [182], " I would revenge the Hellenes of your behaviour, you most " wicked wretch! who, after having received the blessings of " hospitality, have dared to commit so flagrant a crime. Not " only have you suborned the wife of your own benefactor; " that was not enough to content you; but you must carry " her off [183], steal her person: nay, even that does not satisfy

---

[181] Lit. " What he came, having." —Τευκρὸς, which I have rendered Trojan, means an inhabitant of Teucris or Troas. νότερα ὄντα - - - - - ἤ. Matt. 609, 2d parag.

[182] ὑπ᾽ ἀνέμων ἴθυ ἀπολαμφθέντες, " hindered from pursuing their course by the winds."

[183] ἀναπτερώσας αὐτὴν, οἴχεαι ἔχων ἐκκλίψας. The verb ἀναπτεροῦν (from πτερὸν) signifies ' to raise the feathers or wings:' thus the peacock, spreading his tail, is said ἀναπτεροῦσαι τὰ κάλλη. Metaph. ἀναπτεροῦν τινα means ' to fill one with longing desire—hope.' Schneid. Lex. Gr. Germ. ἔχων need

" your cupidity, but you must even rifle your friend's house,
" ere you depart. Now, therefore, though I hold it of great
" consequence not to take the life of strangers, I shall not
" allow you to take away this woman, or this treasure; but
" I will keep them for your Hellenic friend, until he choose
" himself to come and fetch them away. My commands are,
" that you yourself and your shipmates shall quit my land,
" and go to some other, within three days[184]: if not, you
" shall be treated as enemies."

Thus the priests described the arrival of Helen at Proteus's court. Homer also, I think, must have heard the same account: but it was not so well adapted to the epopœïa, as that which he made use of: for this reason[185], he rejected it, although he has given proofs that he was aware of the above history as well. This is evident; for, as he sings in the Iliad (and no where else does he retract) the wanderings of Paris, how, when carrying away Helen, he was driven out of his course, and strayed to various countries; among others, to Sidon of Phœnicia[186]. He hints at the same thing in the exploits of Diomedes[187]; and these are his words:

" Where the variegated robes, works of the Sidonian dames, were
" found, that the god-like Paris himself brought from Sidon,
" sailing on the wide sea, what way he took the high-born
" Helen." *Iliad*, vi. 289—292.

He alludes to the same also in the Odyssey, in these words:

" Such drugs of healing excellence had Jove's daughter, gift
" from Polydamna, Thonis' spouse of Egypt, where the nurtur-
" ing field breeds drugs numerous, some for salutary, others for
" poisonous potions." *Odyss.* iv. 227.

These words, also, are spoken by Menelaus to Telemachus:

"In Egypt the gods retained me, though anxious to return hither,
"because I had not offered to them complete hecatombs." *Od.* iv. 351.

In these verses, Homer proves that he knew of Paris's wanderings: for Syria confines on Egypt; and the Phœnicians, to whom Sidon belongs, inhabit Syria. From these verses, and the last passage especially, it may be evidently concluded[188], that Homer was not the author of the Cypriac verses, but some other poet. For in that poem it is said, " On the third day, Paris reached Ilium, with Helen, from " Sparta, wafted by a favourable breeze over a calm sea:" whereas it is said in the Iliad, that he wandered far and wide with his prize.—But now bid we farewell to Homer and the Cypriac verses.

I inquired of the priests, whether it was a vain fable, or not, that the Hellenes narrate of the Trojan war. To this they made the following answer, obtained, they said, by inquiry from Menelaus himself: That, after the rape of Helen, a vast army of Hellenes invaded the land of Teucria, in Menelaus's cause: after the host had landed, and pitched their camp, they sent a deputation to Ilium, which Menelaus himself accompanied: when admitted within the walls, they claimed back Helen, and the treasure that Paris had stolen from the Hellenic prince, and demanded satisfaction for that unjust deed. But the Teucrians, both then and ever after, persisted in the same declaration, whether put to the oath or not, that they had not Helen, nor the treasure thus claimed, but, that all these things were in Egypt;—that it would not be right they should make retribution for what Proteus, the Egyptian king, had in his possession;—that the Hellenes, fancying the Trojans were laughing at them, therefore besieged the town, and at last[189] captured it. Having stormed the city, they found no Helen there, but received the same account as before; so that the Hellenes, giving at last credit to the report, sent Menelaus himself to Proteus. Menelaus, on his arrival in Egypt, sailed up to Memphis; where he described the true events that had taken place, met with a sumptuous reception[190], and received back Helen unhurt;

and, together with her, all the treasure. Thus successful, Menelaus, notwithstanding, behaved very iniquitously towards the Egyptians. Foul winds hindered him from heaving anchor and taking his departure: this having continued a long time, he had recourse to the following nefarious expedient: he seized two Egyptian children, and sacrificed them. From the moment that it was known he had been guilty of such a murder [191], he became an object of hatred and persecution, and fled with his ships to Libya. Whither he directed his course from thence, the Egyptians confessed they could not tell: but that of the above particulars, some they had ascertained by inquiry; others had occurred before their eyes, and they were able to vouch for their accuracy. Such was the Egyptian account: and I myself accede to the truth of these events having happened in respect of Helen, to which I will subjoin the following remarks. If Helen had been in Ilium, she would have been restored to the Hellenes, whether at or against the consent of Paris; for surely Priam, at all events, could not have been so distraught, nor could all belonging to his family be so infatuated, as to expose to destruction their own persons, their children, their city, in order that Paris might still be united to Helen. Indeed, though they might in the earlier times have followed that counsel, yet, when so many, not only of the Trojan subjects, were cut off, whenever they engaged with the Hellenes, but whenever a battle was fought [192] it was not without the slaughter of one, two, three, or even more of the sons of Priam, if we are to give credit to the accounts of the epics—if, I say, such was really the case, it is my decided opinion, that had Priam himself been married to Helen, he would have given her back to the Achæi, with a view, at any rate, of putting an end to such dire consequences. Neither was Paris even heir to the throne, so as in the old age of Priam to have assumed the management of affairs. Hector was the real heir, being the senior of Paris, and more of a man, and was to succeed to the power at Priam's decease: it would not have been expedient in him to side with his brother, in his iniquities; and to do this, when such calamities, through Paris's agency, oppressed himself and his family, together with all the rest of the Trojans. But they had really no Helen to give up; and, although they spoke the truth to the Hellenes, no faith was put in what they said: the cause of which, in my opinion,

[191] Matt. 296.
[192] οὐκ ἔστι ὅτε οὐ, non est (vel non fuit) quam non, etc.; id est, nunquam non, semper quoties factum prælium est.—Schweig. Lex. Herod.

was, that Providence arranged that the destruction of the Trojan nation, by one general massacre, should convince all men, that for great misdeeds great are the punishments at the hands of the gods.

121. Rhampsinitus, said the priests, was the successor of Proteus: he left, as a memorial, the western propylæa of Vulcan's temple; in front of which he set up two statues, twenty-five cubits high: that standing to the north, the Egyptians call summer; the other, to the south, they call winter: before that called summer they prostrate themselves, and offer sacrifice, but behave just in the contrary way to the other called winter[193]. They added, that this king possessed a vast quantity of money, such as none of the kings that came after him[194] could ever surpass, or even approach to. Wishing to store up his treasure in safety, he gave orders that a chamber should be built of stone, with one of the walls standing against the outside wall of the palace. The builder, after some consideration, devised the following artifice: he laid one of the stones in such a manner, that it might be easily taken out by two men, or even one. When the chamber was completed, the king deposited his treasure in it: but the builder, some time after, being at the point of death, called into his presence his sons, for he had two[195]; and described to them, how, in order to provide for their plenteous subsistence, he had managed in the construction of the king's treasury[196]. Having accurately explained to them all the particulars about the extraction of the stone, he gave them the measures[197]; and said, that, if they observed his directions, they would become the stewards of the royal riches. The builder accordingly died; and his sons did not long tarry to put in practice their father's advice; they came to the palace at night, ascertained the stone alluded to in the wall, pulled it out without any difficulty, and came away with great booty. But, when the king came to open the chamber, he saw, to his astonishment, that the vases containing the money

---

[193] Matt. 407. and 606, 3.

[194] ἐπιτραφέντων, from ἐπιτρέφω equivalent to ἐπιγενομένων, 'none of the kings since born and educated;' 'none of the succeeding kings.'—*Schweig. Lex. Herod.*

[195] ὅπως γὰρ αὐτῷ δύο, "for he had two:" this infinitive, like a great many more, in this old woman's tale particularly, is governed by ἔλεγον.

[196] Lit. ' that being anxious (προορώμενος, looking forward) for them, that they might have abundant means of subsistence, he had used an artifice (τεχνάζων, 'artificiis uti') in constructing the treasury of the king.' τεχνᾶν governs the genitive of the person, and the accusative of the thing, which is here represented by the proposition, ὅπως βίον ἄφθονον ἔχωσι. See Matt. 377.

[197] That is to say, not only the dimensions of the stone, but its distances from the bottom and sides of the edifice. *Schweig.*

were deficient in contents: he could not, however, lay the blame to any one: the seals were all unbroken [198], and the chamber well secured. Having two or three times more opened the treasury, the money visibly decreased (for the thieves continued their rapine): the king therefore adopted this expedient: he ordered some traps to be made, which he set around the vases in which the money was stored: the thieves coming, as was their custom, and one of them having entered the treasury, went straight up to one of the vases, and was immediately caught in the trap: as soon as he found himself in this predicament, he called to his brother, explained to him what had happened, and bade him enter as quickly as possible, and cut off his head, lest he should be seen and recognised, and thereby cause the destruction of the other also. The brother on the outside thought he spoke to the purpose, and did as he was advised. The surviving thief returned the stone carefully, and proceeded home with his brother's head. At day-break, the king entered the chamber, and was amazed to behold the decapitated thief's body in the trap; while the room remained unviolated, and presented no means of entrance or exit. Thus circumstanced, the king, the priests add, acted as follows: he hung the dead body of the thief over the wall; and stationed sentinels underneath, giving them orders to seize and bring before him whomsoever they might see weep or mourn at the exhibition. The mother, it is said, was greatly exasperated at the exposure of the corpse: she spoke to the surviving son, and enjoined him, in all possible ways, to contrive to get possession of the body of his brother, and bring it to her; but, should he neglect to execute her order, she threatened to go herself to the king, and impeach him as in possession of the money. As the mother treated so harshly her surviving son, and he, notwithstanding his many arguments, could not persuade her, he had recourse to the following artifice: he got ready, they say, his asses, and loaded them with skins well filled with wine: he then drove the animals before him; and when he was come to the sentinels set over the suspended body, he pulled two or three of the feet of the skins [199] that hung down; and, when the wine

---

[198] "The seals on the doors." The reader will please to recollect, that locks were not yet invented.

[199] The skins of sheep and goats are used still in the Levant for the storing and conveyance of wine. When one of the animals above mentioned has been slaughtered, the person who officiates as butcher skins the body with a dexterity and rapidity scarcely imaginable: in a few seconds, the whole hide is drawn off, with the hair inside, and may be immediately used for the purpose intended: small apertures are made at the four feet and neck only, and these are tied closely

gushed out, he beat his head, uttering loud cries, as if in doubt which of the asses he should turn first to. The sentinels, seeing abundance of wine flowing away, ran out all together into the road, with cups in their hands, and collected the spilt liquor, which they considered as so much gain [200]. The drover, pretending violent anger, pursued the soldiers with all kinds of abuse [201]: the men, however, soothed him, and he pretended to mollify, and relax in wrath: at last, he drove his asses out of the road, and put their loads all right again: as the soldiers continued to chatter with him, one of them cracked a joke that excited him to laugh, so he gave them one of the wine-skins. The soldiers immediately stretched themselves on the ground, and attended only to drink, and make a friend of the drover, whom they invited to stay and join their revel: the man suffered himself, forsooth [202], to be persuaded, and remained. As the soldiers behaved so civilly towards him, he gave them another of the skins of wine. The men having partaken abundantly of the beverage, became completely intoxicated; and, overpowered with sleep, laid down, and slept on the same spot where they had been drinking. The drover, then, as the night was far advanced, took down the body of his brother, shaved the right cheeks of all the sentinels as a sign of his contempt, then threw the body on the back of the asses, and drove 121 home, having accomplished the orders of his mother. The priests represented the king as sorely irate, when informed that the carcase of the thief had been thus stolen away: fully determined to find out who was the author of this piece of trickery, he is said—although I give no credit to the tale— to have done as follows: he placed his own daughter in a brothel, with orders to receive all comers without exception, and not to admit their embraces until she had compelled each to tell to her what he had done most ingenious and nefarious in his life: him that might relate the same things as were known about the thief, she was to arrest, and keep from going away. The daughter acted according to her father's orders: but the robber (so the priests said) having ascertained why the king had recourse to such an expedient, determined to overreach the king himself in trickery, and

---

up: when untied, the four legs serve as cocks, and the neck as the bunghole.

[200] ἐν ἀλφοῖς ποιευμένοι, 'lucro apponentes,' as Horace has expressed himself, Lib. i. Od. 9.—*Larcher.*

[201] Matt. 383, 6, *obs.* 2.

[202] The particle δὴ is not an expletive: it answers to 'nimirum,' or 'scilicet,' of the Latin; and is used in a jeering or ironical manner, as in Terence, 'populus id curat scilicet.'— *Larcher.*

proceeded thus: he cut off, at the shoulder, the arm[203] of a fresh corpse, and, concealing it under his cloak, went into the king's daughter[204]; and being questioned, as all the others had been, related, as the most nefarious thing he ever did, the cutting off his brother's head, when he was caught in a gin within the king's treasury, and, as the most ingenious, the manner in which he intoxicated the sentinels, and extricated the suspended body of his brother. As soon as the girl heard this, she laid hold of him; but the thief presented to her, in the dark, the dead man's arm, which she took, fancying she grasped her visitor's hand. In the mean while, the thief let go the dead limb to the woman, and escaped by the door. When this also was reported to the king, he was amazed at the skill and audacity of the thief: finally, he sent round to all the towns, and proclaimed pardon to the culprit, and promised a great reward, if he would come into his presence. The thief trusted to the pledge, and went to the king; who greatly admired the man, and united in marriage to him the same daughter, considering him the wisest husband he could select; since this Egyptian surpassed all other Egyptians, who are so preeminent for wisdom among nations.

Subsequently to the above, according to the priests, this king descended into the place which the Hellenes think to be 'Haïdes,' and there played at dice with Ceres; sometimes beating the goddess, at others the goddess beating him. At his return, he received a present from her hands—a gold napkin. The priests say, also, that the Egyptians have instituted a festival, which lasts from the time of the descent of Rhampsinitus to that of his return. I am aware, indeed, that such a festival was celebrated by them, down to my time; but whether for the above, or any other reason, I cannot say: on that day, the priests weave a cloak, and bind the eyes of one of their number with a handkerchief: they conduct the person, thus bound about the eyes, and wrapped in the cloak, to the road that leads to the temple of Ceres, where they leave him, and return. The blindfolded priest is taken, they say, by two wolves, to the temple of Ceres, twenty stades' distance from the city; and is afterwards brought back, to the place he started from, by the same animals. Those who can believe such tales are at liberty to adopt what the Egyptians relate: my business, throughout this History, is to write down what I hear from all persons. The Egyptians assert

---

[203] Larcher proves, beyond question, that χείρ is frequently taken to signify the arm, together with the hand.

[204] See Matt. 578, last parag.

that Ceres and Bacchus are the princes of the infernal regions. They are, likewise, the first people that promulgated the immortality of the human soul; and the doctrine, that, when the body is consumed, the soul enters some other animal, rising into existence always at that moment; and that after it has passed through the bodies of all terrestrial, marine, and aërial creatures, it again animates a human body, born at that time; the circuit being made in three thousand years. This doctrine has been adopted by many Hellenes, some at one period, and others at another, as being their own invention: their names, although known to me, I do not mention.

124 Accordingly, until the reign of Rhampsinitus, by the priests' account, Egypt enjoyed the advantages of universal justice[205] and of great prosperity. After that king's reign, and under that of Cheops over the Egyptians, the country was reduced to the utmost misery[206]: for he shut up all the temples, in the first place, and forbade them to offer sacrifice: in the next place, he ordered all the Egyptians to labour in his own service; some of whom he accordingly appointed to the task of dragging, from the quarries in the Arabian mountains, the blocks down to the Nile[207]: others he stationed to take the said blocks, when brought across the river in vessels, and drag them to the range called the Libyan mountain. They were compelled to labour in this manner by one hundred thousand at a time, each party during three months: the time during which the people were thus ground down[208], lasted ten years on the road which they constructed for the conveyance of the stones; a work hardly less laborious, in my opinion, than that of building the pyramid itself; for in length it is five stades; in breadth, ten orgyæ; in height, at the loftiest part, eight orgyæ; the materials of polished stone, covered with all kinds of carved figures. On this road, therefore, ten years were spent, besides the works on the hill where the pyramids stand; namely, underground apartments, which Cheops ordered to be made, as repositories for himself, in an island formed by the canal drawn from the Nile. The time expended in erecting the pyramid itself was twenty years: its

---

[205] πάσης εὐνομίης: the latter word means, "that state of the commonwealth in which good laws and institutions prevail."

[206] ἐλάσαι may be made intransitive, equivalent to ἐλθεῖν; and then κακότητος must be translated *wickedness*: if it be taken transitively, supplying ὁδὸς, or τὴν Αἴγυπτον, *to lead to, to hurl to*, then κακότητος must be turned into *calamity.—Schweig.*

[207] Matt. 407, 2 b.
[208] Matt. 390, c.

dimensions are, each face eight plethra, the edifice being on a quadrangular plan: the height is the same: it is composed, for the most part, of polished stones, nicely jointed, and none of the blocks less than thirty feet. This pyramid 125 was erected in the manner which I shall now describe[209]: they adopted, for their plan, a flight of steps; called, by some, stairs: by others, a pile of altars. Having laid the first course of steps for the buildings, they hoisted the remainder of the blocks to a proper height, by means of machines consisting of short wooden spars[210]. From the ground, then, they lifted them up to the first course; and when the stone had reached that height, they placed it on another contrivance of the same nature prepared for the purpose on the first course, and dragged it up to the second; and thus the machines must have been the same in numbers as that of the steps: or else they had but one machine, and that moveable, which was taken from step to step[211], as they

[209] The annexed diagram is intended to represent the plan on which the Pyramid is constructed:

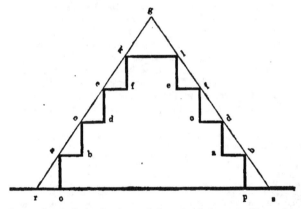

It was first built in the shape of steps: these steps, *a b c, d e f, k l*, were, by some, called κρόσσαι, by others, βωμίδες: the stones for finishing the structure, that is to say, to fill up the vacuities *a c, c e, e k*, &c. were first raised by machinery, to *a b*, from *a b* to *c d*, and so on. They finished, in the first place, the top, *k g l*, and then proceeded to *e f k*; and thus continued descending till they reached the bottom; so that the section of the pyramid, when complete, was an isosceles triangle, *r g s*. The largest of the pyramids consists of about two hundred tiers, or steps, varying in height from two to four feet.

[210] Placed together, probably, so as to form an inclined plane; a machine, which, even in the present day, is the only one used for raising enormous blocks, which would break the cranes and other instruments used for less ponderous objects.

[211] It is probable, that, after ἀνάγει, some such words as ἐπὶ τοῦ δευτέρου ἐπὶ τὸν τρίτον ἀνάγει have been omitted. *Schweig.*

hauled the stone up: for it is proper I should state both modes [212]; as they are related. The highest parts were accordingly the first finished off [213]; after which, they proceeded down to the other parts, step by step; and so, at last, came to the course resting on the ground, and completed also the footing. On the pyramid, an inscription, in Egyptian letters, shews how much was expended in supplying the workmen with radishes [214], onions, and garlic; and I recollect perfectly [215] the interpreter's reading to me the inscription, and saying the amount was one thousand six hundred silver talents. If this statement is correct, how much more must have been expended for the iron tools that they worked with, for the provisions, and clothing of the labourers? when they occupied so long a time as I have said in erecting the pyramid itself, besides that, I suppose, passed in cutting the stone, conveying it, and building the underground places [216], which 126 must have been of no small duration. So deeply had Cheops, it was said, sunk into infamy, that, being in want of cash, he placed his daughter in a brothel, enjoining her to extort a certain sum of money: what that was, however, is not told; but the damsel not only extorted what her father prescribed, but contrived to leave for herself separately a memorial, by asking every one that paid her a visit to give one stone towards the building. And with these stones, it is said, she built the pyramid that stands in the middle of the three [217], in front of the great pyramid: its sides are each one and a 127 half plethron long. This Cheops, according to the Egyptians, reigned fifty years: at the decease of this prince, his brother Chephren assumed the power, and acted after the

---

[212] Literally, " for let it be told by us in both manners, as it is related."

[213] λεκῶσαι signifies to 'finish,' 'to complete,' ' to ornament,' ' to put the last stroke to a work.' Herodotus is speaking of the coating of the pyramid. *Larcher*, from *Wess*.

[214] This word is rendered, by Pliny, " raphanus," i. e. *radish;* by which is to be understood, not the delicate radishes we have in our gardens, for which we are indebted to the Chinese, but a large black sort of turnip, called in English the Black Spanish Radish, which grows, in hot countries, to an enormous size.

[215] Respecting ὡς with the infinitive, consult Schweig. Lex. Herod. voc. ὡς, iv.; and Matt. Gr. Gramm. p. 823, or sect. 543, in which last, the translation given by Blomfield of ὡς μὲν ἐμὲ εὖ μεμνῆσθαι is " as far as I recollect rightly:" Schweighæuser's version is " recte memini." Literally, " and as I perfectly remember what the interpreter, when he read the inscription, said to me," &c.

[216] Probably for the foundation of the pyramid; since, according to Schweighæuser's text, the time passed in excavating the vaults on the hill is comprehended in the ten years employed on the causeway.

[217] According to Herodotus, the first pyramid was that of Cheops; the second, that of Chephren; and the third, that of Mycerinus. The fourth pyramid, or that erected by the daughter of Cheops, was in the middle of the three first, and opposite that of her father.—*Larcher*.

same manner as his predecessor; and, among other things, built a pyramid, which, in size, falls very short of his brother's in its dimensions, for I measured both myself. Neither are there any under-ground apartments [218] attached to it; nor is it watered, like the other, by a canal from the Nile; which, in the latter case, flows by means of an artificial drain round the island, where Cheops himself is said to be deposited. The first story of Chephren's pyramid consists of Ethiopian stone of various colours, forty feet less in height than the other, contiguous to which it stands [219]. Both are erected on one and the same hill, about a hundred feet high. Chephren is stated to have reigned fifty-six years. Thus one hundred and six years are reckoned, during which the greatest calamities visited the Egyptians: during that time the temples were closed, and never opened. In consequence of the detestation the Egyptians have for these two princes, they are not very anxious to mention their names; but call the pyramids after a herdsman, Philition, who at that time grazed his herds about this place.

The king that succeeded Chephren on the throne of Egypt was, they said, Mycerinus, the son of Cheops; who disapproved the conduct of his father. This prince reopened the temples; and restored to the people, ground down to the greatest misery, the privileges of working for themselves, and offering up sacrifice: he adjudged also their suits in the most equitable manner of any of the kings: in consequence of this mode of acting, the Egyptians praise this monarch far above all others of their kings: for not only did he judge in equity, but even, when any one complained of his sentence [220], he gave him a remuneration from his own possessions [221], and pacified his anger. But the first beginning of the calamities that befel this meek prince, one who took so much care of his subjects, was the death of his daughter, the only child that remained to him. He was stricken sorely with sorrow by such a visitation; and desirous of entombing his deceased daughter in a more sumptuous manner than was customary, he gave his commands that a hollow wooden image of a cow should be prepared, which he covered with gold, and in it enclosed the body of his departed daughter. This image, accordingly,

---

[218] Matt. 593, c.

[219] Constr. [Χεφρὲν] ᾠκοδόμησε [τὴν πυραμίδα] ἐχομένην τῆς μεγάλης [πυραμίδος,] ὑποβὰς τὸν πρῶτον δόμον λίθου Αἰθιοπικοῦ ποικίλου, [κατὰ] ταὐτὰ μεγά- λος ὑποβὰς τεσσεράκοντα πόδας τῆς ἑτέρης [i. e. τῆς μεγάλης].

[220] Matt. 574; end of first parag.

[221] Matt. 588, 4.

was not concealed under-ground, but was an object of inspection even in my time; being found at Saïs, standing within the palace, in a hall sumptuously decorated. Perfumes of all sorts are burnt, every day[122], before her; while, through the whole night, a lamp is kept burning. Adjoining the place of this image, in another apartment, are seen the images of Mycerinus's concubines; such the priests of Saïs assert them to be: in fact, several wooden colossuses are placed here standing, to the number of about twenty perhaps, all represented as naked: as to who they 113 are, I can say no more than was said to me. There are, however, some people who give the following account of this cow, and of the colossuses;—that Mycerinus was in love with his daughter, whom he deflowered by violence: the young woman, they say, strangled herself through anguish: accordingly, he entombed her in this cow; while the mother cut off the hands of the attendants who had betrayed her daughter to the father: and even now these statues bear evidence of the punishment they underwent when alive. But I think all these things are mere fables, more especially that about the amputation of the hands: for I myself saw that the hands had dropped off in the lapse of time, and remained in 132 full view at the feet of the images, even in my day. This cow is covered with scarlet trappings: all but the head and neck, which she exhibits, covered with a very thick plate of gold[123]; between the two horns is placed a gold circle, the representation of the sun: the cow herself is not represented standing on her legs, but crouching on her knees: in size, the image is about that of a large living cow. It is carried every year out of the apartment where it is kept: at the time that the Egyptians beat their bosoms in honour of a deity whose name I must not mention here, then they bring out the cow into the light[124]: for it is said the princess, on her death-bed, requested her father, Mycerinus, to let her see the 133 sun once in every year. After the decease of his daughter, the following was the second misfortune that befel the monarch. An oracle was received from the city of Buto, announcing, that " he was to live six years only, and die in " the seventh." It is related, that the prince, vexed at this doom, sent to the oracle; and upbraided the deity, urging, that " his father and uncle had closed the temples, and " slighted the gods, but had enjoyed a long life, in spite of

[122] Matt. 579, 1; second parag.
[123] Matt. 441, 2, a.
[124] Matt. 419, 5.

" their oppressions; while he, though pious and religious,
" was to die so soon." There came, then, a second communication from the shrine; stating, " for that very reason his
" life was abridged, as he had acted contrary to what he
" ought to have done: for it was fated that Egypt should
" be oppressed with calamity during one hundred and fifty
" years; which the two preceding kings were aware of,
" whereas he himself was not." It is added, that Mycerinus
having received this intelligence, and seeing that his fate
was already decided[225], ordered a vast number of lamps to
be made, which he lighted up whenever night came; during
which he drank and enjoyed himself, never ceasing night nor
day, and travelled over the marshes, the groves, and all
places where he ascertained voluptuousness might be gratified. This mode of acting was devised by the king, for the
purpose of convicting the oracle of falsehood; because, by
changing night into day, he should gain twelve years in the
place of three[226].

This king also left a pyramid; greatly inferior, however, in size to that of his father[227], being twenty feet less than three plethra on each side: it is of a quadrangular form, and built half-way up of Ethiopian stone. Some Hellenes assert, falsely, that this pyramid is that of Rhodopis the harlot: these persons are evidently to me quite ignorant who Rhodopis was; otherwise they could not have attributed to her the erection of such a pyramid as this, on which, to use such an expression, thousands of talents innumerable were expended: moreover, Rhodopis flourished in the reign of Amasis, and not at the epoch we are now alluding to: for she was very many years posterior to the kings that left these monuments: by birth, she was a Thracian, a fellow-slave with Æsop the fabulist[228], in the service of Iadmon, the son of Hephæstopolis, a Samian. For Æsop, there can be no doubt, belonged to Iadmon; a fact clearly proved by this circumstance: the Delphians, according to the behest of the oracle, had frequently applied, by herald, for information, " who would claim satisfaction for Æsop's life;" nobody appeared, but the son of Iadmon's son, another Iadmon, who took the fine: therefore Æsop must have been the property of Iadmon[229]. Rhodopis arrived in Egypt, under the con-

[225] Matt. 568.
[226] Matt. 562, 1.
[227] Matt. 397, a, obs.
[228] Matt. 453.
[229] Crœsus sent Æsop to Delphi with a great quantity of gold, in order to offer a magnificent sacrifice to the god, and to distribute to each citizen four minæ. Having, it would seem, some dispute with the Delphians, he performed the sacrifice, but sent the money back again to

duct of a Samian, called Xanthus: she came there to exercise her profession; but was ransomed by a native of Mitylene, Charaxus, the son of Scamandronymus, and brother of Sappho the poetess. Thus Rhodopis was set at liberty, and stayed in Egypt; and, being much sought after, amassed great wealth for a woman of that class, but, at all events, not enough to erect such a pyramid[220]: any one who wishes, may see, to this day, what the tithe of her property amounted to, and would not attribute to her such immense wealth: for Rhodopis, anxious to leave in Hellas a monument of herself, had the following articles made; which she dedicated at Delphi, as a memorial; such as it never occurred indeed to any individual to think of, and present in the temple. Out of the tenth of her whole property, therefore, she made as many iron spits to roast oxen upon, as were equivalent to the tenth of her possessions, and sent them to Delphi. They still lie, in a heap, behind the altar erected by the Chians, opposite the temple.—The harlots of Naucratis are generally very fascinating: for, in the first instance, this woman made herself so famous, that the name of Rhodopis became familiar to all the Hellenes. The second example, subsequently to Rhodopis, was given by a harlot called Archidice, celebrated throughout Hellas, but less notorious than the other.—Charaxus, after having ransomed Rhodopis, returned to Mitylene; and was often the subject of Sappho's gibes, in her verses.—But I will say no more about Rhodopis.

136   Next to Mycerinus, the priests mention, as his successor on the throne of Egypt, Asychis, who erected the eastern porch of Vulcan's temple, which is by far the largest and most beautiful. Each of the porches is covered with engraved figures, and vast numbers of architectural ornaments; but this one more abundantly than the rest. In the reign of this king, it is said, the circulation of money was so straitened, that a law was instituted by the Egyptians, that

---

Sardis, deeming the inhabitants unworthy of the prince's munificence. The Delphians, urged by anger, unanimously accused him of sacrilege; and put him to death, by dashing him from the rock Hyampæus. The god of Delphi, offended at such a deed, made their lands to be barren, and sent them all manner of dire diseases. Wishing to stay the scourge, they proclaimed at the different festivals of Greece, that if any one could be found to demand satisfaction for the death of Æsop, they would grant it him. In the third generation, a native of Samos presented himself, named Idmon [the same with the Iadmon of Herodotus]: he was no relation to Æsop, but one of the descendants of those who had purchased him at Samos. They of Delphi made some satisfaction to him, and so were delivered from the calamities with which they had been afflicted.—*Larcher's trans. from Plutarch.*

[220] Matt. 453.

to redeem a debt, the person that owed the money was to pledge the dead body of his father: to this law was appended another, that the creditor should have the power of seizing the whole of the sepulchral deposits belonging to the debtor. He who, after giving this pledge, failed to cancel the debt, was subjected to the following punishment: he was not himself to receive burial at death, whether in the family sepulchre or any other; neither was any of his posterity to be deposited in a tomb. Asychi, ambitious of surpassing his predecessors, left, as a monument of himself, a pyramid composed of bricks, with an inscription carved on stone, running as follows: " Despise me not in comparison " with the stone pyramids, for I exceed them as much as " Jove does the other gods. They plunged a pole into the " lake[221]; and collecting what silt adhered to the pole, made " of it bricks, and built me in that manner."—Such was the work of this prince.

Next to him, I was informed, ruled a blind man belonging to the town of Anysis; and himself called Anysis. Under his reign, Sabacus the Ethiopian king, followed by a mighty force of Ethiopians, invaded Egypt: accordingly, the blind prince took refuge in the marshes, while the Ethiopian extended his sway over Egypt during fifty years; and, while he held the power, performed the following actions. Whenever any Egyptian was found guilty of a crime, Sabacus would not have him put to death; but, in proportion to the magnitude of the offence, adjudged each to labour at throwing up a mound before the city to which the culprit might belong. By this means, the towns were raised to a still higher level than before; for under king Sesostris, the prisoners of war, who dug the canals, had already thrown up mounds about the cities; and under the Ethiopian prince, these were elevated to a much greater height. Although every town in Egypt now lies high, the most extensive mounds must have been, I think, made about Bubastis, a city which possesses a temple of Bubastis, well deserving to be mentioned: other temples may be larger and more sumptuous, but none is more grateful to the eye. Bubastis is an Egyptian word, answering to Diana. This holy precinct may be thus described. With the exception of the road leading to it, the situation is a complete island; for two canals from the Nile running inland, without mingling their waters, extend each to the entrance: one flows around this

---

[221] *ὑποτίσσων* signifies " to put something flat under another, in order to raise it." *Larcher*. Literally, " for placing a pole under *the mud* in the lake, all the mud that stuck to it, that," &c.

side, the other that: each is one hundred feet in breadth, and shaded with trees. The quadrangle before the temple is ten orgyæ in height; and decorated with beautiful figures, six cubits high. As the sacred precinct stands in the centre of the town, it is visible on every side, from top to bottom, when you go round it; for the town itself having been raised considerably above the old level, by means of the works thrown up, while the temple remained untouched, it is still conspicuous as when first built: a wall runs all round the precinct, covered with figures cut in the stone. In the inside is seen a grove of very large trees, growing round an extensive temple, where the divine image stands. The dimensions of the holy precinct, both length and breadth, are five stades: near the entrance is a causeway of stone, about three stades long, leading through the public square, eastward: the breadth of this causeway is four plethra: on both sides of the road which takes to the temple of Mercury 139 lofty trees are planted. Such, then, is this precinct. The final departure of the Ethiopian prince is thus described by the priests: they say that he saw a vision of the following nature in his sleep: he fancied he beheld a man standing over him, who admonished him to collect all the priests in Egypt, and cut them down the middle. Sabacus having had this dream, said that he regarded it as a suggestion sent him by the gods, in order that he should attack the religious rites, and thereby draw upon himself some calamity at the hands of the gods or men. He determined not to act so, but to take his departure from the country; as the period during which he was fated to rule over Egypt was gone by: for before he quitted Ethiopia, the oracle frequented by the Ethiopians declared that he was to reign over Egypt fifty years. As, therefore, that time was come, and he was alarmed at his dream, he, of his own accord, withdrew from 140 Egypt. After the departure of Sabacus from Egypt, the blind king resumed the authority; and came forth from the morasses, where, during a sojourn of fifty years, he had formed an island of ashes and earth: for the Egyptians being wont to come to him with provisions according to what was imposed on each individual, unknown to the Ethiopian[222], Anysis commanded them to bring with the tribute a certain quantity of ashes, as a present. Prior to Amyrtæus, nobody was able to find out this island: during more than seven centuries the predecessors of Amyrtæus

---

[222] Th. Magist. explains this very ταῦτα (Ἡρόδοτος) τὸ σιγῇ ἀντὶ τοῦ ἀγνοίᾳ. well, at the word σιγῇ. Τίθεται δὲ ὑπ. Larcher.

were unable to ascertain where it lay. The name of this island is Elbo: its extent, in every direction, is ten stades.

Next to this last, it was stated, that a priest of Vulcan 141 ascended the throne: his name was Sethon: he neglected, and held in no account, the fighting caste of the Egyptians, not feeling any necessity of their services. In consequence, he took various opportunities of inflicting disgraces on these people; and, among other things, he deprived them of their lands, which had been picked out and given them by his predecessors, to the amount of twelve acres [233] every man. A short time after, Senacherib, king of the Arabians and Assyrians, led a mighty host against Egypt; in this emergency, the Egyptian warriors would not come forward: but the priest, thus beset with difficulties, entered the temple, and, in front of the sacred image, poured forth his wailings at the danger he was exposed to. After making this complaint, sleep came upon him, and in a vision he fancied the deity was standing by and cheering him, assuring him that he should suffer no discomfiture in facing the Arabian host; for he himself would send assistants to him. Trusting to this dream, the king took such of the Egyptians as chose to follow him, and encamped with his troops at Pelusium, where the entrance into Egypt lay. Not one of the warrior caste, however, joined him: his army consisted of trades-people, mechanics, and market-people. Having arrived at the above place, the field-mice poured in legions against the foe during the night, and devoured the quivers and the bows of the enemy, together with the shield-thongs; so that, on the following day, a multitude of the invading troops, reft of their arms, fell in their flight. And even to this day the stone image of this king stands in Vulcan's temple, with a mouse in his hand, saying, as is shewn by the inscription, " Let " him that looks at me, pay homage to the gods [234]."

Up to this portion of our history, the Egyptians, as well 142 as the priests, shew that the time elapsed from the first king to the death and end of the reign of this priest of Vulcan

---

[233] The ἄρουρα is a land-measure, equal to 100 Egyptian πήχυς. Schneid. Lex. Constr. (ἔλεγον αὐτὸν) ἀτέλειαν τὰς ἀρούρας σφίας. (see Matt. 412, 5.) τῶν (ἔλεγον) ἀρούρας δίδοσθαι ἐπὶ τῶν προτέρων βασιλέων δυώδεκα ἀρούρας.

[234] λέγων διὰ γραμμάτων, means that there was on the statue an inscription, importing &c. The verb λέγων is frequently used with γράμματα, thus, τὰ γράμματα ἔλεγε τάδε, γράμματα λέγοντα τάδε: and many other instances might be produced. I should not have thought it necessary to make this explanation, had I not seen in one of the published translations of Herodotus, that the above is rendered, " and these words issuing from his mouth." It would be highly impertinent to enter into any long disquisition to prove that words cannot issue from the mouth of a marble statue, particularly as Herodotus says no such thing.

was three hundred and forty-one generations of men, and during these generations were as many hierarchs and kings. Now, three hundred generations of men are equal to ten thousand years; for three generations of men amount to one hundred years; and the forty-one generations, still remaining over and above the three hundred, make one thousand three hundred and forty years: thus, in eleven thousand years, together with the addition of three hundred and forty, according to their assertion, no god assumed the human form; neither, said they, had such a thing happened before, nor after, among the other kings of Egypt. But during this period, they asserted, that four times the sun had risen out of his usual seats: and that twice he rose where he now sets, and twice he set where he now rises [235]. They add, that, in consequence of these revolutions, no alterations in regard of Egypt, whether land or river, occurred: nor likewise with respect to diseases, or the things pertaining to death. In former days, Hecatæus the Historian, being at Thebes, was rehearsing his genealogy, and connecting his family with some god in the sixteenth remove: but the priests of Jupiter behaved to him as they did to myself, although I did not mention my genealogy; they took me into the interior of the edifice, which is of considerable extent, and reckoned up, one by one, accurately, a number of wooden colossuses which they shewed me: for every high priest there sets up the image of himself in his lifetime: after reckoning the whole series, and shewing them to me, they proved that every one was the son of his predecessor, commencing at the image of the last deceased, and proceeding along the line till they had got through the whole. When Hecatæus, as I said before, reckoned up his ancestors, and connected them with some god in the sixteenth generation, the priests objected to him the genealogies of their hierarchs, whom they enumerated [236], without admitting in the list that any man was ever sprung from a god: but described their genealogical table in this manner; saying, that each of the colossuses was a Piromis, born of a Piromis, until they had pointed to four hundred and forty-five colossuses Piromis, sons of Piromis, and connected the line with no god or hero. Piromis is an Egyptian word, that means ' a noble and good

---

[235] Three hundred and forty-one. See chap. 142.

[236] ἐπὶ τῇ ἀριθμήσει. Postquam omnes enumeraverant. *Schweig.* Dont ils lui firent l'énumération. *Larcher.* It would be the height of presumption not to bow to such authorities; otherwise I should have taken ἐπὶ in the sense of, *with regard to*: they opposed his genealogy in regard to number, *i. e.* they reckoned up three hundred and forty-five for Hecatæus's sixteen.

man.' Thus, accordingly, the priests proved to me that all 144
those belonging to these images were far from any thing like
a god; but that, prior to these men, Egypt had had the gods
for its rulers, who resided among men; and one of whom
was always invested with the supreme power. The last, they
asserted, that ruled over Egypt, was the son of Osiris, Orus,
the Egyptian name for Apollo: this god deposed Typhon,
and was the last of the immortal beings that reigned in
Egypt. Osiris is the Egyptian for Bacchus.

Among the Hellenes, the most modern of the gods are 145
held to be Hercules, and Bacchus, and Pan. With the
Egyptians, Pan is regarded as extremely ancient, and one of
the eight gods called original; Hercules is said to belong
to the second gods, called the twelve gods; and Bacchus to
the third, sprung from the twelve [227]. I have stated above,
how many years the Egyptians say have intervened from
Hercules to the reign of Amasis [228]: it is said, that in the
case of Pan the number of years was still greater: the
least of all Bacchus, from whom, down to king Amasis, they
reckon fifteen thousand years. All the above dates the
Egyptians profess to know exactly, having at all times kept
an account, and registered the years. From my time, therefore, to that when Bacchus, it is said, was born of Semele,
Cadmus's daughter, is about one thousand six hundred
years: to Hercules, born of Alcmena, nine hundred years:
to Pan, born of Penelope (the Hellenes give to her and
Mercury the title of parents to Pan), the years are not so
many as to the beginning of the Trojan war; that is to say,
about eight hundred years at my time. Of these two sys- 146
tems, every one is at liberty to adopt that of either nation
to whom he gives the greater credit: I have therefore put
down what my own opinion on these matters is; for if these
gods had been known in Hellas, and had lived to old age in
that country, I mean Hercules, begotten of Amphitryon,
and especially Bacchus the son of Semele, and Pan, borne

---

[227] In c. 43, Schweighæuser observes, that λωί τι ἐκ τῶν ἐπτὰ θιῶν οἱ δωδικα θιοὶ ἐγίνοντο cannot signify, as Larcher has, "those twelve gods that were born of the eight gods;" and remarks, at the same time, that Jablonski properly observes, that the Egyptians added, in succeeding times, four deities to the eight which they originally worshipped. Schweighæuser has therefore translated in the above case, "postquam ex primis octo diis exstiterunt illi duodecim." It strikes me as indubitable, that the same reasoning applies to the passage, Διόνυσος δέ, τῶν τρίτων, οἱ ἐκ τῶν δυώδικα θιῶν ἐγίνοντο. I have in consequence ventured to deviate from Schweighæuser, whose version gives "qui a duodecim diis generati sunt."

[228] Matt. 390, c. See chap. 43.

by Penelope, any one might say, that, although they were mortal men, they bore the names of the gods long extant before their time. Now the Hellenes affirm, that Bacchus, immediately after his first coming into existence, was sewed up in Jupiter's thigh, and conveyed by that god to Nysa, a place in Ethiopia, situate above Egypt: as to Pan, they do not pretend even to say whither he was taken to at his birth. Hence, therefore, I have come to the conclusion, that the Hellenes obtained information of their names some time after those of the rest of the gods; and that from that epocha the Hellenes reckon by the genealogies the dates of the births of these gods[239]. This accordingly is agreeable to what the Egyptians themselves say[240].

147 What both the Egyptians and other nations agree to have occurred in this country, will be the subject-matter of the following part of this History; to which will be added some things from my own personal observation. The Egyptians having become independent, after the reign of the priest of Vulcan, established (for they could not live a moment without a king) twelve kings, and divided Egypt into twelve parts. These twelve kings connected themselves by intermarriages, and entered into the following stipulations; that they should not destroy the kingdoms of one another, nor should any one endeavour to get more than another, and that they should all keep on the most friendly terms: the reason which induced them to adopt the above resolutions

---

[239] The question considered by Herodotus in this chapter is, "Whether did the Greeks receive their gods from the Egyptians, or not?" This some affirmed, and others denied: hence the ἀμφότερα, "the two opinions," he alludes to. Herodotus is of opinion, that the "Greeks took their gods from the Egyptians:" which he endeavours to prove by the following line of argument.—No one can deny but that the *gods* Hercules, Bacchus, and Pan, are much more ancient than the *men* bearing their names, who were born in Greece, and are worshipped by the Grecians among the gods. Now, if in ancient times there had been known to the Grecians any Hercules, Bacchus, or Pan, real *gods*, who had reigned among them, then indeed such as affirm those gods to be of Grecian, and not Egyptian origin, might allege that the other Hercules, Bacchus, and Pan, had succeeded them in name and in honours; but, on the contrary, the Grecians know of no Hercules more ancient than the son of Alcmena: and with respect to Bacchus and Pan, not only are the original ones unknown to them, but they are not sufficiently acquainted with the latter ones. Hence it is fair to infer, that the names and worship of Hercules, Bacchus, and Pan, were not known among the Grecians till about the time when the *men* who bore those names took birth. —*Schweig*.

[240] Ταῦτα μὲν νυν αὐτοὶ Αἰγύπτιοι λέγουσι, "These things accordingly the Egyptians themselves say;" that is to say, all that he has mentioned respecting the three orders of gods who ruled over Egypt before the sceptre fell into the hands of men; as likewise the account he has given of the ancient kings of the human race.—*Schweig*.

among one another, was, to fortify themselves strongly. At the very beginning of their accession to the different governments, it was declared by the oracle, " that, of the " twelve, he who should in Vulcan's temple make a libation " from a brazen cup would be king of all Egypt;" for they were wont to hold general assemblies at all the temples. Accordingly, they determined upon leaving, in common, a monument of themselves; and, agreeably to that resolution, caused a labyrinth to be built a little above the lake of Mœris, and not far from the town called the City of the Crocodiles. This edifice, which exceeds all powers of description, I have myself seen; for it is such, that if one could collect together all the Hellenic edifices, all the works they have wrought, the collection would be evidently inferior, as respects the labour employed, and the expense incurred. The temple of Ephesus is undoubtedly magnificent, and so is that at Samos: the Pyramids likewise were noble structures, each equal to many of the mighty works achieved by the Hellenes put together: but the labyrinth beats the Pyramids themselves. The labyrinth consists of twelve court-yards, surrounded by piazzas; two opposite doors constitute the entrances, six looking to the north, six to the south, all in line: one and the same wall on the outside closes in the twelve courts. In the interior are two sorts of rooms, those underground, and those above, the latter raised upon the former: they are three thousand in number, fifteen hundred of each kind. I myself passed therefore through, and saw the upper apartments, which I describe from ocular inspection. I was obliged, however, to confine my acquaintance with the subterranean parts to the information I could get by inquiry; for the Egyptians appointed over the labyrinth would not shew me these apartments by any means, alleging, that in those places were deposited the relics of the monarchs who erected the edifice, and those of the sacred crocodiles. Thus what I say of the lower apartments is taken from hearsay; but all about the upper parts is from actual observation, and I consider them the noblest works of men: for the passages leading out through the piazzas, and the paths across the courts, so varied in their windings, present very many wonders to those that pass by the court to the chambers, and from the chambers to the porches, and from the porches to other piazzas, and other courts from the chambers: all these have a roof of stone: the walls are of the same materials, but full of carved figures. Round every court-yard is a colonnade of white stones, nicely joined. At the extremity of the labyrinth rises a pyramid, forty orgyæ high, on which some gigantic figures are carved: the way into this pyramid is by a subterranean passage[241].

149 A still greater wonder than this labyrinth even is seen in its vicinity: I mean the lake of Mœris; the circuit of which comprises three thousand six hundred stades, or sixty schœnes, a number equal to the length of Egypt on the seaside. This lake stretches, in its length, from north to south; its depth, where it is deepest, is forty orgyæ: there can be no doubt that it was excavated by hand; for about the middle stands two pyramids, each rising fifty orgyæ above the surface of the water, with a foundation to the same depth under water: on both is placed a stone colossus, seated on a throne. These pyramids have therefore one hundred orgyæ in total height, which are exactly equal to one stade of six plethra; for the orgya measures six feet or four cubits, each foot being equal to four palms, and the cubit to six. The waters of this lake are not the spontaneous produce of the soil, which is particularly dry in this quarter: they come from the Nile by means of a canal; and flow six months from the Nile into the lake, and six months from the lake into the Nile: during the six months from the time that the stream begins to flow out, the lake brings in to the royal exchequer one silver talent daily, on the fish; but at the other times, the daily contribution is only twenty minæ.

150 The people belonging to that country told me, also, that this lake discharges its waters into the Libyan Syrtis, by an underground tunnel[242], running westward into the interior, along the mountain above Memphis. As no mound was to be seen resulting from this excavation, a fact which struck me forcibly, I inquired of the people that reside nearest to the borders of the lake where the ground thrown up was to be found: they informed me, that it was carried away; and I readily gave credit to them: for I had heard that in

---

[241] The following explanation of the different parts of the labyrinth is taken partly from Larcher, and partly from Wyttenbach:—

1. αὐλαὶ κατάστεγαι are not covered courts, but courts enclosed with walls. Those courts were surrounded with a peristyle or colonnade of white marble, αὐλὰ δὴ ἑκάστη, στερίσυλος, λίθου λευκοῦ ἁρμοσμένου τὰ μάλιστα.

2. There were twelve ranges of buildings, the same number as of courts. These buildings Herodotus calls αἱ στέγαι.—The ταῦταῖς and ἴλυγμοὶ were parts of the αὐλή: the οἰκήματα and ἐξόδοι were parts of the στέγη.

3. The ἴλυγμοὶ were winding passages, leading out of the court, or αὐλὴ, to the

4. παστάδες, or vestibules of the στέγαι, from which one passed into the

5. οἰκήματα, or apartments; through which ran the

6. ἔξοδοι, or straight passages, leading again to the αὐλαὶ, or courts.

Lastly, ἰροφὴ δὲ πάντων λιθίνη must be referred to εἰσηγμένων, immediately preceding.

[242] Matt. 596, a.

Niniveh, the Assyrian town, a similar thing had taken place. Some thieves determined to make an attempt to carry off the riches of Sardanapalus, king of Niniveh, which were considerable, and deposited in underground treasuries: they accordingly commenced in their own houses, and opened a mine leading direct to the palace: every night they conveyed away the mould proceeding from the excavation, and cast it into the river Tigris, which passes by the city of Niniveh; and this they continued to do, until they had compassed their object. I now heard a similar account respecting the excavation of the Egyptian lake; with the exception, that it took place by day, and not by night: for the Egyptians, after making their excavations, carried the matters thrown up to the Nile, which seized the deposit, and presently dispersed it abroad. Such, therefore, was the manner in which this lake, it is reported, was dug out.

The twelve kings, however, conducted their governments with justice, until the time when they met to offer sacrifice in Vulcan's temple: on the last day of the festival, as they were about to make libations, the high priest brought them golden beakers, which they were wont to use in this ceremony, but made a mistake in the number, bringing eleven only for the twelve. Thereupon Psammitichus, who stood last of all, seeing that he had no beaker, doffed his brazen helmet, stretched it out to receive the wine, and made his libation: all the rest of the kings wore helmets, and at this time had them on. Psammitichus accordingly stretched out his helmet with no sinister motive; but the rest took into consideration what Psammitichus had done, and how the oracle pronounced to them that he who should make a libation from a brass beaker would be sole king of Egypt: reminded of the oracle, however, they could not, in justice, decree death to Psammitichus, being convinced, on their inquiry, that the deed was not purposely committed; but decided to banish him to the marshes, after divesting him of the greatest part of his power. It was added, also, that he should never come out of the marshes, to have any communication with the rest of Egypt. This Psammitichus had fled into Syria previous to the retreat of Sabacus the Ethiopian, who had put to death his father Neco; and, after the Ethiopian, in consequence of his dream, had withdrawn from the throne, was brought back by the Egyptians belonging to the Saïtic nome. Some time after, being appointed one of the kings, he was thus once more compelled, by the eleven kings, to fly to the marshes[243]. Feeling, therefore, that he had been wronged by his colleagues, he contemplated revenge on his persecutors; and sent to the shrine of Latona at Buto, where the most veracious oracles are received by the Egyptians. The answer of the oracle was, that vengeance would come when men of brass appeared rising from the sea: but Psammitichus was loth to give credit to brass men ever being his coadjutors. Not long after, however, some Ionians and Carians, who had embarked for purposes of piracy, compelled by necessity to bear away for Egypt, came on shore, clad in brass armour: an Egyptian (who had never before beheld men accoutred in brass) went to Psammitichus in the marshes, and reported, that some brass men had come from the sea, and were plundering the country. Psammitichus, seeing that the oracle was thus fulfilled, made friends with the Ionians and Carians; and having recourse to great promises, brought them over to join with him. Having effected this, he accordingly, with such Egyptians as volunteered in his service, and these auxiliaries, dethroned the eleven kings.

153 Psammitichus having reduced all Egypt under his dominion, erected the porch of Vulcan at Memphis which looks to the south; and built for Apis a court, where he is fed whenever he appears: it stands opposite the porch, is surrounded with a piazza, and covered with emblems: colossal statues, twelve cubits high, instead of pillars, support the
154 piazza of the court. This prince gave to the Ionians, and those who had assisted him, some lands to occupy, on opposite banks of the Nile: to these two tracts of land he assigned the names of camps; and, accordingly, not only presented them with land for their subsistence, but fulfilled all the other promises he had made them. Among other things, especially, he entrusted to the care of these aliens some of the sons of the Egyptians, to be taught the Hellenic tongue; and from these pupils descend the present interpreters in Egypt. The Ionians and Carians remained for a long time in those quarters, which extend along the seashore, a short distance below the city of Bubastis, on the Pelusiac mouth, as it is called, of the Nile. These colonists were subsequently transferred from hence, and settled at

---

[243] Construction: τὸ δίδυμον φυγεῖν ἐς τὰ ἕλεα καταλαμβάνει μιν πρὸς τῶν ἰνδίκα βασιλέων διὰ τὴν κυνέην. The expression, καταλαμβάνει τινα ποιεῖν, or πάσχειν τοῦτο, and similar instances, are frequent in Herodotus: " it befals or happens to so and so, to do or to suffer so and so." See *Schweig. Lex. Herod.*

Memphis, where they served as a body-guard to king Amasis against the Egyptians. From the period of the settlement of these people in Egypt, the Hellenes have kept up with them such a close connexion, that we know for certain, beginning from the reign of Psammitichus, every occurrence that has since taken place in Egypt; for these Ionians and Carians are the first persons speaking a foreign tongue that settled in Egypt. Down to my day, the dock for ships, and the ruins of houses, were still seen in the country, from whence they were transplanted. Such was therefore the manner in which Psammitichus obtained possession of Egypt.

I have already made frequent mention of the Egyptian oracle[241]; but shall here extend my remarks on this subject; for it well deserves distinction. The holy precinct of Latona, situate in a large town, presents itself to your view, when you sail up from the sea by the mouth called the Lebennytic mouth of the Nile: the name of the city, where this shrine stands, is Buto, as I have before observed. Within this city are seen not only the precincts sacred to Apollo and Diana, but the temple likewise of Latona, in which, accordingly, the oracle is located: it is of considerable extent, and the front portico rises to the height of ten orgyæ: but what struck me as the most marvellous of all, that was to be seen at this place, was, the temple of Latona itself, made, length and height, of one single block of stone: the sides are all equal, each dimension measuring forty cubits: the roof consists of another flat stone, the eaves of which project beyond the walls, on every side, by four cubits. This edifice, therefore, is the most admirable of all the things that are to be seen about this precinct: the next to this is an island called Chemmis: it lies in a deep and broad lake, close by the holy precinct in Buto, and is said by the Egyptians to float. I myself, however, never saw it swim or move, and was struck with astonishment when I heard of the existence of floating islands. In this one, accordingly, is seen a large temple of Apollo: here, also, three altars have been erected: palm-trees grow in abundance in this island, as well as many other fruit-bearing and forest trees. The Egyptians give the following explanation of the floating properties of this island: that Latona, one of the eight gods first existent, and who resided at Buto, where her oracle stands, saved Apollo, whom she had received from Isis as a sacred deposit, by concealing him in this island, now said to float, but in early days known to be fixed. This happened at the time that Typhon,

---

[241] Chapp. 59; 83; 133.

searching on all sides, came in the expectation of finding the son of Osiris. For the Egyptians assert, that Apollo and Diana were the offspring of Bacchus and Isis, and that Latona was their nurse and saviour: for Orus is the Egyptian for Apollo, and Isis for Ceres, and Bubastis for Diana. From this tradition, and none other, Æschylus the son of Euphorion adopted the following tenet, in which he is singular among the earlier poets; that Diana is the daughter of Ceres[245]. In consequence of the event described above, this island was made to float. Such is the account the Egyptians give.

157 Psammitichus occupied the throne of Egypt fifty-four years; during twenty-nine of which, that prince besieged Azotus, a large town in Syria, which he at last captured. This town of Azotus is that, which, of all we know, stood the
158 most protracted siege. Necos was a son of Psammitichus, and succeeded to the throne of Egypt. This prince was the first that began the canal leading to the Erythræan sea; an undertaking which Darius the Persian, in later times, continued. The length of this cut is a voyage of four days: its breadth is made such, that two triremes may pull abreast: the waters that feed this canal come from the Nile: it begins a little above the city of Bubastis, and ends in the Erythræan sea, not far from the Arabian town of Patumos. This work was dug first through the parts of the Egyptian plain that are contiguous to Arabia: above the plain rises the mountain that stretches down to Memphis, in which the quarries are. Accordingly, at the foot of this mountain the canal takes a long reach, from the west to the east; then stretches to the defiles; from whence, taking its course towards the south, it proceeds to the Gulf of Arabia: The shortest way from the Mediterranean sea, to the southern, called also the Erythræan, is from Mount Casius, the frontier of Egypt and Syria, whence to the Gulf of Arabia is one thousand stades: the above is the most direct road; but the canal is considerably longer, inasmuch as it is more winding. One hundred and ten thousand Egyptian delvers perished on this undertaking, during Necos's reign: that prince, therefore, ceased in the middle of the work, in consequence of an oracle, that came warning him that "he was working for an alien;" for the Egyptians call every body aliens who do not use the
159 same language as themselves. But Necos having put a stop to his excavations, turned his attention to war: triremes

---

[245] Herodotus, it is probable, alludes to some piece of the tragic poet which time has withdrawn from the admiration of the world.

were constructed; some on the shore of the Mediterranean; others on the gulf of Arabia, which is a part of the Erythræan sea: the docks for the ships are still seen: these fleets were ready for use whenever required. Necos engaged by land the Syrian forces near[246] Magdolus, and conquered: after the battle, he took Cadytis, a large city of Syria. The garb worn by the king in these achievements was sent to Branchidæ in Milesia, and dedicated to Apollo. He died sometime after, having reigned, in all, sixteen years; and bequeathed the throne to his son Psammis.

Under the reign of Psammis, a deputation from the people 160 of Elis arrived; boasting that they had established the Olympic lists on the most equitable and fairest principles[247] in the world; and fancying that the Egyptians, the wisest of mankind, would be unable to devise any thing better. The deputies of Elis, on their arrival in Egypt, explained for what purpose they had come: in consequence, the king convened those esteemed the wisest of the Egyptians. The assembly met, and heard the ambassadors describe all the regulations respecting the lists which they had thought proper to make: after explaining every particular, the Eleans declared they had come to ascertain, " whether the Egyptians " could devise any improvement in these institutes." The Egyptians held council; and asked the Eleans, whether their fellow-citizens were allowed to contend in the games: the deputies made answer, that the lists were open to any of themselves or the Hellenes, who chose. In consequence, the Egyptians observed: " that, enacting such rules, they swerved " wide of every thing like justice: for it could not be " otherwise than that they would give the preference to " their own citizen, and so do an injustice to a stranger; " but that if they really wished to found just laws, they would " advise them to institute the games for candidates of other " cities, and exclude from the list every citizen of Elis." Such was the admonition the Egyptians ministered to the people of Elis.

Psammis, having reigned alone six years, died imme- 161 diately after an attack on Ethiopia: he was succeeded by his son Apries, who, next to his great-grandfather, Psammitichus, was the most prosperous of former sovereigns, during a reign of five-and-twenty years; in the course of which he marched his army against Sidon, and engaged the Tyrian king by sea. As he was, however, doomed to be visited with calamity, this came to pass on an occasion that I shall

---

[246] Matt. 577. [247] Matt. 446.

describe more largely in my Libyan History, but shall now touch lightly upon. Apries having sent an expedition against the Cyrenæans, met with a sore defeat. The Egyptians attributing the blame to the king, rebelled against him; being convinced that Apries, in furtherance of his own views, had sent them to evident destruction, in order that such a destruction of them should take place, as would enable him to reign undisturbed over the rest of the nation. Highly exasperated at this, the men that escaped from the

162 rout, and the friends of the slain, openly rebelled. Apries, informed of what had occurred, sent Amasis to the insurgents, who was to repress the sedition by persuasives. On his arrival, he endeavoured to appease the Egyptians, exhorting them not to behave in that manner; when one of the insurgents, standing behind him, put an helmet on the speaker's head, saying, " that he crowned him as their king[248]:" this was not very repugnant to the wishes of Amasis himself, as he plainly shewed; for the insurgents having appointed him king of the Egyptians, he prepared to march against Apries. But Apries, informed of his intention, despatched Patarbemis, one of his suite, and a man of great repute, with orders to bring before him Amasis alive. At the arrival of Patarbemis, he called Amasis; but Amasis (who happened to be then mounted) lifted up his thigh, and broke wind, and bade the messenger take that back to Apries: nevertheless, as Patarbemis begged him to come before the king, who had sent for him, Amasis answered him thus: "He had "long been preparing to do that very thing; and that Apries "should have no cause to blame him, for he would forthwith "make his appearance, bringing others in his train." Patarbemis, fully apprised of the intention of Amasis, both from what had been said, and the preparations he himself saw making, hastened to take his departure, for the purpose of communicating, as speedily as possible, to the king, tidings of what was going on: but, as he presented himself before Apries unaccompanied by Amasis, the king, without taking time to deliberate, and excited by anger, ordered the ears and nose of Patarbemis to be cut off. The rest of the Egyptians who still adhered to the king's cause, witnesses of the shameful treatment of so distinguished a fellow-citizen, hesitated not an instant, but forthwith went over to the

163 insurgents, and gave their allegiance to Amasis. Apries,

---

[248] The helmet was, in Egypt, the mark of sovereign power. See c. 151, ἐπὶ βασιλήϊ, " to put him in possession of the crown." The examples of ἐπὶ, in this sense, are very frequent: ἐπὶ βλάβῃ, " nocendi causâ, to injure."—*Larcher.* So ἐπὶ δηλήσει, i. 41; but see Matt. 585, β.

informed of this, placed his auxiliaries under arms, and led them against the Egyptians: his army amounted to thirty thousand auxiliaries, made up of Carians and Ionians; and his palace was in the city of Saïs, a vast and admirable structure. Apries' party took the field against the Egyptians, while that of Amasis marched against the auxiliaries: they both met near [249] the town of Momemphis, and prepared for the conflict.

The Egyptians are divided into seven classes: these are respectively called, priests, soldiers, herdsmen, swineherds, tradesmen, interpreters, pilots: such are the Egyptian classes: their names are derived from their professions. The military are called either Calasiries or Hermotybies: they belong to the following nomes—for the whole of Egypt is divided into nomes: the following are the nomes of the Hermotybies: Busirites, Saïtes, Chemmites, Papremites, the island of Prosopitis, the half of Natho: to the above nomes the Hermotybies belong: they amount at the highest to one hundred and sixty thousand: none of these is ever apprenticed to any handycraft, but all are devoted to war. The Calasires belong to the other following nomes: Thebais, Bubastites, Aphthites, Tanites, Mendesius, Sebennytes, Athribites, Pharbæthites, Thmuïtes; Onuphites, Anysius, Myecphorites—this nome consists of a part of the island lying off the city of Butis [250]: the above are the nomes to which the Calsires belong: they amount, at the highest, to two hundred and fifty thousand: none of these are allowed to apply to any trade, but to military pursuits alone; the son inheriting his father's calling. Whether the Hellenes borrowed this custom likewise from the Egyptians, is a question which I cannot describe for certain, inasmuch as I see Thracians, Scythians, Persians, Lydians, and nearly all foreigners, esteem as a lower class of their fellow-citizens such persons as profess any handycraft trade and transmit it to their posterity; while those who keep aloof from trade are esteemed noble; such, above all, as distinguish themselves in war. These principles are instilled among all the Hellenes, and the Lacedæmonians especially: the Corinthians are the people that shew the greatest respect for mechanics. With the exception of the priests, the military are the only Egyptians

---

[249] Matt. 577.

[250] In the text, "this nome is in an island," but as the nome occupies the whole of the island, I thought it better not to translate quite literally. The expression of the Historian is remarkable: "this nome dwells in an island," instead of " is situated in an island." This is an imitation of Homer, whom Herodotus always follows as his model in style. Il. ii. 625, οἳ δ᾽ ἄρ Δουλίχιον, 'Εχίνδων θ᾽ ἱεράων νήσων, αἳ ναίουσι πέρην ἁλός.—*Larcher*.

entitled to any privileges: to each of this class are awarded twelve choice arouras of ground: the aroura, throughout Egypt, is equal to one hundred cubits, the Egyptian cubit being the same as that of Samos: this privilege extended to all, without discrimination: the following perquisites, they participate in turn, never the same as before. One thousand Calasires, and the same number of Hermotybies, were appointed as body-guards every year to the king: to these, besides the lands above mentioned, the following largess was given every day; to each man, five minæ of roasted corn, two minæ of beef, four arysters of wine.

169 After the arrival of Apries near Momemphis, at the head of the auxiliaries, and Amasis at the head of all the Egyptians, the two parties engaged battle: the auxiliaries behaved gallantly: they were, however, far inferior in numbers, and consequently defeated. Apries is represented as being convinced that even a god might not dethrone him, so firmly did he conceive himself seated: but in this battle he was beaten: taken prisoner, he was conveyed back to Saïs, to his former palace, now that of Amasis: here, for some time, he was kept at the palace, and Amasis treated him very kindly: but at last, the Egyptians blaming Amasis for such unjust behaviour, in thus cherishing the greatest enemy both of themselves and himself, he delivered Apries up to them, who put him to death by strangulation, and then interred him in his paternal tombs. These receptacles are in Minerva's precinct, close to the temple, on the left hand as you enter: the Saïtæ are wont to bury all kings, born in their nome, within this precinct; for the monument of Amasis [251] is seen there at a greater distance from the temple than the tombs of Apries and his forefathers. In the sacred quadrangle stands a great hall, adorned with pillars made to imitate palm-trees, and decked with various embellishments: within the hall stands a niche, with folding-doors, within which is the 170 sepulchre [252]. At Saïs, also, is seen, in Minerva's precinct, the depository of one whose name I do not hold it lawful to mention in this matter: it stands behind the temple, and occupies the whole of that wall of the sacred building: large stone obelisks are found in the precinct; near which is a pond adorned with a border of stone-work; it is in shape circular, and, as far as I can judge, is about the size of that of Delos, 171 called the trochoïd. On this sheet of water the Egyptians

---

[251] Amasis belonged to the Saïtic nome: see c. 172.

[252] I have followed Larcher's translation, which Schweighæuser approves.

represent the adventures of him mentioned above [253]: this spectacle is called the mysteries, by the Egyptians; concerning which, although informed of every detail, I shall hold a decent silence; as well as what concerns the initiation of Ceres, called by the Hellenes the thesmophoria; which I am well acquainted with, but shall withhold describing, excepting so far as it may be lawful to speak of it [254]. It was the daughters of Danaus that imported this ceremony of the initiation, and communicated the same to the Pelasgian women: in subsequent times, the whole of the Peloponnesus being reft of its former occupants by the Dorians, these rites became extinct, except with the Arcadians, the only Peloponnesians that remained and preserved their remembrance.

Apries thus cut off, Amasis ascended the throne: he belonged to the Saïtic nome, and was a native of the town called Siuph. At first, accordingly, the Egyptians slighted Amasis, and held him in little account, as having been previously nothing but a private man, and of no very distinguished family: Amasis, however, soon brought them over [255] to him, by his skill and affability. Of the many precious things that he possessed, there was a golden foot-bason, in which Amasis himself, and all his guests, were wont to wash their feet: accordingly, he broke up this vase, had it converted into an image of the god, and set it up in the most prominent [256] part of the city. The Egyptians, crowding round the image, devoutly worshipped it. Amasis, hearing how the citizens acted, called a meeting of the Egyptians, and explained to them, " that the image had been made out of the " foot-bason in which the Egyptians were wont to vomit, to " make water, and to wash their feet; and now it had become " a special object of their adoration." He added, " that he

172

---

[253] That is to say, of him whose name Herodotus has just informed us he does not think himself at liberty to divulge.

[254] Herodotus is probably the first who made use of this expression, εὔστομα κεῖσθω, as most of those that have used it, add καὶ 'Ηρόδοτον, " to use the expression of Herodotus." The critics blamed the expression, and placed the mark X by the side of it, to shew that it was not to be imitated, because Hellanicus, in reading it, said εὔστομα ἴστω εὔστομα, without dividing the word, which then signifies " let these things be of good taste." Wesseling very properly doubts whether we ought to read εὔ στόμα in two words, as the grammarians would lead us to believe. Sophocles (Philoct. 201) writes it in the same manner as Herodotus; εὔστομα ἴσχι, παῖ, " be silent, son." The scholiast, who relates the joke of Hellanicus, says, τίθασιν οὕτω λέγων, ἀντὶ τοῦ σιῶπα. Larcher. The expression in Herodotus cannot, however, be resolved otherwise than by dividing the word εὔστομα, thus: περὶ τούτων (τὸ) στόμα μοι εὖ κείσθω, i. e. εὖ ἐχέτω. Schweig. Lex. Herod.

[255] προσάγεσθαι, " to bring to their duty," as in Plut. πολέμῳ προσάγεσθαι ἔθνη. Schweig.

[256] Lit. " fittest, most opportune." τῆς πόλεως ἴσον, see Matt. 357.

"himself now had undergone the same change as the foot-
"bason; for previously he was but a private man, whereas
"at present he was their king:" and he then proceeded to
exhort them to honour and respect him: in this manner he
173 brought the Egyptians to brook his rule. He adopted the
following arrangement in his affairs: from the dawn of day,
to the usual time when the public square is full of people[257],
he applied closely to the affairs brought before him: the
remainder of the day he passed drinking and joking with his
guests, throwing aside all thought, and abandoning himself
to fun and frolic[258]. His friends, displeased at this behaviour,
remonstrated with him, in these words: "My liege," said
they, "you do not hold restraint enough on yourself; and
"debase your rank by such levity. It behoves you to sit
"venerated on your venerated throne, and attend through
"the day to affairs: thus the Egyptians might be convinced
"they are ruled by a great man, and you yourself obtain
"more repute: your conduct now is in no manner kingly."
His answer to this was: "They who make use of bows are
"wont to brace them when they wish to shoot; but unbrace
"them, when they have done: for were the bow to remain
"constantly strung, it would surely snap; and so the archer
"would not be able to use it, in case of need. Such is the
"case with man: were he to be incessantly engaged in
"serious business, nor abandon himself sometimes to sport
"and pastime, he would gradually[259] become either mad or
"stupid: this I know, and allot, accordingly, a portion of
"my time to both." Such was the answer he returned to
174 his friends. Amasis is represented, when a private man,
as a giddy youth given to drink and mockery: when the
means failed him to drink and carouse, he went about pilfer-
ing. The persons who accused him of having their property, were wont, in consequence of his denial, to bring him
before the oracle that happened to be in their neighbourhood: in many instances, he was convicted by the oracles;
in others, he escaped: in consequence of this, when he came
to the throne, he acted in the following manner: of all
such gods as absolved him of theft, he neglected their tem-

---

[257] Dio Chrysost. de Gloriâ, Orat. lxvi. περὶ, 'sun-rise,' 'early in the morning;' περὶ πληθώραν ἀγορὰν, 'the middle of the morning,' that is to say, the third hour; τὰς μεσημβρίας, 'noon;' περὶ δείλην, 'the middle of the after-noon,' that is to say, 'the ninth hour of the day;' ἑσπέρα, 'the evening,' 'the sun-set.'—*Larcher*.

[258] εὐτραπέλων is said of a man that exercises the wit of a gentleman; μάταιος, of him whose jokes offend decency and good morals; εὐτραπέλων, 'witty;' μάταιος, 'smutty.' See Larcher and Valckenaer.

[259] On the use of λανθάνων with the participle, see Matt. 552. and Viger. c. v. sect. viii. reg. 3.

ples, and contributed nothing to their repairs; neither did he present sacrifice in them, considering them unworthy of any remuneration, and having false oracles: such as declared him guilty of theft, he attended to with the greatest care, as being truly gods, and proffering true answers.

In the temple of Minerva at Saïs, he erected[260] a wonderful 175 portico, far surpassing all, in height and size, as well as in the bulk and quality of the stones: he likewise dedicated, not only large colossuses and huge sphinxes[261], but also brought, to repair the sacred edifice, stone blocks of extraordinary dimensions: some of these he took from the quarries in the vicinity of Memphis; but the largest blocks of all came from Elephantine, a place twenty days' voyage from Saïs. But of all these masses, that which struck me with the greatest astonishment was a chamber brought from Elephantine, and hewn out of one single block of stone: this enormous mass occupied three years in its conveyance; two thousand men, all belonging to the caste of the pilots, being specially appointed for that purpose. The length of this chamber is, on the outside, twenty-one cubits; its breadth, fourteen; its height, eight. Such are the dimensions of this chamber, measured on the outside: in the inside, they are, in length, eighteen cubits; breadth, twelve; height, five. This stone chamber lies near the entrance into the precinct: the reason why it was not drawn into the sacred inclosure is stated to have been, that the architect, wearied by the labour, seeing what a long time had been taken up, breathed a sigh as the chamber moved forward[262]. Amasis, considering the 176 sigh ominous, forbad the stone to be drawn any further: but others say, that one of the workmen employed at the levers was crushed beneath the mass, and consequently the chamber was not moved any further. Amasis dedicated, in all the renowned temples, works of gigantic size: at[263] Memphis, in particular, he dedicated, in front of Vulcan's temple, a colossus, reclining on his back, seventy-five feet long: on the

---

[260] If the reading *d* is correct, it must be referred to τῇ Ἀθηναίῃ, being put pleonastically, as may be observed in different parts of our Historian. *Schweig.* There is in the text τοῦτο μὲν, corresponding to τοῦτο δὲ a little lower down; "on the one hand—on the other."

[261] Monstrous figures, which had the body of a lion and the face of a man. The Egyptian artists represented commonly the sphinx with the body of a lion and the face of a young woman.

[262] τὸν δὲ Ἀμασιν ἐνθυμεεῖν ποιησάμενον, which the Latin translator has rendered "id advertens Amasis."—That is not correct. Ἐνθυμεεῖν, or ἐνθύμιον ποιεῖσθαι, signifies " in religionem, in omen, vertere:" see Duker on Thucydides, vii. 18. *Larcher.*— ἐνθυμίῳ ποιεῖσθαι, Gall. " faire conscience de faire ou dire quelque chose." Æ. Port. Lex. Ion.

[263] On the repetition of ἐν, see Matt. 594, 1.

same base [204] stand two colossuses of Ethiopian stone, each twenty feet high; one on one side, and the other on the other side of the temple. There is at Saïs a similar colossus, lying, as at Memphis, on the back. It was Amasis also who erected at Memphis the temple to Isis, a vast edifice, deserving to be seen.

177 Under the reign of Amasis, Egypt, it is said, enjoyed the greatest prosperity, both in regard to the advantages accruing to the land from the river, and to mankind from the land; the towns in that period amounted to twenty thousand, all inhabited. Amasis it was that gave to the Egyptians the law, that every year each Egyptian should make known to the governor of his nome [205], from whence he got his living: if he failed to do so, and could not produce an honest livelihood, he was condemned to death. Solon the Athenian borrowed this law from Egypt, and instituted it at Athens: that nation still observe this law as an excellent

178 enactment. Amasis, being fond of the Hellenes, not only conferred various favours to different persons of that nation, but gave to the Hellenes, that came into Egypt, the town of Naucratis for their residence: to such as did not wish to settle in the country, but carry on traffic with Egypt, he bestowed places where they might erect altars and precincts to their gods. The most extensive of these holy precincts, the most renowned and frequented, was the Hellenium: it was erected at the common cost of the following states: of the Ionians, Chios, Teos, Phocæa, and Clazomenæ; of the Dorian, Rhodes, Cnidus, Halicarnassus, and Phaselis; of the Æolians, the Mytilenæans alone: to the above cities this sacred precinct belongs, and they appoint the presidents of the factory [206]. Whatever other cities may claim a share, claim what is not their own. The Æginetæ, however, have erected a temple to Jupiter, apart to themselves: the Samians have

179 done the same to Juno; and the Milesians to Apollo. Originally, Naucratis was the only factory; there was no other in Egypt: if any one arrived at another mouth of the Nile, he was obliged to take an oath, "that he did not enter of "his own accord:" and having done so, he was to proceed round to the Canobic mouth: in the case only of contrary winds impeding navigation, the cargo was to be conveyed, in

---

[204] I suppose that βάθρον is used here to express one of the tiers of steps by which people ascended to the temple.

[205] The provinces of Egypt were called Nomes, and the governor, or chief magistrate of each of those provinces, a Nomarch. *Larcher.*

[206] ἐμπόριον means a commercial place: προστάτης τοῦ ἐμπορίου, signifies the judge of such a town, and not a private judge for commerce, what we call a "consul," as Chishull (Antiquitat. Asiatic.) thinks. *Larcher.*

barises, round the Delta, until it reached Naucratis. Such was the privilege bestowed to Naucratis. The Amphictyons 180 having entered into a contract to build, for three hundred talents, the temple now standing at Delphi—for the former one had been burnt down accidentally, and the Delphians were taxed to furnish one quarter of the costs—the people of Delphi undertook a begging excursion to different places, from which they obtained subscriptions: in this way they brought from Egypt a very great contribution: for Amasis gave them a thousand talents of alum; and the Hellenic settlers contributed, on their part, twenty minæ.

Amasis contracted a league of friendship and alliance 181 with the Cyrenæans: he determined, also, to take a wife from thence;—whether he desired to unite himself to an Hellenic lady, or wished to give thus a proof of his attachment to the Cyrenæans. He espoused, therefore, the daughter of Battus; some say, Arcesilaus; others also Critobulus, a respectable citizen: the lady's name was Ladica. When Amasis lay with his bride, he found himself unable to consummate, although he could enjoy other women: this had lasted a considerable time, when Amasis sent for Ladice herself, and addressed her thus: "Ladice, you have used some "charm upon me, and now you have no means of escaping "the most miserable death of all women." Amasis, in spite of all Ladice said in her defence, relaxed not his stern intention: the princess prayed mentally[287] to Venus, that Amasis might be gratified that night, which would be the only preventive of the calamity that awaited her, and vowed she would send to the goddess an image at Cyrene: immediately she had made this vow, Amasis was made happy: his happiness continued, and his affection for his consort increased. Ladice fulfilled her vow to the goddess: she ordered the image to be made, and sent it off to Cyrene; where it remained safe and sound to my time, with its back turned to Cyrene[288]. Cambysis, after his conquest of Egypt, when he discovered who Ladice was, sent her back, unhurt, to Cyrene. Amasis dedicated offerings in Hellas: first, a 182 gilt statue of Minerva at Cyrene, and his own portrait painted: secondly, at Lindus, two stone statues to Pallas,

---

[287] Wesseling reads τῷ, "in the temple of Venus."

[288] It is probable that this statue was placed within the town; if so, the text means, that it was turned towards the country; and this is the sense that I have adopted. But the text may, with equal propriety, be taken to signify that the statue was outside of the town, and turned towards it. The reader may choose which he likes. *Larcher.*

together with an admirable corset of linen[20]: he dedicated, moreover, to Juno, at Samos, two wooden images of himself, which stood to my days in the great temple behind the doors: those dedications at Samos he made out of regard for the compact of friendship entered into between himself and Polycrates the son of Ajax: the dedication at Lindus was not in consequence of any similar compact, but because it was related that the daughters of Danaus, in their flight from the sons of Ægyptus, having touched at Lindus, founded there the temple of Minerva: such were the dedications of Amasis. He was the first that ever conquered Cyprus, and subjected that island to tribute.

[20] Probably something of the kind, of diaper or damask. See iii. 47, *fin*. This is the last note I find it necessary to append to this most important and interesting part of ancient history: the object that I have kept in view, in the composition and compilation of these observations, has been to explain the meaning of Herodotus;—an object of no small moment, when we consider that this Historian is unquestionably the best authority with regard to ancient Egypt, which he seems to have examined and studied with the curiosity of a traveller and the genius of a philosopher. Had I followed the plan I originally proposed to myself, which was, to illustrate my author by the works of subsequent historians and the journals of modern travellers, the comments upon this single book would have extended to two volumes; indeed, those of Larcher occupy four hundred pages of matter closely printed in very small type: considerations, not within the control of an author alone, have hindered me from carrying into effect my design; but I regret it the less, as a Geographical Dictionary to the Works of Herodotus, translated from Larcher, and accompanied with illustrations from various authors and travellers, is about to make its appearance; which will, at least, assist the reader in those parts of Herodotus where illustration is of the greatest consequence; I mean, with regard to the relative situations of the places he mentions, and the state of the world at the time the Muses were written.

EGYPTIAN CHRONOLOGY.

The Chronology of Egypt, given upon any well-founded authority by Herodotus, according to his own avowal, begins with the Dodekarchia, and is thus arranged:

```
                                    B.C.
     Dodekarchia ................671..656
     Sole rule of Psammitichus......656..617
     ........ Necos ............617..601
     ........ Psammes ........601..595
     ........ Apries...........595..570
     ........ Amasis .........570..526
     ........ Psammenitus .....526..525
```
Egypt conquered by Cambyses.

BOOK III.

THALIA.

SUMMARY OF BOOK III.

The causes of the war between Cambyses and the Egyptians, 1—9. King Psammenitus, son of Amasis, is conquered near Pelusium, 10 seq. After the surrender of Memphis, the Africans, Cyrenæans, and Barcæans surrender, of their own accord, 13. Psammenitus is at first treated liberally; but soon after, being caught intriguing, is put to death, 14, 15. Having subjugated Egypt, Cambyses resolves to carry war against the Carthaginians, Ammonians, and Ethiopians; but the Phœnicians refuse to carry war against the Carthaginians, their fellow citizens: the expedition, therefore, is dropped, 19. Spies are sent from the Ichthyophagi to the Ethiopians, 20: they bring back a threatening answer from the king. The army, marching against the Ethiopians, is compelled to return, by famine, 25. Those sent against the Ammonians, are swallowed up, under mountains of sand, 26. Cambyses is wroth against the rites and the priests of the Egyptians, fancying that the Egyptians rejoice on account of his failure, 27 seq. He refrains not even from his own subjects; but puts to death his brother Smerdis, and his sister, who was likewise his wife; slaughters many, both of the Persians and Egyptians; and gives various other proofs of his insanity, 30—39. In this place is inserted the history of Polycrates, tyrant of the Samians, against whom the Lacedæmonians undertook, about this time, an expedition, 39 seq. The Corcyræans assist in this expedition, in consequence of a grudge against the Samians from the time of Periander: concerning Periander, 49 seq. In the mean time, Smerdis the Magus takes possession of the Persian throne, 61: he sends a herald into Egypt, to summon the troops to abandon the standard of Cambyses, 62. Cambyses, seized with great anger, is about to lead his army against the Magi; but is accidentally wounded, as he is leaping on his horse, and dies, 64 seq. The cheat of the Magus having been discovered by the daughter of Otanes, seven of the chief men among the Persians conspire the death of the usurper, 68 seq. The Magi are put to death, 78. A consultation is held on the most expedient form of government to be adopted; and finally, Darius the son of Hystaspes is pointed out king by the neighing of his horse, 80 seq. He divides the empire into twenty satrapies; the revenue from each of which is stated, 89, 96. Some other nations furnish free gifts to the king; among whom the Indians, whose country and manners are described, 98—101. The advantages of Arabia are then enumerated, 107—113; as well as those of Ethiopia, and the distant tracts of Europe, 114 seq. Intaphernes, one of the seven conspirators, is put to death by Darius's order, 118 seq.; and afterwards Orœtes, 128, who had compassed, by perfidy, the death of Polycrates, the tyrant of Samos, 120—125; who had likewise put to death Mitrobates, a noble Persian, together with his son Crassaspes, and had ordered the murder of a messenger to him by Darius, 126. Democedes, a physician of Croton, having been found among the slaves of Orœtes (125) cures the king and Atossa: he is sent as a guide with some Persians, to reconnoitre Greece and Italy: he makes his escape: and the Persians who had accompanied him are taken, and ransomed by Gillus, an exile of Tarentum, 129—138. The manner in which the Persians took Samos, 139—149. But, at the same time, the Babylonians secede; and, after a siege of twenty months, are subdued by the art and valour of Zopyrus, 150 to the end.

THE THIRD BOOK OF HERODOTUS.

THALIA.

It was against the above Amasis that Cambyses, son of Cyrus, prepared for war, at the head of an army, consisting not only of all the various tribes under his dominion, but also of Ionians and Æolians from among the Hellenes: this expedition was undertaken from the following motive. Cambyses had sent a herald into Egypt, and requested the hand of Amasis's daughter[1]. This request was made at the suggestion of a native Egyptian; who, having a grudge against Amasis, acted in this manner, because the king of Egypt had selected him alone from among the Egyptian physicians, and, forcibly tearing him from wife and children, had made a present of him to the Persians, when Cyrus sent to Amasis, and asked for an ophthalmist, that should be the best in Egypt. This being, accordingly, the reason of the Egyptian's ill-will, he instigated Cambyses, by his counsels, to ask Amasis for his daughter; in order that the king of Egypt either should, to his great mortification, give his daughter, or refuse her, and so become the object of Cambyses's hatred. But Amasis, alarmed, and dreading to be oppressed by the power of the Persians, knew not whether he should give or refuse his daughter; as he was well aware that Cambyses did not intend to take the lady for his wife, but to make her his concubine. After revolving in his mind this subject, he decided to act thus. Apries, the preceding king, had left one daughter, a stately and handsome woman, the only remaining offspring of the family: her name was Nitetis. Accordingly, Amasis decked this damsel in cloth of gold[2], and sends her

---

[1] Constr. ἐπὶ τῇ συμβουλίῃ Καμβύσεα, αἰτέειν [αὑτὸν] αἰτίην "Αμασιν θυγατέρα. Schweig. See Matt. 411, 4.
[2] The Greek is, ἐσθῆτί τε καὶ χρυσῷ.

It is, I think, the figure which the grammarians term διὰ δυοῖν, as in this verse of Virgil: "Pateris libamus et auro." Georg. ii. 192. *Larcher.*

off into Persia, as his own daughter. Some time after, on Cambyses's saluting her by her paternal name, the lady addressed him thus: " Sire," said she, " you know not that " you are deceived by Amasis³, who sent me away to you " thus richly adorned, and gave, as his own daughter, me, " who am in reality the daughter of Apries, whom Amasis " rose up against, with the Egyptians, and killed, although " his sovereign lord." This information, and the desire of avenging that murder, induced Cambyses, violently exasperated, to invade Egypt. Such is the Persian account.
2 But the Egyptians, on the other hand, claim Cambyses as their countryman; affirming, that he was born of this very same daughter of Apries; for Cyrus was the person that sent to Amasis for his daughter, and not Cambyses: but in so saying, they mistake the truth; for it cannot have escaped the Egyptians—indeed, if any nation in the world is well conversant with the Persian customs, that nation is surely the Egyptian—that, in the first place, among the Persians it is not customary that a bastard should reign, while there still exists a legitimate heir; and, secondly, that Cambyses was the son of Cassandane, the daughter of Pharnaspes, one of the Achæmenidæ, and certainly not sprung from Egypt. But the Egyptians pervert history, in claiming
3 any connection with the family of Cyrus. The following tale is likewise told, but I give no credit to it. Some Persian woman paid a visit to Cyrus's wives; and beholding the tall and beautiful children standing by Cassandane, praised them highly, as one filled with astonishment. Cassandane, one of the wives of Cyrus, answered thus: " Although the " mother of such children, Cyrus slights me; and honours " the foreigner from Egypt." Such was the language of Cassandane, who was envious of Nitetis: and the eldest son, Cambyses, hereupon said: " And therefore, mother, when I " become a man, I will, I assure you, turn Egypt upside " down." This speech was made by a boy of ten years of age only, and was held as a prodigy by the women. Cambyses, when he grew up, remembered accordingly his vow; and, having become king, entered upon a campaign⁴ against Egypt.
4 The following other occurrence also took place, and contributed towards the furtherance of this expedition. Among the mercenaries of Amasis was an officer, a native

---

³ Matt. °548, 3.
⁴ Valckenaer observes, that, in Herodotus, στρατηία means an expedition, and στρατιά an army. Thucydides and Xenophon make the same difference between στρατεία and στρατιά. See Schweig. Lex. Herod.

of Halicarnassus, and called Phanes; he was both a wise counsellor and gallant soldier. This individual, disgusted at the behaviour of Amasis, made his escape by sea out of Egypt, with the intention of having an interview with Cambyses. As he was of no humble rank among the mercenaries, and moreover was perfectly acquainted with every thing appertaining to Egypt, Amasis pursued him, making every effort to capture his person: for this purpose he despatched after the fugitive one of his most faithful eunuchs, on board a trireme. The eunuch overtook the deserter, and made him prisoner; but did not convey him back to Egypt; for Phanes cheated dexterously his keeper, made the guards drunk, and went over to the Persians. Cambyses was on the eve of marching against Egypt, and in doubt[5] how he should get his forces across a country wholly without water; when Phanes came over to him, communicated every particular relating to Amasis's affairs, and explained how the passage over the desert was to be performed: he advised that an embassy should be despatched, to request the king of the Arabians to give him a safe passage across his territories. The only practicable entrance into Egypt is by this road: 5 from Phœnicia, down to the confines of the city of Cadytis, the land appertains to the people called Syrian Palæstinians: from Cadytis, which, in my opinion, is scarcely inferior in size to Sardis, the staples along the shore to Jenysus belong to the Arabian prince: from Jenysus, on to Lake Serbonis, the coast is again possessed by the Syrians. Adjoining the above lake, Mount Casius extends down to the sea: and from Lake Serbonis, in which tradition says Typhon is concealed, Egypt begins. Accordingly the country between the city of Jenysus and the Lake Serbonis with Mount Casius, no inconsiderable space, for it is a three days' march[6], is dreadfully scant of water. I am now going to describe 6 what very few of those who have performed the voyage to Egypt know any thing about. Earthenware, filled with wine, is imported twice a year into Egypt, from all parts of Hellas as well as Phœnicia; yet not so much as one wine-jar—if I may use the expression—is to be seen in Egypt. How then, you may say, are they consumed?[7] To this question I give the following answer. Every magistrate is held to collect all the earthen-jars of his own town, and transmit them to Memphis: from Memphis they are trans-

---

[5] Constr. καὶ ἀπορίητι (κατὰ τὴν ἔλασιν. *Schweig.*
[6] Matt. 433. obs. 4.
[7] κῶς for τοῦ may be taken as equivalent to ὡς εἰ: it may also be taken in the sense of *ubi;* "where, then, are they consumed?" *Schweig. Lex. Herod.*

ported full of water, to those dry parts of Syria. Thus all the earthen jars imported into Egypt, and exhibited for sale, find their way into Syria, and go to increase the old stock. This mode of facilitating the ingress into Egypt, by supplying the above-mentioned desert with water[8], was adopted by the Persians, as soon as they had got possession of Egypt. At the time, however, we are speaking of, no store of water was at hand: Cambyses, in consequence of information received from the stranger of Halicarnassus, sent ambassadors to the king of Arabia, and requested a safe passage; which he obtained, after a mutual interchange of pledges.

The Arabians respect their oaths as religiously as any other people[9]: they plight their faith with the following forms:—when two persons are about to plight their faith, a third stands between the two parties, and, with a sharp-edged stone, makes a slight incision in the palms of both, near the two middle fingers: he then takes a shred from the cloak of each, and rubs the blood upon seven stones placed between the two; in doing which, he invokes both Bacchus and Urania. This ceremony being gone through, the person that plights his faith tenders his friends, as a bond[10], to the stranger or the countryman, if the ceremony take place with such; and these friends consider themselves bound to observe the compact. They acknowledge no other gods than Bacchus and Urania; and affirm, that they cut their hair the same as Bacchus does; that is to say, they shear off the hair all around like a wheel, and cut away all the corners about the temples. They call Bacchus, Orotal; and Urania, Alilat. Accordingly, the Arabian prince, after pledging his word to the deputies coming on the part of Cambyses, proceeded to act as follows:—he filled some camels' skins with water, and placed them on the backs of all his living camels: this done, he proceeded to the desert, and there awaited the arrival of Cambyses' army. The above is the more credible of the two accounts given; but it is proper to mention the other also, inasmuch as it certainly does exist. There is in Arabia a great river, called the Corys: it falls into the sea known under the name of Erythræan. From this river, therefore, the Arabian king is represented to have made, by tacking together the hides of oxen and various other animals, an aqueduct, stretching in length to the desert, and thus conducted the water: he is

---

[8] Constr. ἀξαντες (τὴν λοβυλὴν ἐν' Αἰγυπτον) Dorv. *Schweig. Lex. Herod.*
[9] Matt. 289.
[10] σαριγγυῆ, " donne ses amis pour garants." *Larcher.*

likewise said to have dug deep wells in the desert, to preserve the water thus obtained. The road from the river to the desert is a twelve-days' march; and the water was conducted, by three aqueducts, to three different stations.

Near[11] the mouth of the Nile called the Pelusiac, Psammenitus the son of Amasis pitched his camp, and awaited the coming of Cambyses: for Cambyses found Amasis no longer alive, when he marched against Egypt: that king, after a reign of forty-four years, had departed life. During this period, no great calamity befel him: after his decease, he was embalmed, and his remains deposited in the sepulchral chambers he had built in the temple for himself[12]. Under the reign of Psammenitus the son of Amasis, a mighty prodigy occurred to the Egyptians—rain fell at Thebes; an event that never came to pass before, nor since, to my time, according to the Thebans; for no rain whatever falls in the upper part of Egypt; but in the present instance, a drizzling shower was seen at Thebes[13]. The Persians, after crossing the waterless desert, halted close to the Egyptians, for the purpose of engaging: at this moment, the mercenaries of the Egyptian prince, who consisted of Hellenes and Carians, laying it to the charge of Phanes that he had brought a foreign host upon Egypt, devised the following act against him. Phanes had left his sons in Egypt: they, therefore, brought the youths to the camp, and within view of their own father; then, placing a wine-bowl in the mid space between the two camps, dragged the youths, one by one, and cut their throats over the bowl. Having thus slaughtered the whole, they poured wine and water into the bowl; and all the mercenaries, having quaffed of the blood[14], engaged battle. A bloody conflict ensued: great numbers fell on both sides, and the Egyptians were put to flight. In consequence of information from the people resident about the field of battle, I had an opportunity of seeing myself a very surprising thing. The bones of the fallen in this battle are scattered about; those of each party separately—for the bones of the Persians lie by themselves, as they were at first; opposite to which are seen those of the Egyptians:—and the

---

[11] ἐς does not here signify *at*: the country *at* the Pelusian mouth was by no means fit for the encampment of an army. Matt. 557.

[12] See Book ii. 169.

[13] Lit "Thebes of Egypt was watered with rain:" such is the meaning of the passive ὕεται: thus, ἵεται ἡ γῆ ὀλίγῳ, understand ὕδατι: so, a little lower down, καὶ ὕσε ὀλίγοις ψακάσι, "at that time Thebes was watered with drops of rain."—*Valckenaer. Schneid.*

[14] ἐμπιόντες δὲ τοῦ αἵματος: literally, "having drunk of the blood." τοῦ αἵματος is the partitive genitive.—*Larcher.*

sculls of the Persians are so soft, that you may easily make a hole in them by throwing a pebble; while those of the Egyptians are so hard, that you can scarcely break them by repeated blows with a stone. The reason of this, assigned by the people, I at least readily acceded to: it is, that the Egyptians, immediately from their infancy, begin to shave their heads, and the bone of the scull is thickened by exposure to the sun. This accounts likewise for there being few instances of baldness among the Egyptians; for you see less bald men in that country than any other: such, therefore, is the reason of the Egyptians having such strong sculls. With respect to the Persians, the cause of their having such thin sculls is this: from early youth they are brought up with the head shaded by turbans, which they wear in the place of felt caps[15]. I witnessed the same thing also at Papremis, in the sculls of the Persians, under Achæmenes the son of Darius, who were cut off by Inarus, the Libyan prince[16].

13 The Egyptians, routed in the battle, fled in great confusion, and shut themselves in Memphis. Cambyses sent up the river a ship belonging to Mitylene, with a Persian of rank on board as a herald, inviting the Egyptians to terms: the inhabitants, seeing the ship enter Memphis, poured forth in a mass from their city, destroyed the vessel, and tore, limb from limb, the crew, carrying the fragments into the town. Siege was then laid to the place, and the Egyptians at last surrendered[17]. The Libyans on the borders, in fear of receiving the same treatment as Egypt, gave themselves up without fighting, submitted to tribute, and sent gifts: the Cyrenæans and Barcæans, equally alarmed with the Libyans, acted in the same manner. Cambyses received graciously the Libyan gifts; but found fault with those of the Cyrenæans, on account, I suppose, of their insignifi-

---

[15] πίλους τιάρας φορέοντες. The πίλος was the generic name for a *hat*: the particular sort of hat or covering to the head worn by the Persians was the τιάρα, a sort of turban, if we may rely on Quint. Curt. iii. 3, 19. regium capitis insigne, quod coerulea fascia albo distincta circumibat. *Schneid. Gr. Germ. Lex.*

[16] I have called this Inarus "king of Libya," although Herodotus gives him only the appellation of τοῦ Λίβυος, "the Libyan;" first, because Herodotus generally calls kings by the name of the nation over which they rule. He says constantly 'the Persian,' 'the Egyptian,' instead of 'the king of Persia,' 'the king of Egypt.' Ὁ Αἰγύπτιος, 11, is Psammenitus, king of Egypt. Ὁ Ἀράβιος, 9, is the king of the Arabians. Secondly, I have so called him because this acceptation is clearly determined by Thucydides, i. 104. *Larcher.*

[17] In the verb ἵερμαι, and its compounds, the perf. and aor. 2, are taken in a passive sense. *Larcher*; whose translation is "furent enfin obligés de se rendre."—παραστῆναι signifies, properly, "to stand by;" but is often taken by Herodotus in the sense of "to surrender," "to deliver one's self up." iii. 13; v. 86; vi. 99, 140.— *Schweig. Lex. Herod. Wess.*

cancy; for the present sent by the people of Cyrene was only fifty minæ of silver. The king, grasping the money, scattered, with his own hand, the coins among the soldiers.

On the tenth day after the capture of Memphis, Cambyses 14 placed in the suburb, for the purpose of insult, the king of the Egyptians, Psammenitus, whose reign had lasted six months, together with other Egyptians, and made trial of his constancy, behaving to him in the following manner. He dressed the king's daughter in the garb of a slave, and sent her down to the river with a pitcher: she was accompanied with other young maidens, whom Cambyses selected from the first families, all clad in the same manner as the king's daughter. As the damsels passed before them[18] in tears and with lamentable cries, all the fathers answered with similar cries and moans, when they beheld their children thus debased; excepting Psammenitus, who, although he saw and knew them, merely cast his eyes to the ground. After the water-carriers had passed by, the procession was continued by the king's son, with two thousand other Egyptians of the same age, each with a halter tied round his neck, and a bridle in the mouth[19]: these young persons were then conducted to death, as a revenge offered to the Mitylenæans who had come to Memphis on board the ship: for the royal judges had pronounced their sentence, that, for each murdered man, ten of the chief Egyptians should be, in return, put to death[20]. When Psammenitus saw his son passing by, and was informed that he was being led to the scaffold, he behaved in the same manner as he had done to his daughter; although the rest of the Egyptians, seated by his side, wept and bewailed. After these had passed, it so happened, that an old man, one of his drinking companions, fallen from his former state, possessing nothing more than a common pauper, and asking alms from the soldiers, came to Psammenitus the son of Amasis, and the Egyptians seated in the suburb: Psammenitus, at the sight of the beggar, gave vent to his tears, and, calling his old companion by name, smote his head. Some guards, placed over the Egyptian king, communicated to Cambyses all the particulars of his behaviour, as each procession passed by: surprised at

---

[18] κατὰ τοὺς ταφέας. Matt. 581, b, fifth parag.

[19] I thought, at first, that Herodotus had alluded to the "gag;" but a passage in 118 of this book convinces me that it is a real bridle, which was fastened as a mark of disgrace round the neck.—*Larcher.* Herodotus, iv. 69.

uses the word ερυμὸν in the sense of *gagging*; φιμοῦν and ἐπιστομίζειν are the more usual expressions; the former in particular.

[20] Consequently, the crew of the Mitylenian ship, massacred by the Egyptians, must have amounted to two hundred.

this conduct, he sent a messenger, to make inquiries of the king in the following words:—" Psammenitus, your sovereign "lord, Cambyses, asks, Why, seeing your daughter so humi-"liated, and your son proceeding to death, did you refrain "from mourning and weeping; but seeing the beggar, who "is no ways connected with you, honour him as they tell me "you did?" Thus questioned, the king gave the following answer: "Son of Cyrus; the calamities of my own family "are too great to be deplored[21]; but the misery of my com-"panion claimed a tear, he having fallen from happiness "and prosperity, to beggary, on the threshold of age[22]." This being reported[23], Psammenitus appeared to Cambyses to have spoken properly: and Crœsus, according to the Egyptians, shed tears; for the Lydian prince had followed Cambyses to Egypt: the Persians, also, that were present, wept. Such compassion, it is said, took possession of Cambyses[24], that forthwith he gave orders for the son of the Egyptian prince to be reprieved[25] from being executed with the others doomed to death, and the prince himself should be taken 15 from the suburb, back to his home. The persons sent on this commission[26] found the youth no longer in existence, having been the first executed: they removed Psammenitus himself, and brought him to Cambyses; with whom he passed the rest of his life, without being subjected to any further violence; and, had he been prudent enough to refrain from meddling with affairs[27], might have been restored

[21] Matt. 448, b. Cf. Aristot. Rhet. ii. 8.

[22] This Homeric expression appears to admit of two meanings, the commencement and the end of old age. See Larcher's note.

[23] καὶ ταῦτα ὡς ἀπενιχθέντα. The infinitives δοκέειν and δακρύειν are governed by λέγουσι, understood from ὡς δὴ λέγεται. Instead of what would have been the common expression, καὶ ταῦτα ὡς ἀπενίχθη, Herodotus might, therefore inasmuch as the infinitive runs through the sentence, have used the infinitive mood; for we know that in similar phrases, ἐπεὶ, and such like particles, may be construed with the infinitive, ii. 32; iii. 35: but in this instance the author has chosen to construe the particle ὡς with a participle, instead of either an infinitive or indicative, taking ταῦτα ὡς ἀπενιχθέντα as equivalent to ταῦτα ὡς ἀπενίχθη.—*Schweig. Not.*

[24] Matt. 394, c.

[25] οἱ is expletive: a similar pleonasm is equally common in French, that is to say, in familiar language: "faites-moi lui faire telle chose."—*Larcher.*

[26] μέτιεμαι signifies "eo petitum, arcesso."—*Larcher.*

[27] Schweighæuser, after H. Stephen, refers ἐνεωτέρα to the theme ἀνωτέω, and explains this phrase by the pleonastic negative of the Greek idiom: one lying in the α privative of the verb, the other in the particle μή. Literally, "If it had been disbelieved that he was planning innovations." *Schweig. Not.; et Lex. Herod. voc. ἀνωτέω.* Æm. Portus refers ἐνεωτέρα to ἐνεωτεραμαι, of which he regards it as the aor. pass. 1. Att.; and, taking it as an impersonal verb, gives the following translation: "If it had been known that he was not planning innovations." *Port. Lex. Ion. voc. ἀνωτέω.* Werfer, a young man of great hopes, whose premature death Schweighæuser deplores, compares this passage

to the rule of Egypt, and appointed governor of that province; for the Persians are wont to shew honours to the sons of royalty; to whom, although their fathers may have revolted, they still give back the power. That such is their practice, can be shewn by many instances; more especially, Thannyras the son of Inarus, the Libyan prince, who was restored to his father's power; and so was Pausiris the son of Amyrtæus; and this was the case, notwithstanding the Persians were more annoyed by Inarus and Amyrtæus than by any other princes. But now Psammenitus having worked mischief, received his reward: he rose against the Persian king, and roused the Egyptians to revolt: having been convicted, he was sentenced by Cambyses to be put to death instantly, by swallowing a draught of bull's blood: thus, accordingly, this prince came to his end.

Cambyses proceeded from Memphis to the city of Saïs, 16 for the purpose of accomplishing an object he had in view. As soon as he reached Amasis's palace, he commanded the corpse of the deceased to be dragged forthwith out of the sepulchre. When this order had been executed, he gave directions that the carcass should be scourged, the hair pulled out, the body pierced in all parts, and insulted in every manner. When they were tired of performing these operations (for the body, being embalmed, resisted, and did not give way [28]), Cambyses commanded that it should be consumed by fire. It must be observed, that the Persians believe fire to be a god: it is therefore by no means consonant to the customs of either nation to burn the dead—to the Persians, for the reason above assigned, as they say it is not right a god should feast on a man—to the Egyptians, because they believe fire to be a wild living animal, that devours whatever he can seize upon, and, when satiated with food, dies together with what he has consumed; and consequently it is not right, by any means, to give him a human body; and that on this account they embalm their dead, in order that, being placed underground, they should not be eaten by worms. Therefore, in this instance, the injunctions of Cambyses were equally criminal in the eyes of both Persians and Egyptians. However, according to the Egyptian account of this event, it was not Amasis that underwent this treat-

with one in vii. 29, *ἐπίστασο ὅπως ἀεὶ τοιοῦτος*, 'know how,' *i. e.* 'contrive, have a care, to be always such:' hence is deduced a very happy mode of explaining this phrase, 'If he had known how,' *i. e.* 'If he had been prudent enough, not to meddle with innovations,' &c. This translation I have adopted without hesitation. See *Schweig. Lex. Herod. in voc.* ἐπίσταμαι.

[29] καὶ οὐδὲν ὑπείκοντο, was by no means soft and yielding, as a putrid carcass would have been.

ment, but some other Egyptian, of the same age as Amasis, whom the Persians abused, fancying they were insulting Amasis[30]. They add, that Amasis was warned, by an oracle, of what would happen to him after his death; and, in order to avert the forthcoming calamities, he deposited, close to the doors of the sepulchral repository, the very man that was scourged after his death, and gave charge to his son to deposit his own body in the deepest recess of the vault. In my opinion, there is not the least shadow of truth in these orders of Amasis, or in these events connected with his sepulture and with the other man: these things are all embellishments of the Egyptians[33].

17 Subsequently to the above events, Cambyses projected three different campaigns against the Carthaginians, the Ammonians, and the Macrobian[31] Ethiopians dwelling on the southern coast of Libya. He determined to send his fleet against Carthage; to despatch a portion of his infantry against the Ammonians; and to send first spies to the Ethiopians, who were to see the table of the sun, said to be in Ethiopia, if report was true; and, besides, to reconnoitre all the rest; these spies were to carry, as a pretext, gifts to the

18 Ethiopian sovereign. The table of the sun is described as a meadow stretching before the city, full of the boiled flesh of all sorts of quadrupeds, which are spread there by night by the individuals that hold the civic charges: in the day-time, whoever chooses, may come and eat. The inhabitants, it is said, affirm that the earth itself produces all these good things. Such, therefore, is the description given of what is

19 termed the table of the sun. Cambyses, having resolved to send spies immediately, summoned from Elephantine some of the Ichthyophagi acquainted with the Ethiopic tongue. While they were fetching these persons, Cambyses issued orders for the fleet to sail against Carthage: but the Phœnicians refused to obey, being bound to the Carthaginians by the most sacred oaths, and determined not to act so wickedly as to carry war against their own offspring[32]. As the Phœnicians refused to join, the fleet was no longer sufficient for the undertaking: and, accordingly, the Carthaginians thus escaped thraldom at the hands of the Persians: for Cambyses considered it would be unjust to employ main force

---

[29] Matt. 384.
[30] Construction: (δεικνύαι μοι) Αἰγυπτίου σημεῖον εἶναι ἄλλου (falsely).
[31] Macrobians is not the name of a nation, but an epithet given by Herodotus to that portion of the Ethiopians by reason of their longevity. *Larcher.*
[32] Every one knows the Carthaginians were a colony of the Phœnicians: the endearing appellation of children, παῖδες, was given by the mother country to her colonies.

against a people who had voluntarily submitted themselves to the Persians, and were the mainspring on which the naval armament depended[33]. The Cyprians had also given themselves up to the Persians, and joined the expedition against Egypt. When the Ichthyophagi had arrived from Elephantine, Cambyses despatched them to the Ethiopians, prescribing what they were to say; and carrying gifts, consisting of a purple cloak, a golden neck-chain, armlets, a stone jar filled with myrrh, and a flask of date-wine. These Ethiopians, to whom Cambyses was sending, are described as the most gigantic and the handsomest of men: their customs, it is added, are totally different from those of other nations, and especially so far as regards the royal power; these people investing with the sovereignty that citizen whom they regard as of most gigantic stature, and of strength commensurate to his size.

The Ichthyophagi having reached to this nation, presented the gifts to the king, saying as follows: " Cambyses, king of " the Persians, desirous to become your friend, has sent us,with " his behests to us to have an interview with you, and present " you with these gifts, in the enjoyment of which he himself " delights." The Ethiopian, already informed that spies were coming to him, made this reply to them: " It is false " that the king of the Persians," said the prince to them, " sent you with gifts, esteeming it such an honour to have " me for his friend: neither do you speak the truth, for you " have come hither as spies upon my kingdom. If your king " were an honest man, he would neither covet another's " territory besides his own, nor would he reduce to thraldom " men from whom he has never received any offence. Now, " therefore, do you give to him this bow; and say to him " these words: 'The Ethiopian, king advises the Persian " king, when the Persians can thus easily string a bow of " this size, then to head his overwhelming multitudes against " the Macrobian Ethiopians: until that time, let him thank " the gods they have never turned the minds of the sons of " the Ethiopians to possess themselves of any country than " their own.'" He spoke thus, unstrung the bow, and gave it to the new-comers: then he took up the purple cloak, asked what it was, and how it was made. The Ichthyophagi describing to him all the exact particulars respecting purple, and the mode of dyeing; the king said, "The men are full of deceit; and

---

[33] That is to say, the Phœnicians were not only the most considerable part of Cambyses' fleet, but the most skilful in tactics and war; so that without them, Cambyses could compass no undertaking by sea. *Geinoz* quoted by *Larcher*.

full of deceits also are their garments." Then he asked about the neck-chain and the armlets[34]: the Ichthyophagi representing the beauty of such ornaments, the king burst into laughter: he knew, he said, they were chains, and observed that the Ethiopians had stronger ones than those. Next he inquired about the myrrh; and when informed how that ointment was manufactured, he made the same remarks as he had done respecting the cloak. But when he came to the wine, and was informed how it was obtained, he was beyond measure delighted with the beverage; and then asked, what was the chief food of the king, and what the greatest extension of life among the Persians. The spies replied, that the king eat bread, and described the nature of wheat; and stated, that the longest duration of life prescribed to man is eighty years. Whereupon the Ethiopian prince observed, he was not at all surprised that, living upon dung and muck, they should be so short lived; nor indeed would they even be able to attain to that age, if they did not refresh their vigour by the use of the beverage[35]—pointing to the wine, and confessing that, in that particular, the Ethiopians were 23 inferior to the Persians. The Ichthyophagi, in their turn, questioned the king on the length of life, and the diet of his people: he told them, that most of his subjects reached their hundredth year, and some even exceeded that; their food was boiled meat; their drink milk. The spies expressed their astonishment at the number of years; and the king, it is said, took them to a spring, in the water of which they wash and glisten, as if it were oil; afterwards, they smell as of violets. The water of this spring, according to the report of the Ichthyophagi, is so little buoyant, that scarcely any object floats on the surface, not even wood, or things lighter than wood; every thing sinks to the bottom[36]. If what they say concerning this water is true, it is probable that the constant use of it may contribute to their longevity[37]. When they quitted the spring, the king took them to a prison for men, where all were confined in golden shackles; brass, with these Ethiopians, being the scarcest and most esteemed of the metals. The Ichthyophagi, after they had 24 viewed the prison, visited also the table of the sun. Lastly, they were shewn the sepulchral repositories of the dead, which they describe as made of rock-crystal, in the follow-

[34] Matt. 411, 3.
[35] Understand λαυτοὺς after ἀνέρωσι.
[36] It is in allusion to this passage, that the illustrious Boerhaave lends his important testimony to the veracity of Herodotus: "Enim vero hodiernæ observationes probant fere omnia *magni viri* dicta."
[37] Matt. 514.

ing manner. After the body has been desiccated, either in the Egyptian or any other manner, they spread plaster over every part, and paint it, to imitate the original as far as possible; and then lay the corpse in the inside of a hollow crystal cylinder; great quantities of which are dug up in the country, of a beautiful kind. The relics contained within the cylinder are seen through the crystal: they eject no bad smell, and have nothing forbidding about them: thus the whole body is visible in each part[39]. During twelve months, the relations keep, generally, the body by them in their houses, presenting to it the firstlings of all, and offering sacrifice. After that time, they bring out the mummy, and place it somewhere about the town.

The spies having examined all the above things, returned 25 from whence they came: they made their report; and Cambyses, fired with anger[39], instantly commenced his campaign against the Ethiopians, without announcing any previous orders for preparing provisions, or once giving it a thought that he was about to take his army to the extremities of the world; but, as if mad and unsound of mind[40], began his march, as soon as he had heard what the Ichthyophagi had to say. The Hellenes present were ordered to remain where they were: the whole land army[41] he took with him. When he came with his forces to Thebes, he set apart about fifty thousand men; and gave them his commands, to enthral the Ammonians, and set fire to the temple of Jupiter; then, at the head of the rest of the army, he set out for Ethiopia. But before the troops had proceeded one fifth of the way, all the provisions they had brought with them were consumed[42]; the sumpter-beasts then became food, but the supply was soon exhausted. If, therefore, Cambyses, when he saw this, had vouchsafed to alter his mind, and led back the army, he would have proved himself, even after committing this first error, to be a man of sense: the Persian king, on the contrary, paid no attention to this; he pursued his march onwards. The men, so long as they could find any thing growing upon the ground, lived on roots and vegetables;

---

[39] Literally, "*the column* has every part visible, as well as the body:" that is to say, the case was not put up against a wall like the Egyptian mummies, ii. 86. of which latter the fore part was consequently all that could be seen. *Schweig.*

[39] ὀργὴν ποιησάμενος, i. e. ὀργισθείς.

[40] Matt. 444, 5.

[41] ὁ πεζὸς στρατὸς signifies, in Herodotus, a land army, and not infantry or foot. *Larcher.* This is not always the case: it is sometimes opposed to ὁ ἱππος, and at others to ὁ ναυτικὸς στρατός.

[42] σιτίων ἐχόμενα, "the provisions:" this expression is very common in Herodotus. See the *Lex. Herod.* of Schweig. voc. ἔχω, *in fin.*

but when they entered upon the desert sands, some of them had recourse to a horrid expedient: they drew lots, ten by ten, and eat the flesh of one. Cambyses being made acquainted with this, and horror-stricken by these instances of cannibalism, gave up the expedition against the Ethiopians, marched back on his steps, and came to Thebes, having lost great numbers of his men. From Thebes he descended down to Memphis, and gave permission to the Hellenes to sail away. Such was the success[43] of the Ethiopian cam-

26 paign. Those who had been despatched on the Ammonian expedition, departed from Thebes, and proceeded on their march, accompanied by guides: there is no doubt that they reached the city of Oasis, inhabited by Samians, said to belong to the Æschrionian tribe, and seven days' distance from Thebes, across the sands. This place is called by us the Isle of the Blessed. Accounts are given therefore of the arrival of the Persians so far; but from this spot nobody knows what became of them, nor did the Ammonians, or any other people, hear of them: for they never reached Ammon, neither did they return back. The following particulars, however, are stated in addition by the Ammonians;—that when the Persians were on their march from the Oasis to their country through the desert, and had reached about halfway between themselves and the Oasis, just as they were at breakfast, a furious and powerful south-wind arose, bringing mountains of sand, which spread over the army, and thus made it disappear. The Ammonians relate, therefore, that such was the fate of this army.

27 On the arrival of Cambyses back to Memphis, Apis, called by the Hellenes Epaphus, appeared to the Egyptians: in consequence of this manifestation, the Egyptians forthwith donned their best cloaks, and addressed themselves to festive enjoyments. Cambyses observed what the Egyptians were about, and, convinced that they were making these rejoicings in exultation of his ill success, summoned into his presence the magistrates of Memphis: when they appeared before him, he put these questions: " Wherefore " the Egyptians had not done these things on his first visit " at Memphis, but had waited till he now come, having lost " a great number of his troops?" They explained to him, that a god had appeared to them, who was wont to manifest himself only at long intervals of time; that when this happened, all the Egyptians rejoiced and celebrated a feast.

---

[43] οὕτω ἔπρηξε: " adeo cessit infeliciter." The verb πρήξαι is frequently used to signify a calamity, without the addition of κακῶς. See *Wess. Not.*

Cambyses having heard this answer, said they were liars, and as liars sentenced them to death. After the execution of the above persons, he next called before him the priests, who gave the same explanation. Cambyses said he would soon find out whether so familiar a god had come to the Egyptians [44]: having thus spoken, he ordered the priests to bring Apis before him; and they went away, to fetch him.— This Apis, or Epaphus, is a steer, born from a heifer, which is never more allowed to have young. The Egyptians assert, that the moon descends from the sky on the heifer, and that from thence Apis is produced. This steer, bearing the name of Apis, has the following marks: he is black, but carries a square white spot on his forehead: on his back is figured an eagle; in the tail the hairs are double; on the tongue is a chaffer.—When the priests had brought Apis to Cambyses, that prince, as if distraught in mind, drew his dagger, and aimed at the belly of Apis, but wounded him in the thigh; then, bursting into laughter, addressed the priests: " O you stupid fools! are gods such as this, of flesh and " blood, and sensible to steel? A god this, worthy indeed of " the Egyptians! At all events, however, you shall not get " off unpunished [45], for making sport of me." Having so spoken, he ordered the executioners to flog the priests soundly, and to put to death all the other Egyptians they caught feasting. Accordingly, the feast of the Egyptians was put an end to; the priests were punished; and Apis, wounded in the thigh, lay pining in the temple: he died soon after of his wound, and was entombed by the priests, unknown to Cambyses.

But Cambyses, according to the account of the Egyptians, forthwith became raving mad in consequence of this crime; although even previously he had not his right senses. And his first misdeed was committed upon his brother Smerdis, born of the same father and mother as himself: he sent this prince back from Egypt into Persia from jealousy, because he was the only Persian who could string, within two fingers' breadth, the bow brought from the Ethiopian king by the Ichthyophagi; a feat which none of the other Persians could perform. After the departure of Smerdis for Persia, Cambyses had the following dream in his sleep: He fancied a messenger came to him from Persia, announcing that

---

[44] οὐ λήσειν αὐτὸν, κ. τ. λ. Literally, "It should not be concealed from him whether any god tractable to the hand had come among the Egyptians."

[45] χαίροντες. This expression, χαίρων, so common in all the Greek authors, has generally been the stumbling-block of translators: it signifies "with impunity."—*Larcher.*

Smerdis was sitting on the royal throne, and touched with his head the sky. In consequence of this, dreading that his brother might kill him, and become king, he despatched Prexaspes into Persia, his most faithful servant among the Persians, with orders to make away with Smerdis. Prexaspes, accordingly, went up to Susa, and put Smerdis to death; taking, as some say, the prince out to a hunting-party[46]; or, as others relate, conducting him down to the sea-side, where he drowned him. The above, therefore, was the beginning of the evil deeds of Cambyses. His wickedness was next directed against his sister, who had followed him into Egypt; and to whom he was united in marriage, although she was his sister by his father as well as his mother. The manner in which he contrived to form this connection was as follows; for hitherto the Persians had strictly refrained from all intermarriages of brothers and sisters. Cambyses became enamoured of one of his own sisters: having afterwards determined to espouse her, and aware that such a precedent was contrary to custom, he called together the royal judges, and inquired of them whether there was a law authorizing any one who wished to marry his sister. The royal judges are Persians, appointed for life, or till such time as they be convicted of injustice: these individuals pronounce judgment to the Persians, and are the expounders of the laws of their forefathers: to them all matters are referred. When questioned, accordingly, by Cambyses, they consulted, in their answer to him, both justice and their own safety: they declared, they knew of no law that advised a brother to marry his sister; but that they had found, indeed, another one, saying it is permitted to the Persian king to act in every thing as he chooses. Thus they evaded an abrogation of the law, from the fear of Cambyses; and, in order they might not bring destruction to themselves by maintaining that law, found for their purpose another in support of the king's wish to marry his sisters. Then, in consequence of this decision, Cambyses married the object of his love: not long after, he took as a wife another sister. The younger of these, who had accompanied him into Egypt, was, accordingly, the victim of his fury. As in the case of Smerdis, two accounts are given of the death of this princess. The Hellenes say, that Cambyses placed the whelp of a lion to fight with that of a dog, and this lady was a spectator of the combat. The puppy being beaten by the young lion, his brother puppy broke the chain, and rushed to his assist-

---

[46] Constr. οἱ μὲν λέγουσι (Πρηξάσπεα) ἐξαγαγόντα . Σμέρδιν ἐπ' ἄγρην (ἀπίστωσαι).

ance: the young dogs, now two against one, soon overpowered the lion's whelp. At this sight, Cambyses was greatly pleased; but the lady, sitting by his side, shed tears. Cambyses observed her tears, and asked why she wept. Her answer was, that she cried at seeing the puppy come to the assistance of his brother; being thereby put in mind of Smerdis, who she knew would have no avenger. For this remark, Cambyses accordingly, as the Hellenes state, murdered his sister. But the Egyptians, on the other hand, affirm, that they were sitting at table, when the lady took up a lettuce, pulled off the outside leaves, and asked her husband whether the lettuce was more beautiful when stripped, or when accompanied with all its foliage. On Cambyses answering, when with its leaves—she retorted, " Then, indeed, " you have done what I did to this lettuce, in your treat- " ment of Cyrus's family." This enraged the king, who kicked her, although she was with child; in consequence of which, she miscarried, and died.

Such were the excesses committed by Cambyses on his own family, in this state of madness; whether that madness had its origin in the insult to Apis, or any other cause among the many calamities that visit mankind: for it is said, that Cambyses was from his birth afflicted with fits, or what some people call the sacred disease[47]: if such was the case, therefore, it was unlikely that the body being oppressed with such a grievous disorder, the mind should remain uninjured[48]. The following are instances of his mad phrensy, shewn towards the rest of the Persians. It is related, that he once addressed Prexaspes, whom he esteemed highly;— the office of this person was to present all messages; and his son was cupbearer to Cambyses, no inconsiderable dignity; —he addressed, it is said, this officer thus: " Tell me, Prex- " aspes, what is the opinion the Persians have of me? " What are the discourses they hold about me?" " Sove- " reign lord," replied Prexaspes, " in every respect they " extol you highly; excepting, as they say, your too great " fondness for wine." Thus Prexaspes spoke concerning the Persians; but Cambyses went into a passion, and said: " Well, the Persians say, do they, that I lose my senses " through my passion for wine? surely, then, their former

---

[47] The Greek is μεγάλη νόσος, which I at first thought might be translated, literally, " great disorder:" but Hesychius informs us that μεγάλη νόσος signifies the " epilepsy:" consult his Lexicon, voc. μεγάλη νόσος, and νόσος μεγάλη. *Larcher.*—If we adopt Larcher's version of these two words, I cannot see what will become of the qualificative *τινα.*

[48] Matt. 423.

"praise was false." For, previously to this, Cambyses had asked the Persians who sat in his council, and Crœsus, what sort of a man they thought him to be, in comparison with his father Cyrus. The Persians answered, that he was superior to his father; as he possessed not only the whole of the dominions of Cyrus, but had increased them by the addition of Egypt and the empire of the sea. Crœsus, who was present, and disapproved this decision[a], addressed Cambyses in these words: "Son of Cyrus," he said, "in my "opinion you are not equal to your father; for you have "not yet a son, like him that he left." Cambyses was pleased at this observation, and approved highly of Crœsus's 35 decision. Recollecting, therefore, what was then said, he spoke thus in his anger to Prexaspes: "Behold now your-"self, whether the Persians speak the truth, or whether they "themselves do not act as if reft of their senses, when they "hold such language! for if I shoot at your son that stands "yonder in the porch, and hit him just in the heart, that "will shew that the Persians talk nonsense: if, however, I "miss my mark, that will prove the Persians to be right, "and me to be out of my senses." He spoke, and, bending the bow, shot the youth, who instantly fell. Cambyses ordered the body to be opened, and the wound examined; and when the shaft was found sticking in the heart, he said to the father of the boy, laughing, and seeming highly gratified: "Prexaspes, you must at present be convinced that it "is not I that am distraught, but the Persians themselves "that are so: pray, tell me now, did you ever see mortal man "take such good aim[50]?" Prexaspes, who saw the prince was mad, and feared for his own safety, said: "Sovereign lord, "I do not think the god himself could take so steady an "aim." Such was the crime he then committed: at another time he seized twelve Persians of the first rank[51], without any righteous cause, and buried them up to the neck[52].

36 The king acting in the above manner, Crœsus, the Lydian prince, thought it his duty to advise him in the following

---

[a] Matt. 383, 5.

[50] ἐπίσκοπα is a neuter plural, taken adverbially for ἐπισκόπως. ἐπίσκοπον ἰόντος is an arrow that hits the mark, as in Theocritus, Id. xxiv. 105, ὄφρα δ᾽ ἱπταμένας καὶ ἐπισκόπον ἴσαι ἰόντων, which Warton unnecessarily corrects ἐπίσκοπος. There is a great difference between ἐπίσκοπα τοξεύειν and ἐπὶ σκοπόν, κατὰ σκοπόν, κατὰ σκοποῦ τοξεύειν. The first expression signifies, to hit the mark; the others, to shoot at the mark, whether it is hit or not.—Larcher.

[51] Lit. "twelve Persians of the same rank as the highest." Ὅμοια is for ὁμοίως. These were of the class called by Xenophon, in many places of the Cyropædia, the ὁμότιμοι. Larcher.—Schweig., however, translates ὁμοίᾳ τῆς πρώτοις "non dissimili ratione." Schweig. Ver. Lat.

[52] ἐπὶ κεφαλήν, "jusqu'à la tête," Larcher; "inverso capite;" Schweig.

discourse: "Sire, I earnestly beseech you, not to commit "yourself entirely to passion and the warmth of youth; but "restrain and govern yourself. Foresight and prudence "are valuable and wise qualities⁵³. Whereas you put to "death your own fellow-citizens, seizing them for no just "cause: you even slay children. If you continue to act "in this manner, beware lest the Persians rise up against "you. Your father Cyrus enjoined me expressly to ad- "vise you, and to suggest whatever I might think expe- "dient." These observations evidently proceeded from a spirit of benevolence; but Cambyses gave the following answer: "Do you, also, dare to give counsel to me; you, "who so wisely managed your own country; and gave "such excellent advice to Cyrus, exhorting him to cross the "Araxes, and march against the Massagetæ, although they "were willing to cross over themselves into our territory? "You have ruined yourself by your bad government of "your own country: you have ruined Cyrus, who listened "to your advice⁵⁴: but you shall pay for it, as I have long "been wishing to find a pretext to lay hands on you." So saying, he took up his bow, and prepared to aim an arrow at the Lydian prince: but Crœsus escaped, and ran out. Cambyses, disappointed in his intention to shoot him with his own bow, ordered the attendants to lay hold of him, and put him to death: the attendants, however, aware of the king's humour, concealed Crœsus, with a view, in case of Cambyses repenting of what he had done, and inquiring for Crœsus again, to shew him, and thereby get a reward for saving his life: in case the king did not repent, or regret his loss, they might even then put him to death. No long time elapsed before Cambyses did, in fact, express his regret for Crœsus: the attendants seeing this, announced to him that the Lydian prince was still alive. Cambyses observed; "that he was much gratified to find he survived: but that "he would shew no mercy⁵⁵ to those who disobeyed his "orders, and would have them put to death:" in fact, he did so.

Many other instances of the king's phrensy, shewn in his behaviour to the Persians and their allies, occurred during his stay at Memphis. He broke open the ancient repositories of the dead, and examined the dead bodies. He went even to Vulcan's temple, and derided the sacred image⁵⁶: for the

⁵³ Matt. 427.
⁵⁴ See Matt., observation on the separation of the preposition from the verb (δεῖ from ἕλωας), 594, 2.
⁵⁵ παντάπασιέσεσθαι, "to do any thing with impunity:" this verb is construed with the participle.—*Schweig. Lex. Herod.*
⁵⁶ Matt. 394, a. obs. 1.

image of Vulcan is exactly similar to the Phœnician Pataics, which the Phœnicians carry at the prows of their triremes: for the information of those who have never seen this figure, I may say, it is the semblance of a dwarf. Cambyses also entered the temple of the Cabeiri, which is unlawful to all, excepting the priest alone: he consumed by fire the images, after insulting and deriding them in various ways. These images are like that of Vulcan[57], of whom the Cabeiri are said to be the children. I am clearly of opinion, therefore, that Cambyses was in every respect raving mad[58]; for otherwise he would never have thought of insulting and deriding religious things and general customs[59]. Indeed, were an offer made to all mankind to select the best of all laws and customs, after considering those of every country, each would prefer those of his own; so fully convinced is every one of the excellence of his country's usages: consequently, it is out of the question that any but a lunatic would ever hold such things in derision. That all have the same sentiments in respect of national practices, is a fact that may be established by abundant proofs, the following in particular. Darius, at the beginning of his reign, called into his presence the Hellenes resident in his vicinity, and inquired, " at what " price they would resolve to eat the flesh of their deceased " fathers:" they all declared, they would not do so for any compensation whatever. Darius afterwards sent for some Indians called Callatiæ, who feast on the dead bodies of their parents, and, in the presence of the Hellenes, inquired of them, " at what price they would adopt the practice of " consuming by fire their deceased fathers:" the Indians expressed their horror by loud exclamations, and implored the king to use more seemly language. Such is the general persuasion[60]: and, in my opinion, Pindar the poet says justly, " Custom is the king of all."

[57] Matt. 386, 5.
[58] The reader who, after perusing the nine books of Herodotus, closes the volume, and finds that he remembers but this one chapter, will surely not deem his time ill spent. The Historian gives here a wholesome lesson, which, sooner or later, all men learn from a master far more severe than our honest author; I mean, from the world, whose instructions are often purchased at the expense of character and fortune. " These," says Major Rennel, contrasting the character of a true lover of liberty with that of the demagogic scoundrels of the French Revolution, in a strain highly characteristic of the English gentleman, " are the sentiments of a republican, who, in order to enjoy a greater degree of civil liberty, quitted his native city, Halicarnassus, when its system of laws was violated by the tyrant Lygdamis." p. 7.
[59] Matt. 394. obs. 2.
[60] οὕτω μὲν τοι ταῦτα νενόμισται: this, I think, relates to ὡς δὲ οὕτω νενομίκασι τὰ περὶ τοὺς νόμους, a little higher up; being one of those repetitions so common in Herodotus, and most ancient writers. Larcher translates " tant

At the time of Cambyses' expedition against Egypt, the 39 Lacedæmonians were likewise engaged in a war against Samos, and Polycrates son of Ajax, who had risen up and taken possession of that island. At the beginning, he had separated the state into three portions, and divided it with his brothers Pantagnotus and Syloson: subsequently, he put to death the former, and drove away the younger brother Syloson, so that he came into sole possession of all Samos. Having thus established his power, he framed a contract of friendship with Amasis, the king of Egypt, sending gifts to that sovereign, and receiving others in return. In a short time, the power of Polycrates increased all at once, and became renowned [61] over Ionia and the rest of Hellas: for wherever he directed his forces, every thing succeeded happily to him. He was in possession of one hundred penteconters, and had a thousand archers. He attacked and rifled [62] every one without distinction; alleging, that the restoration of what he took away, gave a greater gratification to those who had been plundered, than if he had not taken it away at first. He became, accordingly, master of several islands, and of many continental towns: among others, he defeated, and took prisoners, in an engagement, the Lesbians who were coming with all their forces to the succour of the Milesians: these Lesbian prisoners, loaded with shackles, dug out the moat that surrounds the walls of Samos. Amasis was well aware of the extraordinary good fortune of 40 Polycrates, but it was a subject of uneasiness to him. As his prosperity continued to increase, the king of Egypt made the following communication, by letter, which he sent off to Samos.—" Amasis to Polycrates says this: It is sweet to " hear of the prosperity of a friend and ally: but, convinced " as I am of the divine jealousy [63], I feel little gratified by

la coutume a de force;" and Schweig. " ita igitur hæc constituta sunt."

[61] καὶ (τὰ πρήγματα) ἦν βεβωμένα, κ. τ. λ. " and *his power* was celebrated," &c.

[62] See note 197, in p. 46.

[63] τὸ θεῖον - - - ἐστὶ φθονερόν. This passage, and a similar one in the discourse of Solon to Crœsus, i. 32, have been the subject of much disquisition; as it would seem, at first sight, that Herodotus attributes to the divinity one of the worst passions of human nature; I mean, envy: and, indeed, Plutarch accuses the Historian of so doing, in direct terms. We must not expect to find among the ethnicks those sublime ideas of the divinity for which we are indebted to the immediate revelations of the Almighty. I cannot, however, but be of the opinion of Larcher, that by φθονερὸν Herodotus means the hostility of the divinity against that pride so often engendered by success in the human heart, and not the regret which too many men feel at the prosperity of their fellow-creatures. The epithet " jealous" is not of unusual application to the Almighty in the Scriptures, where the sense of the word is known to every reader: Exod. x. See *Schweig. Lex. Herod.* voc. φθονερὸν.

VOL. I.

"your great good fortune: I would fain myself, and such
"as I cherish, should be at one time exalted by prosperity,
"and at another time humbled by disappointment; and
"thus have life chequered by the alternation of success and
"failure, rather than prosper in every occasion: for never
"have I heard of an individual, constantly successful, that
"did not come to a most miserable end. Listen, therefore,
"to the advice I now offer you; apply this palliative to
"your good fortune: Consider well, and decide on some-
"thing that you hold to be of the greatest worth, and the
"loss of which would most bitterly pain your soul; cast it
"away far from you, so that it may no more be seen of
"man: and if, after this, good fortune and bad do not in
"turn befal you, have recourse to the remedy I have pro-
41 "posed." Polycrates read over this communication; and
having debated carefully in his own mind, how he should
exactly follow the advice of Amasis, considered which of his
rare treasures would, by its loss, inflict the greatest sorrow
on his soul: after due consideration, he decided upon this.
He had a seal which he wore, set in gold; it was an emerald
stone, the work of a Samian, Theodorus son of Telecles:
he resolved, therefore, to cast away this jewel; and for that
purpose equipped a penteconter, on which he embarked;
and gave orders for the ship to stand out for deep water.
Having reached to a considerable distance from land, he
took off his ring from his finger, and cast it into the deep,
before the eyes of all on board, and then sailed back again:
when returned to his palace, he assumed the demeanour of
42 one stricken with great misfortune. Five or six days after
this, a fisherman, having caught a fine large fish, bethought
himself that it would be a present worthy of Polycrates: he
accordingly went with the fish to the palace-gates, and
made known his wish to be admitted into the presence of
Polycrates. His request was granted[64]: he presented the
fish, and said: "Sire, I have caught this fish, but did not
"think it right to take it to market. Although I am a poor
"labouring man, that earns his bread by his hands, I said to
"myself, it is worthy of Polycrates and his empire; and
"therefore I have brought it for your acceptance." Polycrates, pleased with the man's address, answered: "You have
"gratified me much; and I am doubly obliged to you[65],

[64] χωρήσαντος δὲ οἱ τούτου, "cum hoc ei successisset," i. e. having succeeded in obtaining what he asked. The verbs χωρέω, and the compound προχωρέω, are frequently taken in this sense, without the general addition of εὐτυχῶς. Larcher; Schweig. Les. Herod.; Wesseling. Not.

[65] Lit. "and the favour is double, both of the address and the gift."

"for your compliment and your present. I invite you to "supper." The fisherman, considering this a very great honour, went home: and the servants proceeding to cut up the fish, found in its belly Polycrates' ring. As soon as they descried the precious jewel, they took it out, and forthwith, full of exultation, carried it to Polycrates; and gave him the ring, explaining in what manner they had found it. This event seemed to Polycrates fraught with something divine[66]; he described in writing all the particulars of what he had done; mentioned what was the result; and sent off the letter to Egypt[67]. Amasis read over the letter that came from Polycrates, and felt persuaded that it is quite impossible for a man to save a man from his fate; and that, without doubt, Polycrates, constantly so fortunate, would not come to an happy end; for he even found again the very things that he cast away. He therefore despatched a herald to Samos, to renounce his compact of alliance. His motive for acting in this manner was, in order that, in case of any dire misfortune falling upon Polycrates, he should not himself be afflicted with pain at heart in consequence of his friendly connexion.

It was against this Polycrates, so successful in all things, that the Lacedæmonians were now waging war, at the solicitation of a party of the Samians, who, subsequently to these events, founded Cydonia in Crete. Polycrates had sent to Cambyses, who was at that time collecting forces for the Egyptian campaign, and requested that prince to send to him at Samos, and ask for men[68]. Cambyses, on this intelligence, eagerly grasped the offer, and asked Polycrates to send a naval armament to join in the expedition against Egypt. Polycrates, therefore, selected such of the citizens as he most suspected of an intention to rebel; put them on board of forty triremes, and despatched them; enjoining Cambyses, at the same time, never to send them back again. According to some accounts, the Samians, thus despatched by Polycrates, never came to Egypt; but, after reaching the Carpathian sea, held council among themselves, and resolved to proceed no longer in their voyage: other accounts represent them as having arrived in Egypt; and, finding themselves watched there[69], taking to flight; then directing

---

[66] τὸν δὴ (i. e. Πολυκράτεα) ἐσῆλθε τῶν ἴδεαι τὸ πρῆγμα: "the thought entered Polycrates, that the event was superhuman." ἐσέρχομαι, in this sense, sometimes governs the dative; as, Κροίσῳ ἐσελθὸν τὸ τοῦ Σόλωνος, i. 86.

[67] See the same expression in v. 95.
[68] Matt. 531. obs. 2.
[69] φυλασσομένους admits of two meanings, "observatos," and "in custodiâ habitos." Schweig. Lex. Herod. voc. φυλάσσω.

their course towards Samos. It is further stated, that Polycrates went out to meet them with his fleet, and gave them battle: the returning party conquered, and made a descent upon the island, where, in a land engagement, they were repulsed, and so made away for Lacedæmon. There are some persons who assert that these Samians, on their return from Egypt, vanquished Polycrates: but this statement appears to me incorrect; for there would have been no necessity for their application to the Lacedæmonians, if they had been sufficient of themselves to get the upper hand of Polycrates[m]. Besides, reason will not admit, that a sovereign, whose paid auxiliaries and native archers were so plentiful, should have been worsted by such an insignificant band as these Samians, returning from Egypt, constituted. Moreover, Polycrates had collected the children and wives of the citizens under his dominion, in the naval storehouses; and held himself prepared, in case of any treachery on the part of his subjects, or tampering with the returning party, to set fire to the storehouses[71], and consume all the inmates.

46 When these Samians, repulsed by Polycrates, arrived at Sparta, they stood before the magistrates; and made a long speech, exposing, in prolix words, their requests. At this first interview, the Spartans answered, that they had forgotten the commencement, and did not understand the conclusion. Afterwards, in a second interview, the Samians brought a leather-bag[72], and said not one word more than this: "The bag wants flour." The Spartans observed, that these words were superfluous, the bag was enough[73]; but

47 resolved to give them assistance. When the Lacedæmonians had made the necessary preparations, they set out for Samos. The motive, according to the Samians, was to repay them for their former services in assisting the Lacedæ-

---

[70] παρίσταμαι, in the preterite and 2d aorist, signifies, 'I am subdued,' 'I am compelled to yield:' see iii. 13. In the middle voice, this verb is taken actively, and signifies, 'I subdue,' 'I compel to surrender:' except in the first future, where it is taken in a passive sense, as in iii. 155. *Larcher.*

[71] Matt. 400, *f*.

[72] θύλακος is, properly, a "leathern sack:" Hesychius explains it by δοράν διφθέρινος. It is also explained *in Glossis* MSS. "vas ad ferendum panem ex corio, quod milites ferunt." *Larcher.*

[73] περιεργάζομαι signifies, literally, "to do something superfluous and useless:" hence this phrase admits of two meanings; the first is that given by Schneider, in his Gr. and Germ. Lexicon; "that they had done something superfluous with the bag, inasmuch as they shewed it, while it was sufficient to mention it, [mit dem Sacke hätten sie etwas Ueberflüssiges gethan, dass sie ihn gezeigt hätten;"] the second is, "that they had done too much," *i.e.* "had been too garrulous in using words at all: it would have been sufficient to shew the empty bag." *Schweig. Lex. Herod.*; *Schneid. Gr. Germ. Lex. voc.* περιεργάζομαι.

monians with some ships, in their contest with the people of Messene: but, according to the account of the Lacedæmonians themselves, it was not so much to furnish the assistance craved by these Samians, as to gratify a desire of revenge for the robbery of the wine-bowl which they were sending to Crœsus, and that of the corselet sent to them as a present by Amasis, king of Egypt, the year before the plunder of the wine-bowl. This corselet was made of linen, and decorated with abundance of inwoven figures of animals, in gold and vegetable wool[74]. Every thread of this corselet richly deserves our admiration; for, although of very delicate texture, each consists of three hundred and sixty twines, all of which are distinct: such another corselet is that dedicated by Amasis to Minerva at Lindus.

The Corinthians likewise eagerly abetted the expedition against Samos; for they had been insulted by the Samians in the generation preceding this war, and about the same time that the wine-bowl was taken by violence[75]. Periander, the son of Cypselus, sent three hundred of the sons of the chief men of Corcyra to Sardis, where they were to be emasculated. The persons charged with conveying the boys touched at Samos: the inhabitants, having an inkling of the purpose for which the children were conveyed to Sardis, first tutored them how to embrace the temple of Diana; and then forbade that any person should tear the suppliants from the temple. As the Corinthians refused all food to the children, the Samians instituted a feast, which they still celebrate in the same manner. At nightfall, during the whole time the children stayed as suppliants, they instituted choirs of virgins and young boys, enacting, that they should carry baked cakes of sesame and honey, in order that the Corcyræan children might lay hold of them for food. This continued until the Corinthians, appointed to superintend the lads, took their departure[76]; and then the Samians conveyed the children back to Corcyra. If, therefore, after the decease of Periander, friendship had existed between the Corinthians and the Corcyræans, the former would not, for the above cause, have taken any part in the expedition against Samos: the fact is, that, ever since the foundation of Corcyra, the Corinthians and the colonists have constantly been at variance: on this account, therefore, the Corinthians still preserved the remembrance of the insult they had received at the hands of the Samians. Periander selected the sons of

---

[74] Cotton, beyond a doubt.
[75] Matt. 386, 1.
[76] ἐς τοῦτο - - - ἐς ὅ, "eo usque - - - - donec."

the first families of Corcyra, and sent them to Sardis to be
castrated, in revenge of an insult previously offered to him
50 by the colonists. For after Periander had killed his consort
Melissa, another calamity was added to the first: he had
two sons by Melissa, of the respective ages of seventeen and
eighteen years. Their maternal grandfather, Procles, the
usurper of Epidaurus, sent for his two grandsons on a visit,
feeling naturally an affection for the offspring of his daughter: and when he sent back the youths, and bade them farewell, said, " My sons, do you know who murdered your
" mother?" The elder boy took no notice of this speech; but
the younger, whose name was Lycophron, was so stricken
with grief at having heard this, that on his arrival at Corinth,
knowing his father to have been the murderer of his mother,
he would not speak to him, nor enter into conversation with
him; nor would he return any answer, when questioned by
him. At last Periander, setting himself against the boy,
51 turned him out of doors. Having expelled the younger
son, he questioned the elder about what his maternal grandfather might have conversed with him. The youth described
to him how affectionately he had received them: as to the
very words that Procles pronounced when he sent them
away, he had not taken notice what they were, and could
not call them to mind. Periander observed, that it was impossible that he should not have given them some advice;
and continued to examine his son, till, at last, the young man
recovered his memory, and mentioned the above observation of Procles. Periander having considered the subject,
and determined no longer to shew any indulgence to his
younger son, sent people round to the persons at whose
houses his runaway son ate, and forbade them any longer to
receive him under their roofs. The youth, when turned away
by one, sought refuge at another's house; but was soon obliged
to leave that also, in consequence of Periander threatening the receivers, and insisting upon their turning him
away; and thus the banished son went[77] from the house of
one to that of another: and the proprietors, although in fear,
52 still opened their doors to Periander's son. At last, Periander proclaimed, that whoever received him into their houses,
or spoke to him, should pay a holy fine to Apollo, the
amount of which was specified. In consequence of this proclamation, no person would speak to Lycophron; every one
refused him admittance into their houses: besides, Lycophron
himself did not offer any resistance to his father's prohibi-

[77] See Matt. 598, a. Hermann. ad Viger. n. 286.

tion, but began to haunt continually the porticoes. Four days after this, Periander, seeing him reduced to misery, unwashed [78] and unfed, took pity on him; his anger relaxed; he approached him, and said: "My son, which would you choose for yourself, your present mode of life, or the supreme power and luxuries which I now enjoy—and the same are yours, if you but respect your father? Although my own son, and the king of wealthy Corinth, you have chosen a vagrant's life, resisting, and treating in anger, him to whom you ought to behave thus the least of all. If any misfortune has occurred in the family [79], and produced suspicions against me in your mind, know, that this calamity has recoiled on myself, and I bear all the burthen, being the perpetrator of the deed [80]. Now that you have learnt how much better it is to be envied than pitied, and know what it is to evince anger against parents, and parents endowed with power, come back home." By such language, Periander endeavoured to win the affection of his son; but the youth made no reply; and merely observed, that his father owed a fine to Apollo, for having spoken to him. Periander, seeing the youth's distemper was obstinate and incurable, equipped a ship, and sent him away to Corcyra, out of his sight. Having so done, Periander marched against his father-in-law, Procles, as the chief author of his present misfortunes: he captured Epidaurus, and made a prisoner of Procles. In the course of time, Periander, 53 stricken in years, feeling himself no longer competent to superintend affairs and conduct the government, sent to Corcyra, and invited Lycophron to assume the power; for he could discern nothing but stupidity in his eldest son [81]: Lycophron, however, did not even vouchsafe an answer to the bearer of the message. But Periander, who tenderly loved the young man, sent a second message by his daughter,

---

[78] The Greek expression ἀλουσίην means, that 'he had not bathed.' Before the use of linen, frequent bathing was as necessary for health as for cleanliness, more particularly in hot climates. *Larcher.*

[79] ἐν ἀτρείῃ. Wesseling and Coray supply πρήγμασι. Schweighæuser, after Reiskius, takes it to be equivalent to ἐν ἡμῖν, "apud nos, in familiâ nostrâ:" so likewise in iv. 97. *Schweig. Lex. Herod.* voc. ἀτρείη, 3.

[80] There is no necessity of changing τὸ πλίων into τῶν πλίων, according to the conjecture of Coray, because that correlative is commonly understood.

See Hoogeveen de Particulis Græcis, lix. 8. There is no doubt whatever that ἐξεργασάμην signifies, "I have killed:" σφι is a personal pronoun, signifying 'ipsum,' 'ipsam.' Periander dares not say to his son, "I have killed thy mother:" he merely says, "I have killed her;" wishing, perhaps, to diminish the horror of his crime. *Larcher*, and *Schweig. Lex. Herod.* voc. ἐξεργάζεσθαι.

[81] Construction: οὐκ ἐνώρα γὰρ ἐν τῷ πρεσβυτέρῳ τῶν παίδων (τὸ εἶναι δυνατὸν τὰ πρήγματα ἐνιπέειν): the ellipsis being supplied from what goes before. *Schweig.*

the sister of Lycophron, fancying that he might be more effectually persuaded by her. On her arrival at Corcyra, she spoke to her brother thus: "Brother, would you have "the supreme power fall into other hands, and suffer your "father's property[a] to be squandered away, rather than "come and take possession of it yourself? Return home; "cease to punish yourself: obstinacy is but a sorry tenure: "seek not to cure evil by evil. Many place mildness before "mightiness: many, consulting a mother's rights, have cast "away the rights they claimed at a father's hands. The "usurper's power is a slippery holding: the suitors for it "are many: our father is now old: give not to strangers "what is your own." Tutored by her father, the damsel used every persuasive art; but the brother would give no answer, but this: "that he never would return to Corinth, "so long as his father survived." The lady reported all to her father; and Periander sent a third message by a herald, signifying his intention to go himself to Corcyra; and exhorting his son to come to Corinth, and succeed to the throne. The son consented to these terms: the father prepared to sail for Corcyra; the son for Corinth. But the Corcyræans, informed of this arrangement, put the youth to death, in order to preclude the father's coming to their island. These were the reasons that moved Periander to wreak vengeance on the people of Corcyra.

54 The Lacedæmonians, on their arrival at Samos with a powerful force, laid siege to the town: and attacking the walls, left in their rear the tower situated on the sea-side, near the suburb. Afterwards, Polycrates himself, with a strong party, fell upon the besiegers, who were driven back: at the same time, the auxiliaries, together with crowds of the Samians themselves, poured down, from the upper tower erected on the declivity of the mountain, upon the Lacedæmonians, and, after engaging the enemies a short time, put them to flight: the conquerors pursued the fugi-
55 tives, and killed great numbers. If the rest of the Lacedæmonians had behaved on this day with the same gallantry as Archias and Lycopas, Samos would have been taken; for those two heroes, all alone, rushing into the city with the Samian fugitives, and shut out from all retreat, fell within the town itself of the Samians. I myself once met, at Pitane, with another Archias, the third descendant of the

---

[a] οἴκια, 'paternal possessions,' 'patrimony:' ϝοι, like μιν, is equivalent to αὐτόν, αὐτήν, αὐτό: and, consequently, may here be referred to οἴκων. *Schweig. Larcher.*

above-mentioned warrior[53], son of Samius, and grandson of Archias; he belonged to that canton. He respected the Samians more than any other strangers; both because his father received the name of Samius, and was the son of the Archias who displayed such valour at Samos, where he perished; and because, as he said, his grandfather was buried by the Samians at the public expense. The Lacedæmonians, after spending forty days in besieging Samos, saw that matters were none the forwarder[54], and returned to Peloponnesus. As a rather silly tale runs, Polycrates is said to have struck a great quantity of the country coin in lead: this coin he had gilt, and gave to the Spartans[55], who accepted it as a bribe to depart.—This was the first warlike expedition undertaken by the Lacedæmonian Dorians into Asia.

Those of the Samians who had kindled the war against Polycrates sailed away to Siphnos, when the Lacedæmonians shewed an intention to forsake them. The affairs of the Siphnians about this time were in the most flourishing state: they were the richest of the islanders; having in their island, mines of gold and silver, so productive, that out of the tithe of the coin accruing from them a treasury is dedicated at Delphi, comparable to the richest. They divided among themselves, every year, the product of these mines[56]. While they were erecting this treasury, they consulted the shrine, whether such riches would stay by them a long time[57]. The Pythia replied:

" When the Siphnian Prytaneum will be white, and the public
" square white too, then will you stand in need of an intelligent
" man to defend you from a wooden ambush[58] and a crimson
" herald."

But at that time the Prytaneum and public square were made of the Parian marble. The Samians, however, were unable to expound this oracle, neither at the time it was

---

[53] i. e. the grandson of the Archias who was slain at Samos. In speaking of genealogical degrees, the Greeks comprised the two extremes: thus the son was the second descendant, the grandson the third, and the great grandson the fourth. See note 201, p. 48.

[54] Construction: οὐδὲν τι τῶν πραγμάτων προαίνεσθαι ἐς τὸ πρόσω, " and as nothing of their affairs was advanced any the further."

[55] Matt. 457, 3.

[56] The Siphnians, as Larcher observes, became, in the sequel of time, as miserable as they had been opulent; affording another instance, that the monopoly of the precious metals, sooner or later, produces the downfal of nations.

[57] Lit. " whether it was possible (εἰ οἷά τέ ἐστι) that the present advantages should abide with them."

[58] Larcher translates ξύλινόν τι λόχον, by " une embûche de bois :" authorizing himself on Euripides, Troad. 534, who, speaking of the wooden horse before Troy, says, φόνιον ἐν οἰκείῳ ἔχοντα λόχον Ἀργείων - - - Θιᾷ δώσειν.

pronounced, nor even after the coming of the Samians. As soon as the Samians reached Siphnos, they sent up to the city one of their vessels, with ambassadors on board: now, of yore, all ships were painted with red lead; and that was what the Pythia meant, when she declared, the Siphnians ought to guard against a wooden ambush and crimson herald. The ambassadors having arrived, requested the Siphnians to give them ten talents[89]. On their refusal to advance such a sum, the Samians began to plunder their lands: the citizens, informed of this, immediately sallied forth to repel the enemies; they engaged in battle, and were beaten. Many of them were cut off, in their retreat to the city, by the Samians;

59 who, after this, extorted one hundred talents. These Samians purchased, with their money, from the people of Hermione, the island of Hydrea, on the Peloponnesian shore, and pledged it to the Trœzenians; and they themselves went to Crete, and there founded Cydonia: not that they had gone for that purpose, but to expel the Zacynthians from the island. Here, however, they remained; and during five years prospered greatly, so much as to be capable of building the sacred precincts now seen at Cydonia and the temple of Dictyna. In the sixth year, the Æginetæ, assisted by the Cretans, conquered them in a naval engagement, and reduced them to slavery. The conquerors sawed off the prows of their vessels, which carried at the head the figure of a boar, and consecrated them to the temple of Minerva in Ægina. This exploit was achieved by the Æginetæ in revenge of an injury done to them by the Samians: for the Samians, under the reign of Amphicrates at Samos, had first attacked Ægina, and caused much mischief to the inhabitants; but suffered severely in return.

60 I have been the more prolix on the subject of the Samians, as three of the mightiest works of the Hellenes were effected by this people. The first is, the excavation of a mountain one hundred and fifty orgyæ in height, beginning at the foot, and constituting a tunnel with two mouths: the length of this tunnel is seven stades; its height and breadth, each eight feet. Through the whole of this tunnel runs another excavation, twenty cubits deep, and three feet broad; along which, through conducting pipes, water is conveyed to the city from a copious spring[90]. The architect was Eupalinus,

---

[89] χρῆσαι, to give as a gift, not to lend. See Schweig. Lex. Herod. voc. χράω, I. 1.
[90] This work seems to have been a large tunnel dug through a mountain; along the middle of which an aqueduct was made. The tunnel was eight feet high, and as many broad; the aqueduct was three feet broad; so that on either side was a

son of Naustrophus, of Megara: this, accordingly, is one of the three great works. The second is a breakwater, thrown up in the sea, around the harbour: its depth, about one hundred orgyæ; its length, better than two stades. The third work is the most extensive temple, of all that I ever beheld; the first architect of which was Rhœcus son of Phileus, a native of the place.

While Cambyses son of Cyrus was tarrying in Egypt, reft of his senses, two brothers, of the order of the Magi, revolted. Cambyses had left one of them to be steward of his property: he it was that, accordingly, rose up; having ascertained the death of Smerdis, which was kept secret, and aware that the Persians acquainted with that circumstance were few in number[91], the majority fancying the prince to be still alive: he turned over these things in his mind[92], and resolved to seize the opportunity, and take possession of the throne. He had a brother; who, as I before observed, followed his example, and revolted likewise: this brother, in his appearance, resembled greatly Smerdis, and bore the same name as the deceased prince, the son of Cyrus, whom Cambyses had put to death, although he was his own brother. The other Magus, Patizeithes, well aware that this individual would in every thing do as he wished, seated him on the throne: and immediately sent heralds to all quarters, but to Egypt particularly, and proclaimed to the army, that the commands of Smerdis son of Cyrus were henceforward to be obeyed[93], and not those of Cambyses. The different heralds pronounced the above proclamation: the one that was appointed to proceed to Egypt, met Cambyses and the army at Ecbatana in Syria, and, standing forth, in the midst of the congregation, read the proclamation issued by the Magus. Cambyses, having heard this from the herald, thought the man spoke the truth, and that he himself had been betrayed by Prexaspes (that is to say, that, although sent for the purpose of putting Smerdis to death, he had not obeyed the order): he therefore turned his eye to Prexaspes: "Prexaspes," said the king, "is it "thus you execute the orders that I give you?" Prexaspes replied: "My liege, it cannot be true, that Smerdis should

61

62

---

path within the tunnel two feet and a half broad; serving, proba'.ly, as a passage, to repair the works, in case of need. *Wesseling. Larcher.*

[91] Matt. *548, 3.

[92] ταῦτα ταῦτα βουλεύσας ταῦτα, "hæc ille reputans." *Schweig. Vers. Lat.* "Cette mort, jointe aux circonstances dont je vais parler — *this death, coupled with the circumstances I am about to mention.*" ταῦτα ταῦτα relates to the death of Smerdis; ταῦτα, to what follows, viz. the resemblance of the Magus Smerdis to the Prince Smerdis. *Larcher.*

[93] Matt. 443, 1. 2d parag.

"ever have rebelled against you; and you need not have any altercation, great or little, with this man: for I myself, after I had executed your orders, buried Smerdis with my own hands: if, therefore, the dead rise again, you may also expect Astyages, the king of the Medes, to rise up again. If it is now as formerly, nothing can accrue to you from this, at all events. Now, therefore, I think we ought to pursue the herald, question and examine him as to the person from whom he comes here to proclaim that we are to do homage to king Smerdis." Thus Prexaspes spoke: Cambyses took the advice: forthwith the herald was pursued, and came back; and, when he arrived, Prexaspes questioned him: "My good man, since you have told us that you come with a message from Smerdis the son of Cyrus, speak the truth now, and you shall be let go harmless. Did Smerdis himself, appearing before you, give you your orders; or was it one of his attendants?" The man made answer: "I have never seen Smerdis the son of Cyrus, since king Cambyses departed for Egypt. It was the Magus, whom Cambyses appointed his steward, that gave me my orders; saying, that Smerdis the son of Cyrus charged me to make this communication to you." So spoke the man, without recourse to any subterfuge: and Cambyses then said: "Prexaspes, you have done your duty as a faithful servant, and are blameless: but who can be, then, the individual that has risen up against me in Persia, and falsely assumed the name of Smerdis?" Prexaspes replied: "I think, my liege, I can tell you how this comes about. The Magi are the rebels, one of whom you left your steward: I mean Patizeithes, and his brother Smerdis."

64 Cambyses, on hearing the name of Smerdis, was struck with the fulfilment of his dream, and the warning that accompanied it: it was, that he fancied he saw in his sleep a man who announced to him that Smerdis was seated on the throne, and that his head touched the skies. Seeing now that he had by mistake destroyed his own brother, he mourned the fate of Smerdis. Having so done, and bitterly complaining of the many calamities that oppressed him, he leaped on his horse, intending forthwith to proceed to Susa and attack the Magus: but, as he jumped upon his horse, the ferrule of his sword-sheath[94] dropped off, and the sword,

---

[94] μύκης, "a mushroom." This word is metonymically used to signify several things bearing some resemblance in shape to a mushroom: it means here the knob at the end of the sheath. *Schneid. Gr. Germ. Lex.* Nicander expresses himself in the same manner, μύκης ὑπὸ καίριον ἄορος. But as long as we are so little acquainted with the shape of the

thus uncovered, entered his thigh. Struck thus in the same part where he had before pierced Apis the god of the Egyptians, Cambyses, conceiving that he was mortally wounded[95], inquired what was the name of the town; and was told it was Ecbatana; a place where, according to an oracle some time before pronounced at Buto, he was to end his days. Cambyses, accordingly, had thought that he was to die in old age at Ecbatana of Media, where all his riches were deposited; but the oracle meant, in truth, the Ecbatana of Syria. No sooner had the king heard the name of the town, than, oppressed by the combined calamities of the revolt of the Magus and his wound, he was restored to his senses; and, applying to himself the oracle, exclaimed: " Here it is " that Cambyses the son of Cyrus is doomed by fate to die."

Such were the events at the time we are now speaking of: 65 but twenty days after this, Cambyses convened an assembly of the chief Persians, and addressed them as follows:—" Men " of Persia, something had occurred to me, which I kept the " most secret of all, but must now disclose to you[96]. I was " in Egypt at the time, and beheld a vision in my sleep: and " would that I had never seen such! I imagined that I saw " a messenger coming from my home, and informing me, " that Smerdis was seated on the regal throne, and with his " head touched the canopy of heaven. I feared that I should " be reft of my power by my brother, and acted with more " precipitation than prudence[97]; for it belongs not to human " nature to avert what is fated to happen: I mistook " the sense of the warning, sent Prexaspes to Susa with " orders to destroy Smerdis: having committed this wicked " deed, I lived tranquil, never giving it a thought, now as " Smerdis was taken off, that any other individual would " dare to rebel. But I was completely deceived in my views " of futurity: dreadful to say, I murdered my own brother, " and nevertheless am deprived of my kingdom; for the " person whom the god foreshewed me, in my dream, was to " rise up against me, was Smerdis the Magus. Being now " informed of what I have done, do not you fancy that " Smerdis the son of Cyrus is still alive. I tell you, the " Magians are in possession of the crown; him that I left to " administer my private property, and his brother Smerdis:

Persian and Greek words, we can say nothing certain respecting this word. *Larcher.*

[96] ὃς ἐι καιρίῃ βέβληται ἐτύρθαι. The word πληγῇ must be understood from ἴσηθε; an ellipsis of frequent recurrence. *Larcher. Bos Ellips. Gr.* 176.

[96] κατελάβησαί με. "Invasit me," *i. e.* " Impetus invasit animum meum." —*Commode Larcherus*: je ne puis m'empêcher. *Schweig. Lex. Herod.* voc. καταλαμβάνω.

[97] Matt. 456.

"that prince, therefore, whose duty it would have princi-
"pally been to avenge me of this disgraceful insult of the
"Magians, has died a most unjust death, at the hands of his
"nearest relative: he is no more; therefore it is highly
"necessary I should give my commands to you, the rest of
"the Persians⁹⁹, as to what I wish you should do, when I
"depart life. I accordingly call to witness the sovereign
"gods, and enjoin you all, and more especially the Achæme-
"nidæ here present, not to allow the power to go back to
"the Medes: if by craft they have possession, by craft also
"do you dispossess them: if they have wrought by force, so
"do you recover the upper hand by force⁹⁹. If you obey
"my injunctions¹⁰⁰, may your land be fruitful! may your
"women and your children multiply, and yourselves be
"free for ever! But unless you recover the supremacy, and
"exert yourselves for independence, I pray the contrary
"may befal you, and, moreover, that every Persian's death
"may be like mine!" After Cambyses had thus spoken, he
66 deplored the practice of his life. The Persians, seeing their
king weep, rent their garments, and did not spare the cries
of mourning: soon after, caries attacked the bone: the
thing forthwith began to fester, and carried off Cambyses¹⁰¹,
who had reigned, in all, seven years and five months, and
died without leaving any offspring, male or female. Great
disbelief pervaded the Persians that were present of the
Magians being at the head of affairs: they were persuaded
that Cambyses had said what he did of the death of Smerdis, in order that the whole Persian nation should become
his enemies. These persons, accordingly, were under conviction that Smerdis the son of Cyrus had revolted and
ascended the throne: for even Prexaspes strenuously denied
that he had been the perpetrator of Smerdis's death; as it
would have been dangerous for him, now that Cambyses
was dead, to have said that he killed Cyrus's son with his
own hand.

⁹⁹ τῶν λοιπῶν is the same as τοῦ λοιποῦ, and signifies, "tandem, quod ad reliquum attinet, cæterum."—*Larcher*. It is evident that the genitive, τῶν λοιπῶν, is here governed by the superlative ἀναγκαιότατον; the sense being: "Secundo loco, reliquorum præceptorum, quæ mihi vobis danda supersunt, maxime necessarium hoc est." *Schweig Lex. Herod.* voc. λοιπός.

⁹⁹ παστεργασάμενοι τὴν (Περσῶν) ἡγεμονίαν may, perhaps, mean, " if they have put an end to the empire of the Persians." I have followed Schweighæuser's Latin version.

¹⁰⁰ καὶ ταῦτα μὲν ποιεῦσι ὑμῖν · · · · ἐοῦσι τε τὴν ἄπασαν χρόνον ἐλευθέροισι. " Si vous faites ce que je vous recommande, et si vous conservez votre liberté.—*If you act according to my injunctions, and preserve your liberty, may,*" &c. *Larcher*.

¹⁰¹ Supply, to govern ἰοῦσι. the words, ἢ τούτος, or ταῦτα τὰ ποιεῖ —*Schweig.*

Accordingly, the Magus, after the death of Cambyses, 67 pursued his rule undisturbed, taking advantage of his name, which was the same as that of Cyrus's son Smerdis, during the seven months that remained to complete the eight years of Cambyses' reign. During this period, he lavished his benefits on all his subjects: so that, at his death, all in Asia, with the exception of the Persians, bewailed his loss: for the Magus had promised to every nation in his dominions, exemption from all levies for war and payment of tribute for three years; a boon which he pledged himself to, at his first rise to power. In the eighth month the fraud was discovered, as I 68 now shall describe. Otanes was the son of Pharnaspes, equal in blood and opulence to the first of the Persians [101]: he was the first, also, that suspected the Magus not to be the Smerdis son of Cyrus, but what he really was: he inferred this from the fact, that the king never came out of the citadel, and never called into his presence any of the Persians of rank. Having conceived these suspicions, he set to work in this manner. Cambyses had married his daughter Phædima: the Magus, accordingly, had taken her, together with all the rest of Cambyses' women; and she was to him as a wife. Otanes therefore sent to this daughter, and inquired with what man she was wont to sleep; whether with Smerdis the son of Cyrus, or any other man. The lady sent back, in answer, that she did not know; for she had never seen Smerdis the son of Cyrus, and knew not the person who visited her. Otanes sent a second time, with this message: 69 "If you do not yourself know Smerdis the son of Cyrus, ask "Atossa who it is that visits both her and you; for no "doubt she must, at all events, know her own brother." Phædima returned this answer: "I cannot have any con- "versation with Atossa, or see any of the other women with "whom we used to sit all together at work [102]: for as soon "as this man came, whoever he may be, he dispersed us, "and placed us women, one here, another there." When Otanes heard this, the business seemed to him clearer than before: he despatched a third message to his daughter, to this purport: "Dear daughter, high-born that you are, it "becomes you to face what perils your father may expose "you to. For if this man be not the Smerdis son of Cyrus,

---

[101] Matthiæ makes a remark on this passage; but he follows the old reading, ἴσαιος. Sect. 289, 3.

[102] συγκαιρυσίαν, from συγκαιρύστω, "to sit together:" in the Harems of the Medes and Persians, the women used to sit together spinning and conversing, as we may gather from the history of queen Esther. *Wessel*. This interpretation is approved by Schweighæuser; although he gives in his Latin version, "quæ mecum hic unà habitant." See *Schweig. Lex. Herod.* voc. συγκαιρύστω.

"but him that I surmise, he ought not certainly to keep
"company with you and the other women, or to hold the
"Persian empire and escape unpunished, but must satisfy
"justice. Now do, therefore, as I tell you. When he lies
"down by your side, and you have ascertained that he is
"fast asleep, then feel for his ears: if it appears that he has
"ears[103], let that convince you that you are with Smerdis
"the son of Cyrus; but if he has none, you are with Smer-
"dis the Magus." Phædima sent back word, and said,
"she should be exposed to great danger; for if he hap-
"pened not to have any ears, and she was detected feeling
"for them, she knew very well he would put her out of the
"world; nevertheless, she would run the chance." Thus
she pledged herself to do what her father required.—It
must be observed here, that Cyrus the son of Cambyses, the
first Persian king, had cropped the ears of the Magus
Smerdis, as a punishment for some serious crime.—Phædima, this daughter of Otanes, determined to fulfil her promise to her father: accordingly, she waited till it came to
her turn to be the bed-companion of the Magus; for in
Persia, it is the custom that the men should visit their wives
in regular succession: accordingly, she went and slept with
him: when the Magus was fast asleep, she felt for his ears,
and easily[104] ascertained that the man had none; and at the
first dawn of day, she sent and let her father know how
matters stood.

70   Otanes invited Aspathines and Gobryas, Persians of the
highest rank, in whom he placed the highest confidence, and
explained the whole business to them. They themselves
had their suspicions, also, that such was the case; and when
Otanes had produced his reasons, adopted his opinion.
They agreed, among themselves, that each should add to
himself a partner, a native Persian, in whom he put his
greatest trust. Otanes, accordingly, associated to himself[105] Intaphernes; Gobryas, Megabyzus; Aspathines,
Hydarnes. They were therefore six in number, when Darius the son of Hystaspes arrived at Susa from Persia[106],
of which his father was viceroy: the six Persians accord-
71 ingly agreed to add Darius to their number. These seven

[103] Matt. *548, 5.
[104] Matt. 444, 5.
[105] *προσέταιρι*, " proponit." *Schweig.
Vers. Lat.* This translation the learned
scholar has since disapproved; and
proposed to replace that of L. Valla,
" adscivit sibi;" the Greek word being
equivalent to *προσεταιρίσασθαι*, a little
before. *Schweig. Lex. Herod.*
[106] Susa, though one of the capitals of
the Persian empire, was not in Persia,
but in Cissia: cf. 91 in fin. See the
Geographical Index to Herodotus, voc.
SUSA.

met, and mutually exchanged pledges and opinions: and when it came to the turn of Darius to disclose his ideas on the subject: " I thought," said he, " that I was the only " person who knew that the Magus was on the throne, and " that Smerdis the son of Cyrus was dead: and on that ac- " count I came hither, with all speed, to concert the death of " the Magus. But it appears that I am not the only one " acquainted with this secret; you know as much as myself. " I am therefore of opinion, that we ought, forthwith, to " act, and not interpose any further delay [107]." To this Otanes made reply: " Son of Hystaspes," said he, " you are " sprung from a gallant sire, and appear likely to prove " yourself not second to your father. I beseech you, however, " not heedlessly to precipitate things as you do; and consi- " der with more prudence our undertaking; for we must be " more numerous, to compass our object." To this Darius retorted: " Gentlemen, be assured that you will all perish " most miserably, if you adopt the plan proposed by Otanes. " Some one, consulting his own private ends, will report " every thing to the Magus. It is therefore your bounden " duty immediately to strike the blow yourselves. But if " you have determined to wait for greater numbers, and " compel me to it, listen to me: either let us act this very " day; or be assured, if you let slip the present day, no one " shall have the start of me [108]: I will myself become the " informer, and impeach you all to the Magus." Otanes, 72 seeing Darius so decisive, spoke thus: " Since you bind us " down to such despatch, and forbid all delay, come [109], ex- " plain yourself in what manner we can penetrate into the " palace, and fall upon the usurpers; for you yourself must " know, and, if you have not seen, have heard, that sentinels " are stationed on all sides: by what means shall we pass " through them?"—Darius's reply to this objection was in these words: " Otanes, there are many things not suscep- " tible of proof by words, but by facts: there are others " adapted to the powers of description, but, when put in " practice, produce no brilliant result. Be assured, all of you, " that the guards at the different stations will present no " obstacles to our passage: for, in the first instance, none " will impede the entrance of such persons as we are, " partly from veneration, partly from fear: in the second " place, I myself have a very palpable excuse for our " entrance, in saying that I have just come from Persia, " and wish to deliver to the king a message from my father.

[107] Matt. 457, 3.
[108] See the learned Bishop of Lon- don's observation, Matt. p. xlviii.
[109] *Ih*, ' age,' ' come.' Vig. viii. 5, 9.

"When a falsehood is expedient, let it be used; for we have all the same object in view [110], whether we say what is false or what is true. In that case, they who tell the falsehood, do so, at all events, in order that they may gain by making others believe what is false: they who tell the truth, do so likewise to gain and attract confidence, so that more trust may be put in them. Thus taking different ways, we tend to the same scope. If gain were not intended, it would be indifferent whether truth were falsehood, or falsehood truth [111]. The door-keeper, therefore, that lets us civilly pass by, shall hereafter be placed in a better situation: he that attempts to push us back, shall forthwith be declared a foe [112]. Then let us go in, and address

73 ourselves to work."—Hereupon, Gobryas rose: "Dear friends," he said, "when will a better opportunity present itself, to recover the throne; or die, should we fail in our attempt? now that we Persians are under the rule of a Medic Magus, and him cropped of his ears too. You, who were present at the sick-bed of Cambyses, forget not what curses the dying king pronounced on the Persians who would not exert themselves to recover the empire: at that time we did not believe him, but thought he spoke through hatred of his brother. Now, therefore, I give my vote, that we follow the advice of Darius, and, without breaking up our present meeting, straight attack the Magus." Thus spoke Gobryas, and all approved the proposal.

74 At the same time they were debating these things, the following occurrence came to pass. The Magi had determined to conciliate the support and friendship of Prexaspes; as he had suffered such infamous treatment at the hands of Cambyses, the murderer of his son with his bow, and was the only person that knew of the death of Smerdis the son of Cyrus, put away by his own hand: he was, besides, in the highest repute among the Medes. For these reasons they accordingly called him into their presence; and brought him over to their side, insisting, upon his pledge and oath [113], that he would keep to himself, and not divulge to any living being, the deception they were practising on the Persians; and pro-

---

[110] *οὐ ταὐτὰ ἀσκέοντες.* "non eadem exercentes." *τωυτοῦ εἱνεχόμεθα,* "we are anxious for the same," i. e. "we have the same thing at heart."

[111] The veneration for truth among the Persians (see i. 136.) will account for Darius using these sophistic arguments.

[112] Matt. 548, 5. Matthiæ follows the old reading, *διωκότω,* which Schweighæuser has very properly changed for *διδωκότω.* See Lex. Herod.

[113] *λαμβάνειν ὑπὸ πίστει καὶ ὁρκίων,* "fide data et juramentis aliquem obstringere:" the simple verb *λαμβάνειν* being used for the compound *παραλαμβάνειν. Schweig. Lex. Herod.*

mised to him thousands upon thousands[114]. Prexaspes consented to their offer: and the Magians having prevailed upon him, proposed, in the next place, to assemble all the Persians under the walls of the palace, and ordered him to ascend a tower and proclaim that Smerdis the son of Cyrus, and no other person, occupied the throne: they enjoined him to do this, as he was esteemed by the Persians a most honourable man, and had frequently asserted his opinion that Smerdis was still alive, and denied his being the person that killed him. Prexaspes said he was ready to accede to these 75 wishes; and the Magians assembled the Persians, sent Prexaspes up the tower, and bade him proclaim. But he, of his own accord, chose to forget the request of the Magians: he began from Achæmenes, and went through the genealogy of Cyrus's family: coming down to that prince, he finished by rehearsing the services Cyrus performed for the Persians[115]; and then proceeded to disclose the truth, saying, that heretofore he had kept it secret, as it would not have been safe for him to have mentioned what had taken place; but in the present emergency, necessity forced him to speak openly. He then stated, that, compelled by Cambyses, he had himself made away with Smerdis the son of Cyrus, and that the Magians were in possession of the throne. After pronouncing many imprecations on the Persians if they did not recover the empire and wreak vengeance on the Magians, he threw himself, head foremost, from the top of the tower to the bottom[116]. Prexaspes thus put an end to himself, having always been a man of great repute.

The seven Persian noblemen, accordingly, having decided 76 to fall immediately on the Magians and to admit no further delays, proceeded, after prayers to the gods, to their undertaking, knowing nothing of what had been done by Prexaspes. In the middle of their way to the palace, they were informed of what had taken place with respect to Prexaspes: in consequence of this, they stepped out of the highway, and again consulted among themselves. Otanes[117] earnestly advised delay, and not to effect their purpose in the present stir of affairs. Darius contended they should go on, and do as they had agreed, immediately and without any delay. In the midst of their altercation, appeared seven couples of hawks pursuing two couples of vultures, pecking and clawing

---

[114] Lit. "that they would give to him tens of thousands of all manner of things." See *Schweig. Lex. Herod.* voc. πᾶς, 4.
[115] Matt. 500.
[116] Lit. "cast himself (demisit se) head foremost, to be dashed from the tower to the ground."
[117] οἱ ἀμφὶ τὸν Ὀτάνην, i. e. Otanes. See Matt. 271, 2.

them [118]. The seven saw this, unanimously approved the sentiment of Darius, and went on towards the palace, encouraged by the omen. With respect to the sentinels stationed at the gates, the same behaviour nearly was shewed that had been anticipated by Darius in the statement of his opinion; the guards evinced great respect to the Persian nobles; and not suspecting any such attempt on their part, permitted them to pass on, as under the guidance of the gods: and none put any questions. When they reached the front court, they met with the eunuchs appointed to take in all messages; who inquired what their business was; at the same time threatening the door-keepers for letting them in; and endeavoured to hinder the seven conspirators from going any further. The noblemen cheered one another on, and, grasping their dirks, stabbed all their opponents on the spot, and then made a rush to the men's apartment [119]. The Magians happened to be both there, debating the conduct of Prexaspes: they saw the eunuchs in tumult, and heard them shriek: they both ran up to them, and, when informed what had been done, resolved to defend themselves: one, in his hurry [120], took up his bow; the other had recourse to his lance. A scuffle then ensued: the bow was of no service to him that took this weapon, the foe pressing too close upon him; but the other, with his javelin, resisted, and wounded Aspathines in the thigh, and Intaphernes in the eye:— Intaphernes did not die of his wound, but was deprived of the sight of that eye. Accordingly, one of the Magians wounded two of the conspirators: the other, finding his bow of no use, made for an alcove contiguous to the men's apartment, intending to close the doors; and was followed in by two of the seven, Darius and Gobryas. Gobryas grappled the Magus; and Darius stood uncertain, wishing to avoid wounding Gobryas in the dark. Gobryas, seeing him stand idle, asked wherefore he did not make use of his hand: the reply was, "I am anxious not to hurt you yourself." "No matter," exclaimed Gobryas, "drive your sword through both, if "necessary." Darius acted accordingly, made a thrust with his dagger, and luckily hit the Magus only.

79 Having killed the Magians, and cut off their heads, they left their wounded men there, on account of their feeble condition, and for the purpose of keeping guard on the citadel:

---

[118] Lit. 'pursuing,' 'tearing,' and 'clawing two couples of vultures.'

[119] ἀνδρεῶνα, "the apartment of the men;" in distinction of the γυναικωνῖτις, or apartment of the women, the Harem.

[120] Sometimes the idea of rapidity only is contained in φθάνω. See Matt. 559, b.

the other five, with the heads of the Magians[121], rushed out, and, making loud cries and great uproar, called up the other Persians, shewed them the heads, related what they had done, and cut down every Magus they fell in with. The Persians, informed of what had been done by the seven, and the fraud of the Magians, resolved to follow the example of the noblemen, and, dagger in hand, slaughtered every Magus they could find.—This day the Persians in common honour more than any other; and, on its anniversary, celebrate a magnificent festival, called by them the Massacre of the Magians. On that day no Magus must appear out of doors; all stay in their houses till sunset.

After an interval of five days, and when the tumult had 80 subsided, the nobles who had deposed the Magians held council on the situation of public affairs; and speeches were then made, which some of the Hellenes disbelieve, but which were certainly spoken. Otanes advised that the management of affairs should be committed to the whole Persian nation. " I am of opinion," Otanes said, " that we
" should no longer be governed by one single man; such a
" kind of rule is neither good nor desirable: for you know
" to what a height the presumption of Cambyses rose: you
" have likewise experienced the insolence of the Magus.
" How, indeed, could the government of one man alone be of
" any worth[122], when he is allowed to do as he likes? For,
" suppose the very best of all men invested with such power,
" he would be soon thrown out of the sphere of his former
" and habitual ideas: the advantages he enjoys brings inso-
" lence: envy is innate in man: these two vices constitute
" the sum of human wickedness. The despot, filled with in-
" solence, is guilty of many nefarious deeds: envy likewise
" drives him into iniquities. You would think, that, in the
" possession of so many good things, the despot should, at
" all events, be void of envy: just the contrary is his beha-
" viour to his subjects[123]. He hates the virtuous that sur-
" vive, and is pleased with the most wicked of his citizens:
" he listens graciously to slander[124], and is the most incon-
" sistent of men[125]. Shew, in moderation, respect for him,
" he is offended because you did not honour him greatly:

[121] ἔχοντες, 'having,' 'bearing,' 'gestantes.' Larcher translates "tenant à la main."
[122] Matt. 437, second parag.
[123] ἡ γ ἐναντίον τούτω (the contrary of this *conduct*), ἐς τοὺς πολίτας (towards the citizens), εἴωθε (is wont to occur).
[124] Lit. " he is excellent to admit calumnies."
[125] Schweighæuser reads ἀναρμοστότατον ἡ ἀνθρώπων, " quod vero maxime omnium incongruum est:" *mais ce qu'il y a de plus bizarre*. Larcher. Dr. Gaisford reads ἀναρμοστότατος, with Schæfer.

"honour him greatly, he is offended at what he calls adula-
"tion. I come now to his worst qualities: he overturns the
"laws of our fathers; he offers violence to our women; and
"puts to death individuals unheard. The sovereign people,
"in the first place, bears the fairest of names, 'equality of
"justice'[126]: in the second place, this government brings
"not the same evils as the monarch. The sovereign people
"appoint the magistrate,. by the cast of the die[127]; he is
"answerable for all he does: all deliberations are referred
"to the commons. I am therefore of opinion, that we should
"do away with monarchy, and exalt the people; for on the
"many all things depend." Such was the opinion that
81 Otanes laid before the council.—Megabyzus thought it expedient to establish an oligarchy[128]: his words were: "I say
"the same as Otanes said on putting down tyranny[129]; but
"he strayed far from the right judgment, when he urged
"us to confer the power on the multitude[130]. There is
"nothing more stupid than a useless mob[131]; nothing more
"insolent. It is indeed most insufferable, that men, anxious
"to escape the insolence of a tyrant, should expose them-
"selves to the insolence of an uncurbed people. The tyrant,
"when he does act, knows what he does; the mob cannot:
"for how should they know, who have never been taught,
"who are ignorant alike of what is virtuous and proper[132]:
"they rush headlong into things, unguided by reason,
"like a winter torrent. Let those who brood evil to the
"Persians adopt a democracy; while we elect a board of

[126] "Liberté et Egalité" was the cry of the bloodhounds of the French Revolution; whose only object, fatal experience has shewn, was the ruin of the good, and the elevation of the wicked. I am sorry that the narrow limits which confine these illustrations will not allow me to present my reader with the excellent notes of Larcher on these three chapters of Herodotus: his remarks are those of a good scholar and a virtuous man. I can only observe, that I hope no Englishman will read this portion of history, without feeling thankful that his country is blessed with a constitution that knows neither the insolence of the mob, the oppression of the few, nor the tyranny of one.

[127] "Le Magistrat s'y élit au sort; il est comptable de son administration, et toutes les délibérations s'y font en commun." *Larcher.* The subject to ἄρχει is πλῆθος ἄρχον, " po- pulus summum imperium tenens - - - gerit magistratus qui sorte obtigerunt." *Schweig. Lex. Herod.* voc. ἄρχων, 3.

[128] Constr. Μεγάβυζος ἐπέλεσε ἱστορίαν (τὰ πράγματα) ἐλιγαρχίᾳ.

[129] Lit. "The things that Otanes has said, proposing to put an end to royal government, let the same be said by me also."

[130] Matt. 478, a.

[131] ἀχρεῖος: this word, which signifies, literally, "useless," Larcher translates "pernicious:" the Latin, "inutilis," is, he says, taken in the same sense by Horace, Sat. i. 4, 124.

[132] Coray, in a note inserted in Larcher's translation, takes αἰδοῖον to be equivalent to πρέπον: the reader is probably aware that the καλὸν and πρέπον of the Greeks conveyed ideas which cannot be succinctly rendered in English.

"the best men, and commit to them the power; for we shall "be ourselves of the number, and it is probable the best "counsels will spring from the best men." Megabyzus accordingly brought forward the above opinion.—The third was Darius: he explained his opinion in these words: "I "cordially agree to what Megabyzus has said respecting the "mob: in what he says on oligarchy, he is wrong. Of the "three forms of government offered to our consideration, I "suppose each composed of the best men, the best people, "and best oligarchy, and best monarch. The last[133], I "say, far exceeds the two others: nothing surely can be "better than one man, the best of all. When of such prin- "ciples, he will govern his subjects in a manner that shall "call for no complaints; and thus will keep his designs as "secret as possible from the evil-minded. But in an "oligarchy, among the many that exert their talent for "the public good, obstinate private feuds are wont to "arise[134]: for each, anxious to be at the head of all, and to "carry his own measures, becomes an object of enmity "to the rest: hence rebellions arise: from rebellion, mur- "der; and from murder, the passage to monarchy[135]: by "this is proved how much the best that government is. "When the people rule, it is impossible that wickedness "should not exist somewhere: when corruption, however, "rises among the commons, powerful coalitions, not private "feuds, are formed among the bad: for those who seek to "destroy the state, conspire together. This lasts till some "one of the people stands forth to put down the evil-doers: "the champion of the people becomes an object of admi- "ration: thus admired, he soon is therefore evidently sole "ruler[136]; and in this he proves the strength of monarchy. "To comprehend in one word all, let me ask, whence came "our freedom; from the people, an oligarchy, or a monarch? "My opinion therefore is, that, enfranchised by one man, "we should stand by the same constitution: besides, it be- "comes us not to subvert the institutions of our fathers: "that would be a perilous experiment[137]."

The above were the three opinions submitted: accord-

---

[133] ταῦτα, understand χρῆμα: so, lower down, καὶ ἐν τούτῳ διδάξω ἔσυ ἐστὶ ταῦτα ἔχοντα.

[134] φιλέω in the sense of "solere," of which we have seen previous instances.

[135] ἀσίβη. "abire solet." This is one of the peculiarities of the aorist, as I have before observed. *Larcher.* Understand τὸ πρῆγμα, or τὰ πρήγματα, to govern ἀσίβη. *Schweig. Lex. Herod.* voc. ἀποβαίνω.

[136] δι' ὧν ἐφάνη μούναρχος ἐών. The particle διά is separated by tmesis from the verb ἐφάνη (Matt. 594. 2): "he is declared sole ruler."

[137] Matt. Gr. Gram. 457. 3.

ingly, four out of the seven acceded to the last. Otanes, defeated on this question—for he was anxious to see a democracy[138] established in Persia—rose, and spoke thus: "My companions in the late stand for freedom[139], it is clear "that one of us, at all events, must become a king[140], "whether chosen by lot, or by reference to the choice "of the Persian people[141], or by any other device; and I "therefore inform you that I do not intend to enter the "contest with you. I wish neither to rule, nor to be ruled: "on this condition, I give up my claim to the throne; and "on this condition, also, I am, myself and my posterity, to "be for ever independent of all of you." To this proposal the six consented: he ceased to be a candidate, and retired from the meeting. To this day, his family is the only one in Persia that continues independent; and subject to the government so far only as the members of it choose, provided 84 they do not violate the Persian laws. The rest debated in what manner they might deal the most honourably in appointing the future king. They resolved, to whichever of the six remaining candidates the throne might eventually fall, he should present to Otanes, and Otanes' posterity for ever, annually, a Medic dress, and the gifts which might hereafter be considered in Persia the most honourable. They voted this yearly present, because this nobleman was the first to advise the thing, and roused them all: this distinction was given, accordingly, to Otanes. With respect to themselves in common, they decided, that, at all times, any one of the seven should have the privilege of going into the royal presence unannounced, unless the king were sleeping with one of his wives: the king was also to be bound not to marry, except in the families of the conspirators: as to the mode of appointing to the throne, they settled, that he whose horse, at the next sunrise, when they rode out in company, would neigh in the suburb, should have the crown.

85 Darius had a groom, a clever fellow, whose name was Œbares. As soon as the meeting had separated, Darius

[138] The word ἰσονομίη has, I think, this meaning here, and in v. 37.

[139] στασιώται. If we reflect, that Otanes would not have given to himself and associates the odious epithet of seditious, it is clear we must seek some other signification for this word. Hesychius interprets στασιώται, οἱ ἐν τῇ αὐτῇ τάξει, or rather στάσει, as I think we ought to read: this meaning applies very well to the present. The same meaning, perhaps, applies to στασιώται at the beginning of i. 60. Larcher. Ἄλλα γὰρ δή. See Matt. 615. vii.

[140] Constr.: ἢ (ἡμῶν) ἐκστρεψάντων τῷ Περσέων πλήθει κ. τ. λ. in the genit. absolute.

[141] ἐς τοῦ πλέου καθίστε. An idiomatic expression: "took his seat separate from among them."

said to this man: "Œbares, we have decided, with respect
"to the throne, that he whose horse shall neigh the first at
"sunrise, when we ride out on horseback, is to be king.
"Now therefore, if you have any secret to effect this, con-
"trive that I, and no one else, may gain this honour."
Œbares replied: "If, my lord, your election to the throne
"depends on that alone, be of good cheer, and keep up your
"spirits; for I will take care none but yourself shall be
"king[142]: I have several such secrets[143]." "If you know,"
said Darius, "any such art, see that you put it into practice
"directly, as the trial is to take place to-morrow morning."
Œbares therefore acted in this manner: as soon as it was
dark, he took to the suburb a mare, the great favourite of
Darius's stallion, and there tethered her: he then fetched
out the stallion, and walked him round and round the spot
where the mare stood[144]; gradually approaching her: at
last he allowed the stallion to cover. At the dawn of day, 86
according to agreement[145], the six assembled on horseback: they trotted through the suburb; and when they
reached the spot where the mare was tethered the night
before, Darius's horse arriving there, neighed: at the same
moment came a flash of lightning from heaven, followed by
a clap of thunder. This coincidence, as if it were the
result of a premeditated arrangement, consecrated Darius
king[146]: the others dismounted from their horses, and prostrated themselves before Darius, as their sovereign. It is 87
said by some (for two accounts are given by the Persians)
that the artifice to which Œbares had recourse was this: he
passed his hand over the genitals of the mare, and kept it
close under his breeches[147]: as soon as the sun rose, and the
horses were about to start, Œbares pulled out his hand, and
rubbed it over the nostrils of Darius's horse, which, sniffing
up the smell, began to snort and neigh.

Accordingly, Darius the son of Hystaspes was appointed 88
king; and all in Asia were, excepting the Arabians, subject to him, having been reduced by Cyrus, and again by

---

[142] Lit. "No one else shall be king, in preference to thee."

[143] ταῦτα φάρμακα. Φάρμακον is a middle term, taken sometimes in a good and sometimes in a bad sense. *Larcher.*

[144] The Greek adds ἀγχοῦ, *near*: observe, that the dative τῇ ἵππῳ is governed by ἐγγύς, and not by ἀγχοῦ.

[145] κατὰ Ion. for κατά *Larcher.*

[146] ἐνηνεγμένα ταῦτα τῷ Δαρείῳ (these things befalling Darius) ὥσπερ ἐκ συν-τέου του γενόμενα (as if happening ac-cording to some settled plan), ἐτελέωσέ μιν (consummated him, and, as it were, consecrated him king).

[147] "In his anaxyrides." The anaxyrides were a sort of full trow-sers, reaching down to the ancles. *Larcher.* This word has occurred before, i. 71; from which we may gather, that this covering was made of skin; hence the Greek expression for them was θύλακοι.

Cambyses. The Arabians never bent to the Persian yoke: the two nations were on friendly terms, the Arabians having given a passage to Cambyses, through their territories, into Egypt; for without the assent of the Arabians, the Persians could never have invaded Egypt. The first matrimonial connexions that Darius formed with the Persians, were the most illustrious, being with Cyrus's two daughters[148], Atossa and Artystone. Atossa had previously been wife to her brother Cambyses, and subsequently to the Magus: Artystone was still a virgin. He married likewise another lady, the daughter of Smerdis the son of Cyrus, named Parmys: he took also the daughter of Otanes, who detected the Magus: every part was filled with his power[149]. The first thing he did was to set up a stone image of himself, representing a man astride on a horse: on this he put the following inscription: DARIUS THE SON OF HYSTASPES, BY THE INSTINCT OF HIS HORSE (mentioning his horse's name), AND THE SKILL OF ŒBARES HIS GROOM, OBTAINED THE PERSIAN EMPIRE. Having acted in this manner in respect of the Persians, Darius proceeded to establish twenty governments, called, by the Persians, satrapies: having established the above satrapies, and appointed the respective satraps, he determined the amount of tribute that he was to receive from the different nations: to some of these he appended the bordering people; while in the case of others, omitting the names of the neighbouring states, he placed in one and the same department different nations at a considerable distance from one another[150]. I shall now describe the manner in which the governments were distributed, and how the yearly contingency of tribute in each was settled. Such as contributed silver, were ordered to pay according to the Babylonian standard of the talent: such as gave gold, were to pay according to the Euboïc talents. The Babylonian talent is equal to seventy Euboïc mines. Under Cyrus[151], as subsequently under Cambyses even, nothing had been established as to tribute; each nation brought donations; and, in consequence of this imposition of

---

[148] Γάμους τε τοὺς πρώτους ἐγάμει Πέρσῃσι ὁ Δαρεῖος: "Ce fut avec des femmes Perses que Darius contracta ses premiers mariages—*Darius entered into marriage first with some Persian women.*"—*Larcher*. Darius was bound not to marry out of the families of the seven (84): he could not, therefore, have married any but Persian women: I have for this reason preferred the translation of Schweighæuser, "Uxores duxit nobilissimas inter Persas."

[149] Lit. "And all parts were filled with his power."

[150] Larcher translates: "Et à cet effet, il joignait à une nation les peuples limitrophes; et quelquefois, omettant ceux qui étaient voisins, il mettait dans un même département des peuples éloignés l'un de l'autre." This translation is disapproved by Schweighæuser.

[151] Matt. 613. vii.

tribute, and other similiar enactments, the Persians say that Darius was a tradesman, Cambyses a master, and Cyrus a father: the first, because he looked after money in every thing; the second, because he was a stern and supercilious man; the last, because he was good-natured, and had done all the good he could for them. Accordingly, from the 90 Ionians, Asiatic Magnetes, Æolians, Carians, Lycians, Milyans, and Pamphylians, on all these one and the same tribute was imposed: the produce was four hundred talents of silver: this was the first satrapy. From the Mysians, Lydians, Lasonians, Cabalians, and Hygennenses, came five hundred talents: this was the second satrapy. From the Hellespontians, on the right hand as you go up the straits[152], the Phrygians, the Asiatic Thracians, Paphlagonians, Mariandynians, and Syrans[153], came a tribute of three hundred and sixty talents: this was the third satrapy. From the Cilicians, three hundred and sixty white horses, one every day; and five hundred talents; one hundred and forty of which were expended on the cavalry to guard Cilicia, and the three hundred and sixty went to Darius: this was the fourth satrapy. The country beginning from the town of 91 Poseideïum, built by Amphilochus on the frontier of the Cilicians and Syrians, down to Egypt[154], except a part of Arabia which was exempted from taxation, produced a tribute of three hundred and fifty talents: this is the fifth satrapy, and comprises the whole of Phœnicia, and Syria, called Syria of Palæstine, and Cyprus. From Egypt, and the Libyans adjoining to Libya, from Cyrene and Barca (all of which were annexed to the Egyptian department), came seven hundred talents, besides the money proceeding from the fish, the produce of the Lake Mœris: thus, without taking even into account that sum, or the corn supplied, the tribute alone amounted to seven hundred talents; for, in addition, the Egyptians had to furnish to the amount of 100,000 measures of corn for the Persians and their auxiliaries[155], garrisoned at the White Castle in Memphis: this was the sixth satrapy. The Sattagidæ, Gandarians, Dadicæ, and Aparytæ, placed in one and the same division, contri-

---

[152] Herodotus wrote at Halicarnassus, or in Ionia. *Larcher.*

[153] *i. e.* the Leucosyrans, or Cappadocians.

[154] δεξαμενον is an impersonal participle; as, δεον, "cum deceat," ἐξὸν, "cum sit permissum," παρὸν, "cum adsit facultas," ἐνδεχόμενον, "cum fieri possit," &c. *Larcher.*

[155] As in Latin, one might say, without any impropriety, "metiri militibus frumentum tali aut tali mensura, tali quantitate;" so in Greek, which, instead of the ablative of the Latin, uses the dative, the number of measures distributed to the soldiers might be expressed in the dative.

buted one hundred and twenty talents: this was the seventh satrapy. From Susa, and the rest of the Cissian territory, came three hundred talents: this was the eighth satrapy. From Babylonia, and the rest of Assyria, came one thousand talents of silver, and five hundred young eunuchs: this was the ninth satrapy. From Ecbatana, and the rest of Media, together with the Paricanians and Orthocorybantes, five hundred and fifty talents: this was the tenth satrapy. The Caspians, together with the Pausicæ, Pantimathians, and Daritæ, all collected into one government, brought four hundred and forty talents: this was the eleventh satrapy. From the Bactrians, and the nations between them and the Aiglæ, came a tribute of three hundred and sixty talents: this was the twelfth satrapy. From Pactyïca and the Armenians, and the nations extending to the Euxine sea, proceeded four hundred talents: this was the thirteenth satrapy. From the Sagartians, Sarangeans, Thamanæans, Utians, and Mycians, and the inhabitants of the islands in the Erythræan sea, to which the king sends the exiles; from all the above came a tribute of six hundred talents: this is the fourteenth satrapy. The Sacæ and Caspians brought in two hundred and fifty talents: this is the fifteenth satrapy. The Parthians, Chorasmians, and Sogdians, together with the Arians, three hundred talents: this was the sixteenth satrapy. The Paricanians, and Asiatic Ethiopians, furnish four hundred talents: this was the seventeenth satrapy. Two hundred talents' contribution were imposed on the Matienians, Saspeires, and Alarodians: this was the eighteenth satrapy. Three hundred talents were claimed from the Moschians, Tibarenians, Macronians, Mossynœcians, and Marsi: this was the nineteenth satrapy. Of the Indians, the population is by far the most numerous of all nations we know; their tribute amounted to more than that of any other nation [155], six hundred and thirty talents' weight of gold-dust: they constituted the twentieth satrapy. Commuting the Babylonian standard talent into the Euboïc talent, the silver amounts to nine thousand five hundred and forty talents: if we reckon the gold at thirteen times the value of silver, that article is found to amount to four thousand six hundred and eighty Euboïc talents: consequently, the sum total of the tribute, drawn from all the nations together by Darius, amounted

---

[155] πρὸς πάντας τοὺς ἄλλους. "Ils payoient autant d'impôts que tous les autres ensemble—*they paid as many taxes as all the rest put together.*"— Larcher. Schweighæuser disapproves of this mode of translating the passage. "Contra quam (or, supra quam) reliqui omnes." *Schweig. Lex. Herod.*

every year to fourteen thousand five hundred and sixty talents[136]. I do not comprise in this estimate the sums smaller than a talent[137]. Such was the income of Darius, from the tribute in all Asia, and a small portion of Libya. In the course of time, however, this was increased by contributions from the islands, and the people of Europe inhabiting the country down to Thessaly. The king deposits the produce of the tribute in his treasury, after this manner: the precious metals are poured, in a state of fusion, into earthenware moulds: when those moulds are full, he turns the masses out; and whenever he wants a supply, he cuts off the necessary quantity.

Such are the various departments, and the amount of tribute affixed to each. Persia only has been omitted by me, as contributing nothing : the fact is, the Persians are exempt from taxation on the lands they have in cultivation ; nevertheless, they send gifts, although they are not bound to pay any impost. The branches of the Ethiopians, namely, those confining on Egypt, reduced by Cambyses in his expedition against the Macrobian Ethiopians ; those who reside about the sacred city of Nysa, and observe the festivals of Bacchus, all of whom, together with their neighbours, make use of the same kind of pulse as the Callantiæ Indians[138], and live

---

[136] As is generally the case where numbers are mentioned in ancient authors, this passage offers great difficulty: there is no doubt that some mistake must have been committed, either in this chapter or one of the foregoing.

According to Herodotus's calculation, as the text now stands in c. 95, the sum ought to be—
Silver.... 9540 Euboïc talents.
Gold .... 4680 ───────
                  ─────────
                  14220
Instead of which, we have 14560.

Making our calculations from the list of the satrapies, we have 7740 Babylonian talents; which, as the Babylonian talent was to the Euboïc as 70 to 60, (see c. 89,) make,
                 9030 E. talents.
The gold from India 4680 ───────
Revenue from the lake 240 ───────
                  ─────────
                  13950

It is clear there must be an error somewhere. Larcher, without sufficient authority, reads in c. 95, instead of 9540, the number 9880, which does away with the difficulty.

Silver.... 9880 Euboïc talents.
Gold .... 4680 ───────
          ─────────
          14560

Larcher's reason for making this alteration is, that the Sancroft Manuscript has in the margin *ιω*, which stand for 9880; but Dr. Gaisford informs us, that this marginal note proceeds from the hand of some corrector ; it can, therefore, be considered of no authority. See Schweighæuser's note.

[137] τὸ δ᾽ ἔτι ἐλάσσον ἱκανῶν ἐκλείπω. Rather obscurely expressed, " omitting what is less than (or in) these." What is meant is sufficiently clear, namely, that he omits the lesser number of units, wanting to complete the true sum. *Schweig.*

[138] ὄσπριον, a seed of which Herodotus makes mention, c. 100. Valckenaer reads ὄσπρι, in which he is followed by Larcher, " they have the same rites of sepulture "—Some give to ὄσπριον a signification remarkable for its filthiness and inaccuracy: to express that idea, Herodotus uses λαχή or γονή.

under ground; brought every third year, as their gift in common, two chœnixes of unmolten gold[159], two hundred blocks of ebony, five Ethiopian boys, and twenty large elephants' tusks: this custom continued down to my day. The Colchians, and their neighbours up to the Caucasus—so far the Persian dominion extends—taxed themselves to furnish a gift: those north of the Caucasus were independent of the Persians. The Colchians, therefore, taxed themselves, and, down to my day, brought every five years one hundred boys and one hundred girls. The Arabians supplied a thousand talents' weight of incense every year. Such were the gifts brought to the king, over and above the tribute[160].

98   The Indians collect the vast quantity of gold-dust, which, as I have already observed, they bring to the king, in the manner now to be described[161]. Eastward of the Indian territories lies a sandy desert; for, of all nations in Asia that we know, or have heard of to a certainty, the Indians are situated the farthest in the east: beyond the Indians, towards the east, the country is a desert, in consequence of the sand. There are several races of Indians, whose respective languages vary: some of them are nomades, others not; some live in marshes formed by the river: they eat raw fish, which they catch on board boats made of a kind of reed, so large that one joint alone is sufficient to make a boat. They reap down and pick up in the river a sort of bass; from which they plait something like a mat, worn by

99 them as a habergeon[162]. Others of the Indians, residing towards the east, are nomades, eaters of raw flesh: they are represented as having the following usages: every citizen that is sick, whether man or woman, they kill: if it be a man, his male relations and connexions slaughter him, because, as they say, illness would bring down his flesh, and deteriorate its qualities[163]. In vain he denies that he is ill: they do not listen to him, but kill him, and feast on his body. If a woman be sick, her nearest female acquaintances do with her the same as the men do to one another. They

---

[159] *i. e.* gold, such as it was found in the mine, or collected in the streams: being measured by the chœnix, it was, probably, gold-dust.

[160] Major Rennel makes the aggregate of the Persian king's revenue amount to about £3,650,000, or somewhat more than three millions and a half of our money.

[161] τρόπῳ τοιῷδε. This operation is described in c. 102; the four intervening chapters containing some observations respecting the different tribes of Indians.

[162] The φλέως of the Attics, or φλοῦς of the Ionians, was a sort of rush: the Arundo ampelodesmon. *Schneid. Gr. Germ. Lex.*

[163] " Carnem ipsis corruptum iri;" the flesh which they themselves intend to eat would become corrupt, lose its flavour. *Larcher.*

sacrifice those who have reached old age, and eat them; but there are very few that live to such years [164]: for they kill, before then, every one that is seized with any disorder. There are other Indians whose mode of life is very different: they kill nothing that breathes; they sow no crops, and are not wont to have houses; they live on vegetables; and in their country grows a sort of seed [165] about the size of the panicum, in a cod; it rises spontaneously, and the people gather it, boil it, cod and all, and eat it as their usual food. Whoever is visited with sickness among them, goes and lies down in the desert; and none take any account, either of the dying or sick. With the above-mentioned Indians the intercourse of the two sexes takes place openly, in the same manner as with the brute creation. They are all of a colour closely approaching to that of the Ethiopians: their seminal liquor is not white, like that of other men, but black, as well as the skin: the case is the same with the Ethiopians. These Indians are very remote from the Persians; they reside in the southern parts of the country, and were always independent of Darius.

But there are other Indians, at no great distance from the city of Caspatyrus and the country of Pactyïca: they lie north of the rest of the Indians, and resemble closely, in their mode of life, the Bactrian people. These are the most warlike of the Indians, and are the people that are sent to procure the gold. In the vicinity of their territory the land is desert, being covered with sand: in these sandy tracts, accordingly, are found pismires of a size between the dog and the fox, specimens of which are seen in the menagerie of the Persian king, which have been caught, and imported from that country. These pismires, accordingly, burrow under ground; and, in excavating their habitations, throw up hillocks of sand, just the same, and in the same manner, as the ants do in Hellas: they are likewise very similar to our own pismires: the sand that they throw up contains abundance of gold-dust. For the purpose of collecting this sand, therefore, the Indians are despatched to the desert. Each man harnesses together three camels; two males fastened by traces on the off and near sides, and one female in the middle [166]. The Indian rides the female camel, taking

---

[164] Ἢ δὲ τοιούτων λόγον οὐ πολλοί τινες αὐτῶν ἀνύουσιν. "But few of them reach to this state of things (in hujus rei rationem:") i. e. not many reach so far as to be put to death by their friends on account of old age.—*Schweig.*

Lex. Her. voc. λόγος, ii. 3, 2.

[165] Supply σπέρμα after ἰον.—*Schweig. Lex. Herod.*

[166] συμφέρει, applied to any draught animal, signifies one that is harnessed by the side of the yoke, as is done

care to choose one that has lately dropped her young; for their female camels are not inferior in speed to the horse, and, besides, are stronger, and much better adapted to carry burthens. I do not intend to describe the shape of the camel, which is well known to the Hellenes; but will mention one particular, which they are not aware of: the camel has in his hinder-legs four joints and four knees: the organ of generation passes between the hinder legs, and terminates about the tail. The Indians, therefore, provided each with a yoke of the above kind, proceed in quest of the gold; having arranged so, as to be able to commence collecting the sand at the time when the sun is most violent; because, during the parching heat, the pismires keep out of sight, under ground. In the country we are speaking of, the sun is hottest in the morning, and not at mid-day, as in other places, but from the time that the sun is fully risen, to about the breaking up of market [167]: during this time, the sun burns much more vehemently than at noon in Hellas; and the heat is so oppressive, that the inhabitants say they swim in water [168] then: about the middle of the day, the temperature in India is not much higher than in other places Having crossed the Meridian, the sun becomes mild, as at its rise in other countries; and then, gradually sinking, refreshes the atmosphere, until it sets, and the weather becomes quite cool. When the Indians are come to the proper place, they fill with sand the leather-bags they have brought with them, and then retire at the most rapid pace they can: for the pismires, according to the Persians, detect the strangers by the smell, and forthwith enter upon a pursuit: the fleetness of the camels exceeds that of all other animals; for if the Indians did not get a good way a-head of the pismires, while those animals are collecting, not one of the men would escape. They add, that the male camels would not only flag, being inferior in velocity to the female, but would not pull together; while the female, mindful of the young she has left, does not allow the males to tarry behind. Such, according to the Persians, is the manner in which the Indians obtain most of their gold: the other sort of gold is not so abundant, and is dug up in the country.

sometimes in this country with an additional horse to a gig; and is technically called *an out-rigger*.

[167] ἐπιστίλλων of the sun, is equivalent, in Herodotus, to ἀνατίλλων.— *Schweig. Lex Herod.*

[168] As the Latin word *sudor* is manifestly the same with the Greek ὕδωρ, confined by the usage of the Latins to a less extensive signification; so Herodotus, no doubt, has taken the Greek word ὕδωρ in the sense of *sudor*, iii. 104. *Schweig. Lex. Herod.* " Pendant ce tems-là ils se tiennent dans l'eau—*During that time they keep themselves in water.*" *Larcher.*

The extremities of the inhabited earth, for some reason 106
or other, are blessed with the most beautiful productions, as
Hellas is with the best-tempered seasons [109]. India, as I
have just observed, is situated at the verge of the habitable
world: here the living quadrupeds and birds are far greater
than those of other countries; with the exception of the
horses, which are surpassed by the Medic breed, called the
Nisæan horses. Here, again, gold is found in the most
lavish abundance; some brought down by the rivers, some
obtained in the manner I have described: here, also, there
are wild trees which bear, instead of fruit, a kind of wool,
superior in beauty and service to that shorn from the sheep.
The Indians use the product of these trees for their clothes.
Again, in the southern verge of the habitable world lies 107
Arabia: here alone incense grows, and in no other places;
so does myrrh, cassia, cinnamon, and ladanum: all the above
articles, except myrrh, are obtained with considerable difficulty by the Arabians. They collect the incense, which
the Phœnicians import into Hellas, by means of the smoke
from gum-styrax: for the incense-bearing trees are guarded
each by vast numbers of winged serpents, diminutive in
size, and varying in colour: they are of the same sort as
those that invade Egypt. These winged reptiles can be
driven off the tree by nothing but the smoke of the styrax.
According to the Arabians, the whole world would be filled 108
with these serpents, if the same thing did not occur to them
as I know happens with vipers. It is a wise contrivance,
no doubt, of Divine Providence, that all living creatures
which are timid and fit for food should have been made very
prolific, and that those which are noxious and ferocious
should bring forth few young. As an instance of the
former, the hare, hunted alike by beast, bird, and man, is
accordingly so prolific, that she is the only animal that
admits of superfetation: some of the young, when still in
the belly of the dam, are rough with hair; others are quite

---

[109] Herodotus, according to his manner, which is now, no doubt, pretty familiar to the reader, makes a digression on the various productions of the extreme lands of the world then known: the history is resumed at c. 118. I need not observe, that almost all he says in the following chapters is now known to be fabulous; but the reader must remember, that natural history is a science founded on experience alone: no wonder, therefore, that a generation more than two thousand years subsequent to Herodotus should be better acquainted with the secrets of nature than the cotemporaries of our Historian. Even the works of the great natural philosophers of our own day, if I may use the expression, are not free from blunders: for instance, the immortal Buffon asserts that cows shed their horns once a year; a most extraordinary mistake, which was copied by Dr. Goldsmith.

smooth, and without hair; the latter having been but just conceived by the mother, while the others are of their full size [170]. As an instance of the more sterile animal, the lioness, which is very powerful and daring, brings forth whelps but once in her life; for at the time of her ejecting the offspring, she discharges the womb also. This proceeds from the following cause: when the whelp in her inside begins to be endowed with the faculty of motion, being armed with claws much sharper than all other animals, he lacerates the womb; and as he increases in size, he continues to inflict the same injury in a greater proportion: so that when the birth approaches, not one part of the whole 109 envelope remains entire. A similar thing occurs also to vipers, as well as to the winged serpents of Arabia. If these reptiles were to multiply according to the course of their nature, there could be no possibility of the existence of mankind [171]: but when they copulate, the female seizes the male by the neck, and grasps him fast, even after she has conceived; nor does she let go her hold till she has devoured him: in this manner the males are destroyed. The female, however, is punished for her ill-treatment of the male: the young offspring avenge their father, by devouring her womb; and thus effect their entrance into the world by gnawing their way through the abdomen. The snakes that do no harm to men [172] bring forth eggs, and so leave an immense posterity. Vipers are found, indeed, in all parts of the world; but these winged serpents are seen in Arabia, and no where else; there they exist in great numbers.

110 The above, then, is the mode by which the Arabians obtain their incense [173]: they procure the cassia thus: they inclose their whole body in the skins of oxen and other animals; they cover likewise their face, except the eyes only; and, thus accoutred, approach the cassia-tree, which grows in a shallow lake, in and around which winged animals harbour, nearly the same in shape as bats: their voice is appalling [174], and their strength formidable: the Arabians accordingly endeavour to keep them away from their eyes, 111 and so gather the cassia. But they collect cinnamon in a manner still more wonderful: they are unable to explain where this spice comes from, and what land it grows

---

[170] What Herodotus says of the hare is exactly true. *Larcher*. Superfetation does not occur either in the rabbit, hare, or cat: I have been at some trouble to ascertain the fact.
[171] Matt. 443, 1.
[172] Matt. 329, A. 1.
[173] τιότι, "de quo verba facere cœperam." *Schweig. Vers. Lat.*
[174] τίνργυς, from τρίζων, stridere.—The subject is θηρία πτερωτά.

in; except that some relate, probably in accordance with fact, that it is indigenous to the land where Bacchus was nursed: they add, that those little tubes, which we call, after the Phœnicians, cinnamon, are brought by large birds to their nests, which are constructed of mud-plaster on the face of the overhanging cliffs of certain mountains. As it is not in the power of men to climb to such an height, the Arabians have recourse to the following expedient: they cut up into very large joints, the oxen and asses, and other draught animals, and convey them to the mountains, and, laying them down near the nests, go away to some distance: the birds pounce immediately on the pieces of carrion, and carry them up to their nests: the nests, however, are not strong enough to support the weight; they break, and fall to the ground: and the Arabians run up, pick out the cinnamon tubes [175], and export them to other countries. The mode of obtaining what the Hellenes call ledanon, and the Arabians ladanum, is still more extraordinary; for although a most odoriferous substance, it is found in a most stinking place: it is obtained from the beards of he-goats, in the same manner as gum from trees [176]: it is used in several perfumes, and is the principal ingredient of the Arabian fumigation of the person. So far upon perfumes: to which it may be added, that a sweet and divine fragrance breathes from the

112

---

[175] The reader will please to observe, that by *cinnamon* is not understood that which we generally use now-a-days: both the *κασία* and the *κινάμωμον* were (as is proved by Larcher, although Herodotus seems not to have been aware of it) the produce of one and the same plant: the *cassia* was the dry hollow bark of the tree (the real cinnamon of our shops); from its shape it received the names of *κασία σύριγξ, συρίγγιον, cannella cassia*, and in French, *cannelle*; all which names signify a *reed* or *pipe*. The *cinnamomum*, on the other hand, was the branch, together with the bark: this latter is now no longer an object of exportation, probably because enough of the more delicate produce, that called *cassia* by the ancients, is afforded to supply a market, the demands of which cannot be nearly so great as in former days, when perfumes and spices were much more used than at present. I have seen, in the possession of a friend of mine, who is in the East-India service, a piece of the cinnamon-wood: the odour was very grateful, and in taste it might answer as a rough substitute for the common *cannella*, or cinnamon.

[176] ἀπὸ τῆς ὕλης, "from the shrubs." The brevity of the Greek would not be intelligible in English. The ledanon is a production of the ledum, a species of cistus: it is a sort of gummy exudation, collected now-a-days in the Levant, by rubbing the branches with a piece of leather, to which the viscous matter sticks: it is afterwards scraped off, rolled into balls, and dried. I have seen goats browsing on the leaves in the interior parts of the island of Ceos, and have no doubt that what Herodotus states respecting the ancient mode of collecting this drug may be true. The ledum is cultivated in our gardens under the name of the gum-cistus (cistus ladaniferus, *Linn.*); the viscidity of the foliage is not so great as in the plants that grow on the coast of Asia Minor, although it is sufficient to produce a very disagreeable clamminess on the fingers of those that handle it.

113 Arabian regions. These people possess, likewise, two species of sheep, highly deserving of our admiration, and seen no where but in Arabia. One of these has an excessively long tail, three cubits in length at least; which, if they were allowed to trail, might be ulcerated, rubbing continually on the ground: every shepherd, however, of the present day, knows how to turn carpenter, to avoid this misfortune; and makes a little chariot, to one of which he binds each tail. The other race of sheep has broad tails, above a cubit
114 across. Westward, towards the setting-sun [177], is found Ethiopia, the last inhabited country in that quarter: it produces abundance of gold, elephants of huge size, all kinds of wild trees, and ebony in particular, and gigantic, handsome, long-lived men.
115   Such accordingly are the verges of Asia and Libya. Concerning the extreme western parts of Europe, I can say nothing to a certainty; for I do not assent to the report, that there exists among barbarians a river called the Eridanus, that discharges its waters into a northern sea, from whence amber comes; nor am I acquainted with the Cassiterides islands [178], from which tin is imported to us: for, on one hand, the appellation Eridanus of itself betrays an Hellenic, and not by any means a foreign origin, and was fabricated by some poet: on the other hand, I have never been able to hear, from an eye-witness, in spite of all my efforts, how a sea exists in the extremity of Europe. Tin, however, as well
116 as amber, comes from the utmost bounds of Europe. And, moreover, the north of Europe evidently produces a vast quantity of gold: how it is procured I am at a loss to say: the tale goes, that some one-eyed men, called Arimaspi, steal it from the griffons [179]. I by no means accede to the opinion that there exists a race of one-eyed men, in every other respect similar to the rest of mankind. The extremities of the world, therefore, seem to enclose and confine within themselves the rest of the land, and to possess the things we hold to be the most beautiful and rare.
117 There is in Asia a plain enclosed on all sides by a range of mountains, the defiles of which amount to five. This plain formerly belonged to the Chorasmians [180], and lay on the

---

[177] Construction; ἀποκλημένης μεσαμβρίης πρὸς δύνοντα ἥλιον: the literal meaning of which I take to be, "Where the southern tract of heaven declines towards the setting-sun, i. e. the SSW."

[178] The Scilly Islands, if not England itself. See *Geographical Index to Herodotus*, voc. CASSITERIDES.

[179] ὑπαιρέζων, subripere. The preposition is separated from the verb by tmesis, of which we have already seen several instances.

[180] See Matt. 371.

confines of the Chorasmians themselves, the Hyrcanians, the Parthians, the Sarangæans, and Thamanæans: since the Persians have had the empire, it is the appurtenance of the king. Out of the basin, formed by the mountain, flows a considerable river, called the Aces, which, at its commencement, divides into various directions, and waters all the lands of the above-mentioned nations, one of the arms flowing through each defile respectively. Since this quarter has been subject to the Persian monarch, the following change has been wrought there: the king has thrown up dykes across each gorge, with flood-gates in each: the water, thus curbed in its course, converts the plain enclosed in the mountain into a deep sea; the river constantly discharging its stream into it, and having no longer any egress. Those who in former days were wont to use that water, no longer enjoying that blessing, are exposed to a great calamity: in winter, the ground is refreshed by the rain from heaven, like other countries[181]; but in summer, when they sow their millet and sesame, they suffer from drought. Receiving no boon of water, they go themselves, and their wives, into Persia, and, standing at the palace-gates, scream and moan. The king orders the flood-gates to be thrown open that lead into the lands of the supplicants; and, when the ground is soaked through with water, shuts them again, and orders other sluices to be opened for the rest that want particularly. These, I am informed, are not opened before a large sum of money has been extorted, over and above the tribute.

Almost immediately after the rising against the Magians, one of the conspirators, Intaphernes, was put to death[182], for the following insolence: he wished to enter the palace, having some affairs to transact with the sovereign; and, as it had been arranged by the conspirators that free entrance to the royal presence, without being announced, should be a privilege of each, unless the king were conversing with one of his wives, Intaphernes accordingly resolved not to send in any one to announce his arrival, but, as one of the seven, to enter at once. The doorkeeper and usher[183] would not, however, let him pass; alleging, that the king was

[181] ὕει σφι ὁ θεός: lit. "the god (Jupiter) rains to them;" a usual mode of expression. Τί γὰρ ὁ Ζεὺς ποιεῖ; "What sort of weather have we?"— Aristoph. Av. 1501.—*Larcher*.

[182] κατέλαβε Ἰνταφέρνεα ἀποθανεῖν. See note 243, p. 182, of this volume.

[183] ἀγγελιαφόρος. This, says Larcher, was one of the most important and honourable offices among the Persians: the duty of this person was to receive petitions, and introduce persons to the royal presence. This note will serve to rectify the inaccuracy of my translation.

engaged with one of his wives. Intaphernes, fancying these people wished to deceive him, drew his scimetar, and cut off their ears and noses; and hanging them to the bridle of his horse, placed the bridle round the necks of these men, 119 and sent them about their business. The disfigured men presented themselves before Darius, and explained the reason why they were so maltreated. The king, apprehensive that this had taken place with the connivance of the six, sent for each separately, and sounded their opinions, whether they approved or not the transaction: he discovered they were not privy to the outrage; and immediately arrested Intaphernes, and his children and his relations, having many reasons to assume that this nobleman, with the support of his family connexions, was plotting an insurrection against himself. As soon as he had their persons in custody, he put them in fetters, and condemned them to death[184]. And the wife of Intaphernes came to the palace-gates, weeping, and uttering lamentable cries[185]: she persisted in acting thus, and Darius was moved to pity; and sending a messenger to the lady, he spoke thus: "Madam, king Darius gives you one "of the prisoners, your kinsmen, to be reprieved: take "which you choose." The lady reflected a little, and answered: "If the king grants the life of one only, I choose, above all, my brother." Darius, informed of this, and wondering at the choice, sent to ask this question: "Good "lady, the king wishes to know, for what reason, omitting "your husband and your children, do you elect your brother, "who is a more distant relative than your own children, "and less dear than your husband[186]." She answered in these words: "Sire, I may perhaps get another husband, if such "be the divine will; and other children, if such be my lot: "but now that my father and mother are no longer living, "it is impossible I should ever have, by any chance, another "brother: taking this into consideration, I spoke as I did." Darius thought that the lady spoke with judgment; and, pleased at her conduct, released not only the prisoner she asked for, but added to the boon her eldest boy: all the rest he put to death. And thus he made away immediately with one of the seven.

120 Pretty nearly about the same time as the sickness of Cambyses, the following event took place. Orœtes, a Persian, appointed viceroy of Sardis by Cyrus, conceived a very

---

[184] Construction: ἔθετο (σφέας) τὴν ἐπὶ θανάτῳ (scil. δίκην). See *Schweig. Not.* on i. 109.

[185] The particle ἄν is here used to express repetition. See Matt. 598, a.

[186] μεχαιρωμένος, 'acceptus,' 'gratus,' 'jucundus.' *Schweig. Lex. Herod.*

wicked desire of getting possession of Polycrates, and doing away with him; although he had never suffered at the hands of his victim, either in word or deed, nor had he even previously seen him. According to the report which is the most rife, this was his motive: Orœtes was sitting in the king's portal[187], with another Persian gentleman called Mitrobates, the satrap of Dascyleium[188]: these two gentlemen, from conversing before, fell to quarrelling with one another: the dispute was upon their respective merits; and Mitrobates threw out this reproach on Orœtes: "Are you to be ranked "among deserving men, you, who have not even added to "your sovereign's dominion the island of Samos, that lies "close to your own province, on which you might so easily "lay your hand? an island which one of the inhabitants, "assisted with but fifteen soldiers, rose up and took, and is "now its tyrant." According to this account, then, as soon as Orœtes heard this reproach, he took so to heart the disgrace, that he wished not even so much to be avenged of the person who had made this remark, as he longed to destroy utterly Polycrates. There are a few people, however, who 121 relate, that Orœtes sent a herald to Samos, to make some request or other, which, at all events, is not mentioned, whatever it was; and that Polycrates happened to be reclining in the men's apartment, in company with Anacreon of Teos; and whether he did so purposely, foreseeing that Orœtes was about to make some request, or it happened so by chance, when the herald came into the room and advanced to deliver the message from Orœtes, Polycrates, having his face to the wall, neither turned round, nor made any answer[189]. The above two different motives are assigned for the murder 122 of Polycrates: every one may abide by which he likes. Accordingly, Orœtes, who was staying at Magnesia on the river Mæander, sent Myrsus the son of Gyges, a native of Lydia, to Samos, with a message to Polycrates, whose cha-

---

[187] The great lords waited at the gates of the kings of Persia. This practice, established by Cyrus, lasted as long as the monarchy itself; and even to the present day, in Turkey, the court is called the Ottoman *Porte* or Gate. *Larcher.*

[188] νομῷ τῷ ἐν Δασκυλείῳ, i. e. the province round the city of Dascyleium, that of which Dascyleium was the capital, Bithynia.

[189] The construction is rather intricate: the infinitives depend on οἱ δὲ Πλεύνεσσι λέγουσι. Wess. Construction: οἱ δὲ πλεύνεσσι λέγουσι, πέμψαι 'Οροίτεα ἐς Σάμον κήρυκα, ἔστιν δὴ χρήματος δεησόμενον· (οὐ γὰρ ὦν δὴ τοῦτό γε λέγεται): [λέγουσι] καὶ τὸν Πολυκράτεα τυχεῖν κατακείμενον ἐν ἀνδρεῶνι, παρεῖναι δέ οἱ καὶ Ἀνακρέοντα τὸν Τήιον· καί κως, (εἴτ᾽ ἐκ προνοίης αὐτὸν (i. e. Πολυκράτεα) καταλογέοντα τὰ Οἰροίτεω πρήγματα, εἴτε καὶ συντυχίη τις τοιαύτη ἐπεγένετο·) τόν τε γὰρ (see Matt. 394, c.) κήρυκα τὸν Ὀροίτεω παρελθόντα διαλέγεσθαι, καὶ τὸν Πολ. (τυχεῖν γὰρ [λέγουσι αὐτὸν] ἐστραμμένον πρὸς τὸν τοῖχον) οὔτε τι μεταστραφῆναι, οὔτε ὑποκρίνασθαι.

racter he had been informed of. For[190] Polycrates is the first of the Hellenes, we know of, that projected to have the rule over the sea; with the exception of Minos from Cnossus, or some other before him, if any. In respect to what is called the Historic Times[191], Polycrates was the first that conceived any hopes of attaining to the empire of Ionia and the isles[192]. Orœtes therefore, informed of the views of the Samian usurper, sent him a message in these terms. "ORŒTES TO "POLYCRATES SPEAKS THUS: I understand that you project "mighty things, and have not the means compatible to your "views. Now, then, act as I advise you: you will exalt "yourself, and save me: for Cambyses is meditating my "death, as I am informed, beyond all doubt. I beseech you "to convey me away from this land, with my riches: take "one-half for your own, and allow me to keep the rest: by "wealth you will obtain the empire of Hellas. If you do "not give credit to what I say concerning my treasures, "send over the most trusty of your servants: to him I will 123 "shew them." With this communication Polycrates was highly gratified, and resolved to accept the offer; and, as perhaps he was too fond of money, sent first Mæandrius the son of Mæandrius, to examine the treasures of Orœtes: this Mæandrius was a native of Samos, and held the office of secretary to the usurper: he was the same that, some time after these events, dedicated at Juno's temple all the beautiful ornaments of Polycrates' audience-chamber[193]. Orœtes, informed that a person was expected to come and examine his treasures, filled eight chests, almost to their brims, with stones, and over the surface strewed a layer of gold; corded the chests, and held them in readiness[194]. Mæandrius soon

[190] This γὰρ introduces an explanation of τοῦ Πολυκράτεος τὸν νόον; Polycrates's ambition being, to be lord over the sea, and to extend his empire.

[191] ἀνθρωπηίη γενεὴ, the times of men, i. e. those to which historical and true records reach, in opposition to μυθικὴ, the fabulous times. *Scaliger*, quoted by *Larcher*.

[192] Lit. "Polycrates is the first that had great hopes that he should rule over Ionia and the islands."

[193] ἀνδρεὼν, a word of which we have met instances once and again: it is equivalent to ἀνδρεὼν, or ἀνδρεωνῖτις, in opposition to γυναικεῖον or γυναικωνῖτις, the former the apartment of the men, the latter that of the women. The word ἀνδρεὼν was used likewise to signify, in the houses of the Romans, a walk between two contiguous quadrangles of the building. I have used the word *audience chamber*, in order to avoid a periphrasis; for the civilized languages of the present day have no terms indicative of that seclusion of the fair sex, which marks barbarism in the man, and want of virtue in the woman.

[194] Before the invention of locks, it was the custom, in ancient times, to secure the doors, chests, &c. with knots. Some of these knots were so difficult, that no one who was not in the secret could unfasten them.—Every one has heard of the Gordian knot: and Homer frequently alludes to the practice. Odyss. viii. 447.— *Larcher*.

after arrived, made his survey, and sent his report to Polycrates. The Samian prince, in spite of divine warnings from 124 the shrines, in spite of the representations of his friends, prepared to set out himself for Orœtes' residence: to all these admonitions was added that of his daughter, who had dreamed that she saw her father high aloft, washed by the rain[195], and anointed by the sun. The young lady having received such a vision, had recourse to every expedient in order to avert her father from going over to Orœtes: even at the moment he was stepping on board the penteconter, she pursued him with her evil omens. Polycrates meanwhile threatened his daughter, that, if he returned safe home, he would take care she should long remain a spinster: the young woman prayed it might come to pass; as she would prefer waiting a long time to be married, to being reft of her father. Polycrates, however, regardless of all advice, 125 sailed away to Orœtes, taking with him several companions; and among others, Democedes the son of Calliphon, a native of Croton, and by profession a physician and surgeon, the most skilful in his art of all his cotemporaries[196]. On his arrival at Magnesia, Polycrates perished in a horrid manner, wholly unworthy of himself or of his exalted mind; for not even the Syracusan usurpers, nor one of the Hellenic tyrants, was ever deserving of comparison with Polycrates. Orœtes put him to a death too dreadful to describe, and crucified him afterwards[197]. Such of his followers as were Samians Orœtes dismissed and let go, bidding them be thankful to him for their liberty: such as were aliens and servants, he considered as mere slaves. Thus Polycrates, crucified, fulfilled every particular of his daughter's dream; for when it rained, he was washed by Jove; and he was anointed by the sun, which drew out the oily juices from his body. The frequent good fortune that attended Polycrates, therefore, brought him to this end; as Amasis, the king of Egypt, had portended[198].

Not long after, due vengeance was awarded[199] to Orœtes, 126

---

[195] Lit. "by Jove." See note 181, p. 253, of this volume. So in the next chapter: "He was washed by Jove, whenever he rained."

[196] Lit. "and who exercised his art the best of those in his time."

[197] ἀνεσταύρωσε "exposed his body on a stake or cross, i. e. gibbet." This passage shews that the verb ἀνασταυρόω is not used by Herodotus to express any particular mode of execution: it is probable, from what goes before, that the unfortunate Polycrates was flayed alive. The words *impaling*, and *breaking on the wheel*, although understood by many to express particular manners of executing criminals, apply only to the exposition of the carcass after death.

[198] See c. 43.

[199] Lit. "The Furies, avenging Polycrates, pursued Orœtes even."

for the murder of Polycrates. For after the death of Cambyses, and the reign of the Magians, Orœtes had remained at Sardis without rendering any support to the Persians, who had wrested the empire from the Medes: seizing the opportunity of those days of confusion, he compassed the death of Mitrobates, the viceroy of Dascyleium, who had upbraided him with his conduct towards Polycrates, and assassinated Mitrobates' son Cranaspes, Persians of high rank. He exhibited many other instances of gross insolence; and murdered one of Darius's couriers[200] who had brought him disagreeable intelligence, on his return; posting on the road some ruffians, who killed the man and his horse, and put 127 the bodies out of sight. After his accession to the throne, Darius longed to be avenged of Orœtes, for all his iniquities; but principally for the murder of Mitrobates and Mitrobates' son: he thought it, however, not expedient to send an expedition immediately against him, for matters were not yet quite settled: he himself had but just attained the sovereign power; and he knew Orœtes had a body-guard, consisting of a thousand Persians, and held the governments of Phrygia, Lydia, and Ionia. Darius therefore devised the following stratagem: he convened the Persians of the highest rank, and addressed them thus: "Persians," said he, "who among you will pledge himself to accomplish an
"object which requires skill, not violence or great numbers?
"for where skill is required, force is of no avail. Who
"among you, then, will kill Orœtes, or bring him to me
"alive? him, who never rendered any service to the Per-
"sians, but has been guilty of great crimes. In the first
"place, he has made away with two of us, both Mitrobates
"and his son: secondly, he slays even those who summon
"him in my name, and are sent by my order; such intole-
"rable insolence does he shew. Ere, therefore, he work
"any greater evil to Persia, let death prevent him, at our
128 "hands." Such was the proposal made by Darius: thirty champions pledged themselves to the new king, as prepared each to do according to his bidding. Darius put a stop to their contestations[201], by ordering recourse to lot: the lots were drawn: the prize fell to Bagæus the son of Artontes. Bagæus, thus chosen, proceeded thus: he wrote several letters, concerning various matters, and affixed to them Darius's

---

[200] ἀγγαρήϊος, a courier, or *tartar*, belonging to the Persian service of the ἀγγαρήϊον: concerning which, see viii. 98.
of a similar expression occurs in vii. 9, where Portus explains καταλαμβάνειν διαφοράς, by διαλύειν διαφοράς. Æ. Port. Lex. Ion.

[201] καταλάμβανε ἐρίζοντας. Something

seal; and, with these letters in his possession, departed for Sardis. At his arrival, and introduction to Orœtes' presence, he took out the letters one by one, and gave them to be read out by the king's secretary [202]; for an officer of that kind is always appended to the train of a viceroy. These letters were delivered by Bagæus, with a view to try whether body-guards were inclined to revolt from Orœtes: and observing that they paid great respect to the letters themselves, and still more to their contents, produced another, which ran thus: " Persians, it is the behest of king Darius that you be " no longer the guards of Orœtes [203]." On hearing this, they immediately grounded their javelins. Bagæus, seeing they obeyed this order, even took courage, and handed over the last letter to the secretary, in which was written: " King " Darius commands the Persians at Sardis to put Orœtes to " death." The guards no sooner heard these words, than, drawing their scimetars, they killed him on the spot. Thus Orœtes, the Persian, paid forfeit for the murder of Polycrates, the Samian.

The property of Orœtes having been confiscated, and conveyed to Susa, an accident happened to king Darius shortly after: in leaping from his horse at the chace, he strained his foot: so violent was the twist, that the ankle was forced out of its socket: and, at first, presuming that he had at his court some of the Egyptians regarded as the first men in the profession of the healing art, he trusted his case to their treatment: these doctors, however, violently twisting the foot back, did but increase the evil. During seven days and seven nights, Darius, in consequence of this accident, was kept awake: and on the eighth day, accordingly, the king being still no better, some one, who had already heard, at Sardis, of Democedes the Crotoniat's skill, make a communication to Darius, who ordered Democedes immediately into his presence. They found him among the slaves of Orœtes, where he was held in no estimation; and took him before the king, bound in fetters, and clothed in rags. As the man stood before him, Darius asked him whether he knew the

---

[202] στιμαιρειν signifies, to take away the wrapper of any thing: in this sense we have previously seen Polycrates, iii. 41, στεμαιρεαμενος την σφραγιδα, "taking off the signet which encompassed his finger." The letters sent by Turkish gentlemen are always wrapped in silk bags or cases, sealed with their signet: the ancient Persians most probably had some similar usage, which will account for the expression here used by Herodotus, which signifies, literally, " having taken off the wrapper of each separately."

[203] The superfluous negative, which is, no doubt, too familiar to the reader to require any comment. See Matt. 533, obs. 3.

medical art: Democedes, fearing to discover himself, lest he should be separated for ever from Hellas, denied that he knew any thing about it. But Darius saw enough to convince him that he was dissembling[204], and perfectly acquainted with medicine; so he ordered the persons who had brought him, to fetch the whips and spurs. Democedes then discovered himself; declared, that he had learned the art, but imperfectly, and that he had a smattering only of it, having been intimate with a physician. Immediately, Darius entrusted himself to his treatment[205]; and he made use of the Hellenic medicines; and, by substituting emollients instead of violent means[206], procured some sleep to the patient; and in a short time restored him to perfect health and soundness of body, although the king himself had given up all hopes of ever being able to step on that foot. In recompense for this service, Darius presented his medical attendant with a pair of golden shackles. Democedes, upon this, asked the king if he had purposely doubled his sorrows because he had restored him to health. Darius, much pleased at this answer, sent him to his own wives: and the eunuchs, taking him round to see them all, said to the ladies, "This is the man who "restored life to our liege lord." Each of the ladies dipped a vase[207] into a chest of gold, and presented it to Democedes;

---

[204] The sense is the same as if there was παυσάμενόν τι τῷ Δαρείῳ τυχνάζειν, καί τις ἐπιστάμενος, "It appeared to Darius that he dissembled being a physician, though he was so in fact." *Larcher.*

[205] ἐπέτρεψε: understand ἰαυτόν, or τὸ πρᾶγμα. *Schweig.*

[206] I take ἥτω as relating to the treatment of Democedes, and ἰσχυρὰ to that of the Egyptians, as being the first signification that would be given to the passage by a non-medical reader. Coray understands both ἥπια and ἰσχυρὰ of the treatment adopted by Democedes: "the injury," says he, "was a luxation of the foot, that had been unskilfully treated by the Egyptian physicians: the first operation Democedes had to perform, must have been, therefore, to luxate again the joint. Immediately after that operation, μετὰ τὰ ἰσχυρὰ, in order to calm the pain, he administered to his patient some narcotic, ἥπια, as, for instance, opium, to make him sleep. This practice is still followed in all violent surgical operations." The translation, according to this illustrious editor of Strabo, must be, therefore, "And, by administering some narcotic after the operation, procured," &c.

[207] ὑποτυπτουσα δὲ ἀβτίων ἰαδοσε φιάλῃ ἐς τοῦ χρυσοῦ τὸν θῆκαν. A most difficult passage. For the different emendations proposed by various scholars, the notes of Schweighæuser may be consulted. Construction: ἑκάστη αὐτῶν, each of them, ὑποτυπτουσα φιάλῃ, dipping under with a saucer, (no ii. 136, αὐτῇ ὑποτυπτοντες ἐς λίμνην) ἐς τὸν θῆκαν τοῦ χρυσοῦ, into the chest or repository of gold, &c. We have likewise, vi. 119, ὑποτύψας γαυλῷ ἀνελέει, "shaking under with a bucket draws from the well." I have followed the reading of Dr. Gaisford, proposed by Porson. Schweighæuser gives ὑποτυπτουσα δὲ ἀβτίων ἰαδοσε φιάλῃ, τοῦ χρυσοῦ σὺν θῆκιν ἰδωρήσατο Δημοκήδεϊ οὕτω δή τι δαψιλέϊ δωρεῇ, κ. τ. λ. The translation of which must be, however, lame: "each of them dipping in with a saucer, presented to Democedes such an abundant gift of gold together with the vase," &c.—Leaving the

thus conferring such a munificent gift, that the servant who followed him, named Sciton, picked up the gold staters that fell from the vases, and thus collected a great quantity of gold for himself.

This Democedes, coming thus from Croton, had proceeded 131 to the court of Polycrates. Being at Croton harshly treated by his father, a man prone to anger, and unable to brook any longer such usage, he forsook his home, and proceeded to Ægina. Settling in that island, he surpassed, in the first year, the first physicians, although unprovided with instruments, and having none of the necessary adjuncts to the arts of medicine and surgery[908]. In the second year, the Æginetæ rewarded him by a yearly fee of one talent from the public chest: in the third year, the Athenians allowed one hundred minæ: in the fourth year, he arrived at Samos, where Polycrates allowed him two talents annually. From this man the people of Croton became not the least celebrated physicians[909]; for it soon came to pass, that they were spoken of, all over Hellas, as the first medical men: the Cyrenæan physicians were but the second. So, about the same period, the Argeians were exalted to the first rank among musicians. At the time 132 we are now speaking of, Democedes, having completely cured Darius, was in possession of a large house at Susa, and was the companion of Darius's table: he enjoyed every luxury, with the exception of his being far away from Hellas. Of his intimacy with the king, the first instance is, that he obtained from Darius the reprieve of the Egyptian doctors who had first administered to the king: they were about to be impaled, because they had proved themselves inferior to one Greek physician: secondly, he rescued from bondage a soothsayer of Elis, who had followed Polycrates, and remained among the slaves, not thought of. In short, Democedes was all in all with the sovereign.

reader to search for further information on this passage from the various commentators, I shall proceed to give Larcher's illustration of the meaning of φιάλη.—The word φιάλη belongs to the office of the cup-bearers. In order to have a correct idea of what it means, it is necessary to be acquainted with what regards this service. 1st, A certain quantity of wine and water, in proportion to the strength of the wine, or according to the taste of the drinkers, was poured into large vases. These vases, from the mixture of the two liquors, were called craters.— 2dly, The mixture was dipped out of these craters with a cyathus (κύαθος), a sort of deep pitcher, and the drink was poured out into a cup which was called ἔκπωμα. 3dly, The ἔκπωμα was presented to the guest on a φιάλη: this latter, therefore, was a saucer or plate: I mean, a flat, broad vessel, on which the cup was presented. See Xen. Cyrop. i. 3, 8. *Larcher.*

[908] Surgery was not, in former times, separated from medicine.

[909] C'est à lui que les médecins de Crotone doivent la plus grande partie de leur réputation—*To him the Crotonian doctors are indebted for the greatest part of their reputation.—Larcher.*

133 A short time after these events, the following occurrence took place. Atossa, the daughter of Cyrus, and wife of Darius, was afflicted with a tumor on the breast. After some time, it broke; and ate away by degrees, until it had increased to a considerable size: she concealed it through shame, and mentioned it to no one. However, as it continued to get worse and worse, she sent for Democedes, and shewed it to him. He told her, that he could heal the tumour; but insisted she should pledge herself[210] to remunerate him fairly for his service, by granting a request which he hereafter would make; and added, that he had no intention to ask any 134 thing that a lady would blush to grant. When he had healed the tumor, and restored her to health, Atossa, instructed by Democedes, thus addressed Darius, who was in bed with her. "My liege," said Atossa, "possessing such power, you "sit down tranquil, and attempt not to add by conquest any "nation or empire to the Persians. It behoves, I think, a "monarch, young, and master of such riches, to give proof "of his valour, so that the Persians may know they are "commanded by a gallant king. There are two motives "which should urge you to act in this manner; that the Per- "sians may be convinced they are headed by a valiant hero; "and that they may taste the toils of war, and not abide in "idleness, brooding conspiracies against yourself. Now "that you are in the bloom of life, you should achieve some "brilliant deed: for, as the body grows, so the mind grows; "as the body becomes old and infirm, so it is with the mind; "it is blunted for all purposes." Thus, at the suggestion of Democedes, Atossa spoke. Darius answered: "All that you "suggest, my dear love, I have myself already resolved to "do: for I intend to throw a bridge from this continent to "the other[211], and carry war into Scythia: my designs will "be accomplished ere long." Atossa then spoke thus: "Look you now! I beseech you not to march first[212] against "the Scythians; for, when you choose, they will be yours: "but, for my sake, invade Hellas. I so long, from what I "hear, to have, in my train, Laconian girls, and others from "Argos and Attica and Corinth. You have, besides, the "best man in the world to tell you every thing about Hellas, "him that cured your foot." Darius answered: "My love, "since you prefer I should make my first essay on Hellas, "I think it better previously to send some Persians, with the "man you speak of, and survey the country. They will see

---

[210] Ἠ μὲν, used Ionically, in forms of swearing, for μὴν
[211] That is to say, from Asia to Europe: see iv. 88.
[212] Matt. 281, 2.

" and hear all particulars, and make their report: and then,
" fully informed, I will march directly against the Hellenes."

Thus he spoke; and no sooner said, than done. As soon 135
as day dawned, he summoned fifteen Persians of rank; and
commanded them to follow Democedes, and visit the shores
of Hellas: but cautioned them not to let Democedes escape
out of their hands, but, by all means, to bring him back with
them. Having issued these commands, he next summoned
to his presence Democedes himself; requested him to act as
a guide to the Persians, shew them the whole of Hellas, and
return: he likewise ordered him to take with him all his
moveable property, as a present to his father and brothers,
promising that he would make it up to him liberally: to this
he would add a merchant-ship, to convey the gifts; and stow
her with all kinds of precious things, to accompany him on
his voyage. I have no doubt myself[212] that Darius made
these offers without any secret sinister motives: but Democedes, being afraid that Darius was only making a trial of
him[213], accepted the gifts without any apparent eagerness[214],
but observed, that he would leave his own things behind, in
order he might find them again on his return: he said he
would accept the merchant-ship, which Darius promised him,
to convey the gift to his brothers. Darius having given
these orders to Democedes, despatched the party down to the
sea-side.

They proceeded down to Sidon in Phœnicia; forthwith 136
manned two triremes, together with a large Phœnician
round craft, and loaded them with precious things. Having
made all the proper preparations, they sailed for Hellas:
they touched at various points of the coast, surveyed it,
and wrote down their observations[215]: after visiting many
places of the greatest celebrity, they proceeded to Tarentum
in Italy. There the king of the Tarentines, Aristophilides,
out of kindness to Democedes[216], first took away the rudders
of the Medic vessels; and next cast into prison the Persians,
alleging, it is pretended, that they were spies. While these
were in durance, Democedes proceeded to Croton; and when
safely arrived at home, Aristophilides liberated the Persians,

---

[212] See Matt. 543.

[213] *ib* for *ἰὸ, οὗ, of him.*

[214] ἐπτοίχυς signifies *to seize greedily.* Larcher. Construction. ἤλασε
πάντα τὰ ἰδίμεια, ὥστε ἐπιδραμεῖν αὐτοῖς.
Schweig. Lex. Herod.

[215] Larcher says, "et levèrent le
plan:" the passage, however, may
be translated, and "wrote down a
description of them."

[216] ἐν ἱκεσίαις τῆς Δημοκήδεος: the
genitive must apply to Aristophilides.
Coray makes it refer to Democedes,
giving to ἱκεσίαις quite another
meaning, " By the artifice of Democedes:" his proofs in support of this
meaning are too long for insertion in
this work. See Larcher, iii. 399.

137 and gave back the rudders which he had taken away. The Persians then sailed away, in pursuit of Democedes, and arrived at Croton; and, meeting with him in the market-place, seized his person. Some of the citizens of Croton, apprehensive of drawing upon themselves the vengeance of the Persians, would fain have winked at this outrage [217]; but the rest fell upon the fifteen, and thrashed the Persians with clubs. The Persians, in the mean time, hallooed out to them: "Citizens of Croton, have a care what you do! you are "rescuing a runaway from our sovereign. And do you "imagine king Darius will put up with such insolence [218]? "How sweetly will he handle you, if he come upon you? "Will he not attack your city the first of all? Will you not "be the first reduced to bondage?" But the Crotonians listened not to what they said, but rescued Democedes, and seized the merchant-ship the strangers had brought with them. The Persians sailed back to Asia; and did not attempt, now they were reft of their guide, to prosecute their researches into Hellas. Democedes, at their departure, enjoined them to inform Darius, that Democedes was on the point of marrying the daughter of Milo: for the name of that wrestler was well known and celebrated at the court of Darius. And, in truth, I am of opinion that Democedes hurried this union, and expended much, in order to prove to Darius that
138 he was a man of rank, even in his own country. The Persians unmoored, and departed from Croton; but were driven with their ships to Iapygia, where they were made prisoners. Gillus, a Tarentine exile, ransomed, and took them over to Darius; who was ready to give, in return, whatever he might ask. But Gillus related to him his misfortune, and implored the king to ensure his return to Tarentum: in order, however, not to disturb and alarm the whole of Hellas by a grand armament sailing on his account to Italy, he said the Cnidians would be sufficient to re-establish him; being convinced, that, in consequence of the friendship existing between the Cnidians and Tarentines, he should easily obtain permission to return. Darius promised him he would do so; and kept his promise; for he sent a messenger to the Cnidians, requesting them to convey Gillus to Tarentum: the Cnidians, following the recommendation of Darius, were not able to prevail on the Tarentines, and not powerful enough to compel them by force. Such, therefore, was the result of this

---

[217] Construction: οἱ μὲν ἐποίμεν ἦσαν περιῖδαι (αὐτὸν τοῖς Πέρσαις).

[218] πῶς βασιλεῖ ἰσχύσειν ταῦτα περιορίσθαι: Lit. "quomodo sufficere poterit regi tali contumelia affici?" *i. e.* How can he be content to be insulted in this manner?

undertaking: the above were the first Persians that came from Asia to Hellas, and they came for the purpose of reconnoitering the country.

After the above events, king Darius took possession of Samos: this was the first city, whether of the Hellenes or Barbarians, that he captured; and it was from the following motive. In the expedition made by Cambyses son of Cyrus against Egypt, a great number of Hellenes followed him to that country; some, of course, for commercial speculations; others for taking a part in the military operations; some few also for the opportunity of seeing the country. Of these last, Syloson was one: he was the son of Æaces, and brother to Polycrates, and an exile from Samos. The following piece of good luck befel this Syloson: he threw a scarlet mantle about his shoulders, and took a walk into the market-place at Memphis: he was remarked by Darius, at the time belonging to Cambyses' guards, and as yet held in no account: Darius had a longing for the cloak, and accosted Syloson, trying to purchase it from him. Syloson, seeing that the young man was so anxious to become the possessor of the cloak, urged by some extraordinary infatuation, said: "I do not intend to sell my cloak for any sum "of money; but, nevertheless, as things are thus, it shall be "yours[219]." Darius praised his liberality, and accepted the cloak. Syloson, accordingly, made up his mind to having lost his cloak by his own simplicity: but in the course of time, Cambyses died, the seven conspirators rose up against the Magus, and Darius, one of their number, ascended the throne. Syloson being informed that the power had passed into the hands of the very same man at whose request he had once given him his cloak in Egypt, went up to Susa; where he seated himself in the portal of the royal palace, and stated that he had been the benefactor of Darius. The gatekeeper, hearing this, communicated it to the king; who was surprised, and said to himself [220]: "Have I then received any "favour from a Hellene, to whom I am indebted, having so "lately come to the throne? Scarcely has one of that na"tion appeared before me[221]. I have contracted no debt "with any Hellenic man. Nevertheless," said Darius to the

porter, " send the man in: let me ascertain what he means " by this." The porter introduced Syloson: as he stood in the presence, the interpreters inquired of him who he was; and what he had done, to say that he had been a benefactor of the king. He replied, by describing what had occurred with respect to the cloak; and stated, that he was the individual who made the present to him. At this, Darius exclaimed: " What, most generous of mortals! are you the " person that did me that service, when I was but an humble " soldier, small as it was? At all events, my gratitude shall " be equal to what I should now feel for the most magnifi- " cent gift. In recompense, I will give you gold and silver " with a lavish hand; so you shall never repent the service " you have done to Darius the son of Hystaspes." To this Syloson made reply: " Sire, give me not gold nor silver: " recover and give me back Samos, my country, now usurped " by one of our slaves, since the murder of my brother Po- " lycrates by the hands of Orœtes: give it without blood-
141 " shed or bondage." Darius listened to this petition; and despatched an army, under the command of Otanes, one of the seven; enjoining him to accomplish what Syloson asked for: accordingly, Otanes went down to the sea-side, and embarked [222] the troops.

142 The sovereignty of Samos was in the hands of Mæandrius the son of Mæandrius, who had been left as regent by Polycrates: he was desirous to prove himself the most just of men, but did not succeed in his project; for when the death of Polycrates was announced to him, he acted in the manner I am now going to describe. In the first place, he erected an altar to Jupiter Liberator, and fixed the boundaries of the sacred precinct that surrounds it, as is still seen in the suburb: having done this, he convoked an assembly of all the citizens, and addressed to them the following speech: " You all know," said he, " that the sceptre and the whole " power of Polycrates was entrusted to me; and now it de- " pends upon my will, whether I shall assume the power " over you. I intend to do my utmost to avoid what I re- " probate in my neighbour: for I cannot approve the con- " duct of Polycrates, or any other person who assumes " despotic sway over men equal to himself. Polycrates, " then, has fulfilled his destiny; and I will place the power " in the hands of you all: I proclaim liberty and equality of " laws. I think it just, however, that I should receive some

---

[222] στέλλω is said of the sea as well as of the land. Eurip. Iphig. in Aul. 661; Æschyl. Pers. 175.—*Larcher.*

"remuneration for my sacrifice: let me choose to the value
"of six talents, out of the property of Polycrates. I claim,
"moreover, for myself and my descendants for ever, the
"priesthood of Jupiter Liberator, to whom I have erected
"a temple; while on you I confer the boon of freedom."
Such was his address to the Samians: but one of the assembly rose up, and said: "You, sir, are certainly very unfit to
"rule over us, pernicious and wicked man that you are.
"You ought rather to give us an account of the moneys
"that have passed through your hands[233]." Thus spoke one 143
of the influential citizens, whose name was Telesarchus.
Mæandrius, convinced by this, that, if he himself let go the
power, some tyrant would arise in his place, thought no
longer of giving it up; but retired to the citadel; and sending
for each of the principal men of the Samians, under pretence
of giving an account of the sums he had expended, arrested
them, and threw them into chains. Soon after, Mæandrius
fell sick: his brother, called Lycaretus, expecting he would
die, put to death all the prisoners, with a view of facilitating
his assumption of the Samian government; for it appears
the people of Samos were not at all inclined for liberty.

Accordingly, when the Persians arrived at Samos, bring- 144
ing with them Syloson, not one was found to lift up his
hand against them: Mæandrius himself, and his partisans,
declared they were ready to come to terms, and to leave
the island. Otanes acceded to these conditions, accepted
and gave the pledges; and the most distinguished Persians placed themselves before the citadel, seated upon
chairs. The tyrant Mæandrius had a brother that was not 145
quite in his senses[234], whose name was Charilaus: this brother
of his, accordingly, having done something wrong, was confined in a dungeon. The lunatic having heard what had
been done, looked through the grating of his dungeon, and,
seeing the Persians thus quietly seated, made a loud exclamation, and declared that he wished to speak to Mæandrius[235]. Mæandrius, informed of this, ordered him to be
unchained, and brought before him. As soon as he was
brought in, he began to abuse and vilify his brother, urged
him to fall on the Persians, and spoke thus: "You, the
"greatest scoundrel of the world, have doomed me to be
"chained down in a dungeon, I, that am your own brother,
"and had committed no offence deserving of fetters; yet,

[233] Construction: ἀλλὰ μᾶλλον [ᾗ οὐ ἔχεις] ἴχνος λέγειν δόσιως, κ. τ. λ Herod. λίγων, 2. Matt. 613; and Bp. Blomfield's observation, Matt. Gr. Gram. p. 1.
[234] See Matt. 457, 1.
[235] ἰὸν λίγων. See Schweig. Lex.

"even when you see the Persians expelling you by violence,
"and bereaving you of your home, have not the heart to
"seek revenge, easy as it would be to defeat them. If you
"are afraid of them, give me your mercenaries; I will hurl
"vengeance on them for coming here[226]: and as for your-
146 "self, I will presently send you out of the island." So spoke
Charilaus. Mæandrius took him at his word: not that he
was, in my opinion, such a fool as to fancy his forces would
be a match for those of the king, but that he envied Syloson's good luck, if he should, without any toil, get possession
of the town unscathed. By exasperating the Persians, he
sought accordingly to clip the power of Samos, and so deliver it up; well aware, that if the Persians suffered any discomfiture, they would be bitterly inveterate against the Samians: he knew, moreover, of a safe retreat from the island,
whenever he chose to avail himself of it; for he had ordered
a secret passage underground to be excavated, beginning
at the citadel, and terminating at the sea. Accordingly, Mæandrius himself sailed away from Samos; and Charilaus, after
putting all the auxiliary troops under arms, threw open the
gates, and rushed upon the Persians; who were far from expecting such an attack, and fancied that all matters were
settled and arranged. Meanwhile, the mercenaries massacred the above-mentioned Persians of rank, whom they found
sitting before the citadel[227]. While they were engaged in
this slaughter, the rest of the Persians came up, to bear
a hand: the mercenaries, broken, ran back, and shut them-
147 selves up in the citadel. Otanes, the commander, a witness
of the blow inflicted on the Persians, forgot the injunctions
given him by Darius, not to kill or take prisoner any of the
Samians, but to deliver up the island unscathed to Syloson:
on the contrary, he made known to the army, that they were
to cut down alike every man or boy: in consequence, one
portion of the army proceeded to lay siege to the castle;
while the rest went about, putting every one they met to the
148 sword, whether on sacred or profane ground.—Mæandrius,
having made good his escape from Samos, sailed for Lacedæmon: on his arrival there, he carried up to the capital the
things he had brought with him, and acted in the following
manner: he set out his different vases of silver and gold, and

[226] τῆς ἰσάδα ἀείξας. Matt. 345, a.
[227] ἀφροφορευμένος is taken by Coray in the middle voice. It was, he says, a luxury, known even among the Athenians, to be followed by a servant carrying a seat, which he presented to his master whenever he wished to sit down. "Those among the Persians who were the most respected, and had seat-bearers in their train," &c. Coray, quoted by Larcher.

his attendants proceeded to wipe them clean. He, being at the time in conversation with Cleomenes the son of Anaxandrides, one of the Spartan kings, took him into his house. Cleomenes was struck with wonder and amazement at the sight of so much plate, and Mæandrius urged his visitor to carry away with him what articles he chose [298]: twice or thrice this offer was made; but Cleomenes behaved as an honest man; he spurned the gift, and, being informed that Mæandrius was courting support from others by such means, presented himself before the ephori, and declared that it was better Sparta should dismiss this Samian stranger from the shores of Peloponnesus, so that he might no longer persuade himself or others to become a pander to his views. The ephori, in consequence of this communication, proclaimed, by herald, the expulsion of Mæandrius.—But the Persians 149 having captured all the Samians, as in a net [299], gave up to Syloson the island, reft wholly of population: some time after, however, Otanes re-peopled the land, in consequence of a dream that occurred to him, and a disease that attacked his natural parts.

As the naval armament was on its way to Samos, the Baby- 150 lonians, having made vast preparations, rebelled. During the whole time of disorder that lasted through the reign of the Magus, and the insurrection of the seven, they had been providing to resist a siege; and, by some means or other, were enabled to do so, unknown to any one. When they openly threw off their allegiance, they acted in the following manner. With the exception of their mothers, every one of the citizens chose one of the women in his house, whom he liked the best; all the rest were gathered together in one place, and strangled: the one preserved by each citizen was for the purpose of cooking his provisions; the rest were strangled, to decrease the consumption of provisions. Darius, having received intelligence of this, collected all his 151 forces, and marched against them: having reached Babylon, he laid siege to the place; but the inhabitants took little account of this: they ascended to the battlements of their wall, and there danced, and laughed at Darius and his host: one of them even hallooed to the besiegers, saying: "Why sit you there, Persians? had you not better go about "your business? for you will never catch us, until mules "breed." This was said by one of the Babylonians, who never expected to see a mule with a foal. After a lapse of 152 one year and seven months, both Darius and his whole army

---

[298] ἰὼ ἂν ᾖς τῶν χρόνων τούτων .... ἰὼ ἂν ἰσιλίσσων. See Matt. 598, a.

[299] Cf. vii. 64. where Herodotus explains this mode of capture.

were sorely annoyed, that they could not yet capture Babylon. Darius tried every stratagem, every artifice, against the place; and, with all his exertions, could not get possession, even by resorting to the mode in which Cyrus had succeeded: but the Babylonians kept guard, and it was impossible to surprise them [230].

153 In the twentieth month from the opening of the siege, Zopyrus, the son of the Megabyzus who was one of the seven conspirators against the Magus, was witness to a very extraordinary occurrence: one of his own mules, belonging to the baggage-train, brought forth a young mule: Zopyrus, informed of the event, scarcely could give credit to the report, but went and saw the foal himself; charged the [231] grooms to say nothing of what had happened, and revolved the prodigy in his own mind. He recalled to his mind the speech of the Babylonian, pronounced at the beginning of the siege—that when mules, barren as they are, should procreate, then should their city be carried: he concluded, from this omen, that now the time was come when Babylon was to be taken; for this seemed to have been spoken by divine inspiration, and had actually occurred to one of his
154 own mules [232]. Having made up his mind that now was the time appointed by fate for the capture of Babylon, he presented himself before Darius; and inquired of his majesty, if he regarded it as of paramount importance that Babylon should be taken. When informed that the king considered the thing as of the first consequence, Zopyrus considered how he should alone make the capture of the place, so that the achievement should be his deed and work: for with the Persians, such gallant exploits conduce greatly to the promotion of the authors [233]. Accordingly, having debated within himself how he should be able to attempt what he proposed, he could not devise any other expedient, than to disfigure dreadfully his person, and then desert over to the enemy. Holding this of little consequence, he lacerated himself in a most dreadful manner: he cut off his own nose and ears, sheared his hair all round, lashed his body with
155 whips, and presented himself before Darius. The king was sorely grieved at seeing his chief nobleman thus disfigured: he started up from his throne, and with loud exclamations,

---

[230] See i. 151.

[231] I have endeavoured to express the force of the particle τις, which is by no means an expletive. *Larcher.* See Matt. 591, 8.

[232] Lit. "and that the mule had foaled to himself."

[233] ἐς τὸ πρόσω μεγάλως τιμῶνται, "Honorantur et ad insignem magnitudinis gradum evehuntur," i. e. τιμῶνται, ὥστε αὐτοὺς (τοὺς ἀγαθοεργοὺς) ἐς τὸ πρόσω μεγάλως ἀνήκειν. See Matt. 818.

demanded who had treated him thus, and who had disfigured him in this manner. "The man lives not, my liege, that "dares," said Zopyrus, "or has the power to treat me thus, "except yourself. No stranger, sire, has wrought this: I "myself am the perpetrator of this deed, indignant to be- "hold Assyrians deride Persians." "O most miserable of "men!" retorted Darius, "you give the fairest of names to "the foulest deeds, in saying that you have thus treated "yourself, in order to get the upper hand of the enemy: "how, simple man, will the foe relax his insolence, in con- "sequence of your disfiguring yourself? Are you reft of "your senses, to have ruined yourself in this manner?" Zopyrus made reply: "If I had communicated to you what "I was about to do, you would not have allowed me to act "so: but now I have had the resolution to do it myself; "and therefore, if you do not fail on your part, we shall get "possession of Babylon. As I am now, I will desert over "to the city; tell the people that I have suffered this treat- "ment at your hands; and, by persuading them to that, shall, "I expect, get the command of the garrison. Do you, "reckoning from the time that I enter the rampart, count "the tenth day; and choose a thousand of the men, the loss "of whom would be of little moment, and post them at the "gates called after Semiramis: seven days after, post for "me, at the gates called those of Nineveh, two thousand: "then wait twenty days more[224], when you will command "four thousand more, to their station at the gates called the "Chaldæan. Let the first, and the others, have no arms of "defence but their swords; leave them those. And after "twenty days more have elapsed, without delay order the "whole army to encircle the city, and storm the wall; and "station my Persians at the gates of Belus, and those of "Cissia: for I expect, that, in consequence of my heroic "deeds, the Babylonians will, among other things, confide "even the cross-bars[225] of the gates to my keeping: and "then I and the Persians must address ourselves to work."

Having thus explained what he wished to have performed, 156 he proceeded up to the city gates, turning himself round to look behind, as if he were a real deserter. The persons

---

[224] See Matt. 544: likewise the Bishop of London's remark in the same work, p. xlviii.

[225] βαλανάγρας. This word signifies a sort of hook used to pull out the βάλανος, a small round piece of iron driven through the jamb of the gate, and the extremity of the μοχλὸς or cross-bar, to keep it in its proper situation: in case of opening the gates, the βαλανάγρα was indispensable to release the fastening of the bar, so that it might be shot back. I have adopted the English word *key*, for want of a better term.

stationed on the towers, to keep a look-out, ran down below, and, putting one of the large folding-doors ajar[236], inquired who he was, and what he wanted. He informed them, that his name was Zopyrus, and that he had come over to them as a deserter: the door-keepers no sooner heard this, than they took the new-comer before the common-council of the Babylonians. Standing before the members of that assembly, he deplored his misfortune, saying, that Darius had served him in this cruel manner, because he advised him to raise the siege, as there was evidently no means of securing a capture: "And now," said he, continuing his discourse, "I be-
"come a great accession to yourselves, men of Babylon, and
"a great defalcation to Darius and his army: for he shall
"pay me for having mutilated me in this manner: I am
157 "acquainted with all the secrets of his counsels." So he said. The Babylonians, seeing a man of that rank among the Persians deprived of his nose and ears, and covered with weals and stripes, were completely convinced of the truth of what he said, and that he was come to their support: they therefore were inclined to grant him whatever he might ask. He asked for the command of the military force. Having so far succeeded, he proceeded to act as he had arranged with Darius: on the tenth day, accordingly, he made a sally with the Babylonian troops, surrounded the thousand men whom he had commissioned Darius to station, and cut them to pieces. The Babylonians, finding he was a man to act up to his words, were all overjoyed beyond measure, and were eager to obey his commands. He let pass the number of days appointed; and again, with a chosen party of the Babylonians, made a sally, and cut to pieces every one of the two thousand men stationed, according to agreement, by Darius. The Babylonians, witnesses of the gallant exploits of their new commander, had all of them Zopyrus's name at the end of their tongues[237], extolling him highly. Once more, after letting the appointed time pass over, he led on the above-mentioned band, surrounded the four thousand, and destroyed them to a man. Having achieved this glorious action, he became the idol of the Babylonians: they proclaimed him their commander-in-chief, and governor of their

---

[236] τὴν ἑτέρην πύλην. That is to say, one of the folding-doors of which the gates (πύλαι) was composed. The gates of the ancient towns consisted of two folding-doors, each fixed to a round bar, turning within sockets hewn in the sill and lintel: these folding-doors were fastened by a cross-beam, the ends of which ran into cavities made in the jambs. Such, at least, were the gates of Mycenæ, the stupendous ruins of which I saw some years since.

[237] See Matt. 438.

city. Finally, Darius having, according to previous agree- 158
ment, made a general assault on the wall, Zopyrus displayed
the whole of his stratagem: for the Babylonians that
ascended to the battlements were all hurled head-foremost
down. Zopyrus, with his own hands, opening wide the gates
of Belus and Cissia, admitted the Persians within the wall.
Those of the Babylonians who saw what had been done took
refuge in the temple of Jupiter Belus: the rest kept each to
his post, till he also was informed of the treachery which had
been practised [238].

Thus was Babylon a second time captured. Darius, 159
having now the Babylonians in his power, in the first place
rased the walls, and tore down all the gates; for at the first
capture by Cyrus, nothing of the kind had been done. Next,
he impaled about three thousand of the chief citizens, and
gave the town to the rest of the Babylonians to inhabit. In
order that the citizens might not be without women, and
their race become extinct, Darius made the following provision. The Babylonians had, as I before observed, strangled
their wives at the commencement of the blockade, with a view
to spare their stores: the Persian monarch, therefore, taxed
the neighbouring nations to send a certain number of women
to Babylon: the contingency from all these nations amounted,
in the whole, to fifty thousand women. From these women
the present Babylonians descend. None of the Persians, 160
whether previous or subsequent—with the exception, however, of Cyrus, to whom no Persian would presume to compare himself—ever surpassed Zopyrus, in Darius's opinion [239],
by his heroic deeds in the service of the state. It is related,
that Darius frequently expressed his opinion, that he would
rather that Zopyrus had not disfigured his person than have
received the accession of twenty Babylons. He treated him
with magnificent honours; sent to him every year the gifts
deemed the most honourable by the Persians; and gave him
Babylon to rule, without any contribution to the royal exchequer, during the whole of his life: he enriched him by
very many other donations. From this Zopyrus descended
Megabyzus, who held the command in Egypt during the war
with the Athenians and allies: from Megabyzus descended
Zopyrus, who voluntarily emigrated from Persia to Athens.

[238] Matt. °548, 3.—Ἱμασιν, plural, with Ἱμασσι, singular, Matt. 301, a. [239] παρὰ Δαρείῳ κρίσῃ. See Matt. 389.

BOOK IV.

MELPOMENE.

SUMMARY OF BOOK IV.

AFTER *the capture of Babylon, Darius marches against the Scythians, because they had invaded Asia, and held possession of it for twenty-eight years,* 1. *The country and the origin of the Scythians,* 5—36. *Concerning the three quarters of the world, Asia, Libya, and Europe,* 37—45. *Concerning the rivers of Scythia,* 47—57. *Darius, having started from Susa, crosses the Thracian Bosphorus by a bridge of boats; compels the Thracians to submit to his yoke; (digression concerning the Getæ and Zalmoxis,* 94—96*;) crosses the Ister, and, leaving the Ionians to guard the floating-bridge over the river, marches up the country,* 83—98. *The situation and dimensions of Scythia: its various tribes,* 99—177. *The art by which the Scythians elude the efforts of Darius,* 118—134. *After pursuing the Scythians without success, the king at last returns to the Ister; from whence he passes over into Asia,* 134—143. *At the same time, another army of the Persians attacks Barce, in order to avenge the death of Arcesilaus, king of the Cyrenæans, and son of Pheretime. The Historian takes the opportunity of inserting the history of Cyrene, from the time that a colony was settled in Libya by the Minyæ of the island of Thera,* 145—164. *A description of the tribes of Libya,* 168—199. *The Barcæi are taken, by the perfidy of the Persians; and Pheretime cruelly avenges the death of her son. The Persians make a vain attempt on Cyrene; and, on their return into Egypt, are harassed by the Africans,* 201 *to the end.*

THE FOURTH BOOK OF HERODOTUS.

MELPOMENE.

The next expedition undertaken by Darius, subsequent to 1 the capture of Babylon, was against the Scythians[1]. As Asia flourished in population, and vast revenues poured in on all sides, Darius conceived a desire of visiting the Scythians with his vengeance; they having been the original promoters of hostility, by breaking into the territory of the Medes; and, after defeating that nation in battle, unjustly usurping the supreme power: for, as I have already observed, the Scythians had been, during eight-and-twenty years[2], the sovereign lords of Upper Asia. In their pursuit of the Cimmerians, they broke into Asia, and put down the power of the Medes[3], who, previously to the irruption of the Scythians, had obtained the whole empire of Asia. The Scythians, however, after their absence from home during eight-and-twenty years, and at their return to their own country, met with toils scarce inferior[4] to those they had experienced at the hands of the Medes, for they found themselves opposed by no inconsiderable multitude of enemies. The wives of the Scythians, in the long absence of their husbands, had sought the company of their slaves. I shall take 2 this opportunity of observing, that the Scythians put out the eyes of all their slaves, in order to make use of them in the preparation of the milk which constitutes their only beverage.

---

[1] Lit. "An expedition of Darius again took place against the Scythians." If we follow the old reading, *αὐτοῦ* instead of *αὖ τοῦ*, the meaning will be, that Darius marched in person against the Scythians. See *Schweig. Not.*

[2] See Matt. 141.

[3] See i. 103, 105. *Wess.* See likewise c. 12. of this Book.

[4] "Scythas---excepit labor non minor," etc. *Schweig. Lex. Herod.*—Understand *πόνος* after *Μηδικοῦ*: thus the battle of Marathon is called *πόνος*, vi. 114.

These slaves use tubes of bone, similar to our musical fifes, which they thrust up the vulva of the mare, and so blow in air by their mouths: some are employed in milking the mares, while others are busy thus blowing: as they assert, this practice is adopted for the purpose of inflating the veins of the mare, and making the dug sink lower down. When the milk has been procured, they pour it into wooden vases; around which the blind slaves are stationed, to keep agitating and shaking violently the milk: they skim off the substance that swims on the top, and consider it the most delicate: the rest is deemed inferior [5]. For the above purpose, the Scythians put out the eyes of every slave they can procure: of course, I do not mean the Scythians that apply to agriculture, but those that are nomades or pastors [6]. From these slaves, accordingly, and the Scythian women, had sprung a band of youths; who, when informed of their origin, resolved to go forth and face the Scythians, at their return from Media: but previously they cut off their own territory by a broad trench, extending from the Tauric mountains to the vast lake called the Mæotis [7]: after having accomplished this work, they opposed the Scythians in their efforts to make good their ingress, and engaged battle: many encounters took place, but the Scythians were unable to advance a step, in spite of their fighting: at last, one of the returning party addressed his comrades: "What are we about," said he, "men of Scythia? We engage in equal fight with our "slaves; thus decreasing our own numbers by our own

---

[5] On this passage, Larcher has the following note. This is the cream. It is very astonishing that neither the Greeks nor the Latins had any word in their language to express this idea. Fortunatus, who flourished in the sixth century, has made use of the word *crema*, derived from *cremor*, which the Latins use to express the thick slime that swims on water in which any pulse has been soaked. *Larcher.*—I do not think that the shaking the tube would have been the readiest way to obtain cream, which, as every one knows, is procured by suffering the milk to settle for some time. τὸ ἐπιστάμενον ἀυτοῦ appears to me to allude to the curd or butter, which always swims in the churn; and τὸ ὑπιστάμενον, to the whey or butter-milk

[6] There were Scythians whom Herodotus especially designates ἀροτῆρες, in distinction of the νομάδες. The meaning of the Historian must be, therefore, that none but the nomade or pastoral tribes among the Scythians have this cruel practice with their slaves. See *Valck.* and *Schweig.* As these nomades led a roaming and vagabond life, the most effectual mode to prevent their slaves from escaping, was to blind them; and this probably is the meaning of the conjunction γάρ.

[7] Ἐκ τῶν Ταυρικῶν ὀρέων. These mountains must not be confounded with the Mount Taurus of Asia. See the *Geographical Index to Herodotus*. See, respecting this trench, the note on c. 28. If we were to read ἐκ τῶν Ταύρων ὀρέων, "from the confines of the Tauri," the position of this trench would be much more easily understood.

" deaths, and diminishing that of our slaves that are left by
" destroying them. Believe me, therefore: let us dismiss
" javelin and bow; let each take his horsewhip, and make a
" rush upon them. So long as they have seen us armed,
" they have fancied themselves our equals: but when they
" shall see us grasping the whip instead of the bow, they
" will feel they are our slaves, and, convinced of that, will
" offer no more opposition." The Scythians, hearing this, 4
adopted the advice: the opposing party, surprised at the
alteration, forgot to fight, and took to their heels. Thus
the Scythians not only ruled over Asia, but, being driven
back by the Medes, returned to their country in the above-
described manner: this was the motive which urged Darius
to be anxious to wreak vengeance on the Scythians, and
induced him to collect his force for the purpose of invading
them.

According to the account given by the Scythians[8], they 5
must be the most modern of all nations in the world: the
origin of their race, as they say, was this: the first man that
existed in this country, previously a complete desert, bore
the name of Targitaus. The progenitors of this Targitaus
are represented as being Jupiter and the daughter of the
river Borysthenes: I put no faith, however, in this report[9].
From Targitaus sprang three sons, Leipoxaïs, Arpoxaïs,
and, the youngest, Colaxaïs: under the reign of these three,
some instruments of gold fell from heaven[10], a plough with
its yoke, a battle-axe[11], and a cup; all these alighted on the
Scythian territory. The first that espied them was the
elder brother: he approached the things with the intention
of picking them up; but on his coming up, the gold caught
fire. He retired: the second brother went up, and the gold
again flamed[12]: thus two of the three were driven back
by the fiery gold[13]. Thirdly, the youngest coming up, the

---

[8] *Ὡς δὲ Σκύθαι λέγουσι* ..... *εἶναι*
κ. τ. λ. See Matt. 538, 2. In the
time of Herodotus, there were four
opinions respecting the origin of the
Scythians. 1st, That of the Scythians
themselves, mentioned in c. 5. 2dly,
That of the Greeks on the Euxine,
which begins c. 8, and continues to
the end of c. 10. 3dly, That common
to the Greeks and Barbarians, and
adopted by Herodotus. This opinion
is mentioned c. 11 and 12. 4thly,
That of Aristeas of Proconnesus, which
begins at c. 13.

[9] The Greek adds, " But they do say it."

[10] *φερόμενα.* Consult Matt. 557; and
the Bishop of London's note, p xlviii.
of the same work.

[11] A double-edged battle-axe; the
francisck of our northern forefathers.

[12] Lit. " And it (*i. e.* the gold) did
again the same."

[13] *ἀπώσασθαι,* à se repellere, repu-
diare. *Schweig. Lex. Herod.* I take
καιόμενον τὸν χρυσὸν, as the subject
of the sentence: it may otherwise be
translated, taking *τοὺς μὲν* for the subject, " These, accordingly, refused the
burning gold."

fire went out, and he took the things home. The elder brothers, in consequence of this[14], it is said, of one accord made over the whole kingdom to their youngest brother.

6 From Lipoxaïs, accordingly, sprang those Scythians that are called the Auchatæ horde: from the second, Arpoxaïs, proceeded those called Catiari and Traspies: from the youngest arose the royal horde, called Paralatæ[15]. All these hordes bear one general common name, Scoloti, from the king's
7 cognomen. By the Hellenes they are called Scythes. Such the Scythians state to be their origin: the years, from the first beginning, amount in all, from the first king, Targitaus, to the invasion of their country by Darius, to just one millennium[16], and no more. The above gold, which is sacred, is watched with the greatest care by the royal horde: they approach it, propitiating with great sacrifices, every year[17]. He that is appointed at this festival to bring the sacred gold into day-light, should he fall asleep, cannot, according to the account of the Scythians, pass through the year: in consequence of this, he is presented with as much ground as he can compass in one day on horseback[18]. The land being very extensive, Colaxaïs, according to their account, divided it into three kingdoms, among his sons. The largest portion, being appointed to that where the

---

[14] πρὸς ταῦτα ('in consequence of this event:' see Matthiæ's remark on the meaning of πρὸς ταῦτα, 591, β.) τοὺς πρεσβυτέρους ἀδελφεοὺς συγγνόντας (assenting to its being fated that the younger brother should reign), παραδοῦναι κ. τ. λ. —Schweighæuser, however, gives in his Latin version, "quâ re intellectâ:" a similar signification is attributed to πρὸς ταῦτα συγγ. by all the translators, English and French.

[15] The reading τοὺς βασιλῆας is surely not the right. If we read τοῦ βασιλέος, the translation will be, "From the youngest of them, who was king, those that are called Paralatæ." If we follow the conjecture of Schweighæuser and Wesseling, τοὺς βασιληίους, the meaning will be, that "from the youngest sprung the Royal Scythians, of whom mention is hereafter made."

[16] The text adds, "But so many."

[17] Had Herodotus meant only that the Scythians offered great sacrifices to this gold, he would merely have said, θυσίησι μεγάλῃσι μετέχονται: so in vi. 69. ἱερῷ τε μάλιστα μετέχεται. Wesseling is of opinion that μετέχονται ἀνὰ πᾶν ἴσον, signifies that "the kings bring every year this gold, each into his own individual states." I think he is right, and this is the sense I have followed. Larcher.—My translation follows that of Schweighæuser, who, I think, overthrows the argument of Wesseling.

[18] The whole of this is unintelligible to me: reason cannot but allow, that if so great a quantity of land was given to the sentinel for remaining awake only one day, as Larcher explains it, the task was by no means commensurate to the reward. I see that one of the manuscripts gives ὡς ἂν, instead of ἵνα: if we adopt this reading, might not the sense be, "And for that reason they give it (i. e. the sacred gold) to him, that he may ride about with it on horseback during one day?" Every one will allow that the guard would not be so inclined to drowsiness, while on horseback.

sacred gold was kept. Above, towards the north, beyond the inhabitants of this tract[19], the land cannot be seen to any considerable distance, or be travelled over, by reason of showers of feathers that fall down[20]: for the earth and air are filled with feathers, which is the cause that precludes all prospect.

Such is the account the Scythians give of themselves[21], 8 and of the countries above them. The Hellenic settlers on the shores of the Pontus[22] make the following statement: that Hercules, driving before him the herds[23] of Geryon, arrived in this country, now inhabited by the Scythians, but at that time completely desert. Geryon they represent as residing far from the Pontus[24], in an island, called, by the Hellenes, Erytheia, situate beyond Gades, without the Pillars of Hercules, on the Ocean, a river. Concerning the Ocean they have an idle tale, saying, that it begins in the east, in the quarter where the sun rises, and flows completely round the earth—this however they do not shew by fact: from thence Hercules had come to the country now called Scythia. The Hellenes go on to state, that, visited by a storm[25], and chilled by the cold, he drew over himself the lion's skin, and fell asleep: that, in the mean time, his horses, unyoked for the purpose of grazing, disappeared, by some

---

[19] Join πρὸς βορῆν ἀνέμων τῶν ὑπεροίκων. *Wess.* I have followed Larcher: "Quant aux régions situées au nord et au dessus des *derniers habitans* de ce pays, les Scythes," &c.

[20] Herodotus explains what is meant by these feathers, that is to say, they are nothing more than flakes of snow, c. 31.

[21] διὲ in the sense of περὶ: see Matt. 582.

[22] See the note on the word Πόντος, lower down.

[23] The Ionians make use of the feminine with the name of the animal, to express a herd, or congregation of animals: ἡ ἵππος, cavalry: ἡ ὄνος, a herd of asses. *Larcher.*

[24] Herodotus, and most of the ancients, understood by πόντος, the sea in general; nor must that word be taken to signify the Pontus Euxinus, unless circumstances affix to it that sense, that is to say, when Herodotus is speaking of the countries in the neighbourhood of the Euxine. In this case he is speaking of the Scythians, and of their country, situate on the Euxine. The circumstances, therefore, require that we should understand by the Greeks of the Pontus, those on the Euxine, and not the Greeks of Greece. *De la Nauze.*—This note, Larcher tells us, is taken from a letter addressed to Bellanger, who understood the words 'Ελλήνων δὲ οἱ τὸν Πόντον οἰκέοντες, at the beginning of this chapter, of the Greeks on the Mediterranean. In the present instance, it would appear, from the mention of the proximity of Gades, that ἔξω τοῦ Πόντου must signify "without the sea," that is to say, without the Mediterranean. If the reader choose to adopt the reading κατοικημένην, according to Schweighæuser's conjecture, the translation will be: "Geryon, they say, inhabited an island which the Greeks call Erytheia, situate (κατοικημένην) without the sea, (*i. e.* the Mediterranean) near Gades, on the Ocean, beyond the Pillars of Hercules." Respecting the signification here given to κατοικημένην, the reader is referred to p. 187, note 250, of this volume.

[25] See Matt. 613, vii.

9 superhuman influence. When Hercules awoke, he proceeded in search of his steeds; went all over the land; and at last came to the country called Hylæa; where, in a cavern, he found a monster of two natures, one half a woman, the other a serpent[26]. The upper part, down to the buttocks, presented the form of a woman: below, that of a serpent. Hercules saw this monster: he was surprised, but inquired if she had seen his strayed horses. She replied, that they were in her possession; and she would not restore them until she had conversed with him: to that condition Hercules assented; but the creature still put off the restoration of the horses, wishing to enjoy a longer time the company of Hercules, while he himself was anxious to depart: at last she restored them, and said: "I have saved for you these "horses, which had strayed to this place. You have re- "turned the service; for I have by you three sons. Pray, "tell me what I am to do with them, when they grow up; "whether shall I establish them here; for here I am sove- "reign queen; or shall I send them to you." To this, as the Hellenes represent, Hercules made this reply: "When you "see my sons grown to manhood, fail not to do as I now tell "you. He, whom you see bend, as I do, this bow, and gird "himself in this manner with the belt that is here, keep him "in your country. Send away from hence him that shall "fail in what I now enjoin. In so doing, you will be con-
10 "tented; and you will have obeyed my orders." Hercules, accordingly, bent one of his bows—for till then he carried two; shewed his paramour how the belt was to be girt[27]; then gave her the bow, and the belt, from the top of the clasp of which hung a gold cup; and took his departure. When the children were grown up to manhood, she gave them their respective names[28]; Agathyrsus to the first; Gelonus to the second; and Scythes to the youngest. Then, mindful of her commission, she acted conformably to the behests of Hercules. Accordingly, two of the young men, Agathyrsus and Gelonus, not being equal to the appointed task, were driven away by their mother, and left the country: but the youngest of the three, Scythes, having accomplished the conditions, remained in his country: and from Scythes the son of Hercules sprang the Royal Scythians of subsequent generations: from the above-mentioned cup came also the custom, still in vogue, of Scythians wearing a

---

[26] ἔχιδναν, *viper*.
[27] προδεικνύειν signifies to shew first, by one's own example, how any thing is to be done.
[28] τοῦτο μὲν (λέγουσι αὐτοὶ) σφι ἐποίησαν. --- τοῦτο δὲ ταῦτα, on *the one hand* --- *on the other hand*.

cup at their belt. This accordingly [29] was done for Scythes only, by the mother. Such is the account given by the Hellenes settled on the shores of the Euxine.

There is also another account given, to which I myself attach some credit: it is this [30]: they relate, That the nomade Scythians, who once resided in Asia, being defeated in war by the Massagetæ, crossed [31] the Araxes river into the land of the Cimmerians: for it is added, the country now occupied by the Scythians belonged in former times to the Cimmerians. That on the approach of the Scythians, the Cimmerians held council, the invading army being so numerous [32]. The opinions were accordingly divided between them; both were warmly supported: that of the kings was the best: for the opinion of the people was, that expediency suggested they should not hazard themselves before such a multitude [33]: that of the kings was, to fight for the soil with the invaders. But the people did not choose to yield to the kings, nor did the kings choose to bend to the people: accordingly, one party resolved, without striking a blow, to retire, and abandon the country to the invaders: the kings voted to remain in the country of their fathers, and there meet death, rather than join the people in their flight; arguing, how many blessings they had hitherto enjoyed, and what evils they might expect in flying from their native soil. Such being the opinions on the two sides, they separated, and, being equal in numbers, fell to blows. Every man among the kings having been slain by the opposite party, the Cimmerian people buried them all on the bank of the river Tyras, where the grave is to this day seen. After they had buried the fallen kings, the remaining people departed from the country; and the Scythians, coming up, took possession of a deserted land. Even now we find in Scythia, Cimmerian castles and Cimmerian ferries [34]; we find, also, a quarter called Cimmeria; and there is a Cimmerian Bosphorus. It is likewise evident, that the Cimmerians [35], fleeing out of

---

[29] τὸ δὲ, relating, I believe, to κατα-
παύεται ἐν τῇ χώρῃ. Schweighæuser
clearly shews that μοῦνος is an adverb.
[30] ἔχων δὲ. See Matt. 604.
[31] διαβάντας διαβάντας, Matt. 559, c.
[32] See Matt. 568, 2.
[33] διάμενον. Most commentators regard σφῆγμα ἴδη and διάμενον (ἴδη) as a tautology. But Schweighæuser is of opinion that the common formula, σφῆγμα ἴδη ἑωυτε ἑωυτῶν, is equivalent, by ellipsis, to σφῆγμα διαμενὸν ἔστι. The construction, therefore, will be: (λέγουσι) τὴν τοῦ δήμου γνώμην φέρειν, ὡς εἴη σφῆγμα διαμενὸν ἀπαλλάσσεσθαι, μηδὲ κινδυνεύειν πρὸς πολλούς.

[34] Πορθμήια is here a proper name: it was the name of a town from whence the Cimmerian Bosphorus was crossed. There are many places in this country called, by a similar reason, Hithe.
[35] Matt. 547.

Asia before the Scythians, colonized the Chersonesus on which the Hellenic town of Sinope now stands. It is likewise certain, that the Scythians, in the pursuit of the Cimmerians, missed their road, and fell unawares upon the Medic territory: for the Cimmerians, in their flight, kept constantly to the sea-shore; while the Scythians pursued, keeping Caucasus to the right; and so fell upon the Medic territory, having wandered into the interior, out of their right way. This different account is common both among Hellenes and aliens.

13 Aristeas the son of Caystrobius, a native of Proconnesus, mentions in his poems; That he came as far as the Issedones, inspired by Apollo. That above the Issedones dwell the Arimaspi, men with but one eye: above these latter are found the gold-keeping griffons: above them are the Hyperboreans, extending to the sea. He adds, accordingly, that all these, with the exception of the Hyperboreans, have, commencing with the Arimaspi, successively advanced on their next neighbours[36]: and that by the Arimaspi the Issedones were pushed out of their country; the Scythians, by the Issedones; the Cimmerians, by the Scythians; the former of whom, residing on the southern sea[37], were obliged to forsake their country. Thus even that poet does not
14 coincide in respect to this country with the Scythians. I have[38] already mentioned of what country Aristeas was, who sings these things: I will now detail what I have heard concerning him at Proconnesus and Cyzicus. It is related, that Aristeas, who did not belong to any very humble family, had gone into a fuller's shop at Proconnesus, and there suddenly fell dead. The fuller directly closed his workshop, and hastened to carry the tidings to the nearest kinsmen of the deceased. The report of the death of Aristeas having quickly spread over the town, a citizen of Cyzicus, coming from Artace, contradicted the rumour; declaring, that he had met Aristeas going to Cyzicus, and conversed with

[36] αἰεὶ τοῖσι σ. λεπτίθεται, "font continuellement la guerre à leurs voisins." *Larcher.* I should have preferred taking αἰεὶ in the sense of *uniformly*, making the meaning to be, "all these nations, the Arimaspi beginning, successively fell on their neighbours."

[37] ἐπὶ τῇ νοτίῃ θαλάσσῃ; this must be the Euxine, which was really to the south, in respect of the Arimaspi, &c. The words ἐπιόντας ἐπὶ θαλάσσαν allude, perhaps, to some sea, which probably Aristeas represented as bounding the northern extremity of Europe: the existence of this sea was, as we shall see hereafter, doubted by our Historian.

[38] The description of Scythia is resumed in c. 16. The two intervening chapters are a digression, respecting Aristeas, a celebrated poet, of whose works only twelve verses are now extant; six of which are preserved in Longinus, the others in Tzetzes. See Larcher, iii. 422, 3.

him. This person continuing pertinaciously to give the lie to the report, the relations of the deceased proceeded to the fuller's, with the intention of taking away the body for interment: they opened the workshop, but no Aristeas appeared, dead or alive. However, in the seventh year after, he appeared again at Proconnesus, and composed the poem now called, by the Hellenes, the Arimaspea: after he had written that poem, he disappeared a second time. Such are the accounts given at Proconnesus and Cyzicus. The following particulars I heard from the people of Metapontium in Italy. Three hundred and forty years after the second disappearance of Aristeas, as I find by comparing the statements made both at Proconnesus and Metapontium, an event connected with the above poet occurred. The Metapontines declare, that Aristeas appeared personally in their country, ordered them to erect an altar to Apollo, and place close by a statue of himself, giving it the name of Aristeas of Proconnesus: for he affirmed, that theirs was the only country of the Italiots[39] whom Apollo had visited, and at the time he himself[40], who was now Aristeas, followed the god, under the form of a raven. Having said thus much, he disappeared. The Metapontines add, that they sent to Delphi, to inquire what spectre of a man it might have been: and the Pythian answered, by bidding them attend to the phantom; if they did so, they would prosper[41]. The Metapontines, having received the response, obeyed the injunction: and now there stands a statue, bearing the name of Aristeas, close by the image of Apollo, around which bay-trees spring: the second image is found in the market-place. So much, therefore, concerning Aristeas[42].

Concerning the country, however, of which this history proceeds to speak, no one knows any thing for certain about the parts that are situate above it: for I have never been able to obtain any account of them from an eye-witness: nor even does Aristeas, of whom I have just made mention, pretend, in his poem, to have reached any further than the Issedones: what he heard about the country higher up to north was, he says, taken from the description given by the

---

[39] There is the same difference between the 'Ιταλιῶται and the 'Ιταλοί, as between the Σικελιῶται and the Σικελοί. The 'Ιταλοί and the Σικελοί were the ancient inhabitants of Italy and Sicily: the 'Ιταλιῶται and the Σικελιῶται were the Greeks who had established themselves in Italy and Sicily. *Larcher.*

[40] See Matt. 535.

[41] Matt. 457.

[42] Lit. " Let so much be said, accordingly, about Aristeas."

Issedones. I shall however mention[43] here whatever I have heard as certain concerning the most distant parts. Taking our departure from the staple of the Borysthenïtæ, which is the central point of the sea-coast appertaining to Scythia, the first occupants of the land are the Callipidæ, who are husbandmen, and Hellenic Scythians. Above these is a different nation, the Alazones, as they are called: they, as well as the Callipidæ, have the same usages as the Scythians, but sow, for home consumption, corn, onions, garlic, lentils, and millet. Above the Alazones are the Scythian husbandmen: they grow corn, not for their own use, but for exportation: north of these lie the Neuri. Farther on, towards the north of the Neuri, the land, as far as we know, is desert[44]. Such are the nations on the Hypanis river, and west of the Borysthenes, as you ascend that stream. If you now cross[45] over the Borysthenes, the first country from the edge of the sea is Hylæa: advancing northward from thence, you come to the territory of the Scythian Georgi, whom the Hellenes, dwelling on the banks of the Hypanis, call Borysthenïtæ, but give themselves the appellation of the Olbiopolitæ: these Scythian Georgi accordingly occupy the land for three days' journey to the east, extending to a river that bears the name of Panticapes: their territory extends northwards, for a space of eleven days' navigation up the Borysthenes. The land immediately above them is, for the greater part, desert. Having crossed the desert, you reach the Androphagi, a distinct nation, quite unconnected with the Scythian: beyond these, the land is wholly desert[46]; no human beings are seen there, that we know of. Eastward of these Scythian Georgi, after crossing the Panticapes, you meet, for the first time, with Scythians nomades (pastors), who neither sow nor plow: all this country is wholly destitute of trees, except Hylæa: these nomades occupy a space of fourteen days' journey across to the east, and stretching to the banks of the river Gerrhus. On the opposite side of the Gerrhus are the quarters called the Royal: the inhabitants are the most valiant and numerous of the Scythians: they regard the rest of the Scythians as their vassals. This race extends down, southward, to Taurica: eastward, along the trench[47] dug by the progeny of the blind slaves, and to

---

[43] Lit. " But what we have been able to come at accurately by hearsay, as far as possible, all shall be mentioned."

[44] Construction: (κατὰ τὸ πρὸς βορέην ἔρημον Νευρῶν, (ἡ γῆ) ἔρημος ἀνθρώπων. See Matt. 437. obs. 3.

[45] διαβάντι: see Matt. 390, b.

[46] Understand χώρα with ἔρημος.

[47] This is the meaning of the par-

the staple called Cremni on the Lake Mæotis: some of them stretch even to the river Tanaïs. Northward of, and above the Royal Scythians, are found the Melanchlæni; not a Scythian, but a distinct nation. Finally, above the Melanchlæni, are lakes; and the land, as far as we know, is desert and uninhabited.

After crossing the Tanaïs river, you are no longer in 21 Scythia: the first region is that of the Sauromatæ: they commence at the top of the Lake Mæotis, and occupy the land northward, for a space of fifteen days' journey, all destitute of trees, whether wild or cultivated. Beyond the Sauromatæ are the Budini, dwelling in the second tract: they occupy a land thickly studded with all sorts of timber. Above the Budini, advancing to the north, lies first a desert seven days across: at the extremity of the desert, inclining more to the west, are found the Thyssagetæ, a numerous and distinct nation, living by the chace. Contiguous to 22 these are the Iyrcæ, residing in the same quarter: they live also by the chace[48], which is managed in the following manner: the country being well clothed with forests, every hunter climbs up a tree, and puts himself in ambush[49]: he is provided with a horse, trained to lie down on his belly, in order to appear very small; and with a dog. Whenever he spies any game from the tree, he shoots it with his bow, immediately mounts his horse, and pursues, followed closely by his dog. Beyond these, inclining[50] eastward, dwell a distinct race of Scythians, which at one time seceded from the Royal Scythians, and so settled in this country. So far 23 as the land of these Scythians, the above-described regions are level, and the soil is deep: beyond, the face of the country becomes stony and rugged. After travelling over a good distance of this rocky country, a nation is found, they say, at the foot of some lofty mountains; who are all, male and female, bald from the birth, have snub noses, and long chins[51]. They speak a distinct language, but wear the Scythian costume. They live on the fruit of a certain tree, the name of which is ' Pontic:' it is, in size, about equal to the fig-tree, and bears a fruit similar to a broad-bean, with a stone inside. When this fruit is ripe, they squeeze it through cloths: a thick black juice exudes, which they call

---

ticle 34. The trench of the sons of the blind slaves appears, from this passage, to have been situate somewhere between the Tauric Chersonesus, and the mouth of the Tanaïs.

[48] ἐπὶ θήρης, " on game." Matt. 573.

[49] Understand ἡ ἄγρεσις before λοχᾷ.

[50] I do not see very clearly the precise force of the article τὸ, in this instance. With regard to the general expression of ἀνακλίνωντι in the dative, see Matt. 390, b.

[51] Or, beards, if the reader chooses: see Schweig. Lex. Herod. voc. γένυσι.

'Aschy:' this they sip, and mix with their milk, the general beverage. From the thickest sediment of this pulp they mould lozenges, which serve them as food; for they have little cattle[52], the pastures not being very excellent in these regions. Every one of these people lives beneath a tree: in the winter, they hide the tree under a white woollen stuff[53], which in summer they take off. No one does them any injury; for they are considered as sacred: they possess none of the instruments of war. They[54] not only settle the differences that happen among their neighbours, but whoever takes refuge with them is safe from all violence: these people are called Argippæi.

24 Up to these bald-headed men, we have a very accurate knowledge of this country[55], as well as of the nations that precede them; for some of the Scythians are in the habit of going thither, from whom information may be procured, as well as at the staple of the Hellenes on the Borysthenes, and the other places of the same kind in Pontus. The Scythians who perform this journey transact business in seven different languages, through seven different interpreters.

25 No one can say any thing certain about what is beyond the bald-headed race, for lofty mountains of very difficult ascent cut off communication: however, the Argippæi say, what appears to me incredible, that these mountains are inhabited by men with goats'-feet. When you have passed through[56] these people, you meet with another race of men, who sleep six months at a time: this appears to me quite impossible[57]: but the parts east of the bald race are well known; they are inhabited by Issedones: as to the countries that lie north, both of the bald Argippæi and Issedones, all remains totally unknown, with the exception of what those

26 two nations report[58]. The Issedones are said to have the

---

[52] πρόβατα signifies not only sheep, but likewise all kinds of cattle, in Herodotus. πάντα τὰ τετράποδα ἰνδάλλειν οἱ παλαιοὶ πρόβατα. Schol. Hom. Il. xiv. 154.

[53] εἶλῳ στεγνῷ λευκῷ. This was not a woven stuff, but wool squeezed and stuck together; in short, felt. The word στεγνὸς, firmus, joined to εἶλος, appears to me decisive; and I think we must understand here a felt tent. Larcher.

[54] τοῦτο μὲν ---- τοῦτο δὶ, on the one hand ---- on the other.

[55] ἐπιφανέια τῆς χώρης πολλή ἐστι, lit. "the knowledge of (i. e. our acquaintance with) the country is great;" that is to say, the country is sufficiently known.

[56] See Matt. 390, b, for the rule by which διεξβάντι is in the dative.

[57] τὸν ἀρχήν. See Hermann. ad Viger. Not. 67.

[58] The following is Larcher's translation, which the reader is at liberty to adopt: "But what is above, towards the north, is known neither to the Argippæi nor the Issedones, who give no further account than what I have stated from them:—Mais celui qui est au-dessus, du côté du Nord, n'es connu ni des Argippéens ni des Issédons, qui n'en disent que ce que j'ai rapporté d'après eux." Larcher.

following customs: When the father of one of them dies, all the kinsmen bring to him some of their kine: after they have slaughtered these animals, and cut up the flesh, they proceed to cut up as well the deceased father of their host, and, mixing together the different kinds of flesh, spread it forth as a banquet. With respect to the head of the deceased, they strip it to the bones, scour it clean, and plate it with gold[59]; and afterwards use it as a sacred ornament[60], at the great annual sacrifices they make. The son acts thus with regard to his father, and so the Hellenes celebrate the anniversary of the death of theirs: the Issedones, however, are reckoned honest: the women have with them the same authority as the men[61].

The Issedones themselves pretend, that above their country 27 are the one-eyed men, and the gold-watching griffons: from them the Scythians borrow the same tale which we Hellenes have adopted from the Scythians, and call the above people, as the Scythians do, Arimaspi; 'arima' being the Scythian word for 'one,' and 'spou' that for 'eye.' All the 28 country I have been speaking of is visited with a hard winter; during which, eight months, the frost is intolerable[62]; such, that if you pour water on the ground, you make no mud; but kindling fire, you produce it. The sea concretes, and so does the whole of the Cimmerian Bosphorus. The Scythians residing within the trench[63] make warlike[64] expeditions on the ice, and drive their waggons across to the Sindi: thus the winter lasts[65] during eight months;

---

[59] It is pretended that there is a difference between κατάχρυσος and ἐπίχρυσος; the former signifying *gilt*, and the latter, *plated with gold*.

[60] Hesychius explains ἄγαλμα by πᾶν ἐφ᾽ ᾧ τις ἀγάλλεται. Larcher translates it, in this instance, by *comme d'un vase précieux*, and Schweighæuser by *pro sacro vase*; but, says the latter, in his Lex. Herod. 'satius fuerat ponere *pro ornamento quo gloriantur.*'

[61] The text adds: "these accordingly are likewise known."

[62] ἀφόρητος ἐστι. See Matt. 445, b.

[63] Herodotus means, no doubt, the trench dug by the sons of the blind slaves mentioned in c. 3. Most geographers place this trench on the isthmus that joins the Chersonesus to the continent: if their position is right, Herodotus must allude in this place to the Scythians of the Chersonesus, which signification Larcher has adopted in his translation. I shall prove hereafter, that it is by no means clear that there were any Scythians at all established in the Chersonesus. I have therefore preferred a literal translation. I see, that in a small volume of maps, &c. lately published to illustrate Herodotus, the trench of the sons of the blind slaves, a very important position in the ancient geography of Scythia, is placed at the bottom of the Palus Mæotis, near the mouth of the Tanaïs: I am not however aware by what authority the conjecture of Major Rennel is neglected.

[64] Instead of στρατεύονται, it has been proposed to read στραγγεύονται, "they sojourn." We have seen booths, waggons, and even a printing-office, in full activity on the frost bound Thames.

[65] ἐκστάσιες ἰών. See Matt. 552, 1.

during the four remaining months, the cold is still perceptible in that country. This Scythian winter is different from those of other countries, in many respects: in the first place, while that season lasts, it rains hardly worth speaking of[66]; but in summer, rain never ceases. When there is thunder elsewhere, there is none in Scythia; but in summer, the thunder is most awful: if this phænomenon occur in winter, it is regarded as a most extraordinary prodigy. The same is the case with respect to earthquakes; whether in summer or winter, they are reckoned wonderful occurrences in Scythia. The horses bear through this winter: mules and asses are totally unable to stand the severe cold: and yet, in other countries, horses get frost-bitten when they stand out in a severe cold, while the asses and mules resist. I think that the same cause may account for the oxen being a mutilated race, inasmuch as they have no horns in Scythia: my opinion is borne out by this line in Homer's Odyssey[67], which runs thus:

29

" And Libya, where the rams quickly shoot their horns:"

expressing, justly, that the horns grow rapidly in hot countries; but in rude climates the horns of cattle are not produced at all, or if so, scarce grow to any size. But—as, indeed, my narrative from the beginning has sought continually for excursional subjects—I am surprised that in the whole country of Elis no mules can breed; although the cold is not great, nor can any other evident cause be assigned. The people of Elis themselves attribute to some curse the impossibility of breeding mules in their territory; but when it is the season for the mares to be impregnated, they drive them to the neighbouring districts, and there have them covered by the asses; until the males are with foal, when they drive them back. As to the feathers with which the Scythians say the atmosphere is so replete, that they hinder them from all possibility of seeing the extension of the continent, or going over it, my opinion is this: In the upper part of this country there is a constant fall of snow, smaller[68], of course, in summer, than in winter: any one that has seen snow fall thick, close to him, knows what I mean; the snow looks just like feathers; and on account of

30

31

---

[66] ἐν τῷ (i. e. ἐν ᾧ scil. χειμῶνι), in the winter, τὴν μὲν ὡραίην, at the usual time (in other countries), οὐκ ἔω λέγειν ἄξιον ὄμβρῳ, it rains nothing deserving mention (or, if the reader choose, nothing to signify). Schneider, however, takes τὴν ὡραίην in the sense of, in the spring. See Schneider's Gr. and Germ. Lexicon.

[67] Lib. iv. vers. 85.

[68] ἐλάσσων. See Matt. 404.

such a severe winter, the northern parts of this continent are uninhabited: and therefore the Scythians and their neighbours, I think, say feathers[69], comparing the snow to them. The above is the account of what is related of those very distant tracts.

Concerning the Hyperboreans nothing is related, whether by Scythians or the other nations residing in that country, except perhaps the Issedones: and, in my opinion, even the Issedones have nothing to say on the subject; for in that case the Scythians would make after them the same statements as they do in respect of the one-eyed men. But Hesiod mentions the Hyperboreans; and so does Homer in the Epigoni, if indeed Homer be really the author of that poem. The people of Delos, however, are those that have the most to say about the above race of men. They state, that certain sacred things, packed in wheat-straw, presented by the Hyperboreans, passed through the hands of the Scythians; by whom they were transmitted to the adjoining people, and so on from nation to nation, till they came to the farthest point of their western progress, on the Adriatic: thence, received first by the Dodonæans, they were forwarded into the south; and descended to the Maliac Gulf, where they crossed over to Euboea, and were sent from one town to another on to Carystus. From that port, the Carystians, without touching at Andros[70], took them direct to Tenos; and the Tenians delivered them at Delos. This was the manner in which the sacred things reached Delos, according to the account of the people of that island. They add, that, the first time, the Hyperboreans sent, as bearers of the sacred things, two virgins, whose names, the Delians say[71], were Hyperoche and Laodice; and that, for the security of the two virgins, the Hyperboreans sent five of their citizens to attend them: these are now called Perpherees, and receive great honours at Delos. In consequence of the persons thus despatched not coming back to their country, the Hyperboreans conceived that it would be a grievous calamity for them never to be able to greet again[72] the deputies

---

[69] Lit. " I think, therefore, the Scythians and the neighbouring people call the snow feathers, by comparison (εἰκάζοντας, comparing)" - - - - 'Who sendeth His snow like wool.' Psalm cxlvii. 16. quoted by *Larcher*.

[70] Lit. οἳ δ' ἀπὸ ταύτης (τῆς Καρύστου πόλεως), in their progress from this place (i. e. from Carystus), λαλεινοὺς (λέγουσι) "Ἀνδρον, they say they (i. e. the offerings) passed by Andros, that is to say, did not touch at Andros: Καρυστίους γὰρ (λέγουσι) εἶναι τοὺς κομίζοντας εἰς Τῆνον, for they say it was the Carystians that conveyed them to Tenos.

[71] εἶναι, redundant, see p. 128, note 73, of this volume. Consult, likewise, Matt. 414, 1, a.

[72] " That it should happen to them always not to," &c.

that they sent: they wrapped therefore, for the future, the sacred things in wheat-straw; and took them to the people on their borders, requesting[73] them to forward the parcel from themselves to some other nation: and by this mode of conveyance, according to the Delians, it reached their island. I myself am aware of a practice similar to that adopted with these sacred objects. The Thracian and Pæonian women, when they offer sacrifice to Royal Diana, will not 34 slaughter the victims[74] without wheat-straw. In honour[75] of these Hyperborean virgins, who died at Delos, the young women and men of the island are wont to cut their hair: the girls, previous to their wedding, cut off a lock of hair, twist it round a spindle, and place it on their sepulchral monument, which stands in Diana's precinct[76], on your left-hand, as you go in: on the top of the monument grows an olive-tree. The young men twist some of their hair round a plant, and do the same. Such is the honourable tribute the 35 virgins receive from the Delian youth. The islanders add to the above account, that, previous to Hyperoche and Laodice, two virgins, Arge and Opis, travelled through the same nations, and came to Delos: they brought to Ilithya a contribution which their countrywomen imposed on themselves, in return for easy labours in child-birth[77]. Arge and Opis, they say, came, accompanied by the gods themselves[78]; and other honours, too, were shewn to them by the Delians: for, they say, the women collect gifts[79] for them, and invoke them by name, in the hymn composed in their praise by Olen the Lycian: and that, borrowing the custom from the Delian women, those of the islands and Ionia celebrate Opis and Arge, invoking them by name, and making

---

[73] I read τοὺς πλησιοχώρους, in the accusative. Construction: κελεύοντας, they were earnest in enjoining, τοὺς πλησιοχώρους, their next neighbours, προπέμπειν σφία (i. e. τὰ ἱρὰ), to forward them, to send them forward, ἀπὸ ἑωυτῶν. from themselves, &c.

[74] θύειν τὰ ἱρὰ signifies " to sacrifice the victims." The accusative governed by εἶδα.

[75] See Matt. 387, 2.

[76] 'Αρτεμίσιον can have no other signification, since it must be evident to all that an olive-tree could not grow within the temple itself. *Larcher.*

[77] I suppose that, according to this second account of the Delians, Hyperoche and Laodice were not represented as virgins. Larcher translates, without his usual accuracy: "They brought to Ilithya the tribute they were commissioned to offer for the speedy and happy delivery of the women of their country—Celles-ci apportoient à Ilithye le tribut qu'elles étoient chargées d'offrir pour le prompt et heureux accouchement des femmes de leur pays." ἀντὶ, see Matt. Gr. Gram. p. 877.

[78] Apollo and Diana. *Larcher.*

[79] ἀγείρειν signifies ' to collect contributions,' as in i. 62. In Catholic countries, the practice of collecting money, in the name of some saint, at mass, is still followed: to this Wesseling alludes, in his note on the word.

collections. This Olen, coming from Lycia, composed also the other old hymns that are sung at Delos. The Delians add, that when the thighs of the victims have been consumed on the altar, the ashes are thrown and spread [80] on the tomb of Arge and Opis; which is placed behind the temple of Diana, towards the east, and close to the banquet-hall of the Ceians. The above observations are sufficient concerning the Hyperboreans: for I need not rehearse the tale of Abaris, represented to have been an Hyperborean, and who says that he carried an arrow all over the world, without eating. If there be Hyperboreans, there must be Hypernotians [81]. I can but laugh, however, when I see many persons making outlines [82] of the world, without possessing the slightest knowledge to serve them as a guide: they draw the ocean flowing all around the earth, as if it were a circle made on a turner's lathe [83], and trace Europe and Asia as equal: but I will now explain, in a few words, what is the size, and what the figure of each [84].

The middle part of ASIA [85] is occupied by Persians, conti-

---

[80] Ἀναιρεούσθαι ἐπιβάλλομένων, "are expended by being thrown upon," &c. The adjective *all*, I think, conveys the idea with sufficient distinctness.

[81] Ὑπερβόρειοι signifies those dwelling under the extreme northern tract of the heavens; ὑπερνότιοι, those under the extreme southern tract. The reasoning of Herodotus, which amounts to a denial of the existence of Hyperboreans, is therefore pretty nearly the same as though we should say: If Captain Parry finds the north pole inhabited, we may conclude the south pole to be so likewise.

[82] Otherwise, " who have described in *words* the periphery of the earth." The reader will collect, from v. 49, that brass maps were not unfrequent in the time of Herodotus.

[83] ἐκ δοῦ τόρνου. See Matt. 573. The τόρνος was certainly nothing more than a carpenter's compass, as Schneider has taken great pains to prove in a most acute and erudite article on the word τορέω in his Gr. and Germ. Lex.

[84] This leads our Historian to a very curious and interesting digression on the world as then known. The continent of Africa was known to be bounded all round by the sea; the southern coasts of Asia had been visited; but the western and northern tracts of Europe remained undiscovered, as well as the eastern parts of Asia and Europe.

[85] Schweighæuser is of opinion, that Herodotus wrote Ἀσίην, or Ἀσίης εἰ μέσον Πέρσαι εἰσίωσιν. In this description, he supposes a straight line to be drawn, as it were, from the Erythræan Sea, that is to say, from the Gulf of Persia to the Euxine or Black Sea: along this line dwelt four nations, occupying the whole country between the two seas: these nations were, reckoning from the south, the Persians, Medes, Saspires, and Colchians; which latter extended to the Phasis, the admitted boundary of Asia and Europe. He now proceeds to describe the continent westward of this imaginary line: from the line, two vast tracts of land jut towards the west; the first, that is to say, the northern one, in the shape of a rough quadrangle, the north side of which runs along the Euxine, Propontis, and Hellespont, to Cape Sigeum; the western down the Ægean; and the southern from Cape Triopium along the Myriandric gulf: the second, that is to say, the southern tract, in the shape of a rough triangle, the western side of which runs along the coast of Phœnicia and Syria, cuts athwart the isthmus that joins Africa

guous to the Erythræan sea: above these, on the north, are the Medes: north of the Medes are the Saspires: above the Saspires lie the Colchians, resident on the shore of the northern sea, into which the Phasis discharges its waters.

38 These four nations extend from sea to sea. Westward of this middle tract [86] project two regions, bounded by the sea, which I shall now proceed to describe. The coast of the first begins in the north from the Phasis; it stretches along the Euxine and the Hellespont, to Sigeum in the Troad: in the south, the shore of this projecting region commences from the Myriandric gulf adjoining Phœnicia, and extends to Cape Triopium. In this tract dwell thirty different nations.

39 The shore of the second projecting region begins in Persia, and is formed by the Erythræan: along this coast, first comes Persia, then succeeds Assyria, next Arabia: it terminates (not really, but by custom [87]) at the bottom of the Arabian gulf, and the spot to which Darius conducted the canal from the Nile [88]. The remaining shore extends on the Mediterranean: between Phœnicia and Persia, the country is broad and extensive; and below Phœnicia, the shore stretches along Syria of Palæstine, to Egypt, where it termi-

40 nates. In the eastern quarters, beyond the middle tract of the Persians, Medes, Saspires, and Colchians, extends the Erythræan sea: in the north lies the Caspian; and east of that sea the stream of the Araxes. In this direction, Asia is inhabited as far as India: from that country begins already the eastern desert, and no one knows any thing about the rest. Such are the outlines and dimensions of Asia.

41 LIBYA belongs to the second of the projecting tracts [89] above

---

to Europe, and continues along the Red Sea, while the southern side is washed by the Erythræan. Having thus described the continent westward of the four nations, he proceeds to those eastward, the names of which he does not mention, contenting himself with stating, that on the north they are bounded by the Caspian Sea and the Araxes, and on the south by the Erythræan; and that all beyond the Indians is desert and unknown.

[86] *ἀπ' αὐτῆς*, i. e. *Ἀσίης*. It is a pity that the collators have not found sufficient authority for *ἀπ' ἀντίης*, *opposite*. *ἀπτὰ* signifies a tract stretching along the sea: the context shews clearly that peninsula, taken in its usual acceptation, would not be a proper interpretation.

[87] I have followed Schweighæuser's interpretation, *Lex. Herod.* voc. *νόμος*, 1. Larcher's translation is, "Elle aboutit, mais seulement en vertu d'une loi—*it terminates, but only in virtue of a law.*"

[88] See ii. 158.

[89] The meaning is, that Libya is an immense peninsula, jutting from the second *ἀκτὴ* at the Isthmus of Suez. The breadth of this neck of land is one thousand stades from this sea, i. e. the Mediterranean, to the Erythræan Sea, i. e. the Red Sea. It appears, from different passages, that Herodotus applied the name of Erythræan to all the sea south and southeast of the Isthmus of Suez, comprehending the Red Sea, the Persian Gulf (of the existence of which, however, Herodotus seems to have been ignorant), and the Indian Ocean.

described; for from Egypt, Libya begins: in Egypt, this tract is confined to a narrow isthmus; for from the Mediterranean sea to the Arabian gulf is a space of but one hundred thousand orgyæ, which make one thousand stades: at a short distance from the isthmus, the tract, which now takes the name of Libya, becomes exceedingly wide. I am surprised, therefore, that persons make such mistakes in defining and dividing Libya, Asia, and Europe; for there is an immense difference between those parts: Europe, in its length, extends along both that of Libya and Asia; but in breadth it is, evidently, not to be compared[90]: for Libya proves of itself[91], that it is surrounded by the sea, with the exception of the part that is connected with Asia. Neco, king of Egypt, is the first we know to have demonstrated this fact. When he had ceased his works on the canal between the Nile and the Arabian gulf, he despatched some Phœnician sailors, with orders to return through the Pillars of Hercules into the Mediterranean, and to reach Egypt. The Phœnicians accordingly took their departure from the Erythræan, and navigated the southern sea. When autumn came, they landed[93]: and sowed a crop, whatever part of Libya they might have reached, and awaited the harvest. They then reaped their wheat, and set sail. Having thus continued their excursions during two years, in the third year they doubled the pillars, and arrived in Egypt; and declared, what to me appears incredible, but may perhaps seem to others probable, that, in their circumnavigation of Libya[93], they had the sun on their right hand. Thus the limits of Libya were first ascertained[94]. The Carthaginians relate that,

42

43

---

[90] Or, what would, perhaps, be a better translation: "In respect to breadth, it does not appear possible to make a comparison." The meaning of Herodotus is, that Europe extends in length, that is to say, from west to east, the whole of Africa and Asia; Europe being supposed, according to the geography of our author, to extend eastward, into unknown tracts beyond the Caspian, as far as Asia did: but in respect to breadth, that is to say, the dimensions from south to north, Europe was not yet defined, (see c. 45); whereas Neco's expedition had determined that of Africa, and Scylaxes that of Asia.

[91] See Matt. 548, 5.

[92] Ἄν, with the imperfect of the indicative, to express the repetition of the action: I think the auxiliary *would* convey the same idea in English. The Phœnicians, being two whole years on their voyage, probably performed the operations of sowing and reaping twice. See Matt. 598, a.

[93] That is to say, when they had crossed the Equator.

[94] Οὕτω μὲν αὕτη ἐγνώσθη τὸ πρῶτον, lit. "Thus it (i. e. Libya) was for the first time known." Herodotus does not mean that the interior of Africa was made known, but only that it was discovered that this quarter of the globe was surrounded by the sea, except on the side where it confines on Asia. The fact is, we must supply from the beginning of this chapter, στεἰλλοντες ἰόντας, πλὴν ὅσον αὐτῆς πρὸς τὴν Ἀσίαν ὁρίζει. Larcher.

subsequently [94] the following circumstance occurred: Sataspes the son of Teaspis, one of the Achæmenidæ, was sent on the same expedition, but, at all events, did not circumnavigate Libya: terrified at the length of the voyage, and the deserted appearance of the shore, he returned without accomplishing the task imposed on him by his mother:—for Sataspes had violated the maiden daughter of Zopyrus the son of Megabyzus: being sentenced, in consequence of this crime, to be impaled [95] by king Xerxes, the mother of Sataspes, a sister of Darius, besought the life of her son, declaring she would inflict on him a greater punishment than the king himself [96] proposed: she would bind him down to circumnavigate Libya, until he had completed the task, and returned by the Arabian gulf. On these conditions, Xerxes granted the request. Sataspes proceeded into Egypt, and, taking a ship manned by Carthaginians, sailed through the Pillars of Hercules; and, after doubling the foreland of Libya, called Cape Solœis, steered for the south: having passed over many leagues of sea, in many months' voyage, seeing that there still remained a greater distance before him [97], he turned about ship, and sailed away for Egypt. After this, he presented himself before Xerxes; and related to the king, that at the furthest extremity of his voyage he had sailed along a shore inhabited by pygmies, dressed in clothes of date-leaves; who, when he steered from their coast, forsook their towns, and fled to the mountains: his crew had entered the towns, but had done no harm, taking nothing but a few heads of cattle. He assigned, as the reason for not continuing his progress, and completing the circumnavigation, that his ship was stopped, and it was impossible to go any farther. Xerxes, however, convinced he did not speak the truth, and as Sataspes had not completed the task imposed, he impaled him, in accordance with the original sentence [98]. An eunuch belonging to Sataspes no sooner heard of his master's fate, than he fled to Samos with

---

[94] Μετὰ δὲ, subsequently to the circumnavigation of these Phœnicians, Καρχηδόνιοί εἰσι οἱ λέγοντες, the Carthaginians affirm [that they know Libya is surrounded by the sea]. This is to be supplied from the last words of the foregoing chapter. See Schweighæuser's note. Larcher translates, "Les Carthaginois racontent que, depuis ce temps, Sataspes, fils de &c.— *the Carthaginians relate, that, since then, Sataspes, the son of,*" &c. There can be no need of shewing the superiority of Schweighæuser's punctuation and interpretation.

[95] See p. 257, note 197, of this volume.

[96] Ἰασίων relates to ἀνασκολοπ. and to Xerxes. See Matt. 448.

[97] Construction: ἐπὶ (ὁ Σατάσπης), αὐτὸ Δεῖ τοῦ πλεῖνος (τῆς θεοῦ). See Matt. 296.

[98] Lit. "executing the former sentence."

great riches, which were seized by a Samian citizen, whose name I am acquainted with, but do not choose to divulge.

We are indebted to Darius for many discoveries respecting Asia. This king, anxious to ascertain into what sea the Indus disembogues, the only river besides one[99] that has crocodiles in its stream, sent an expedition by sea to determine the truth: it consisted of various individuals in whom he could place his confidence, but more particularly Scylax, a citizen of Caryande. This expedition embarked at Caspatyrus, a city in Pactyice; and proceeded down the stream, in an eastern direction, till it reached the sea: then, steering on the sea westward, arrived in the thirtieth month at the same place[100] from whence the Egyptian king, as I before observed, despatched the Phœnicians to circumnavigate Libya. After the completion of this voyage of discovery, Darius subdued the Indians, and took advantage of the sea for his own service: the whole of Asia, with the exception of the eastern side, was found to present the same circumstances as Libya[101]. As to Europe, however, it is completely unknown to every one[102] whether this part of the world is bounded by the sea on the east or north: in length, it is known to exceed that of the two other continents together. I cannot conceive why[103] the earth, being one and undivided, ever came to receive three names, and those of women; or why the Nile, an Egyptian river, and the Phasis, a river of Colchis, should have been fixed upon as the boundaries of Asia: (some give, instead of the Phasis, the Tanaïs, Mæotis, and Cimmerian Hythe[104]:) neither can I furnish any information as to the names of the persons who assigned the above limits, or whence they borrowed[105] the names of the three parts of the world. Libya, according to the account of the Hellenes in general, takes its name from Libya, the name of a native woman: and Asia, from[106] that of Prometheus's wife. But the Lydians claim the latter, affirming that Asia was so called after Asias, son of Cotys, and grandson of Manes; from whom the tribe called Asias take their name in Sardis. As to Europe, however, no one in existence knows whether it is encircled by the sea: whence it

---

[99] *i. e.* the Nile: see Matt. 467, 2 *a.* 468, *obs.* 3.

[100] Patumos, unquestionably.

[101] παρεχομένη, "affording." The reading proposed by Schweighæuser, in his note on this passage, gives a much better sense, τὰ ἄλλα ἀνεύρηται ὁμοίη τῇ ἐχομένῃ τῇ Λιβύῃ, "the rest of *Asia* is explored, alike with Libya, which adjoins it."

[102] See Viger. p. 66.

[103] ἰσ' ἴστω. See Matt. 584.

[104] See note 35, on this word, p. 283.

[105] Larcher observes, that θέιντο is not, in this instance, taken in the reciprocal sense usual in the middle voice. *Larcher.*

[106] See Matt. 584.

obtained its name, or who gave it, remains a mystery; unless we say that this continent takes its name from Europa of Tyre, having previously been nameless, as well as the two others. But Europa, it is known, was at all events an Asiatic woman, and never touched at the country now called Europe by the Hellenes: she passed only[105] from Phœnicia to Crete, and from Crete to Lycia. We shall say no more upon this subject, and shall make use of the names now in common use[106].

46 The Pontus Euxinus, which Darius invaded, exhibits, of all countries in the world, the most uncivilized nations. I except, however, the Scythians: for we cannot mention one nation within[107] the Pontus that has displayed any intellectual powers; nor have we ever heard of a learned man in these quarters, saving the Scythian people, and Anacharsis. The Scythians, among all nations we know of, have invented the wisest mode of securing one of the most important objects of government: this is the only thing I admire among them. This most important invention is an expedient by which those that come with an intention of invading them can never escape: the Scythians not being to be found but when they choose, it is impossible to surprise them; for they have no cities, no fortresses: they carry with them their houses; are all good horsemen and archers; they live not by husbandry, but on the produce of their cattle; and their waggons are their dwellings. How, therefore, could the Scythians be otherwise than invincible; and must it not

47 be very difficult to bring them to engagement? This invention of the Scythians has its origin in the peculiar fitness of the country itself, and the numerous rivers which serve them as bulwarks: for their land is level, and, being well watered, produces an abundant herbage. The rivers that intersect the surface of Scythia are scarcely less numerous than the canals of Egypt: I shall mention only those that are the most celebrated, and such as are navigable from the sea

---

[105] Schweig. Lex. Herod. voc. ἔστι; Viger, p. 102. and Hermann's note, 91.

[106] τοῖσι γὰρ νομιζομένοις (εὐνομάσι) αὐτῶν (i. e. τῶν μερίων τῆς γῆς) χρησόμεθα. Larcher.—"*We shall abide in this respect by the received opinion*—nous nous en tiendrons là-dessus aux opinions reçues."

[107] Herodotus never uses ἐντὸς but in speaking of what is on the hither side, that is to say, between himself and something else. This was not, therefore, written in Asia Minor, at Halicarnassus, Samos, &c. For is that situation, the Scythians, &c. would not have been between himself and the Euxine. He must have written it at Thurium, in the heel of Italy; the Scythians being on the hither side of the Euxine, in respect to the inhabitants of that town. This passage is, consequently, one of those added by our historian after he had settled in Italy. *Larcher.* See Wesselingii Præf. p. v. of Dr. Gaisford's edition of Herodotus.

upwards. They are, the Ister; next, the Tyras; together with the Hypanis, the Borysthenes, the Panticapes, the Hypacyris, the Gerrhus, and the Tanaïs[108]. Their courses are as follows.

The Ister, in the first place, is the mightiest river that we are acquainted with: it is always equal, and of the same depth, both in winter and summer. It is the first river in Scythia: it comes down from the west: and is the largest, by reason of the multitude of streams that contribute their waters[109]: these are the causes of the extraordinary magnitude of the Ister. From the Scythian territory, five rivers[110], at least, pour their waters into this one: the Scythian names of them are, the Porata (the Pyretus of the Hellenes), the Tiarantus, Ararus, Naparis, and Ordessus. The first of the above is large: its stream lies eastward[111] of the others, and mingles its waters with the Ister. The second, called the Tiarantus, is considerably more to the west, and smaller[112]. The Ararus, the Naparis, and the Ordessus, flowing between the courses of the above two, accordingly discharge themselves in the Ister. These are the indigenous rivers of Scythia, that contribute to swell the mass of the waters of the Ister. From the land of the Agathyrsi flows the Maris, another tributary to the Ister. From the pinnacles of Hæmus roll three other large rivers, that pour their waters into this stream, the Atlas, Auras, and Tibisis. Athwart Thrace, and the land of the Thracian Crobyzi, flow the Athrys, Noes, and Atarnes, which also unite with the Ister. From

---

[108] Scythia is, therefore, comprehended between the Danube (Ister) and the Don (Tanaïs). It comprises, accordingly, the Ukraine, the Nogais Tartars, the Don Cossacks, &c.—*Larcher.*

[109] κατὰ τοιούσδε ---- ταυτωσι. I have followed Schweighæuser's Latin version, though by no means satisfactory. Schweighæuser proposes a punctuation which gives a very good sense, and squares pretty well with the rules of grammar: κατὰ τοιούσδε μέγιστος γέγονε· ποταμῶν καὶ ἄλλων ἐς αὐτὸν ἐκδιδόντων, εἰσὶ δὴ οἵδε οἱ μέγαν αὐτὸν ταυτωσι. In which, ποταμῶν καὶ ἄλλων ἐς αὐτὸν ἐκδιδόντων is equivalent to ποταμοί μὲν καὶ ἄλλοι ἐς αὐτὸν ἐκδιδοῦσι. " It is the largest on this account: there are various rivers that roll their waters into its stream, but the following are they that make it large." Herodotus then proceeds to enumerate those rivers.—*Schweig.*

[110] After reading Dr. Gaisford's observation, I have not hesitated to adopt μεγάλοι instead of μὲν οἱ. If this latter reading be followed, the first μὲν, where the author says, διὰ μὲν γε τῆς Σ. may be regarded as having for its respondent the δὴ in ἐκ δὴ Αἵμου, and the second μὲν in ῥέουσι μὲν οἱ βέοντες, as being answered by the δὴ in ἐκ δὴ Ἀγαθύρσων. See Schweighæuser's note on c. 49.

[111] There is no river now-a-days answering to the position of the Pyretus, that flows towards the east: the Pyretus is probably the modern Pruth. I think, therefore, that the words πρὸς ἠῶ ῥέων are to be taken in the same sense as in c. 40. p. 294; that is to say, that they do not signify " flowing towards the east," but rather that the river *lies* east, its stream flowing south.

[112] Supply, after ἐλάσσων, ἀνακοινοῦται τῷ Ἴστρῳ τὸ ῥέος.

Pæonia and Mount Rhodope, the Scios river, bursting through a defile of Hæmus, joins the main stream. From the country of the Illyrians, the Angrus, north of the above, flows through the Triballic plain, and descends to the Brongus, which joins itself to the Ister: thus the Ister receives the tribute of both those great rivers. The Carpis, and another river, the Alpis, north of the Brongus, descend from the land of the Ombrici, and discharge their waters into the Ister: for that river flows across the whole of Europe, rising in the country of the Celts[113], who, next to the Cunetæ, are the last inhabitants to the west of Europe: it flows all across

50 Europe, and enters sloping into Scythia. From the accumulation of the waters of the aforesaid rivers, and a great many more, the Ister exceeds all other rivers in size: for undoubtedly, if you compare the two rivers the one to the other, the Nile must yield to the Ister in the abundance of its waters: for in the case of the Nile, no river, no brook even, contributes to swell that stream. But the Ister invariably flows equal, both in summer and in winter: the reason of which is, in my mind, as follows: the country through which this river runs, is, throughout the winter, visited with but little rain, but all parts are covered with deep snow: in the summer, the snow, that had fallen the winter before in vast quantities, now melts, and gives itself to the Ister, the waters of which are therefore kept at their full: to this must be added the frequent and violent falls of rain that occur in summer: but in proportion as the sun attracts to himself, in summer, more water than in winter[114], so, in proportion, the waters that mingle with the Ister are in summer nearly the same as in winter: from the balance of these two agents, such an equilibrium is produced, that the river, as we see, is constantly one and the same.

51 The Ister, then, is one of the rivers of the Scythians: next is the Tyras, which proceeds from the north, and rises in an extensive lake, out of which it flows: this stream divides Scythia from the land of the Neuri: at its mouth are found

52 Hellenic residents, called the Tyritæ. The third river, the Hypanis, rises in Scythia itself; and flows out of an extensive lake, around which white horses are grazed: this lake is rightly designated the mother of the Hypanis; out of which, accordingly, the Hypanis springs. During a short navigation of five days, the water is still sweet: from that point it becomes, and continues all through its course of forty days

---

[113] See ii. 34. p. 122 of this volume. already been mentioned by Herodotus,
[114] This attraction of the sun has ii. 25.

down to the sea, to be excessively[115] bitter. The cause of this is the discharge of a bitter spring into the stream: this spring is so bitter, that, although insignificant in its size, it pollutes[116] the Hypanis, a river of the second order, but the largest of that. This bitter spring lies on the borders of the Scythian husbandmen and the Alazones: its name, as well as that of the place where it flows, is called, in Scythian, Hexampæus; in the Hellenic tongue, Hiræ-hodi (Sacred Ways). In the country of the Alazones, the Tyras and Hypanis contract the interval that separates one stream from the other[117]: from that spot, each, making an elbow, flows on, tending gradually to expand the mid-space.

The fourth is the Borysthenes; next in magnitude, of these 53 streams, to the Ister, and, in my opinion, the most productive and conducive to comfort and prosperity, not only of all the Scythian rivers, but of all in the world, saving and excepting the Egyptian Nile: to this latter, indeed, no river whatever can be compared, although the Borysthenes is, of the rest, the one that confers the greatest blessings. It rolls through the most beautiful and highly-cultivated meadows, which furnish the cattle with excellent pasture; it gives in great plenty the best sorts of fish; it is sweet to drink of its waters; it flows limpid and clear, amid rivers turbid and muddy[118], the pulse that spring up on its banks are the very best; and in those places where no crops are sown, rises a most vigorous and tall herbage: at the mouth are natural salterns; which produce, spontaneously, immense quantities of salt: this river produces also large fishes[119], without bones, for salting; and a great many other things worthy of admiration. Up to the land of Gerrhus, accordingly, a voyage of forty days, the Borysthenes is known to come from the north; but no one relates any thing about the parts higher up, or the people that inhabit them: it is extremely probable, therefore, that this river passes through desert lands, before it arrives at the country of the Georgian Scythians, who extend along its banks for a voyage of ten days. This, and the Nile, are the only rivers of which I cannot describe the sources; nor

---

[115] ἀλῶς is an Ionism for σφόδρα, valdè. *Larcher.*

[116] μιερῶ signifies to mingle as wine in a crater, μιερῇ κρητῆρι οἴνου, iv. 66. A literal translation would not be sufficiently intelligible. ᾗ μιγάτω, &c. in which the relative ᾗ is put for ὅντι, see Matt. 479, obs. 1.

[117] συνάγουσι τὰ ῥέματα, contrahunt limites, exiguo intervalla distantes fluunt. *Schweig. Lex. Herod.*

[118] Supply ποταμοῖς after ἰλυρῶσι.

[119] This is undoubtedly the sturgeon of the Danube, a large fish, whose spawn, together with that of some other fish, forms, when salted and pressed down, the celebrated caviari. ἀνάκανθα does not signify exactly 'without bones,' but without those bones jutting out on either side of the spine, as is the case with most fish: the eel, therefore, is ἀνάκανθος.

do I consider any of the Hellenes wiser than myself on this subject. Pretty near the sea, the Hypanis mingles with the Borysthenes, and both streams disembogue in one marsh: the space of land lying between the two rivers constitutes a promontory, something like the prow of a ship [120], and is called Cape Hippolaus: here also stands the sacred precinct of Ceres. Beyond the temple, and on the bank of the Hypanis, reside the Borysthenitæ. So much for the above rivers.

54 Next to these is the fifth river [121], the name of which is the Panticapes: this river comes down from the north, and flows from a lake: between the bank of this river and that of the Borysthenes dwell the Georgian Scythians. The Penticapes proceeds down to Hylæa, and, after passing along that region, mingles its waters with those of the Bory-
55 sthenes. The sixth river is the Hypacyris; which takes its origin in a lake, flows through the territories of the Scythian nomades, and falls into the sea near the town of Carcinitis, skirting, on the right, Hylæa, and what is called the Achil-
56 lean Course. The seventh is the Gerrhus river: it branches out of the Borysthenes, in that quarter of the country up to which the Borysthenes is known: the spot where this takes place, bears the same name, Gerrhus, as the river itself. It flows down to the sea; and serves as a boundary, both to
57 the territory of the Nomades and Royal Scythians. The eighth river, therefore, is the Tanaïs; which flows from the upper country, out of an extensive lake, and discharges its waters into a still more vast lake, called Mæotis, which bounds the Royal Scythians and the Sauromatæ. Into the Tanaïs falls another river, the name of which is the Hyrgis.
58 The above are the most renowned of the rivers by which Scythia is enriched. The grass that grows in Scythia, and is grazed by the cattle, is more productive of gall [122] than

---

[120] Ἐν ἰμβόλω τῆς χώρης, lit. "a ship's spur of the land:" the meaning is sufficiently evident, that the land assumed at its termination the shape of the spur or rostrum with which we all know the ships of the ancients were armed at the prow.

[121] Μετὰ δὲ τούτους πέμπτος ποταμὸς ἄλλος, τῷ οὔνομα Παντικάπης: another fifth river. It is in this manner that the ancient Attic writers express themselves. πέμπτος ἄλλος - - - - Ἐὺν βοῇ ναρίστατι. Æsch. Sept. c. Theb. 488. As the Ionians were originally Athenians, they had preserved several of the ancient Attic forms. *Larcher.*

[122] ἐπιχολωτάτη. This word Em. Portus translates *amarissima*; and thinks that Herodotus alludes to a species of wormwood, growing in great abundance in Scythia, with which, according to Pliny, the cattle of the country were fattened. Ovid. de Ponto, 3.—Tristia per vacuos horrent absynthia campos, Conveniensque suo messis amara loco est. The next following words of the author, Portus is of opinion, signify nothing more than that one may convince one's self that the cattle live on wormwood by opening their carcasses [for no gall will be found].

any of the grasses that we know of; a fact easily ascertained, by opening the carcasses of some Scythian beasts.

Thus abundantly are the Scythians provided with the great commodities of life[123]: their various customs are such as I am now going to describe. The following are the only gods to whom they pay worship: to Vesta in particular; next, to Jupiter and the Earth, for they consider Earth as the consort of Jupiter; after these, Apollo and Celestial Venus, Hercules and Mars: all the above the Scythians acknowledge. Those called Royal Scythians offer likewise sacrifice to Neptune. In Scythian, the names of the gods are, Vesta, Tabiti; Jupiter, very properly, in my opinion at least, Papæus[124]; Earth, Apia; Apollo, Œtosyrus; Celestial Venus, Artimpasa; Neptune, Thamimasadas. They are not accustomed to build altars and temples, except to Mars: for that god they do so. The mode of sacrifice is the same with all[125], and in every sacred enclosure alike. The sacrifice is thus made: the victim itself stands erect, his two fore-feet bound: the officiating priest places himself behind the beast, seizes the end of the cord, and throws him down. As the victim falls, he invokes the god to whom the sacrifice is offered; and, after that, throws an halter round the neck of the victim, and, thrusting a stick in the loop, twists

---

Æm. Port. Lex. Ion. Larcher translates "la plus succulente." I have followed Schweighæuser, whose translation is the same as that of Schneider, "Gras, das viel Galle macht." *Schn. Gr. Germ. Lex.*

[123] "The Scythians have then in abundance the most necessary things for life.—*Les Scythes ont donc en abondance les choses les plus nécessaires à la vie.*" Larcher. "Istis igitur maximis commodis quum abundent Scythæ," &c. *Schweig.* In my rough draught of the present work, I had considered the first sentence of this chapter as a repetition, in other words, of τῷ δὲ Σκυθικῷ γένει ὁ μὲν τὰ μέγιστα τῶν ἀνθρωπηίων πρηγμάτων σοφώτατα πάντων ἐξεύρηται, κ. τ. λ. of c. 46, which introduced the digression on the rivers of Scythia. I had, therefore, translated: "The most important objects, therefore, (*i. e.* defence from an invading foe) are thus easily obtained by them."

[124] The fact is, that Herodotus supposed this word to signify, among the Scythians, *father;* which is likely enough to have been the case; for we know that, in all languages, απ, πα, παππα, are the first syllables that children pronounce, and that they use them to designate their parents. *Larcher.*

[125] πάντα τὰ ἱρά. Three different interpretations are given of these words. 1st, "In all their sacred places." Although the Scythians did not erect any temples, it can scarcely be doubted but that they had some open spots set apart for their religious solemnities. This is the translation of Larcher. 2dly, "In all their sacred ceremonies." This is the interpretation given by Wesseling, and followed by Schweighæuser in his Latin version." 3dly, "With every kind of victims." We know that θύειν τὰ ἱρά means to immolate victims; consequently, if the preceding θύειν be taken in that specific sense, ἱρά must signify victims: this interpretation is corroborated by the words at the end of the 61st chapter, where Herodotus informs us that the Scythians sacrifice all kinds of cattle, but chiefly horses. See *Schweig. Lex. Herod.* voc. ἱρὸν 3.

it until the beast is suffocated. He kindles no fire, makes no auspicatory ceremonies[126], no libations; but having strangled the beast, and flayed him, addresses himself to the cooking. As Scythia, however, is wholly destitute of firewood, they have invented the following mode of cooking the flesh: when they have skinned the victim, they strip the flesh from the bones; and then, if they happen to have any of the country caldrons, which are similar to those of the Lesbians, only that they are much larger, they kindle a fire of the bones, and so cook the meat. If they have no such utensil, they stuff all the flesh of the victim into the maw, pour water over it, and kindle a fire of bones: the bones burn beautifully, and the maws hold together efficiently the flesh while it is boiled on the bones: thus the ox cooks himself; and such is the observance for every victim. When the meat is finished cooking, he that sacrifices, throws the firstlings of the flesh and bowels before him as an offering: they sacrifice also different sorts of beasts, and principally horses.

Such is the mode of sacrifice, and such are the victims used by the Scythians to the generality of their gods; but in respect to Mars, their practice is this. According to general usage, in each of the governments a sacred station[127] is dedicated to Mars. Bundles of brush-wood are heaped up, to a length and breadth of three stades, and less in height[128]: on the top of this pile is erected a square platform, perpendicular on every side excepting one, which, to facilitate the ascent, is on a slope: every year they add to the pile one hundred and fifty waggon-loads of fagots, because the heap is constantly sinking, from the weather. On

---

[126] These ceremonies among the Greeks consisted, 1st, In sprinkling the victim with lustral water. 2dly, In throwing on its forehead some whole barley mixed with salt. (The Latins used flour and salt, which they called *mola salsa*.) 3dly, In cutting off some hair from the brow of the victim, and casting it into the fire. The Greeks designated these ceremonies by the word καταχύσται, which is the proper term. See Larcher's note.—The reader will do well to attend to the difference between καταχύσται and ἀπαρχύσται, at the end of the next chapter. *Schweig. Not.*

[127] ἀρχεῖον signifies the senate, the place where the magistrates assemble. As the Scythians had no houses, these places with them were no doubt in the open air, the *fields of Mars* of our ancestors. Besides, a pile three stades long, and as many broad, could hardly be contained within any building. I have consequently expressed in my translation that they were fields of assembly. *Larcher.*

[128] ὕψος ἢ ἔλασσον. The meaning of this is, 'somewhat less in height.' The existence of such piles in a country where wood was so scarce, that it could not be found for the necessary purpose of cooking, must strike every one as improbable. Schweighæuser suspects that Herodotus wrote ὕψος ἢ εὐαλίου ἔλασσον. Perhaps the original reading was ὕψος ἢ ἴσον, meaning "equal in height."

the summit, accordingly, an old scimetar of iron is planted by each Scythian government, and this serves as the symbol of Mars. To this scimetar they offer yearly sacrifices of horses and cattle; and present more sacrifices to these symbols than to all the rest of the gods. Out of all the prisoners they may take of the enemy, they sacrifice one in every hundred: this sacrifice is not performed in the same manner as the beasts; the ceremonies are very different. They begin by making libations of wine on the heads of these victims, and then slaughter them over a bowl: as soon as this has been done, they carry up the bowl to the top of the fagot-pile, and pour the blood over the scimetar. While this is doing on the pile, others below, about the foot of the pile, cut off the right arms, with the shoulders and hands of the slaughtered prisoners, and throw them aloft in the air. When they have performed these ceremonies [129] on each victim, they retire: wherever the limb cut off may have fallen, there it lies, apart from the body. Such are, then, 63 the sacrifices instituted among the Scythians: they never use swine for the purpose, nor will they suffer one of those animals to be reared in their dominions.

In what concerns war, they have the following institutions. 64 Of the first enemy a Scythian sends down, he quaffs the blood: he carries the heads of all that he slays in battle to the king; for when he has brought a head, he is entitled to a share of the booty that may be taken; not otherwise. To skin the head, he makes a circular incision from ear to ear; and then, laying hold of the crown, shakes out the skull: after scraping off the flesh [130] with an ox's rib, he rumples it between his hands, and, having thus softened the skin, makes use of it as a napkin: he appends it to the bridle of the horse he rides, and prides himself on this; for the Scythian that has most of these skin napkins is adjudged the best man. Several among them make coverings also of the entire skins, tacked together like shepherds' coats [131], and wear them, instead of cloaks, over all: others flay the right hands of their slain enemies, and, taking off the nails with the skin, make covers for their quivers. The human skin is thick and shining, and about the most brilliant white [132]

---

[129] ἀσίξαντες. If this word comes from ἀσίγγω, it is taken in a very extraordinary meaning. See Schweig. not. and Coray's remarks in Larcher's translation, vol. iii. 485.

[130] See note i. p. 496. of Dr. Gaisford's edition of Herodotus, borrowed from Wesseling.

[131] These shepherds' coats were made of skins sewed together; and were probably not unlike the capote of the Albanian peasants in the present day.

[132] Supply ἐν ἄρα ἢ λευκοῦ δοκέοντο

of all hides. Many among them take the whole skin of a man, stretch it on a wooden frame[133], and use it as horsecloths: such are their customs. The skulls themselves, that is to say, not all, but those of their most inveterate enemies, they prepare thus: they saw off the parts beneath the eye-brows, and scour out the top. If the owner be a poor man, he merely covers the outside with leather, and so makes use of it: if a rich man, he not only covers it with leather, but plats it with gold in the inside, and uses it as a drinking-cup. He prepares in the same manner the skulls of his relations, if they had any quarrel with him, and he has gained the day over them in presence of the king[134]. When any guest, for whom he has respect, visits him, he brings forth these skulls, and narrates, how they were relations of his, and acted as foes[135], and how he overpowered them: this they call heroism. Once in every year, the provincial governor, each in his government respectively, mingles[136] wine and water in a bowl, of which drink all the Scythians by whom foes have been captured. Those who have never achieved such a deed, taste not of the wine, but sit apart in disgrace: this is, with them, considered as the greatest opprobrium. All who have made very many prisoners of war drink two cups[137] for one.

67   The soothsayers among the Scythians are in great numbers: they foretell the future by the help of several willowrods; and perform in the following manner. They bring with them large bundles of rods, lay them on the ground, and untie them; arrange separately each rod, and prophesy. As they pronounce their predictions, they gather up sticks, and again make up the bundle. Thus is the indigenous art of soothsaying practised among them. But the Enarees, the half men and half women[138], are said also to be endowed by Venus with the divining faculty: they predict by the help of bass, the inner bark of the lime-tree: they split the bass into three parts, twist it round their fingers,

---

ἄγμα. Schweig. Lex. Herod. Previously to Schweighæuser, the reading was ἐν ἄρα σχιδῶν, κ. τ. λ.

[133] I understand Herodotus to mean, that these skins were stretched out on a wooden frame to dry; and, when dry, were used as saddle-cloths for the horses.

[134] ἢν ἐπικρατήσῃ αὐτοῦ, si vicit illum, παρὰ τῷ βασιλεῖ, apud regem, *i. e.* judicio regis, lite a rege judicata. *Schweig. Lex. Herod.* This is the same interpretation as that of Larcher.

Schweighæuser gives, in his Latin version: " atque regis judicio alter alteri in potestatem est traditus."

[135] Lit. " excited war against him."

[136] See note 207, p. 260, of this volume.

[137] σύνδυο κύλικας is generally translated, " two cups joined together."— Schweighæuser follows the general interpretation in his Latin version, but corrects it, in his notes, to " *bina* pocula singuli habentes."

[138] He alludes to i. 105.

and then, unrolling it, prophesy. Whenever the king of the 68
Scythians is stricken with illness, he sends for the three most
renowned soothsayers, who divine in the manner just
described: they assert, that there is no doubt but that so
and so[139], mentioning accordingly some one of the king's
subjects, must have sworn falsely by the king's hearth: for
it is customary with the Scythians, in general, to invoke the
royal hearth, when they wish to pledge themselves by the
most solemn of oaths. Forthwith the accused, whom the
diviners thus impeach of perjury, is brought before the king:
the soothsayers accuse the prisoner of having, as is evidently
shewn by divination, forsworn, by invoking the royal hearth,
and in consequence the king is visited with pain. The
accused denies his guilt, declares that he has not forsworn
himself, and spurns the impeachment: then the king, summons twice the number of soothsayers, different from the
former; and if they, likewise, recurring to their art, convict
the prisoner of perjury, he is immediately beheaded, and the
first soothsayers share by lot his possessions. If the soothsayers sent for, after the first, by the king, acquit the prisoner, others, and again[140] others, are convened: accordingly,
if the majority agree in acquitting the man, the first soothsayers themselves are condemned to death. They execute 69
therefore these men in the manner I shall now describe:
they load a waggon with fagots, and harness to it some
oxen; then fetter the legs of the soothsayers, tie their hands
behind, put a gag in their mouths, and stick them in the
middle of the brush-wood. They next set fire to the
apparatus, and, frightening the oxen, set them off. The beasts
are frequently consumed together with the soothsayers: sometimes they get only a scorching, and escape, when the
pole[141] has been burnt off. In the same manner they burn
to death the soothsayers, for other reasons besides the
above, and call them false prophets. Of those whom the
king puts to death, he spares no males, but does not touch
the females. The Scythians, whomsoever they pledge their 70
oaths to, practise the following ceremonies: they pour wine
into a large cup of earthenware, and mingle with it some of
the blood of the contracting parties: the blood is procured
by a slight cut on the body with a pricket or knife: they

---

[139] Matt. 484, b.

[140] ἄλλοι - - - καὶ μάλα ἄλλοι, alii—iterumque alii. *Schweig.*

[141] The ῥυμὸς was a pole fastened to the front of the carriage: at the extremity of it, a bar (the ζυγὸς) was fixed crosswise: to this bar the horns of the oxen were fastened. This simple mode of harnessing kine is still in use abroad, and is found to answer every purpose.

then plunge into the cup a scimetar, an arrow, a battle-axe, and a javelin. Having made all these preparations, they pronounce long prayers; after which, the contracting parties drink a portion of the wine and blood, and afterwards the most distinguished of their followers do the same.

71 The tombs of the Scythian kings are seen in the land of the Gerrhi, at the extreme point to which the Borysthenes is navigable. Here, in the event of a king's decease, they dig a deep square fosse. Having made this preparation, they envelope the body[142] in wax; open the belly, and cleanse it out; then stuff it full of turmeric and aromatics, together with parsley and anise-seed[143]; sew it up again; and convey it in a waggon to some neighbouring Scythian nation. The people receive the dead body, and act in the same manner as the Royal Scythians, that is to say, cut off the tips of their ears, shave their hair around the head, make incisions in their arms, lacerate their faces and noses, and drive arrows through their left hands. From thence they convey the royal corpse, by waggon, to another province of his dominions, and the people first visited accompany the procession: when they have paraded the corpse through all the provinces, they find themselves in that of the Gerrhi, the most distant of the king's dominions, and where the royal tombs are situated. And then, having placed the dead body in its grave, on a bed of grass, and planted spears on both sides, they lay some wooden beams across, and complete the roof by covering in with osier twigs[144]. In the vacant space left round the body in the fosse, they now lay one of the king's concubines, whom they strangle for this purpose; and his cup-bearer, his cook, his groom, his page, his messenger, some horses, in short, samples of all his things, together with gold cups, for they use no silver or brass. Having so done, all fall to work at throwing up an immense mound, striving and vying with one another who shall do the most.

72 After an interval of twelve months, the following additional duties are performed. They take the most useful of the deceased king's servants;—these are all native Scythians, and by the late king's orders waited on him; for

---

[142] Construction: ἀναλαμβάνουσι τὸν νεκρὸν, κατακεκηρωμένον μὲν (κατὰ) τὸ σῶμα, (ἔχοντα) δὲ τὴν νηδὺν ἀνεσχισμένην, κ. τ. λ. See Matt. 427, b.

[143] Schneider takes ἄννησον to be equivalent to ἄνηθον, dill or fennel.— Others take it to signify anis, the proper term for which is ἄννησον. The seeds of both plants are highly aromatic, so that the difference can be of very little importance. Schneider, Griechisch—Deutsches—Wörterbuch. voc. ἄννησον.

[144] ἰτυΐ. The same lexicographer, whom I have just quoted, is of opinion that this word should be translated, 'with reeds.'

the king possesses no purchased slaves;—of these they strangle fifty, together with fifty beautiful horses. They take out the bowels from the dead bodies, scour out the bellies, stuff them with straw, and sow them up again. They next place half the felloe of a wheel[145], the outside downwards, between two posts, and stick in the ground many other frames of the same sort. They then run thick poles through the whole length of the bodies of the horses, up to the shoulders, and set them across the felloes: the foremost felloe supports the shoulders of the horse, and the hindermost holds up the belly and the hind-quarters: while the four legs, unsupported, dangle in the air. They put a bit and bridle to each horse; and pull the bridle forward, fastening it up to a post[146], for that purpose. Accordingly, they seat upon one of these horses each of the fifty attendants they have strangled, after driving a wooden spar along the back-bone of each, up to his throat: this spar projects at the bottom; and that part is pushed into a socket[147] made in the pole that passes through the horse's belly. Having fastened this sort of horsemen around the mound[148], they take their departure.

Thus the Scythians inter their kings. When any other 73 Scythians die, their nearest kinsman lay them out in a waggon, and take them round to their friends: each of whom receives and feasts the followers of the funeral, presenting to the dead man the same dishes as to the rest: during forty days, private individuals are in this manner paraded, and then interred. The Scythians who have buried a dead body make use of the following mode of purification: they

---

[145] The ἄψις is the exterior wooden periphery of the wheel, what we call the *felly*.

[146] ἐκ πασσάλων δῆσαν. The reader must attend to the construction of δῆσαν with ἐκ, in which case it means *to fasten and suspend from*. The πάσσαλοι, to which the bridle was fastened, was, therefore, higher than the horse's head: it was probably so arranged in order to keep the head and neck in their proper position; since, otherwise, those parts would have fallen down, from want of support. This remark may appear trifling; but I am induced to make it, from seeing that the text has not been sufficiently attended to in delineating a figure illustrative of this part of Herodotus, which has lately made its appearance.

[147] If we adopt Dr. Gaisford's punctuation, I do not see very clearly what is to become of the particle δὲ: I would, therefore, preserve the comma after τούτου, and with Schweighæuser give the following construction: ἐπεὰν διελάσωσι ξύλον ὀρθὸν παρὰ τὴν ἄκανθον μέχρι τοῦ τραχήλου ἱππέων τινέων, κάτωθεν δὲ (in the sense of γὰρ, *quum*, see Matt. Gr. Gram. 613, v.), ὑπερέχει (μέρος) τοῦ ξύλου τούτου, τὸ (in the sense of τοῦτο, i. e. τοῦτο τὸ μέρος τοῦ ξύλου) παγγνύουσι ἐς τόρμον τοῦ ἑτέρου ξύλου, κ.τ.λ.

[148] I have endeavoured to express the force of ἐπὶ in the verb ἐπιστήσαντες.

soap and wash their heads[149], and, sticking up three sticks inclining to a point, stretch a woollen cloth[150] about them, making all as tight as possible; they then throw red-hot stones into a vase[151] placed inside of the sticks and the 74 clothes.—Hemp grows in this country. Except in size and thickness, it is extremely similar to flax. Hemp, however, is greatly superior to flax, inasmuch as it springs self-sown. The Thracians manufacture, from this plant, garments which equal even those of linen: nor can any one, not very conversant in these matters, distinguish whether the garment is made of hemp or flax; while he who has never before 75 seen hemp articles takes them to be linen.—The Scythians accordingly provide themselves with a certain quantity of hemp-seed: they creep under the clothes, and strew the grains on the red-hot stones; the seed smokes, and sends up such a steam as no Hellenic vapour-bath can exceed. The Scythians, dizzy through the vapour, shout with pleasure: this stands them in place of a bath, for they never wash any part of the body with water[152]. The women pound on a rough stone the wood of the cypress, cedar, and incense-tree, pouring water on the mixture: when they

---

[149] I do not see the necessity of adding the words "with a kind of soap," more here than in ii. 37, διασμώντες (τὰ σωμάτια), or in iii. 148, ἐξέσμων τὰ σωμάτια.

[150] See note 53, p. 288 of this volume.

[151] This vase was used to burn hemp-seed, as Herodotus informs us in c. 75; the intervening chapter being a description of the hemp-plant.

[152] There is no doubt that this was done by the Scythians in order to procure that state of drunkenness to which all savage nations are so much inclined: the Historian mistook the object. The *hasisha al fokara*, which consists of the leaves and seeds of the hemp-plant, are much used in the East as a substitute for opium; and deplorable objects are frequently seen in the towns of Turkey, burthened with diseases produced by the use of that plant. I copy from Sacy's Chrestomathie Arabe, ii. 155, the following ordinance, published to the French army soon after the opening of the Egyptian campaign:—

"1. The use of a strong liquor manufactured by some Mussulmen from a certain strong herb called *hasish*, as also the practice of smoking hemp-seed, are prohibited throughout Egypt. Those that are in the habit of drinking the above liquor, and smoking the aforesaid seeds, lose their senses, and fall into violent delirium, which often leads them to commit all kinds of excesses.

"2. The distillation of the *hasish* is prohibited throughout Egypt: the doors of the coffee-houses, or public or private dwellings, in which it may be retailed, shall be walled up; and the proprietors shall be condemned to three months' imprisonment.

"3. All the bundles of *hasish* that may be brought to the custom-houses shall be confiscated, and publicly burnt."

I am sorry to see that the smoking of the *hasish*, that is to say, of a sort of paste (called *chillum*) made by the Turks from hemp-seed and opium, is becoming fashionable in this country, particularly among young men. This will account for the insertion of a note which is rather inconsistent with the plan of illustration that I have hitherto followed.

have thus procured a thick paste [153], they smear it over the body and face, and by this means a sweet smell attaches to them; and when, on the second day, they take off the cataplasm, their skin is clean, and adorned with a beautiful lustre.

The Scythians shun, with the greatest abhorrence, strange customs; not only the customs of other nations, but most of all those of the Hellenes [154]: of this, both Anacharsis, and next to him again Scylas, afford abundant proof. In the first, the events connected with Anacharsis were as follows: Having visited many countries, and displayed every where [155] his wisdom [156], Anacharsis was on his road back to the seats of the Scythians: sailing through the Hellespont, he touched at Cyzicus; and finding [157] the inhabitants engaged in a pompous celebration of the festival to the Mother of the Gods, he made a vow to the goddess, that if he returned home safe and sound, he would not only offer sacrifice to her with the same ceremonies as he had witnessed the citizens of Cyzicus doing, but institute also a vigil in her honour. On his arrival in Scythia, he hid himself in the country called Hylæa: this quarter is close to the Achillean Course, and is full of trees of all sorts. Anacharsis retired secretly to this place, and went through all the ceremonies of the feast to the goddess, having a tambourine in his hands, and images fastened on his person. He was observed, when thus occupied, by a Scythian; who went and informed Saulius the king; who himself seeing what Anacharsis was about, aimed an arrow, and shot him dead. Even now, if you inquire about Anacharsis, the Scythians will not allow that they know such a person, because he migrated to Hellas, and observed foreign practices. I was informed by Timnes, the guardian of Ariapithes, that Anacharsis was [158] the paternal uncle of Idanthyrsus, king of the Scythians; that he was the son of Gnurus, grandson of Lycus, great-grandson of

---

[153] See Matt. 423, 5.
[154] The construction of this passage presents several difficulties. 1st, The use of ἕκαστα, where we should have suspected the writer would have used μάλιστα. 2dly, The meaning of the parenthetical clause, μά τι γι ἀλλήλων. Werfer and Schweighæuser account for the use of ἕκαστα by regarding φεύγειν as one of those verbs mentioned by Matthiæ, 533, 2, which take the infinitive with μά: this being granted, one can easily see why the Historian says χρᾶσθαι φεύγουσι Ἑλληνικοῖσι ἕκαστα, when, according to the structure of most languages, μάλιστα might be thought more proper. With regard to the second difficulty, it remains hitherto unconquered: if we read μά τι γι ὦν ἄλλων, the construction becomes comparatively easy. I have followed the interpretation of Larcher and Schweighæuser, although by no means satisfactory.

[155] κατ᾽ αὐτὸν, i. e. γῆν, ibi.

[156] τοῦτο μὲν, which is answered by πολλοῖσι δὲ κάρτα ἔτεσι, κ. τ. λ. at the beginning of c. 78. *Schweig.*

[157] γὰρ. See Matt. 613.

[158] See Matt. 538, 2.

Spargapithes; if, therefore, Anacharsis was of that house, he was surely [159] killed by his own brother: for Idanthyrsus was the son of Saulius; and Saulius was the murderer of Anacharsis. I have, however, heard some Peloponnesians who give a different account; That Anacharsis, despatched by the Scythian king into foreign lands, became a disciple of the Hellenes; and, on his return, said to the prince who had sent him on this expedition, that all the Hellenes applied to universal wisdom, with the exception of the Lacedæmonians, but these only understood how to speak and reply rationally and prudently. But this is nothing more than pure invention on the part of the Hellenes; for this philosopher undoubtedly perished, as I said before. Accordingly, he suffered this cruel treatment for his adopting strange customs, and his intercourse with the Hellenes.

78 Very many years subsequently, Scylas, the son of Ariapithes, underwent a fate nearly similar to that of Anacharsis. Ariapithes, king of the Scythians, had, beside other sons, one called Scylas: he was born of an Istrian [160] woman, a foreigner. His mother taught him the Hellenic language, and letters. In the course of time, Ariapithes met with his death by the treachery of Spargapithes, king of the Agathyrsi. Scylas succeeded to the throne, and to his father's wife, whose name was Opœa: she was a native of Scythia, and had brought Ariapithes a son, named Oricus. Scylas, although king of the Scythians, was wholly averse to the customs of that country, and much more inclined to those of the Hellenes, in consequence of his early education. He was wont to act in the manner I am now going to describe. Whenever he brought the Scythian army to the city of the Borysthenitæ (who assert that they descend from the Milesians), Scylas entered the town, leaving his troops in the outskirts; and as soon as he was within the walls, he closed the gates, cast off the Scythian dress, and assumed the Hellenic. Thus clad [161], he walked about the public square, unaccompanied by guards or any other person. He kept a strict watch at the gates, lest he should be seen by the Scythians in this apparel. Besides adopting, in various respects, the Hellenic practices, he observed also the ceremonies used by the Hellenes in the worship of their gods. After passing thus a month or more, he would take his departure, and assume again the Scythian costume. In this manner he acted frequently: he built himself also a palace

---

[159] ἴστω, "let him know, he was killed by his own brother."
[160] A city of the Milesians, near the mouth of the Danube.
[161] ἄν, to express the repetition of the action, Matt. 598, a.

at the Borysthenes, and espoused there a woman of the country[162]. He was doomed however, by fate, to perish miserably: and so it came to pass on the present occasion. He was anxious to be initiated in the Bacchic mysteries: at the moment he was about to be admitted to the sacred rites[163], a mighty prodigy occurred. As I before observed, he had, in the city of the Borysthenitæ, a large and magnificent mansion, around which stood sphinxes and griffons in white stone. The god hurled his shafts against this edifice; and the whole was reduced to ashes. Scylas, nevertheless, went through the sacred rites. The Scythians reproach the Hellenes with their Bacchic ceremonies; for, say they, it is not consonant to reason, to devise a god such as this, that impels men to madness. When Scylas had been initiated in the Bacchic mysteries, one of the Borysthenitæ escaped over[164] to the Scythians, and said: "You Scythians laugh "at us[165], because we celebrate the Bacchanal feast, and "the god takes possession of us: now, that very god has "taken possession of your king: he worships Bacchus, "and by the god is distraught of his senses. If you disbe- "lieve what I say, follow me, and I will shew you." The chief men among the Scythians followed the man: the citizen of Borysthenes led the way, and secretly placed them on a tower: soon after, Scylas passed by with the Bacchanalian crew, and was seen by the Scythians. They considered this as a sore insult; and, returning, acquainted the whole army with what they had witnessed. When, afterwards, Scylas returned home to his own states, the Scythians revolted from Scylas; and, in his stead, proclaimed his brother Octamasades, born of the daughter of Teres. Scylas, informed of what had taken place, and of the cause alleged, fled to Thrace. Octamasades, hearing this, marched against Thrace: when he reached the Ister, the Thracians advanced to meet him: as both parties were about to engage battle[166], Sitalces sent to Octamasades, saying: "Why should we try "the fate of battle? you are my own sister's son; you have

---

[162] καὶ γυναῖκα ἔγημε ἐς αὐτά. This last word refers to οἰκία, "uxorem duxit in istas ædes." *Larcher.*

[163] Ἔρχεσθαί τι ἐς χεῖρας signifies to undertake, to commence upon any thing. *Schweig. Lex. Herod.* Larcher translates " et qu'on alloit lui mettre les choses sacrées entre les mains." I do not think that τελετὴ is ever taken in the sense of sacred things.

[164] I read with Schweighæuser and Schneider διαδρήντων, the meaning of which can be more easily guessed than that of διαφέροντος, particularly as Hesychius gives δρατίνη, *fugitivus*, a deserter, a runaway slave, as the explanation of δεδρὼς. *Schneider, Gr. Germ. Lex.* voc. διαδρηστίω. Herodotus uses the expression ἄδρηστα ἀνδράποδα, iv. 142. *Schweig.*

[165] See Matt. 394, a. obs. 2.

[166] Understand μάχης after συνάψειν.

"in your power my brother. Restore to me my brother; "and I will give you back Scylas, yours: thus neither you "nor I shall expose our troops to danger[167]." This message Sitalces communicated by a herald; for his brother had fled from him, and taken refuge with Octamasades. The Scythian acceded to the contract: he surrendered his maternal uncle to Sitalces, and received in exchange his brother. Sitalces, as soon as he had his brother in his power, retired with his army; while Octamasades, on the spot, beheaded his brother Scylas. Such is the veneration of the Scythians for their customs, and such the punishment they award to those that adopt foreign institutions.

81. I have never been able to obtain correct information as to the Scythian population: the accounts I have heard all vary in numbers, some representing the Scythians as immensely numerous, others as very few, reckoning none but real Scythians[168]. There is one thing connected with this, of which I myself have been an eye-witness. Between the Borysthenes and Hypanis' rivers, there is a spot called the Exampæus; which I mentioned a little above, observing that a bitter spring was seen there, the stream from which, running down into the Hypanis, renders the waters of that river undrinkable[169]. In the above spot lies a brass caldron, six times more capacious than that consecrated, at the mouth of the Pontus, by Pausanias the son of Cleombrotus. If the reader has never seen this Scythian vase, I must inform him, that it will hold easily six hundred amphoræ, and that the brass of which it consists is six fingers' thick: it was made, according to the account of the people in the vicinity, out of arrow-heads. The king, whose name was Ariantas, wishing to know the amount of the Scythian population[170], ordered all his subjects, under pain of death in case of neglect, to bring each one arrow-head, without the shaft. Such a prodigious quantity of arrow-heads was in consequence collected, that the king resolved to make of them a

monument to posterity; and accordingly this caldron was cast out of the brass, and dedicated at Exampæus. Scythia displays no other wonders than [171] her mighty rivers, which are very numerous. But there is one thing, over and above the rivers and the vast plain, which I consider worthy of admiration, and shall mention: it is, the footstep of Hercules impressed on a rock; it resembles a man's step, but is two cubits long: it is seen near the Tyras river.—I now return to the subject which I was discoursing on [172] at the beginning.

Darius, preparing to march against Scythia, despatched messengers, with his commands to some, that they were to contribute troops; to others, that they were to furnish ships of war; to others again, that they were to take proper measures to lay a bridge over the Thracian Bosphorus. Artabanus, son of Hystaspes, and brother to Darius, advised the king by no means to enter upon an expedition against the Scythians, alleging the poverty of that nation. Seeing that his good counsel would be of no avail, he ceased to press the matter; and Darius, having made all due preparations, placed himself at the head of his army, and commenced his march from Susa. It was then that Œobazus, a Persian, the father of three sons, all enlisted in the expedition, implored the king to leave one to him: the king answered, as to a friend whom he considered to have made a moderate request, that he would leave all three. Œobazus was therefore highly gratified, fancying that his son would be discharged from the service: but Darius gave orders to the head executioners to put to death all the sons of Œobazus; and, after their death, left them on the spot.

Darius proceeded in his march from Susa, till he reached Chalcedon on the Bosphorus, where a bridge had been thrown across the strait: here he went on board a ship of war, and sailed up to the Cyanean islands, which, according to the Hellenes, floated of old on the surface. The king took his seat in the temple, and cast his eyes on the Euxine sea; a sight deserving of admiration; for this, of all the high seas of the world, is the most wonderful in its nature. Its length is eleven thousand one hundred stades: its breadth, at the greatest, three thousand three hundred stades. The mouth of this wide expanse is four stades across: the length of this entrance, the neck [173], called the

---

[171] Construction: χωρὶς ἢ ὅτι (ἔχω) ποταμοὺς, κ. τ. λ.
[172] ᾖα. See Matt. 214, 4.
[173] The article τὸ relates to μῆκος τοῦ στόματος; the words ἡ αὐχὴν being, as it were, in parentheses.

Bosphorus, where the bridge stood, measures about one hundred and twenty stades in length, and leads down to the Propontis. The Propontis, on the other hand, is five hundred stades in breadth, in length fourteen hundred, and discharges its waters into the Hellespont; a strait that in its narrowest part is but seven stades broad, in length four hundred. The Hellespont terminates in a vast expanse of waters, called the Ægean sea. These seas have been measured in the following manner. A ship, in the long days of summer[174], on an average, makes seventy thousand orgyiæ in the day, and sixty thousand in the night. Now, from the mouth of the Euxine to the Phasis (in this direction the greatest length of the Pontus) is a voyage of nine days and eight nights: these make one hundred and ten thousand one hundred orgyiæ, equivalent to eleven thousand one hundred stades. From Sindica to the river Thermodon (in this direction the greatest breadth of the Pontus) is a voyage of three days and two nights: these make thirty thousand three hundred orgyiæ[175], or three thousand three hundred stades. The Pontus, therefore, and the Bosphorus, together with the Hellespont, were thus measured by myself: they are such as I have described. To the Pontus[176] belongs a lake, whose waters it receives, but little inferior to itself in magnitude: it is called the Mæotis, and the mother of the Pontus.

87 Darius, having viewed the prospect of the Pontus, sailed back to the bridge, which had been constructed under the direction of Mandrocles, an architect of Samos. The king examined the Bosphorus also; and erected on the shore two pillars of white stone, with inscriptions in Assyrian letters on one, and Hellenic letters on the other, expressing the names of all the nations[177] he had under his command; and they were all those over whom his dominion extended. Seven hundred thousand men, with the cavalry, were reckoned in

---

[174] μακρημερίη, that season of the year in which the days are longer than the nights. *Schweig. Lex. Herod.* If the numbers are right in this chapter, it must be allowed that the Historian expresses himself in a very loose manner; the difference between the voyage by day and that by night being only one seventh; and, as many circumstances always retard navigation in the dark, the days and nights must have been, it would seem, pretty nearly equal.

[175] ἰνδικα μυριάδες καὶ ἑκατὸν ὀργυιῶν: these words Larcher understands to signify 110,100 orgyiæ: he therefore proposes to read ἰνδικα καὶ ἑκατὸν μυριάδες ὀργυιῶν, but Schweighæuser proves satisfactorily that both readings are equivalent, and signify 1,110,000 orgyiæ.

[176] ὁ Πόντος οὗτος: *this Pontus*, probably to distinguish it from the neighbouring Hellespont. *Schweig.*

[177] γράμματα must be taken in the sense of inscriptions, and ὅσα construed in apposition with γράμματα.

the land-army alone, without taking into account the fleet, consisting of six hundred sail of the line. The Byzantines, accordingly, brought these pillars, at a subsequent period, to their city, and made use of them in the erection of an altar to Orthosian Diana; excepting one block covered with Assyrian characters, which was left near the temple of Bacchus in Byzantium. The spot where Darius caused the bridge to be thrown over the Bosphorus must have been, I conjecture, half-way between Byzantium and the temple at the mouth of the Euxine sea. Darius, satisfied with the manner in which the bridge [178] had been constructed, rewarded the architect, Mandrocles, of Samos, with a magnificent present [179]: with the first-fruits of which, Mandrocles caused a picture to be made of the bridge over the Bosphorus, with Darius seated on his throne, and the army passing over: this painting he dedicated at Juno's temple (in Samos), accompanied with the following inscription:—

"Mandrocles, having thrown a bridge of boats across the fishful
"Bosphorus, has dedicated this monument to Juno; in re-
"membrance of the crown which he has gained for himself, the
"glory which he has shed on the Samians, and the gratification
"he has afforded to king Darius."

Darius, having rewarded Mandrocles, passed over into Europe; enjoining the Ionians to proceed on the Euxine sea, as far as the river Ister; and, when they should have reached so far, to await till he came up, and meanwhile join the two banks of the river with a bridge of boats. The Ionians, Æolians, and Hellespontines, were the leaders of the naval armament. The fleet accordingly stretched between the Cyanean islands, and stood direct for the Ister. The ships ascended the river two days' voyage from the sea to the main stream; and moored a floating bridge across the Ister, at the place [180] where that river

---

[178] σχέδιος signifies "temporary:" when σχεδία is used to express a bridge, the word γέφυρα must be understood. The bridge over the Bosphorus was of boats.

[179] The Greek is, ἐδωρήσατο πᾶσι δέκα, 'he made him a present of ten things of every kind;' that is to say, he gave him ten of all the kinds of things his present consisted of. *Larcher.* We have met with πᾶς in a similar sense, i. 50. iii. 18.

[180] αὐχὴν signifies, literally, *a neck:* hence, metaphorically, it is applied to an isthmus, the continent being regarded as the body, and the peninsula as the head, united by the isthmus or neck: so again it is applied to a strait, the main sea being regarded as the body, and the interior sea as the head, united by the strait or neck. In this passage the word is used to express that part of the river where the different embouchures branch out like so many heads from the main body of the stream. See *Schweig. Lex. Herod.*

branches out into various mouths. Meanwhile Darius, having crossed the Bosphorus by the floating bridge, marched through Thrace; and coming to the sources of the Tearus 90 river, encamped there for three days. The Tearus is represented by the people residing on its banks as the best of rivers: it is not only good for various diseases, but is moreover a perfect cure for the itch in man and horse: the sources of this river are thirty-eight in number; they all gush out of the same rock; some are cold, others hot. They are found at equal distances from the town of Heræum, near Perinthus, and from that of Apollonia on the Euxine; two days' journey from either. The Tearus unites to the Contadesdus; the Contadesdus joins the Agrianes; and the Agrianes falls into the Hebrus, which discharges its waters 91 into the sea, near the town of Ænos. Darius, therefore, having reached this river, and pitched his tents, was delighted with the stream, and erected a pillar there, with this inscription: " The sources of the Tearus produce the best " and finest water of all rivers: the best and finest of men " visited them, on his expedition against the Scythians, " Darius the son of Hystaspes, king of the Persians and of 92 " the whole continent." Darius, having taken his departure from this spot, came to another river, the name of which is the Artiscus; it flows through the land of the Odrysæ. On his arrival at its banks, he pointed out a spot to the troops, and ordered every man, as he passed by, to throw a stone on the appointed place. The army obeyed the order; and Darius continued his march, leaving at this spot large heaps of stones.

93 Previous to arriving at the Ister, Darius reduced first the Getæ, who call themselves immortal. The Thracians of Salmydessus, and those residing above Apollonia and Mesembria, called Scyrmiadæ and Nipsæi, surrendered without resistance. But the Getæ, making an obstinate stand, were forthwith enslaved: this nation is the most valiant and the 94 most equitable of the Thracians. They call themselves immortal, for this reason, they are of opinion that they never die, and that the departed go to join their god Zalmoxis: some among them believe that Zalmoxis is the same as Gebeleizis. Every five years, they choose one of their number by lot, and send him as messenger to Zalmoxis, each charging him with his own requests to the god. Their mode of despatching this person to Zalmoxis is as follows. Some are appointed to keep erect three javelins; others lay hold by the hands and feet of the man who is to be despatched to Zalmoxis; they swing him backwards and for-

wards a few times, then toss him in the air, so that he may fall on the points of the javelins. If, accordingly, the man die sticking on the lances, they fancy the god is propitious; but if he do not die, they lay the blame on the messenger himself, and declare that he is a bad man: they despatch another, and, while he is yet alive, give him their commissions. These same Thracians, in case of thunder and lightning, hurl their shafts against heaven, and threaten the god: they think, likewise, there is no god but theirs. According to information which I received from the Hellenes residing on the coast of the Hellespont and the Euxine, the above Zalmoxis was in reality a man, and a slave at Samos: he belonged to Pythagoras the son of Mnesarchus: here, when made free, he amassed great riches; and, subsequently, went home. But, as the Thracians led a bad and rude way of life, Zalmoxis—who was acquainted with Ionic customs, and more civilized manners than his countrymen[181], and had long been connected with Hellenes, and with the most learned[182] of the Hellenes in particular, Pythagoras—built a hall, in which he received the chief citizens at his table; and informed them, that neither he himself, nor his guests, nor any of their posterity for ever, would die; but that they would go to a place where they should still live, and enjoy all kinds of bliss. While[183] Zalmoxis was behaving in the manner I have described, and communicated such lessons, he excavated an underground apartment for his own residence, under the hall. When the work was completed[184], he disappeared from the sight of the Thracians, and descended into his subterranean chamber, where he abode three years: his friends mourned him as dead: but in the fourth year he made his appearance to the Thracians: and thus Zalmoxis brought them to give faith to what he said. In this manner the Hellenes represent him to have acted. I do not exactly disbelieve this tale about Zalmoxis, and his underground chamber: I must say, however, that I have my doubts: it is my opinion, that this Zalmoxis lived many years before the birth of Pythagoras. Whether there ever was a human Zalmoxis, or whether he is the native god of the Getæ, I shall say no more about him. The people who practise the

---

[181] See Matt. 449, c.

[182] The Greek is, *οὐ τῷ ἀσθενεστάτῳ σοφιστῇ*, not the weakest philosopher.—An example of the figure called λιτότης, μείωσις, and which is very common in the Greek and Latin authors. *Larcher*. See Matt. 463.

[183] *ἐν ᾧ ----- ἐν τούτῳ, dum—interim.* Schweighæuser, in his Latin version, takes these words as relating to *διωρύσσων*, but retracts his opinion in the Lex. Herod.

[184] *συντελέων ἔχι*, equivalent to *συντελῶς ἦν.* See Matt. 604.

ceremony I have described were subdued by the Persians, and followed in the train of Darius's army.

97 On the arrival of Darius, accompanied by the whole land army, at the banks of the Ister, all the forces passed over: and Darius gave orders to the Ionians to unmoor the craft composing the floating bridge[185], and to follow him, skirting the shore with the naval armament. As the Ionians were preparing to obey these orders, and unmoor, Coes the son of Erxandrus, the leader of the Mytilenæans, addressed Darius in the following words, having first ascertained whether the king would vouchsafe to listen to the advice of one who was desirous to explain what he thought. "Since[186] " your Majesty," said he, " is about to carry war into a land " of which no part is, we know, cultivated, and where no " cities are found, I beseech you, let the bridge remain as it " is; and leave those who have built it, to watch over it. " Then, whether we meet with the Scythians, and succeed " to our mind, or find it impossible to meet the enemy, a " safe road back will, at all events, be open to us. Not " that I fear, in any manner, that we can be defeated in open " field by Scythians; but I do fear, that, seeking in vain to " bring them to the fight, the calamity of losing our way " may befal us. It may be objected, that what I say is for " my own advantage, that I may stay behind; but I propose, " my liege, what I conceive the best suggestion for your- " self: I, however, will follow, and beg that I may not be " left behind[187]." Darius approved highly the suggestion, and gave the following answer: " My Lesbian friend, if I " return home safe and sound, fail not to come before me, " that I may make you a return for your good advice, by

98 " my good deeds." Having so said, he made sixty knots in a leather thong, and, convening the Ionian rulers, spoke thus: " Ionians[188], I have changed my intentions with respect " to the bridge, which I have before explained to you: take " this thong, keep it, and do as I bid you. As soon as you " see me depart to attack the Scythians, then begin, and " shake out one of these knots every day: if, in that time, " I do not appear again before you, but if as many days have " elapsed as there are knots, make away for your respective " homes[189]. Until then, however, as I have altered my mind, " I command you to watch the float vigilantly, and exert

---

[185] λύσαντας τὴν σχεδίην (γέφυραν)— "having unfastened the temporary bridge." The bridge was made of boats.

[186] γὰρ, used in the sense of which we have already seen so many instances, Matt. 613.

[187] ἐν λειφθίην. See Matt. 514, 3.

[188] Matt. 430, 7.

[189] Matt. 466, 1.

" yourselves to the utmost to preserve it whole and unin-
" jured: in so doing, you will gratify me extremely." Darius
finished speaking, and gave orders to march onwards.

Thrace projects considerably in front of the coast of 99
Scythia[190]: at the extremity of the indenture in Thrace made
by this bay commences the Scythian domains[191], into which
the Ister pours its waters, towards the south-east, where it
falls in the sea. I am now going to describe the extent[192]
of Scythia, along the sea, from the mouth of the Ister. From
the Ister begins Old Scythia[193]: this country lies south; it
extends up to a town called Carcinitis: from this place, advancing still along the same sea, the land is mountainous,
and juts forward into Pontus: it is occupied by the Tauric
people to the town of Chersonesus Trachea[194]: this tract
extends also to the eastern sea[195]: for the two parts of the
Scythian boundaries, that range along the southern as well
as the eastern seas, are like the land of Attica. And in this
case, the Tauric race, occupying their portion, is pretty nearly
the same as if some alien race, and not the Athenians, had
possession of the Sunian promontory (supposing that foreland to project more to a point in the sea) from the Thoric
canton to the Anaphlystic canton:—I am here comparing
small things to big things:—such is Taurica. For the satis-

---

[190] This sentence admits of two constructions; first, ἡ Θρηΐκη (κατὰ) τὸ ἐς θάλασσαν πρόκειται τῆς Σκυθικῆς γῆς, 'that part of Thrace that goes down to the sea lies before Scythia:' secondly, ἡ Θρηΐκη πρόκειται τῆς Σκυθικῆς γῆς (κατὰ) τὸ ἐς θάλασσαν, 'Thrace lies before that part of Scythia that extends to the sea.'

[191] κόλπου δὲ ἀγομένου κ. τ. λ. The meaning of this is by no means clear. Larcher translates, "à l'endroit où finit le Golfe de Thrace—*at the spot where the Gulf of Thrace terminates.*" Schweighæuser explains it, " ubi sinus ducitur hujus regionis, (*i.e.* ubi in sinum circumducitur hæc regio,) ibi Thraciam excipit Scythia."

[192] ' I proceed to describe the part of Scythia with regard to measure.' ἐς μέτρησιν, Matt. 578.

[193] ἀρχαίη Σκυθική, that is to say, Old Scythia, the territory occupied by the Scythians previously to their expulsion of the Cimmerians, and the extension of their frontier eastward. *Schweig.* Placing one's self at the north extremity of Scythia, and turning one's face towards the Chersonesus Taurica, or Crimea, Scythia will lie to the south. *Larcher.*

[194] Herodotus is not here speaking of a peninsula, but of a Greek city which bore the name of Chersonesus Trachea. Stephanus Byzant. says so expressly, and even quotes this passage of our Historian. *Larcher.* It must, however, be observed, with Schweighæuser, that κατήκειν can be predicated only of a country, and that the city of Chersonesus stood on the western part of the peninsula; whereas Herodotus says of the Chersonesus Trachea, that ἐς θάλασσαν τὴν πρὸς ἀπηλιώτην ἄνεμον κατήκει. The reader must likewise remember, that μέχρι expresses a boundary of time, place, or number; that boundary being either included or excluded.

[195] Larcher is of opinion that Herodotus means, by the eastern sea, that portion of the Euxine east, in relation to Scythia, beginning at the Ister. Others are of opinion that he meant the Palus Mæotis.

faction of those who have not navigated about these parts of Attica, I will illustrate the thing by another example: it is as if some distinct nation, not the Iapygians, beginning at the port of Brundusium, should cut off the rest of Iapygia to Tarentum, and have possession of the foreland. I mention these two examples: I might produce many, which Taurica
100 resembles[196]. Taking from Taurica, the Scythians are found above the Tauric people, and possess the country along the eastern sea, and the parts west of the Cimmerian Bosphorus and the Palus Mæotis, up to the Tanaïs river, which discharges its stream at the farthest extremity of that lake. From the Ister, Scythia stretches accordingly inland; and in its upper parts, is enclosed first by the Agathyrsians; next, by the Neurians; then by the Androphagians; and lastly,
101 by the Melanchlænians. Scythia, therefore, being of a quadrangular form, with two parts contiguous to the sea[197], extends every way inland equally to what it does along the coast. For, from the Ister to the Borysthenes is a ten days' journey; from the Borysthenes along the Lake Mæotis is another ten days' journey. The day's journey I take at an average of two hundred stades: thus the measure of Scythia, taken parallel to the coast, would be four thousand stades: taken transversely, it would still be four thousand stades. Such is the extent of this land.
102 The Scythians, aware that alone they were not equal to the discomfiture of Darius's forces in a pitched battle, sent ambassadors to the bordering nations. The respective kings of those countries met, and held council in consequence of the approach of such a numerous army. To the meeting came the kings of the Taurians, Agathyrsians, Neurians, Androphagians, Melanchlænians, Gelonians, Budinians, and
103 Sauromatæ. The people of Tauris have the following usages: they sacrifice to the Virgin[196], both shipwrecked mariners and Hellenes, that are cast away on their shores, and fall into their hands: the preparatory ceremonies of this sacrifice being finished, they strike the victim on the head with a club. Some persons affirm that they then impale the head, and throw the body down the precipice on which the temple stands: others agree with these as far as respects the head, but deny that the dead body is thrown

---

[196] This is equivalent to δύο δὲ λόγων ἐχόντα, πολλὰ ἄλλα λόγω παρόμοια, οἷς Ἰαπὺς ἡ Ταυρική. *Schweig.*

[197] σὺν δύο μερέων πατυμένεων ἐς θάλασσαν: this Larcher translates, "et deux de ses côtés (a mistake of the press, probably, for côtés), s'étendent le long de la mer."

[198] τῇ Παρθένῳ. This *virgin*, as we are informed at the end of the chapter, was Iphigenia the daughter of Agamemnon.

down the cliff; on the contrary, they say it is put under ground. The Taurians themselves state, that the goddess to whom they offer these sacrifices is Iphigenia the daughter of Agamemnon. To the foes that fall into their hands they behave thus: they cut off the enemy's head, and carry it with them home; and there stick it on a tall pole, which they place high above the roof, and even the chimney of the house. They allege, that they place thus aloft the heads of their foes as a protection to the whole house. These people live by pillage and war. The Agathyrsians are of the most 104 effeminate[199] of men, and all excessively fond of gold ornaments. With them, women are made public property, in order that all the Agathyrsians may be connected by blood, and, being akin to one another thus, may not be affected by mutual hatred and envy. In other respects, their usages approach nearly to those of the Thracians. The Neurians 105 have the same customs as the Scythians: the generation before Darius's invasion, the whole nation, was forced to migrate, on account of the abundance of serpents; their own territory producing many, and vast numbers invading their lands from the deserts in the north. Thus oppressed, they forsook their native land, and took refuge with the Budinians. It appears that these people are wizards[200]; for it is affirmed[201] by the Scythians, and by the Hellenes residing in Scythia, that, once every year, each Neurian becomes a wolf for a few days, and again resumes his original form: this, however, they will never make me believe, although they affirm even by oath that they speak true. The Andropha- 106 gians have the wildest manners of all men in the world: they are totally ignorant of the principles of justice: are nomades; and wear a garb similar to the Scythian: their language is singular[202]; and they are the only eaters of human flesh among these tribes. The Melanchlænians all 107 wear black mantles, whence their appellation: they practise the same usages as the Scythians. The Budinians are a 108 great and populous nation: they stain their whole bodies of a deep blue and red[203]. A town built of wood is seen in their country; its name is Gelonus: each side of the wall

---

[199] This epithet does not, one would think, apply to a nation that acted with so much readiness and vigour, when the Scythians applied to them for assistance.

[200] ἀνδροφάγοι ἵπποι. This expression is very common in Plato and Xenophon. Καίτοι σοφὸς τις ἵπποι, "It appears he is a philosopher."— Plat. in Eutyph. quoted by Larcher. —See Viger, p. 358.

[201] See Matt. 538, 1.

[202] See Matt. 612, iii.

[203] This is understood, by some, to be the natural colour of the eyes, hair, and skin: by others it is taken to allude to the substances with which they smeared their bodies.

extends thirty stades, is lofty, and made of wood solely: of the same materials are the houses and temples; for here you find temples of the Hellenic gods, adorned, after the Hellenic fashion, with images, altars, and chapels of wood. In fact, the Gelonians were originally Hellenes: banished from the staples, they settled among the Budinians, and 109 speak a language partly Scythian and partly Hellenic. The Budinians have not the same language as the Gelonians; neither do they follow the same mode of life: these people, being aboriginals, are nomades: they are the only inhabitants of that region who eat vermin; while the Gelonians plough the ground, eat corn, have gardens, and are quite different in features and complexion: the Budinians, however, are erroneously denominated by the Hellenes as Gelonians. Their whole country is abundantly studded with trees of all sorts: in the thickest of the forests is found a spacious and wide lake, and in its vicinity a marsh surrounded with reeds. In this place they catch otters, beavers, and other animals with square snouts: their skins are sewed on the hem of the cassocks: their testicles are used in medicine, for the cure of uterine diseases.

110 Concerning the Sauromatæ the following account is given. After the battle between the Hellenes and the Amazons,— the Scythians give to the Amazons the name Oirpata, a word that may be translated 'manslayer,' for *oir* is the Scythian for *man*, and *pata* for *to slay*,—after that battle, as the report goes, the Hellenes, having won the day on the Thermodon, sailed away with three ship-loads of Amazons, whom they had succeeded in capturing alive: when at sea, the women fell on the men, and massacred them all: but the Amazons, wholly ignorant of the art of navigation, not knowing the use of a rudder, or a sail, or an oar, were borne at the will of wind and wave, after they had destroyed their conquerors: they reached, at last, Cremni on the Lake Mæotis, a town belonging to the country of the free Scythians. Here the Amazons landed from their vessels, and, advancing into the inhabited parts, took the first stud of horses they fell in with, mounted on their backs, and pillaged the Scythian posses- 111 sions. The Scythians knew not what to make of this event: they were not acquainted with their language, their costume, or their nation, and were in amazement whence they came. They fancied the Amazons were young men of one and the same age[204], and consequently prepared to give them battle.

---

[204] That is to say, I think, "taking them to belong to a race of men of a diminutive stature:" if the Amazons had been mixed with men, they might have guessed their sex, from the inferiority of their stature.

After the battle, the Scythians got possession of the slain, and so ascertained their sex. They debated this circumstance; and resolved to refrain from thus killing them, and to send out their young men to them, amounting to the same number as the women themselves. The young men were to go, and encamp opposite the Amazons, and do as they would do: if the women pursued them, they were not to fight, but to run away; and, when they ceased, were again to come up, and pitch their camp near the enemy. This resolution was adopted by the Scythians for the purpose of procuring children from the Amazons. The youths sent on 112 this mission acted according to order. When the Amazons saw that the young men had not come to hurt them [205], they did not disturb them: meanwhile, day by day the two camps approached nearer and nearer; the youths, as well as the Amazons, had nothing but their arms and horses, but lived alike on the chase and pillage. The Amazons were wont 113 about noon to scatter themselves away from the camp in parties of one or two, in order to satisfy the wants of nature: the Scythians, observing this, did the same; when one of the young men crept up to an Amazon parted from the rest: the girl, far from driving the youth away, granted her favours to him; but she did not speak, for the two parties could not make themselves mutually understand by word: she made known to him, however, by signs with her hand, that he should come the next day to the same spot with a companion; making sign, they should be two, and she would bring a companion. On his return to his comrades, the young man communicated to them what had occurred: on the day following, he went with a friend to the rendezvous, and there found the Amazon of the day before, waiting with another [206] woman. As soon as the rest of the young men were apprised of this, they also sought the good graces [207] of the other Amazons. Soon after, they united their camps, 114 and lived together: each man taking to wife her with whom he had first conversed. The men were not able to learn the language of their wives, but the women soon attained that of their husbands. When they were able to understand one another, the men said to the Amazons: "We have fathers " and mothers; we have property: let us therefore no longer

---

Larcher and Coray prove satisfactorily that ἁλικία signifies stature.

[205] See Matt. 585, β, second parag.

[206] See Matt. 472, 12.

[207] ἱππιλώσαντε, lit. "tamed to themselves." This word comes from κρί-λος, a 'ram.' As that animal was accustomed to the shepherd's hand, and was tame, κρίλος came to be used adjectively, to signify any tame animal. Hence the verb κτιλόω.— *Larcher.*

"lead this sort of life: let us join with the Scythians in common, and live with them. We will have no other wives than you." To this proposal the women replied: "We should not be able to live with your women; for their customs and ours are at direct variance: we shoot with the bow, hurl the lance, and ride the horse; we have never learned women's arts: your women, on the other hand, never practise the exercises we allude to; they attend to the works of women, stay under the tilts of their vehicles, and go not to the chace, or any where else. It is impossible for us, therefore, to agree with them. But if you desire to have us for your wives, and to prove your love of justice, go to your parents; claim your share of the patrimonial possessions[208]: then return, and let us live 115 by ourselves." The young men assented to this advice, and acted accordingly: having received the share of their patrimony, they came back to the Amazons; and the women addressed them thus: "Both fear and decency[209] forbid us to sojourn in this country: in the first place, we have bereaved you of your fathers: in the second place, we have committed many ravages on your lands. If you vouchsafe to take us as wives, do with us what we now advise: come, let us leave this land, cross the Tanaïs, and there 116 dwell." To this the young men acceded also: they crossed the Tanaïs; and advancing three days east from the Tanaïs, and three days north from Lake Mæotis, arrived in the country where they still reside, and there settled: from that day, the Sauromatan women have preserved their original mode of life; they go a hunting on horseback, with or without their husbands; join in war; and wear the same 117 garb as the men. The Sauromatæ use the Scythian dialect, corrupted[210] in early times by many grammatical incongruities, arising from the superficial manner in which the Amazons learnt that speech. Their institutions in respect of matrimony are these: no virgin is allowed to marry until she have killed one of her male enemies: some of the women, however, die of old age before they marry, not being able to fulfil the condition.

118 The Scythian ambassadors, introduced[211] to the assembled

---

[208] τῶν κτημάτων τὸ ἐπιβάλλον.—Understand μέρος.

[209] φόβος is a sudden fright, δέος the permanent dread of some future evil. See Amm. in the Append. to Scap. Lex.

[210] σολοικίζοντες αὐτῇ, lit. "speaking it corruptly, making solecisms in it."

[211] The Historian now resumes the thread of the history; which he had interrupted at c. 103, to give a slight description of the nations adjoining the Scythians.

princes of the before-mentioned nations, informed them, that the Persian king, after reducing the whole of the other continent, had laid a bridge over the neck of the Bosphorus, crossed into this continent, and, having subdued the Thracians, was now bridging the Ister, with the intention of subjecting to his dominions all these countries: "By no means, "therefore," said they, "do you sit aloof, and witness our "destruction; but, with common accord, let us unite to oppose "the invader. If you refuse to act, as we suggest, and we "needs must bend, either we shall forsake our country, or, "remaining, submit to Persian terms: for what would you "have us to do[212], if you withhold assistance? The calamity "will fall not a whit lighter on you than us; for the Persian "sovereign has arrived with the intention of enthralling "us all, and without exception; nor will he be content to "hold us in subjection, and respect you. We can produce "undoubted proof of the truth of what we now say: if the "Persian leader had directed his arms against us alone, he "would have refrained from touching any others, and would "have marched straight across their country into ours; to "shew to all, that his expedition had for its object the "Scythians, and none others: no sooner, however, had he "crossed over to this continent, than he begins to quell all "he falls in with, and accordingly has reduced under his "sway the Thracians, and more particularly our neighbours, "the Getæ." When the Scythian ambassadors had finished [119] their representations, the kings, who had come from the various nations, debated the question. Opinions were divided: the Gelonian, Budinian, and Sauromatian sovereigns, of common accord, promised assistance to the Scythians; but the Agathyrsian, Neurian, Androphagian, Melanchlæmian, and Taurian princes, returned the following answer to the Scythians. "Had you not yourselves been the "aggressors on the Persians, and the first to begin war, and "should you have made the same request as you now make, "your application would not only have appeared to us "reasonable, but we would have listened to it, and would "have joined our exertions to yours[213]. But now you have, "unauthorized by us, invaded the country of those people; "you have ruled over the Persians, so long a time as their "god permitted; and they, roused by the same god, are "preparing to give you like for like. But, on our part, we

---

[212] τί γὰρ πάθωμεν; See Matt. 515, 2. Schweighæuser, in the Lex. Herod. corrects the Latin version which he had given.
[213] ταυτὰ ἂν ὑμῖν ἐσχάνομεν, lit. "we would do the same as you."—

" have never injured, in any manner, these men; nor do we
" intend to try the experiment for the first time now. If,
" however, the Persian should come against our country, and
" commence deeds of injustice, we certainly will not bend to
" the yoke: until we see this come to pass, we will stay at
" home; for we cannot think the Persians will ever march
" against us, but against such only as have been guilty of
" previous atrocities to them."

120 When intelligence of this reached the Scythians, they resolved not to give battle, or make any open attack, as they had no allies to support them; but determined to recede gradually, and draw back, filling in the wells they passed by, disturbing the springs, and destroying the grass on the ground: for this purpose, they divided their forces into two battalions. It was agreed that the Sauromatians should be joined to that which composed the kingdom [214] of Scopasis: and if the Persian should direct his steps towards the domains of Scopasis, this detachment was to retire quietly, retreating straight to the Tanaïs river, along the Palus Mæotis: and when the enemy should wheel back on his steps, they were to follow, and pursue, in the rear. This, which was one of the divisions of the Scythian empire [215], lay on the road above described: the grand division, consisting of two kingdoms, one ruled by Idanthyrsus, the other by Taxacis, which were to be united in one battalion, was increased by the accession of the Budinians and Gelonians, and appointed to keep one day's march a-head of the Persians, retreat quietly, and act as had been arranged in council: they were accordingly to retire straight to the states of those powers who had refused support to the Scythians, in order that they also should be entangled in war, and, however unwilling they might be to share in the war against the Persians, be driven to it in spite of themselves. Both divisions were afterwards to return home, and attack the invaders, if it appeared meet

121 to the council. The Scythians having come to the above resolutions, went to meet Darius's host, sending in the van their best horsemen, as out-riders. In respect of the waggons which their children and women lived in, and all their herds, excepting so much as was necessary for their own subsistence, and consequently was left behind, the whole,

---

[214] τὴν μίαν τῶν μοιρῶν. This does not relate to one of the bodies into which the whole forces of the Scythians were divided, but to one portion of the Royal Scythians: that tribe, it appears, consisted of three portions, one commanded by Scopasis, one by Idanthyrsus, and one by Taxacis.

[215] τῆς βασιληίης, regni, id est, regiorum Scytharum. *Schweig.*

both of the waggons as well as of the cattle, were sent away, with orders to proceed to the north.

The outriders came up with the Persians about the third 122 day's march from the Ister: having thus ascertained the exact position of the enemy, the Scythians advanced a day's march ahead, encamped, and destroyed all the produce of the land: as soon as the Persians caught a glimpse of the Scythian horse, they followed on the steps of their retiring opponents. After this, the Scythians[216], directing their retreat straight to the territory of Scopasis, the Persians followed on in pursuit eastward, and to the Tanaïs: the retiring party crossed the Tanaïs; the Persians followed their example, and pursued: having passed through the country of the Sauromatians, they reached that of the Budinians. During all the time, accordingly, that the Persians were 123 marching over Scythia and Sauromatia, they found nothing to pillage, the country being dry and sterile; but when they came to the territory of the Budinians, and fell upon the wooden town, which the citizens had emptied of all its contents and forsaken, they set it on fire; and having committed this outrage, they continued to follow on the footsteps of the Scythians. At last, passing through this country, they came to the desert, which is unoccupied by any inhabitants, and extends seven days' journey above the Budinian frontier. Beyond this desert reside the Thyssagetans; from whose quarters four great rivers rise, and, flowing through the lands of the Mæotians, fall into the Lake Mæotis: their names are, the Lycus, the Oarus, the Tanaïs, the Syrgis. When therefore Darius had reached the desert, he ceased the 124 pursuit, and halted his army on the bank of the Oarus. Having so done, he began erecting eight extensive forts, at equal distances from one another, on a line extending about sixty stades, the ruins of which were in existence to my day. During the time he was thus employed, the Scythians, who had been the object of his pursuit, made a circuit round the upper parts of the desert, and returned home: these having completely vanished, and no longer making their appearance, Darius accordingly left his castles half finished, and directed his march to the west, feeling convinced that the Scythians he had been pursuing constituted the whole nation, and had fled to the west.

Leading on his forces at a quick march, he met, on his re- 125 turn into Scythia, with the battalion, consisting of two united portions of the Scythian empire; and directly commenced

---

[216] Those commanded by Scopasis.

pursuit, the enemy keeping at a distance of one day's march ahead. The Scythians—for Darius did not choose to relax the pursuit—followed the orders given in council, and took their route into the countries which had refused them support; and first to the land of the Melanchlænians: both Scythians and Persians harassed this country. The Scythians next led the way into the territories of the Androphagians: after harassing these also, they removed to Neuris, where they acted in the same manner, and were proceeding in their flight to the Agathyrsians; but these latter, who had witnessed the dismay and flight of the bordering nations, sent a herald to the Scythians, previously to any attempt on their part, to warn them from crossing their frontier; informing them, that if they were determined to force an entrance, they must first meet the Agathyrsians on the field of battle. The Agathyrsians, having made known their intentions, immediately proceeded to the defence of their frontier, for the purpose of resisting the invaders. The Melanchlænians, Androphagians, and Neuri, offered no resistance to the irruptions either of the Scythians or Persians: unmindful of their former threats, they fled, in great dismay, towards the northern desert; but the Scythians, warned off by the Agathyrsians, gave up all intentions of invading that country [217], and enticed the Persians out of Neuris, on their own lands.

126 This mode of warfare having lasted a considerable time, and not being likely to cease, Darius sent a horseman over to the Scythian king Idanthyrsus, with orders to address him in these words: "Strange man that you are! wherefore do you continue thus to retire from before me, when you have the choice of two modes of proceeding [218]? If you fancy yourself equal to resist my power, stand your ground, cease to wander, and join battle with me [219]. If, on the other hand, you confess yourself inferior, then cease thus to run away; and bring to your lord and master the boon of earth and water, and come to terms with me."

127 To this message, Idanthyrsus sent back the following reply: "Things are with me thus, Persian. I have never yet fled before man through fear, nor do I now flee before you: neither am I doing any otherwise than I am wont to do in times of peace. Why I do not give you battle forthwith, I

---

[217] Construction: οἱ δὲ Σκύθαι οὐκίτι ἀνεπλέοντο ἐς τοὺς Ἀγαθύρσους ἀντίπαντας. [218] ἴξῃς from ἴκειν. See Matt. Gr. Gram. 564. [219] μάχεσθαι, the infinitive for imperative. See Matt. 544. See likewise Bishop Blomfield's remark, p. xlviii. of the first volume of Matt. Gr. Gram.

"will now explain to you. We possess no cities; we have no crops growing on the land, for which we dread pillage or devastation, and therefore should hasten to engage in conflict with you. Yet, if you must immediately proceed to extremes, we have our paternal tombs; come on: find out where they lie, and attempt to disturb them: and then you may discover whether we will fight for our tombs or not. Ere this, unless reason prompt us, we will not engage in battle with you. Thus much have I to say in answer to your challenge. I consider Jove my progenitor, and Vesta, the queen of the Scythians, to be my sovereign rulers, and them alone. Instead of the boon of earth and water, I will send you such as it more behoves to present you with: in reply to your boast, that you are my lord and master, I bid you weep."—'I bid to weep,' is a Scythian form of speech[220]. Such therefore was the answer the herald carried back to Darius.

The kings of Scythia were filled with indignation, at hearing the word 'slavery;' and accordingly sent the detachment under the command of Scopasis, to which the Sauromatians were adjoined, to hold a conference with the Ionians stationed as a watch on the bridge over the Ister: they resolved that the rest[221] of the Scythian forces should no longer entice the Persians about the country, but should fall upon them whenever they were taking their meals[222]: observing, therefore, at what hours the Persian soldiers ate their victuals, these orders the Scythians executed. The Scythian cavalry invariably repulsed that of the Persians; but the horsemen, falling back on the infantry in their flight, were supported by the foot-soldiers; and the Scythians, after driving back the cavalry, were obliged to turn back, for fear of the infantry. The Scythians, however, repeated their onsets at night.—I cannot pass under silence a very extraordinary occurrence, that was very favourable to the Persians, and equally baneful to the Scythians, in their attacks on the picquets of Darius's camp: it was, the effect of the braying of the Persian asses, and the shape of the mules; for Scythia produces no asses nor mules, as was before observed; and indeed, throughout the whole of Scythia, not one of

---

[220] τοῦτό ἐστι ἡ ἀπὸ Σκυθῶν ῥῆσις: that is to say, a form of speech used by the Scythians, and from them copied by the Grecians. See *Schweig. Not.* Consult likewise Matt. 279.

[221] That is to say, the main body of the army commanded by Idanthyrsus and Taxacis.

[222] I have followed Schweighæuser's explanation: see his note. Larcher translates " toutes les fois qu'ils prendraient leurs repas —*whenever they should be at their meals.*"

those animals is to be seen, by reason of the cold. The braying of the asses, accordingly, startled the Scythian horses. It frequently happened, that at the moment they were charging the Persian line, the noise of the asses was heard by the horses; which immediately pricked up their ears, and started back, affrighted and amazed, at a sound which they then heard, for the first time, from animals whose form was unknown to them. This circumstance, accordingly, had some slight influence in the skirmishes between the Persians and Scythians [223].

130 The Scythians, seeing that the Persians were in great distress, adopted the following measures to induce the enemy to remain a longer time in Scythia; and, though already reduced to the greatest want of all necessaries, be exposed to still greater misery and calamity. They left behind some of their herds [224] with the herdsmen, and retired themselves to other quarters: the Persians fell upon the herds, took possession of them, and exulted in their prize.

131 This occurred several times; but at last Darius was reduced to the extreme of want: the Scythian kings, informed of this, despatched a herald with gifts to Darius—a bird, a mouse, and a frog, with five arrows. The Persians inquired of the bearer what was the meaning of the presents. This man stated, that he was commissioned only to present the gifts, then return immediately; and advised the Persians, if they were prudent men, to find out what the gift meant. The Per-

132 sians, in consequence, held council on the subject. Darius's opinion was, accordingly, that the Scythians thus delivered themselves up to him, by presenting earth and water: explaining the mouse to be a figure for the earth, in which he lives, feeding on the same food as man [225]; while the frog is

---

[223] Construction: (οἱ Πέρσαι) ἐφέροντο ταῦτα ἐπὶ σμικρόν τι τοῦ πολέμου, taking φέρεσθαι in the sense of *sibi ferre*, ' to gain,' ' to receive:' " By this the Persians gained some small advantage in the war." *Schweig. Lex. Herod.* voc. φέρω, 6.

[224] The intention of the Scythians was, to make the Persians prolong their stay in Scythia. Had they kept their flocks completely without the reach of the invaders, the Persians, not finding any thing whatever in the country, would have immediately retreated, to avoid perishing by hunger. The Scythians, consequently, had recourse to this stratagem: they abandoned a small part of their flocks; for the genitive, τῶν προβάτων τῶν σφετέρων, is a genitive of partition (Matt. 356.) The Persians, exalted by this success, ἐπηρμένοι τῇ εὐπραγίῃ, expected still greater, and hoped to find at last the place where the Scythians had secreted all their flocks. This slight advantage was no effectual relief to the famine that raged in the Persian camp, but made them conceive hopes of soon enjoying abundance. This hope induced them to prolong their stay; and the more that was prolonged, the more their misery was increased, according to the desire of the Scythians. *Larcher.*

[225] Matt. 386, 1.

begotten in the water; and the bird was very like to the horse: lastly, the arrows were a type, signifying that the Scythians surrendered their power. Gobryas, one of the seven conspirators against the Magus, gave a very different interpretation: "Persians," said he, explaining the meaning of the gifts, "unless like birds you fly in the air, or like "mice hide yourselves in the earth, or like frogs leap in the "marshes, you will never get back to your homes, but will "be pierced by those shafts." Such were the explanations of the Persians with respect to the signification of the gifts.

The Scythian detachment[227] which had before been appointed to guard the country about the Lake Mæotis, and now was sent down to the Ister to confer with the Ionians, having arrived at the bridge, addressed the Ionians thus: "Men of Ionia, we have come the bearers of freedom to "you, that is to say, if you listen to us. We are told that "Darius enjoined you to keep guard on the bridge for sixty "days only; and in case of his not appearing in that in- "terval of time, permitted you to return to your homes. "Now, therefore, we advise you to do as we will tell you; so "you will subject yourselves to no blame, either on the part "of Darius or of us Scythians: now that you have waited the "stipulated days, return to your own country." The Ionians agreed to do so, and accordingly the Scythians immediately marched back.

After the presentation of the gifts to Darius, the Scythian forces[228], exclusive of the above detachment, drew up foot and horse, as if about to engage battle with the Persians. In the midway between the Scythian line and that of their enemies, a hare started, and ran along: all the Scythian soldiers, as soon as they saw the game, joined in the pursuit: all the men, in confusion, shouting vehemently, Darius inquired the cause of the uproar among his adversaries; and being informed that the Scythians were pursuing a hare, he observed to those with whom he was wont to converse on other subjects: "These men appear to me to have a great "contempt for us: I am convinced now that what Gobryas "said about the Scythian presents was correct: as mat- "ters[229], therefore, seem at present, even to myself, to "stand as he said, we are in great need of some wise counsel, "how we may secure a safe retreat back to whence we

---

[227] ἡ ἣ Σ. μία μοίρα, the body commanded by Scopasis.

[228] That is to say, the two bodies under the command of Idanthyrsus and Taxacis.

[229] Lit. "As, therefore, matters appear to me also to stand thus."

"came." At this, Gobryas spoke: "My liege," said he, "I knew previously, by report, nothing but a little about the poverty of this people: having come so far, I am wiser than I was, and I see them laughing at us. I think, therefore, now, that at nightfall we ought to kindle the fires, as we have always hitherto done, practise some deceit on the soldiers who are, through weakness, unfit for laborious exertions, and persuade them to remain in the camp: we ought also to tether all the asses, and depart, ere the Scythians march direct to the Ister, and break up the bridge, or the Ionians adopt a resolution likely to bring destruction upon us all." Such was the advice of Gobryas. And as soon as night came, Darius acted accordingly: the sick men, and those of whom the loss would be of the least account, he left on the spot in the camp; and, having tied up all the asses, marched away. The asses were left for the purpose of making a noise: the men were left really on account of weakness, but under pretence that Darius himself, with the healthy troops, intended to make an attack on the Scythians, and that they were in the mean time to keep a watch over the camp. Having thus persuaded the men he left behind, and lighted fires, Darius marched with all despatch towards the Ister. The asses, deprived of company, accordingly made more noise than usual: the Scythians heard that, and fancied the Persians were still in their old position. At the dawn of day, the men left behind, convinced that they had been betrayed by Darius, stretched out their hands to the Scythians, and told them what had occurred: as soon as they received this intelligence, the two combined divisions, and the detached division[220] of the Scythians, together with the Budinians, Gelonians, and Sauromatians, united in a body, and pursued the Persians by the direct road to the Ister. But, as the Persian army consisted, for the most part, of infantry, and was unacquainted with the roads, which are not cut out in that country; while the Scythian army was composed of cavalry, and well aware of the short cuts on the way; the two parties missed one another, and the Scythians outstripped a considerable time the Persians in arriving at the bridge. Informed that the Persians had not yet arrived, they hailed the Ionians that were on board: "Men of Ionia," said they, "your appointed days have elapsed[221]; you cer-

---

[220] Lit. "The two portions of the Scythians and the one:" that is to say, the bodies commanded by Scopasis, Idanthyrsus, and Taxacis, had united into one army.

[221] αἱ ἡμέραι ὑμῖν τοῦ ἀριθμοῦ διοίχωνται, by enallage for ὁ τῶν ἡμερῶν ἀριθμὸς διοίχεται. Schweig. Lex. Herod.

"tainly do not right in staying any longer. If, however,
"until now you have been afraid, break up immediately the
"passage across, and, glad to obtain your freedom, away,
"and thank the gods and the Scythians. As for your
"former lord and master, we are going to handle him in
"such a manner, that he shall never again levy war against
"any nation."

In consequence of these summons, the Ionians held council. The opinion of Miltiades the Athenian, who was the commander-in-chief and governor of the Hellespontines residing on the Chersonesus, was, to take the advice of the Scythians, and deliver Ionia from thraldom. Histiæus the Milesian, in opposition to this, observed: ." Although we now "each of us enjoy the power over our respective states by "the indulgence of Darius, if the supremacy of Darius be "abolished, I myself will no longer be able to hold my own "sceptre, nor will any one else[232]; every one of the states "will prefer a democracy to an usurped dominion." Histiæus having broached this opinion, all who had first been of the side of Miltiades went over to that of Histiæus. The voters at this meeting[233], each high in esteem with the king, were, the tyrants from the Hellespont; Daphnis of Abydos, Hippocles of Lampsacus, Herophantos of Parium, Metrodorus of Proconnesus, Aristagoras of Cyzicus, Ariston of Byzantium. Those from Ionia were, Strattis of Chios, Æaces of Samos, Laodamas of Phocæa, and Histiæus of Miletus, whose proposal was opposed to that of Miltiades. The only person of rank on the part of the Æolians, present at this assembly, was Aristagoras of Cyma[234].

The above personages, accordingly approving the advice of Histiæus, resolved moreover to act and speak in this manner[235]; to break up the bridge on the Scythian side of the river, to about the distance of a bow-shot, in order that, although they did nothing, they might appear very active, and so the Scythians would not think of forcing a passage

---

[232] One might have expected οὔτε ἄλλος οὐδεὶς οὐδαμῶν: instead of which, the author has given οὔτε ἄλλον οὐδένα οὐδαμῶν, as if the preceding words had been οὔτε αὐτὸς οἷόν τε εἶναι, governed by ἔλεγε. See Wess. Not.

[233] οἱ διαφέροντες τε ἐὰν ψῆφον, who voted. Διαφέρω is here taken for φέρω, the preposition adding nothing to the signification of the simple verb. Larcher.

[234] All these petty princes had given shackles to their country, and were upheld in their usurpations merely by the means of the Persians, who had good reasons to prefer a despotic form of government to a democracy.— It was, therefore, neither generosity on their part, nor commiseration for the misfortunes of the Persians, that dictated their resolution, but rather ambition. Larcher.

[235] Lit. "To add the following works and words besides that, πρὸς ταύτῃ, i. e. πρὸς τῇ Ἱστιαίου γνώμῃ.

across the Ister by the bridge. After they had broken up the bridge on the Scythian side, they agreed to say, they would do all that the Scythians pleased. This having been done, Histiæus, in the name of all, spoke thus: "Scythians, "you have come to us seasonably, and have brought[236] us "good counsel. You have put us in the right road, and we "will exert ourselves to satisfy you[237]. For, as you see, we "are breaking up the bridge, and will work with the greatest "ardour to secure our liberty. While we are breaking up "the bridge, you have a good opportunity to go after the "Persians, find where they are, and wreak on them that "vengeance which they deserve for their treatment of us 140 "and of yourselves." The Scythians, trusting once more to the sincerity of the Ionians, wheeled back in search of the Persians, but failed completely in taking the same road as the enemy. The Scythians were indebted to themselves for this, having destroyed the pastures for the horses, and filled in the wells and springs: had they refrained from doing that, they might have easily found the Persians. In the present instance, they were deceived in what they had determined upon as the best mode of proceeding. The Scythians, accordingly, taking that road on which fodder and water might be found for the horses, kept a look out for the enemy, fancying that he would make his retreat over the same tract: but the Persians proceeded back, carefully following the footsteps of their former progress[238]; and thus with some difficulty reached the ferry across the Ister. They arrived in the night, and, finding the bridge broken up[239], were in great consternation, thinking that the Ionians had 141 left. But there was in the train of Darius an Egyptian, whose voice was the most sonorous ever heard: this man stood on the bank of the Ister, and, by the command of Darius, hailed Histiæus of Miletus. Histiæus heard the summons at the first call, and, bringing all the ships, completed 142 the float for the passage of the army. The Persians, there-

---

[235] Matt. 557.

[237] τά τε ἀπ' ὑμέων ἡμῖν χρηστῶς ἰδοῦσαι, καὶ τὰ ἀπ' ἡμέων ἐς ὑμέας ἐπιτηδέως ὑπηρετέεται. "Your actions, conduct, quæ a vobis proficiscuntur, are directed to our advantage, ea benigne nobis administrantur, reguntur, and our actions, quæ a nobis proficiscuntur, carefully lend assistance to you."

[238] That is to say, they retreated by the same way they had commenced their invasion of Scythia.

[239] See Matt. 382, 4. obs. This grammarian accounts for the use of the genitive γεφύρης, instead of the dative, usually governed by ἐντυγχάνειν, by supposing that the compound is put for the simple verb, τυγχάνειν, which, every one knows, takes the genitive. Schweighæuser, regarding such an enallage as a poetical licence, not used by prose writers, proposes to take λελυμένης τῆς γεφύρης as a genitive absolute, and understand τῷ οἴκῳ after ἐντυχόντες.

fore, in this manner made their escape: but the Scythians, in their search, again missed the Persians. And now the Scythians consider the Ionians, if regarded as freemen, as the most dastardly and effeminate of all mankind; but if, on the other hand, they are looked upon as slaves, they hold them to be the most cringing thralls of their lord, and the least inclined to run away.

Darius, passing through the country of the Thracians, 143 arrived at Sestos in the Chersonesus; whence he crossed on shipboard into Asia, leaving the Persian Megabazus commander-in-chief in Europe. Darius once paid a great honour to this general, by an observation which he made in the presence of the Persians. Darius was about to eat some pomegranates: as soon as he had broken open the first, he was asked by his brother Artabanus, what the king could wish for in such abundance as the kernels of that pomegranate. To which Darius replied, that he would prefer the possession of an equal number of Megabazuses to having the dominion over Hellas. Such was the compliment the king paid to his general. At the time we are now speaking of, he left him behind as commander-in-chief, with an army of eighty thousand men. This same Megabazus left an 144 everlasting memorial of himself to the Hellespontines, by making this observation. When at Byzantium, he was informed that seventeen years had elapsed between the settlement of the Chalcedonians and the foundation of Byzantium: Megabazus, hearing this, remarked, "At that time the "Chalcedonians must have been blind; since, having the "choice of the better situation, they had taken the worst[240], "which could only be accounted for in consequence of blind- "ness." Megabazus, thus appointed to the command of the troops stationed in the Hellespontine territory, reduced all to the Medic rule[241].

---

[240] Megabazus alluded probably to the disadvantages of the situation for trade, the current flowing out of the Bosphorus into the Propontis rendering it extremely difficult of access to ships of any burthen. Otherwise, a more magnificent situation for a city than that of Chalcedon, opposite to Constantinople, could hardly be found in the world.

[241] A recapitulation of the principal events in this unsuccessful expedition of the great king may be of some use to the reader. Darius builds a bridge of boats across the Bosphorus, somewhere between Byzantium (Constantinople) and the mouth of the Euxine (Black Sea): he marches his army into Europe, and despatches the vessels which had composed his floating bridge up the Bosphorus and Euxine, to the Ister (Danube): meanwhile the Persian army advances by land towards the Ister, reducing the different tribes they meet with to the dominion of the Medes. A floating bridge is thrown by the Ionians across the Ister, and Darius passes into Scythia. During the approach of the invaders, the Scythians had made preparations for their defence: their main body is stationed somewhere in

145 At this time, another important expedition was undertaken against Libya; the motive of which I am about to describe, prefacing the following observations. The children's children of the Argo's crew, driven out of Lemnos by the Pelasgians, who had violated the women of Brauron [242], belonging to the Athenians, sailed away for Lacedæmon; and, seating themselves on Mount Taÿgetus, kindled fire. The Lacedæmonians, seeing this, sent a messenger, to inquire who they were, and whence they came: their answer to the questions put by the messenger was this; "that "they were Minyans, sons of the heroes that had manned "the Argo; who, touching at Lemnos, had given rise to "their generation." The Lacedæmonians, hearing this account of the descent of the Minyans, sent to them a second time, and asked what motive had urged them to come to Lacedæmon, and to kindle fire: they explained, that they had been driven away by the Pelasgians, and had come over to their fathers: they requested likewise to be admitted among the Spartan citizens, to participate in civic honours [243], and to receive allotments of land. The Lacedæmonians decided to admit the Minyans on the terms that the exiles themselves proposed: their chief motive for acting in this manner was, the share that the Tyndarides had taken in the navigation of the Argo. They received the Minyans, gave them allotments of ground, and drafted them into the tribes: the Minyans forthwith contracted marriages, and gave to others the wives they had brought from Lemnos.

the north of their territory, and their cattle, women, and moveables, are sent still further northward: a detachment marches down to the Ister. The Persians, descrying this detachment, fancy they have before them the whole of the Scythian army, and pursue them vigorously: the Scythians, however, retire, destroying every thing on their passage along the shores of the Euxine and Palus Mæotis: the pursued, as well as their pursuers, cross the Tanaïs, and, after marching through the country of the Sauromatæ and Budini, come to a desert, where the Scythians, wheeling round the higher parts of the country, return into Scythia, and join themselves to the main body. Darius, who (although the Historian does not mention the circumstance) probably supposed that the Scythians had taken their flight to the eastward, builds several forts on the river Oarus, with the intention, it may be conceived, of hindering the inhabitants from returning to their territory: informed of his mistake, he turns to the right about, and, for the first time, descries the main body of the Scythians, who, in order to harass the Persians by continual marches and want, retreat before them from one frontier country to another. Darius, being at last reduced to total want, abandons a part of his army, and with the rest marches back towards the Ister. The Scythians send a detachment to urge the Ionians to break the bridge across the Danube, and likewise to cut off the retreat of the Persians: in both these objects the Scythians fail, and the Persians thereby are enabled to make their escape.

[242] See vi. 188.

[243] See Matt. 359. obs. 1. Consult, likewise, 585.

After no long interval of time, the Minyans gave proof of 146
their insolence: they claimed a participation in the throne[244],
and committed other nefarious deeds. The Lacedæmonians
accordingly determined to put them all to death; and,
making them prisoners, placed them in confinement. With
the Lacedæmonians, public executions take place by night,
never by day[245]. As they were doomed to death, the wives
of the Mynians, who were citizens and daughters of the
principal men in Sparta, asked permission to be admitted
into the prison, to have an interview with their respective
husbands. No fraud being suspected on the part of these
women, permission was granted them. After they had got
admittance into the gaol, they acted as follows: each woman
gave her own clothes to her husband, and the women took
those of the men. The Minyans, put on the clothes of their
wives, and by these means got out as women, escaped, and
again stationed themselves on the Taÿgetus.

At the time of this occurrence, Theras, the son of Aute- 147
sion, grandson of Tisamenes, great-grandson of Thersander,
who was the son of Polynices, was preparing to depart from
Lacedæmon on a migratory expedition. This Theras was
a Cadmeian, brother to the mother of the sons of Aristode-
mus, called Eurysthenes and Procles: during the minority
of these children, Theras had acted as regent in Sparta.
When his nephew had come to man's estate, and succeeded
to the throne, Theras, indignant to be under the rule of
others when he had tasted himself of power, refused to
remain at Sparta, but proposed to set sail to join his relations who resided in the island now called Thera, the same
known by the name of Callista in earlier times: they were
descendants from Membliarus the son of Pœciles, a Phœnician: for Cadmus the son of Agenor, in his search after
Europa, touched at the island now called Thera, and, whether
pleased with the country or with some other object in view,
left in this island some Phœnicians, and, among others, one
of his kinsmen, Membliarus. These Phœnicians occupied
the island, then called Callista, during eight generations of
men, before the arrival of Theras from Lacedæmon. Theras, 148
therefore, departed for that island, with many emigrants
from various tribes, intending to settle among the inhabitants;
not by any means to drive them away, but regarding

---

[244] See Matt. 360.
[245] The Attics use μεθ᾽ ἡμέραν instead of ἐν ἡμέρᾳ. *Schol. Aristoph.*
quoted by Larcher. See also Matt.
587, c.

them as his near connexions[246]. The Lacedæmonians, persisting in their determination to put to death the Minyans who had escaped from prison and stationed themselves on the Taÿgetus, Theras begged that their lives might be spared, and offered to take them out of the country. The Lacedæmonians acceded to his prayer: he departed with three triconters, to join the descendants of Membliarus. He did not, however, take with him all the Minyans: most of them went over to the Paroreates and Caucones, and, driving them from their country, divided themselves into six tribes; and afterwards founded the following towns, Lepreum, Macistus, Phrixas, Pyrgus, Epium, and Nudium; most of which were destroyed by the Elians, in my days. The island itself took the name of Thera, from its founder. His son refused to accompany him[247] in his voyage; and therefore Theras observed, that he was leaving him a sheep among wolves; and from this remark the name of Oïolycus (sheep-wolf) was given to the young man, an appellation which in time prevailed. Oïolycus had a son called Ægeus; from whom the Ægidæ, a numerous tribe in Sparta, have borrowed the denomination: the children of the men belonging to this tribe not surviving[248], they built, by divine admonition, a temple to the furies of Laïus and Œdipus: after this, their children survived. The same calamity visited[249] their descendants in Thera.

150   Up to this place in the history, accordingly, the Lacedæmonians agree with the people of Thera. For the following events, the latter are our only authority. Grinus the son of Æsanius, a descendant of this Theras, and king of the island of Thera, visited Delphi, to offer an hecatomb on the part of his city. He was followed by several citizens; among others, by Battus the son of Polymnestus, one belonging to the line of Euphemus the Minyan. Grinus the king of Theron, consulting the shrine, was making various inquiries, when the Pythia bade him "found a city in Libya." The prince replied: "I, O sovereign god, am now old, and weighed "down by years[250], to undertake such an enterprise: bid

---

[246] I read συνοικήτων, from συνοικεῖν, in the same sense as in c. 159.

[247] γάρ. Matt. 613.

[248] See the foregoing note.

[249] I have translated from the reading ταὐτὰ ταῦτα συνέβη καὶ ἐν Θήρῃ, κ. τ. λ. In the previous sentence, Schweighæuser reads ὑτίμων, unless the passage is misquoted in his Lex. Herod. According to the reading in Dr. Gaisford's edition, ὑτίμων must be supplied after ταὐτὰ ταῦτα: "the same (probably the same evil) abode by the descendants," &c.

[250] βαρὺς ἀείρεσθαι, too heavy to rise, bent down under the weight of years. Larcher. gravis ad me loco movendum. Schweigh. Lex. Herod. gravis ad majus quidpiam moliendum. Schweig. Vers. Lat.

" some of these younger men to perform the thing :" in so saying, he pointed to Battus: there the matter ended at that time. The Theræans, having returned home, took no further notice of the oracle; and not knowing where Libya lay, were loth to send a colony on so rash an undertaking. During seven years from that year, not a drop of rain fell 151 on Thera: every tree in the island, but one, perished by the drought. When the inhabitants consulted the oracle, the Pythia reproached²⁵¹ them with their neglect of the behest to plant a colony in Libya. As there was no remedy for the evil, they despatched messengers to Crete, who were to inquire whether any of the Cretans, or the foreigners resident there, had ever gone so far as Libya: as they were wandering about the island, they came at last to the town of Itanus; there they became acquainted with a dyer, whose name was Corobius; this man related, that once, driven by the winds, he arrived in Libya, at the island called Platea. The ambassadors enticed this man by a reward, and took him with them to Thera. A few men, sent at first to reconnoitre, set sail from Thera, and, by the guidance of Corobius, made accordingly the said island of Platea; left Corobius there, with provisions for some months; and sailed away with all despatch, to announce the discovery of the island to the Theræans. These persons having been longer absent 152 than was agreed upon, Corobius was at last reduced to the greatest want; but a Samian vessel, commanded by Colæus, bound for Egypt, touched at Platea: the Samians, informed of the whole history of what had occurred, left him provisions enough for twelve months' consumption. Anxious to arrive in Egypt, they bore away from the island, and were driven from their course by a violent and long-lasting gale from the east: they were impelled through the strait bordered by the Pillars of Hercules, and came at last safe to Tartesus, by Divine Providence. In those days, that staple was not yet frequented by the merchants: so that, on their return home, they made the greatest profit by their cargo, of any Hellenes that we know of, saving and excepting however Sostratus son of Laodamas, of Ægina, with whom none other can be put in comparison. These Samians set apart the tithe of their gains, namely, six talents; out of which they caused a wine-bowl of brass to be made, after the fashion of an Argolic vase; around which are seen griffins' heads in quincunx order²⁵²: three brass colossuses, seven cubits

---

²⁵¹ Hesychius explains πρόφις, Iliad. iii. 64, by ὀνείδει. *Coray.*

²⁵² πρόκροσσαι. I have followed Schneider's interpretation, " ringshe-

high, on their knees, served to support this vase, which was dedicated in the temple of Juno. This was the first origin of the close alliance that existed between the Samians on one hand, and the Cyrenæans and Theræans on the other. The

153 Theræans having left Corobius in the island, went back to Thera, and announced that they had founded a settlement in an island contiguous to Libya. The Theræans, hereupon, resolved to send men from each canton, of which there were seven; the brothers drawing lots. They appointed also Battus king and leader of the colony; and fitted out two penteconters for Platea.

154 The above things are related by the Theræans only: in the rest of the history, the Theræans agree with the Cyrenæans; but the latter give a very different account, as far as respects Battus. The Cyrenæans relate as follows. Etearchus was king of Axus, a city of Crete: this prince having lost his wife, was left with a motherless daughter [253], but married a second time: the new bride had no sooner entered her husband's house, than she showed herself to be a true step-mother, by her conduct towards her daughter-in-law Phronima; she did every mischief she could devise to injure the girl; and at last, charging her with unchastity, made her husband believe that such was the case. Etearchus, talked over by his wife, behaved with great cruelty and iniquity to his daughter. There was at that time in Axus, a Theræan merchant, Themison by name: Etearchus entered into a covenant of friendship with this man, and made him swear to serve him, in whatever he might require: the merchant took the oath; and Etearchus then delivered to him his daughter, and requested him to take her away, and throw her into the sea. Themison, indignant at being thus cheated in his oath, dissolved the compact, and acted in the manner following: he took the young lady aboard a ship, and set sail: when he was come into deep water, wishing to acquit himself of his oath to Etearchus, he fastened her with ropes, and let her down into the deep;

155 then, drawing her up again, made for Thera. There Polymnestus, one of the principal citizens of Thera, took Phronima as a concubine: in the course of time, a son was born to him: the child was afflicted with an impediment in his

---

rum stehen, wie κρίσσαι, erhoben Greifenköpfe hervor." *Schneid. Gr. Germ. Lex.* The meaning is not at all clear: Schweighæuser translates, " in quincuncem disposita gryphum capita." Larcher, " des têtes de gryphons, l'une vis-à-vis de l'autre." This same word occurs in vii. 188.

[253] ἐπὶ θυγατρὶ ἀμήτορι. See Matt. 586, γ.

speech[254], and received the name of Battus, as both Cyrenæans and Theræans say: in my opinion, however, it was some other appellation: he must have obtained the name of Battus after his arrival in Libya, both in consequence of his elevation, and of an oracle pronounced to him at Delphi. For the Libyans call a king ' battus[255];' and on that account it was, I surmise, that the Pythia called him so in the Libyan tongue, knowing that he was to be a king in Libya. For, when he had risen to man's estate, he went to Delphi, to consult about his voice; when the following response was given by the Pythia:

" Battus, you are come about your voice. Apollo, my sovereign
" lord, sends you to Libya, abounding in fleeces, to establish
" a colony."

This was the same as if she had said, in Hellenic, " O king, " you have come about your voice." His reply to the oracle was: " Sovereign lord, I came to consult you on my voice: " you command me impossibilities, and bid me colonize " Libya. With what power? With what forces?" This observation drew no further answer from the Pythia; and, as she persisted in the same declaration as at first, Battus abruptly quitted her, and proceeded back to Thera[256]. After 156 this, great calamities visited both Battus himself and the rest of the Theræans. The inhabitants of the island, ignorant of the cause of these visitations, sent to Delphi, to inquire respecting their present sufferings: the Pythia's answer was, they would be more successful if they united with Battus, and founded Cyrene in Libya[257]. Immediately after this, the Theræans sent off Battus with two penteconters: they sailed for Libya, because it was impossible to do otherwise, but returned to Thera. The Theræans, however, beat them off, when they attempted to land, and insisted, that they should sail back to where they came from, and determined they should not be allowed to set foot on the shore. Impelled by necessity, they set sail back again, and settled on an island contiguous to Libya, the name of which, as I before observed, was Platea. It is reported, that this island is equal in size to the present city of Cyrene.

157 Having resided on this island two years, they set sail for Delphi, leaving but one of their number behind: they undertook this voyage in consequence of nothing prospering with them. On their arrival at the shrine, they consulted the oracle; stating, that they had settled in Libya, but had not improved in circumstances since their settlement. The Pythia to this made the following response:

"If you know fleece-rife Libya better than myself, who have
"been there, although you have not, I verily admire your
"sapiency."

When Battus[258] and his people heard this speech, they forthwith sailed back to Platea; for according to the response, the god would not hold them acquitted till the colony had settled in Libya itself. On their return, therefore, they gave up the one that they had left on the island; and established themselves opposite, on the Libyan coast, in a place called Aziris, enclosed on two sides by delightful hills, 158 with a stream on the other. Here they remained six years. In the seventh year, the Libyans promising to take them to a better situation, they were prevailed upon to forsake Aziris. The Libyans conducted them from thence towards the west: they arranged the journey according to the times of the day, so that the Hellenes could not see the finest part of the country, but passed it by in the night: that tract is called Irasa: and brought them to a spring, called that of Apollo, and said: "Hellenes, it behoves you to settle 159 " here; for in this place the sky is open[259]." So long, therefore, as Battus, the founder, was alive, and he reigned forty years, and during the life of Arcesilaus his son, who ruled sixteen years, the Cyrenæans remained at the same standard as they were in the commencement of the settlement. Under the third king, called Battus the Fortunate, the Pythia urged all Hellenes to take ship, and join the Cyrenæan settlers in Libya; as the Cyrenæans invited them to a share of the land. The Pythia's warning was this:

"Whoso to much-prized Libya comes too late to share the land,
"he some day[260] shall repent."

---

[258] See Matt. 271, 2.

[259] This sentence is thus paraphrased by Larcher: "Le ciel y est ouvert pour vous donner les pluies qui rendront vos terres fécondes"—*Here the heavens are open, to give you the showers necessary to fertilize your fields.*—Valckenaer conjectures βεινός, instead of *ὀβρανός*: here the mountain, *i. e.* the land, is pierced; that is to say, here is a spring.

[260] κδικα, Dor. for κοτέ.

A great multitude of people having collected at Cyrene, the neighbouring Libyans, with their king, called Adicran, were deprived by them of a large tract of land: conceiving themselves insolently treated by the Cyrenæans, they sent to Egypt, and gave in their submission to Apries, the Egyptian king. Apries levied a mighty army of Egyptians, which he despatched against Cyrene. But the Cyrenæans drew up in the country of Irasa, at the Thestes spring, and engaged with the Egyptians, and gained the day. The Egyptians, who had never before made trial of the Hellenic prowess, and held that nation in contempt, were totally defeated; and so routed, that very few of them made good their return to Egypt. In consequence of this defeat, the Egyptian people were so exasperated against Apries[261], that they rebelled against him.

Arcesilaus was the son of the said Battus: after his accession, he quarrelled with his brothers, who consequently forsook him, and proceeded to another part of Libya: and having held consultation among themselves, they founded the city still called, to the present day, Barca: while thus occupied, they roused the Libyans against the Cyrenæans. Arcesilaus soon after marched against the supporters of the Libyans, and the rebels themselves: the Libyans, alarmed at his approach, fled over to the eastern Libyans; and Arcesilaus followed in pursuit, until he reached Leucon in Libya, where the Libyans determined to fall upon him: they engaged the Cyrenæans; and beat them with such bloodshed, that seven thousand of the Cyrenæan heavy-armed men fell on the spot. After this blow, Arcesilaus fell sick; and, having taken physic[262], was strangled by his brother Learchus; who, in his turn, was destroyed by the artifice of Arcesilaus's wife, Eryxo. Arcesilaus was succeeded by his son Battus: he was lame, and incapable of using his feet. The Cyrenæans, in consequence of the calamity by which they had been visited, sent to Delphi, and inquired what form of government they ought to adopt, more conducive to their happiness. The Pythia directed them to procure an arbitrator from Mantinea in Arcadia: the Cyrenæans, accordingly, supplicated the citizens of Mantinea to send them such a man: the Mantineans appointed one of the most respected of their townsmen, Demonax. This person proceeded to Cyrene, and examined every thing: in the first

---

[261] Construe together κατὰ ταῦτα ἐπιμεμφόμενοι Ἀπρίῃ. in the same sense as in ii. 161. Αἰγύπτιοι ταῦτα ἐπιμεμφόμενοι.

[262] Or, perhaps, "having fallen sick in consequence of poison which he had swallowed." See *Schweig. Not.*

place, he divided the inhabitants into three tribes, making the first division to consist of Theræans and their neighbours; the second, of Peloponnesians; the third, of all islanders. In the next place, he set apart for Battus certain lands [263], together with the sacerdotal office; and restored to the people all the former possessions of the kings.

162 This arrangement subsisted under the reign of Battus. Under that of his son Arcesilaus, much confusion arose on the subject of office: for Arcesilaus, the son of Battus the Lame and Pheretime, refused to abide by the enactments of Demonax of Mantinea, and reclaimed the privileges possessed by his forefathers: on this account, he excited factious insurrections, and was obliged to take refuge at Samos; while his mother fled to Salamis in Crete. Euelthon at that time held the power in Salamis: he was the same as dedicated a beautiful censer, now deposited in the treasury of the Corinthians at Delphi. Pheretime, at her arrival in Salamis, requested troops, to reinstate herself and her son [264] in Cyrene; but Euelthon would rather give her any thing than troops. Pheretime, at every present she received, said, "This is beautiful; but it would be still more beautiful to "give me the armed men I ask for." At last, Euelthon sent her, as a present, a golden distaff and spindle, together with a stock of wool; and, upon Pheretime's still giving the same answer, the bearer on the part of Euelthon said, "Such are 163 " the gifts we send to ladies; not troops." Arcesilaus meanwhile, staying at Samos, enlisted every body that he could persuade by a promised grant of land: having collected a great number, he proceeded to Delphi, to consult the oracle on his return. The Pithya's response was this: "Under four "Battuses, and four Arcesilauses [265], during four generations "of men, Apollo vouchsafes to you the dominion of Cyrene: "he warns you not to attempt any more; but bids you to be "quiet, and go home: if you should meet with a furnace "full of amphoræ, kindle no fire to bake, but rather spread "them to the breeze of heaven: but should you bake them,

---

[263] τιμένεα. I have given Schweighæuser's translation; who explains the word to mean, "sacred fields, on the income from which the priests subsisted." Wesseling's translation is merely, "certain portions of the land;" in which he is followed by Larcher.

[264] σφίσι, them.

[265] The sovereigns of Cyrene, belonging to the family of Battus, reigned in the following order:—
1. Battus, the founder of the colony. 2. Arcesilaus. 3. Battus, surnamed the Happy. 4. Arcesilaus. 5. Battus, the Lame. 6. Arcesilaus, murdered by his brother. 7. Battus, deposed by the Mantinean arbitrator, Demonax. 8. Arcesilaus, the same to whom this answer was given by the Pythia.

" enter not the water-girt place: if you do, you will die,
" yourself, together with the finest bull[206]." Such was the 164
answer returned by the Pythia to Arcesilaus: he then took
those he had enlisted at Samos, and passed over to Cyrene;
took possession of the power; and, forgetting the oracle he
had received, called to account[207] the fomenters of the com-
motion which had caused his flight. Many of the accused
withdrew wholly from the country: some few were captured
by Arcesilaus, and were sent to Cyprus to be put to death.
These prisoners, accordingly, were conveyed to Cnidos;
where they were rescued by the citizens, and sent to Thera.
Some few more of the Cyrenæans, having taken refuge in
the great tower of Aglomachus, which was private property,
Arcesilaus surrounded the edifice with wood, and set it on
fire. After committing this piece of wickedness[208], perceiving that he had fulfilled the oracle in which the Pythia
warned him from baking the amphoræ in the furnace, withdrew, of his own accord, out of Cyrene, dreading forthcoming
death, and considering Cyrene to be the water-girt place.
He had espoused a relation, the daughter of the king of the
Barcæi, whose name was Alazir: with this prince he took
refuge; but the citizens, assisted by some Cyrenæan fugitives, recognised him in the market-place, and slew not only
Arcesilaus himself, but his father-in-law, Alazir, also. Thus
Arcesilaus therefore, having unwittingly infringed the oracle's
behest, fulfilled his fate.

His mother Pheretime, during the time of Arcesilaus's 165
voluntary sojourn at Barca for the purpose of warding off
the threat of the oracle, held her son's place at Cyrene,
managed the government, and presided over the council.
As soon, however, as she heard of the death of her son at
Barca, she immediately directed her flight to Egypt: for
Arcesilaus had performed some services for Cambyses, the
son of Cyrus; as it was he that delivered Cyrene up to Cambyses, and subjected his states to the payment of tribute.
On her arrival in Egypt, Pheretime seated herself as suppliant of Aryandes, calling upon him to revenge her;
alleging that her son had met with his death in consequence
of his affection for the Medic supremacy[209]. Aryandes 166

---

[206] This prediction of the death of the bull seems, says Wesseling, to hint obscurely at Alazir, the father-in-law of Arcesilaus. See the end of c. 164.
[207] αἰτίην ἔχε τι. See Matt. 411. 4.
[208] ἐπ' ἐξεργασμένοις. See a similar expression, viii. 94. and ix. 77; respecting which, consult Matt. 565, obs.
[209] That is to say, the Persians: the reader will see the confusion of these two terms very frequently in the following Books.

was the governor of Egypt, appointed by Cambyses: some time subsequent to these events, he was executed for his presumption, in attempting to rival Darius. Having been informed, and having seen, that Darius conceived the design of leaving a monument behind him such as had been accomplished by no other sovereign, he took an opportunity of mimicking his liege lord; for which he was richly rewarded. For Darius having purified some gold to the highest degree of fineness, struck coins from it: Aryandes, therefore, as ruler of Egypt, made the same of silver[270]; and to this day the Aryandic is the purest silver coin. Darius, when informed of this, brought another charge against Aryandes, that of rebellion;

167 and put him to death. But at the time we are speaking of, the said Aryandes took pity on Pheretime, and gave her the whole standing forces of Egypt, army and navy; appointing Amasis, a Maraphian, to the command of the land army, and Badres to that of the shipping: this admiral was, by birth, one of the Pasargades. Previously, however, to despatching the forces, Aryandes sent to Barca a herald, to inquire who had murdered Arcesilaus; but the Barcæans, by common accord, took the responsibility on themselves, in a body, having suffered much from the cruelties of the deceased king. When Aryandes heard this, he forthwith gave orders to the army and fleet to depart, taking with them Pheretime. That princess, it appears, was merely a pretence[271]: the expedition was fitted out, in my opinion, for the purpose of effecting the subjection of the Libyans: for the nations of Libya are many and various; few of which were subjects of the great king, while the greater part took no account of Darius[272].

168 The Libyan nations thus lie in their respective situations[273]. Beginning from the frontier of Egypt, the first Libyans one meets with are the Adyrmachidæ, who follow the same customs as most of the Egyptians, but wear the same dress as the other Libyans. The women carry a brass ring on each leg; let their hair grow long[274]; press between the teeth the vermin they catch on their persons, and throw it away: in this respect they are singular among Libyans:

[270] See Matt. 409, b.

[271] πολίμου and ονέλου have been proposed instead of λόγου, either of which gives a better sense than the present reading, ὡς ἐμοὶ δοκέειν, see Matt. 543.

[272] The narrative is here interrupted, to make place for a description of Africa, that is to say, the northern parts: it is resumed in c. 200.

[273] Lit. "The Libyans dwell in this manner."

[274] τὰς κεφαλὰς δὲ κομῶσαι, "suffering the hair to grow long on their heads." κομῶσαι, in the plural with ἑκάστη, see Matt. 301, a.

they are likewise the only Libyans that introduce their girls, who are about to be married, to the king; who, if pleased with the bride, culls the firstlings of her charms. These Adyrmachidæ stretch from Egypt to the lake called Plunos. Adjoining to them are the Giligammæ, occupying the western tract, on to the isle of Aphrodisias. Half-way along the shore lies the island of Platea, which was colonized by the Cyrenæans: inland lies the port Menelaus and Aziris, which the Cyrenæans likewise inhabited. Here commences the growth of the silphium[175], and continues from the island of Platea to the mouth of the Syrtis: the Giligammæ have nearly the same customs as the others. Next to them, on the west, are the Asbystæ, lying above Cyrene, and not extending down to the sea; for the sea-side is occupied by Cyrenæans: they are, of all the Libyans, those that make the greatest use of four-horse chariots: they copy most of the customs of the Cyrenæans. After the Asbystæ follow, on the west, the Auschisæ: these reside above Barca, and extend to the sea, near the Hesperides. About the middle of the country of the Auschisæ are found the Cabales, an inconsiderable nation, which stretches along the sea, near Tacheira, a town in Barcæa: they have the same customs as those resident above Cyrene. On the western border of the Auschisæ come the Nasamones, a numerous race, who in summer forsake their herds, which they leave on the sea-side, and go up to the land called Augila, where they collect dates: the palms that produce that fruit are there seen in vast quantities, all fructiferous. These people give chase to and catch the locusts, dry them in the sun, pound them to dust on which they pour milk, and drink the mixture. Each man has several women, and converses with them promiscuously, after the same manner nearly as the Massagetæ, sticking his staff in the ground. When a Nasamonian, accordingly, first marries, it is the custom for the bride to grant her favours to all the guests, each of whom makes[176] her some present which he has brought from home. The pronouncing of oaths and professing of divination take place according to these forms: in taking an oath, they touch with their hands the tombs of men said to have been the most equitable and best[177], and swear. They prophesy, by going to the tombs

---

[175] The Greek says only "the silphium:" I have added a few words, for the sake of clearness. The sap of this plant was used by the ancients in cookery and medicine. The African or Cyrenæan silphium is the same with the *ferula tingitana*, or *fennel giant* of our gardens; the inspissated juice of which is now called asafœtida.

[176] See Matt. 521.

[177] See Matt. 419, 3; 467, c.

of their progenitors; and, after offering prayers, lie down and sleep; and take for their guide any dream that they may have in their sleep. The pledge of faith between different parties is conducted thus: one party gives the other to drink out of his hand: this form is observed reciprocally: if there is no water at hand, they take up a handful of sand[278], and mutually lick up some.

173 The Psylli are borderers to the Nasamonians: these perished in the following manner. The south wind had dried up their tanks, and the whole of their country, lying within the Syrtis, was wholly reft of water. The Psylli, therefore, unanimously agreed to wage war against the south wind, (I mention this as the account of the Libyans[279],) and, when they reached the desert, a storm of sand from the south poured down upon them: the Psylli thus cut off, the Nasa-
174 monians occupied their territory. Above these, towards the south, in the wild tract, dwell the Garamantes, who avoid society, or conversation with all men: they possess no warlike weapons, and know not even how to defend themselves.

175 The above, therefore, lie above the Nasamonians: westward, along the shore, reside the Macæ: these people dress their heads so as to give them the appearance of wearing a crest; for this purpose, they let the hair on the middle of the head grow long, and shave, close to the skin, the right and left sides: they carry, in war, the skins of ostriches[280] as bucklers. Through their country flows the Cinyps river, which rises on the hill called that of the Graces, and falls into the sea: the hill of the Graces is thickly studded with trees, while no tree whatever is seen in any other quarter of the parts above described: this hill is two hundred stades' distance
176 from the sea. Adjoining to the Macæ are found the Gindanes, among whom every woman wears leathern rings on the calves of her legs: it is said, that from every man she receives, she asks a similar leathern ring. The woman that has the

---

[278] The genitive partitive: see Matt. 356, b.

[279] The wise (and who, in the present day, is not, in his own estimation, wise?) will laugh at the fables which Herodotus tells with so much gravity: it should, however, be recollected, that, in the state the world was in when he wrote his history, the most useful thing he could do for posterity was to give all the accounts he heard from the various people he travelled among. One of those nations, it must be recollected, informed Herodotus, that they had circumnavigated Africa; and it was reserved to Vasco de Gama to prove, by actually doubling the Cape of Good Hope, that that tale, at any rate, was not so false and ridiculous as philosophers asserted.

[280] The στρουθός is any bird, particularly those of the sparrow kind; the στρουθὸς μεγάλη, or κατάγαιος, or Λιβυκὸς, the ostrich; κατάγαιος, because the ostrich, though it has wings, cannot fly.

most of these rings is deemed the best, as being the favourite of most men. The Lotophagians occupy a foreland 177 projecting from the land of the Gindanes into the sea: they live upon the fruit of the lotus-tree, which, in size, is the same as the lentisk, and in sweetness similar to the date: from this fruit the Lotophagians make wine also[281].

Contiguous to the Lotophagians, on the sea, are the 178 Machlyes; who make use of the lotus likewise, but less abundantly than the former people. They stretch along the bank of a large river called the Triton, which discharges its waters into the Lake Tritonis: in that lake lies the island called Phla, and which, it is said, an oracle declared was to be colonized by the Lacedæmonians. The following tale is 179 told. When Jason had built the Argo at the foot of Pelion, he shipped on board a hecatomb[282], and a brass tripod; set sail; and doubled the Peloponnesus, shaping his course to Delphi: and when off Malea, he was assailed by a gale from the north, which drifted him to Libya. Before he came in sight of land, he found himself on the Tritonian sands; and, in the midst of his embarrassment, how he should extricate himself, Triton, we are told, appeared before him, and asked for the boon of the tripod; promising, that he would pilot him through the passage[283], and would bring him out safe and sound. Jason gave credit to his visitor; and, accordingly, Triton shewed him how to direct his course among the quicksands, and placed the tripod in his own temple: then,

---

[281] Mungo Park gives the following description of this lotus, which, as I have before observed, is very different from the plant mentioned in ii. 92.—"It bears small farinaceous berries, of a yellow colour, and delicious taste. The natives convert them into a sort of bread, after pounding them gently in a wooden mortar, until the farinaceous part of the berry is separated from the stone. The stones are afterwards put into a vessel of water, and shaken about, so as to separate the meal which may still adhere to them: this communicates a sweet and agreeable taste to the water, and, with the addition of a little pounded millet, forms a pleasant gruel called *fondi*, which is the common breakfast in many parts of Ludamor, during the months of February and March. This fruit is collected by spreading a cloth upon the ground, and beating the branches with a stick."

Desfontaines, a French botanist, has given a scientific description of the lotus. It is a sort of jujube-tree, *Rhamnus Lotus*. Linnæus had given the specific *lotus* to a plant of the genus *Rhamnus*; but as he had not seen the plant, his description is incorrect. The Rhamnus Lotus is a thorny shrub: its fruit is not unlike that of the cultivated jujube-tree, *Rhamnus* Ziziphus, but it is spherical, and smaller.

[282] It does not appear that the word Hecatomb is to be taken here in its usual sense of "a solemn sacrifice of one hundred oxen, or other animals," but rather of a victim, any thing that is to be offered: the term seems to be used, in the same sense, in o. 50 of this Book.

[283] This is the usual acceptation of the word διεκπλοος, and that in which it is to be taken in the description of the bridge of boats, vii. 36.

seated in the tripod[284], he prophesied, and pointed out to Jason and his followers the whole course of the adventures that were to befal them;—that, " when a descendant of one " of the Argo's crew would carry off the tripod, then " would the Hellenes, fate impelled, found one hundred towns " about the Tritonis lake." The Libyans, informed of this 180 prophecy, hid the tripod. Adjoining these Machlyes are the Auseans: both nations lie around the Tritonis lake, and the Triton river serves as the boundary between the two. The Machlyes let their hair grow on the back of the head: the Auseans let it grow on the forehead. At an annual festival of Minerva, the girls, divided in two parties, fight with stones and clubs; saying, that they conform to the practice of their forefathers, in honour of the native goddess, whom we call Minerva. The girls that die of their wounds are said to have been false virgins. Previous to the cessation of this fight, they perform the following ceremony: they deck the girl who by common consent has behaved the most gallantly, with a Corinthian helmet and the panoply of an Hellene, place her in a chariot, and drive her round the lake. In what manner they dressed the girls before the coming of the Hellenes, I cannot say: I suppose, however, that it was in Egyptian armour; for I know to a certainty that the buckler and helmet were introduced among the Hellenes from Egypt. They assert that Minerva is the daughter of Neptune by the Tritonis lake; and that, irritated at the behaviour of her father, she gave herself to Jupiter; who, accordingly, made her his adopted child. These people have no wives united to them in wedlock: they practise promiscuous concubinage, after the manner of the brute creation: when any woman's child is become adult, he is brought before the assembly of men, held every three months[285]; and whichever the young man may be alleged to resemble, to him the youth is adjudged.

181   The above are the nomade or pastoral Libyans that reside in the vicinity of the sea. Inland, and higher up, lies the wild-beast tract of Libya: above that stretches the sandy brow of the desert, extending from Thebes in Egypt to the Pillars of Hercules. In that sandy brow are found, every ten days' distance, salt in large clumps, on hills: from the top of each hill gushes, in the midst of the salt, a spring of fresh sweet water. Around, dwell people who are the last inhabitants on the verge of the desert, and above the wild-

[284] ἐπιθεσπίσαντα τῷ τρίποδι, i. e. θεσπίσαντα ἐπὶ τῷ τρίποδι.

[285] τρίτου μηνὸς must be taken as equivalent to διὰ τρίτου μηνός.

beast track. The first of these nations thus situated is that of the Ammonians, at ten days' journey from Thebes: they possess a temple of Thebaïc Jupiter: for, as I before observed, the Jupiter of Thebes is likewise represented with a ram's head[286]. These people have in their country another kind of spring-water; which early in the morning is lukewarm; rather cooler at the time that the market is full; but at mid-day becomes quite fresh; and at that time, accordingly, the Ammonians water their gardens. Towards the fall of day, this spring gradually loses its freshness; until, at sunset, the water becomes again lukewarm; then increases gradually in heat till midnight, at which time it boils and bubbles: midnight gone by, it gets cooler until the dawn of day:—this spring takes its name from the sun. After the Ammonians, still ten days further, along the sandy brow, is seen another salt-hill, with a stream of water: the vicinity is inhabited: this country bears the name of Augila; and to this quarter the Nasamonians proceed, for the purpose of gathering dates. Ten days from Augila, farther on, is another hill, with water, and whole groves of fruit-bearing date-trees, as in the other parts of this sandy brow: this place is inhabited by a people called the Garamantes, a powerful and numerous race: they bring up mould on the salt earth, and sow their crops. Here is the shortest cut to the Lotophagi, to whom the distance is thirty days' journey: in this country the kine graze backwards: their horns jut forward, and that is the cause of this retrograde motion; for they are unable to advance forward, as they would stick their horns in the ground: these animals are in no other respect different from other kine, except in this, and their skin, which is very thick and tough[287]. These Garamantes hunt the Ethiopian Troglodytes with their four-horse chariots. The Troglodytes are the swiftest of all men we are acquainted with: they live on serpents, lizards, and such kinds of creeping things.

Ten more days' journey beyond the Garamantes, you meet with another salt-hill and stream of water: the people residing in the environs are called Atarantes: they are, of all men we know of, the only people who have not personal names: the name for the whole nation is Atarantes, but no name is given to any individual: these people curse the sun at his

---

[286] See ii. 54.
[287] It is very evident that τρίψις is taken in a very extraordinary sense: what that sense, however, is, is by no means so clear. Schweighæuser interprets it as signifying, " Firmitas attritui frictionique resistens." Larcher, " Souplesse." Schneider, " Die Härte im Anfühlen—*hardness to the touch.*"

greatest elevation; and add much abusive language, because he burns them and their country. Another ten days' journey, and there is another salt-hill with water, and inhabitants residing around: adjoining the salt-hill[268] rises a mountain, called the Atlas: it is steep, and round on every side; and so lofty, it is said, that it is impossible to discern the summit, which is eternally surrounded with clouds, summer and winter: this mountain, the inhabitants say, is the pillar of heaven, and from it the people take their name, calling themselves Atlantes. The Atlantes are said not to eat any living

185 thing, and never to have dreams. Up to these Atlantes, accordingly, I am enabled to give the names of the nations residing on the sandy brow; but my information extends no further: this brow, however, extends to the Pillars of Hercules, and even outside of them. Every ten days' journey there is a salt-mine, and people residing around it. The houses of all are built of lumps of salt; for these parts of Libya are never visited with rain; indeed, if rain ever fell, salt-walls could not last. The salt dug out of the mines of these countries is white and purple. Above this brow, towards the south and interior parts of Libya[269], the land is without animals, refreshed with no rain, shaded by no trees; and no moisture is found in any part.

186 Thus, therefore, as far as the Lake Tritonis from Egypt, extend the Libyan pastors, men that eat the flesh and drink the milk of their cattle: they never eat of the female kine, nor breed up any pigs; similar in those respects to the Egyptians. The women of Cyrene not only refrain from cow's flesh out of respect for Isis in Egypt, but observe fasts and celebrate feasts in her honour: the women of Barca refrain not only from cow-beef, but also from pig's-flesh. Such is

187 the case, accordingly, with the above parts. But west of Lake Tritonis, the Libyans are no longer pastors; nor do they use the same practice with their children as the nomades do—I cannot say for certain all the nomade Libyans, but many of them do thus: when their children have attained their fourth year, they burn, with an uncombed flock of wool, the veins at the top of the head, and some of them perform the same operation on the veins of the temples. This is done for the following purpose, in order they should never

---

[268] There is no doubt that all this tract abounds in mineral salt. Shaw speaks of whole hills and tracts of salt in this country: the regular distances from salt-hill to salt-hill seems, however, to be an embellishment of the truth: we are not, however, nearly enough acquainted with the interior of Africa to affirm that what Herodotus states is false.

[269] See Matt. 437. obs. 3.

suffer from humours flowing from the head [290]: and by this means, they assert, the children become most healthy. In fact, the Libyans are the healthiest of men we know of; whether from the above cause, I cannot vouch for certain. If the children they are thus burning have convulsions, the remedy they have discovered is, to sprinkle them with the urine of a he-goat [291]. I give this statement on the authority of the Libyans themselves. The mode of sacrifice with the nomades is as follows: they begin by cutting off the ear of the victim, and throw it over their house: this done, they twist the neck of the victim. Sacrifice is offered to the sun and moon alone. The above religious ceremonies are accordingly common to all the Libyans; but those who graze their cattle about Lake Tritonis sacrifice besides, principally, to Minerva, Triton, and Neptune. The Hellenes have taken the attire and spencer of the images of Minerva from the Libyan women; except that those women wear a dress of leather, and the fringes on their ægis are composed, not of serpents, but of leathern cords; in other respects, the dress is wholly of the same fashion. Moreover, the name itself proves that the attire of the images of Pallas comes from Libya; for the Libyan women throw over the rest of their clothes, tanned goat-skins [292], bordered with red-tinged fringe: from these goat-skins the Hellenes have borrowed the ægis (or spencer). I believe, likewise, that the piercing shrieks heard in temples first took their origin in that country. The Hellenes learnt from the Libyans, also, how to harness and equip a fourhorse chariot. All the Libyan nomades, with the exception of the Nasamonians, bury the dead in the same manner as the Hellenes; except the Nasamonians, who bury their dead in a sitting posture; taking care, when the sick man breathes his last, to put the body in that position, and not on the back. The houses are constructed of asphodel-stalks, wattled with rushes, and portable. Such are the usages of these people.

Westward of the River Triton, on the confines of the Ausenses, the first Libyan husbandmen are met with: they are accustomed to reside in houses, and are called Maxyes: they let the hair grow on the right side of the head, and shave the left side: they paint their bodies with vermilion, and declare they are descended from the Trojans. This country,

---

[290] The same custom is said to hold among the Abyssinians.

[291] The urine, by the volatility of its alkali, may have, in spasmodic affections, the same effect as the spirits of hartshorn, which we use in similar cases.

[292] From αἴξ, αἰγός, 'a goat,' the Greeks made αἰγίς, αἰγίδος, which signifies a goat's-skin, and Minerva's ægis. *Larcher.*

and the rest of western Libya, are not only more abundant in animals, but likewise more thickly wooded than that of the nomades: for eastern Libya, where those pastors graze their cattle, is low and sandy, on to the River Triton; while western Libya, occupied by husbandmen, is mountainous, well-wooded, and abounding in animals: among these people, enormous serpents and lions are frequent, as well as elephants, bears, aspics, and horned-asses; together with dog-headed and creatures without a head, which have eyes in the bosom, according to the account at least of the Libyans: they have also wild men and women, and many other wild animals that really exist[293]. With the pastoral Libyans, this is not the case; but they have other animals[294], pygargi, and antelopes, and bubali, and asses not horned, but others that never drink; oryes, of the size of oxen, the horns of which are used for the curves of the Phœnician citherns: they have also foxes, hyænas, porcupines, wild rams, dictyes, thoes, panthers, boryes; land crocodiles, three cubits long, similar to lizards; ostriches; and small serpents, each with one horn. These are the animals in nomade Libya, together with those found in other countries; except the stag and wild-boar, neither of which is ever found in Libya. In this country there are three sorts of rats: those called bipeds; others called zegeries, a Libyan term equivalent to ours of hillock: the third sort is called hedgehogs: there are likewise weasels in the silphium, similar to those at Tartessus. Such are the animals found in the land of the pastoral Libyans, so far as I was able to collect, by most careful inquiries.

Contiguous to the Libyan Maxyes are the Zaveces, whose

---

[293] ἀπατέψαντα. Herodotus means, that he does not believe about the cynocephali, acephali, but that he does know there are in their country many sorts of wild beasts.

[294] Nothing very certain is known respecting any of these animals: the distance of time since Herodotus wrote, the imperfect knowledge we have of the country, and the probability that some of the species here mentioned may have retired more to the south, are insuperable difficulties in the way of a correct translation. I shall, however, present my reader with the most probable conjectures made by modern Naturalists:

πύγαργος—a sort of antelope; its buttocks white. Deuteron. xiv. 5.

ζόρκας—another sort of gazel, or antelope.

βούβαλις—buffalo, or perhaps the antelope bubalus.

ὄρυς — unknown: Cuvier takes it to be the same as the oryx, now called antelope oryx.

βασσάρια—foxes, according to Hesychius.

ὕαιναι—hyænas.

ὕστριχες—porcupines.

δίκτυες—unknown.

θῶες—jackals, or tigers.

πάνθηρες—panthers.

δίπους—the jerboa, a sort of diminutive kangaroo.

The others have not even been the object of conjecture.

wives drive the chariots to war. Contiguous to these are the Gyzantes: in their country the bees make a vast quantity of honey; but much more still, we are told, is made by men. The Gyzantes paint their bodies with vermilion; and eat monkeys, which breed on the mountains in immense numbers[295]. Not far from the above, according to the account of the Carthaginians, lies an island called Cyraunis: its length is two hundred stades; its breadth exceeding narrow: it is full of olive-trees and vines. There is in this island a lake, out of the mud of which the girls of the country collect gold-dust, by means of feathers daubed with pitch. I know not whether this is true: I write merely what is said: this account, however, may be perhaps correct. I myself have seen how at Zacynthus[296] the pitch is got up from the water in a certain lake there; that is, the land contains many lakes, the most extensive of which is seventy feet square by two orgyæ in depth: they thrust into that basin a myrtle-branch at the end of a pole, and then pull it out again, with the pitch sticking to the myrtle: this pitch has a smell of bitumen, and in other respects is better than the Pierian pitch: they dig a hole near the lake, in which they pour the pitch; and when they have collected a sufficient quantity, turn it out into amphoræ or wine-jars. Whatever falls into this lake goes under ground; and re-appears on the surface of the sea, which is four stades distant from the lake itself: thus, therefore, it is probable, that what is related of the Libyan lake may be accordant to truth. The Carthaginians relate, also, that there is a place in Libya with a nation residing outside of the Pillars of Hercules; that they carry on trade with this people; and when they arrive at that country, they take out their cargo, and, spreading the wares in regular order upon the sea-side, return to their ship, and raise a smoke. The natives, when they see the smoke, come down to the shore, deposit gold for the articles, and retire to a certain distance from the wares. The Carthaginians then land from their ships, and look at the gold: if the amount appears sufficient for the goods, they take it up, and go away: if not sufficient, they return aboard, and await patiently. The natives come forward, and deposit more gold, until they have satisfied the Carthaginians: neither party ever cheats: for the Carthaginians never touch the gold, until its amount is made up equal to the price; nor

---

[295] See Matt. 445, c.
[296] This is confirmed by modern travellers. There is in Trinidad a lake of pitch covering above a hundred acres.

do the natives touch the goods till the sellers have accepted and taken away the gold[297].

197 Such are the Libyan tribes whose names I am able to enumerate: many are still, and were formerly, independent of the king. As to what I have to say in addition concerning this region, is, that four distinct races, and no more, occupy the whole continent of Libya, so far as we know: two of these are aboriginal, the other two are not so: the Libyans and Ethiopians are aboriginal: the former dwell in the north, the latter in the south of Libya. The nations of
198 foreign origin are Phœnicians and Hellenes. I am of opinion that Libya is not to be compared either with Europe or Asia, in excellence of soil; if we except only the district of Cinyps, for both river and land bear one and the same name: the soil of that part of Libya may compete with any corn-country whatever, and in this respect it differs from all the rest of Libya. The soil here is black, and well watered by springs: it has nothing to fear, either from drought or from too much rain; for in this quarter of Libya rain falls. The products here equal those in Babylonia. The Euesperitæ possess also an excellent soil; for the product, in the best years, is one-hundred-fold; but in Cinyps it
199 reaches to three-hundred-fold. The land of Cyrenæa, the most elevated of that part of Libya which is occupied by the nomades, has three seasons worthy of admiration. First, the fruits growing on the sea-side swell, and the harvest and vintage take place: when these crops have been collected, those of the middle region become ripe, and fit for gathering; this part of the territory is called the mountain: no sooner is the middle crop harvested, when in the highest region of the country the fruits swell and ripen; so that the first fruits and wine are being consumed when the last are being gathered. Thus harvest-time lasts eight months with the Cyrenæans.

200 On the arrival of the Persians[298], despatched from Egypt, by Aryandes, to Barca, for the assistance of Pheretime, they laid siege to the town, summoning by herald the inhabitants to deliver up the authors of the murder of Arcesilaus. As the whole body of the citizens were implicated in the deed, they refused terms: in consequence, the Persians besieged Barca during nine months, digging mines under ground that reached to the inside of the fortress, and making violent

[297] This same mode of trafficking is carried on between the Moors and Nigretians of the present day, according to Shaw.

[298] Herodotus here resumes the narrative, which he had interrupted, 168, to speak of Libya.

assaults. With respect to the underground excavations, a coppersmith discovered a mode of ascertaining the direction of the mines, by means of a brazen shield: this shield the man carried round, within the city wall, keeping it in contact with the surface of the ground: in the parts where the mines extended, the brass shield sent forth a sound; in the other parts it was wholly silent. In this manner the citizens were enabled to countermine and slay the Persian delvers; and the Barcæi repelled all assaults. After a long time passed thus, and many on both sides having fallen— not the fewest on the part of the Persians—Amasis, the commander of the land-forces, devised the following: seeing that the Barcæi were not to be captured by force, but might be so by artifice, he acted thus. In the night, he dug a wide fosse, over which he laid a floor of thin planks: this he covered with a coat of mould, and levelled the ground about. At the break of day, he invited the Barcæi to a conference. The citizens were delighted at this information, being pleased at the idea of making a compact; and they entered into an agreement of the following nature, binding themselves by solemn oaths[200], pronounced on the brink of the hidden abyss: " So long as this land lasts as it is, so long shall " this oath last as respects the town: the Barcæi declare they " will pay the due tribute to the king; and the Persians declare " they will never renew their attempt against the citizens of " Barca." After taking the oath, the Barcæi, putting their trust in the Persians, went themselves out of the town, and, opening all the gates, permitted any that chose, among the besiegers, to visit the fortress. But the Persians now broke down the concealed bridge, and rushed into the town: they broke down the bridge they had just built, for the following purpose, that they might keep their oath; having sworn to the Barcæans that they would keep the oath for ever, so long as the land should remain as it was: and thus, by breaking down the bridge, the oath would no longer hold respecting the country.

Pheretime, accordingly, as the citizens of Barca had been delivered up to her by the Persians, crucified the most culpable among them around the city; and cutting off the breasts of their wives, stuck them upon the walls: the rest of the Barcæi she ordered to be given as booty to the Persians, excepting such as were Battiadæ, and not implicated in the murder: to these Battiadæ, Pheretime gave permission to remain in the town. The Persians, having made slaves of the

[200] See p. 188, note 267, of our second volume.

rest of the Barcæi, took their departure: and when they were near the city of Cyrene, the citizens, to preserve themselves from some oracle, let them pass through the town. As the army was passing through the place, Bares, the commander-in-chief of the fleet, advised that the town should be captured; but Amasis, the commander-in-chief of the land forces, refused, " because Barca was the only Hellenic city he had " been sent to attack:" in consequence, having passed through Cyrene, and encamped on the hill of Lycæan Jove, they began to repent they had not taken possession of Cyrene, and tried to enter it again; but that, the citizens would not allow. A panic seized the Persians, although attacked by no enemy; and they ran away, to the distance of about sixty stades. When the army had encamped in that place, a messenger arrived from Aryandes, recalling the forces. The Persians asked the Cyrenæans to give them provisions for their march, and their request was granted: taking these with them, they proceeded to Egypt. Quitting Cyrene, they were received by the Libyans, who slew all stragglers and
204 laggers for the sake of their clothes and accoutrements. This Persian army penetrated no farther than the Euesperides in Libya. The Barcæi, whom the troops had made slaves of, were transported out of Egypt, and sent to the Persian king; and Darius gave them a village in Bactria for their residence: to this village the slaves gave the name of Barca; and it was still, down to my time, one of the inhabited places of Bactria.
205 But neither did Pheretime end prosperously her life; for immediately after she had wreaked her vengeance on Barca, she quitted Libya, and returned to Egypt, where she met with a miserable death, swarming with maggots that devoured her flesh while yet alive. Thus the too eager gratification of vengeance draws down the indignation of the gods on mankind. Such, therefore, was Pheretime the wife of Battus: and thus dreadful the vengeance that visited the Barcæi!

END OF VOL. I.

CPSIA information can be obtained
at www.ICGtesting.com
Printed in the USA
BVHW040029060120
568598BV00007BA/81/P